THE PAPERS OF
ZEBULON BAIRD VANCE

Zebulon Baird Vance ca. 1870. Photograph courtesy of Mrs. Graham A. Barden, New Bern; copy by State Archives, Division of Archives and History, Raleigh.

The Papers of Zebulon Baird Vance

· Volume 2 ·

1863

Joe A. Mobley

Editor

Raleigh
Division of Archives and History
North Carolina Department of Cultural Resources
1995

North Carolina Department of Cultural Resources
BETTY RAY MCCAIN
Secretary
ELIZABETH F. BUFORD
Deputy Secretary

Division of Archives and History
WILLIAM S. PRICE JR.
Director
LARRY G. MISENHEIMER
Deputy Director

To William C. Harris

CONTENTS

ILLUSTRATIONS

FOREWORD

Publication of volume 2 of *The Papers of Zebulon Baird Vance* is particularly gratifying. Volume 1, edited by Frontis W. Johnston, appeared in 1963 during the centennial of the Civil War. Over a period of three decades several editors attempted to continue the project. In 1983 Gordon B. McKinney, then a member of the history department at Western Carolina University, agreed to assume responsibility for producing a letterpress edition of the Vance Papers. A grant from the National Historical Publications and Records Commission delayed work on the letterpress edition so that Dr. McKinney and Dr. Richard M. McMurry could prepare a microfilm edition of the Vance Papers. *The Papers of Zebulon Vance* (Frederick, Md.: University Publications of America, 1987), consisting of thirty-nine reels, brought the microfilm edition to a successful conclusion.

Upon accepting a position in Washington, D.C., Dr. McKinney was unable to begin work on the letterpress edition. No progress occurred until Joe A. Mobley assumed responsibility for the Vance Papers in 1991. Mr. Mobley, a senior editor with the Historical Publications Section and a careful student of the Civil War, brought years of editing experience and research to the project. He faced a formidable task. From more than three thousand potential documents, he had to choose a small fraction to transcribe, edit, and annotate for printing. Mr. Mobley's astute judgment is evident throughout this volume.

Students of North Carolina history, southern history, and the Civil War need no introduction to Zeb Vance. Arguably the most popular figure in the state's history, Vance was elected governor in the midst of a conflict that deeply divided North Carolina. The problems Vance confronted as the state's chief executive in 1863 challenged his vast political and administrative skills. Internal dissent, demands from the Confederate government in Richmond, military operations, war-weariness and poverty at home, shortages, slave unrest, and reversals on the battlefield combined to make Vance's governorship one of unrelieved crisis. With great skill Mr. Mobley offers researchers and readers of this volume a vivid portrait of Vance's forceful leadership at a tumultuous time in the state's history. Mr. Mobley received both his B.A. and M.A. in history at North Carolina State University. He is author of a number of other works published by the Division of Archives and History, including *James City: A Black Community in North Carolina, 1863–1900* and *Ship Ashore! The U.S. Lifesavers of Coastal North Carolina.*

Other members of the Historical Publications Section who helped in the preparation of this volume include Lisa D. Bailey and Sandra T. Hall. Besides the State Archives in the North Carolina Division of Archives and History, the following repositories gave permission to reproduce Vance papers from their collections: William L. Clements Library, University of Michigan, Ann Arbor; Special Collections Department, Duke University Library, Durham, N.C.; Manuscript Department, Harvard College Library, Harvard University, Cambridge, Mass.; Library of Congress, Washington, D.C.; and the Southern Historical Collection, University of North Carolina Library, Chapel Hill. Special thanks are due those repositories for their cooperation and the staff of the Historical Publications Section for its superb work.

Jeffrey J. Crow
Historical Publications Administrator

January 1995

ACKNOWLEDGMENTS

The editor of volume 2 of *The Papers of Zebulon Baird Vance* wishes to acknowledge several persons who helped ensure the completion of the book. Colleagues at the Historical Publications Section to whom he owes thanks include Jeffrey J. Crow, Kathleen B. Wyche, Robert J. Cain, and Jan-Michael Poff, all of whom rendered sound editorial advice. Weymouth T. Jordan Jr. provided information on North Carolina soldiers in the Confederate army. Sandra T. Hall typed the calendar from index cards, and Lisa D. Bailey lent her proofreading skills to the entire volume. Among archivists and manuscript curators, Charles Edward Morris and the staff of the State Archives search room deserve recognition for their help in locating and copying documents. The same credit is due Richard A. Shrader of the Southern Historical Collection, University of North Carolina Library, Chapel Hill. Martin K. Winchester, presently a graduate student at the University of Minnesota, Minneapolis, made an invaluable contribution to the project as a state government intern in the summer of 1992 by transcribing manuscripts and performing a number of important research assignments. Volunteer intern Beth Lowery, formerly at Meredith College, Raleigh, contributed in the spring of 1993 by comparing transcriptions from the Governors Letter Books of Vance. The editor also acknowledges his debt to Gordon B. McKinney and Richard M. McMurry for their microfilm compilation *The Papers of Zebulon Vance* (Frederick, Md.: University Publications of America, 1987).

INTRODUCTION

The year 1863 marked a turning point in the fate of the Confederate States of America and the history of the state of North Carolina. The year also constituted a milestone in the career of Zebulon Baird Vance. In 1863 the Confederacy came face-to-face with the reality that in all likelihood it could not win its independence through battlefield victory. The Army of Northern Virginia's failure at the Battle of Antietam and the subsequent issuance of the preliminary Emancipation Proclamation in September 1862 had ended for all practical purposes any possibility of foreign intervention on behalf of the Southern cause. Resounding Confederate defeats at Gettysburg and Vicksburg in July 1863 reinforced that fact and proved the power of the Federal army, which—with the aid of the Federal navy—began tightening its coils upon the Confederacy from the north and west and along the Atlantic coast.[1]

In North Carolina conscription, wholesale desertion from Confederate ranks, fears that the Emancipation Proclamation would incite slaves to insurrection, inflation, shortages, speculation, illegal distilling, a tax in kind, battlefield losses, and Federal raids into the state's interior all contributed to a decline in the will of North Carolinians to wage civil war. Amid such sudden change and disruption, the young Zebulon Baird Vance found himself confronting a myriad of problems and challenges the like of which he had never faced before and could not have foreseen when he became governor of North Carolina in early September 1862.

The problem of conscription into the Confederate army excited more discontent among North Carolinians and caused more difficulty for their governor than perhaps any other single issue in 1863. The Confederate Congress passed its first two conscription laws in April and September 1862. The first act drafted into the army all white men between the ages of eighteen and thirty-five, and the second extended the age limit to forty-five. Many Southerners considered the laws a violation of individual liberty, and they bridled under the exemption legislation that immediately followed each of the acts. Some attempted to use the exemption laws to avoid military service. The poor considered the provision for the hiring of substitutes to favor the wealthy; and in North Carolina, following the enactment of the second conscription act, the issue of substitution led to confusion and controversy over the draft's constitutionality. The trouble began when Chief Justice Richmond M. Pearson of the North Carolina Supreme Court ruled that substitutes were not liable for conscription according to the act of September 1862, and moreover the men for whom they had substituted could not be legally drafted either. Pearson issued writs of habeas corpus and ordered the discharge of a number of men who had previously hired substitutes.[2] The nonslaveholding populace also proclaimed its outrage over the Twenty-Negro Law, which exempted from military service the owner or overseer of any plantation of twenty or more slaves and increasingly led the lower classes to view the war as a struggle to preserve slavery and benefit the rich.[3] "The poor Soldiers is fiting for the rich mens Negroes," complained one farmer to Vance in January 1863.[4]

When Vance spoke after the war about Confederate conscription, he acknowledged the devastating impact it had on Southern morale and commitment to the war effort. "It was," he declared in a speech in Boston in 1886, "perhaps the severest blow the Confederacy ever received, as it did more than anything else to alienate the affections of the common people, without whose support it could not live for a day. It was not only regarded as a confession that the new government was not able to depend upon the voluntary support of the people, with which it so triumphantly started out ... but it opened a wide door to demagogues to appeal to the non-slaveholding class, and make them believe that the only issue was the protection of slavery, in which they were to be sacrificed for the sole benefit of the masters."[5]

Closely associated with the disruption wrought by conscription was the immense problem of desertion. From the time Vance took office as governor, the difficulty of controlling desertion unmercifully plagued him. He first authorized the militia to arrest deserters but soon was thwarted by Chief Justice Pearson, who issued writs of habeas corpus and ordered the release of those arrested on the ground that the state militia had no authority to arrest Confederate soldiers. Such action, Pearson argued, was the responsibility of the Confederate government.[6] In response to Pearson's ruling, the governor applied to the legislature for authority to arrest deserters and asked for a law against harboring them. But the state lawmakers denied his request "on much the same grounds as those assigned by The Chief Justice, to wit, that it was the business of Congress to provide for the execution of its own laws." Vance then ordered the militia just to "aid the Confederate officers as a *posse* when requested" in the apprehension of deserters. "In the meantime," Vance wrote Jefferson Davis on May 13, 1863, "news of Judge Pearson's decision went abroad in the Army in a very exaggerated and ridiculous form, soldiers were induced to believe that it declared the conscript law unconstitutional and that they were entitled if they came home to the protection of their civil authorities—Desertion ... broke out again worse than before."[7] When the Home Guard, composed of men not eligible for the draft, supplanted the militia in July and attempted to make arrests, the chief justice ruled that the Home Guard also had no authority to apprehend Confederate deserters and conscripts. In December 1863 the legislature passed a bill that authorized the governor to use the Home Guard to arrest deserters and recusant conscripts. Meanwhile Vance's public proclamations urging deserters to return to their regiments had brought some success.[8]

Yet the difficulties of conscription and desertion continued to weigh upon Vance. The protest, civil unrest, and armed conflict excited by those problems reached a pinnacle in the Quaker Belt of the state's Piedmont, where such peace societies as the Heroes of America defied conscription, concealed deserters, and called for a return to the Union.[9] Equally disruptive was the violence that took place in the Mountains of North Carolina, where a strong unionist element also resisted Confederate authority. At Shelton Laurel in the Mountain county of Madison, the clash between Confederate supporters and tories or unionists resulted in a massacre in which Confederate troops summarily executed a number of prisoners suspected of guerrilla activity.[10]

Like the chaos and resentment created by conscription and desertion, the issuance of the Emancipation Proclamation in its final form by the Federal government in January 1863 did much to instill disillusionment and weaken war support among the common people in North Carolina. The proclamation alarmed the nonslaveholding citizenry by reinforcing the concept that the war was not being fought for independence or states' rights but for the preservation of slavery.[11] Abraham Lincoln's edict for black freedom also created within the state—among slaveholders and nonslaveholders alike—a chilling and widespread panic that slaves would be incited by news of the proclamation to rise up and murder whites.[12] Such fears were enhanced when Federal troops, who had occupied eastern North Carolina since March 1862, began enlisting slaves into black regiments.[13] As a result of the white fear of slave violence, the General Assembly in February 1863 passed a special law that gave the governor authority to order the immediate convening of special courts of oyer and terminer for the swift trials of slaves accused of murdering whites.[14]

The Confederate government's enactment of a tax in kind led to further public disaffection with the war. In April the Congress passed a law designed to overcome growing inflation in Confederate and state paper currency. The act provided for a graduated income tax and a 10 percent tax in kind on agricultural products. The Southern public generally acquiesced in the income tax, which was low and ineffectually collected. The tax in kind, however, resulted in considerable protest, as agents of the Confederate bureaucracy efficiently canvassed the states to appraise crops and to collect large quantities of foodstuffs.[15] "The Confederate Tax in Kind will produce dissatistion if not oppersition from the people," wrote one Caswell County farmer to Vance. "There seems to be no escape for us from these sore troubles but to make peace with the North on the best terms we can."[16] Shortages of various kinds—cloth and cotton and wool cards, for example—were a part of day-to-day life in the Tar Heel State, although an anticipated food shortage failed to occur in 1863. The Impressment Act passed by the Confederate Congress in March allowed Confederate officers to impress, with compensation to owners, food, forage, livestock, and other private property, as well as blacks (slaves and free). Those resources were used for the subsistence and assistance of the army.[17] Many North Carolinians objected to the measure as a violation of states' rights. To ensure that North Carolina retained enough food to feed its poor, the legislature passed a law permitting the state to purchase supplies and hold them in reserve "to prevent suffering in the families of soldiers and consequent disquiet and desertion in the army." But an abundant harvest and citizens' hoarding in response to the Impressment Act produced a surplus "that the fear of famine kept out of the market." Consequently, Vance wrote to Secretary of War James A. Seddon, "It affords me great pleasure to assure you that the crisis in regard to provisions in this state has passed over, and the conviction is now firm in all minds that there is not only enough but to *spare*. I hope to be able to turn over some 250,000 lbs bacon and some corn to the Confederacy."[18] The problem of shortages also was partially alleviated by Vance's deployment of purchasing agents to England and his skillful management of several state-owned blockade-runners, including the famous *Advance*, to obtain supplies for North Carolina's soldiers and civilians.[19]

Still, the impressment of supplies and of slaves to work on fortifications continued to alienate many North Carolinians from the Confederate cause. In addition to impressment and certain shortages, speculation, inflation, and illegal distilling of corn and grain particularly rankled the poor. Fueling the dissatisfaction were the heartfelt losses of loved ones on distant battlefields and the raids and threat of full-scale attack by the Federal troops occupying eastern North Carolina. As statewide disillusionment grew, more and more North Carolinians began to favor peace negotiations with the North. Their ever-increasing concern ultimately forced Vance to confront the peace issue.

In fact, the greatest personal quandary that Vance faced in 1863 was deciding whether to support the movement within his state to end the war with a negotiated peace or to continue to back the administration of Jefferson Davis in its effort to carry on the conflict until a war-weary North cried "enough" and acquiesced to an independent Confederate States of America. "The decision filled many anxious days," historian Richard E. Yates has written, "for the popular young governor knew well that his political future was at stake."[20] Since the beginning of the war, support for secession and the Confederacy had been far from unanimous among North Carolina citizens. As the people became increasingly despondent and disgruntled over battlefield losses, conscription, desertion, threat of slave attack, tax in kind, impressment, and other issues, they began to agitate publicly for an immediate peaceful conclusion to the fighting. Those who sought peace with the Federal government found a spokesman in William W. Holden, editor of the Raleigh newspaper the *North Carolina Standard*. Holden began calling for peace negotiations, and organized peace meetings convened in many communities. Resolutions adopted at the meetings denounced Confederate despotism and advocated peace talks with the Federals. North Carolinians staunchly loyal to the Confederate cause (supporters of the Confederate party) saw the peace movement as a treasonous effort to reconstruct the old Union and demanded that Vance subdue Holden and his followers. Confederate officials in Richmond also became alarmed at the unrest stirred up by the editor of the *Standard*.[21] Jefferson Davis wrote to the governor on July 24 to inquire whether rumors were true that "Holden is engaged in the treasonable purpose of exciting the people of North Carolina to resistance against their government, and co-operation with the enemy."[22]

In early August Vance traveled to Richmond to confer with Davis about Holden and the peace advocates. Returning to Raleigh, the governor composed a letter to be made public that denounced the peace movement but did not attack Holden personally.[23] Dissuaded from publishing the letter by the prominent politician William A. Graham, Vance instead called a meeting of Graham and other Conservatives (the party to which both Holden and Vance belonged) to develop a policy to combat the peace initiatives. Principally on the advice of Graham, Vance issued a public proclamation discouraging peace meetings but not criticizing Holden.[24]

Shortly after the proclamation appeared, Georgia troops passing through Raleigh broke into the *Standard* office and scattered Holden's papers and the ink and type from his press. The ransacking soldiers, from the command of General Henry Benning, were responding to resolutions adopted in Virginia by Confederate army officers most of whom were from North Carolina. The resolutions called for the suppression of Holden and the peace proponents. On the day following the attack on the *Standard* office, allies of Holden sacked the office and destroyed the presses of the *State Journal*, a Raleigh newspaper that had joined the campaign to gag the *Standard*. The trouble intensified when angered soldiers from a passing Alabama brigade announced plans to seize Holden, whose friends vowed to protect him. During all three altercations Vance personally managed to calm mobs and restore quiet in the capital.[25]

Holden himself expressed gratitude for the governor's actions in preventing bloodshed and preserving public order. He promised to support Vance as long as the state's chief executive adhered to the true principles of the Conservative party. No more local peace conventions convened, but in the November elections the peace faction of the Conservative party—again urged on by the *Standard*—won six of the ten seats in the Confederate Congress. Holden renewed his attacks on the Confederate government, protesting such violations of personal liberty as conscription and impressment. In December he began calling for a state convention to initiate peace negotiations directly with the Federal government in the hope of bringing an unpopular and devastating war to an end. He vowed to oppose Vance in the gubernatorial election of 1864 unless the incumbent governor supported the state convention. Vance, however, refused to endorse the calling of a state peace convention, and he soon broke off relations with Holden.[26]

Despite his break with Holden and the peace proponents and his general support of the government in Richmond, Vance frequently quarreled with Jefferson Davis, Secretary of War Seddon, and other Confederate authorities over the conscription of state officials, deployment of North Carolina troops, the impressment of forage and supplies, and the general intervention of the Confederate government into state affairs. Although the governor disagreed with Chief

Justice Pearson's interpretations and attempted to have them overturned by the full court, he nonetheless defended them as state law and refused to allow Confederate officers to ignore the writs of habeas corpus. That posture brought him into considerable conflict with the government in Richmond. Displaying an impetuous and stubborn temperament, Vance also was quick to take offense at policies and acts that he felt slighted him or his state. Outraged that North Carolina's soldiers were not receiving the recognition they deserved from the War Department and the Virginia press, he angrily told Seddon that "such things are hard to bear" but "The troops from N.C. can afford to appeal to history: I am confident that they have but little to expect from their associates."[27]

Nevertheless, by the end of 1863 Vance clearly had confirmed his loyalty to the total Confederate war effort. Although at times he may have seemed publicly in favor of peace negotiations between the Confederate and Federal governments, his motivation for endorsing those talks was merely to quiet the growing dissatisfaction within his state over continuing hostilities. Vance was convinced that the Lincoln government would never agree to a peace that included Confederate independence and left slavery intact—a condition upon which the Davis government uncompromisingly insisted. Therefore, the governor sincerely believed that peace meetings between representatives of the governments in Richmond and Washington had no real chance of success, even if the Lincoln administration would agree to negotiations. But despite that belief, Vance maintained that the Davis government should make a propaganda show of trying to hold such talks in order to regain the declining support of the populace. "After a careful consideration of all the sources of discontent in North Carolina," he wrote Jefferson Davis on December 30, "I have concluded that it will be perhaps impossible to remove it except by making some effort at negotiation with the enemy. . . . I am promised by all men who advocate this course that if fair terms are rejected it will tend to greatly strengthen and intensify the war feeling and will rally all classes to a more cordial support of the government. . . . I have not suggested the method of these negotiations or their terms, the *effort* to obtain peace is the principal matter."[28] Thus as the year drew to a close, Vance remained committed to the Confederacy and its resolve to win its independence. With that position firmly in mind, he turned his attention to the coming gubernatorial campaign for his reelection in 1864.

---

[1]J. G. Randall and David Donald, *The Civil War and Reconstruction*, 2d ed. (Lexington, Mass.: D. C. Heath and Co., 1969), 363–364, 506; James M. McPherson, *Battle Cry of Freedom: The Civil War Era* (New York: Oxford University Press, 1988), 556–558, 664–665.

[2]Memory F. Mitchell, *Legal Aspects of Conscription and Exemption in North Carolina* (Chapel Hill: University of North Carolina Press, 1965), 3–60; J. G. de Roulhac Hamilton, "The North Carolina Courts and the Confederacy," *North Carolina Historical Review* 4 (October 1927): 366–371. See also Albert Burton Moore, *Conscription and Conflict in the Confederacy* (New York: Macmillan Co., 1924).

[3]Patricia L. Faust et al., eds., *Historical Times Illustrated Encyclopedia of the Civil War* (New York: HarperCollins, 1991), 767.

[4]L. K. Walker to Zebulon B. Vance, January 16, 1863, Zebulon B. Vance, Governors Papers, State Archives, Division of Archives and History, Raleigh.

[5]The speech is reprinted in Clement Dowd, *The Life of Zebulon B. Vance* (Charlotte: Observer Printing and Publishing House, 1897). See pp. 447–448 for quote.

[6]Hamilton, "North Carolina Courts and the Confederacy," 368–370.

[7]ZBV to Jefferson Davis, May 13, 1863, Zebulon B. Vance, Governors Letter Books, State Archives.

[8]Mitchell, *Legal Aspects of Conscription and Exemption*, 59; Hamilton, "North Carolina Courts and the Confederacy," 376–377; *Public Laws of North Carolina, 1863* (called session), c. 10; Proclamations by ZBV, January 26, May 11, 1863, Vance, Governors Letter Books, State Archives.

[9]William T. Auman and David D. Scarboro, "The Heroes of America in North Carolina," *North Carolina Historical Review* 58 (October 1981): 327–363; William T. Auman, "Neighbor against Neighbor: The Inner Civil War in the Randolph County Area of Confederate North Carolina," *North Carolina Historical Review* 61 (January 1984): 59–92.

[10]Phillip Shaw Paludan, *Victims: A True Story of the Civil War* (Knoxville: University of Tennessee Press, 1981).

[11]Harold D. Moser, "Reaction in North Carolina to the Emancipation Proclamation," *North Carolina Historical Review* 44 (January 1967): 53–71.

[12]Moser, "Reaction to the Emancipation Proclamation," 69; Paul C. Cameron to ZBV, February 19, 1863, and Daniel H. Hill to ZBV, July 10, 1863, Vance, Governors Papers, State Archives; ZBV to Jefferson Davis, May 21, 1863, Vance, Governors Letter Books, State Archives.

[13]Richard Reid, "Raising the African Brigade: Early Black Recruitment in Civil War North Carolina," *North Carolina Historical Review* 70 (July 1993): 266–297; William T. Dortch to ZBV, January 7, 1863, and John Pool to ZBV, July 25, 1863, Vance, Governors Papers, State Archives.

[14]*Public Laws of North Carolina, 1863*, c. 35. Although the law also applied to whites who committed capital crimes, it was invoked almost exclusively in cases in which slaves murdered whites.

[15]E. Merton Coulter, *The Confederate States of America, 1861–1865* (Baton Rouge: Louisiana State University Press, 1950), 149–182. See also Richard C. Todd, *Confederate Finance* (Athens: University of Georgia Press, 1954).

[16]Philip Hodnett to ZBV, July 30, 1863, Vance, Governors Papers, State Archives.

[17]Faust et al., *Encyclopedia of Civil War*, 379.

[18]ZBV to James A. Seddon, April 27, 1863, Vance, Governors Letter Books, State Archives.

[19]Glenn Tucker, *Zeb Vance: Champion of Personal Freedom* (New York: Bobbs-Merrill Co., 1965), 216–238; Richard E. Yates, *The Confederacy and Zeb Vance* (Tuscaloosa, Ala.: Confederate Publishing Co., 1958), 68–84.

[20]Yates, *Confederacy and Zeb Vance*, 85.

[21]William C. Harris, *William Woods Holden: Firebrand of North Carolina Politics* (Baton Rouge: Louisiana State University Press, 1987), 127–136.

[22]Jefferson Davis to ZBV, July 24, 1863, Zebulon Baird Vance Papers, Private Collections, State Archives.

[23]Yates, *Confederacy and Zeb Vance*, 88; ZBV to John H. Haughton, August 17, 1863, Vance Papers, Private Collections, State Archives. (In the present volume the Haughton letter appears as an enclosure in ZBV to William A. Graham, August 19, 1863, William Alexander Graham Papers, Private Collections, State Archives.)

[24]Max R. Williams and J. G. de Roulhac Hamilton, eds., *The Papers of William Alexander Graham*, 8 vols. (Raleigh: Division of Archives and History, Department of Cultural Resources, 1957–1992), 5:322–323; Proclamation by ZBV, September 7, 1863, Vance, Governors Letter Books, State Archives.

[25]Harris, *William Woods Holden*, 138–140.

[26]Harris, *William Woods Holden*, 140–142.

[27]ZBV to James A. Seddon, July 26, 1863, Vance, Governors Letter Books, State Archives.

[28]ZBV to Jefferson Davis, December 30, 1863, Vance Papers, Private Collections, State Archives.

EDITORIAL METHOD

The documents currently known to exist in the papers of Zebulon Baird Vance for the year 1863 total approximately 3,606. The largest single repository for those materials is the State Archives, North Carolina Division of Archives and History, Raleigh. That facility houses three major collections pertaining to Vance: the Governors Papers, the Governors Letter Books, and Vance's private papers. The rest of the Vance papers reside in various collections throughout the United States. Of the number extant, 406, or about 11 percent of the total, have been transcribed and printed in this volume. The rest are listed in a calendar at the end of the book. The calendar catalogs the papers chronologically in the order in which they are arranged within a collection. Listed first are the Governors Papers, then the Governors Letter Books, followed by Vance's private papers, and lastly all other repositories.

Perhaps the most difficult task in editing a selective volume of papers of a significant historical figure is the problem of determining what to include. Any selective process is necessarily subjective. Nevertheless, the editor has established and adhered to certain guidelines in deciding which documents to include in *The Papers of Zebulon Baird Vance*. Because volume 2 deals exclusively with the year 1863, those letters and other manuscript items that best reveal Governor Vance's actions, thoughts, and ideas during that crucial period of the Civil War have been chosen. More specifically, the editor has transcribed materials that pertain to the major political, military, and administrative decisions of the state's chief executive. The topics of states' rights, war disillusionment and peace, conscription, desertion, habeas corpus, and fear of Federal attack predominate. Letters written *by* Vance received priority over those written *to* him. Of the 406 letters, telegrams, proclamations, and memorandums published herein, 203 are *from* Vance. Virtually all surviving correspondence known to have been created by Vance in 1863 has been printed. The few exceptions include routine commissions, appointments, proclamations, and other documents merely requiring his signature.

The editor has made transcriptions for this volume from manuscript sources only. None comes from printed matter such as newspapers, published records, or other documentaries, although some of the same documents may be found in other printed works. For example, Vance's addresses to the General Assembly, which already appear in *Legislative Documents* published by the state of North

Carolina, are not contained herein unless they also exist in manuscript form in the original records of the General Assembly.

Although in deciding which items to publish in volume 2 the editor has concentrated on materials that deal with major decisions and problems of a governor and state at war, he could not exclude entirely letters from ordinary folk—farmers, businessmen, soldiers' wives, and troops in the field—if the reader was to derive an accurate and complete picture of the tumultuous circumstances amid which Vance led his state in 1863. Therefore, the editor has transcribed and printed a sampling of documents that he considers representative and graphic in describing the deprivation, fears, and war support of ordinary North Carolinians—at home and on the battlefield—who constantly bombarded Vance with their complaints and pleas for help. The quantity of such correspondence is so large that the incorporation of all of it alone would have required several volumes. The editor hopes, however, that researchers seeking further sources on the home front and war sentiment among the populace will find assistance by consulting the calendar for such subjects as destitution, poor relief, salt, distilling, blockade, tax in kind, disaffection, conscription, desertion, peace, habeas corpus, and civil unrest.

The difficulty of selection also involves some technical decisions. In cases where multiple copies of the same document exist, the editor has used the copy of earliest origin. For instance, a letter in Vance's own handwriting would be transcribed rather than a clerk's copy of the same correspondence. Along these same lines, an explanation of the Governors Letter Books, located in the State Archives, needs to be made. During Vance's years as governor, clerks penned into large books copies of many of the letters that he sent and received. Often, those letter book entries are the only known surviving copies of the correspondence. Soon after the Civil War Federal troops confiscated the letter books, which had been moved from Raleigh to Greensboro for safekeeping. Union officers shipped the books to the War Department in Washington, D.C. North Carolina's subsequent efforts to recover them proved unsuccessful until 1886, when the federal government agreed to provide the state with certified handwritten copies of the letter books. Then in 1962 the North Carolina Department (later Division) of Archives and History applied for and received the original books. In volume 2 of *The Papers of Zebulon Baird Vance* the transcriptions from the letter books are made from the original versions prepared by Vance's clerks, although the federal copies occasionally were used to aid in deciphering difficult handwriting. Researchers who compare the letter book entries contained in this volume with those in the microfilm publication entitled *The Papers of Zebulon Vance* (Frederick, Md.: University Publications of America, 1987), compiled by Gordon McKinney and Richard McMurry, will find that they sometimes differ. The microfilm edition was filmed not from the original letter books but from the federal copies made in 1886. The differences usually are minor but at times are serious, as in instances of misspellings and of words or sentences left out by the Washington scribes.

Although the Vance papers have been transcribed and printed as exactly as feasible, a number of editorial adjustments and devices appear throughout volume 2 to provided continuity and assist the reader. Margins, indentation, and placement of elements have been standardized. Misspellings and punctuation have been retained except when the misspelling was so flagrant or the punctuation so erratic or bizarre as to be unintelligible or misleading. In such cases silent emendations have been made. Commas, double commas (,,), colons, or semicolons clearly intended to end a sentence or indicate an abbreviation have been replaced by periods. Small dashes, at the bottom of a line and end of a sentence (_), also have been converted to periods. Long dashes (—) are retained whether they come within or at the end of a sentence. Flourishes and other extraneous marks have been eliminated. [Sic] indicates only factual errors and words that are repeated in error ("the the," for example). Superscript characters have been brought down to the line and followed by a period. Angle brackets (< >) enclose letters and words canceled by the writer but still legible. Interlinear insertions appear within solidi (/ /), and all editorial insertions have been italicized and placed in square brackets ([ ]). Inferred readings also are in square brackets but in roman type. [Illegible] indicates words that cannot be deciphered, and such terms as [faded] and [torn] appear where appropriate. All notes follow immediately the document to which they refer.

Zebulon B. Vance frequently made endorsements on the backs of letters he received. In those notations he usually gave instructions to clerks or aides for responding to the letter or for filing the correspondence. Because those endorsements (some brief, others having several sentences) include significant information about Vance and his mind-set, the editor has placed them—with the designation [Endorsed]—at the end of the document on which they were written. Some letters received have been published herein mainly on the basis of what Vance's endorsement reveals. Endorsements other than those by the governor also have been included when they provide information not already given in the item. The editor has noted enclosures with the heading [Enclosure] and placed them immediately after the correspondence that they accompanied, regardless of the date on which the enclosure was written.

LIST OF PAPERS PRINTED IN THIS VOLUME

ABBREVIATIONS OF REPOSITORIES

A&H:Ashe   Samuel A'Court Ashe Papers, Private Collections, State Archives, Division of Archives and History, Raleigh

A&H:GA   General Assembly Session Records, State Archives, Division of Archives and History, Raleigh

A&H:GLB   Zebulon Baird Vance, Governors Letter Books, State Archives, Division of Archives and History, Raleigh

A&H:GP   Zebulon Baird Vance, Governors Papers, State Archives, Division of Archives and History, Raleigh

A&H:Gra   William Alexander Graham Papers, Private Collections, State Archives, Division of Archives and History, Raleigh

A&H:Hale   Edward Jones Hale Papers, Private Collections, State Archives, Division of Archives and History, Raleigh

A&H:Hill   Daniel Harvey Hill Sr. Papers, Private Collections, State Archives, Division of Archives and History, Raleigh

A&H:Pet   Pettigrew Papers, Private Collections, State Archives, Division of Archives and History, Raleigh

A&H:Set   Thomas Settle Jr. Letters, State Archives, Division of Archives and History, Raleigh

A&H:VanPC   Zebulon Baird Vance Papers, Private Collections, State Archives, Division of Archives and History, Raleigh

A&H:Whit   John D. Whitford Papers, Private Collections, State Archives, Division of Archives and History, Raleigh

Duke:Sed   James Alexander Seddon Sr. Papers, Special Collections Department, Duke University Library, Durham

Duke:Van   Zebulon Baird Vance Papers, Special Collections Department, Duke University Library, Durham

Duke:Wor   Worth Family Papers, Special Collections Department, Duke University Library, Durham

Har:Hill   Daniel Harvey Hill Papers, Manuscript Department, Harvard College Library, Harvard University, Cambridge

Har:Van   Zebulon Baird Vance Papers, Manuscript Department, Harvard College Library, Harvard University, Cambridge

LC:CSA — Confederate States of America Papers, Library of Congress, Washington, D.C.

LC:RBV — Robert B. Vance Papers, Library of Congress, Washington, D.C.

Mich:Sch — Schoff Collection, William L. Clements Library, University of Michigan, Ann Arbor

SHC:Ben — Henry Lewis Benning Papers, Southern Historical Collection, University of North Carolina Library, Chapel Hill

SHC:Car — David Miller Carter Papers, Southern Historical Collection, University of North Carolina Library, Chapel Hill

SHC:Clar — William John Clarke Papers, Southern Historical Collection, University of North Carolina Library, Chapel Hill

SHC:Clin — Thomas Lanier Clingman Papers, Southern Historical Collection, University of North Carolina Library, Chapel Hill

SHC:Dav — John Mitchell Davidson Papers, Southern Historical Collection, University of North Carolina Library, Chapel Hill

SHC:Gra — William Alexander Graham Papers, Southern Historical Collection, University of North Carolina Library, Chapel Hill

SHC:Law — Evander McIvor Law Collection, Southern Historical Collection, University of North Carolina Library, Chapel Hill

SHC:McD — Thomas David Smith McDowell Papers, Southern Historical Collection, University of North Carolina Library, Chapel Hill

SHC:Mall — Peter Mallett Papers, Southern Historical Collection, University of North Carolina Library, Chapel Hill

SHC:Palm — William P. Palmer Collection, Southern Historical Collection, University of North Carolina Library, Chapel Hill

SHC:Pea — John R. Peacock Collection, Southern Historical Collection, University of North Carolina Library, Chapel Hill

SHC:Rob — Marmaduke Swaim Robins Papers, Southern Historical Collection, University of North Carolina Library, Chapel Hill

SHC:Sau — Joseph Hubbard Saunders Papers, Southern Historical Collection, University of North Carolina Library, Chapel Hill

SHC:Sha — John McKee Sharpe Papers, Southern Historical Collection, University of North Carolina Library, Chapel Hill

SHC:Sil — Jacob Siler Papers, Southern Historical Collection, University of North Carolina Library, Chapel Hill

SHC:Tate — Samuel McDowell Tate Papers, Southern Historical Collection, University of North Carolina Library, Chapel Hill

SHC:Van — Zebulon Baird Vance Papers, Southern Historical Collection, University of North Carolina Library, Chapel Hill

SHC:Yel — Edward Clements Yellowley Papers, Southern Historical Collection, University of North Carolina Library, Chapel Hill

THE PAPERS OF ZEBULON BAIRD VANCE

State of North Carolina
Executive Department
Raleigh, Jany. 1st. 1863

Mr. Geo. V. Strong[1]
C. S. District Attorney
Goldsboro' N.C.

Dear Sir

The Rev. R. J. Graves, who was arrested & sent to Richmond, as a spy or something of that kind, has been returned to this State in accordance with a joint resolution of the Legislature, & bound over for examination before Judge Manly at Hillsboro' on the 15th. inst.[2]

The Secretary of War[3] has been notified & requested to send such evidence as he may have against the defendant. I also desire your attendance & solicit your action, on behalf of the Confederate States.

Very resptly
Z. B. Vance

[1]George Vaughn Strong, Confederate district attorney, had been a Wayne County delegate to North Carolina's secession and constitutional conventions, 1861–1862. John L. Cheney, Jr., ed., *North Carolina Government, 1585–1979: A Narrative and Statistical History* (Raleigh: Department of the Secretary of State, 1981), 387, 825.

[2]In 1862 the Reverend Robert J. Graves, pastor of the Bethlehem Presbyterian Church in Orange County, had published a letter in the Richmond (Va.) *Enquirer* challenging the Confederacy's propaganda that antiwar sentiment and war weariness prevailed among

Northerners. Fearing that Graves's letter would undermine the war effort, Confederate authorities, who also accused Graves of being a spy, ordered the minister arrested and transported to Richmond, where he was imprisoned. ZBV and the state legislature demanded his return to North Carolina—stating that both personal and states' rights had been violated by the Confederate government in arresting Graves without a warrant or specific charges and in taking him from the state without authorization. The War Department ordered the prisoner returned to North Carolina, where at Hillsborough in February he appeared before State Supreme Court Justice Matthias Evans Manly. Manly bound Graves over to the Confederate court at Richmond to stand trial for treason. A Confederate grand jury, however, found insufficient evidence against him, and he never came to trial. Frontis W. Johnston, ed., *The Papers of Zebulon Baird Vance*, 2 vols. to date (Raleigh: Department of Archives and History, 1963—), 1:444–445, 449–452, 454–455; Glenn Tucker, *Zeb Vance: Champion of Personal Freedom* (New York: Bobbs-Merrill Co., 1965), 279–282; Richard E. Yates, *The Confederacy and Zeb Vance* (Tuscaloosa: Confederate Publishing Co., 1958), 52–53; *North Carolina Standard* (Raleigh), February 20, June 19, 1863; Max R. Williams and J. G. de Roulhac Hamilton, eds., *The Papers of William Alexander Graham*, 8 vols. (Raleigh: Division of Archives and History, Department of Cultural Resources, 1957–1992), 5:433–436, 445–449, 451–452, 455–456, 473–474, 483–484, 492–494.

[3]James Alexander Seddon, Confederate secretary of war, November 1862-February 1865. *Dictionary of American Biography*, s.v. "Seddon, James Alexander."

ZBV to James A. Seddon   A&H:GLB

State of North Carolina
Executive Dpt
Raleigh, Jany. 2d. 1863

Hon J. A. Seddon
Secy. at War

Sir

Your letter by Mr. Cowles[1] concerning the surrender of R. J. Graves to the civil authorities of this State has been received, and with it also the person of the said Graves, in compliance with a resolution of the General Assembly of North Carolina, a copy of which I had the honor to enclose the President.

Allow me Sir, to express my gratification not only at the prompt compliance with the wishes of our Legislature, but also at the manner & spirit manifested in the deed by yourself acting in the absence of the President.[2] Nothing tends more strongly to preserve harmony and cordial feeling, than for a state, naturally & properly jealous of its rights, to perceive such a courteous disposition to respect and defend them, on the part of the General Government.

Graves has been bound over to appear before Hon. M. E. Manly one of the Justices of the Supreme Court of North Carolina, at Hillsboro, on the 15th. inst. for examination. I will this day notify Mr. Geo. V. Strong C.S. District Attorney, and ask him to cause the attendance of such witnesses as he may deem proper,

& would thank you to order the attendance of the soldiers mentioned in the letter to the Richmond Enquirer, a copy of which you were good enough to enclose me.

I trust Sir, it is not necessary for me to assure you that the greatest motive actuating me in this matter is my earnest desire to see all the forms of law and liberty observed, so long as I have the honor to preside over the destinies of a people, distinguished as law loving and law abiding, and in nowise to screen the guilty.

Reciprocating in the highest degree, the sentiments of esteem and consideration proposed in your letter.

> I am, Sir,
> Your obt. Svt.
> Z. B. Vance

[1] Andrew Carson Cowles, Yadkin County legislator, delivered to Richmond North Carolina's resolution protesting the arrest of Graves. Cowles returned to Raleigh with the secretary of war's reply. Johnston, *Papers of Vance*, 1:444n.

[2] Jefferson Davis was visiting the armies in the West.

William A. Smith to ZBV　　　　　　A&H:GP

> Boon Hill Johnston County NC.
> Jan 3rd. 1863—

To His Excellency Gov. Vance,

Sir,

The people of Johnston County owe allegiance first to *North Carolina* secondly to the Confederate States, and accordingly, to my Humble judgement *protection* is due from North Carolina to her Citizens even against the injustice of the Confederate authorities; but so far from the State protecting Johnston County and equalizeing her among her sister Counties, the State itself seems at the present time to be almost as injust as the would be Aristocratic and demanding Horse leeches of the Confederate Service. Not long since a man, who said he had authority from the Commander at Goldsboro, but who could not read his own instructions, having never had the blessing extended to him of learning his letters came to this his native County with and armed force to press and take our wagons & mules from us, his particular friends he passed by lightly, those whom he before had old grudge against, he robed of all they had in the way of teames, and if they objected he threatened them should they not hush there complaints to take <them> and force them into the Confederate Service thereby implying it was a *bad* place; which according to *Assy Biggs*[1] is *treason.* Such men appear at our homes with bayonets and demand that we /feed them

&/ give them quarters and tell us if we refuse the[y] will press what they demand, and in addition to this when every wagon mule &c is gone comes the Governor with his bob tail malish demanding half of our able bodied slaves, which the Confeds have had for seven weeks, when they released those from *Wayne in two*, to work at a place which a yankee, as mean as they are positively refused to have; and then we have the Editor and scribling correspondent declareing that the slave owners must feed all the poor, and sustain the Confederative Government & Gov Vance: afterwards comes the sheriff in loud tones demanding his taxes, and the speculator demanding his profits, and after the whole set is done with us, we are left beggars: but this is not the worst; if they can take what we have in the way of teames and make us feed them while on such expeditions we fear it will not be long before they will demand what we have provided for our families & the poor. We would feel safe if we could get to *Wake* County or others of our neighboring Counties, above or further *below*, as it appears all the mallice is against old *Johnston*, but we will first appeal to you our noble and good Goveror to do us justice and protect us in our personal liberties and let us fair eaqualy with our sister Counties; should you fail comply, we must as a free people either move to *Wake* or to *Orange* where I am happy to say, I would feel secure. Should we not be granted that boon, having not returned our teames where with to move, we must throw ourselves upon the back of the great *Humbug* and seceed from our good old mother North Carolina which we so much love Of course no one at this day, will deny our right, Garenteed to us by the noble *blood* of *South Carolina* Please let me know wether we shall plant any crops this year, or shall we all plunge head long into anachy & confusion and the strongest take all and let the helpless perish as they deserve for being helpless and Weak.

> With Great Respect I am
> Your obt Servant
> W. A. Smith[2]

[*Endorsed*] Ansr. Mr. Smith that the Govr. has no intention to oppress Johnson Co. The former call was made by Confed. authorities & their call for labor was made general on the country nearst the works &c. Will try to see that they suffer no more than the others. They have promised to dismiss all the hands in about two weeks

Z B V

---

[1]Asa Biggs, Confederate district judge and ardent secessionist and defender of slavery. *Dictionary of North Carolina Biography*, s.v. "Biggs, Asa."

[2]William Alexander Smith, planter who owned twenty-four slaves in 1860 and member of the state secession and constitutional conventions, 1861–1862, and the legislature, 1864–1865. After the war he became a Republican with service in both state and national governments. Eighth Census of the United States, 1860: Johnston County, North Carolina, Population and Slave schedules, National Archives, Washington, D.C. (microfilm,

State Archives, Division of Archives and History, Raleigh); *State Chronicle* (Raleigh), May 18, 1888.

ZBV *to James A. Seddon*   A&H:GLB

State of North Carolina
Executive Department
Raleigh Jany 5th. 1863

Hon. J. A. Seddon
Secty at War

Sir

I beg to trouble you in regard to a matter of great importance to the Army—The increase of desertion—In most of the midland and lowland counties of this state I shall be able to make arrests and prevent serious combinations of them by means of the local militia with the occasional assistance of the regiment of conscripts at this place. But in the mountains of the West the case is different. The enforcement of the Conscript law in East Tennessee has filled the mountains with disaffected desperadoes of the worst character, who joining with the deserters from our Army form very formidable bands of outlaws, who hide in the fastnesses, waylay the passes, rob, steal, and destroy at pleasure. The evil has become so great that travel has almost been suspended through the mountains. The Militia has become too feeble to resist them, as that section has turned out its proportion for the war with the greatest patriotism & unanimity. I propose to organize about two hundred men, put them under the command of experienced officers, arm and equip them at State expense, if the President will accept them into Confederate Service, and pay them only when actually engaged.

I hope the Department will accede to the proposition, the impunity which the deserters enjoy and the contagion of their example is operating most ruinously upon the efficiency of the Army to say nothing of the injury to property and citizens of that section.

I am now maturing a vigilant system of general police for the whole state for the prompt arrest of deserters and conscripts, which my Adjutant General[1] will submit for your approval soon and perhaps ask your assistance. I also intend to urge upon our Legislature, soon to re-assemble, the passage of a law disfranchising all who illegally avoid their duty in the public defence

I am Sir
Very respectfully
Yr. obt. Svt.
Z. B. Vance

---

[1]James Green Martin. *Dictionary of North Carolina Biography*, s.v. "Martin, James Green."

ZBV *to James A. Seddon*   A&H:GLB

Executive Office
Raleigh, N.C. January 6th. 1863

Hon. J. A. Seddon
Secty at War

Sir

Some time since when in Richmond,[1] I had the honor to mention to the President the subject of enforcing the conscription in Counties wholly or in part under the control of the enemy.[2] In view of the difficulty of the case, I asked his consent to raise by volunteering all the troops I could in such of our eastern counties.

To this he consented, and under my authorities some four or five companies have been raised and the volunteering is still going on.

The enrolling officers have however applied to me for instructions, thinking it their duty under orders to conscript all they find of the proper age and to prevent any more from volunteering.

Having only a verbal understanding with his Excellency, I thought it best to lay the matter before you and have the written consent of the Department, so as to avoid any appearance of conflict, and relieve the enrolling officers—

The policy is so obvious that, I need not dwell upon it. A large proportion can & have been obtained where it would be impossible to enforce the law. Where it can be vigorously executed of course it is best that it should be done.

Allow me to hope that it may not be inconvenient for you to give me an early reply

Most respectfully
Yr. obt. Svt.
Z. B. Vance

[1]ZBV had visited Richmond early in October 1862, ostensibly to deliver—in company with Surgeon General Edward Warren—medical supplies to North Carolina troops returning from the recent Battle of Antietam. Johnston, *Papers of Vance*, 1:275n; Tucker, *Zeb Vance*, 207.

[2]A number of eastern counties came under Federal control following the capture of Roanoke Island and New Bern in February and March 1862. The presence of Union troops remained a threat throughout the remainder of the war. John G. Barrett, *The Civil War in North Carolina* (Chapel Hill: University of North Carolina Press, 1963), 66–148.

James A. Seddon to ZBV   A&H:GP

[*Telegram*]

Richmond 6th. Jany [1863]

Raleigh

Gov Vance

Could you not give aid against the invasion of your State[1] by calling out the Militia who would embrace the exempts as well as those over forty five (45). We are straining to send forces to you

J. A Seddon
Secy of War

[*Endorsed*] *Copy of Answer*

Raleigh Jany 7th.

Hon J A Seddon
Richmond Va.

I can call out malitia if desired. The General in command[2] has not seen fit to communicate with me, and I was not aware of any movement of the enemy

Z B Vance

---

[1]Union troops occupying eastern North Carolina periodically raided the interior.

[2]Gustavus Woodson Smith, commander of the Department of North Carolina and Southern Virginia. Mark Mayo Boatner III, *The Civil War Dictionary* (New York: David McKay Co., 1959), 771–772.

William T. Dortch to ZBV   A&H:GP

Goldsboro, Jany 7th. 63

Gov. Vance:

Dear Sir:

My object in writing is to call your attention to our laws in regard to the punishment of armed slaves & Yankees who may be found with them. My books have been sent up the country, but according to my recollection our statutes are not sufficient to embrace cases which may occur under the proclamation of Lincoln & our President.[1]

The mere fact of finding a colored person armed ought to be made a capital offence, & the presence of a Yankee with an armed negro ought also to be made capital.

After examination if you think necessary, I hope you will bring the subject to the attention of the Legislature.

Genl Smith returned last evening. Latest report from below is that the Yankees are 50,000 strong at Newberne.

Yours &c
W. T. Dortch[2]

[1]In response to the Emancipation Proclamation, President Davis announced to the Confederate Congress that he would deliver all captured Federal commissioned officers to the states to be tried and sentenced as "criminals engaged in exciting servile insurrection." But he never carried out his threat. E. Merton Coulter, *The Confederate States of America, 1861–1865* (Baton Rouge: Louisiana State University Press, 1950), 265–266.

[2]William Theophilus Dortch, legislator and Confederate senator, lent support to programs to strengthen the Confederacy and opposed peace schemes. *Dictionary of North Carolina Biography*, s.v. "Dortch, William Theophilus."

William B. Rodman to ZBV   A&H:GP

Richmond Va Jany. 7 1863

Dear Sir

I deliberately forebore voting in the Governor's election—because I could not satisfy myself how I ought to vote. I foresaw your election. Your being in the army was a strong reason for thinking that we felt and thought essentially alike on public affairs. My only source of hesitation was in the conduct of some who were supporting you. Your Inaugural removed all my fears. It seemed plain that your election under the very circumstances which had attended it was the most fortunate event for the State. From that time I have ranked myself among your supporters. You have a difficult position to fill and the support you are entitled to in endeavoring to fill it properly, is not a suspicious cautious and critical one but a hearty and generous one. You have to combine two hostile parties into energetic and successful resistance to the common enemy—to carry/the State/ triumphantly and as safely as possible through this great revolution—save her from internal truly patricidal war—and leave her with a record of wisdom and valor and patriotism which shall be a new and enduring base for a united proud and glorious career in the future; Our State has heretofore lacked unity of feeling and State pride. These spring mostly from a community of inheritance in great names and glorious memories—and that this war and your administration must supply her with. The attempt to realize this idea will be itself a title to fame, and success will give you a place in history such as no previous Governor of N.Ca. has been in a position to think of. Circumstances have made possible to you what would have been impossible to another. You can keep alive patriotism and crush treason boldly without fear of consequences Boldness will conquer and confirm the attachment of all friends of Southern Independence and if there be among your present supporters any who are not so (which I do not assert) they dare not desert you for in that event they could only go to the enemy who is not/now/strong enough to protect them—desert you they will when that opportunity occurs do as you may. I am in a position which is agreeable to me and as I have no favor to ask of you I feel no delicacy in addressing you as I do. I wish to aprise you that until I shall see strong proof that your purposes have become different from what I now believe them to be you may rely on my disinterested sympathy and co-operation.

very truly
Your friend
Will. B. Rodman[1]

[Endorsed] File

Z B V

[1]Jurist William Blount Rodman, appointed by President Davis in 1863 to a military court in Richmond with jurisdiction to try military offenses by soldiers below the rank of brigadier general. Although considered a staunch Democrat and states' rights and secession supporter before the war, after the conflict he cooperated with the Republicans, serving as a member of the state's Constitutional Convention of 1868 and supreme court, 1868–1879. Samuel A. Ashe, Stephen B. Weeks, and Charles L. Van Noppen, eds., *Biographical History of North Carolina*, 8 vols. (Greensboro: Charles L. Van Noppen, 1905–1917), 3:344–354; Cheney, *North Carolina Government*, 575, 588n.

—————

James A. Seddon to ZBV　　　　A&H:GP

[*With enclosure*]

Confederate States of America,
War Department,
Richmond, Va. Jan 8, 1863.

His Excellency Z. B. Vance,
Governor of North Carolina,
Raleigh, N.C.

Sir,

　　I have the honor to enclose a copy of a letter addressed to the Governor of Virginia, which will indicate to you the measures which have been agreed upon between his Excellency and the Department, to meet the existing emergency.

May I not suggest to your Excellency the importance of similar action in North Carolina, to aid in repelling the threatened movement of the enemy upon the Railroad connections in your State?

> With high consideration
> Your obt. servt.
> James A Seddon
> Secretary of War

[*Enclosure*]

James A. Seddon to John Letcher   A&H:GP

> (Copy.)

> Confederate States of America,
> War Department,
> Richmond, Va. Jan 8th. 1863.

His Excy. John Letcher,
Govr. of Va

Sir,
    In view of the menacing movements of the Enemy in North Carolina, with the intent of striking at the Railroad connections in that State, and perhaps of invading Virginia, I am instructed by the President respectfully to suggest to your consideration the propriety of calling out the militia in all the counties near to the North Carolina Line, in preparation to aid in repelling any such enterprise. The call might be limited to those of the exempted classes and those above the age of forty, at the same time this Department will call on all subject to the Conscript law in such counties to come forward and report at suitable places of rendezvous. Thus the whole arm bearing popoluation may be promptly commanded for the temporary emergency.

> With high consideration & esteem
> Most respectfully Yrs
> James A. Seddon
> Sec of War

James A. Seddon to ZBV   A&H:VanPC
[*With enclosure*]

Confederate States of America,
War Department,
Richmond, Va. Jany. 8th. 1863

His Excy.
Z. B. Vance
Govr. of N.C.

Sir

I send you herewith an extract from a letter of Genl. Ro E. Lee just received. It explains his visions in relation to the threatened movements of the enemy in your State and his mobility to supply the reinforcements which would be desirable for your defense. You will observe that he like myself relies in the existing deficiency of regular troops on the patriotism and valor of the citizens of your State and seeks to know whether the presence of one of his most distinguished Generals, General D. H. Hill[1] of your State might not prove advantageous in moving and stimulating the people and in counselling and cooperating with the State Authorities. On this subject, I wish to defer to your judgment and wishes of which I should be pleased to be advised. Before receiving this letter from Genl. Lee, I had taken the liberty respectfully to suggest for your consideration a call I had made on the Govr. of Va. for the aid of the militia and to request if it met your approbation, that a similar call should be made in N C by the State on its militia and by the Con. Governmt. on the conscripts—By such means, I hope adequate aid may be obtained to repel the threatened invasion of your State

With high respect & esteem
Very Truly Yrs
James A Seddon
Secy of War

[1]Daniel Harvey Hill soon assumed command in eastern North Carolina. He was called to defend Richmond during the Gettysburg campaign of July and then transferred to the Army of Tennessee. *Dictionary of North Carolina Biography*, s.v. "Hill, Daniel Harvey."

[*Enclosure*]

Robert E. Lee to James A. Seddon A&H:VanPC

Copy

Head Quarters Army N. Va.
5th. January, 1863

The Hon. Secretary of War
Richmond,

Sir,

I have to thank you for your long explanatory letter of the 3d. inst. In relation to operations in North Carolina, owing to the positions of the enemy, the features of the country, and the strength of our army in that State, we can only at present expect to act on the defensive. I hope we shall be able to obtain troops for that purpose. I have relied much on the troops of that State turning out for its defense, and have heretofore found that they have cheerfully and promptly done so, when necessity required. If you think any benefit will be derived by sending an officer to Raleigh to inspirit or encourage the people, I will detach from this army, Major Genl. D. H. Hill, a native of North Carolina, and a most valuable officer, for the purpose. By cooperating with the Governor and State authorities, great advantage might be gained. At this distance, I do not see how offensive operations could be undertaken with advantage, as the most we could hope for would be to drive the enemy to his gunboats, where he would be safe. The assignment therefore of any of our active force to North Carolina would be to withdraw them from the field of operations where, as far as I can yet discover, they may be / much/ needed. Genl. Burnside's[1] army is increasing rather than diminishing. The troops from in front of Washington, and the Upper Potomac, that have not made a junction with him have been moved down towards Stafford. Genl. [*Henry W.*] Slocum's Division is at Accoquan and Dumfries, General [*Franz*] Sigel's corps is at Stafford C. H., Genl. [*Robert H.*] Milroy has moved down as far as Martinsburg. From the letter of Mr. Jones,[2] which you sent me, it seems that reinforcements from Yorktown and Gloucester are being forwarded to him. I have not however yet heard of their arrival. It is very clear that Genl. Burnside will not advance towards Richmond unless he is reinforced. If he determines to go into winter quarters, I think it probable that a part of his force may be sent South of James river, but if he does not, he must be strengthened rather than weakened. Before the battle of the 13th. of Dec. I think his force could not have been less than one hundred and twenty thousand men. It may have been more. Since then, Genls. Sigel's, Slocum's and [*John W.*] Geary's forces have joined him. Taking the lowest number, his force is double that of this army. You can judge then of the propriety of weakening it, if it is to keep the field. I have always believed that Genl. Foster's[3] force has been much overrated. The reports from citizens, however intelligent and honest, cannot be relied on. Had Genl. Foster received all the reinforcements that have been reported since this army recrossed the Potomac, he ought to have the largest /Federal/ army now in the field. I am not certain that he will attempt any expedition, except those of a predatory character. I think he will rather be deterred, than encouraged, by the result of his late expedition, especially when he considers the probability of reinforcements being sent to North Carolina. It is as natural that he should be preparing for defense as offense. It is proper, however, that we should be prepared, and we ought to concentrate there as large a force as possible; and to be successful in our operations our officers must be bold and energetic. Information should be obtained by our own scouts, men accustomed to see things as they are, and not liable to excitement or exaggeration.

> I have the honor to be
> With great respect
> Your obdt. servt.
> (signed)   R. E. Lee
> Genl

[1]Ambrose Everett Burnside commanded the Federal army in eastern North Carolina until July 1862, when he left with 7,000 troops to reinforce General George B. McClellan threatening Richmond. After the Battle of Antietam in autumn 1862 he replaced McClellan as commander of the Army of the Potomac. Boatner, *Civil War Dictionary*, 107; Barrett, *Civil War in North Carolina*, 128.

[2]John Beauchamp Jones, War Department clerk and diarist. *Dictionary of American Biography*, s.v. "Jones, John Beauchamp."

[3]John Gray Foster replaced Burnside in North Carolina.

James A. Seddon to ZBV   A&H:GP

> Confederate States of America,
> War Department,
> Richmond, Va. Jany 9 1863

His Excellency
Z B Vance
Governor of N.C.

Sir

Your letter of the 6th Inst[1] has been rec'd. By an act of the late Session of Congress (No [illegible]) the President was authorized & empowered to receive into the service companies or regiments that might be formed in such places as to which the conscription acts had been suspended or could not be enforced by reason of the occupation of the enemy, under & according to the 1st. & 2nd. sections of the act of the 8th. of May 1861 providing for the raising of additional forces to serve during the war. The department will under the terms of that act accept companies or other organisations that may be formed under it, by the direction of your Excellency.

Very Respectfully
Yr obt Sevt
James A Seddon
Secretary of War

¹In this volume.

ZBV to James A. Seddon   A&H:GLB

[Telegram]

Telegraphic
Raleigh Jany 10th. 1863

Hon James A. Seddon
Richmond Va.

Genl. Smith don't favor calling out the Militia. Can you furnish Arms if I call them out?

I can do so if you prefer it. Answer at once.

Z. B. Vance

John M. Worth to ZBV   A&H:GP

Wilmington N.C. Jany 12/63

Gov. Z. B. Vance

Dear Sir

I herewith report to you the result of my operations as Salt Comr. I have rec'd

from the State Treasury	$ 61,741.07
Sales of Salt	83,668.55
	$145,409.62
I have paid out	142,083.01
& have cash on hand	3,326.61
	$145,409.62

I have on hand Provisions that cost about $3,000.00

Debts due from County Agents $20,000 & Salt enough on hand to pay all the debts against me. I am now making 300 bushels per day—with pans enough up to reach 350 Bus per day—At present and for the past week the Military

Authorities have had my Steam Boat that supplies the Riverside Works with Water—it is a drawback of 80 bushels per day. I hope they will soon return the Boat, but have no assurance of that. I am selling the Salt now at $5, per bushel, and if allowed to go on without interruption believe that in four months I can pay back all the money drawn from the Treasury.

At a meeting held on the coast—at your request—by the Salt makers—it was decided that it costs $8, pr bushel to make Salt. I have no advantage over them except the labor of conscripts—which cannot amount to 50 on the bushel.

For some time it has been impossible to ship Salt on either the Wiln. & Weldon or Wiln. & Manchester Roads, and I have sent none than the proper proportion of Salt to Counties that could be reached by the Cape Fear River and the Wiln. Charlotte & Rutherford R. Road.

I will make up to the other counties as soon as it can be shipped. I deemed it unwise to keep Salt here while threatened by the enemy. I have and shall still make every exertion to make all the Salt I can—it is now abundant in this Market and selling from 8 to $10, pr bushel.

Several of the Counties on and near the Wiln. & Weldon R. Road are suffering for Salt and cannot get it for the want of transportation. If you could send a train for that purpose it would be a very great relief to the people

> Very Respectfully
> Your Obt Servt
> J M Worth[1]
> Salt Comr.

[Endorsed] Copy & file For Salt Committee—

ZBV

[1]John Milton Worth, state salt commissioner, former state senator, and postwar treasurer of North Carolina. Ashe, Weeks, and Van Noppen, *Biographical History*, 3:454–560.

ZBV to James A. Seddon   A&H:GLB

> State of North Carolina
> Executive Department
> Raleigh Jany. 15th. 1863

Hon J. A. Seddon
Richmond Va.

Sir

My Adjt. Genl. J. G. Martin had the honor to enclose you on the 13th. a copy of an order issued from his office for the organization of the Militia force of twenty seven counties, being all east of this place. Genl. Smith has been notified of this action and if desired they will be promptly sent to report to him. You are aware, I suppose that he does not desire them.

Permit me to ask your concurrence in a plan we desire to adopt here for the arrest of deserters and recreant conscripts. It is to ask you to send home some one of our weakest regiments with yet a complement of efficient officers, to be stationed at some central point, where it could cooperate with and take charge of our Militia Patrols. We need an addition to a few regular troops, especially efficient officers to take charge of the various detachments. In this way the regiments could soon fill up its own ranks with conscripts and if necessary return to duty and another one sent.[1]

Should this be practicable and meet your approbation I would respectfully suggest the sending of the 16th. No. Ca. Regt., Col. John S. McElroy,[2] now near Fredericksburg

> Most Respectfully
> Yr. obt. Svt.
> Z. B. Vance

[1]Not until autumn 1863 did the War Department adopt ZBV's suggestion and dispatch North Carolina troops, commanded by Brigadier General Robert Frederick Hoke, back to the state to arrest deserters and draft-dodgers. Barrett, *Civil War in North Carolina*, 191–192. See also James A. Seddon to ZBV, February 9, in this volume.

[2]Continued to command the Sixteenth Regiment in Virginia. He was wounded at Chancellorsville in May and absent wounded until his resignation, December 8, 1863. Louis H. Manarin and Weymouth T. Jordan, Jr., comps., *North Carolina Troops, 1861–1865: A Roster*, 13 vols. to date (Raleigh: Division of Archives and History, Department of Cultural Resources, 1966–), 6:10.

John L. Peyton to ZBV   A&H:GP

Paris January 15th. 1863.

His Excellency
Gov Vance
Raleigh N.C.

Sir

In accordance with the terms of an agency conferred upon me for & in behalf of the State of N.C. the nature of which may be seen from a copy of the papers on file in the Executive department at Raleigh, I left Charleston S.C. on the 26th. of Oct 1861 under authority from the Secretary of the Navy in the Confederate States Steamer "*Nashville*" & arrived in England on the 21st. of November.

No arms were then to be had, but I gave an order to a Manufacturer, who delivered to me on two separate occasions 1760 long Enfield Rifles, with bayo-nets, nipple keys, moulds etc: etc: for which, including freight to Nassau & in-surance I paid out the sum of £6500. sterling placed in my hands by the State authorities £6285.11.6 which left a ballance of £211.2.6 in my hands after paying £3.6.0 to the Bank the English tax on the foreign bills of exchange, which sum of £211.2.6 I retained in part payment of the last half of the sum of £500. agreed to be paid to me for my services & one half of which, to wit; $1250 had been paid to me before leaving Raleigh, which leaves due to me from the State, £38.17.6. But this is not the object of my letter.

I shipped the arms from London nearly twelve months ago, viz on the 30th. of Jany 1862, on board the Steamship "Southwick" bound for Nassau New Prov-idence, where they were consigned to Henry Adderly & Co, from whom I have a letter informing me of their safe arrival there, & that they were reshipped for the Confederacy & I presume for Charleston (tho they do not say so) in the vessels & at the times following, that is to say,

76 cases 20 rifles each in the	"Nashville"	5	April/62
5 " " " " " "	"Mi[nks]"	19	May "
7 " " " " " "	"Cecile"	20	" "

They do not state whether they reached the Confederacy nor have I ever recd. from Gov Clark[1] or yourself any acknowledgment of their receipt, tho' I hope & believe that they have reached their destination, as I have never seen mentioned the capture of any of the vessels above mentioned. I should feel better satisfied however to be aprised by Your Excellency.

I was not able to carry out that portion of the contract providing for the purchase of arms & munitions to the extent of $200,000 on credit, & to be paid for on delivery in a Confederate port. The fact that the State refused to take any part of the risk of running the Blockade, but threw the whole of it upon the sellers of the articles, while the Confederacy was taking the *whole risk*, defeated this matter. Had the State sent out a few hundred thousand dollars of her six pr. ct. bonds having 30 yrs to run I might have bought the articles by depositing them as collateral security or sold them at about 35 pr.ct discount. I could do the same now. N.C. bonds can be so used when Confederate bonds wd. not be available. The first will be taken, but not the last, until our independence is acknowledged. I mention these facts that you may know how to proceed if the State sd. now or at any future time desire to buy in Europe either arms, munitions, Blankets, hat, shoes uniforms or the like & I avail my self of the opportunity of writing to tender my services to the State if she should need any arrangements to be made—any such stocks sold any such purchases made. A letter will always reach me addressed to the care of "*John Wilson Esq 93 Great Russell Street Blooms-bury London*".

The intelligence of the defeat & flight of Burnside[2] has been recd. here with every demonstration of pleasure; & the backbone of the Northern war party is considered as broken. Lincoln's proclamation declaring the negroes free where his edict will be about to use his own language, as effective as a "Papal bull against a comet" & retaining men in slavery where he has power to give them liberty is regarded as on a par with the rest of his <*illegible*> acts & has excited the most general & profound detestation. But there will not yet be a recognition of the South. England is the stumbling block in our way. The English people, I believe sympathize with us, that is to say all but the Exeter Hall Party,[3] but the government is too well pleased to see both North & South exhausted to stop the strife. Besides the longer it lasts the greater will be the development of the cotton production of India & the rest of the world, which England delights to witness, as it tends to make her independent of the Confederacy. The people of the South will I trust be no longer deceived by such false hopes–will realize that they have no friends among the crown heads of Europe—that they must rely upon themselves for deliverance from the hated thraldom of the Yankee Union Similar success to that of Fredericksburg will do more to bring about the solution of our difficulties than all the powers of the Earth. None of the governments of Europe have ever prosposed to mediate because they cared any thing for either North or South, but simply because of the distress among their cotton operatives, which /Excited/ their serious alarm. This is what has stimulated the Emperor Napoleon for starvation and revolution are synonymous terms in France. But that he may not be urged faster than he desires in his scheme of American mediation lest it may embroil him with the U.S. & affect his *role* in Mexico he has just demanded of his Chamber of Deputies a large grant of funds to relieve the distress prevailing in the cotton manufacturing districts, & he & all the leading men of the Country are heading lists for voluntary subscriptions, by which enormous sum will no doubt be raised, where the accumulations of wealth are so vast as in this country. I regret to say therefore that I see no prospect of any efforts being made in Europe to bring the war to a close for an indeffinite period in the future.

> With sentiments of respect
> I have the honor to be
> Your Obt Sevt
> John L. Peyton[4]

P.S. Feb. 15th. 1863.

The views above expressed a month ago are confirmed by the speeches at the opening of the British Parliament & when they are seen at Richd. I think the C.S. govt. will feel that self respect demands the recall of our commissioner.[5] I think it would be our best policy to withdraw the whole. It is simply rediculous to have them in Spain & in Brussels when Europe has agreed to wait for the action of England & France.

---

[1]Henry Toole Clark preceded ZBV as governor. *Dictionary of North Carolina Biography*, s.v. "Clark, Henry Toole."

[2]At Fredericksburg, Va., December 1862.

[3]An evangelical antislavery group.

[4]John Lewis Peyton, agent in England to purchase arms and supplies for North Carolina. See John Lewis Peyton, *The American Crisis: Or, Pages from the Note-Book of a State Agent during the Civil War*, 2 vols. (London: Saunders, Otley, and Co., 1867).

[5]James Murray Mason remained Confederate diplomatic commissioner to England until the war's end. *Dictionary of American Biography*, s.v. "Mason, James Murray."

Duncan K. McRae to ZBV   A&H:GP

Nassau—
Jany. 19th./63

Governor

I have an opportunity to write you by a vessel to leave to morrow—

After all sorts of detentions and difficulties I at last have succeeded in reaching this place and shall proceed as soon as possible to the place of destination—There I expect to join Mr. S.[1]

There are some articles of importance here which I might send by an early opportunity if I can dispose of some of the scrip—which I have a fair prospect of doing—Should I dispose of it—I shall take the responsibility of doing so as the prices will be cheaper when put to you at a Confederate port than if sent by the terms of the contract—I am assured by the most substantial news that I shall find a good market for the script—tho it may be necessary to go beyond the point named—I am satisfied that the *plan started on, is not* practicable—The blockade is now so successfully run by *certain owners*—with steamers—as to make it unwise to adopt any other mode—These owners and their agent here have in the most cordial terms assured me—that freight destined for the use of the state shall always have preference of private freight and at half price—say at present 15 pounds sterling per ton. A calculation on this basis will discover that the cost taking into consideration the insurance of said vessels will be less than by that mode—The regular & numerous steamers from Europe direct to this place and the facility afforded Govt freight—*or state*, renders it easy to put goods here & at reasonable prices—and when here—the same facilities daily increasing–if we hold Wn. & Ch—will put them in port at home—

So if Mr S. has not satisfactory evidence of his ability to execute the contract in terms—I shall in the discretion allowed me urge a change so as to put the goods in separate parcels here and from here by several steamers—in limited quantity on each to confederate ports. There is no news here–except the stranding of a Yankee transport near here with a loss of a large number of horses.

I shall probably be obliged to go to Europe to sell the scrip—I shall at once advise you of my success—and as soon as I can be more useful in the state I beg you will advise me that I may hasten my return We have just learned today of the advance on Wilmington and we feel the deepest anxiety. I shall write you by another opportunity in a day or two by which time I expect to be able to leave here.

I am very Respty
D K McRae[2]

[1]George Nicholas Sanders, a promoter of questionable motives who contracted with North Carolina to go abroad to sell state naval store bonds and assist McRae in the purchase of supplies. *Dictionary of American Biography*, s.v. "Sanders, George Nicholas."

[2]Duncan Kirkland McRae, lawyer, politician, and Confederate colonel appointed by ZBV as special envoy to Europe to sell North Carolina cotton bonds and procure supplies. *Dictionary of North Carolina Biography*, s.v. "McRae, Duncan Kirkland."

ZBV to James A. Seddon   A&H:GLB

Raleigh 20th. Jany 1863

Hon. Jas. A. Seddon
Secty at War
Richmond

Let me beg you to send every available man, as I am sure the crisis is upon us in North Carolina[1]

Z. B. Vance

[1]A response to a Federal raid toward Goldsboro.

Henry Heth to ZBV   A&H:GP

[*Telegram*]

Knoxville
Jan 21 1863

Raleigh

Gov Vance
Capt Nelson attacked the tories of Laurel Killing thirteen (13) & capturing Twenty (20). He says the whole force does not exceed Sixty (60).[1] Should this estimation of their force be True I do not think it advisable to alter our plans

H. Heth[2]
Brig Genl Comdg

[*Endorsed*]

Answer.

Gen Heth,
Knoxville Tenn.

Yours recd. I hope you will not relax until the tories are crushed, but do not let our excited people deal too harshly with these misguided men. Please have the captured delivered to the proper authorities for trial.

Z. B. Vance

Mr Battle[3] will copy

[1]Early in 1863 a band of tories (Union sympathizers) and Confederate deserters from Shelton Laurel in Madison County pillaged the seat of Marshall, and Captain Nelson's company—part of the detachment led by Brig. Gen. William George Mackey Davis from the Department of East Tennessee—retaliated against the raiders. Later, units of the Sixty-fourth Regiment North Carolina Troops, commanded by Lt. Col. James A. Keith, massacred a number of unarmed prisoners and tortured their relatives. ZBV received news of the massacre in a letter of January 31 from Augustus S. Merrimon (in this volume). State and Confederate investigations ensued. For an account of the expedition and subsequent massacre, see Phillip Shaw Paludan, *Victims: A True Story of the Civil War* (Knoxville: University of Tennessee Press, 1981).

[2]Henry Heth, commander of Department of East Tennessee, ordered the Confederate troops to Madison County. Barrett, *Civil War in North Carolina*, 197–198; Paludan, *Victims*, 87–89.

[3]Richard Henry Battle, ZBV's private secretary. *Dictionary of North Carolina Biography*, s.v. "Battle, Richard Henry."

Gustavus W. Smith to ZBV   SHC:Palm

Goldsboro Jany. 21st. 1863

Gov. Z. B. Vance
Raleigh

My Dear Sir,

I send with this copies of two orders, one sending officers into the different Counties and Districts of the State. The other an order in regard to officers and soldiers, absent without leave or remaining away after their leave of absence has expired. Please give me the aid of your great personal influence with the people of the State, and also require the civil and military officers of the State to assist in bringing back to their places in the ranks all /who are/ absent without orders or legal authority.

I would suggest a Proclamation from you, and a stirring appeal to the soldiers and the people to rally now for the defense of their own homes and maintain the high and honorable distinction already acquired by North Carolina in this war upon the battle fields of Virginia and Maryland.

A strong and united effort on the part of the men of North Carolina will enable to drive the invader out of the State. Appeal to the ladies to make the unwilling men take their places at this hour upon the field of battle, under this influence actively exercised, the ranks will soon be filled and we can then bid defiance to the combined abolition cohorts of the world. I remain Governor with great respect

> Very Truly Your friend
> G. W. Smith
> Maj. General

ZBV to James A. Seddon   A&H:GLB

> Executive Department of N.C.
> Raleigh—Jany 22d. [1863]

Hon. Jas. A. Seddon
Secy of War,

My dear Sir,
   Your timely suggestion in regard to procuring the services of Gen. D. H. Hill[1] has been already acted upon. I have to thank you for it.

Permit me to call your attention to the matter of appointing officers in the N.C. Troops—The Executive of this State has heretofore exercised the right of filling all vacancies occurring in regiments originally raised for the War (not conscripted), which right has been acquiesced in by the War Department—A State Law provides how it shall be done. Latterly commissions have issued from your office to several of these regiments, producing some confusion, and rendering many dissatisfied because the order prescribed by our law was not observed.

Should the claim asserted by the Executive of this State to make these appointments, continue to be recognized, I beg to express the hope that you will permit no more such commissions to be issued

> With sincerest respect and Esteem
> I remain Yr. obt. Svt.
> Z. B. Vance

---

[1]January 8, in this volume.

ZBV to James A. Seddon   A&H:GP

Copy

Executive Department of No. Ca
Raleigh Jany. 22d. 1863.

Hon James A Seddon
Secty. of War

Dear Sir

It pains me to have to communicate with you so often in the character of a complainant The necessities of the case must be my apology.

There are a large lot of broken down Cavalry horses belonging I think to Genl Jenkin's[1] command, quartered in the Counties of Wilkes, Yadkin, Ash and Surry in this State. The officers controlling them are pressing corn and forage at prices less by one half than the current rates in that country. As that country was almost ruined by drouth last season, there will be the greatest difficulty in feeding the wives and children of the absent Soldiers.

I respectfully submit sir, that these horses ought not to be quartered in Sections, where they will cause distress. I am now purchasing corn at State expense in the East for the relief of that country. I would suggest that horses to recruit be sent to that region where there is a great abundance likely to fall into the hands of the enemy, to forage under the protection of our troops. Earnestly hoping that you will see proper to order the removal of these horses, I remain

Most Respectfully
Yr. obt servt.
Z. B. Vance

[1]Albert Gallatin Jenkins, commanding a cavalry brigade in western Virginia. *Dictionary of American Biography*, s.v. "Jenkins, Albert Gallatin."

Jacob C. Barnhardt to ZBV   A&H:GP

Headquarters 84th. Regmt N C M
Pioneer Mills NC Jany 23rd./63

Gov Z B Vance

Dear Sir

Some two months ago I ordered two deserters from the Army to meet me, to return to their Regmt The Capt of the Co in which they resided reported that they had gone to rejoin their Cos. But never reported /as I learned afterwards/ The Captain to-day informs me that it is *Suspected* that they are secreted in the neighborhood & at their home and are probably kept under lock & key to prevent any one from seeing them He asked me whether he should break locks & doors where he suspected them to be secreted and could not get admittance otherwise Not being able to answer the question with certainty I told him I would refer the matter to you for instruction as I did not wish to get him into any dificulty You will please answer as early as practable and your orders will be obliged

> Your Humble Servt.
> Jac. C. Barnhardt Col
> 84th. Regmt N C M

[*Endorsed*] The Captain can not break locks & doors unless he *knows* the parties are in—He ought to have arrested them at the start

> Z B V

ZBV to Gustavus W. Smith   A&H:VanPC

> *Copy*

> State of North Carolina
> Executive Department
> Raleigh Jany. 24th. 1863.

Genl. G. W. Smith
Goldsboro

My Dear Sir

Yours accompanying the orders &c received this morning.[1] My proclamation[2] will appear in the morning papers, and every thing that I can, shall be done.

I recd. information this morning from Wilmington that Genl. Whiting[3] had Seized all the teams, hands and boats belonging to the State Salt Agent and completely stopped the works. This is a great calamity to our people, to stop the making of 350 bushels of Salt per day right in the midst of pork packing season.

I can scarcely conceive of any such emergency as would justify it. A little trouble on the part of Genl. Whiting's Quarter Master would have enabled him to press teams in the adjacent counties, and a requisition upon me for labor would have furnished as much as he wanted, as was done with Col. Sterns.

Let me ask you to have these hands and teams restored to the Agent, unless it be impossible to supply their places in time. It is almost as important to the State, as the safety of the city, as our people cannot live without the Salt.

> Most Truly Yrs.
> (Signed)   Z. B. Vance.

---

[1]January 21, in this volume.

[2]January 26, in this volume.

[3]William Henry Chase Whiting, commander of military district of Wilmington. *Dictionary of American Biography*, s.v. "Whiting, William Henry Chase."

Milledge L. Bonham to ZBV A&H:GP

State of South Carolina.
Head Quarters.
Columbia January 25th. 1863

To His Excellency
Governor Z. B. Vance

Dear Sir

Yours of January 3d. enclosing Proclamation of November 26th. 1862[1] has been received. Governor Pickens[2] doubtless had not seen a copy when he used the expression attributed to him if any such was made. You are correct in supposing that I know you too well to believe you capable of wishing to act unneighborly or unjustly towards a Sister State. It is not improbable that other States will have to adopt the same means of repressing speculation which you have adopted. I take this occasion to say to you that I shall be glad to receive from you by telegram and otherwise the earliest information of the movements of the enemy in your State, wherever made, compatible with the press upon your time and the public interest and I will cheerfully reciprocate. It occurs to me it is desirable we should preserve such relations during our terms. Such information promptly conveyed may prove mutually beneficial to our States.

Yours very truly
M. L. Bonham[3]

[1]Proclamation by ZBV prohibiting the export of certain provisions and essential articles from North Carolina. See Johnston, *Papers of Vance*, 1:404–405.

[2]Francis Wilkinson Pickens, South Carolina governor, 1861–1862. *Dictionary of American Biography*, s.v. "Pickens, Francis Wilkinson."

[3]Milledge Luke Bonham, South Carolina governor, 1863–1864. *Dictionary of American Biography*, s.v. "Bonham, Milledge Luke."

Gustavus W. Smith to ZBV SHC:Van

Goldsboro Jany. 26th. 1863

Governor Z. B. Vance
Raleigh

My Dear Sir

Your letter calling attention to the impressment of transportation &c. by Gen. Whiting[1] was recvd. yesterday and copy at once forwarded to Gen. Whiting, requesting that he would except in expectation of immediate attack not hold the transportation, and that he would allow the Salt manufactory to proceed whenever practicable.

The letter of your Aid Mr. Barnes,[2] has been forwarded to the Dept. at Richmond approved, requesting authority to raise the guides referred to.

I was at Kinston yesterday. Nothing important from the enemy, except they have doubled the guards, and our secret agents have found it impossible to pass. I will keep you informed of important news. A cavalry company will be ordered to report to you, and I have authorised Gen. French[3] to send a force to Wilkes County & that section—[4] A man has been caught attempting to get there with his arms, ammunition &c. last Wednesday I think. He has been tried, convicted and will be executed today.

> Very Respectfully & Truly Yours
> G. W. Smith
> Maj. Gen.

[Endorsed] Copy & file

Z B V

¹January 24, in this volume.

²David Alexander Barnes. Dictionary of North Carolina Biography, s.v. "Barnes, David Alexander."

³Samuel Gibbs French, district commander in the Department of North Carolina and Southern Virginia. Boatner, Civil War Dictionary, 315.

⁴The area that included eastern Wilkes County was known as the Quaker Belt and became the locale for civil disobedience and violence by deserters, dissenters, and unionists. See William T. Auman, "Neighbor against Neighbor: The Inner Civil War in the Randolph County Area of Confederate North Carolina," North Carolina Historical Review 61 (January 1984): 59–92.

ZBV to James A. Seddon   A&H:GLB

> State of North Carolina—
> Executive Department
> Raleigh Jany. 26th. 1863

Hon James A. Seddon
Sec'y of War
Richmond, Va.

Sir

I had the honor to complain to his Excellency the President, and your immediate predecessor Mr. Randolph,[1] in regard to the manner of enforcing the

Conscript Act in this State, & of disposing of the men in regiments, during the month of October last.[2] I am compelled again, greatly to my regret, to complain of the appointment of Col. August[3] as Commandant of Conscripts for North Carolina, who has recently assumed command here.

Merely alluding to the obvious impropriety and bad policy, of wounding the sensibilities of our people by the appointment of a citizen of another State to execute a law, both harsh & odious, I wish to say Sir, in all candor that it smacks of discourtesy to our people to say the least of it. Having furnished as many (if not more) troops for the service of the Confederacy, as any State, and being, as I was assured by the President, far ahead of all others in the number raised under the Conscript law—the people of this State have justly felt mortified in seeing these troops commanded by citizens of other States to the exclusion of the claims of their own. This feeling is increased & heightened into a very general indignation when it is thus officially announced that North Carolina has no man in her borders fit to command her own Conscripts, though scores of her noblest sons & best officers are now at home with mutilated limbs and shattered constitutions

Without the slightest prejudice against either Col. August or the State from which he comes, I protest against his appointment as both unjust & impolitic. Having submitted in silence to the many, very many acts of the Administration, heretofore, so calculated to wound that pride, which North Carolina is so pardonable for entertaining, it is my duty to inform you that if persisted in, the appointment of strangers to all the positions in this State and over her troops, will cause a feeling throughout her whole borders, which it is my great desire to avoid.

Trusting Sir, that you can appreciate the feelings of our people, and will pardon the frankness with which I have spoken, I have the honor to remain—

> Most respectfully
> Yr. obt. Svt.
> Z. B. Vance

[1]George Wythe Randolph. *Dictionary of American Biography*, s.v. "Randolph, George Wythe."

[2]See Johnston, *Papers of Vance*, 1:252–253. The second Confederate conscription act, of September 1862, superceded the first, passed in April, by increasing the draft ages from 18 through 35 to 18 through 45.

[3]Thomas P. August, of Virginia. Barrett, *Civil War in North Carolina*, 185.

Proclamation by ZBV   A&H:GLB

A Proclamation

Whereas, it has been made known to me that a large number of soldiers from our Armies are absent from their colors without proper leave in this /the/ hour of our greatest need, and it being confidently believed that a large majority of such, were impelled to this by a natural and almost irresistable desire to see their friends & homes once more after so long an absence, and not because of a cowardly determination to leave their brave comrades to share all the dangers and hardships of the field alone. And whereas, Maj Genl. G. W. Smith in command of the Department of North Carolina, by consent of the Secretary of War, has published an order declaring that all who may voluntarily return to duty by the 10th. day of February next, shall be received into their several commands with no other punishment than a forfeiture of their pay for the time they have been absent without leave: and declaring further that all who do not so return by the said 10th. day of February, shall, when apprehended, be tried for desertion, and upon conviction be made to suffer death:

Now therefore, I, Zebulon B. Vance Governor of the State of North Carolina, do issue this my proclamation to all soldiers from this State, serving in the Army of the Confederacy, who are now illegally absent from their colors, commending them to return to duty with their comrades, and exhorting them to avail themselves of this opportunity of saving their friends from the disgrace and infamy which will cling forever to the name of a deserter from his country's cause and themselves from a felons death. Many after carrying their country's flag in triumph through various bloody conflicts and making themselves a name, of which their childrens, children might have been justly proud, have forfeited it all by absenting themselves at a moment when their own State is invaded, and about to be desolated by a brutal, half savage foe—Now is the time to reinstate themselves, by a prompt return to duty. I appeal to them to stand by their country yet a little longer, and not to sully by desertion the bright and glorious reputation of the State, which they have helped to win on a hundred hard fought fields: And I appeal to all good and loyal citizens throughout the State to give their influence to induce these men to return—Let no one unmoved by this appeal to his patriotism and honor, suppose that he can remain at home with impunity; the full powers of the State authorities, aided if need be by the Confederacy, shall be put in force to arrest him and bring him to punishment after the 10th. day of February next,[1] and there shall be no rest for the deserter in the borders of North Carolina. And let none excuse their desertion by declaring that they go home to take care of their families, they will add nothing to the comforts of their families by hiding like guilty men in the wood by day and by plundering their neighbors by night, they only bring shame and suffering upon the heads of the innocent, and their little children, when grey headed old men, will have the finger of scorn pointed at them, and the bitter taunt will ring in their ears, "Your father skulked in the woods, to keep from fighting for his country.

The State is now trying to provide food for your families, and each county is making a similar provision, and as your Chief Magistrate, I promise you that the wife & child of the soldiers who are in the Army doing his duty, shall share the last bushel of meal & pound of meat in the State.

Let ever patriot in the land assist with all his influence in the execution of this proclamation, and our victorious ranks will again be filled, and our country soon be rid of the enemy

In witness thereof Zebulon B. Vance, our governor, Captain General and Commander-in-chief hath signed these presents and caused the Great Seal of the State to be affixed.

Done at our City of Raleigh on the 26th. day of January in the year of our Lord 1863

Z. B. Vance

[1]Subsequently extended to March 5.

ZBV *to John Letcher*   A&H:GLB

State of North Carolina
Executive Department
Raleigh Jany. 27th. 1863

To His Excellency
John Letcher
Governor of Virginia

Dear Sir

I have recently received information that a Captain Oliver of the Virginia State Line is recruiting conscripts in Ash County in this State, and that a Captain Pauly in the same service is recruiting conscripts and deserters in Ash and Alleghany Counties. It is important that such proceedings should not be permitted to continue and I am satisfied that your Excellency will cheerfully aid me in attaining this result.

I have therefore to request that your Excellency will direct such orders to be issued as will cause all such men hereafter enlisted to be returned to their appropriate commands and will prevent others being hereafter recruited by these officers[1]

With assurances of high regard
I am your obedient Servant
Z. B. Vance

[1]For responses, see William H. Richardson to ZBV, January 31, and David A. Barnes to William H. Richardson, February 2, in this volume.

ZBV to William J. Hawkins   A&H:GLB

State of North Carolina
Executive Department
Raleigh Jany. 27th. 1863

Dr. W. J. Hawkins[1]
President &c

Sir

After looking at the working of things I have concluded that the State Cotton and Corn at Halifax and Enfield will never be hauled. As it is of the very greatest consequence to the state that both should be got away, I want you to stop the night train and *haul* the Corn and Cotton, let the consequences be what they may unless it can be done speedily without stopping this train

Very respectfully
Yr. obt. Svt.
Z. B. Vance

[1]William Joseph Hawkins, president of the Raleigh and Gaston Railroad. *Dictionary of North Carolina Biography*, s.v. "Hawkins, William Joseph."

Robert B. Vance to ZBV   A&H:VanPC

Shelbyville, Tenn.
Jany 28th. 1863

Dear Brother:

Your letter afforded much pleasure, and bro't vividly to mind times that are past & gone never to return. In all the ups and downs that have befallen us in this life, I have never forgotten our boyhood. The Old farm & orchard, the roaring French Broad, the rocky mountains, the fishing frolics and mad swimming spells in the river—these all occur to my mind often, and I think how changed things are now. "When I was a child, I tho't as a child & spake as a child, but now that I am a man, I have put away childish things." Previous to getting your letter I had written you touching the Brigadiers place, stating that 39th. N.C. was with me.[1] Since then I have also asked for the 60th. N.C. approved by Maj Gen McCown[2] & I judge by Gen Cheatam,[3] comdg our corps at present. I am obliged to you for getting the Legislature to interfere, altho the petition may not carry the point. A letter from you to Genl Bragg[4] would have weight. If it did not get my Brigadier commission, it would at least (I think) keep me in command of the Brigade. We have no news of importance. There was pretty warm firing this morning on Murfreesboro pike, but what caused it we cannot tell. Morgan, Wheeler, Forrest & Wharton[5] are on the alert & it will be hard to trap them.

The Yankees will find it difficult to advance now, as the roads are awful. This shows the wisdom and sagacity of Gen Braggs movements. It would seem as if our falling back was unfortunate, but I think it was wise. The enemy to Murfreesboro had fine pikes from all directions & was closer to his *base*. Here he will soon strike dirt roads & the worst in the world, besides the country is eat up. Well we are of necessity *now* a defensive army, and when the enemy advances he will have to bring his supplies 55 miles, which is a heavy job & gives our cavalry a chance to give them "fits." So mote it be. Gen Bragg's Head qrs /are/ at Tullahonia Tenn. I am very pleasantly situated now—have a nice tent, stove, bedstead, table &c. and a fine Adjutant General. John Davidson[6] is near by & is as cheerful as ever. Harvey[7] is at Murfreesboro sick & wounded. I will write again soon. Judge Davidson[8] says never to mind that "waning"; that all will be right. Go ahead as you have began & my word for it all will be right. Tell sister Hattie[9] to write if you are busy.

> My love to all,
> affectionately
> Robert

[*Endorsed*] File private

Z B V

---

[1]Robert Brank Vance, brother of ZBV, commanded the Twenty-ninth Regiment North Carolina Troops, until January 1863 when he temporarily assumed command of the Second Brigade (including the Thirty-ninth Regiment) of his division of the Army of Tennessee. He was promoted to brigadier general and given permanent command of the brigade in March. Manarin and Jordan, *North Carolina Troops*, 8:235; Boatner, *Civil War Dictionary*, 866; Walter Clark, ed., *Histories of the Several Regiments and Battalions from North Carolina in the Great War, 1861–'65*, 5 vols. (Raleigh: State of N.C., 1901), 2:486–494.

[2]John Porter McCown, division commander. Jon L. Wakelyn, *Biographical Dictionary of the Confederacy* (Westport, Conn.: Greenwood Press, 1977), 295–296.

[3]Benjamin Franklin Cheatham, I Corps, Army of Tennessee. Wakelyn, *Biographical Dictionary of Confederacy*, 128–129.

[4]Braxton Bragg, commander of Army of Tennessee. *Dictionary of American Biography*, s.v. "Bragg, Braxton."

[5]John Tyler Morgan, Joseph Wheeler, Nathan Bedford Forrest, and John Austin Wharton. Wakelyn, *Biographical Dictionary of Confederacy*, 189–190, 325–326, 433–434.

[6]John Mitchell Davidson, paternal cousin of ZBV. Johnston, *Papers of Vance*, 1:7n.

[7]Hugh Harvey Davidson, brother of John Mitchell Davidson. Johnston, *Papers of Vance*, 1:7n.

[8]ZBV's cousin Allen Turner Davidson, lawyer, Confederate congressman, and member of the Council of State, 1864. *Dictionary of North Carolina Biography*, s.v. "Davidson, Allen Turner."

[9]Harriette Espy Vance, ZBV's wife. Johnston, *Papers of Vance*, 1:16n.

ZBV to John D. Whitford   A&H:Whit

State of North Carolina
Executive Department
Raleigh Jany. 28th. 1863

Col J D Whitford[1]
Prest. A & NCRR.
Goldsboro

My dear Sir,
   The bearer Lt Poindexter C.S.N. has been again to see me about the iron at B[*illegible*]'s Station. I have offered the Secy. of the Navy[2] all the iron on your Road from Kinston to New Berne, if they would only go & get it—That at B[*illegible*]'s station, I have understood you to say was necessary for repairing the roads & have refused to let it go on that account—I have referred the Lieutenant to you, if the iron is necessary to the efficiency of our roads, refuse to let it go, if you can do without it, let them have it. It seems to me though that the Government is able to get up that from below Kinston if half an effort was made.

Truly Yrs
Z. B. Vance

   [1]John Dalton Whitford, president of Atlantic and North Carolina Railroad. Johnston, *Papers of Vance*, 1:397n.
   [2]Stephen Russell Mallory. *Dictionary of American Biography*, s.v. "Mallory, Stephen Russell."

ZBV to William F. Lynch   A&H:GLB

State of North Carolina
Executive Department
Raleigh Jany. 28th. 1863

Flag Officer
W. F. Lynch[1]
Wilmington

My dear Sir
   Yours by Lieut. Commanding Poindexter C.S.N. has been recd. in regard to iron for the completion of the gun boats on the Roanoke.
   The question is an interesting one to me indeed. I have offered the whole of the iron of the Atlantic and N.C. Road within our lines below Kinston, some fifteen miles, but this you say cannot be got for want of transportation

The small amt. at [blank] Station, not enough for your purposes, is held by Col Whitford the Prest. for the repairs of his own and our other roads who have no reserved iron: and our roads as you are aware are fast wearing down under the great amount of running they are compelled to do. Such being the case, you may percieve my embarrassment—I am of course exceedingly anxious for the completion of the boats And the railroad men say to give up this Iron would soon render it impossible for them to repair and in case of such an accident (by no means unusual) as the burning of a bridge they would be powerless to rebuild. I have referred Lt. P. to Col Whitford again instructing him to give up the iron if in his opinion it can be safely done, otherwise to retain it.

I know what else to do for the best.

I am still confident in the opinion that on a proper application to Gen Smith, the iron below Kinston could be sucured and if so the whole difficulty would be solved

> Most Respectfully
> & Truly Yrs
> Z. B. Vance

[1]William Francis Lynch, commodore and commander of the Confederate naval force on the coast of North Carolina. *Dictionary of American Biography*, s.v. "Lynch, William Francis."

ZBV *to Jacob Siler*   SHC:Sil

> Executive Office
> Raleigh Jany 28th. 1863

Jacob Siler Esq
Agt for Cherokee Lands

My dear Sir

Your letter for the 19th.[1] has been received, making enquiry as to the manner of disposing of the funds in your hands under different acts of the Legislature.

I am of the opinion that you should meet the appropriation made by the act of the present Session, the language of the act itself would seem to imply as much, and the purpose of the appropriation—the repairs of certain bridges &c— would seem to intend an immediate and absolute expenditure of the money, and not that it should depend on some contingency.

I will sustain you in this construction at all events.

> Most respectfully & truly
> Z. B. Vance

[1]A&H:GP.

Albert G. Jenkins to ZBV   A&H:GP

Head Quarters Cavalry Brigade
Salem, January 28, 1863.

His Excellency Z. Vance
Governor of N. Carolina.

Sir:

I desire to call your attention to a matter of much concern to the public interest.

In order to enable the armies at Fredericksburg, Richmond and other points having R. Road communication with this section to obtain the necessary supplies of Corn &c, all the horses, mules &c of this Dept. have been sent to a considerable distance—to be foraged until Spring—from the line of this R. Road (Va & Tenn Road). In thus distributing these animals–after over-stocking almost every part of Virginia—it became a matter of necessity to send some of them to portions of North Carolina, where both grain and long forage were abundant. But unfortunately there is a great indisposition on the part of the people there, to sell their produce for Confederate money, at any price, and I desire to ask relief at your hands, in the form of authority of some kind, for impressment. This authority you can limit with such restrictions as will make it entirely certain that no injustice will be done to your people. If some step of this sort is not taken promptly, and we should be compelled in this portion of S.W.Va. to bring the horses in the service of the Govt. back to this section, and thus consume the forage which is essential to the wants of our armies elsewhere, it is manifest that the most serious detriment to the public service, must occur.

Knowing your disinterested patriotism not only from your public character, but also from a personal acquaintance, which I had the pleasure of having, while we were both members of the old Federal Congress, and your full and entire devotion to our cause, which is not the cause of a State but of the whole South, I have taken the liberty of addressing you upon this subject.

I shall forward this to you, after having referred it for the consideration of the General Commanding this Military Dept.

I am, Sir, Respectfully
Your obt. Servant.
A. G. Jenkins
Brigadier General

Samuel B. French to ZBV A&H:GP

Executive Department
Richmond January 30, 1863

To His Excellency
Z. B. Vance
Govr. of N.C.

Sir

I am instructed by Gov. Letcher to acknowledge the receipt of your favor of the 27th inst[1] & to inform your Excellency that the Adjutant General of the State has been directed to issue such orders as will require the return to your authority of any conscripts from North Carolina which may be in the State Line, also to prevent the further enlistment of conscripts from your State.

The Governor bids me to give to your Excellency the assurance of his high consideration

Most respectfully
S. Bassett French[2]
Col & A.D.C.

[*Endorsed*] Copy—

Z B V

[1]In this volume.
[2]Samuel Bassett French, also "extra aide-de-camp" to generals Robert E. Lee and Thomas J. Jackson. See Glenn C. Oldaker, comp., *Centennial Tales: Memoirs of Colonel "Chester" S. Bassett French, Extra Aide-de-Camp to Generals Lee and Jackson, the Army of Northern Virginia, 1861–1865* (New York: Carlton Press, 1962).

James A. Seddon to ZBV A&H:VanPC

Confederate States of America,
War Department,
Richmond, Va. Jany. 30th. 1863

His Excy. Z B Vance
Govr. of N.C

Sir

I am surprised to hear from one of your late letters[1] that you consider the Department to have interfered irregularly with the appointment of officers to some State Regiments from N. Carolina for the war—I am unconscious to what regiments or appointments you refer and certainly have had no intention of trenching on your perrogatives. One appointment alone that of Lieut Col Moore[2] to a Regiment to be composed, as at the time was directed, of a North Carolina battalion and of some conscripts then at Raleigh, was made by me, as from subsequent information I have, without sufficient care but it was done in supposed deference to your own wish on the representation you had desired the Regiment to be so formed and the particular officer appointed. If in this a mistake has been committed, it will be cheerfully corrected, but I should be pleased to learn first that you had not desired the appointment. You will also gratify me by informing me what regiments you regard as State Regiments to which your powers of appointment extend and on what ground the claim rests. I do not find or the Adj. G office any distinction of the kind made, nor can I learn that a claim of appointment has been appealed by you to any. I have the Honor to be with high consideration & esteem

Respectfully Yrs
James A Seddon
Secy of War

[1]January 22, in this volume.

[2]Benjamin R. Moore, adjutant, Sixteenth Regiment North Carolina Troops. Manarin and Jordan, *North Carolina Troops*, 6:10. See also Johnston, *Papers of Vance*, 1:456–459.

ZBV to Joseph E. Brown   A&H:GLB

State of North Carolina
Executive Department
Raleigh 30th. Jany. 1863

To Joseph E. Brown[1]
Governor of Georgia

Dear Sir

I have the honor to enclose herewith a copy of a Resolution passed by the Legislature of North Carolina in reference to the purchase of Machinery for the Manufactory of Cotton and Woollen cards.

I beg the favor of your early attention to this subject and request you will furnish me with the information desired, in relation to this important manufactory, which I learn has been in successful operation in your State

I am very respectfully
Your obt. Servt.
Z. B. Vance

[1]Joseph Emerson Brown. *Dictionary of American Biography*, s.v. "Brown, Joseph Emerson."

ZBV to John M. Davidson　　　　　　SHC:Dav

Executive Office
Raleigh N C Jany. 30 [1863]

Dear John:

Your letter of 7th. December was not opened until this moment. It with a large pile has been on my table sometime and the pressure on my time caused by the recent advance of the enemy has prevented its being attended to.

I have only time now to say that the Legislature has failed to comply with my recommendations about State troops and it is therefore out of my power to favor you with a position as I should have gladly done. I was very glad to hear from you—hope you got safely through the great battle, and should be pleased to receive news from you often. Hattie and children are well and send love. My regards to everybody.

Truly yours
Z. B. Vance

Augustus S. Merrimon to ZBV　　　　　　A&H:GP

Asheville N.C.
Jan'y. 31st. 1863.

Gov. Z. B. Vance.

Governor;

The Arms &c. have at length reached Asheville and I have turned the whole over to Col. W. R. Young,[1] in persueance of your instructions. I have forwarded his recp't. to Maj. T. D. Hogg.[2]

I learn that the Laurel expedition is about over. I can't give you any of the details of the affair. I suppose the proper officers will report to you. I learn that a number of *prisoners* were *shot* without any trial or hearing whatever. I hope this is not true, but if so, the parties guilty of so dark a crime should be punished. Humanity revolts at so savage a crime. Our Militia had nothing to do with what was done in Laurel. I am glad of this. It turns out that the Militia were not really needed. So I thought in the outset and advised our people, but they & Genl. Polk[3] Could not be satisfied without calling out the Militia.

Nothing new—All well.

I Am &c Yrs. Truly,
A. S. Merrimon[4]

[*Endorsed*] File

Z B V

[1]William R. Young, commander of 108th Regiment, North Carolina Militia. Johnston, *Papers of Vance*, 1:341n.

[2]Thomas Devereux Hogg, chief commissary of the Subsistence Department of North Carolina. *Dictionary of North Carolina Biography*, s.v. "Hogg, Thomas Devereux."

[3]Leonidas Polk, corps commander, Army of Tennessee. *Dictionary of American Biography*, s.v. "Polk, Leonidas."

[4]Augustus Summerfield Merrimon, lawyer and future U.S. senator and chief justice of the state supreme court. As solicitor of the Eighth District, he prosecuted the marauders who raided Marshall. *Dictionary of North Carolina Biography*, s.v. "Merrimon, Augustus Summerfield." This letter was the first news that ZBV received of the Shelton Laurel massacre. See also ZBV to Merrimon, February 9, in this volume.

William H. Richardson to ZBV   A&H:GLB

Adjutant Generals Office
January 31st. 1863

To His Excellency
Z B Vance
Governor of North Carolina

Sir

Pursuant to the instructions of the Governor of Virginia, I have the honor to transmit herewith, orders for the officers referred to in your letter of the 27th. inst.[1] to the Governor. And as the proper address of these officers is not known here, to request that your Excellency will cause them to be delivered.

These proceedings were without authority and unknown to the Governor, who begs your Excellency to be assured that no officer of the State of Virginia will be permitted to do any act in the State of North Carolina which is not sanctioned by yourself

I have the honor to be
With high respect
Your obt. Servt.
Wm. H. Richardson
A. G. V.

[1]In this volume.

ZBV to Jefferson Davis   Har:Van

State of North-Carolina—
Executive Department
Raleigh, Feb 2d. 1863

His Excellency
President Davis,

Sir,

I was both surprised and grieved to learn to day that it was your intention to [remove] Maj. Gen G. W. Smith from the command of this Dept.

It is rumored here that he is to be sent to Texas at the request of the [*faded*]tatives of that State. I know not [of] course how that is, but hope that the wishes of the people of this State will meet with as much consideration from your Excellency as any of [her] Sisters. The unanimous sentiment here, so far as it can be ascertained, is adverse to the removal of Gen Smith.

His great zeal in acquainting himself with the localities of our <of> coast; his thorough efforts to organize both our forces and transportation, together with his evident knowledge of and respect for our people had inspired universal confidence and esteem. Between himself and the State authorities there existed the most con[*faded*] and thorough accord in all respects, giving promise of the most beneficial results in the expected invasion of the enemy. A stranger would have to learn all these things over again, and might probably, though it is hardly possible, inspire the same confidence and give promise of the same results.

Permit /me/ to indulge the hope that you may find it not inconsistent with the public service to retain Gen. Smith in command of this Department. Should it be determined however to remove him, I beg we may not be disappointed in his successor. This Department is certainly intitled to a general of approved talent and experience.

I have the honor to be
Your Excellency's obt svt.
Z. B. Vance

[*Endorsed*] Feb 2, 1863 Governor Vance N. Car. Has heard it was intended to remove Genl. G. W. Smith from command of Dept. N. Car. & hopes that the Prest. will retain Genl. S. in the command, as he has the entire confidence of the people of N. Car.

Ans. It is not in present contemplation to remove Genl. Smith from his present position, his return to his Hd. Qrs. from the field was for considerations not connected with any disatisfaction[1] I am happy to receive the within impressions—Genl. D. H. Hill it is hoped will be able to serve his country in N.C.

Jeffn. Davis

Recd. Feb. 11, 1863

[1]Smith resigned his commission on February 17. For the organization and various commanders of the Department of North Carolina and Southern Virginia after his resignation, see Boatner, *Civil War Dictionary*, 599–600.

ZBV to Albert G. Jenkins   A&H:GLB

State of North Carolina
Executive Department
Raleigh Feby. 2d. 1863

Brig. Genl. A. G. Jenkins
Salem Va.

Sir

Your communication of the 28th. ulto.[1] asking for authority from me to impress Corn & forage for the use of a number of Calvary horses belonging to your command has been received.

I am sorry that I cannot consistently with the duty I owe my own people, comply with your request—The horses are unfortunately in the midst of a section which was almost ruined by drouth last summer which concurring with the diminished amount of labor in that region has produced such a scarcity of Corn as to render the certainty of suffering imminent among the women and children unless relief be afforded them. With this view I have been authorized by the Legislature and am now actually engaged in removing Corn from the Eastern counties up the line of our central road to prevent starvation there. So far therefore from granting authority to anyone to impress corn there, I had some days before the receipt of your letter addressed the Secy of War asking for the horses to be removed as a matter of humanity. I at the same time suggested that they be ordered into Eastern North Carolina, where corn is not only abundant but liable to be destroyed by the enemy and it is our object to consume as much of it as possible.

You do me no more than justice in your estimate of my desire to serve the cause in any possible way, which good opinion I hope will be in no wise changed when informed of my great anxiety to protect the wives & children of our soldiers from sufferings for want of bread.

Allow me to say that I am sure you are not aware of the conduct of the men in charge of these horses. I am informed by citizens that they are under no sort of controls. They feed their horses on the ground—wasting more than half in the mud, at night they ride them all over the country, frequently breaking open granaries, drinking & insulting citizens and making themselves a terror to the whole population. I trust you will enquire into these reports, and have the evil corrected if true.

Assuring you of my gratification in hearing directly from you after having read so much of your gallant exploits in N. Western Virginia, and hoping that some day we may be able under happier auspices to renew old associations

I have the honor to remain

> Most respectfully & Truly
> Yr. obt. Srvt
> Z. B. Vance

[1]In this volume.

David A. Barnes to William H. Richardson   A&H:GLB

> State of North Carolina
> Executive Department
> Raleigh Feby 2d. 1863

Adjutant General W H Richardson

Dear Sir

His Excellency Gov. Vance has received your communication of the 31st. of January[1] in reply to his letter,[2] and he directs me to say in reply that he is willing that conscripts who have been already recruited by Officers of the Virginia line and are now in actual service may remain. He desires however that the deserters may be returned and that your officers may in future desist from recruiting persons subject to conscription and deserters

I herewith return your orders to Captains Parsley and Oliver and you can modify them accordingly

> Yours very respectfully
> David A. Barnes
> Aid de Camp to the Governor

[1]In this volume.
[2]January 27, in this volume.

ZBV to William G. M. Davis   A&H:GLB

> State of North Carolina
> Executive Department
> Raleigh Feby 2d. 1863

Gen. G. W. M. Davis [sic]
Warm Springs N.C.

Sir

Yours giving an account of operations of yr. command in the mountains of this State[1] has been received. The result is quite satisfactory and I am especially

pleased to learn that there appears to be no regular organization of enemies to
the Government in that country. I was loath to believe so, and from the first was
of the opinion that the raid[2] was only for plunder and that the whole matter was
probably exaggerated. I hope now that quiet and order are restored in that region,
and have to return you my thanks for the very prompt and energetic aid offered
by your comand in producing this state of things.

I was fearful in the great excitement prevailing among our people, that the
misguided people of Laurel might be dealt too harshly with, and warned the
officers to be cool & just. I was therefore sorry to learn this morning, that Col
Allen[3] had hanged several of the captured prisoners. I hope this is not true, as it
would be much better to have them dealt with by the law.

In regard to removing them into Kentucky, I approve of the plan, provided
they desire to go. I would not wish however to excite the women & children or
old men, if they desire to remain. As the law ought to be strong enough to keep
them in subjection.

I hope Col. McElroy[4] will take proper steps to prevent the escape of his prisoners—

> With sentiments of regard
> I am Sir
> Yr. obt. Svt.
> Z. B. Vance

[1]William G. M. Davis to ZBV [n.d., ca. January 30], A&H:GLB.

[2]Of the town of Marshall, preceding the Shelton Laurel massacre. See Henry Heth to
ZBV, January 21, in this volume.

[3]Lawrence M. Allen, commander of the Sixty-fourth Regiment North Carolina Troops
and the superior officer of James A. Keith, the officer charged with ordering the massacre
of the Shelton Laurel prisoners. Clark, *Histories of Regiments from North Carolina*, 3:659.

[4]John W. McElroy, Yancey County merchant and father-in-law of Robert B. Vance.
He commanded the Yancey County militia, which operated against unionists and deserters
in western North Carolina. Johnston, *Papers of Vance*, 1:96

David A. Barnes to William H. C. Whiting   A&H:GLB

> State of North Carolina
> Executive Department
> Raleigh Feby th 3d. 1863

Genl. W. H. C. Whiting

Dear Sir

His Excellency Governor Vance has received your communication[1] calling
his attention to the fact of the issuing of writs of habeas corpus to bring the cases

of minors before the courts in distant parts of the State, and he directs me to say in reply that your letter contained the first intimation that such writs had been issued.

The writ of habeas corpus is the common right of every man and he has neither the power or inclination to prevent the issuing of such process

> Yours very respectfully
> David A Barnes
> Aid de Camp to the Governor

[1]January 24, A&H:GLB.

Joseph E. Brown to ZBV   A&H:GP

> Executive Department,
> Milledgeville, Ga.,
> February 4th. 1863.

His Excellency
Z. B. Vance
Governor of N. Carolina,
Raleigh, N.C.

Sir:

I have the honor to acknowledge the receipt of your letter of the 30th. ult.,[1] accompanied by a copy of Resolutions passed by the legislature of your State, in reference to the procurement of machinery and wire for the manufacture of cotton and wool cards; and in reply, beg leave to state that, in December last, pursuant to an act just previously passed by the General Assembly of this State, I purchased, on behalf of the State, a half interest in what was known as the "Pioneer Card Manufacturing Co." then located at Cartersville, Ga., at the price of $60,000. At the time of the purchase, the property of the Company consisted of one machine for setting the teeth of *cotton* cards, and one for card clothing for factories—a lot of wire said to be enough to make some 12,000 pairs of cards; all of which, I believe, had been brought in from the United States, at considerable expense to the enterprising parties /who/ imported and transferred them to the persons of whom the State purchased. They also had a steam engine, and a small stock of leather and other materials necessary in the business of the Company.

The great object the State had in view in purchasing an interest in the Company, was to get the imported machine to duplicate it, and by putting more machines in operation, to be able, after a time, to manufacture cards enough to supply, in a great measure, the wants of the people of our State, for that indispensable implement of domestic manufacture of cloth.

The machinery and stock of the Company have been removed to this city; and the manufacturing is now carried on in the State Armory buildings, which are located inside the Penitentiary walls. We have commenced to make ten new machines in the State Armory Shops; but none of them are yet in successful operation. The old machine when in operation, turns out about 24 pairs of cotton cards per day, which we sell at $6. per pair, *for leather* or *skins* suitable for making others—giving a preference in making sales, to widows of deceased soldiers and wives of soldiers now in service. We cannot yet approximate a supply even to those classes of our people. The original stock of wire has not yet been exhausted; but our Master Armorer, (who is also Superintendent of the card manufactory,) says he can draw suitable wire in the Armory.

The State being only *half owner* of the card manufactory, and as all the machines we can make for a considerable time to come, will be required to manufacture enough cards to supply the wants of our own citizens to sell any of the machines would be considered unfair to the other part owners, and to our own people who have so much need of cards; yet I cannot permit the State to be even a partner in selfishness, and refuse to a sister State the privilege of inspecting, taking the dimensions and making drawings of one of our machines, that she might have others made; and though to grant this privilege may be viewed by the individual part owners, as derogatory to their interests, yet, if your State will send a competent mechanist here to inspect, take the dimensions and make drawings of our machines, he shall have every facility afforded him to accomplish that object. In this way I presume your State could have machines made in some machine shop within her own limits, or elsewhere in the Confederacy.

The machines are small, but quite complicated. A good machinist will, however, find no difficulty in making them. They require but little power to run them.

I regret that I do not have it in my power to do more for your noble State in this regard. I shall at all times, however, be glad to give you any information in my power, and to render you any assistance which my obligations to the other partners in the Company, will allow.

> I am, very respectfully,
> Your Excellency's obt. servt.
> Joseph E. Brown

[*Endorsed*] File & copy

Z B V

[1] In this volume.

ZBV to James A. Seddon   A&H:GLB

State of North Carolina
Executive Department
Raleigh Feby 4th. 1863

Hon. Jas. A. Seddon
Secty of War

Sir

Yours of the 30th ulto.[1] asking what appointment have been made by the War Dept. which pertained to the Executive of this State and what regiments this power extended to and upon what grounds this claim of the Executive rested, has been received.

I have the honor to enclose herewith a list of the regiments which the Governor of this State claims to exercise the right of appointing officers in. This claim rests on the ground that these regiments were organized originally for the period of the War under a state law and the governor was required by that law to commission the officers and to fill vacancies therein. The remaining regiments from this State in Confederate service known as "Conscript regiments" were originally twelve months men and the appointment of these officers is given to the President by an act of the 16th. April 62 and is conceded by the State authorities.

Permit me to remark that whilst there is no particular importance attached to the matter, yet the foregoing distinction has been so far observed by my predecessors and the War Dept. and a departure from it now could only create dissatisfaction and confusion.

The enclosed extract of a letter from Col. Avery[2] 6th. N.C.T. will give you a particular case, to which among others my former letter referred. The case of Lt. Col. Moore was not complained of, as I had thro' a misapprehension recommended him myself.

Allow me to disclaim, Sir, most emphatically, an intention to charge you with a disposition to "trench upon my prerogative". I have seen no evidence of such intention in any part of the official intercourse I have had the honor to hold with you. My former letter was based upon the supposition that you were unacquainted with the status of the troops from this state in the matter of commissioning officers &c

I have the honor to be
Sir most respectfully
Yr. obt. Srvt.
Z. B. Vance

[1]In this volume.

[2]Isaac E. Avery. Manarin and Jordan, *North Carolina Troops*, 4:267.

ZBV to Samuel G. French   A&H:GLB

State of North Carolina
Executive Department
Raleigh Feby 4th. 1863.

Maj. Genl. French
Goldsboro N.C.

My dear Sir

A Mr John Wilson a citizen of Bertie Co. writes that all communication between his county and the contiguous counties beyond the Chowan River has been forbidden by your order and that in consequence large supplies of pork, lard &c are prevented from coming into our lines. He also states that Capt. Newhart of the Cavalry, intrusted with the execution of your orders in that region, has seized some twelve or fifteen thousand pounds of meat, brought across the river by loyal citizens and confiscated to the use of the troops as lawful prize. If all this be *not* according to your orders permit me to request you to look into the matter and to see that no wrong is done to loyal citizens; and if done by your order, I hope you will pardon me for suggesting that no prohibition should be laid on the trade with loyal people across the river & Especially upon the getting out of all manner of provisions and Army supplies.

Supposing that the scope of your orders must be misapprehended and that you intended very properly only the suppression of illegal traffick with the enemy, I am content merely to call your attention to the matter

Most respectfully
Yr. obt. Svt.
Z. B. Vance

James A. Seddon to ZBV   A&H:GLB

Confederate States of America
War Department
Richmond Va. Feby 4th. 1863.

His Excellency
Z. B. Vance

Sir

Some six or eight weeks since I invited your attention to the importance of the Rail Road connection to be made by the Confederate Govt. under act of Congress between Danville Va and Greensboro N.C. and invoked your aid to command the slave labor requisit for its early completion. You then declined any impressment in this request under the conviction that with adequate energy on the part of the contractors a sufficient number of slaves might readily be obtained at not unreasonable rates. Will you excuse my again asking your attention to this subject and soliciting a reconsideration of your decision. I am assured that every effort has been made and that rates exceeding in liberality current prices for hire have been freely offered without success in obtaining the required labor. Some impression has prevailed that Slaves employed in this locality had peculiar facilities of escaping and hence the unwillingness of their owners in Eastern Counties to hire them to the Contractors. Besides there is a general disinclination to hire servants to be employed on works of this character where large numbers are assembled. Serious delay must therefore occur unless the authority of your State can be exercised to provide an adequate number of slave laborers for the work. In consequence it is respectfully submitted to you to determine whether the importance of this work, does not justify, if it does not require such exercise of your authority. Full hire shall be paid and every care possible shall be taken to provide for the comfort and safety of the slaves.

In connection with the same subject allow me to ask your attention to a petition which, I understand has been presented to your Legislature seeking such change in the charter of incorporation for the connecting road as will allow conformity of guage throughout & prevent the necessity of break at Danville.

The importance of this in view of the usefulness of the road for military operations needs no comment, but in reference to the future advantage of the road to your State interest, I may be permitted to suggest that a break at Danville could only operate injuriously as, it would tend to make that place more decidedly a depot and a place of transfer. All considerations seem to recommend the proposed change of charter and it would be gratifying to this Department if you could concur in this view and lend your potent influence to induce the amendment.

> With great esteem
> Very respectfully Yours
> James A Seddon
> Secty of War

James J. Pettigrew to ZBV   A&H:VanPC

> Magnolia
> Feby 5th. 1863.

Gov. Z. B. Vance,

Dear Sir,

I see in your message a recommendation of a means of <abs> settling the very difficult question of suspected characters,[1] which certainly vexes us <very>

much without our being able really to effect any/thing satisfactory/. When they are sent to me, I generally feel inspired to discharge them, <without> but such course is hardly fair to the outposts, whose safety is frequently endangered by a man, against whom nothing positive can be proven. Ours and others are often cut off by means of information thus conveyed, though often time, I admit, by their own negligence

The Legislature is too jealous of power after the present emergency. I sympathise with their jealousy of the Confederate government, because, that <power> /government/ is distant, and overwhelmed with business, so that power entrusted to it must be executed through agents, who are often times, wanting in direction but I do not see the same reason for jealousy of the State authorities. Bad times are coming here, for the Yankees seem to have selected this State and Louisiana for the practical experiment of arming the negroes in the midst of the white population. From all appearances the "[blag flag]"[2] is imm['anent].

Unless there be constitutional impediment in the way, I would take the liberty of suggesting, that the Legislature authorize you <to> not only to suspend the Habeas Corpus as to all persons suspected of siding the enemy, but of declaring Martial Law <in> to such offences, in the invaded portion of the State. Let them stack on as many people as they think necessary to watch you, in the shape of a "Commission" or "Council," only give the power to somebody. It may seldom be necessary to punish people, but it is very frequently necessary to keep them for a while, where they can do no harm to our outposts, for nothing demoralises the outposts men, than to have a man sent back among them, whom they believe, but can not exactly prove, to be friendly to the enemy. Now that the /Yankees/ have openly declared the reign of terror, I fear more of our people, will succumb to fear and be as dangerous to us, as though they were regular traitors.

In view of <the> this enforcement of Lincoln's proclamation, among the negroes, I think that the Legislature should take some step calculated to encourage our people and add to the confusion of the enemy, and [increase] the dissatisfaction, which we know to exist, by adding thereto the powerful notion of /the/ fear of consequences. The Legislature do not seem to understand the cause of dissatisfaction against them in the army. It is not, that we object to this or that, particular measure, for we are not in a position to judge of the advantage or disadvantage of such measure, but it is because they give us no word of encouragement, nor manifest any of that enthusiastic detestation (or hatred) of the enemy <,> for his outrages, which animate us, who witness them. I trust sincerely that they will not adjourn without having a full and free expression of opinion, upon the one subject, upon which we should all agree, viz the conduct of the Yankees i in our State. Surely the letter from Elizabeth City, published in the Standard, ought to make their blood boil.[3] Should the President turn over the officers captured, to the State, the interesting question arises how they are to be disposed off.[4] They are "alien enemies," and as such it is doubtful whether they could be tried by a Civil Court; at all writs according to the form of the <Civil> /Common/ law, it is very doubtful whether they could be convicted.

But they are subject to Martial (not military) Law, and can be tried by a "Military Commission." I think the Legislature should authorize you, /as/ Commander in Chief, to organize such a court and have them tried and executed. Even if it were never done, the authority to do it, would cause the boldest of them to <hesita> waver, at the prospect of capture and ignominious death. The fanatics will be much bolder by <dispotion> disposition, but the vast majority of their officers are not fanatics on the subject of arming the negroes, and all who are not so, will be made cowards.

With <the> best wishes for the success of our joint efforts to drive united [Govt] & Yankees into the Sea, I remain &c [*illegible*]

[Yours truly]
J. J. Pettigrew[5]
[Brig G N.C.T.]

[1]Apparently referring to ZBV's proclamation of January 26 (in this volume) regarding deserters and their return to their army units. Pettigrew believed that some of the deserters coming back to their companies in eastern North Carolina were collaborating with the Federals.

[2]"Black flag," a symbol of uncivilized warfare.

[3]Reportedly by an anonymous woman in Elizabeth City claiming that Federal troops and "Buffaloes" (North Carolinians serving with the Union army, see Barrett, *Civil War in North Carolina*, 174), were terrorizing local citizens. *The North Carolina Standard*, January 30, 1863, published excerpts of her letters.

[4]Referring to Jefferson Davis's response to Lincoln's Emancipation Proclamation. See William T. Dortch to ZBV, January 7, 1863, in this volume.

[5]James Johnston Pettigrew commanded a brigade in southern Virginia and eastern North Carolina from September 1862 to May 1863, when his brigade rejoined the Army of Northern Virginia. Stewart Sifakis, *Who Was Who in the Civil War* (New York: Facts on File Publications, 1988), 502.

Gustavus W. Smith to ZBV   A&H:VanPC

Richmond Feby 5th 1863

Governor Z. B. Vance
Raleigh N.C.

My Dear Governor,

Your kind letter of the 3rd. ins. by the hands of Dr. Manson[1] is received. I shall ever cherish with pleasure the recollection of our intercourse at a trying time for the State of North Carolina of which you are Governor and I at the time was Commander of the Military forces of the Confederate States in that section of our Country.

To whatever of success may have attended my efforts in hurried preparation to meet an enemy already far advanced within the State before my arrival, I am largely indebted to your prompt and effective co-operation, and my success in forming an opinion upon the state of affairs, and /understanding the/ feelings of the people is due mainly to the fact that you without reserve frankly and candidly led me behind the curtain, and enabled me to see and judge.

I shall ever cherish with pleasure, the remembrance of our close friendly relations, official as well as personal during my brief sojourn amongst your people. Meeting almost /as/ entire strangers to each other, I feel that I am parting from a fine friend for whom I have not only strong personal attachment, but great respect and admiration for his character and ability. I do not as yet clearly understand the wishes and intentions of the government in regard to myself, but under the circumstances feel satisfied that I am not to return to North Carolina. And on some accounts it is perhaps fortunate that I am not to go back.[2]

I take a deep interest in all that concerns the welfare of the people of /the State of/ North Carolina, and will rejoice in her successes, and hope that soon under a better leader than I am, the invaders may be driven from her soil, and that we may all enjoy peace, freed from <all> connection with the intermedling fanatical yankee.

The officers of my staff join me in kind regards to yourself. Please present my compliments to Mrs. Vance; and remember me to little Zeb.[3]

> Very Truly Your Friend
> G. W. Smith

[1]Otis Frederick Manson, a physician and Confederate surgeon in charge of a hospital in Richmond for the care and rehabilitation of North Carolina soldiers. *North Carolina Biography*, s.v. "Manson, Otis Frederick."
[2]See ZBV to Jefferson Davis, February 2, in this volume.
[3]Zebulon Baird Vance Jr., ZBV's fourth son.

Samuel G. French to ZBV   A&H:GLB

> Head Quarters Goldsboro
> Feb 5th. 1863

His Excellency
Z. B. Vance
Gov. No. Ca.

Dear Governor

I have your letter of yesterday,[1] I am sorry for you if you are annoyed as much as I have been by such letters as Mr Wilsons to you. My orders are not to let persons known to be disloyal, and persons who are entire strangers in the community pass the Chowan—but all persons of good character and standing for adherence to our cause, can cross—

As regards produce—beef-pork & Salt and other necessary articles to the country and for their own use, my orders are that loyal citizens be encouraged to bring them over or to go for them, and that they be given aid, support and escorts for protection—in short assistance in any way—But I have said men must not be permitted to carry over, wherewith to purchase these things, any Cotton, Tobacco or other produce that is contraband.

The pickets there once captured or claimed to have captured some pork which was sunk[2] by the owners and which they said would have fallen into the hands of the enemy but for them. I have instructed them this was wrong, even had they taken it from the hands of the enemy, because it does not belong to them, but to the Government. On this capture I presume Mr W's letter is founded.

It was ordered to be returned to the owners—My orders give every aid and assistance to all good people in their legitimate pursuit without let or hinderance; and in some instances when trading with disloyal citizens on the other side; countenancing illegal traffic in order to get things absolutely necessary.

Of course I cannot prescribe to Capt Newhead[3] what he shall do in every instance and have told him to use common sense and sound discretion

Yrs Truly
S. G. French
Maj. Genl.

[1] In this volume.
[2] Abandoned.
[3] Appears as Newhart in ZBV's February 4 letter to French.

ZBV to Richard S. Donnell   Duke:Van

[*With enclosure*]

State of North Carolina
Executive Department
Raleigh Feby 6th. 1863

Hon R. S. Donnell[1]
Speaker Hs Commons,

Sir,

In answer to a resolution from your body requesting a tabular statement of the number of conscripts and volunteers from each county of this State, I herewith enclose a letter from Gen. J. G. Martin, Acting A. Genl, & showing the impossibility of accurately complying therewith.

> Very respectfully
> Yr obt svt
> Z. B. Vance

[1]Richard Spaight Donnell, speaker of North Carolina House of Commons, 1863–1865. *Dictionary of North Carolina Biography*, s.v. "Donnell, Richard Spaight."

[*Enclosure*]

James G. Martin to ZBV   A&H:GP

> Executive Department
> North Carolina,
> Adjutant General's Office,
> Raleigh: February 6th. 1863.

To His Excellency Z. B. Vance
Governor of North Carolina,

Governor:—

A copy of a resolution adopted by the House of Commons requesting a statement of the number of Conscripts & Volunteers from each county in the State has been recieved

The information desired cannot be correctly furnished from this office, for the reason that only the original muster rolls of companies are filed here, which do not include either conscripts or recruits, of whom a large number have joined the regts of N.C. Troops

I am, Governor,

> Very Respectfully
> Your Obt. Servant
> J. G. Martin
> Adjutant General

James A. Seddon to ZBV   A&H:GP

> Confederate States of America,
> War Department,
> Richmond, Va. 7th. Feby 1863

His Excellency
Z. Vance
Gov of North Carolina
Raleigh

Sir—

Your letter of the 5th. ult.[1] submitting a plan for the arrest of deserters and the enforcement of the conscription act has been recd.

The subject has been considered of by the President, and this department— The object proposed is very desirable & the department is ready to adopt the most suitable plan for that purpose

The one which would seem to be most simple & which would afford adequate force to accomplish the end, is to enlist two or three companies under the act providing for home defences and to place them at your disposition for the particular service mentioned in your letter Such companies would be received into the Confederate service whenever organized

> Very Respectfully
> Yr obt Svt
> James A. Seddon
> Secy of War

[*Endorsed*] File & copy

ZBV

[1]In this volume.

ZBV to James J. Pettigrew   A&H:Pet

> State of North Carolina
> Executive Department
> Raleigh, Feby 7th. 1863

Brig. Gen Pettigrew
Magnolia N.C.

My Dear Sir,

Yours[1] recd. last night, and I return my thanks for your suggestions—I will write you again in regard thereto. I ask your help now in regard to another matter.

I have accepted three or four companies of State troops, raised inside the enemies lines in Pasquotank County, to operate in that region against the buffaloes & negroes.

I want an officer, with the rank of Major to command. I want him to be No. 1, not a sharp drill master, but a bold, enterprising man of sense & descretion, fit for a separate command. Can you recommend me to the right man? If such an officer is not placed over them they will not earn their salt.

I am raising all the companies I can in those counties where the conscript law can not be executed.

Please write me if you know such a man
In haste

> Yours truly
> Z. B. Vance

[1]February 5, in this volume.

James A. Seddon to ZBV A&H:GP

[*With enclosure*]

Confederate States of America,
War Department,
Richmond, Va. February 9 1863

His Excellency Z. B. Vance
Governor of N.C.
Raleigh N.C.

Sir

Your letter of the 15th ult[1] requesting that the 16th N.C. Regt be sent home to gather up deserters and recusant conscripts was referred to Genl Lee for report and your attention is respectfully called to the annexed copy of his reply

Very Respectfully
Your Obdt Servt
James A Seddon
Secretary of War

[*Enclosure*]

Robert E. Lee to James A. Seddon A&H:GP

"Copy"

Details of officers and men have been made from all N.C. regts to visit the State to obtain recruits & absentees. Two N.C. Brigades Ransom's[2] & Cookes[3] have recently been detached from this army to N.C. with the hope that its ranks may be filled. At this time I do not think it prudent to make further detachments.

(signed)   R E Lee
Genl Commdg

[*Endorsed*] File & copy

Z B V

---

[1]In this volume.

[2]Matt Whitaker Ransom. Ashe, Weeks, and Van Noppen, *Biographical History*, 1:420–429.

[3]John Rogers Cooke. *Dictionary of North Carolina Biography*, s.v. "Cooke, John Rogers."

ZBV to Augustus S. Merrimon A&H:GLB

State of North Carolina
Executive Department
Raleigh, Feby 9th. 1863

A. S. Merrimon Esq
Solicitor 8th. Dist.

Dr. Sir,

I want you to take such steps as may be necessary to secure and prosecute all the prisoners on Laurel taken by the recent expedition.

I desire you also to make an investigation officially into the reported shooting of a number of these prisoners, with all the circumstances, as I intend to look into the matter myself

Very respectfully
Yr. obt. Svt.
Z. B. Vance

ZBV to Richard S. Donnell Duke:Van

State of North-Carolina,
Executive Department,
Raleigh, Feb 9th. 1863

Hon R S Donnell
Speaker Hs Com.

Sir,

I have the honor to acknowledge the reception this morning, of a resolution of your Honorable body making enquiry in relation to the impressment by Gen. Whiting of the teams & hands of Mr. [John M.] Worth Salt Agent, at Wilmington.

I enclose herewith for the information of the House copies of sundry letters in relation thereto, from which it will be perceived that Gen Smith at my request promptly ordered the restoration of the hands & teams.[1] I have not since heard from the agent, Mr. Worth and consequently cannot say whether or not he has resumed operations.

Very respectfully
Yr obt svt
Z B Vance

[1]See Gustavus W. Smith to ZBV, January 26, in this volume.

Burton N. Harrison to ZBV   A&H:GP

Confederate States of America,
Executive Department,
Richmond, Va. Feb 12, 1863

His Excellency
Z. B. Vance
Raleigh N.C.

Sir:

The President would have himself replied to your letter of the 2d. inst.[1] but has been for several days incapacitated for business by illness which keeps him confined to his room.

He directs me to express his happiness upon receiving your expressions of confidence in Genl. G. W. Smith and of satisfaction with his course in North Carolina. Genl. Smith's return to his Head Quarters in this city, from the field, was for considerations not connected with /any/ dissatisfaction on the part of the administration—nor because of any design to remove him from his present command.

Genl. D. H. Hill is now in North Carolina and, though in ill health, it is hoped that he will be able to serve his country in a command in your State.

I have the honor to be, Governor,

Your obt. sert.
Burton N. Harrison
Private Secretary

[1] In this volume.

ZBV to James A. Seddon   A&H:GLB

State of North Carolina
Executive Department
Raleigh Feby 12th. 1863

Hon James A. Seddon
Secty of War

Sir

I have the honor to acknowledge the receiption of your letter of the 4th. inst.[1] invoking the aid of the authorities of the State to procure labor for the completion of the Danville rail-road, & also asking my influence with the Legislature in securing the guage of that road to correspond with that of the Virginia roads.

The object is a most important one and commends itself strongly to my favor. But under all the circumstances I feel compelled to decline *impressing* slaves to aid in its completion. For many months past the Eastern part of this State has been furnishing labour upon all the public works from Wilmington to Petersburg and no less than twenty counties are now so employing their slaves. In the region through which this road runs there are very few slaves and the very existence of the people require them to labor on their farms.

In addition to the fact, that this road is viewed with almost universal disfavor in the State, as entirely ruinous to many east of it, and that the charter never could have been obtained, but as a pressing War necessity. I feel it due to candor, that I should add, there exists a very general impression here that upon the completion of the Danville Connection, as it is termed, the eastern lines of our roads would be abandoned to the enemy. How far this opinion does injustice to the purpose of the War Dept., I am not able to say, I merely state the fact. For these reasons with the additional one that the road is constructing by private contractors I do not feel that I could be justified in forcing the labor of citizens upon it. I assure you I regret this exceedingly, not only on account of the importance of the work itself to our military operations; but also because it is exceedingly unpleasant for me to refuse to do any thing whatsoever which is requested by the Confederate authorities and regarded as important to the General cause. I would suggest however that a large a large [*sic*] number of free negroes might be obtained in the adjoining counties of Virginia and North Carolina. And if this species of labor could be made available my assistance in gathering it up shall be promptly rendered. In regard to the guage of the road, I have to say that the proposition to make it conform with the Virginia Roads, had been disposed of in the negative before yours was received.

> Very respectfully
> Yr. obt. Svt
> Z. B. Vance

[1]In this volume.

ZBV to James Sinclair   A&H:GP

> Executive Office
> Raleigh N.C. Feb 17th./63

Col James Sinclair[1]

My dear Sir,

Your letter[2] was of such a character & required so many questions answered that I could not find time in my office to answer it sooner without slighting important matters as I shall even now be compelled to do to a greater extent than is desirable did leisure permit.

I have persistently regarded you Col, <as> an injured man, and had it ever been in my power it was my intention to have given you such a position as could have enabled you to reinstate yourself in the public estimation. Associated with you in the defense of New Berne, I found you always energetic and efficient. For weeks we laboured almost alone, (with our regiments) in reconnoitering the localities and preparing /the defenses/ on the right of our position. The drill and discipline of your Regt. appeared to equal that of any other of the Brigade (Gen Branches)[3] for the period of its organization. In regard to your conduct on the field, I can say that on Wednesday evening previous to the battle of New Berne your regt. was thrown forward to Fishers landing, four or five miles from the main body, without support, where you sustained a severe fire of shell from the enemys gun boats under circumstances well calculated to demoralize raw troops, which position you left only by orders, falling back in order to the breast works. On the day of battle on the Friday succeeding, I was not in observing distance and therefore did not see you or your regt, but having defended you in the court of enquiry afterwards held to investigate charges affecting you & Lt. Col Craton,[4] I heard most of the evidence given before it, and can say that while there were some things tending to impeach your judgement I heard nothing which I thought could fairly impeach your courage. Nor did any thing appear /up/ on the investigation so far as I remember, which <ought> /might/ not ordinarily have happened to any brave man leading his regt. into their first fight against superior numbers, and through the still more trying scenes of disorderly retreat. Such has been my unwavering opinion, often freely expressed.

The court I think was a fair one, though in as much as there were also charges against your Lt Col Craton there was necessarily some feeling in the regiment which more or less coloured the statements of the witnesses. At that time you had also become unpopular in your regiment from some cause, and the fact of your being a minister, coupled as it generally is in such cases with the idea of such a character being incompatible with a military command, increased the general disposition to censure and criticism which was evinced by almost every one connected with the matter. These things all rendered it difficult indeed for you to get your case fairly stated to the public, and the election for officers coming off so soon thereafter by which you were deprived of your command (apparently (though not necessarily by any means) disgraced you.

That all these things taken together should affect your reputation as an officer and a man of courage, to some extent, I do not wonder, when I consider that in our gallant an chevalrous South the reputation of a soldier is almost as delicate as the virtue of a woman; and especially when we consider that so few will take the trouble to investigate for themselves the facts in the case of a man who is *down*. But why /these/ allegations should affect so seriously your character as a christian and a minister, I confess I am at a loss to know, seeing that they do not *charge* you even, so far as I know with any breach of the decalogue.

Men are sometimes however the victims of circumstances, and such I believe you now to be. Being once under the weather, there are many pious [souls] in the world who think their best way to show a detestation of *bad people* is to kick the man whom every one else kicks. I prefer if I can with justice, to lend a helping hand.

Let me assure you in conclusion that I would rejoice to see you on your feet again, reinstated in the confidence of your people; and wiser from the lessons of the past, serving your country again, with usefulness in this the hour of her need—

Very Respectfully

Z. B. Vance

A true copy of the original

[1]A Presbyterian minister and commander of the Thirty-fifth Regiment North Carolina Troops. A military court of inquiry had charged Sinclair with being "unsoldierly" in his conduct during the Battle of New Bern in March 1862. Although the court later dropped the charges, he was not reelected to command when his regiment was reorganized in April. See Johnston, *Papers of Vance*, 1:121n.

[2]October 27, 1862. Johnston, *Papers of Vance*, 1:282–284.

[3]Brigadier General Lawrence O'Bryan Branch, commander of Confederate forces defending New Bern. He was killed at the Battle of Antietam in September 1862. *Dictionary of North Carolina Biography*, s.v. "Branch, Lawrence O'Bryan."

[4]Marshall D. Craton, lieutenant colonel in the Thirty-fifth Regiment. He resigned that position in April 1862 and became colonel of the Fiftieth Regiment. Manarin and Jordan, *North Carolina Troops*, 9:358.

ZBV *to Samuel G. French*   Mich:Sch

State of North Carolina
Executive Department
Raleigh, Feb'y 18th. 1863

Maj Gen S. G. French

Genl,

I enclose you a batch of letters[1] concerning the desire of a Mrs. Carter[2] who desires to go to her husband[3] at New Berne by the reading of which you will come to a knowledge of the whole matter.

Carter her husband, is a Union refugee from Tenn, a man who before the war occupied a good social position. After he left Tenn, Majr. W. J. Brown[4] her father brought her to his home in Buncombe County where she has remained since, and now wishes to go to her husband & share his fortunes.

Major Brown is a Northern man by birth but has been a resident of N.C. since 1842; he is a man of good social position, has been an intimate friend of mine, his only two sons[5] entered the army with me in April 1862 and both died in the service. The lady I believe sympathises with her husband, but I believe to be honorable and worthy of the permission asked—I hope you may see proper to let her go, and to let her trunks come through if she desires it—

Please return Mrs. Carters letter to me, & read & forward the one to her husband with a note saying to him what your will permit &c

> Very respectfully
> Z. B. Vance

The man C[ag]ier, who also asks for permission to go to Baltimore, I know nothing about.

> Z B V

[1]Surviving relevant letters for 1863 are William B. Carter to ZBV, February 16 and William J. Brown to ZBV, February 25, A&H:VanPC.
[2]Former Mary W. Brown.
[3]William B. Carter.
[4]William John Brown, lawyer and land speculator.
[5]William Caleb Brown, a law partner of ZBV, and Samuel Smith Brown. Actually William J. Brown had a third son, John Evans Brown, who traveled to the California Gold Rush in 1849, and subsequently to Australia and New Zealand. Johnston, *Papers of Vance*, 1:53n, 54n.

Paul C. Cameron to ZBV   A&H:GP

Hillsboro. N.C. Feby 19th. 63—

His Ex Gov Vance.

Dear Sir.

We have at this time 5 negro men in our jail—all committed in the last three days—the two first committed on tuesday—charged with the killing of their Master Mr. Stroud[1] in the south western corner of the County—the other three committed today charged with the killing of their Master Mr. Lockheart[2] in the North Eastern part of the County—. Both are said to be brutal murders without provocation & in *both* cases the slaves *confess* to the killings—

As you might suppose the community is much excited and I am told a strong disposition prevails to take the matter in hand & execute the slaves without waiting the action of a court. I hope no such step will be taken—but I think in times like this it is very desirable that a trial should be had at the earliest day and the punishment should be prompt. I think a letter from you giveing the assurance of an early trial would quiet the excitment and be most acceptable to all.

Yours very truly
Paul C. Cameron[3]

"The Sheriff" resides at Chapel Hill—

H. K. Nash Esqr County Atto—

[Endorsed] Col. B. has ansd. File—

---

[1]Isaac Stroud. See Harold D. Moser, "Reaction in North Carolina to the Emancipation Proclamation," North Carolina Historical Review 64 (January 1967): 69.

[2]John Lockhart. See Moser, "Reaction to the Emancipation Proclamation," 69.

[3]Paul Carrington Cameron, wealthy planter, large slaveholder, state senator, and railroad magnate. Dictionary of North Carolina Biography, s.v. "Cameron, Paul Carrington."

Henry K. Nash to ZBV   A&H:GP

Hillsboro Feb. 20th. 1863—

To His Excellency
Z. B. Vance—

Dear Sir

I have taken the liberty, as the County Attorney for Orange in the absence of the Solicitor for the Circuit, and at the request of many of our citizens, to address you upon the state of affairs in our County; and urge you, if compatible with your sense of duty, to commission some one of our Judges to hold a Court of Oyer & Terminer here without delay—[1] Within the last ten days two most atrocious murders have been committed by slaves upon their masters, both highly respectable citizens of the County, & the excitement among our people is necessarily very great—Seven are now in jail, and three more will be brought up today—[2] Nothing but the hope & expectation of their having a speedy trial prevented their instant execution—Next week is County Court & I fear if this expectation of immediate trial is disappointed, summary justice will be executed upon them, without regard to law—This should by all means be avoided if possible, but cannot, I fear, unless the course suggested can be adopted—

May I ask to hear from you upon the subject, as soon as convenient—

Very respectfully
Your Obt. Sevt.
Henry K. Nash—[3]

[1]The authority of the governor to call special courts of oyer and terminer for swift trials had been inherent since the colonial period. But laws of 1854 and 1863 further specified the governor's power and broadened the jurisdiction of such courts. For information on those laws and their relevance to the Orange County murders, see Paul C. Cameron to David A. Barnes, February 23, in this volume.

[2]Only five slaves were charged with the murders. Nash may be referring to additional suspects or witnesses who were later released.

[3]Henry Kollock Nash, lawyer and former state legislator. Williams and Hamilton, *Papers of Graham*, 5:102n; Cheney, *North Carolina Government*, 312.

William A. Graham to ZBV   A&H:GP

Hillsboro Feb. 21st. 1863

His Excelly. Z. B. Vance—
&c &c &c—

Dear sir

I transmit herewith a communication from John A. McMannen Esqr.[1] relative to a supply of cotton cards for the people of this state—You will observe, that he sent with it to me, a letter from the Executive of Georgia, giving information concerning a Machine for the manufacture of cards in that state, but affording a discouraging prospect of either procuring a machine there, or a supply of cards from that state for the people of this—I do not enclose that letter because I presume your own correspondence has put you in possession of the information it contains, and Mr McM. desired it to be returned to him—If you however shall deem it important it can be sent hereafter—You will observe, that Mr Mc-Mannen's conclusion is, that our only resource for obtaining cards is in foreign importation & running the blockade—If you shall deem it expedient to apply my part of the secret appropriation to this object, and by this means, I know no one, who is better adapted to an enterprize of that nature than Mr McMannen himself—He is intelligent, fertile in resources, and full of zeal in the cause—

With great respect
Your Obedt. servt.
W. A. Graham[2]

P.S. Mr Nash Co. solicitor informs me, he has written you, asking the order of a Court of Oyer & Terminer in this County—[3] I beg to suggest that Judge Gilliam[4] would be an acceptable Judge to commission for this service, and the 2nd. monday in March a proper time—That is the old time of the superior Court of Orange—

Enclosure: 1863, Feb. 9. McMannen to Graham—[5]

[Endorsed] File

Z B V

[1] A Durham County minister and machine manufacturer. Williams and Hamilton, *Papers of Graham*, 5:344n.
[2] William Alexander Graham, planter, lawyer, and political leader in the state—U.S. and Confederate senator, governor, and U.S. secretary of the navy. *Dictionary of North Carolina Biography*, s.v. "Graham, William Alexander."
[3] See Henry K. Nash to ZBV, February 20, in this volume.
[4] Robert B. Gilliam, superior court judge and former speaker of House of Commons. Williams and Hamilton, *Papers of Graham*, 5:117n.
[5] Not extant.

Paul C. Cameron to David A. Barnes   A&H:GP

Hillsboro. N.C. Feby 23rd. 63—

Col. D. A. Barnes

Dear Sir

When I wrote Gov Vance (at the request of some of my neighbors) I was under the impression that at the late Session of the Legislature an act had been passed authorizing the Governor to issue commissions for the holding of Special Courts for the trial of criminal cases.[1]

Gov Graham was under that impression: and I hope it may turn out to be so—. There is *no* pretence whatever that there exist in this community or County any "conspiracy or plot" for rebellion and murder in any part of the slave population—.

The killing of poor Stroud & Lockheart—two slaveholders in our County last week—is to be regarded as far as I can learn—as just a singular coincidence Yet nevertheless our entire population desires an early trial and prompt punishment if to be had—. No "five Justices" can hardly ask for a Court of Jail delivery as provided for in the act mentioned by you—.[2]

Yours very Respectfully
Paul C. Cameron

[1] An act of February 1863 that authorized the governor to call courts of oyer and terminer "to indict and try all white persons, slaves, and free persons of color, and all other persons charged with capital felonies, crimes, misdemeanors, or any violation or offence whatever of the criminal law of which the superior courts at their regular terms, have jurisdiction." *Public Laws of North Carolina, 1863*, c. 35. That statute superseded the 1854 revised law "Slaves and Free Negroes," which empowered the governor to commission courts of oyer and terminer only for trials of slaves accused of conspiracy or insurrection. *Revised Code of North Carolina, 1854*, c. 107, s. 41.
[2] Law of 1854. See note 1 above.

William A. Graham to ZBV   A&H:GP

Hillsboro Feb. 25th. 1863

His Excelly. Z. B. Vance—

Dear sir,

Mr. Nash informs me that he has received a communication from Col. Barnes in reference to the court proposed to be held in this county for the trial of certain slaves charged with capital offences: from which I infer that Col. B. may have overlooked the act of the last session of the Legislature pertaining to courts of oyer & terminer, as he refers to section 41 Chapter 107 of Revised Code for the authority of the Governor to commission a Judge to hold such court—[1] It is possible that a commission under that act may be sufficient for these cases, but I doubt it—From /what/ I learn, they are cases of murder with possible accessories both before & after the fact; and as the statute in the Revised Code relates only to cases of conspiracy &c, it is questionable whether a court with adequate powers can be constituted under it—The act of the last session, according to my recollection gives more ample authority.[2] I beg therefore that you examine it, and if it be as I suppose, that you will make out the commission under it. Or perhaps upon examination you may deem it proper to make out commissions under both Statutes—I trouble you with these suggestions, because it /is/ imperative there shall be no mistake in the holding of the court—For the public excitement against the criminals can with difficulty be controlled—

> I am with high respect
> Your Obedt. servt.
> W. A. Graham

[*Endorsed*] Col. Barnes reply

Z B V

[1] See Paul C. Cameron to David A. Barnes, February 23, in this volume.
[2] See again Cameron to Barnes, February 23.

ZBV to Robert B. Gilliam   A&H:GLB

The State of North Carolina

To the Honorable Robert B. Gilliam

Greeting

By virtue of authority vested in me, by an Act passed by the General Assembly and ratified on the 7th. day of February A D 1863,[1] good cause having been to me shown why a Court of Oyer and Terminer shall be held in the County of

Orange, for the speedy trial of certain persons accused of capital crimes against the laws of this State. You are hereby nominated, appointed and commissioned to hold a Court of Oyer and Terminer in said County of Orange, at such Early time as you may be pleased to designate.[2]

In witness whereof, His Excellency Z. B. Vance, our Governor, Captain General and Commander in Chief hath signed these presents & caused the Great Seal to be affixed.

> Done at the City of Raleigh on the
> 25th. day of February in the year of our
> Lord, One thousand eight
> hundred and Sixty Three
>
> Z. B. Vance

[1]*Public Laws of North Carolina, 1863*, c. 35 records the date of ratification as February 9.

[2]Having received this commission, Gilliam convened court at the March term of the Orange County Superior Court. A jury found four of the slave defendants guilty of murder and the fifth guilty of accessory to murder after the fact. The four were hanged on April 10. The remaining defendant received a new trial in September, was found guilty, and then hanged on October 16. *State v. Solomon, Daniel, and America, State v. Lucian and Allen*, and *State v. Solomon*, Orange County Superior Court Minutes, March and September terms, 1863, State Archives, Division of Archives and History, Raleigh.

ZBV to James A. Seddon   A&H:GP

Copy

> State of North Carolina
> Executive Department
> Raleigh Feby. 25th. 1863.

Hon Jas. A. Seddon
Secty: of War

Sir

I had the honor some three weeks or a month ago to address you, res[p]ectfully asking the removal of a lot of broken down Cavalry horses, from the North Western Counties of this state of Genl Jenkins' command, which were devouring the substance of a people threatened with famine. I have not had the pleasure of receiving a reply to that letter.[1]

I beg leave to inform you that their depredations are still continued and that they have become not only a nuisance, but a terror to the community and enclose you a letter from Col. Forkner[2] of the 73d. N.C. Militia, giving evidence of their behaviour. With every possible disposition to aid in the support of the army, I have the strongest reasons conceivable—the existence of my own people—for declining to permit these horses to remain in that section of the State. When the question of starvation is narrowed down to women & children on the one side and some worthless Cavalry horses on the other, I can have no difficulty in making a choice. Unless they are removed soon, I shall be under the painful necessity of calling out the Militia of the adjoining Counties and driving them from the state. I hope however to be spared such a proceeding

Very Respectfully
Yr. obt. servt.
(Signed)   Z. B. Vance

¹January 22, in this volume.
²See Samuel Forkner to ZBV, January 31, A&H:GP.

James A. Seddon to ZBV   A&H:GP

[*With enclosure*]

Confederate States of America,
War Department,
Richmond, Va. Feby 25th. 1863

His Excy
Z B Vance
Govr. of North Carolina
Sir

Will you permit me to invoke your attention to the enclosed report made through the Quarter Master Genl to me by Major Carrington a most efficient and well informed officer having chief charge of the forage supplies for our Armies in Virginia—The matter of this report has seemed to me so important and so dependant on influences within your power seriously to control, that I have ventured not merely to lay it before you but likewise to direct Major Carrington to bear it in person, that, should you grant him the privilege of an audience, he may more fully give you an exposition of the existing state of our supplies, of the prospects to be anticipated and of the best means in his Judgment of developing and commanding our resources

I commend him to your favourable consideration <and> and hope his visit may not prove unproductive of good to the Public Service by enlisting your active cooperation in the measures his experience suggests

With high Esteem
Most Respy. Yrs.
James A Seddon
Secy. of War

[*Enclosure*]

Charles S. Carrington to Abraham C. Myers   A&H:GP

Richmond February 24th. 1863

Col. A C Myers[1]
Quartermaster Genl.

Col

I ascertain from the reports of Maj Whitfield QM that 133,000 bushels of Corn were in store in this city on the 3d. instant—that his receipts to the 22d. instant inclusive were 26,000 bushels, that his transfers and issues were 74,300 bushels, leaving 84,700 bushels in depot. I further ascertain the daily average of these receipts to be 1,300 bushels and transfers and issues 3,715 bushels and that at the same rates of receipts and issues the stock of Corn in this city <would> /will/ be exhausted in 35 days from the 22d. instant. I apprehend that the transfer of Corn from this city to Genl. Lee's army will be greater in future because of the recent occupation of the "Northern Neck" of Va. by the enemy, and because of the increased remoteness from the army of the Corn remaining in Essex & Middlesex Counties. I also apprehend that under existing arrangements for transporting Corn from Tawboro [*Tarboro*] & Weldon to this city the receipts will be less. Maj Whitfield reports 9,400 bushels as the receipt of Corn for the week ending the 22d. of February, but with the railroad transportation now employed in this service, I believe that the maximum weekly delivery of Corn in this City from Tawboro & Weldon will be 8,200 bushels. I requested Col Wodley A AG, to provide sufficient transportation to secure the daily delivery in this city from Tawboro of 4,000 bus of Corn. I do not doubt but that Col. Wodley has discharged his whole duty in the premises I believe that the want of the necessary rolling-stock by the roads between Tawboro & Richmond is the only reason why the transportation has not been provided.

I am informed that for some months past a portion of the rail-road transportation of North Carolina has been employed under the orders of his Excellency Governor Vance, in removing the surplus Corn of eastern North Carolina to the western portion of that State. The Corn of eastern North Carolina has already been greatly reduced & the amount remaining is not beyond the necessary demands of the armies of the Confederate States. These demands require that 30,000 bushels of Corn shall be brought from this section to Richmond very week. The posts of Wilmington & Petersburg & those intervening must be chiefly sustained by this Corn. The post at Raleigh <is> /should/ depend<dent> upon it. Shipments of Corn are made from Weldon to the army under the command of Genl Pryor[2] & the army in North Carolina cannot be sustained without the Corn of this section.

The officer in charge of the post of Kingston [*Kinston*] reports that "forage is becoming exceedingly scarce as the authorities at this place have allowed too large a quantity to be sent to the western part of the State." When a proper representation of these facts is made to the patriotic Governor of North Carolina I believe that he will arrest the further removal of Corn necessary to the armies of the Confederate States, and give all of the assistance in his power to divert the transportation now employed in this service & necessary to place this Corn within reach of these armies

Very Respectfully
Your obt Servant
Chas. S. Carrington
Maj & QM

[1] Abraham Charles Myers, Confederate quartermaster general, 1861–1863. Wakelyn, *Biographical Dictionary of the Confederacy*, 328–329.

[2] Roger Atkinson Pryor, commanding a brigade in Virginia. Boatner, *Civil War Dictionary*, 674.

ZBV to President and Directors of NCRR   A&H:GLB

State of North Carolina
Executive Department
Raleigh Feby 26th. 1863.

To the Prest & Directors
of the N.C.R.R. Co.

Gentlemen

I regret that a great press of business accumulated by a recent absence from home, renders it out of my power to attend your meeting, especially so, as it was called by Mr Webb[1] at my request. I am compelled therefore to put my proposition before you in writing.

The great necessity, of both the country and Army renders the subject of transportation of the most vital importance and it was with the view of doing something if possible, to increase the power & efficiency of your Road that I asked Mr Webb to call this meeting. Being the main trunk road of the State, into which all the other roads discharge themselves it is not to be wondered at that it should have proved itself unable to meet the demands upon it. Without intending any reflection whatsoever upon the management of the Road, it may, I think be fairly said, it is overtaxed and is clearly unequal to the task of transporting the freight which is waiting upon it. The supreme importance of that required for the use of our Army, is acknowledged, whilst the wants of the State in corn for the poor, and the Cotton bought to redeem our obligations abroad, are scarcely less so. I am able to see but one remedy and that is to permit the Atlantic and N.C.R.R. Company to take charge of and work the Eastern section of your road from this place to Goldsboro for such length of time and under such terms as you may think best. Having the unemployed rolling stock and employees &c. I am convinced that Company can work it well and that it would give the balance of your road the motive power to put new life and vigour into its operations

With my limited experience in railroad matters, I shall not argue the proposition. I could give gentlemen of your experience no new light, I am confident. But I am assured by four fifths of all railroad men with whom I have conversed, that the arrangement could be made without loss to your road and with infinite advantage to the public and would be greatly superior to the plan proposed in lieu thereof—of running cars of other companies over it by permission. I beg leave also to remind you of the very great importance of prompt and regular communication, in a military point of view between this place and Goldsboro, which we now do not enjoy. I am aware Gentleman of the extreme repugnance with which an independent rail road Co would regard a proposition to farm out a portion of their road to another on various accounts. And I should feel great delacy in making the proposition, did I not sincerely believe that the public interest, before which every minor consideration must give way, imperatively demands it.

Trusting that you may so regard it and if so, confident that you will promptly give the proposition at *least a* trial.

I have the honor to be Gentlemen

> Most truly & Respectfully
> Yr. obt. svt.
> Z. B. Vance

[1]Thomas Webb, Hillsborough lawyer and president of the North Carolina Railroad. Allen W. Trelease, "The Passive Voice: The State and North Carolina Railroad, 1849–1871," *North Carolina Historical Review* 61 (April 1984): 186n.

ZBV to James A. Seddon   A&H:GLB

> State of North Carolina
> Executive Department
> Raleigh—Feby. 27–1863

Hon. J. A. Seddon
Secy of War

Sir

I learn that the War Dept has refused to accept the resignation of Col. W. P. Bynum[1] 2d. N.C. Troops who was elected by the Legislature to the office of Solicitor of the 7th Judicial District of this State.

I beg leave to protest against this disrespect towards the civil government of N.C.—The office is an important one and Col Bynum was chosen for it by the Legislature without his solicitation, on a deliberate conviction of his fitness for the place.

Common courtesy, it seems to me, requires that his resignation should be accepted, and I am confident that upon a consideration of the whole matter it will be done at once.[2]

> Very respectfully
> Yr. obt. svt.
> Z. B. Vance

[1]William Preston Bynum. *Dictionary of North Carolina Biography*, s.v. "Bynum, William Preston."

[2]The War Department accepted Bynum's resignation on March 21, 1863. Manarin and Jordan, *North Carolina Troops*, 3:379.

ZBV to William G. M. Davis   A&H:GLB

> State of North Carolina
> Executive Department
> Raleigh Feby 27th. 1863

Brig. Gen. Davis
Knoxville Tenn

Genl

In my last letter to you[1] I referred to a report that a number of prisoners taken on Laurel had been shot in cold blood, and expressed the hope it might not prove true

I fear however that it is even worse than was first reported. I beg leave to ask your attention to the copy enclosed of a part of a letter from A. S. Merrimon Esq. attorney for the State in that district,[2] and to respectfully request you to make enquiry into the truth of the statements therein with a view to proceedings against the guilty parties. Whilst expressing again my thanks for the prompt aid rendered by your command in quieting the troubles in that region, I cannot reconcile it to my sense of duty to pass by in silence such cruel & barbarous conduct as is alleged to have characterized a portion of them, and more especially as the officers mentioned are citizens of this State.

> Very respectfully
> Yr. obt. Svt.
> Z. B. Vance

[1]February 2, in this volume.
[2]See Augustus S. Merrimon to ZBV, February 16, 24, A&H:GP.

ZBV *to Sewall L. Fremont*   A&H:GLB

State of North Carolina
Executive Department
Raleigh Feby 27th. 1863

S. L. Fremont Esqr[1]
Supt. W. & W.R.R.

Sir

The necessities of the Confederate service as represented to me, require more railroad transportation for corn from Tarboro and Weldon to Richmond.

In view of this necessity I have consented that the train of ten cars pledged on the seventeenth inst. through the President of the Wilmington and Weldon Road to the service of the State, shall be used by the Confederate States for the above mentioned service.

You will therefore please hold the said train of ten cars subject to the order of the proper Confederate Officer

Respectfully Yrs
Z. B. Vance

[1]Sewall Lawrence Fremont, army officer and superintendent of the Wilmington and Weldon Railroad. *Dictionary of North Carolina Biography*, s.v. "Fremont, Sewall Lawrence."

ZBV *to James W. Osborne*   A&H:GLB

State of North Carolina
Executive Department
Raleigh Feby. 28th. 1863.

Judge Osborne[1]
Charlotte N.C.

My dear Sir

I am informed upon undoubted authority that there are quite a number of distilleries in operation in Lincoln and adjoining counties in open defiance of the law. People expect me to do *every thing* now a days and have therefore called on me to enforce this law and as there is no Solicitor for that district I am compelled to call on you. It requires a prompt remedy. Will you please to issue bench warrants against the offenders, or take such other steps as to you may seem best to bring them sharp up and put a stop to these operations? I would be greatly obliged

Most respectfully

Z. B. Vance

[1]James Walker Osborne, superior court judge of Buncombe County, politician, and former superintendent of U.S. Mint at Charlotte. *Dictionary of North Carolina Biography,* s.v. "Osborne, James Walker."

ZBV to James A. Seddon   A&H:GLB

State of North Carolina
Executive Department
Raleigh Feby. 28th. 1863.

Hon. Jas. A. Seddon
Secty of War

Sir

Some six months since a disturbance occurred in Madison Co. N.C. near the Tennessee border—by some disloyal persons, capturing the little county town and seizing a lot of salt and other plunder—An armed force was promptly sent from Knoxville under command of Genl Davis to suppress /the/ insurrection which was accomplished before the local militia could get there, though ordered out immediately.

But in doing so, a degree of cruelty and barbarity was displayed shocking and outrageous in the extreme, on the part of Lt. Col. J. A. Keith 64th. N.C.T. who seems to have been in command and to have acted in this respect without orders from his superiors, so far as I can learn—I beg leave to ask you to read the enclosed letter (copy) from A. S. Merrimon, States Attorney for that judicial district,[1] which you will perceive discloses a scene of horror disgraceful to civilization. I desire you to have proceedings /instituted/ at once against this officer, who if the half be true, is a disgrace to the service and to North Carolina.

You may depend upon the respectability and fairness of Mr. Merrimon, who made an investigation officially by my order—[2] I have also written Genl Davis[3]

Very respectfully
Yr. obt. Svt.
Z. B. Vance

[1]See Merrimon to ZBV, February 16, 24, 1863, A&H:GP.
[2]ZBV to Merrimon, February 9, in this volume.
[3]February 27, in this volume.

ZBV to James A. Seddon A&H:GLB

State of North Carolina
Executive Department
Raleigh Feby. 28th. 1863.

Hon. Jas. A. Seddon
Secty of War

Sir

Yrs per Maj Carrington[1] was duly recd. and with enclosures has been carefully considered. The matter has given me much embarrassment. In the interior of the State there is much suffering for bread already and will be more on account of the failure of the crop from drouth. And the Legislature made a large appropriation of money to enable me to purchase corn and transport it west to feed wives and children of soldiers. I had only secured about 50000 bushels very little of which has been removed for want of transportation. To surrender the whole of this and cease buying more, would so effectually close up the chances of the people for bread that I feel great reluctance in doing so even for so vital an object as the feeding of the Army. I however agreed with Major Carrington to exchange corn bushel for bushel at Charlotte, to turn over a part of my transportation and in consideration of the fact that with my Agents and teams now in the field, I could secure much that he could not reach, I agreed to continue purchasing and to turn over to him as the necessities of the service might require.

This arrangement was the very best I could consistently make; for I do assure you Sir that the suffering of my people will be very great indeed if the State should afford them no relief I feel that I ought not to abandon them—and in preventing suffering in the Soldiers families I am greatly promoting the efficiency of the Army itself. I am now organizing a corps of provision Agents throughout the interior to see what can be bought and how much is hoarded that may be seized and trust that the result may be such as to enable me to surrender to the Army the whole crop of the east

Very Respectfully
Z. B. Vance

[1]February 25, in this volume.

James A. Seddon to ZBV   A&H:GP

Confederate States of America,
War Department,
Richmond, Va. Mch 1st. 1863

His Excy.
Z. B. Vance
Gov of N. Carolina

Sir

I regret to learn from your letter of the 25th. ultimo[1] that such serious opposition is entertained by you to the continuance of the Horses of a portion of
Genl. Jenkins Command in the Western Counties of N Carolina—I had commended your previous letter to the attention of the Genl. Commanding that
Department with the hope that the evil complained of would be enquired into
and if found remediable would be corrected. Doubtless it has been continued
only from the necessity of the Case. The truth is that the large number of Cavalry
in the Mountainous regions of East Tenn and Va. could not be subsisted there
during the winter and it was deemed imperatively necessary that most of the
men should be dismounted and the Horses sent to more distant regions, less
exhausted by being ravaged or drained by the struggling armies, for subsistence
and preparation for the approaching Campaign—It was supposed and indeed
strongly represented that the Counties on the Eastern Slopes of the Mountains
in N C would afford abundant supplies and easily had forage for them, <but only
to> and that benefit would result from sending them there not only to the Horses
but to the people around in affording them a market for their surplus grain and
forage—Only a moderate number however were sent there and more were scattered about in the various more distant Counties of Virginia along the valley
and the Mountain <Counties> Districts—Complaints similar to those addressed
to you have come up from various Counties of this State where they have been
collected, for the products of the last season were scant almost everywhere, and
some irregularities are but too apt to occur with the rather irregular and partially
disciplined cavalry men sent with the Horses. But our authorities have been
content with the effort to redress them by appeal to the Officers or the Commanding Generals and no effort has been made or intimated of a purpose to expel
them by force—They are it will be recalled, not as Your Excellency supposes
broken down Horses, nor can they be considered as Va. Cavalry, tho lately engaged in that State—They are Horses of the Cavalry of the Confederate States,
engaged for the common defense as well of N Carolina as <any> /every/ other
State and placed where they are to preserve them in a state of efficiency for our
further struggles in a common cause I trust therefore Your Excellency will forbear
from any forcible explusion of them, should their still longer stay be deemed
indispensable—Your letter however shall be sent to the General Commanding

the Department whence these Horses were sent and his attention especially invoked to your remonstrances

> With high Esteem
> Very Truly Yrs.
> James A Seddon
> Secy. of War.

[1]In this volume.

William H. C. Whiting to ZBV   A&H:GP

> Hd. Qrs. Wilmington
> March 2nd. 1863.

To his Excellency the Governor
Raleigh.

Sir,

Our necessity here for labor is very great & valuable time is pressing—The negroes we now have ought to be discharged—I am very loth to resort to impressment of the hands of the people immediately in this vicinity who have already done so much & made so many sacrifices to promote the defence, but unless I receive some assistance very speedily from elsewhere, I shall be compelled to do it.

> Very Respy.
> W. H. C Whiting
> Brig Genl.

[Endorsed]

> (Ansd. by Telegraph)
> Raleigh Mar 4th.

Gen Whiting
Wilmington

I have ordered 500 negroes for you. Coming from the interior they will be gathered up slowly, but will hurry them as much as possible

> Z B Vance

[Endorsed] Copy & file

> Z B V

ZBV to Richmond M. Pearson   A&H:GLB

Executive Dept. N.C.
Raleigh March 2d./63

Hon. R. M. Pearson[1]
Chief Justice N.C

Dr. Sir

You are aware that the late Legislature by a joint resolution declared the office of Adjutant General vacant by reason of the incumbent having accepted an incompatible office under the Confed. States Govt.[2] and that by a subsequent Act the appointment was conferred on the Govr.

Gen Martin the present incumbent having declared his intention of testing the legality of the action of the Legislature, by an appeal to the courts, I am placed in a position rather Embarrassing.

To avoid the somewhat unpleasant spectacle of a lawsuit for possession of an office confidential in its relations to myself and very important to the public at this time, I have concluded with the consent of Gen Martin to make a case and ask the opinion of the Supreme Court immediately thereon. With this view I should be greatly obliged and I have no doubt but the public interest would be also subserved if you would have the kindness to call the court together and give its opinion upon this question.[3] As early a day as possible is requested

Very resply. &c.
Z. B. Vance

[1]Richard Mumford Pearson, chief justice of the North Carolina Supreme Court. *Dictionary of American Biography,* s.v. "Pearson, Richard Mumford."

[2]As well as serving as state adjutant general, James Green Martin held a Confederate commission as a brigadier general and commanded the District of North Carolina, a territory from the Roanoke River to the South Carolina line. The legislature had declared his office as adjutant general vacant on December 8, 1862, but he continued in that capacity until as late as March 11, 1863. *Dictionary of North Carolina Biography,* s.v. "Martin, James Green"; Cheney, *North Carolina Government,* 198n.

[3]The court upheld the legislature, and Martin left office. On March 13, ZBV appointed Daniel Gould Fowle as the new adjutant general. Fowle soon resigned and served as a legislator and superior court judge. He became governor in 1889. ZBV to Daniel G. Fowle, March 13, A&H:GLB; *Dictionary of North Carolina Biography,* s.v. "Fowle, Daniel Gould."

Daniel H. Hill to ZBV A&H:GP

Goldsboro N.C.
March 3d. 1863

His Excellency Z. B. Vance
Governor of North Carolina

I have been very anxious to have a long talk with you. But as we have a new excitement about immense reinforcements at Newberne, I am afraid to leave here.

The Yankees will be great fools, if they do not try Wilmington simultaneously with Charleston or prior to the attack at that place. Wilmington is poorly fortified. What they have been doing so long is the mystery to me. What a worthless people we are. When millions are at stake, work cannot be got or where the laborers are procured, nothing is done.

Fort Caswell is particularly weak & I fear would be untenable unless the rear traverse is complete. Genl. Whiting has written to me several times in regard to a negro force. He is very urgent to get 500 negroes for two weeks. If you would make the requisition, they would doubtless be procured without difficulty.

Com Lynch is very anxious to get the rail-road iron at or near Laurensburg & belonging to the Wilmington & Charlotte R.R. He thinks that he will have to abandon his gun boats, unless he can get this iron.

If I can safely leave here, I will do so soon

With great respect
D H Hill

ZBV to John D. Whitford A&H:Whit

March 3d. 1863.

Col. J. D. Whitford

Dr. Sir,

It seems I did not fairly understand you in regard to the iron on your road, when we last talked together. In January I gave Robinson[1] a permit to take up the torn up iron below Kinston, and I did not intend to countermand that permission.[2]

This was the first proposition I made to the Sec'y of the Navy which he first declined. Having afterwards agreed to it, I could not well back out. They propose to return it six months after peace, and I see no way to refuse it without laying myself liable to a charge of being indifferent to the public defense.

Very truly
Z. B. Vance

---

[1]Brig. Gen. Beverly Holcombe Robertson, cavalry commander. Boatner, *Civil War Dictionary*, 702.

[2]See ZBV to John D. Whitford, January 28, and ZBV to William F. Lynch, January 28, in this volume.

ZBV to Francis C. Lawley   A&H:GP

State of North-Carolina,
Executive Department,
Raleigh, March 4th. 1863

Francis C. Lawley[1]
29 Berkeley Square
London

It is agreed between Mr. Francis C Lawley of London England, and Gov Z B Vance on the part of the State of North Carolina, that if he can succeed in effecting a loan on behalf of said State for two hundred thousand pounds in England, payable in cotton at the present prices in the Southern Confederacy, delivered at Wilmington N.C. three months after the conclusion of peace, he is to receive fifteen per cent, of such amount, or twenty, should he find it necessary to use more in effecting said loan.

Z B Vance
Govr. of N.C.

Address to Mr. Lawley The Honbl. Francis C. Lawley and inclose the communication within an <En> Envelope addressed Messrs. Leeman & Clark Solicitors York, England.

[1]An English correspondent covering the war for the *Times* (London) and reportedly having "universal acquaintance" with banks in England. A. D. Banks, an Alabama relative of ZBV, had introduced Lawley to the governor. A. D. Banks to ZBV, February 27, A&H:VanPC. See also William Stanley Hoole, *Lawley Covers the Confederacy* (Tuscaloosa: Confederate Publishing Company, 1964).

ZBV to Thomas D. McDowell   SHC:Mall

State of North Carolina
Executive Department
Raleigh, March 4th. 1863

Hon T. D. McDowell[1]
Richmond Va

Dear Sir

Our mutual friend Col P Mallett[2] who will hand you this will also show you an unsealed letter to Mr. Seddon which will show what I have asked to be done for him—He can himself explain the whole matter. It is a hard case indeed, and I desire you to see Mr Dortch, Mr Davis and if necessary the whole of our delegation and ask them oblige me and a gallant officer by seconding my request. It is a splendid body of men, well equipt, well disciplined, and fought with most desperate gallantry, at Kinston. Every body here would grieve to see them scattered & their individuality lost. Besides there are a number of high spirited young officers who would be entirely thrown out and reduced to ranks.

Very truly & respectfully yours
Z B Vance

[1]Thomas David McDowell, lawyer, legislator, and Confederate congressman. Wakelyn, *Biographical Dictionary of the Confederacy*, 296.

[2]Peter Mallett, commandant of conscripts in North Carolina, who led a unit of conscripts into battle at Kinston in December 1862, was wounded, and was then temporarily replaced by Thomas P. August. Johnston, *Papers of Vance*, 1:175n; Clark, *Histories of Regiments from North Carolina*, 4:407–408; ZBV to James Seddon, January 26, in this volume.

ZBV to Nicholas W. Woodfin   A&H:GLB

State of North Carolina
Executive Department
Raleigh March 4th. 1863

N. W. Woodfin Esqr[1]
Saltville Va.

My dear Sir
Your letter[2] by Mr [Joseph] Hine was duly recd. and read as well as my limited education would permit.

I have just seen Col August[3] & he agrees to detail all your hands as desired—I hope by this means you will be enabled to keep, /in wood and keep/ the works going during the summer. We shall need every bushel we can get next fall. Notwithstanding that Salt is now down to $5. per bushel in Wilmington for domestic & $8 for Turks Island,[4] the packing season having passed. I am glad that you have succeeding in getting some of it away. I had entirely dispaired of getting any over the Va roads, seeing how difficult it is to get our own roads to do any thing here at home. I think your suggestion a good one about hauling across the mountains to Morganton or near there. If you should think it indispensable I will order my quarter master to buy up or hire & establish a line of wagons to run regularly from the works during the summer and fall to the R. Road. It would be first necessary however to secure protection from the military along the Tennessee border, as I learn that travel is very insecure there and frequently outrages are perpetrated on passengers. I have no doubt but this could be done. I don't know how your corn is to be got to you when the salt can't be brought here. If no other way be possible it might be taken up the Western Road and the salt waggons might load over with it. This would be slow and precarious but the works must not stop. I will also try the quarter master Genl. if he has any corn in Western Virginia to exchange with you which would be a mutual accomodation. This is the best plan if he should have any in that section.

Rest assured that every thing possible shall be done to keep you going and to sustain your efforts in this most important branch of subsistence.

Most truly

Z. B. Vance

[1]Nicholas Washington Woodfin, lawyer, farmer, and politician, serving as North Carolina's representative at the salt works at Saltville, Va. Ashe, Weeks, and Van Noppen, *Biographical History*, 2:481–486.

[2]February 24, A&H:GP.

[3]As commandant of conscripts, Thomas P. August was in charge of detailing the state's conscripts, as well as their drilling and subsistence.

[4]Salt from Turks Island in the Bahamas.

ZBV to James Longstreet   A&H:GLB

State of North Carolina
Executive Department
Raleigh March 4th. 1863.

Genl Longstreet[1]
Comdg. Dept. N.C.
Petersburg Va

Genl.

I trust you will pardon me for the seeming indelicacy of making a suggestion concerning matters not strictly within my province I allude to the removal of Brig. Genl. Pryor from his command on the Black Water.[2] This line defending the approaches to our most important rail road connection[3] is almost regarded as a N.C. command, hence the interest I feel in it.

From information received daily I am satisfied that Genl Pryor has the confidence of all parties in that region. The citizens of that portion of N.C. for whom only I have the right to speak, I know greatly regret to see Genl P removed. A thorough acquaintance with the people and the country has begotten mutual confidence and good will, and when informed of the fact, I feel sure, that unless the good of the service should require it, you will not disregard the wishes of our people. Of course this is merely a suggestion. Your superior knowledge of our military necessities will enable you to decide for yourself what is best for the country.

Permit me General to Express the Satisfaction of the people of North Carolina, exhibited everywhere, on seeing the announcement that they were to be defended by the gallantry & skill of General Longstreet. With my best wishes and tendering you my cordial cooperation whenever and wherever you may think it available,

I am Genl.

> With highest respect
> Yr. Obt. Srvt.
> Z. B. Vance

[1]James Longstreet, corps commander in the Army of Northern Virginia, had assumed command of the Department of North Carolina and Southern Virginia on February 26. Boatner, *Civil War Dictionary*, 490, 599.

[2]Blackwater River, which rises in Virginia and flows southwest into North Carolina to join the Chowan River a short distance south of the Virginia line. William S. Powell, *The North Carolina Gazetteer* (Chapel Hill: University of North Carolina Press, 1968), 52.

[3]At Weldon.

ZBV to James A. Seddon   SHC:Mall

> State of North Carolina
> Executive Dept.
> Raleigh, March 5th. 1863

Hon. Jas. A. Seddon,
Secy. of War,

Sir

I beg leave to ask your favorable consideration in the case of Col. Mallett, late commanding the Camp of Instruction[1] near this place, who will hand you this, and make known the circumstances of his case.

His conduct whilst in command, I believe, gave general satisfaction: He organized a Camp Guard of some 600 men, who were duly officered by his assistants and drill masters and rigidly disciplined. Ordered suddenly into the midst of the severe conflict at Kinston, their conduct was such as to elicit the praise of veteran troops and the whole country. Their heavy losses show the gallantry of their bearing and their leader. Col. Mallett was severely wounded, from which he is now slowly recovering. On hobbling back to Raleigh, he finds himself superseded by Col. August, and an order directing his command to be disbanded & placed in various regiments as Conscripts! What is to become of him? I respectfully submit that it is a great hardship upon these brave men and their officers, after having been associated together for eight or ten months and fought together on the field, to be now scattered among strange regiments, their officers conscripted and their efficient and gallant Commander turned out of the service.

In view of the hardship of the cause and the meritorious conduct of both men & officers, I am constrained, in spite of my general indisposition to form new regiments, to ask you first to retain Col. M. in command of the Camp as heretofore, whence he could be easily sent to any point where he might be needed; or if this cannot be done I ask that he may be sent into the field with his entire command, having Col. August to form a new guard from the new Conscripts.

It is one of the finest bodies of men in the Southern Confederacy and on their own account should not be separated.

> Very respectfully
> Yr. obt. svt.
> (signed)   Z. B. Vance

[1]The camp of instruction for conscripts—named Camp Holmes for General Theophilus Holmes—had been established in June 1862. Johnston, *Papers of Vance*, 1:175n.

ZBV to Stephen R. Mallory   A&H:GLB

> State of North Carolina
> Executive Department
> Raleigh March 7th. 1863

Hon S. R. Mallory
Secy Navy

Sir

You can have the iron requested by your letter of the 13th. ulto.,[1] to be replaced, if you will permit it to be exchanged for the old iron on the different road of the state[2]

They are rapidly running down and are applying for the same iron. I suppose their worn out rails would answer the same purpose for rolling

> Very respectfully
> Yr. obt. srvt.
> Z. B. Vance

[1]Mallory had requested 707 tons of unused railroad iron from the Wilmington, Charlotte, and Rutherfordton Railroad "to be rolled into plates for protecting the gun boat and battery under construction on Roanoke River." Mallory to ZBV, February 13, A&H:GP.

[2]Atlantic and North Carolina Railroad.

ZBV *to Jefferson Davis*   A&H:GLB

State of North Carolina
Executive Department
Raleigh March 7th. 1863.

His Excellency
President Davis

Sir

In November last I procured the services of Mr John White of Warranton N.C. an extensive and well known merchant, to go to Europe and purchase supplies for the N.C. Troops, on the condition that his son-in-law Sergt. S. P. Arrington 12th. N.C. Troops should be detailed to take charge of his affairs during his absence. As it was a matter of public importance, I made no doubt but so small a favor would be readily granted, on the score of courtesy if nothing else.

To my great surprise however, both Mr [George W.] Randolph and his sucessor have refused my application after a full explanation of the urgency of the case, as Mr White's services could not have been secured without a positive promise of his son-in-law's detail. It is a small matter certainly, a *very small matter*, but I feel it my duty to bring it to your attention[1]

Very Respectfully
Yr. obt. Servt.
Z. B. Vance

[1]Samuel Peter Arrington remained with his regiment until paroled at Appomattox Court House in April 1865. Manarin and Jordan, *North Carolina Troops*, 5:117, 148.

ZBV *to Braxton Bragg*   A&H:GLB

State of North Carolina
Executive Department
Raleigh March 9th. 1863.

Genl. Bragg[1]

Sir

I venture to make a request of you that I think will conduce to the public welfare as it certainly will to the credit of our State.

Quite a considerable body of troops raised in the mountains of N. Carolina are now in East Tennessee, they consist of Col. Allens regt., Col Loves, Col Folks (cavalry) Col Palmers' regt. Col Thomas battallion, in all some 4000 men.[2] Guarding bridges mountain passes and keeping the population in check, they have been subjected to but little discipline necessarily and their proximity to their homes causes constant desertions and in some cases almost complete dis-organization. I ask that they may be sent somewhere else further from home and placed in more active service. Numerous petitions to this effect reach me from both citizens and soldiers and from all I can learn they will reflect but little honor upon the state and do little for the cause unless this is done. I know the men General, and they are as good material for soldier as there is upon the continent and under other auspices would shed as much glory upon the name of North Carolina, as their brothers have in Virginia and Middle Tennessee.

I have the honor to bring this matter to the attention of the President, but he did not think proper to interfere with the disposition of the troops in your Department. Earnestly hoping for your favorable consideration, I beg to assure you that I am with great respect & esteem

Yr. obt. Servt.
Z. B. Vance.

[1] Braxton Bragg (a native North Carolinian), commander of the Army of Tennessee. *Dictionary of North Carolina Biography*, s.v. "Bragg, Braxton."

[2] Lawrence M. Allen, Sixty-fourth Regiment North Carolina Troops; James Robert Love, Sixty-ninth Regiment North Carolina Troops; George N. Folk, Sixty-fifth Regiment North Carolina Troops; John B. Palmer, Fifty-eighth Regiment North Carolina Troops; William Holland Thomas, Sixty-ninth Regiment and Thomas's Legion North Carolina Troops. Clark, *Histories of Regiments from North Carolina*, 3:431, 659, 673, 729–732.

ZBV to James M. Mason   A&H:GLB

State of North Carolina
Executive Department
Raleigh March 11th. 1863.

Hon. James M. Mason
Comsr. C. S. America
London

My dear Sir

Some time since I [*sent*] to Europe, Mr John White as agent for this State for the purpose of effecting a loan and purchasing supplies for the soldiers of N.C. who by agreement with the Confederate Government has undertaken to equip her own troops. I directed him to communicate with you and obtain your advice and assistance which I hope he has done I have not heard from him since he reached Liverpool and therefore know not how he has succeeded. Last week I met with the Hon Francis T. [C.] Lawley—29 Barkley Square London, who suggested that if a power of attorney were sent to you and he were to take the matter in hand, that he could perhaps secure a loan for this state of one million dollars on favorable terms, by the means of some official and family influence which he could bring to bear. Fearing from his long delay that Mr White has been unsuccessful, I have concluded to try Mr Lawley's plan, if you will so greatly oblige me and the State which I represent in the manner he proposes—

I accordingly enclose herewith a power of Attorney[1] authorizing you to represent me in the matter and also letters to Mr White and Col. D. K. McRae (whom I afterwards sent abroad on the same business) instructing them to suspend their own efforts and permit the new attempt to be made.

The terms proposed were eight percent interest on bonds redeemable in Cotton at the present prices in the Confederacy (about 17 to 20 cents) to be delivered at Wilmington N.C. within three months after a treaty of peace &c. You can issue the bonds yourself having them printed &c all at my expense of course. Presuming that you are fully posted on matters of news, I will only add that we are all cheerful and hopeful of our affairs and will go into the Spring Campaign with life & vigor

> Most Respectfully
> Yr. obt. Servant
> Z. B. Vance

[1]Dated March 12 and copied in A&H:GLB.

ZBV to John White   A&H:GP

> State of North Carolina,
> Executive Department,
> Raleigh, March 12th. 1863

John White Esq.

Dear Sir:

If you have not as yet met with success in effecting the necessary loan, to accomplish the purposes of your mission, you will please see the Hon James M. Mason before making any further efforts—I have seen & conversed with a gentleman from England who has suggested a mode whereby we may be able to negotiate a loan through Mr. Mason—on a principle different from that upon which you were authorized to proceed—You will consult with him & he will explain the arrangement I desire to make through him—& I therefore need not give you the details in this note—

Hoping that among you our object may be accomplished & wishing you a safe return to the state & your family I remain—

> Very respectfully yours
> Z. B. Vance

See other side—

P.S. I have intimated to Col McRae that he might purchase some cotton cards. If you get funds enough, I would be glad you would also purchase some and one or two machines for making them with a quantity of wire &c. I do not know what a machine will cost; if but little then purchase several of them. Use your judgment—Cards are now the greatest want of our people—

                              Z B Vance

                    ZBV to Duncan K. McRae   A&H:GLB

                         State of North Carolina
                         Executive Department
                         Raleigh March 12th. 1863
Col. D. K. McRae

My dear Sir
    Circumstances occurring since your departure render it unnecessary for us to purchase the number of arms originally contemplated. I think one fourth (say 2500) will be a sufficient investment at present—the Legislature having declined to raise any State Troops. Should you succeed in effecting a loan on your Scrip, you might invest it in shoes, blankets and gray cloth of the Army and Cotton & Wool Cards for the people.
    If you have not succeeded in getting the loan, please suspend all further efforts and consult with Mr Mason of Va. our Commissioner to England, as I have adopted another plan, to be tried in case you and Mr White have both failed. For various reasons upon reflection, I have concluded that I would prefer you to have the negotiation of the Scrip instead of Mr Saunders [*George N.Sanders*]. I had no intention of letting Mr. S. hawk our paper about through Europe. I know you will appreciate my reasons. Should you be in Europe (and I am writing as though you were) I desire you to act with Mr White, put your fortunes together, Ship your purchases together &c.
    Your family are well. Your various letters from Nassau were duly received

                         Respectfully & Truly
                         Z. B. Vance

James Longstreet to ZBV   A&H:GLB

Hd. Qrs. Petersburg Va.
March 12th./63.

His Excellency
Gov. Z. B. Vance
N.C.

Sir

Your favor of the 4th. inst[1] was received at Wilmington, on the 8th. The removal of Genl Pryor from the Blackwater was made necessary by other move-ments of troops. I can assure you and the good people (in whose behalf you write) that the change will in no way disparage their interest. The officer now in com-mand on the Blackwater is one of our most energetic and enterprising Brigadiers. I can safely assure you that yourself and the citizens will be quite well satisfied with the change after the Officer is known. Genl Pryor's command was only in this Department for the winter. It will soon return to the command where it properly belongs, Western Virginia. I hope that this may be a satisfactory expla-nation of the recent change on the Blackwater.

I thank you sincerely for your kind expressions about myself and trust that I may be able to fulfill your expectations. We have many difficulties to contend with and one of the most serious is the want of system and order in our trans-portation. If you can assist in regulating this, I think /that/ we can promise you important results in our operations

It was my intention to have done myself the honor to make you a flying visit, but I find that I cannot well quit my post.

With the greatest respect
I am Your mt. obt Sert
James Longstreet
Lt. Genl. Comdg.

[1]In this volume.

David A. Barnes to John Pool   A&H:GLB

State of North Carolina
Executive Department
Raleigh March 12th. 1863.

John Pool Esqr[1]

Dear Sir

Several companies of Partisan Rangers, for local defence, have been formed in the counties east of the Chowan River, enough to form a battalion, which may ultimately be increased to a Regiment. His Excellency Governor Vance is desirous of procuring the services of some one to command these forces who has a thorough knowledge of the country, the confidence of the people and such prudence, discretion and energy as will make them effective. Your name has been suggested itself to him as a person possessing these qualifications and he directs me to tender you the command with the rank of Lt Colonel and to express the earnest hope that you will accept it

> With sentiments of great respect
> Your obt. Servt.
> David A. Barnes
> Aid de Camp to the Governor

[1]Bertie County lawyer, legislator, strong unionist, and postwar U.S. senator. *Dictionary of American Biography*, s.v. "Pool, John."

Joseph E. Brown to ZBV   A&H:GLB

> Executive Department
> Milledgeville March 14th. 1863

His Excellency
Z. B. Vance

Dear Sir

I have permitted Mr. Brown[1] to take one of our Card machines apart and take drawings of it to his satisfaction. Though the machine is complicated I trust he may find no difficulty in making one. It affords me much pleasure to have been able to comply with your requests. I trust your energetic efforts may result in much benefit to the people of your Noble State. If we can make a supply of clothing and provisions we can, with the blessing of Providence fight the enemy for a score of years.

Assuring you of my readiness at all times to serve you in any way in my power & have the honor to be

> Very respectfully
> Your obt Servt.
> Joseph E. Brown

[1]Machinist sent to Georgia to learn how to build machinery for manufacture of cotton and wool cards. See Joseph E. Brown to ZBV, February 4, in this volume.

ZBV to Daniel H. Hill   A&H:GLB

[*Telegram*]

Raleigh March 14th. 1863.

Genl. D. H. Hill
Kinston N.C.

I hope you will not send so many cavalry men to Wilkes—a small body of infantry with the Militia would be much better, and the consumption of forage would distress that country generally

Z. B. Vance

ZBV to David A. Barnes   A&H:GP

[*Telegram*]

Kinston [*March*] 16 1863

Col Barnes

Cahoons Cavalry are not under my control I dont want them [*to*] do anything for me they are under Genl Hills orders entirely tell Genl. Fowle he can order them away when he chooses nothing very important our Troops are not attacking Newberne The impression here seems to be that it is a foraging movement only Pettigrew lost four Killed and Twenty wounded at Barringtons Ferry No particulars—show this [*to*] Mrs V

Z B Vance

David A. Barnes to Robert E. Lee   A&H:GLB

State of North Carolina
Executive Department
Raleigh March the 19th. 1863

General Robert E. Lee

His Excellency Governor Vance has received information that certain soldiers, belonging to the brigades of Generals Ramseur and Hoke[1] are now under arrest and are being tried for desertion.

His Excellency is deeply pained to learn this and directs me to communicate to you the facts and circumstances connected with the return by these men to the Army.

While Major General G. W. Smith was in command of this Department he caused an order to be issued extending a full pardon (except forfeiture of pay for the period of unauthorized absence) to all enlisted men absent without leave, who should voluntarily return to their respective commands, on or before the

10th. day of February. Upon consultation between Genl. Smith & the Governor it was thought that a proclamation by His Excellency appealing to the patriotism & State pride of absentees would induce their speedy return to duty. A proclamation[2] was accordingly issued and the reasonable expectation as to its effect was fully realized and hundreds were induced to return to their colors—

The period at first limited was so brief that numbers in remote parts of the State were unable to comply. With a knowledge of this fact and in conformity with an order of Genl. French another proclamation was issued extending the time to the 5th. of March—It is true that General Smith's order could only extend to his own Department, but his Excellency thought it right to extend it to all North Carolina soldiers—

Copies of the order of Gen. Smith and the proclamations of the Governor are herewith enclosed.

In the opinion of His Excellency the punishment of these men would be a gross violation of justice and good faith and he enters his most solemn protest against it.

In issuing these proclamations he was actuated by a sincere and earnest desire to promote the interest of the public service and he had reason to believe that his course would meet the approbation of the Confederate authorities and he trusts and believes that in this reasonable hope he will not be disappointed—He will not allow himself to *doubt* but that your sense of justice and right will induce you to cause all such soldiers to be immediately discharged from arrest

> With sentiments of the
> highest respect
> Your obedient Servant
> D. A. Barnes
> Aid de Camp to the Governor

[1]Stephen Dodson Ramseur and Robert Frederick Hoke. Boatner, *Civil War Dictionary*, 404–405, 677.

[2]January 26, in this volume.

ZBV to Thomas P. August   A&H:GP

Copy

> State of North Carolina
> Executive Department
> Raleigh March 20th. 1863.

Col. T. P. August
Comdg. Conscripts
Raleigh N.C.

Colonel

I desire to have an understanding with the War Dept. in regard to the Conscription of State officers. Applications are made to me almost every day to apply

for the exemption or detail of Such officers and it is proper that the matter should
be defined. Zealous as I have been and continue to be in the enforcement of this
law, I cannot permit my own officers to be conscribed. The ground I shall assume
is, that all state officers and employees necessary to the operation of this government—of which necessity I must judge—Shall not be interferred with by the
enrolling officers and any attempt to arrest such men will be resisted.

This I deem not only necessary, <but due to the> to the dire administration
of the government, but due to the rights and dignity of the sovereign state over
whose destinies I have the honor to preside. If not authorized to decide in the
premises yourself, I respectfully request that you lay the matter before the War
Dept.

> Very Respectfully
> Yr. obt. Servt.
>
> (Signed)   Z. B. Vance

David A. Barnes to Collett Leventhorpe   A&H:GLB

> State of North Carolina
> Executive Department
> Raleigh March 20th. 1863

Col. C. Leventhorpe[1]
Commdg. 11th. Regt. N.C.T.

Colonel

His Excellency Gov. Vance has received your letter[2] suggesting that there are
large tracts of land remaining uncultivated in the counties of Pitt & Beaufort,
which a number of poor people in their immediate vicinity would be pleased to
cultivate by paying a reasonable rent to the owners and giving the names of a
number of the proprietors.

His Excellency Governor Vance directs me to return you his thanks for the
suggestion, that he has no power to grant such authority, but that he will communicate with the proprietors upon the subject[3]

> With sentiments of high respect
> Yr. obt. Svt.
> David A. Barnes
> Aid de Camp to the Governor

[1]Collett Leventhorpe, commanding the Eleventh Regiment North Carolina Troops in
eastern North Carolina. *Dictionary of North Carolina Biography,* s.v. "Leventhorpe, Collett."

[2]March 11, Mich:Sch.

[3]See Barnes to William Grimes, William Blount, and William Blount Jr., March 20,
A&H:GLB; and Grimes to Barnes, March 21, A&H:GP.

Soldiers' Wives to ZBV   A&H:GP

Salisbury, NC
March 21st./63
To His Excellency the Gov of the State of NC

Dear Sir—

Having from absolute necessity been forced into measures not at all pleasant to obtain something to eat by the cruel and unfeeling Speculators who have been gathering up at enormous prices, not only bread stuffs but every thing even down to eggs Chickens & Vegetables to carry out of our State for the purpose of Speculating upon them We feel it /now/ our duty Honored and esteemed Gov to inform you truthfully of our proceedings and humbly pray to inform us whether or not we are justifyable in what we have done—and if not for Heavens Sake tell /us/ how these evils are to be remedied.

We Sir are all Soldiers Wives or Mothers our Husbands & Sons are now separated from us by this cruel War not only to defend our /humble/ homes but the homes & /property/ of the rich man and at the same time that we are grieved at this separation yet we murmur not—God bless them our hearts go with them and our prayers follow them for Heavens protection through all the trials and difficulties that may surround them, but Sir we have to live and we must live while they are gone from us and that too without much or in many cases any assistance from them for how far will eleven dollars go in a family now /when/ Meat /is/ from 75 to $1[.]oo pr pd flour $50 pr bll. wood from 4 to 5$ pr load, meal 4 an[d] 5 dollars pr bushel, eggs 50 to 60 cts pr doz chickens $7[.]oo pr doz, Molasses $7[.]oo pr gal rye 20 cts pr qt. & and, addition to that we are willing and do work early and late to keep off starvation which is now staring us in the face, but the government only allows us 50 cts a pr for lined pants and 75 cts for coats and there are few of us who can make over a dollar a day, and we have upon an average from three to five helpless children to support and still we complain not at Government prices if we can only get bread divided among us and meat at a reasonable price but Sir many of us work day after day without a morsal of meat to strengthen us for our Labors and often times we are without bre/a/d Now Sir how We ask you in the name of God are we to live.

Laboring under all these difficulties Sir we as we have told you in the commencement of this letter were from Stern necessity compelled to go in serch of food to sustain life and some forty or more respectable but poor women started out backed by many citizens to get food we took our little money with us and offered to pay Government prices for what we took but the Speculators refused us any thing or even admittance into their premises We then forced our way in and compelled them to give us something & we succeeded in obtaining twenty three blls of flour two sacks of salt about half a bll of molasses and twenty dollars in money, which was equally divided among us in the presence of our highly esteemed friend and Lawyer Blackmen, besides many other gentlemen of good and high standing in society. Now Sir this is all we done and necessity compelled us to do it and the reason we have addressed you Sir is that we understand that we have been reported to you as plunderers of the town disturbing the peace and quiet of the community, but Sir we have honestly told you the whole proceeding and we now pray your protection or a remedy for these evils—we as much as any one deplore the necessity of such proceeding and do humbly pray you in behalf of our helpless children to so fix the prices of bread and meat that we can by our own labor gain an honest portion of that which sustains life—

To whom else can we go but to you our highly esteemed and cherished Gov to redress these evils. You were the choice of our Husbands and Sons and we too look up to you Sir with perfect confidence as being able and willing to do something for us—we ask not charity we only as[k] for fair and reasonable prices for provisions and leather for Sir many of us have been shoeless this whole winter except the cloth shoes we can make for ourselves which are no protection even against the cold, in conclusion Sir we humbly beg you after carefully and prayerfully considering our letter to let us hear from you—you can address Mary C Moore Salisbury NC and that Heavens richest blessings and a long life may be your portion with your happy family is the earnest and heartfelt prayers of many

Soldiers Wives[1]

---

[1]For descriptions of the so-called food riots involving the women of Salisbury, see Barrett, *Civil War in North Carolina*, 188, and Michael Brown to ZBV, March 18, A&H:GP.

ZBV to James A. Seddon   A&H:GP

Copy

State of North Carolina
Executive Department
Raleigh March 21st. 1863.

Hon Jas. A. Seddon
Secty of War

Sir

I beg to call yr. attention to the statements contained in the enclosed letter[1] from Lt. F. P. Axby, a respectable young Soldier resident in Cherokee County N.C. From it you will perceive that his brother & two other citizens of that county have been arrested by a parcel of armed Soldiers from Georgia & carried off no one knows where or why. My object is to ascertain why these citizens of North Carolina were so arrested, what for, by whose authority, where they are taken to, and what is proposed to be done with them. ? . Presuming that the

whole thing has been without your <authority> /knowledge/, I ask these questions of you because you have the means of obtaining answers to them which I
have not. As such proceedings cannot be tolerated for a moment, I have issued
orders *pendente lite*[2] to the State officers of that County to call out the Militia
and shoot the first man who attempts to perpetrate a Similar outrage without
the authority of the Marshal of that district

Hoping that you may find leasure to answer soon, I am, Sir

With every sentiment of
respect & regard
Yr. obt. servt.
(Signed)   Z. B. Vance

[1]Not extant.
[2]Meanwhile, or while litigation continues.

ZBV to James A. Seddon   A&H:GP

Copy

State of North Carolina
Executive Department
Raleigh March 21st. 1863.

Hon. Jas A. Seddon
Secty. of War

Sir

Yours of the 7th. inst,[1] enclosing letters from Lt. Col. Cook & Genl. Jones,[2]
in relation to impressment of forage by a detachment of Gen. Jenkin's Cavalry,
has been received. I am sorry to see that the charge of impressment is denied
upon the authority of "Sergt. Hale"[3] the concurrent testimony of the citizens of
about twenty Counties, with at least fifty letters to that effect in my office would
seem to be Sufficient to establish a fact of general notoriety. These men were in
service detachments operating in as many different counties and Sergt. Hale
hardly could know what they were all doing at the same time. Their method was
to go to a farmer's house and tell him they wanted corn at $1.50 per bushel and
if he did not sell *they would take it.* In some instances their Quarter Masters
attended public Sales and publicly notified the assemblage (most of them families
of absent Soldiers) that they need not bid for the corn, that they were determined
to have it! Yielding when resistance would have been useless, they (the Cavalry)
took the corn at such prices as they saw proper to pay, and this is not impressment! I beg leave also to assure you that the imputations indulged in by Genl
Jones & Lt. Col. Cook against the loyalty of the people of that region (I suppose

also on the authority of Sergt. Hale) are entirely without foundation in fact. The refusal to take Confederate money (if such was the case) originated solely in the fact that they did not have the corn to sell. Neither North Carolina money or gold could buy an article which was not in the Country. That country to my personal knowledge may safely challenge any Similar region in the South to show a better muster roll in the army. But that is not the matter at issue. I complain that a large body of broken down cavalry horses are in No. Carolina eating up the substance of the people in a region desolated by drouth and reduced to the verge of starvation, impressing it at prices /about/ one half the market rates— the people or the horses must Suffer. I ask for the removal of the horses. It is denied or refused. That is the question. I beg leave to disabuse your mind of the impression which it seems to entertain, that I object to these impressments because they were for *Virginia* cavalry. By no means. I did not term them such, at least did not so intend to term them. I have no prejudice against the troops from any state engaged in defending the common cause. But I *am* unwilling to see the corn taken from the mouths of women and children for the use of *any* troops, when these troops might be easily removed to regions where there is corn to sell. And I earnestly request once more that they may be so removed.

> Very Respectfully
> Yr. obt. servt.
> (signed)   Z. B. Vance

[1]A&H:GP.

[2]A. F. Cooke, Eighth Virginia Cavalry, and Samuel Jones, commander, Department of West Virginia. Their letters are found only with the copy of Seddon's March 7 correspondence recorded in A&H:GLB.

[3]J. C. Hale, serving as agent for impressment of forage.

Leonidas L. Polk to ZBV   A&H:GP

> Camp 43d. N.C.T.
> Kinston N.C.
> March 23d./63

Gov. Z. B. Vance

Governor

About the 1st. of Jany. a call was made in Anson County for slaves to work on the defences around Wilmington. The people very generously responded to the call, with *the distinct understanding that the negroes were to be returned within four (4) weeks.* Many of the largest slaveowners in the county, who have done nothing for the cause, sent none of those sent, many ran away at the expiration of their /time/ & went home. Several of us have negroes in *Fort Caswell* yet &

when, through our agent, we attempt to ascertain <of> the probable length of time they are to be kept, or whether we are to receive compensation for their labor, we receive nothing but insult from self important & impertinent officials. If they had been Called for, for 3 months, they would have been sent as readily, but the bad faith with which it has been managed has caused a great deal of complaint, & if they get anymore negroes from Anson Co. they have them to *steal*. They promised weeks ago, to get slaves from other counties to relieve ours, but it is yet neglected. I am willing & anxious to do all I can for the Cause, but our families have rights & they must be protected, & hence I appeal to you. I understand the most of the negroes yet retained belong to men who are in service. If the rights of our families are to be violated, or they are to be robbed of the means of support, at the pleasure of unfaithful, insolent, & impudent military officials, then the end of this struggle is not far distant. Feeling assured that you will give this matter due attention I subscribe myself with sentiments of very high esteem your most obt svt

L. L. Polk[1]

[1]Leonidas LaFayette Polk, a lieutenant in the Forty-third Regiment North Carolina Troops. After the war he became first commissioner of agriculture in North Carolina, a newspaper editor, leader in the Farmers' Alliance, and founder of the *Progressive Farmer*. *Dictionary of American Biography*, s.v. "Polk, Leonidas LaFayette"; Manarin and Jordan, *North Carolina Troops*, 10:370.

James A. Seddon to ZBV   A&H:GP

Confederate States of America,
War Department,
Richmond, Va. Mar 25, 1863.

His Excellency Z. B. Vance,
Governor of North Carolina,
Raleigh, N.C.

Sir,

I have received your letter[1] with regard to the arrest of citizens of North Carolina by a party of Cavalry from Georgia.

In reply I have the honor to say, that the Department has no information at present concerning the alledged arrest and removal referred to you [sic] by your

Excellency, but will proceed to institute inquiry and require report of all the facts and redress of any injustice done. I will advise you of the result of my inquiries.

With high regard
Your obdt. servt
James A Seddon
Secretary of War

[1]March 21, in this volume.

Gabriel J. Rains to ZBV   A&H:GP

Confederate States of America,
Bureau of Conscription,
Richmond, Va. March 25th. 1863

His Excellency
Z. B. Vance, Govr. of N. Ca.
Raleigh, N.C.

Sir.

Your letter to Col. August, of the 20th. inst.,[1] has been referred to this Bureau, and I regret that circumstances have arisen impairing that harmony necessary for a proper execution of the law of Conscription.

So far from opposition we have calculated on your assistance in this matter, and I had already written to the Commandant of Conscripts for N. Ca. "that whenever the wishes of his Excellency, the Gov'r, can be accorded with, without clear infraction of law, it is desirable so to do." The law exempts Judicial and Executive officers of State Governments, except those liable to militia duty. This you will readily perceive must be the rule of guidance for the agents of this Bureau, and there are no means, short of supernatural power, for them to know, outside of the law, of such employees your Excellency wishes to be exempted. Hence forbearance is respectfully asked until reference can be had with this Bureau, with which you are cordially invited to correspond, believing that between us of the same State, no difference can occur in such matters the legality of which is left to your judgment.

Col. Mallett has been ordered to relieve Col. August in his duties as Commandant of Conscripts in N. Ca.

I am, Sir, very respectfully
Your obt. Servt.
G. J. Rains[2]
Brig Genl. & Supt.

[1]In this volume.
[2]Gabriel James Rains, native North Carolinian, superintendent of Bureau of Conscription, and explosives expert. W. Davis Waters, " 'Deception is the Art of War': Gabriel J. Rains, Torpedo Specialist of the Confederacy," *North Carolina Historical Review* 66 (January 1989): 29–60.

ZBV to James A. Seddon   A&H:GLB

[*Telegram*]

Raleigh March 25 [1863]

Hon Jas. A. Seddon
Richmond Va.

Genl. Pillow[1] has sent a detachment of Cavalry into Western N. Carolina to enroll and arrest conscripts without the shadow of law and in defiance of the proper authorities. Please order it stopped through Col Collant Greenville, Tenn. or there will be resistance and bloodshed

Z. B. Vance

[1]Gideon Johnson Pillow, holding only a minor command in Tennessee because of a reprimand for his conduct at the Battle of Fort Donelson in February 1862. *Dictionary of American Biography*, s.v. "Pillow, Gideon Johnson."

James A. Seddon to ZBV   A&H:GP

[*Telegram*]

Richmond Mch 26 186[3]

Gov Z B Vance

Gen Pillow has been already Expressly forbidden to Interfere with the regular enforcement of the Conscript law by the proper Bureau officers

Jas A Seddon

James A. Seddon to ZBV   A&H:GP

Confederate States of America,
War Department,
Richmond, Va. Mch 26th. 1863

His Excy
Z B Vance
Govr. of N Carolina

Sir
    The application recently made by Genl. Edney[1] of your State, sustained by your endorsement, seeking that effective measures be taken to repress and disarm

the bands of marauding deserters and refugees represented to be collecting in the mountains of your Western Counties, has been submitted to the President and received the attentive consideration of the Department. It is not deemed Judicious to assent to the suggestion of the petition presented by Genl. Edney that the Conscript Law be suspended in the Counties west of the Blue Ridge in your State, and that local organizations of the Militia or State Forces be formed to operate against these marauding Bands. In addition to the objection, that the Conscripts of this District, when safely available, might thus be withdrawn from the calls of the public service, when they are now so needed, it is feared, that the use of these men exclusively or mainly against the marauding and disaffected classes of their vicinity might engender the worst sort of civil strife and lead to inextinguishable feuds and mutual reprisals to the grievous affliction and waste of the whole region. It has been thought a wiser course to order Genl. Donelson,[2] in whose Command the District lies, to send an efficient officer with an adequate command to search through the <Counties> mountainous disaffected localities, capture <and> /or/ disperse all outlying Bands and, seeking the aid of the enrolling officers of the District, to conscribe and send to the remoter Armies all of Conscript ages believed to be dangerous or disloyal. At the same time partly to cooperate with him, but mainly afterwards to report similar manifestations and preserve order, it is suggested that all the loyal citizens, not liable to conscription, should be organized into troops "for local defence & special service" to remain quietly at their Homes when no danger existed, but to be liable be called into service whenever occasion demanded These if promptly formed might act at once with Genl Donelson's Command, but in any event, it is hoped, may be constituted in time effectually to keep down any future uprisings or collections of marauders. Should they prove inefficient or inadequate for such purpose, Conscripts collected from the loyal portion of the neighboring people will be detailed to join and act under such organizations so long as their services may be necessary. In this mode, the Conscripts will be retained at command, nor will they be formed into separate organizations, from which when once formed of Conscripts, experience has shown they cannot be withdrawn without difficulty and seeming injustice, especially to the officers.

Sincere solicitude is felt by the Department for the relief of the District referred to, and it has dictated the measures suggested. It is hoped they will prove effectual and at the same time meet the sanction and cooperation of your Excellency

> With high Esteem
> Very Truly Yrs
> James A Seddon
> Secy of War

---

[1]Bayles M. Edney, a lawyer and former state senator who also had been a general in the militia before the war—hence the title "general." Johnston, *Papers of Vance*, 1:92n.

[2]Daniel Smith Donelson, commanding Department of East Tennessee. Wakelyn, *Biographical Dictionary of the Confederacy,* 172–173.

ZBV to James A. Seddon   A&H:GLB

Raleigh March 26th 1863

Hon. Jas. A. Seddon
Secty of War
Richmond Va

A recent decision of our Chief Justice on a Habeas Corpus renders it impossible for me, without further legislation to aid in arresting conscripts with Militia. I therefore advise that Col Mallett's battalion be not diminished, for the present, as the whole execution of the law will now devolve on him

Z. B. Vance

Robert E. Lee to ZBV   A&H:GLB

Head Quarters Army Virginia
March 26th. 1863

His Excy. Z. B. Vance
Governor of North Carolina

Sir
    Your letter of March 19th.[1] by your A.D.C. with reference to the trial of Soldiers who returned to this Army under your proclamation of Jan. 27th.[2] has been received. I received no copy of that proclamation and only became aware of it upon reviewing the proceedings of Courts Martial before which deserters from N.C. Regiments were tried. Although I supposed that its provisions extended only to the Dept of N.C. Still as it appeared probable that the men might have acted under its promises, I at once remitted the penalties inflicted by the courts and restored the men to duty. I also directed that no charges should be preferred against Soldier who returned to duty under similar circumstances. I am glad to receive a copy of your patriotic call & hope that you will do all in your power to keep our ranks full

I have the honor to be
With great respect
Your obt Servant
R. E. Lee
Genl

[1] In this volume.
[2] January 26, in this volume.

John Pool to David A. Barnes　　　　　　A&H:GP

Cobraine—March 28th., 1863.

Col. David A. Barnes
Aid de Camp &c.

Dear Sir:

Your letter of the 12th. inst.[1] reached me after an unaccountable delay of twelve days. I have taken a few days to consider, & inquire into the condition, personnel, & c. of the forces proposed to be placed under my command. I am fully satisfied that they cannot be rendered efficient. If I were to accept the proposed position, I should meet disappointment & mortification. The Rangers will succeed in limiting the depredations & outrages of the few miserable "Buffalos" who infest that section, by waylaying the roads & killing some of them, now & then. But no military enterprize, that would reflect credit on a commander, is possible. Large forces of the enemy, by land and water, completely environ & possess that whole section of country. There is no room for retreat, except across the Chowan river, near its mouth—& I believe /that no/ emergency could induce the larger part of the Rangers to cross the river. They would sooner disband & go home–leaving the commander to be held responsible for calling down upon the people a raid which could do nothing to repel or punish. These forces are not disciplined, & with their ideas of the conditions & purpose of their organization, could not be rendered obedient to orders, while they remain about home. An officer of military experience, who has seen some actual service, might inspire a degree of confidence & impress them with his authority—& in that way avoid, to some extent, the difficulties that would beset a mere civilian placed over them by the Governor. Allow me to suggest Maj. J. W. Hinton, of Col. Shaw's Regiment.[2] He would, probably, be pleased with a command in the neighborhood of his family. The Rangers are of service to the people East of the Chowan, as a sort of police force, & ought to be kept there for that purpose. But they can do nothing for the Confederacy, at large.

If I were to accept the command of such a force, it would certainly involve my personal ruin, at once; as your knowledge of my location will readily convince you. But I would not let any personal consideration influence my conduct, where I had a reasonable assurance that I could render any substantial service to my country.

Please, express to the Governor my grateful appreciation of the confidence & regard implied in tendering me the command—& my regret that circumstances forbid my accepting it.

With great respect,
Yours, &c
John Pool

[1] In this volume.
[2] James W. Hinton of Henry M. Shaw's Eighth Regiment North Carolina Troops. On July 8, he received command of the Sixty-eighth Regiment then serving in the north-eastern part of the state. Manarin and Jordan, *North Carolina Troops*, 4:521, 523; Clark, *Histories of Regiments from North Carolina*, 3:713–718.

ZBV to Gabriel J. Rains   A&H:GP

Copy

State of North Carolina
Executive Department
Raleigh March 31st. 1863.

Brig Gen. G. J. Rains
Bureau of Conscription
Richmond

Genl.

Your letter of the 25th. inst[1] is to hand, asking my "forbearance" in reference to the conscription of certain officers and inviting my correspondence in reference thereto. I avail myself of that invitation to make myself understood in the matter. You say that you have calculated on my assistance instead of my opposition in this matter. You may so calculate with perfect confidence. The fact that the conscript law has been more faithfully executed in N.C. than any other state in the Confederacy, and that no other Southern executive (So far as I am aware) has used the whole power of the State Militia to execute it, might be taken as an earnest of my intention to sustain the Government, so far as it may be rightfully done. But I cannot go beyond this. Though heretofore I have not belonged to that class of politicians who made the "night (and day) hideous" with cries for *State rights* and was rather accused of Consolidationism. Yet I am not quite willing to see the State of North Carolina in effect blotted from the map and her government abolished by the conscription of her officers The clause of the law quoted by you can easily be made to effect that, for the Militia law of the state expressly provides that in "Case of invasion or ensurrection, *No body* shall be exempt from duty" of course then *every body* is liable to conscription.

The Governor is Commander in chief and all officers of the Militia are of course liable to Militia duty and therefore to conscription also. You are already enrolling our Magistrates who comprise our Courts of Pleas & Quarter Sessions, lay our taxes, assess property for taxation, provide for the poor and preserve the peace generally, and with them their executive officers—the Constables, also the police officers of our cities and corporations. Now Sir, after these and the Militia officers have been taken by the Confederacy, will you please to inform me what remains of the boasted *sovereignty* of the States? Do not reply <that> by saying you have not enrolled the Militia officers—you claim the right to do it and *may* undertake it at any time. God forbid that the rights and honor and the existance /itself/ of the State should rest *only* upon the grace and mercy of a Bureau of Conscription. The rights of the States certainly rest upon a more solid basis than this. You also say that there are no means short of supernatural power by which you can know of the officers & employees of the State, to which my letter to Col August referred outside of the law. That may be. In fact I do not know that it is <necessary> /required/ <for> /of/ you to know what officers are necessary to the ordinary operations of this state government. But it is certainly the business of the Chief Magistrate of the state to know, and it is especially his duty under the Constitution to see that they are not interfer<r>ed with in the discharge of their appropriate functions. I cannot therefore recede from the position before assumed, that it is my duty to resist the conscription of all state officers and agents whose services are necessary to the proper and due administration of the affairs of the State and of which necessity her authorities must of <the> course be the Judges. Neither can the claim, plain and obvious as it is, be permitted to rest upon the grace of Congress as exemplified in the Exemption bill or the discretion and good will of those intrusted with the execution of the law, but upon those high and inalianable rights which by the genius of our government are deemed inherent in and inseparable from the sovereign character of the state. If it is the intention of the Confederate authorities to to carry the execution of the law of Conscription beyond this I should be glad to be so informed at as early a day as possible. This city is to be stripped of its police officers tomorrow and the Magistrates of many of the counties are already ordered into camp, and I desire the question settled. Assuring you of my desire that harmony may continue to exist as heretofore and of my great desire to assist in attaining an Independence by any possible means in the power of the State of North Carolina consistent with the preservation of liberty itself—I am General

Very sincerely & Respectfully
Yours

(Signed)   Z. B. Vance

¹In this volume.

ZBV to Jefferson Davis   Har:Van

State of North-Carolina,
Executive Department,
Raleigh, March 31st. 1863

His Excellency
President Davis,

Sir,

I have this day addressed a letter¹ to Gen Rains, chief of Bureau of Conscription in regard to the enrolling of certain state officers, but as the case is urgent and may assume important proportions, I have thought it best to address you directly and beg your attention thereon at as early a moment as your heavy duties may permit.

The extreme rigour and—I am proud to be able to add—*good faith* with which the conscript law has been executed in North Carolina, has stripped it so bare of its laboring and official population, as to render its further operation a matter of anxiety in various respects. In addition to sweeping /off/ a large class whose labor was I fear, absolutely necessary to the existence of the women & children left behind, the hand of conscription has at length laid hold upon a class of officials, without whose aid the order and well being of Society could not be preserved nor the execution of the laws enforced; and whose conscription is insulting to the dignity, as it is certainly violation of the rights and Sovereignty of the States. Having heretofore exerted the utmost powers with which I am entrusted, and even exceeded them, according to a recent decision of the Chief Justice of the State, in the execution of this law, at this point I deem it my duty not only to pause, but to protest against its enforcement. In my letter to Gen Rains I assumed the position that the Confederate authorities should not conscribe any officers or agents of the State whose services were necessary to the due administration of the government, and that the State authorities—not the Confederate—must judge of this necessity. In this class I should certainly place Justices of the Peace, Constables, and the Police organizations of our towns and cities. There being no attempt made to enroll the officers of the Militia I shall not argue as to them, though I understand the right is claimed under the law, to conscribe them.

The Exemption bill of October 11th. 62, provides that the executive and judicial officers of the States shall be exempt, except such as may by state laws be subject to militia duty. This would render every able bodied man in the State liable to conscription as our laws expressly provide that in case of *invasion* or insurrection *no person* shall be exempt whomsoever. If this construction should prevail you will perceive that /it/ is in the power of the War Dept. to abolish the State government by a very simple process. But taking it for granted that such a construction is not intended, I beg leave to say that the present proceedings of the Bureau go very far toward it. I need not inform you of the character and duties of the magistracy—you can not /but/ be aware of their importance. I will only say in brief, that in addition to their being conservators of the peace generally, they constitute our courts of Pleas & Quarter Sessions and have jurisdiction over a far more extensive and in many respects—more important range of subjects than the Superior Courts—in fact the Superior Courts can not be held without them. They lay more than half the taxes of the State, assess all the property for taxation, provide for the poor (now a doubly important function) and in many cases the law requires a certain number to be present to render their proceedings valid. The constable is the Sheriff of the magistrates court, and as absolutely necessary to the community as the Sheriff himself; since our sheriffs can be compelled to execute no process except those addressed to him by a court of record. It is no answer to all this <by> to say, that we have more justices than are actually necessary and that *some* might be dispensed with. The Legislature of the Sovereign State of N.C. recommended their appointments to the Executive according to the forms of the constitution, and it is /to/ be presumed they deemed them all necessary, and no one has the right to say otherwise.

The municipal officers present if possible a still stranger case. The mayor and police of this city have been enrolled and ordered into camp, which of course abolishes the government of the corporation at once and turns over the inhabitants to a state of lawlessness and anarchy.

With the magistrates, the Militia, and the municipal officers of our incorporated towns, constables & such like officers of the State swept into a camp of instruction, I am at a loss to know what would be left of the power or sovereignty of this State or any other? So obvious is the great damage and disparagement <would> /which/ this lattitudenous construction of the law /could/ work against the States, that I can not believe its framers so intended it. And with all due respect I doubt the wisdom and the policy of the War Department in urging it so far. Having made no question of its constitutionality, and interposed no obstacle to its faithful execution, but on the contrary, acquiesced in it as a great measure of necessity and assisted with zeal in its enforcement, I am content now to state my opinions simply upon a fair construction of its terms. And I am quite confident, that your sense of justice will not fail to perceive the weighty reasons of comity, policy, and respect for States rights—the great democratic doctrine of our revolution—which admonish you of the impropriety of alarming the jealousy of the States, exciting the murmurs of the people and crippling the security of their government, by seizing a few officers who could do little toward increasing the ranks, or officering of the army; but who as a part of the government are deemed necessary at home.

Soliciting again your earliest convenient answer, and begging you to accept assurances of my highest consideration and esteem,

> I am Sir
> Very truly
> Yr. obt svt.
> Z. B. Vance

[1]In this volume.

ZBV to John White   A&H:GLB

State of North Carolina
Executive Department
Raleigh April 1st. 1863

Mr John White
Liverpool England

Dr Sir

Messrs Sterling, Campbell & Albright[1] of Greensboro N.C. desiring to purchase some supplies and fixtures for their book publishing house, have deposited
with me two hundred and two bales of Cotton prime quality, average weight
about four hundred and seventy pounds, and twenty five hundred barrels of Rosin.
If you have been successful in securing a loan upon our Cotton or bonds please
advance to their Agent Mr W Hargrove White the bearer, as much money as
this amt. of Cotton and Rosin may come to according the terms at which you
have sold ours, whatever that may be, or should you not have disposed of all the
Bonds or Cotton Scrip, you might if you should think best, advance him bonds
or scrip at the same rates and let him deal for himself, taking his receipt therefore
of course

Very truly yours
Z. B. Vance

[1]Richard Sterling, James D. Campbell, and James W. Albright, textbook publishers for
North Carolina. Karen C. Carroll, "Sterling, Campbell, and Albright: Textbook Publishers, 1861–1865," *North Carolina Historical Review* 63 (April 1986): 169–198.

James A. Seddon to ZBV   A&H:GP

Confederate States of America,
War Department,
Richmond, Va. Apl. 2, 1863

His Excellency Z. B. Vance,
Governor of North Carolina,
Raleigh, N.C.

Sir,

On the receipt of your telegram[1] with regard to the condition of affairs in
Western North Carolina, I directed Genl. Donelson to send a force to Asheville
and the vicinity to repress the disorder existing there. I have just received from
him the following dispatch:

Knoxville, Apl. 1/63

Hon. J. A. Seddon,

In compliance with your your [*sic*] order a regiment of Cavalry will leave this place for Asheville N.C. to-morrow morning with orders to sweep the mountains in its vicinity of marauders, conscripts and deserters D. L. Donelson, Brig. Genl. Comd'g.

> With high regard
> Your obdt. servt.
> James A Seddon
> Secretary of War

[*Endorsed*] Copy & file

Z B V

[1]March 25, in this volume.

Jesse G. Shepherd to ZBV   A&H:GP

> Fayetteville
> April 3d. 1863.

Hon Z B. Vance.

Dear Sir.

In the company of Fort Fisher lately commanded by Cap McRae—(now Major 1st. N.C Battallion)[1] there is a private soldier from Robeson County whose name is John Walker. He is the owner of twenty slaves—or is the head of a family including his mother and sister—having twenty slaves among them. He is a man of good character—and may be relied on in all that he states. He told me in the utmost frankness that he has now an overseer, from necessity—but would prefer to be at the head of his own affairs. Have you the power to detail or discharge him? This Battallion is in service by State authority.

> With the highest respect
> J. G. Shepherd.[2]

[*Endorsed*] This Govr. does not feel justified in following this feature of the Conspt. Law, believing it to be unjust & unfair—But if he did, the law does not operate to discharge a man already in service, but only exempts those not yet taken.

Z B Vance

[1]Alexander McRae, First Battalion, Heavy Artillery, numbered as Ninth Battalion "merely as a convenience" in Clark, *Histories of Regiments from North Carolina*, 4:303–313.

[2]Jesse George Shepherd, jurist, legislator, and former speaker of North Carolina House of Commons. Johnston, *Papers of Vance*, 1:160n.

ZBV *to John G. Shorter*   A&H:GLB

State of North Carolina
Executive Department
Raleigh April 4th. 1863

His Excellency
John Gill Shorter
Montgomery Ala

Sir

I am in receipt of your favor of the 31st. ulto[1] in relation to procuring a supply of cloth for the Cadets of your University from the factories of this State.

I sincerely regret that it is impossible for me to grant your request without doing injustice to our own soldiers. This state as you are aware clothes her own troops by contract with the Quarter Master General, and we are now so far behind, and our Soldiers are in such great need, that it requires much more than the whole product of our mills to supply them.

Under such circumstances I feel confident you will appreciate the necessity which compels me to decline

Very Respectfully
Z. B. Vance

[1]SHC:Pea.

ZBV *to James A. Seddon*   A&H:GLB

State of North Carolina
Executive Department
Raleigh April 7th. 1863

Hon. Jas. A. Seddon
Secty of War

Dr. Sir

I am in receipt of yours of the 2d.[1] inclosing copy of Genl. Donelsons despatch &c.

There is no need of troops at Asheville—there being no disorder there, except that which is threatened by the illegal seizure of Conscripts by Genl Pillows Independent Conscript Bureau. All that is necessary there, is to order Genl Ps men to cease their operations and permit the regular enrolling officers to perform their duties—

In the adjoining counties of Yancy, Mitchell and Watauga the tories and deserters are in strong force and the force ordered to Asheville, should be sent there at once

Very Respectfully &c
Z. B. Vance

¹In this volume.

Allen T. Davidson to ZBV   A&H:VanPC

Richmond Va.
April 7 1863

Dear Zeb

I Recd. a letter from a friend to day in N.C. saying he was verry desirous to have G. W. Swepson¹ of Graham appointed one of the State directors of the / Western/ N.C.R.R.—

If it is not contrary to your general plan of things I would be glad you would appoint him he is a man of first rate business talent and a verry warm and devoted friend of yours and mine—If you can put him in I will be much obliged—

Congress will not adjourn before the 20th. if then—The Standard² has the vote on the Tax bill all wrong—The vote given was upon the Supplimental bill or machinery of the tax bill—All of the members from N.C. present voted for the Tax bill but one—I wish you would suggest this to him³ for fear he may pitch into us. The vote on the Tax bill was taken in secret and the Secrecy has not been removed—

The bill is under discussion in the Senate—with material amendments—such as an income Tax—[purely] in kind, what do you think of it!

Theo.⁴ was here a few days ago—but has gone home—he wants you to send me the Books he left with you—

I heard from B'ro. Harvey⁵ today by a Col just from Camp Chase where he is doing well and getting well of his wounds

Yours truly
A T. Davidson

¹George W. Swepson, businessman who—in collaboration with Milton S. Littlefield— gained control of the Western North Carolina Railroad after the war and swindled the

state and individuals out of millions of dollars through bribery and bond fraud. Charles L. Price, "The Railroad Schemes of George W. Swepson," *East Carolina Publications in History* 1 (1964): 32–64.

²*North Carolina Standard* (Raleigh).

³William Woods Holden, editor of the *North Carolina Standard* and leader of peace movement. He became provisional governor after the war. *Dictionary of North Carolina Biography*, s.v. "Holden, William Woods."

⁴Theodore Fulton Davidson, son of Allen T. Davidson. He later became attorney general of North Carolina. *Dictionary of North Carolina Biography*, s.v. "Davidson, Theodore Fulton."

⁵Hugh Harvey Davidson.

                         William N. H. Smith to ZBV   LC:CSA

                              Richmond, Va.
                              April 7, 1863

Gov. Z. B. Vance
Raleigh

Dear Sir

I enclose you a correspondence between Mr Ould,[1] Agent of Exchange and myself on a subject of considerable importance to the people of portions of the State under the enemy's control. You can make such use of the letter of Mr Ould as <you> the public interests require. In a few days he will publish in more careful form, for general information, the results of the arrangement between the Commissioners.

                              Very respectfully &c.
                              Yours
                              W. N. H. Smith[2]

¹Robert Ould, Confederate agent for exchange of prisoners of war. Wakelyn, *Biographical Dictionary of the Confederacy*, 336. Ould's letter to Smith is not extant.

²William Nathan Harrell Smith, Confederate congressman, former U.S. representative, and future chief justice of North Carolina Supreme Court. *Cyclopedia of Eminent and Representative Men of the Carolinas of the Nineteenth Century*, 2 vols. (Madison, Wis.: Brant and Fuller, 1892), 2:89–92.

John G. Shorter to ZBV   A&H:GLB

Executive Department
Montgomery Ala. April 7th. 1863.

His Excellency Z. B. Vance
Governor of North Carolina
Raleigh

Sir

I have the honor to aknowledge the receipt of your favor of 3d. inst[1] and in reply would state that previous to the Session of 1862, Justices of the peace were, by the Military Code of Alabama, exempt from Militia duty, but by an act approved December 6th. 1862, they were declared "subject to militia service, unless physically or mentally disqualified for such service". Since the approval of this Act, justices of the peace in the State of Alabama have been enrolled for Confederate Service, when within Conscript ages

Very respectfully
Yr. obt. Servt.
Jno. Gill Shorter
Gov of Alabama

[1]Not extant.

James A. Seddon to ZBV   A&H:GP

Confederate States of America,
War Department,
Richmond, Va. Apl 8, 1863.

His Excellency Z. B. Vance,
Governor of N.C.
Raleigh, N.C.

Sir,

I have the honor to enclose an extract from a letter of Genl. Sam. Jones, to whom I referred your Excellency's communication of the 21st. ult.[1] I trust it will be your pleasure to comply with the suggestion of Genl. Jones, in view of the facts presented.

With high regard
Your obdt. servt.
James A. Seddon
Secretary of War

[*Extract*]

Copy

Hd. Qrs. Dept. W. Va.
Dublin, April 2d. 1863.

Hon. James A. Seddon
Secty. of War.

Sir

x   x   x   x

I desire to say that it [*is*] impracticable to forage them in this Dept. at present.
I hope very soon to receive a supply of corn from Ga. and when that is received
I can bring the horses within my Department, and perhaps send them to forage
in a part of the Country now occupied by the enemy. If Gov. Vance will bear
with me a few weeks longer I can relieve his state of the horses without injury
to the service. If the horses are brought into Va. now they will probably starve.
If they are sent further South they would probably have to go to Ga. before forage
could be found in abundance, and by the time they could reach that country, I
should want them to start back to Va. to enter on active service. I therefore
respectfully suggest that the horses be allowed to /remain/ a few weeks, not more
than two or three, where they are.

x   x   x   x

With great respect
Your Obt. Servt.
(Signed)   Sam Jones
Maj. Genl.

¹In this volume.

Peter Mallett to ZBV   A&H:GP

Conscript Office
Camp Holmes April 8th. 1863

His Excellency
Gov Vance
Raleigh N.C.

Governor.

Your communication of yesterday¹ stating that you had protested against the
conscription of Magistrates in N.C. and asking that no further steps be taken
until the matter is settled, has been rec'd. The orders already issued for their
enrollment were by direction of the Bureau and I am not at liberty to revoke

them, but I will not issue the order for them to be brought to camp until the matter is decided. I have the honor to be, Governor,

> Very Respectfully
> Your obdt servt
> Peter Mallett
> Col Comdr Conscripts

¹Not extant.

ZBV *to James A. Seddon*   A&H:GLB

> State of North Carolina
> Executive Department
> Raleigh April 10th. 1863

Hon. Jas. A. Seddon
Secty. of War

Sir

I have forborn for a long while to ask your attention to a nest of Confederate officers in the town of Salisbury N.C who have long been suspected of speculating at the public expense, & oppressing the people in that region. I was gratified to learn that a commissioner had at length been sent out by the Q. M. General to investigate these alleged abuses, and was not surprised to learn that he had flushed quite a den of scoundrels and speculators who have been imposing on the public for a long time, selling in Charleston and elsewhere supplies bought and often impressed, as though for the government. I have not seen the report of the commissioner, and can only speak from private information, which says that the evidence unmistakeably implicated Captain McCoy,¹ Commanding the Confederate prison there, in these disreputable transactions. If true it would furnish the department sufficient grounds to do an act, that would afford the most lively gratification to the people of North Carolina—the removal of McCoy from his present command.

I assure you Sir, that three fourths of the wide spread dissatisfaction caused by suspension of Habeas Corpus, and the arbitrary arrest of our citizens, has arisen from the insolence and disrespect of the State authorities exhibited by that man. When to this, it is also made known that he is implicated in the villainy which has so long abounded there, his removal will become a matter of necessity. I therefore feel it my duty to advise and request that captain McCoy be removed.

> I am Sir
> Very Respectfully
> Yr. obt. Svt.
> Z. B. Vance

[1]Henry McCoy, commandant of Salisbury prison from September 1862 to October 1863. He also served for a time as quartermaster. Louis A. Brown, *The Salisbury Prison: A Case Study of Confederate Military Prisons, 1861–1865* (Wendell, N.C.: Avera Press, 1980), 43, 110, 168.

Gabriel J. Rains to ZBV   A&H:GP

Confederate States of America,
Bureau of Conscription,
Richmond, Va. Apl. 11th. 1863

His Excellency
Z Vance
Govr. of N. Ca

Governor.

I have the honor to acknowledge /your letter/ of 31st. March last[1] and to explain your views it was laid before the Secty. of War.

He returned it to me with remark that it was read with pain and regret, and directs me to say that the only question is whether the Conscription Law as enacted by Congress is to be executed according to its plain import, and that this Bureau has no authority to modify or dispense with, nor can it recognize such right or discretion in state authority.

The subject is now in abeyance with the Hon Members from N.C of both Senate and House, and I think some modification of the Law will be proposed.

I have the honor to be Governor

Very Respectfully
Your Mo. Obt. servt.
G. J. Rains
Brig Genl.
Supt.

[1]In this volume.

Joseph E. Brown to ZBV   A&H:GP

Executive Department,
Milledgeville, Ga.,
April 11th. 1863.

His Excellency
Z. B. Vance,
Raleigh, N.C.

Dear Sir:—

I have the honor to acknowledge the receipt of your letter of the 3d. instant,[1] and in reply, to say, that no civil or military officer of this State has been enrolled under the conscription acts passed by Congress.

By the new Code of this State, which went into effect the first of January last, "Judges of the Supreme, Superior and City Courts, Justices of the inferior Courts and of the Peace, Sheriffs and Deputies, Clerks of Courts and Ordinaries", are exempted from military duty. But by the Statutes of force in the State before that time, no civil officer of the State was exempted.

In a case brought before the Supreme Court of this State last fall, at the instance of officers or agents of the Confederate government, to test the constitutionality of of [sic] the conscription Acts of Congress, it was decided, though the point was not directly in issue, that a conscription Act passed by Congress requiring the enrollment and forcing into military service of the civil officers of a State, would be unconstitutional.

The decision in that case is quite lengthy, and has not been published, but it has been filed in the Clerk's office here; and I send you a copy[2] of the part of it which relates to that point.

Very respectfully
Your Obt. Servt.
Joseph E. Brown

[1]Not extant.
[2]Not extant.

Braxton Bragg to ZBV   A&H:GLB

Head Quarters Army of Tennessee
Tallahoma Tenn April 12th. 1863

Hon. Z. B. Vance
Governor &c
Raleigh, N.C.

My dear Sir

Your letter of March 9th[1] in reference to the present condition and future disposition of the No. Carolina troops in East Tennessee has been recd. As with most of my correspondence not strictly official, I regret that urgent demands upon my time has compelled me to leave it unanswered until now, for which apparent neglect, I hope the simple explanation will be ample apology.

I fully concur in the views you express in regard to the demoralizing influences to which the troops referred to are exposed in their present location and am satisfied a transfer would be highly beneficial. The Department of East Tennessee has, however, never been under my command and I am unable by my own orders to effect the change, but will endeavor to accomplish the desired object by a reference and recommendation to higher authority. Having had so little to do with the troops of my native State, it will give me great pleasure to secure the services of the Brigade, which, I feel confident would under proper discipline soon equal any in the Service

With assurances of my high regard

> I beg to remain
> Very Respectfully & Truly
> Your obedient Servant
> Braxton Bragg
> General

¹In this volume.

Proclamation by ZBV   A&H:GLB

By the Governor of North Carolina a
Proclamation

Whereas it has become apparent to me and to all who are interested in the welfare of the State and who have any feelings of humanity for suffering among their fellow men, from cries which reach us from the poor in all sections of the land, that starvation will be the fate of many of our heretofore favored people, unless the *crime of speculation in the necessaries of life* can be arrested: And whereas, it is my bounden duty to protect the citizens of the State, of which I have to [sic] honor to be the Chief Magistrate, against the evils consequent upon this crime, for the utmost of my ability.

Now, therefore, I, Zebulon B. Vance, Governor of North Carolina, do, by and with the advice and consent of the Council of State issue this Proclamation, forbidding all persons, for the space of thirty days from the date hereof, from exporting any of the following articles beyond the limits of the State, to wit, any Salt, Bacon, Pork, Beef, Corn, Meal, Flour, Wheat, Potatoes, Shoes, Leather, Hides, Cotton Cloth, and Yarn and Woolen Cloth.

From this prohibition the following persons are to be exempted. All Quarter Masters and Commissary Agents of the Confederate Government and of any State of the Confederacy, exhibiting proper evidence of their official character—

Also all agents of any County, District, Town or Corporation, of other States, who shall exhibit satisfactory proof of their Agency for the purchase of such articles, for public uses, or for distribution at cost and transportation and not for resale or profit. Also, all persons whether residents or non-residents of the State who may purchase any of said articles for their private use, of which, before the articles are removed, their oath before a Justice of Peace, may be taken as Evidence. The exception is to extend to Salt made by non-residents on the sea coast and in their own works and to cargoes entering a port of this State from abroad.

And of said Articles that may be stopped *in transitu* from our borders are to be confiscated to the use of the State.

The Colonels of Militia throughout the State are enjoined to see that this Proclamation is enforced. I Earnestly appeal to all good citizens to sustain and aid me in carrying out the object this Proclamation is designed, as far as possible, to effect—

In witness thereof Zebulon B. Vance, Governor, Captain General and Commander-in-Chief, hath signed these presents and caused the Great Seal of the State to be affixed

Done at our city of Raleigh this the 13th. day of April, A.D. 1863 and in the year of our Independence the 87th.

Z. B. Vance

George Davis to ZBV   A&H:VanPC

Richmond 16 Aprl 1863

Gov. Z. B. Vance
Raleigh N.C.

Dear Sir

Your letter[1] has been duly received.

General Iverson[2] was appointed a Brigadier upon a strong recommendation from Genl. D. H. Hill endorsed by Gen. Jackson.[3]

Mr. Dortch and myself some time ago addressed to the Secy of War a strong protest against Gen Iverson's appointment being made as a *North Carolina,* appointment, inasmuch as he has never been a citizen of our State. I regret to say that the Secy's reply has been highly unsatisfactory, persisting in continuing the nomination as made.

We have heard of a good deal of dissatisfaction with Gen. I. but, so far as I am aware, it all rests upon rumor. Your own letter is the only exception, and that, you are aware, can hardly be of much use to us. I have for a long time been very indignant at the appointment of persons from other States to command Nor Ca Troops. But all our efforts so far have been unable to correct the evil—The reason is, that our recommendations for high military appointments are ignored altogether, and attention is given to nothing but the recommendations of the Generals.

I agree entirely with what you say of Cols Hall[4] and Leventhorpe, and would be glad to aid in their promotion, if my aid were worth anything

Very Truly Yours
Geo Davis[5]

[1]Not extant.

[2]Alfred Iverson Jr. of Georgia, former commander of the Twentieth Regiment North Carolina Troops, appointed brigadier general November 1, 1862. Patricia L. Faust et al., eds., *Historical Times Illustrated Encylopedia of the Civil War* (New York: HarperCollins, 1991), 387.
[3]Thomas Jonathan (Stonewall) Jackson.
[4]Edward Dudley Hall, commanding Forty-sixth Regiment North Carolina Troops. Manarin and Jordan, *North Carolina Troops,* 11:134.
[5]George Davis, Confederate senator, who became last attorney general of the Confederacy in January 1864. *Dictionary of North Carolina Biography,* s.v. "Davis, George."

Joseph C. Pinnix to ZBV   A&H:GP

Hd. Qrs. 47th. Reg NC M
Yanceyville NC
April 17th. 1863

Gov Vance

Dear Sir

On yesterday a load (four Bales, supposed to be about 200 bunches) of Cotton Yarn en route to Virginia markets came to Yanceyville, which in obedience /to/ your—proclamation I Seized and now hold subject to your order. The Said cotton was in the waggon and care of Bedford McCray but belonged to Geo. W Swepson of Alamance County, who I learn has been and is still Sending off to Virginia large quantities at enormous prices, and refuses to sell at home. This article is very much—needed in this County (as we have no Factory in this County) especially by the families of Soldiers. If it meet your approbation, it would be a great accommodation to sell the above article here at whatever price you may see fit to put upon it, which if you conclude to do, please let me know how to dispose of it & the price–whether factory price or the price it sells at here, and also whether to Soldiers families alone or to the Citizens indiscriminately. Probably it would be best to let Soldiers families have it at our price and Citizens another higher price. I hasten to write you concerning this matter as it is very probable that application will be made to you by the party to release said Cotton from my possession.

There can be no doubt but that the owner of this Cotton has been and is still sending off large quanties to other markets than in N.C. at enormous prices. I learn that he expected $15 pr bunch for this lot, a part of which is to Farmville Va. and a part to Robt Swepson in Richmond who is agent to sell for said Geo W Swepson, the Consequence of which is that our people suffer for the want of it, as they are ashamed to asked these prices here & therefore will not sell at all Especially is this the case with the poorer clases of our soldiers families whose wives & Children are suffering & Shivering /while/ their husbands & fathers are exposing their lives to defend our Country and its rights at *only Eleven Dollars* pr month.

I am truly glad to see your proclamation and will Say it meets with the approbation of all I have heard speak of it, only it would have suited us better if it had not been limited to 30 days, but continued in force untill revoked when circumstances would admit, however you can renew it, or else the parties who it is intended to effect will only hoard up till the time expires.

Pardon me for this lengthy communication.

> I remain yours obediently
> & very Respectfully
> Jos. C. Pinnix Col. Com

[*Endorsed*] Before the reception of this letter the owner called & made affidavit that it was started out of State before the proclamation, and I released it— otherwise I should have been glad to let the people there have it—

> Z B V

Joseph C. Pinnix to ZBV   A&H:GP

> Hd. Qrs. 47th. Reg NC. M
> Yanceyville NC April 20th. 1863

Gov Vance

Dear Sir

I write again to inform you that one of my Captains (Wiley) reports to me to day that he has seized five hundred bunches of cotton yarn which was being carried out of the State contrary to your proclamation, he failed to report the party it belong to, or the party who was halling it, but I learn it belong to the same party who owned that I seized last week (Geo. W. Swepson Alamance Coty) who as I stated in my other communication has carried & still carrying off large quantities at enormous prices, when our people are suffering for the want of it. You may be sure if he brings it through this County we'll have a large Share of it for our State—What must be done with it?

> Yours Very Respectfully
> Jos. C. Pinnix Col. Com

[*Endorsed*] Write him that I am gratified at his promptness & efficiency—that I gave Swepson permission to recall some yarn which he alledged was started before the procm. Perhaps this is it!

> Z B Vance

Jonathan Worth to ZBV   A&H:GP

Treasury Department.
Raleigh. Apl 20th. 1863
Govr. Vance

The 2nd. Sec. of an ordinance of the Convention,[1] page 129, requires all State and County Revenue officers to receive Confederate Treasury notes in payment of all public dues.

The late act of Congress relating to the funding of Confederate Currency, provides among other things, that all the issues, dated prior to Decr. 2nd. 1862, shall not be fundable after the 1st. day of August 1863. The object of this act is to induce the holders of this currency to fund it before the 1st. of August, because, after the 1st. of August, it would become less valuable than the new issues fundable in 6 per cent bonds—and thereby diminish the circulation & cause the new issues to appreciate. I do not doubt that this act will tend to accomplish the objects intended to be effected, but I believe a vast amount of the old 8 per cent issue, will not be funded, and will become greatly depreciated below any other currency after the 1st. Augt., if not entirely uncurrent.

If these views are correct, it will follow that our taxes, due to the Treasury the 1st. of Octr. next, will nearly all be paid in this poorest currency.

Another reason why this State will be likely to have afloat, at the season when our Sheriffs are collecting the taxes, a large amount of this old currency, is that the Legislature of Virginia, by a recent act, has made only "The Confederate States non-interest bearing notes of the denominations of or over five dollars dated <dated> and issued on and after the 1 Apl 1863, <shall hereafter be> receivable in payment of taxes and other public dues to the State". This act, by which the old issues are not receivable for public dues in Va, is in furtherance of the purpose of Congress [blotted] impairing the value of the old issues, and will throw many of them into circulation in this State, where they are still receivable in payment of public dues.

I do not think there is any remedy for this evil, excepting by an act of the Legislature; and I therefore respectfully recommend that your Excellency convene the Council of State to consider of this matter

Yours very respectfully
Jona. Worth[2] Pub Tr.

---

[1]The Secession Convention of North Carolina, which met four times in 1861–1862 and passed a number of ordinances, thus acting as a lawmaking body. Although Jonathan Worth hoped the convention would replace the General Assembly during the war, public opinion opposed such a usurpation of legislative power. ZBV urged the convention to assemble a fifth time in the autumn of 1862 to deal with extortion and speculation, but

its president declined and it never convened again. Cheney, *North Carolina Government*, 376, 386–387, 399–401.

²Jonathan Worth, treasurer of North Carolina, 1862–1865, and postwar governor. *Dictionary of American Biography*, s.v. "Worth, Jonathan."

ZBV to Peter Mallett   A&H:GLB

[*With enclosure*]

State of North Carolina
Executive Department
Raleigh April 20th. 1863

Col Mallett

Your note¹ enclosing copy of an Order from Conscript Bureau in regard to conscripting certain officers of this State, and asking certain questions in regard to their functions &c has been recd.—In answer thereto I beg leave to submit the enclosed letter from Mr. Phillips,² Auditor of Public Accounts, which so fully explains the Status and duties of the various State officials whose enrollment is objected to, that I adopt it fully as expressing my own opinions

Very Respectfully
Yr. obt. Svt.
Z. B. Vance

[*Enclosure*]

Samuel F. Phillips to ZBV   A&H:GLB

11th. April 1863
Raleigh N.C.

To His Excellency
Z. B. Vance—

Governor

In the case of the State of North Carolina liabilities to Militia duty affords but a poor test of the question, which of her state and county officers can we spare for the Army of the Confederacy? because, under the Militia law of the State *no man can ever be called beyond the limits of his own county for the purpose of doing Militia duty*—The Code³ (Ch. 70, S-8) gives to every county at least one regiment and provides (S-21) that the place for mustering this body shall be as near the centre of the district as possible. By section 36 (which is the only provision upon the subject) majors [*major generals*] and brigadier generals are to receive their respective corps only "by regiments", "at the usual place of regimental musters". The last Militia Act (September 1861) does not affect these provisions. The only question then which the State has decided in rendering certain of her County and general officers liable to Militia duty is—that there is nothing in the nature of their duties to prevent them from mustering some half-dozen times a year in their respective districts—leaving it to the good senses of the various court martials to excuse any such officer as might fail to attend a muster because of actual engagment in the duties of his office. It is plain that the question as to which of them can be spared for the confederate Army is one altogether different and that some officers should be exempted by the President under that head of the act of Congress which provides for *special exemption* "on account of necessity"— The Confederate government makes no point as to the propriety of changing an officer liable from his age to the Conscription act, for one not so liable. Very properly it leaves the selection of incumbents for necessary civil officers to the discretion & patriotism of the Several States. If the *office* be one necessary in the machinery of the State, no other question is asked and an exemption is granted for that highest of all reasons, recognized in the Act, viz— necessity—

How far that necessity exists in North Carolina with reference to the offices of Constables, Coroners, County Trustees, Justices of the Peace and Registers will now be briefly inquired into.

I *Constables*—Section 38 of the Constitution of North Carolina requires— "That there shall be a Sheriff, Coroner or Coroners and Constables in each county within this State" Accordingly the Code provides that of Constables there shall not be a greater number than one in each Captain's district, with some slight exceptions therein mentioned. They give Bond in the sum of $4000 and take an Oath of office. Their duties are well known. In all countries where the Common law prevails they are the principal and most effective peace officers & whatever may be said (and in some instances truly) of the character of the persons who fill this office in question—much of the good order and the security of English & American society has for centuries depended upon their exertions— The nature of their calling demands that they should be active young men, yet fully one third of them will be found beyond the age of 45 years. In addition to their common law duties, they are required in this State to attend upon trials of civil causes before magistrates—serving process & notices and summoning witnesses and afterwards enforcing the judgments: ch 24 of Code—

II *Coroners*—the Section of the Constitution above cited includes Coroners. The Code provides that the County Courts, a majority of all the Justices in each County being present, shall (respectively) by a majority vote appoint one Coroner for each County, or if necessary more than one. He gives bond in $2000 and takes an oath of office: when he succeeds to the duties of Sheriff he gives the same bond that the latter does. The Coroner is an officer well known to the Common law, honorable and of high antiquity. He holds inquest over persons suddenly dead and when it is *found* that one of these have been slain he sets in motion the machinery of justice. He serves all process that is directed against the Sheriff, and all process which the Sheriff from interest or other cause of *unindif*-

ferency cannot serve: and when there is no person properly qualified to act as Sheriff in any County the Coroner acts as Sheriff. His duties are therefore only occasional, but when required they are of the highest importance. The office is one quite indispensable. There are generally but one to a county, the exception being in a few of the most populous counties. They are generally men of middle age—often physicians, and it is probable there are not fifty of them in the State who are or will probably become liable to conscription—Code, ch. 25.

(a) The above contains a brief summary of the position Constables and Coroners. It seems that upon the merit of the question they should be exempted. But besides this it deserves attention that the State which will be allowed to be the exclusive judge of what is necessary to preserve its peace, has required by a constitutional provision that there shall be Officers of these kinds in each county: and the effect of this declaration (as it could not be really) so has not even in appearances been affected by a declaration upon the part of the Legislature subjecting them to the performance of a military duty which is to be done exclusively within the limits of the respective counties.

III *County Trustees*—These are the Treasurers of the respective Counties, receiving and disbursing every year from $5000 to $25000 applied to various purposes of County policy. The Code provides that there may be one in each County: power is reserved to the County Courts (a majority of the Justices in the County being present) to abolish this office and impose its duties &c upon the Sheriff. This has been done in several instances, but in general it is found impracticable for the Sheriff to discharge this Office in addition to his own. From the nature of the Office it is generally filled by men of mature years. Where it exists it is quite indispensable, and the competency of deciding in what cases it shall exist apart from the office of Sheriff resides exclusively (as must be admitted to be good policy) with the County Court constituted as above. The number liable to conscription must be very small—Code Ch:29.

IV *Registers*—Of these there is one to each County. The office has existed in the State, at least since the year 1715. It is his business to keep a register of ordinary deeds, mortgages, trusts, bills of sale, & other similar instruments. Some of these have a validity for all purposes only from the time of registration and no instrument required to be registered can be given in evidence unless this has been done. The indispensableness of this Office can be seen at a glance.

V *Justices of the Peace.* The Constitution (Sect 33) provides that Justices of the Peace shall be commissioned by the Governor upon recommendation by the General Assembly, and that they shall hold their office during good behaviour. There is no class of State officers, that upon the whole is more important than this—and here as in all other communities governed by the common law, it embraces a very great proportion of the wealth, intelligence and character of society. They exercise to some extent judicial, legislative and ministerial functions. They are single judges in actions of debt for amounts (in general) of $100, they try and decide cases of small infractions of police law: in their assemblies in the County Courts (a majority of their number within each county being present) they elect various County officers, lay taxes and regulate their expenditure in providing for the poor, for bridges, the expense of Courts &c &c. Ministerially they perform a great variety of duties, under the revenue law of the State in administering its general police and other matters. Besides this they hold the County Courts as Judges, at least three being present. In this State the County courts have a large jurisdiction of civil and criminal causes [cases]: and the business done by them is very considerable. With a few exceptions, they have jurisdiction of all civil causes, and can try and decide all criminal matters, the punishment of which does not extend to life or limb. Any Magistrate in commission has a right to assist in holding the County Courts, and in some cases to be decided by a majority of his brethren—it is made his duty to do so. These courts sit quarterly. By the recent State law much of their civil jurisdiction has been suspended. An act of the last legislature allows *one third* of the number of Magistrates in any county the same power of acting which heretofore had required a majority. The number of Magistrates in this State is very considerable, perhaps as many as one in every twenty five of the voting population. It is supposed that from two thirds to three fourths of them are above the age of 45. A full proportion of them are in the ranks of the Volunteers from this State. Much remark has been indulged in as to the number of persons in the State who have been exempted from conscription solely on this account. The number of these has been greatly exaggerated. No one can be familiar with the spectacle of a meeting of the majority of the Magistrates in a county without bearing in mind how large a majority of those present are men of advanced and declining age.

In considering the question whether the Magistrates shall be exempted from Conscription, it is not competent for the Executive Department of North Carolina to indulge in any private views, (even if he had them) as to the necessity for public ends of the present large number of these officers. The Constitution has given to him no right to criticise the manner in which the General Assembly has performed duties that are delegated to the latter. This instrument has vested the power of appointing Justices exclusively in the General Assembly. The duty of commissioning such as may be recommended is merely a ministerial one and has no discretion connected with its performance. In as much then as the Constitution has conferred on the General Assembly exclusive, the power of deciding how many magistrates are necessary in various counties every private citizen of the State and every other department of the Government is bound, in all public action, to believe that this power has been wisely bestowed and as wisely executed. Much more must the Executive, in all correspondence, or other business with exterior Governments act upon this as a presumption, *juris et de jure*.[4] It would be a matter of first offence for him or any other person, within or without the state, in any official transaction to question the good faith, wisdom, or any other circumstance of propriety that marks the deliberations or decisions of another Department of the State Government. Such a principle requires but to be mentioned in order to secure universal acquiescence. Under it is clear that all State Officers which by the Government of the State or any department thereof (vested with the right of deciding) are declared to be necessary to carry out the various functions of the State Government—must be held to be thus necessary by all persons and authorities who are willing, *in any case* whatever to recognize and defer to the will of the State

I am with great Respect &c
S. F. Phillips

[1]April 9, A&H:GP.

[2]Samuel Field Phillips, legislator and former law professor of ZBV, who became state auditor for public accounts in December 1862. After the war he served as speaker of the House of Commons and as solicitor general of the United States. Cheney, *North Carolina Government*, 183, 198n, 321, 323, 331, 333; Tucker, *Zeb Vance*, 47; Elizabeth Gregory McPherson, ed., "Letters from North Carolina to Andrew Johnson," *North Carolina Historical Review* 28 (January 1951): 69n.

[3]*Revised Code of North Carolina*, 1854.

[4]Of law and right, an irrebuttable presumption.

ZBV to Peter Mallett   A&H:GP

Copy

State of North Carolina
Executive Department
Raleigh April 21st. 1863.

Col. Mallett
Comdg. Camp Holmes

Col.

The following named persons placed in my hands by Col. Martin[1] and sent to your Camp for safekeeping, having been retained some three months and no charges of any kind appearing against them as required by law, you are hereby requested to set at liberty, viz

Henry Ha[neberr]ly, Green Manson, W. Jackson, Joshua Lufton, Wm. Hodges, Chamey Kengan, E. H Genkins, M. L. Stransberry and W. A. Foreman

Very Respectfully
Yr. obt. servt.
(signed)   Z. B. Vance

[1]William Francis Martin, commander of Seventeenth Regiment North Carolina Troops, lawyer, politician, and brother of General James Green Martin. Johnston, *Papers of Vance*, 1:273n.

Daniel H. Hill to ZBV   A&H:GLB

Goldsboro' N.C. April 21st. 1863

His Excellency Z. B. Vance
Governor of North Carolina

Dear Sir

I think that Infantry would be of little service in Moore County without the cooperation of Cavalry. I wish to send 25 horsemen and 50 Infantry.[1]

This is however, a bad time to weaken my force. I learn that there are 100 vessels now at Morehead City and that troops are pouring in /from/ Charleston. The Charleston Expedition is abandoned and Wilmington and the Rail Road are the next object of Yankee Cupidity. Genl. Longstreet wrote to me to ask you to call out the militia I don't know that any good could result from it except the Exposure of the skulkers. The men staying at home now are consumers and non producers. They ought to be kicked into ranks by some means. One of your stirring appeals would do good. Your scathing rebuke of deserters and skulkers make even cowards blush. I fear that the discontent and demoralization of the troops have been mainly caused by unwise ebillitions of temper on the part of our local press.

Would to God that our Editors could fight the common enemy and let their private quarrels lie over. If conquered by the Yankees our doom will be the most miserable known in history. There is no insult and no indignity which these infernal wretches will not inflict upon us

I Earnestly hope that you will call out every able bodied man in the State, but especially that you will issue a Proclamation in regard to deserters and skulkers

Yours truly
D. H. Hill
Maj. Genl

[1]To quell antiwar violence and hunt deserters and draft evaders. ZBV had received news of the trouble in Moore County in a letter from local resident R. Street (April 10, A&H:GP). In a brief endorsement on the back of that correspondence ZBV ordered it referred to General Hill with a suggestion that Confederate troops be sent to the area. See also Auman, "Neighbor against Neighbor," 73.

ZBV to James A. Seddon   A&H:GP

Copy

State of North Carolina
Executive Department
Raleigh April 22d. 1863

Hon J. A. Seddon
Secty. of War

Sir

I beg leave to ask your interference in regard to some irregularities connected with the execution of the Act of Conscription in this State. Maj Genl. D. H. Hill Comdg. this Dept. in his very commendable zeal to fill up the ranks of our Army has virtually superseded the enrolling officers. Numerous complaints are made to me that he arrests men and sends them direct to the Army without allowing the proper officers to pass upon their claims to exemption, as required by the act itself and the regulations of the Dept. thereon.

In other instances it is complained that the exemptions furnished by Col. Mallett and his subordinates have been disregarded and the men forced into <into> service notwithstanding. As a matter coming within my own knowledge, I also beg leave to say that a number of men have been seized by Gen. Hill and conscribed, who were members of a State battalion raised under an act of Congress, by volunteers from counties within or near the enemy's line, where the enrolling officers could not go to do their duty. I respectfully ask that these men should be returned to Captain Whitford[1] who commands the battalion, and as for other irregularities complained of I am clearly of opinion and so request, that the best way would be to comply with the law *strictly in all respects*—that all conscripts should pass through the hands of the proper enrolling officers alone And the military authorities should not be permitted to interfere with their duties, except simply to render aid when required in making arrests. This course would, I am confident, give greater satisfaction, be much better for the public good, and is besides, what we are entitled to at the hands of the Government

Very Respectfully
Yr. obt. servt.
(signed)   Z. B. Vance

[1]John N. Whitford, Eleventh Battalion (subsequently Sixty-seventh Regiment) North Carolina Troops. Clark, *Histories of Regiments from North Carolina,* 1:14; 3:703; 4:338.

ZBV to Daniel H. Hill   A&H:GP

Copy

State of North Carolina
Executive Department
Raleigh April 22d. 1863

Genl. D. H. Hill
Goldsboro N.C.

Dear Sir

The papers in relation to the seizure of horses in Moore & Randolph by Lt. Pugh[1] has been received with endorsements &c.

The explanations are very unsatisfactory and disingeneous. It is exceedingly strange that 15 or 20 horses should be taken and the officers not know who they were taken from or who they belonged to! This being so, in all conscience how did he know them to be disloyal. What right had Lt. Pugh to plunder the citizens? By whose authority did he undertake to try these people and decide upon their loyalty, and proceed to confiscate their property? And more especially who authorized him to burn the Still houses of the citizens? I am sure I did not, neither did Genl Smith who sent him to me. I think according to his own confession he has made out a case sufficient for him to be dismissed the service. I dont ask this however, but only that the horses may be returned to their owners or paid for. I have no right however to waive any claim which these men may have against the Government for damages for their houses burnt.

Very Respectfully and
Truly Yours
Z. B. Vance

[1]Commanding troops in operations against deserters and Union sympathizers.

ZBV to William H. C. Whiting   A&H:GLB

Executive Dept. N.C.
Raleigh April 23d.

Maj. Genl. W. H. C. Whiting
Wilmington N C.

General

The Second lot of Negroes are ready to go down, some of them on the road. I[t] seems my duty however to ask you if there is no chance of dispensing with this second lot? They are so greatly needed in the fields, and the matter of provisions is one of such immense importance to us all, that I beg of you to do without them, if the safety of the Country will at all permit. Of course this must depend upon your judgment entirely, and I know I need not argue the matter with you. They shall be sent promptly if you deem it indispensable

> Very Respectfully Yours
> Z. B. Vance

ZBV to Daniel H. Hill   A&H:GLB

> State of North Carolina
> Executive Department
> Raleigh April 23d. 1863

Maj. Genl. D H Hill
Comdg. Goldsboro' N.C.

General

Yours of yesterday[1] is just recd.—In view of the alarming information it conveys of this probable invasion of the State, I will not press for the troops to be sent to Moore County at present. I will at once issue an appeal to the people to send in the Deserters and absentees and do every thing I can to bring up every man to his post. I do not think General that the Militia ought to be called out, for various reasons. Their help would be little, their consumption of rations great, and beyond any sort of doubt, their removal now from their crops would be followed by the most disastrous consequences. If you think it necessary, when the enemy's movement is fully developed I will call out the *Militia Officers* of whom there are some two or three thousand, which will be a larger number, I fear than we can arm and make available—I can bring them to Raleigh at once by *An Order*. I earnestly hope however that such a thing will not be necessary. In accordance with a previous request, I have addressed a note to the City Editors urging them to avoid exciting any panic among the people, and to be cautious not to speak of the movement of troops &c

> Very Respectfully
> Z. B. Vance

[1]April 21, in this volume.

James R. McLean to ZBV   A&H:GP

> Richmond Va
> April 24th 1863

Gov Vance

Sir,

I have seen your several communications to Gen Raines the chief of Bureau of Conscription and also a letter to Col Gaither.[1] In conversation with other members from N.C. I have urgently insisted that your most reasonable requests should be complied with in relation to the Conscription of Civil and military officers of a sovereign state.

From the outset, I have given a cheerful and cordial endorsement <of> /to/ your administration of state affairs. I hold it to be the duty of every patriotic citizen to uphold and sustain both State and Confederate authorities, at all times and especially in the terrible crisis through which we are now passing. It certainly is desirable that harmony and co-operation should exist between state and Confederate authorities, but if an issue is forced upon me, all my sympathies and energies of course will be given to my native state.

It was never supposed by Congress, that the Conscript law included any state officers, Judicial, Legislative [or] ministerial <officers>, necessary to preserve and administer the authority of the State Government. I not only admire and applaud the courage and determination which you have manifested, but I think, with great respect [faded] /[your solemn] duty/ to uphold and sustain the equality, dignity, honor and independence of North Carolina, the good old mother of us all—

At all events you /shall/ have my humble, but cordial support—Excuse this hasty letter—

> Very Respectfully
> Your Obt Servant
> J. R. McLean[2]

[Endorsed] File

ZBV

[1]Burgess Sidney Gaither, Confederate congressman, and a former speaker of the North Carolina Senate, as well as superintendent of the U.S. mint at Charlotte. *Dictionary of North Carolina Biography*, s.v. "Gaither, Burgess Sidney."

[2]James Robert McLean, Confederate congressman, lawyer, and former legislator. *Dictionary of North Carolina Biography*, s.v. "McLean, James Robert."

Thomas S. Ashe to ZBV   LC:CSA

> Richmond
> April 24 1863

Hon Z B Vance

Dear Sir

I have been shown a letter[1] addressed by you to the Hon B S Gaither in reference to the conscription of our Justices which you say you are resolved to resist. I think you are right, and for me, I will sustain your course as much as I should deprecate any collision between the State and Confederate authorities upon a vital question like this. I am on the side of my native State I am clearly of the opinion that Congress has no power to conscript any officer of a State, unless the State Legislature shall declare him to be liable to service in the Confederate [army].

I commit myself therefore readily to your support in this matter because I am [faded] that your course will be marked by that forbearance patience and wisdom which characterizes your whole administration. I hope however that the military committee will propose the amendment to the conscription bill now under consideration before it, as will relieve you from the unpleasant duty of coming in collision with the Confederate authorities.

> With sentiments of high respect
> Your obdt set
> Thos. S. Ashe[2]

[1]Not extant.

[2]Thomas Samuel Ashe, Confederate congressman, former legislator, and postwar U.S. congressman and associate justice of the North Carolina Supreme Court. *Dictionary of North Carolina Biography*, s.v. "Ashe, Thomas Samuel."

Burgess S. Gaither to ZBV   A&H:VanPC

House of Representatives
April 24th. 1863

His Excellency Gov Vance

My Dear Sir

I received your letter[1] a few days since and have had a fine and full interview with our delegation in reference to your position upon the conscript law and your correspondence with the department here on this subject and I have the pleasure to inform you that your course is approved and endorsed by our delegation and they will sustain you before their constituents. I rejoice that you have taken the bold and manly position you have assumed in this matter. It is just and proper in itself and absolutely necessary for the honor of our State. Our state has been snubbed and insulted by the official of this Government, until it has become intolerable and not to be borne any longer and has the effect to wake up our entire delegation, to the point of repelling with indignation any neglect of the rights of our state or of its citizens. The tendancy of things here is toward a consolodated military operation, ignoring all the rights of the states, and the truest and boldest men here in the advocacy of state rights, are the *old line Whigs*, who wish to preserve in tact, the constitution rights of both state and the Confederate Governments. The extremist and ultra friends of state rights, appear to

have lost their resoning and are upon the wild idea of revolution, without com-
pass and are drifting into the vortex of despotism. They shown high capacity for
the destruction of the old government and now exhibit none for the construction
of the new one. They succeeded in establishing the constitutional right of peace-
able secession and recently in the senate they have attempted to organize and
establish by law constitutional & legal nullification of any and all the powers of
the Confederate Government, by the State Courts, by organizing the Supreme
Court without the power of appellate jurisdiction from the State Courts. Fortu-
nately, we were enabled in the House to defeat the bill for the present, but there
is no hope of establishing the Supreme Court, without yielding to this miserable
doctrine, while the senate is composed of its present members. I am disgusted
with matters here and am greatly inclined not to be a candidate again—My
situation here and at home is rather unpleasant for a public man. I am looked
upon here by the peculiar friends of the administration with suspicion and considered too sensitive and factious in all matters connected with my state and
anxious to get up issues with the officials in their treatment towards our state
and our citizens, and at home, if I may judge from the feelings of the last Legislature, and from the opinions of the [illegible] in my district I have not the confidence of the Conservative party of the state. In the remarks I had occasion to
make in the presentation of the resolution of our General assembly, which I
thought historicaly true and just, I excited some of our democratic members to
take issue with me & was unsustained by the rest of our delegation. At the first
session where the attempt was made to disarm our private citizens, when I attempted to indicate their rights by a call upon the President for his authority to
do so I met with oposition from some of our delegation & support from some in
a tangible [shape] But the unkindest cut of all, taking all things into consideration, was the action of the last Legislature in importing from another circuit that
fellow Shipp[2] for the judgeship over me & others of the circuit. I did not really
want the judgeship, but when I found the manner in which things were managed
in that matter by a Legislature composed of my party friends I felt indignant and
now feel disgraced in the state and am here subject to the mortification of having
my course in public affairs repudiated by my own state and party friends. I have
really been so much depressed by it that I have taken but little part or interest
in the matters of this session and feel like leting all public matters go to the D—
and myself to private life I say this much to you, as a personal and political friend
who knows me well and know the success I have rendered this same Conservative
party and how little other gentlemen, (who have been promote[d]), have to boast
of in that way—We are approaching the end of the session & have done but
little for the public good save the refusal to extend the suspension of the writ of
Habeas Corpus & to discourage & denounce martial law. We have passed a
revenue law, which will be [practicaly] oppressive to our Western people and
favourable to the land & slave interest I did not vote for it & intend to denounce
it when necessary We are in the hands of the Cotton states and the grain &
stock farming interest is to be sacrificed to their interest I have scarcely room to

express my entire & unqualified approval of your administration. Please give my regards to Mrs Vance

Yours truly
B. S. Gaither

[1]Not extant.
[2]William Marcus Shipp, superior court judge of Seventh Judicial District and former member of the North Carolina House and Senate and the Secession and Constitutional conventions of 1861–1862. After the war he became chairman of the Shipp Commission for investigating the Swepson-Littlefield frauds and subsequently served as state attorney general and then again as superior court judge. Cheney, *North Carolina Government*, 323, 329, 356n, 371n, 372n, 386, 427, 440n, 578, 595n, 824; Johnston, *Papers of Vance*, 1:71n.

ZBV to William T. Dortch   A&H:GLB

State of North Carolina
Executive Department
Raleigh April 25th. 1863

Hon. W. T. Dortch
Richmond Va

My dear Sir

Permit me to call your attention to a matter of very great importance and which demands immediate action. I urged upon the Legislature as you may remember to pass laws making it punishable to harbor conscripts & deserters or give them aid in any way. The Legislature through the influence of Mr [*William A.*] Graham, declined to do so, on the ground, that it was the province of Congress alone to provide for the enforcement of its own laws &c. This seems to be recognized among legal gentlemen here as the proper ground. Since the adjournment of the Legislature Chief Justice Pearson has decided in effect that it was not legal for the Governor to employ the Militia in arresting Conscripts and deserters—that Confederate officers alone could do so—The effect of these things has justified the fears which I entertained. Desertion is alarmingly on the increase and their friends and relations openly protect and feed them—The Army is loosing almost as many by desertions as it gains by conscription and I am in effect powerless. Now will not Congress take some action in the matter? What is required is the passage of a short statute against all who harbor, feed or in any way aid men to evade the law or to escape capture: and to make some provision for employing the militia of the States, by request upon the Governors in making arrests &c &c. If this were done I could "clean out" North Carolina with my Militia and occasional help from the regular soldiers. Some compensation should be given to the Militia for their services.

Please consult with Mr Seddon and our State delegation, and do what you think best and speedily

> Very respectfully
> Yr. obt. Svt
> Z. B. Vance

ZBV to James A. Seddon   A&H:GLB

> State of North Carolina
> Executive Department
> Raleigh April 27th. 1863

Hon. Jas. A. Seddon
Secy. of War
Richmond

Sir

I received a message from you by Judge Ruffin[1] in regard to supplies for the Army and desiring to know if I could not turn over to the Confederacy the stores on hand belonging to the State.

It affords me great pleasure to assure you that the crisis in regard to provisions in this State has passed over, and the conviction is now firm in all minds that there is not only enough but to *spare*. The passage of the impressment act and the near approach of a harvest which promises to be abundant, have brought to light many hoards that the fear of famine kept out of the market.

The call for aid to the Army has met with a liberal response from our generous people and I trust all fears may be dismissed.

The quantity of provisions on hand were not large belonging to N.C. They were purchased under authority of an Act of our Legislature to prevent suffering in the families of soldiers and consequent disquiet and desertion in the Army. The demand has been much less than I expected, and in a few weeks I shall be able to see what can be dispensed with. I hope to be able to turn over some 250,000 lbs bacon and some Corn to the Confederacy. Precisely how much I can not now say. The purchases of Govt. Agents can also be increased when the State and most of private individuals cease to be in the market

> Very respectfully
> Yr obt Servt
> Z. B. Vance

---

[1]Thomas Ruffin, former chief justice of the North Carolina Supreme Court and member of the state's secession convention. *Dictionary of American Biography*, s.v. "Ruffin, Thomas."

Archibald H. Arrington to ZBV   A&H:GP

House of Reps. Apl. 28th 1863

His Excellency
Govr. Vance,

Sir,

I learn through my colleage Col. Gaither that you have taken the ground, not to permit our state officers to be made subject to conscription, I am fully of opinion that you have assumed the true ground, and I shall most cheerfully sustain you in the stand you have taken—though I trust that an amendment that was added to the Exemption act which was adopted on yesterday will prevent or allay the difficulty that has arisen between the Sectry. of War and yourself—I was satisfied that difficuties would arise from the wording of the Act of Congress and I appealed to Mr. Miles[1] the Chairman of the Committee on Military affairs several times and urged the propriety of wording the act so as either to embrace Justices of the Peace or to exempt /them/ in order that the law might operate uniformly in all the states but I faild to be able to convince him of its propriety, now he sees the necessity of it, and was quite willing to adopt an amendment that will obviate the difficulty between you & him which hope will be concured in by the Senate and put an end to all difficulties of this character—

I am Sir with great Respect
Your obt. St.
A. H. Arrington[2]

[*Endorsed*] File

ZBV

[1]William Porcher Miles, Confederate congressman from South Carolina. Faust et al., *Encyclopedia of Civil War*, 492–493.
[2]Archibald Hunter Arrington, Confederate congressman, former U.S. congressman, planter, and lawyer. *Dictionary of North Carolina Biography*, s.v. "Arrington, Archibald Hunter."

ZBV to James A. Seddon   A&H:GLB

Executive Department N.C.
Raleigh April 28th. 1863.

Hon. Jas. A. Seddon
Secty. of War

Sir

From the best information to be obtained it seems now pretty /certain/ that the enemy has abandoned further attempts upon Charleston and will direct his attention principally to the invasion of North Carolina during this season. I desire to say that the coast of North Carolina is very poorly defended indeed. The Roanoke, the Tar and the Neuse,[1] embracing the richest corn growing region of the State, upon which the Army of Genl Lee has been subsisting for months, have no heavy Artillery for their defence. The attack on Washington[2] recently failed through the defect of artillery and the very alarming inferiority of the ammunition. I very much fear that region will not be planted, so disheartning is the prospect of defense. One fifth of the care taken in rendering Charleston impregnable would be well bestowed in strengthening the defences of Wilmington, which are now confessedly weak. It is a point equally important in a military view, in every respect, and calls as loudly for the protection of the government, and yet nearly all the heavy guns of the Confederacy seem to have been sent to Charleston, and other points are left to take the chances. An attack upon Wilmington by half the number of iron clads which assaulted Charleston would be equivalent to the capture of the city—Can nothing be done to strengthen that point?

From Roanoke Island to the late seige of Washing[ton] the history of the War has been a succession of calamities in North Carolina which none but the ungenerous and untruthful can charge to a want of bravery and patient endurance on the part of her people. I shall not pretend to say that our defence is intentionally neglected, but that it is very poorly provided for is a fact too patent to deny and that it *can* be better provided for, *I hope* is true—from the fact which I am assured is true—that every sea port in our possession is stronger than Wilmington. It is discouraging to know this when we consider what North Carolina has done for the cause in men and means. We certainly ought to fare no worse than our Sisters. I am again called on by Genl. Hill to call out the Militia. Considering that our white male population is already taken to the age of forty, that nearly twenty of our richest counties have been stripped of their slaves, that over 1500 are yet at work on the fortifications, it seems a physical impossibility to prevent a famine should all the balance of our labor be abstracted from the farms in the middle of the planting season. Yet I could call them out with less reluctance and put raw plowman to contend with iron clad ships of war with less regret, if I were honestly convinced that every thing possible to do, had been done, and that such a course was unavoidable. What the precise resources of the Ordnance Department are, of course I do not know. But may I hope, that now that the attack upon Charleston is over, the defences of Wilmington and navagable rivers of this state will receive the Earnest attention of the War Dept., and the requisitions of the Generals in command will meet with every possible fulfillment? Permit me to assure you in the candor which I usually employ in addressing /you/ that an earnest & vigorous effort to defend these exposed points would work a most happy effect in the dissatisfied public mind of this people

I am Sir

Most Respectfully
Yr. obt. Servt.
Z. B. Vance

[1]Rivers.
[2]North Carolina town on the Tar (which becomes the Pamlico) River. Confederate troops had attacked a Federal garrison there. Barrett, *Civil War in North Carolina*, 156–162.

Lewis S. Williams to ZBV   A&H:GP

Charlotte N.C. April 29, 1863

His Excellency Gov. Vance

Sir,

Will you please inform me if the prohibition to send flour and other necessaries of life beyond the limits of the State—recently promulgated by your authority—Extends to flour bought and owned by parties in South Carolina & Georgia when said parties have had the flour in question in transit over the railroads of this state for months before your order was issued—There is flour here in that condition and I would like to know if it is embraced in your proclamation.

With Much Respect
Your Obt. Servt.
L. S. Williams
Col. 85th. N.C.M
pr. R. Tiddy[1]

[*Endorsed*] So many persons have violated my prohibition by pretending to have bought supplies before the proclamation that I made no distinction in their favour, but not wishing to work any hardship I reserve the right to judge of individual cases presented to me

Z B V

[1]Richard Tiddy, apparently dealing in flour. After the war he became co-owner of Wm. & R. Tiddy, Paper Manufacturers, Lincolnton. William L. Sherrill, *Annals of Lincoln County North Carolina*, 2nd. ed. (Lincolnton: United Daughters of the Confederacy, 1967), 104–105; W. and R. Tiddy to ZBV, April 14, 1888, SHC:Van.

John D. Hyman to ZBV   A&H:VanPC

Asheville N C
April 30th. 1863.

Dear Governor

Yours of 23d. inst.[1] is rec'd. I anticipated your letter by paying the $1400 on the Cotton debt. I charge no fee. What I did cost me little trouble, and I did it as a favor to you and others. You & your co-sureties, however, have been saved at least $700 if not $1000 by the sale at this particular juncture.[2] I feel sure no such opportunity would have been again presented. If I had desired to purchase the establishment for printing purposes, $500 is the most I would have given; for the press is an old one and has been very much abused, and as for the type, there was not enough remaining to print a 7x9—in brief the office was a total wreck. The thieving boys about town had broken into the office and stolen nearly all the job-type, rules, composing sticks—and a great deal of the text-type in printing a paper—and the balance was in a most perfect state of *pi*.[3] But the government is rich—in shin plasters—and could well afford to pay a large price for type-metal—to make "gudgeons"—"to catch whales", I suppose.—

You say you hear that [*Allen T.*] Davidson, Love,[4] [*Bayles M.*] Edney, & myself will all be candidates for Congress.—I can only speak for myself. I have said to some of my friends that I would serve, provided I should not sufficiently improve to return to the army. I abandoned that hope some time since and have resigned my commission. I may, therefore, be considered a candidate. I wrote Davidson some time ago that I would be a candidate, and requested him to write me tendering the matter. He did write me and stated that he knew of no gentleman he would sooner support than myself, subject to the condition that he did not run himself. He did not say this in terms, but such I took to be the purport of his letter. He said he did not care much about running, but he was in the hands of his friends and his being a candidate or not depended upon their wishes. Thus the matter stands, so far as he & myself are concerned. You say Davidson & I "must *comp*"—that Davidson being the incumbent is entitled to consideration &c. A compromise in a matter of this kind can be made only by the withdrawal of one <party or the> of the parties in favor of the other. The question then is, which of us shall withdraw? The only answer to this question /is/ who is the stronger man before the people? This latter question being properly answered, the matter is determined. It would become neither Mr. Davidson nor myself to answer this question. Then who is to decide? Shall a convention of our friends be holden? I think it would be unwise and impolitic at this time, or at any time, pending the war, /to hold/ a convention to decide upon the status of different candidates. The soldiers in the service could have no voice in the matter and it would be unjust to them. It is true a few of our friends, the prominent men of the Conservative Party, might hold a consultation in reference to the matter. But such a commission would be a delicate matter to them and they might be influenced by partialities; so that the result of their consultation might be un-satisfactory to the candidate elected to withdraw his name and distasteful to the people at home or the soldiers in the Army.—

Upon the whole, therefore, I have concluded to test my strength with the votes of the district. I may be considered fairly in the field. Mr Davidson says he <n> is not yet a candidate. Upon the matter of being "horned of", I am the ox more likely to be gored than friend Davidson, who admits that he is undecided whether to become a candidate or not. The accident of his being the incumbent does not, in my estimation, of itself, entitle Mr. Davidson to peculiar consideration.—

If there is such a thing as gratitude in this degenerate age, I think I could without impropriety make an appeal to some of my friends to give me the weight of their influence on this the only occasion I have ever asked anything at their hands. But I shall make no special appeal. What I have done in time past was done from the promptings of duty. What sacrifices I made were made cheerfully— with no view to a quid pro quo.—I have learned by experience, that if one does not paddle his own canoe, the same will not be paddled at all.—

Popularities in times like these are deceptive—he that floats on the top of the waves of popular favor to-day may with all his hopes and aspirations be submerged to rise no more tomorrow, however well he thinks he may be watching his corks.

As for Love and Edney, neither of them can make anything like a decent showing. Love is making a few friends, as one of the board of Examination of Conscripts by exempting well men from conscription and by playing the petty demagogue generally in the district. But original secession sticks to him like the shirt of Nessus.[5] Edney is not /worth/ penning a paragraph about. He came home a week or two ago and told the people that he had induced the President to suspend the execution of the Conscription act West of the mountains. But the publication of the Sec of War's letter to yourself[6] has given him the lie direct. The people are now cursing him. Had he succeeded, the thing would have given him no strength in the army, for as you very well know the soldiers are exceedingly anxious to have the Conscription act rigidly executed and enforced while it would have done him little good at home.—

I was unjust to myself at the commencement of the war by volunteering so soon, or I might have obtained a better military position. While my precipitancy was the cause of my not obtaining a military position, yet I am inclined to think I may be able to turn my mistake to advantage. So far as I know I was the first man West of the Blue Ridge that volunteered—I went in as a *private* and served as a *private*, and I continued in the service until I was disabled in battle—it is true my position was an humble one in rank—so much the better with the people, particularly with the soldiers.—Verbum Sap[7] &c

I am here at home with nothing to do—there is no law business. I wouldnt speculate had I the means to do it. Nearly all our friends have some position now but poor me. I am a cripple for life. What shall I do? I would not knowingly endanger the cause of conservatism—for I am an eternal enemy to original secession and desire it to be put under foot and kept there, as I think it will be. If others come into the field & cause our defeat, I could say to them as Macbeth addressed the ghost of Banquo—"Thou canst not say, I did it" &c.

I have written you freely, dear Vance, and what I have written I wish you to regard as confidential. Of course I would like to receive the suggestion of friends and am willing to give their advice and counsel due consideration. I do not mean to say that my purpose to serve is like the laws of the Nudes and Persians.[8] If I had some good berth in the army, I would much prefer remaining in the service during the war. But I know of no position I could likely get. The North Carolina delegation, I learn, have recommended me to the President for the position of one of the members of a Corps Court Martial. But I doubt whether I will be appointed. I shall be happy to hear from you.—

Yours Very Truly
J. D. Hyman[9]

[1]Not extant.
[2]Of the newspaper *Asheville Spectator*, of which ZBV was part owner and had been co-editor in the 1850s. Tucker, *Zeb Vance*, 60–61, 69.
[3]Disorder.
[4]Samuel L. Love, legislator, physician, and postwar state auditor. John Preston Arthur, *Western North Carolina: A History from 1730 to 1913* (Asheville: Daughters of the American Revolution, 1914), 171; William L. Love to ZBV, April 3, A&H:VanPC.
[5]From mythology, meaning source of misfortune from which there is no escape.
[6]March 26, in this volume.
[7]Enough said.
[8]Without consideration or cause.
[9]John Durante Hyman, a friend of ZBV, lawyer, and former co-editor of the *Asheville Spectator*. Johnston, *Papers of Vance*, 1:50n.

ZBV to James A. Seddon   A&H:GLB

State of North Carolina
Executive Department
Raleigh May 1st. 1863

Hon. Jas. A. Seddon
Secty of War

Sir

I enclose herewith a copy of a letter[1] from Lt. Col. S. D. Thurston Comdg. 3d. N.C. Infty. to which I ask your attention

In regard to the complaints of the writer, I have had the honor to express myself heretofore both to yourself and his Excellency the President in general terms. I can now only say that I concur fully with the Sentiments of Col T. and would be much gratified if this regiment and the 1st. N.C.I. could be placed in a North Carolina Brigade without detriment to the service

Very respectfully
Yr obt svt
Z. B. Vance

[1]April 27, A&H:GP. Stephen D. Thurston complained of his regiment having to serve under generals from other states and requested that it be placed in a North Carolina brigade.

William T. Dortch to ZBV   A&H:GP

Goldsboro, May 2nd., 63

His Excellency
Gov Vance
Raleigh

My dear Sir:
In consequence of sickness in my family, I left Richmond last friday (yesterday week).
Early in the Session I introduced a resolution instructing the Committee on the Judiciary to enquire into the necessity of amending & making more stringent the laws in regard to harboring deserters &c. The Committee thought further legislation unnecessary & so the matter ended. I fear we shall have serious difficulties in some sections of the State in regard to the matter. On being informed of your demand that State officers should not be conscripted, I immediately called on Genl Raines & insisted that your wishes should be complied with. I procured a copy of your letter & laid it before the Committee on Military Affairs, having charge of the exemption bill. I have not been informed whether any exemption bill has passed since I left. I judge, however, that your demand will be complied with. Your Brother [*Robert B. Vance*] was confirmed Brigadier before I came home.

Yours &c
Wm. T. Dortch

ZBV to James A. Seddon   A&H:GLB

Raleigh May 4th. 1863

Hon. Jas. A. Seddon
Secy of War
Richmond

Genl Hill advises me to order out the Militia, do you wish it done?

Z. B. Vance

James A. Seddon to ZBV   A&H:GP

[*With enclosure*]

Confederate States of America,
War Department,
Richmond, Va. May 5, 1863.

His Excellency Z. B. Vance,
Governor of N.C.
Raleigh, N.C.

Sir,

I have the honor to invoke your attention to the enclosed letter from Genl. Pender,[1] with an endorsement by Genl. Lee. The subject is one of great importance, /and/ I respectfully urge that you will aid in arresting the progress of desertion among the North Carolina troops, which unless promptly checked, will be destructive of the discipline and morale of our Army. A copy of the letter and endorsement will be sent to Genl. [*D. H.*] Hill, with direction to furnish you a Regiment, should you desire it, to assist in arresting deserters.

Very Respectfully
Your obdt. servt.
James A. Seddon
Secretary of War

[*Endorsed*] File & copy—

Z B V

[1]William Dorsey Pender, brigade commander in General Ambrose Powell Hill's division, Army of Northern Virginia. He was promoted to major general on May 27 but later died from a wound sustained at Gettysburg. Faust et al., *Encylopedia of Civil War*, 569.

[*Enclosure*]

William D. Pender to Walter H. Taylor   A&H:GP

Hd. Qrs. Pender's Brigade
April 23d. 1863

Maj W. H. Taylor
A. A. Genl.
Army N. Va

Major

I would beg leave to call the attention of the Commanding General to /the/ state of affairs that exist in the N.C. Regts of this Army, and the crimes which in my opinion have brought it about. I think I am safe in saying that at least two hundred men have deserted from the Twenty /four/ Regts in this corps, within the last thirty days. This Sir I fear is not the worst of it for unless some prompt means <means> be taken to arrest those already deserted, and severe punish-ment be inflicted after they shall be caught, the matter will grow from bad to worse. In my humble opinion the whole trouble lies in the fact that they believe, when they get into N.C., they will not be molested, and their belief is based upon the *dictums* of Judge Pearson, Chief Justice of the State in a recent trial of persons who killed some militia officers while in the discharge of their duties.[1] I have not seen the Judge's proceedings in the case *but our men are of the opinion* that he held that the Conscript Law was unconstitutional, and hence they draw the conclusion, that enrolled conscripts will not only be justified in resisting the Law but that those who have /been/ held in service by the Law, will not be arrested when <the> they desert. This conclusion is bourne out by the facts. I have heard from a reliable gentleman that conscripts & deserters go unmolested in Yadkin Co. N.C. and Sgt G[rase] of my Brigade, who has just returned, was told by the Militia /officers/ of that County, that they should not arrest any more deserters in the face of Judge Pearson's holding, unless protected by the Govern-ment, and the boldness of the deserters there, proves that they are acting up to their word. Letters are received by the men, urging them to leave, that [they] will not be troubled when they get home.

It would strike me that the holding alluded to, being only the individual *dictum* of one of the three Judges, could be binding only in that particular case.

What I have stated concerning Yadkin I fear holds good elsewhere & unless some check is put upon it, will work great and serious injury to the cause. I would suggest that a Regt. be sent to that section of the state to arrest deserters. Any efforts to apprehend them between here & home, must be only partial at best, & when we get on the march totally impracticable. Unless something is done & quickly, serious will be the result. Our Regts will waste away more rapidly than they ever have by battle.

In writing the above I wish to be just to my State & must say that /I think too many/ troops of /other/ states of the Confederate States would act as ours are, if they thought they could with safety. I am anxious that my State & her troops shall not lo[s]se the credit they have so justly earned in this war, by the conduct of a few bad men.

I am Sir very respectfully
W. D. Pender
Brig. Genl.

[*Endorsed*] Hd. Qrs. 26 April 1863 Respr. forwd. to the Honble. Secy. of War with the request that the attention of the Govr. of <Georgia> N.C. be imme-diately called to this-subject & that a regt. be at once put at his disposal for the duty Genl. Pender states to me that the men go off with their arms in squads—

They can thus band together in the State with other malcontents & produce great trouble, defy the laws &c

R E Lee
Genl.

[1]When the North Carolina Militia arrested deserters in Yadkin County in early 1863, the deserters killed two of the militiamen. Pearson issued writs of habeas corpus and then released all the prisoners on the grounds that the state militia had no authority to arrest Confederate deserters or recusant conscripts. J. G. De Roulhac Hamilton, "The North Carolina Courts and the Confederacy," *North Carolina Historical Review* 4 (October 1927):368–370; Richard Bardolph, "Confederate Dilemma: North Carolina Troops and the Deserter Problem," pt. 2, *North Carolina Historical Review* 66 (April 1989):183–184.

James A. Seddon to ZBV   A&H:GLB

Richmond May 5th. 1863
Gov Vance
Raleigh N.C

Either you or Genl Hill can better judge of the situation in North Carolina than I can The emergency should be very great to justify calling out the Militia at this season. I do not advise it

J. A. Seddon
Secty. of War

[*Endorsed*] Copy from memory of a lost dispatch recd. from Secty. Seddon

Z. B. V.

James A. Seddon to ZBV   A&H:GP

Confederate States of America,
War Department,
Richmond, Va. May 6 1863.
His Excellency Z. B. Vance,
Governor of N.C.
Raleigh, N.C.

Sir,
I have received your letter of the 27th. ult.[1] stating that you hope to turn over some 250,000 lbs. of bacon and some corn to the Confederate Government, in a few weeks.

In reply it affords me great pleasure to acknowledge with grateful appreciation this liberal and patriotic offer. The stores will be received whenever your Excellency deems they can be judiciously transferred, at such appraisement prices as may be fixed by the Assessor appointed under the late Act of Congress, for your State. You will add to the obligation by giving this Department timely notice of the time and place of such contemplated delivery, so that the supplies may be duly cared for and forwarded.

I am happy to hear of the restored confidence of the people of your State in the sufficiency of their supplies for home consumption, although I may not agree with you as to all the reasons that you state as inducing it. The real scarcity was confined to a few districts, but by the unwonted inflation of the currency and the exaggerated apprehensions inspired by the invasion of the enemy, the conviction prevailed that it was very general. The alarm, however, caused extraordinary exertion on the part of all really without supplies to provide themselves, and now the truth begins to be realized, that your extensive and fertile State cannot be easily reduced to serious want. The relief from such apprehension, however unfounded, is a source of great and just satisfaction, and must be specially grateful to your Excellency whose exertions have contributed largely to relieve the public mind.

> With high regard and respect
> Your obdt. servt.
> James A Seddon
> Secretary of War

¹In this volume.

ZBV to James A. Seddon   A&H:GLB

> State of North Carolina
> Executive Department
> Raleigh, May 7th. 1863

Hon. J. A. Seddon
Secy of War
Richmond,

Genl Hill is gathering up all troops in the State. I am furnishing Militia for guarding bridges, provost duty &c—Can not Capt [Henry] McCoys command at Salisbury be sent to the front temporarily? There are only about thirty prisoners there and a Militia battalion can guard them—

> Z. B. Vance

John H. Winder to ZBV   A&H:GP

[*Telegram*]

Richmond May 7 1863

Gov. Vance

Capt McCoy has been instructed to report to you by Telegraph & place his command at your disposal telegraph where you wish

J H Winder[1]

---

[1]John Henry Winder, Confederate provost marshal general. Boatner, *Civil War Dictionary*, 940.

Proclamation by ZBV   A&H:GLB

By the Governor of North Carolina
A Proclamation

Whereas, the time limited by my Proclamation, dated the 13th. of April,[1] forbidding the exportation of certain articles from the State is about to expire

Now, therefore, I, Zebulon B. Vance, Governor of North Carolina, do, by and with the advice and consent of the Council of State, issue this Proclamation, continuing said prohibition thirty days from the 13th. inst subject to the exceptions and restrictions contained in said Proclamation of the 13th. April, with the following alterations The prohibition is not to embrace the article of Salt and Lard is to be added to the articles prohibited

Justices of the Peace are also enjoined to assist in carrying [*out*] this Proclamation

In witness whereof Zebulon B. Vance Governor, Captain General and Commander-in-Chief hath signed these presents and caused the Great Seal of the State to be affixed

Done at the City of Raleigh, this 8th. day of May, A.D. 1863 and in the 87th. year of our Independence

Z. B. Vance

---

[1]In this volume. ZBV extended the time limit of this proclamation for an additional thirty days with a new proclamation on June 8. See A&H:GLB.

Proclamation by ZBV   A&H:GLB

By the Governor of North Carolina
A Proclamation

Whereas, I have learned with great pain that there have been latterly numerous desertions from the ranks of our gallant army and that there are many
persons in the country who incite and encourage these desertions and harbor
and consceal these misguided men at home, instead of Encouraging Them to
return to duty:

Now therefore I, Zebulon B. Vance Governor of the State of North Carolina,
do issue this my proclamation commanding all such evil disposed persons to desist
from such base, cowardly and treasonable conduct, and warning them that they
will subject themselves to indictment and punishment in the civil courts of the
Confederacy as well as to the everlasting contempt and detestation of all good
and honorable men. Certainly no crime could be greater, no cowardice more
abject, no treason more base, than for a citizen of the State, enjoying its privileges
and protection without sharing its dangers; to persuade those who have had the
courage to go forth in defence of their country, vilely to desert the colors which
they have sworn to uphold, when a miserable death or a vile, skulking and
ignominious existence must be the inevitable consequence: no plea can excuse
it. The father or the brother who does it should be shot instead of his deluded
victim, for he deliberately destroys the soul and manhood of his own flesh and
blood. And the same is done by him who harbors and conceals the deserter—
For who can respect either the one or the other? What honest man will ever
wish or permit his own brave sons or patriotic daughters, who bore their parts
with credit in this great struggle for independence to associate, even to the third
and fourth generation with the vile wretch who skulked in the wood, or the still
viler coward who aided him, while his bleeding country was calling in vain for
his help? Both are enemies, sneaking, mean enemies to their country, before
whom our open foes will be infinitely preferred. Both are foes to their own kindred and noble countrymen who are electryfying the world by their gallant deeds,
& pouring out their blood upon the field of battle to protect those very men who
are sapping the vitals of our strength. And woe unto you, deserters and aiders
and abettors when peace being made and independence secured, these brave
comrades whom ye deserted in the hour of their trial shall return honored and
triumphant to their homes! Ye that hide your guilty faces by day and prowl like
outlaws about by night, robbing the wife and mother of your noble defenders, of
their little means, while they are far away facing the enemy, do you think ye can
escape a just and damning vengeance when the day of reckoning comes. And ye
that shelter, conceal and feed these miserable depredations and stimulate them
to their infernal deeds, think you that ye will be spared? Nay: rest assured, observing and never failing eyes have marked you, Every one.—And when the
overjoyed wife welcomes once more her brave and honorable husband to his

home, and tells him how in the long years of his absence in the lonely hours of the night, you who had been his comrades rudely entered her house, robbed her and her children of their bread and heaped insult and indignities upon her defenceless head, the wrath of that heroic husband will make you regret in the bitterness of your cowardly terror that you were ever born. Instead of a few scattered militia, the land will be full of veteran soldiers, before whose honest faces you will not have courage to raise your eyes from the Earth. If permitted to live in the State at all you will be *infamous*. You will you will be hustled from the polls, kicked in the streets, an honest jury will not believe you on oath, and honest men everywhere will shun you as a pestilence, for he who lacks courage and patriotism can have no other good quality or redeeming virtue. Though many of you rejected the pardon heretofore offered you, and I am not authorized to promise it, yet I am assured no man will be shot who shall voluntarily return to duty. This is the only chance to redeem yourselves from the disgrace and ignominy which you are incurring. Again our troops have met the Enemy and a great and glorious victory has been won. But several thousand of our Soldiers fell in achieving it for us. Every man is needed to replace the gallant dead, and preserve an unbroken front to our still powerful Enemy. Unless desertion is prevented our strength must depart from our armies and desertion can never be stopped while either through a false & mistaken sympathy or downright disloyalty, they receive any countenance or protection at home. I therefore appeal to all good citizens and true patriots in the State to assist my officers in arresting deserters and to frown down all those who aid and assist them. Place the brand upon them and make them feel the scorn and contempt of our outraged people. Unless the good and the patriotic all over the land arise as one man to arrest this dangerous evil, it will grow until our Army is well nigh ruined. The danger of starvation having happily passed away—the approaching and apparently bounteous harvest giving evidence of ample supplies for the coming year—our great army in Virginia again jubilant over a mighty victory—I am well assured that our danger now lies in the disorganization produced by desertion—You *can* arrest it my countrymen if you will but bring to bear the weight of a great, a patriotic and united community in aid of your authorities

In witness thereof, Zebulon B. Vance, Governor Captain General & Commander-in-Chief hath signed these presents and caused the great seal of the State to be affixed

Done at the city of Raleigh this 11th. day of May A.D. 1863

Z. B. Vance

John M. Worth to ZBV   A&H:GP

Wilmington N.C.
May 11/63

Gov Z. B. Vance
Raleigh N.C.

Dear Sir

For the month of April, I have to report the shipment of 5,833 bushels Salt to different County Agents—and the exchange of about 500 bushels for provisions, at $5—per bushel.

The average market price during the month was about $9.50 per bushel.

The counties are much better supplied with Salt now than they were at this time last year—

It was quite rainy during April and I did not make as much Salt as I would had the weather been more favorable—The present month promises very well now, and I hope this months report will be much better.

The extreme high prices of Provisions &c—has compelled me to advance the price of Salt to $6—per bushel since the first instant.

Col. [*Robert*] Strange of the 22d. Regt. N.C.M.—informs me that according to his constructions of the late act of the Legislature my employees will not be exempt from Militia duty—unless by special orders from you.

Will you be kind enough to <in> forward the orders to him immediately so that I will not be troubled in the matter.

Very Respectfully
Your Obt. Servt.
J M Worth
Salt Comm

[*Endorsed*] File & Copy—Gen Fowle will exempt all necessary hands for Col Worth

Z B V

William D. Pender to ZBV   A&H:GP

Camp Gregg, Va.
May 12th. 1863.

To His Excellency
Z. B. Vance
Raleigh

Governor:

I have the honor to send by Capt. Summey[1] the sword of Brig. Genl Hays,[2] U.S.A., captured in the battle of Chancellorsville by Lieut Ireland[3] of the 13th.

N.C. Regiment of my Brigade. Lt. Ireland presented the sword to me, and I, deeming it a tribute due to my State, have ventured to forward it to you, to be placed amongst the trophies of the War at our Capital. Lt. Ireland was one of the hundreds of heroes that fought under my command on that memorable day. I feel proud in being the commander of such troops. To give you some idea of the desperate gallantry shown by my Brigade, it lost about 750 out of little more than twice that number. The 13th. also captured a stand of colors. You must not draw invidious distinctions between my regiments because of these trophies, because where /they/ all fought /so/ well it would be difficult to say which fought best.

I am Sir, very respectfully
W. D. Pender
Brig Genl.

P.S. Let me state to relieve the sorrow we all feel at the heavy loss sustained by us, that only about one hundred of my Brigade was killed.

[1]Daniel F. Summey, Sixteenth Regiment North Carolina Troops. Manarin and Jordan, *North Carolina Troops*, 6:10; Clark, *Histories of Regiments from North Carolina*, 4:138, 629.

[2]William Hays, commanding a Federal brigade at Chancellorsville, where he was captured and quickly exchanged. Faust et al., *Encyclopedia of Civil War*, 354.

[3]John Rich Ireland. Manarin and Jordan, *North Carolina Troops*, 5:279, 327.

ZBV to Jefferson Davis   A&H:GLB

State of North Carolina
Executive Department
Raleigh May 13th. 1863

His Excellency
President Davis

I recieve information from our generals in the field that desertion is alarmingly on the increase in the Army, and have called upon me to use my exertions to check it so far as I could among the troops from North Carolina.

Since my assumption of office my best energies have been faithfully addressed to this matter and not without some success. But many difficulties have interposed. In the first place I found great difficulty in organizing a raw and inexperienced Militia so as to make them efficient in arresting armed soldiers, their neighbors, friends and kindred. After getting this organization into some shape, a rencounter between a squad of my Officers and some deserters and conscripts took place in Yadkin County, in which two of the former were killed. The slayers were arrested, placed in prison, obtained a writ of *Habeas Corpus*, returnable before Chief Justice Pearson who discharged the prisoners on the ground that the Governor, in the absence of express enactment, had no authority to arrest deserters and conscripts, which pertained to the Confederate Authorities alone, and therefore these men have committed no offence in resisting an unauthorized arrest &c. I had previously applied to the Legislature for authority to arrest deserters and to pass a law making it penal to harbor and conceal them, which was declined on much the same grounds as those assigned by The Chief Justice, to wit, that it was the business of Congress to provide for the execution of its own laws &c. I then applied to Congress by a suggestion to Mr Dortch Senator from this State, who informed me that Congress had also declined to take action in the matter, for what reason I do not know.

Balked thus on all my attempts, about to incur the imputation of exceeding my rightful authority, and risking my Militia to be shot down with impunity, I could but revoke my orders, and substituted merely a command that they should aid the Confederate Officers as a *posse* when requested. In the meantime news of Judge Pearson's decision went abroad to the Army in a very exaggerated and ridiculous form, soldiers were induced to believe that it declared the conscript law unconstitutional and that they were entitled, if they came home to the protection of their civil authorities—Desertion, which had been temporarily checked, broke out again worse than before. Letters from Genl. D. H. Hill and Brig. Genl. W. D. Pender and others were received imploring me to take some steps to stop this fearful evil and restore the efficiency of the Army. My own observation convinced me of the importance of their suggestions, and though not concurring with them in their estimate of my ability to remedy the evil, I yet resolved to do all in my power. I have therefore reissued my orders to the Militia, have called out considerable bodies of them to guard the roads, ferries &c and issued a proclamation appealing to the people to assist me in the arrest and return of deserters and to the extent of my power shall strive to repress this fearful danger. Inasmuch as you have power to call out the Militia of the Confederacy for certain purposes, and as no one denies your right to arrest deserters from the armies of which you are Commander in Chief, would it not give validity to my action if I proceeded under your request or requisition? I do not know what steps have been taken by other Southern Governors in this matter, and it would seem invidious to make a requisition alone upon North Carolina for the militia for this purpose, as implying that there were more desertions from this State than any other, which I hope and believe is not true, except in so far as our troops are nearer to their homes and therefore more tempted than those further South. I refer of course to our Armies in Va and N.C. those in the South and West I know nothing about. Even this should not however stand in the way of my rendering all possible aid to the Confederacy if necessary that it should be done.

But if you could fall upon some arrangement with the States, all of them by which their militia could be legally employed in this service, I know that its results would be most happy in this State, and I doubt not equally so in the others. I need not argue the matter, knowing a statement of the facts will be sufficient—In this connection I beg leave also to say, that having made arrangements to capture and restore deserters, it is also equally or decidedly more important, rather to remove, as far as possible the causes which move our troops to quit their colors. I do not believe that one case in a hundred is caused by disloyalty—have no apprehensions whatever on that score. Home sickness, fatigue, hard fare &c have of course much to do with it. The promise of the law of Conscription, that the[y] *should* have furloughs, which has never been redeemed is one *principal* cause beyond a doubt. They invariably offer this excuse when arrested.

How this can be removed and this promise redeemed in the present exigencies of the service, I am of course unable to see. Another great cause—in fact almost the only one assigned by the last class of conscripts, is that they were refused permission to enter the regiments of their choice with their neighbors and relations. Large numbers actually threaten to desert before they leave camp and generally make good their threats. I have had the honor to urge this matter upon your attention on a former occasion, and I am now fully convinced that the service loses in attempting to fill up certain regiments first, without regard to the wishes of the Conscripts. The remedy is plain here, and we should no longer neglect it.

Pardon this *long* letter, far exceeding I fear, your ability to read, during the exacting pressure of the great events by which your time is engaged and believe me to be

> Most respectfully
> Your obt. Svt.
> Z. B. Vance

ZBV to Cotton Manufacturers   A&H:Ashe

Copy

> State of North Carolina—
> Executive Department
> Raleigh May 16th. 1863

To the Cotton Manfacturers
of North Carolina

Gentlemen

The recent demonstrations of the enemy at Vicksburg have probably entirely cut off our supply of wool from Texas.

This being so, unless the small quantities throughout the state, are gathered up, and saved, the mills will stop in a short time, and our soldiers will be naked. This is a natural and unavoidable result.

The best and almost the only way I can devise to gather up this wool, which is mostly in small lots, in the hands of families who are keeping it for their own use, is to exchange cotton yarns for it. Preparations are already making for this thing by mill owners from other states.

Now if you will assist by furnishing the yarns, it is confidently believed that enough wool can be obtained *to keep our army clothed through the coming fall & winter otherwise I see no possible way it can be done.* The matter is before you Gentlemen in all its consequences.

Thankfull for the generous assistance which most of you have heretofore given this Department I feel confident that your patriotism and public spirit will not fail now—

Col. H. A. Dowd[1] A.Q.M. visits you in person & will explain our necessities and arrange all particulars—

> Very respectfully—
> Your obt servt
> Z. B. Vance

[1]Henry A. Dowd, colonel in Fifteenth Regiment North Carolina Troops until his resignation in February. He then became one of North Carolina's assistant quartermasters. Manarin and Jordan, *North Carolina Troops,* 5:502.

Augustus S. Merrimon to ZBV   A&H:VanPC

> Asheville N.C.
> May 18th. 1863.

His Excellency
Z. B. Vance
Raleigh, N C.

Governor:

There is a prospect now, that the ring-leaders of the outbreak on Laurel in Madison County will be captured, including William Shelton. One of them was brought to jail two days ago. I do not think it advisable to ask you to order a Court of *Oyer & Terminer* for their trial. I think it most prudent to delay this until the regular term of the Supr. Court. It may be necessary to remove the case from Madison Co. I am informed, that the Military authorities have *allowed* Col. James A. Keith to *resign* his office, and that too, without any trial for, or inquiry into, the alleged Murder of thirteen prisoners in Laurel, by his immediate Command. Am I correctly informed on this matter? I suppose you are advised. If he has not been tried for this offence, he ought to be held to answer for it before our County. He is now at large in Madison County and a highly respectable citizen just from the County, informs me that it is *suspected* that he will *decamp* to a point beyond the reach of the *civil* or any other arm in this country. If no action has been taken against him for the alleged crime, it is important that he be arrested *at once* and held to answer for his crimes according to law.

If you can, please advise me, whether I am correctly informed or not, and make such suggestions touching the matter as you deem advisable. I shall pros-ecute the *"Laurel Men,"* vigorously and he must share the same fate, if no action has been taken against him.

I am &c
Yr. obt. Serv't.
A. S. Merrimon

Peter Mallett to ZBV A&H:GP

[*With enclosure*]

Conscript Office,
Camp Holmes, May 18th., 1863.

Hon. Z. B. Vance,
Governor of N. Carolina,
Raleigh, N.C.

Sir:

I have the honor to enclose herewith copy of instructions of the 11th. inst. from the Bureau of Conscription, relative to the case of John W. [N.] Irwin [*Irvin*],[1] decided by Chief Justice Pearson on a Writ of Habeas Corpas.

I am instructed to disregard this opinion officially.

I am, Governor,
With high regard,
Your obt. Servant,
Peter Mallett Col.
Commdt. of Conscipts for N.C.

[1] In March, Pearson had ruled that Irvin, who had been drafted under the first Con-federate conscription act and hired a substitute, was not subject again to conscription just because the second act had removed his substitute's initial ineligibility based on age. Tucker, *Zeb Vance*, 291–292; Hamilton, "North Carolina Courts and the Confederacy," 369.

[*Enclosure*]

(Copy)

Confederate States of America,
Bureau of Conscription,
Richmond, Va., May 11th., 1863.

Col Mallett,
Supt. Conscription N.C.

Colonel:

I am directed by the Superintendent to furnish for your information and guidance the following decision of the Secretary of War:

To Bureau of Conscription:—

The report submitted by you, of the case of John W. [N.] Irwin [Irvin] decided by Mr. Chief Justice Pearson in a Writ of Habeas Corpas, has been considered by the Department. The act of April 16, 1862, ¶9, (Conscription Act) provides, "that persons not liable for duty may be received as substitutes for those who are, under such regulations as may be prescribed by the Secretary of War."

The regulations made by the War Department are usually promulgated in orders. In Genl. Orders No. 64, (8th. Sept.) the Secretary decided that "a substitute becoming liable to conscription, renders his principal also liable, unless exempt on other grounds." Again, in General Orders No. 82 (3rd. of Nov. 1862) it was published that, "In all cases in which a substitute becomes subject to military service, the exemption of the principal by reason of the Substitution shall expire." These regulations of the War Department on the subject of substitutes are manifestly within the scope of the power confided by Congress, and form a part of the condition upon which every substitute is received. No substitute could have been received otherwise, than as subject to the regulations thus prescribed by the War Department.

In the absence of any regulation the same conclusion would result from a just construction of the legislation of Congress. The conscription act proceeds upon the principle that the State may summon all classes of citizens to the common defence, and in the present instance it authorized the President "To call out" and "put in" the service all those of a class specified in the act, that Congress did not exempt. The 9th. section of the act authorized the conscript to avail himself of the service of the non-conscript for his relief under such regulations as the War Department might prescribe, by engaging him as a substitute. That the principle on which the legislation of Congress is founded, might not be impaired, and that the State should have the services of all for the common defence, it would seem to follow that where the liability of the substitute to perform military service arose under an act of Congress, and he was no longer exempt from military duty, that his faculty of relieving his principal must terminate.

The opinion of Mr. Ch. Justice Pearson is not regarded by the Department as a sound exposition of the act of Congress, and you will not regard it in your official action as such.

By order of the Secretary of War

(Signed)   J. A. Campbell
A.S.W.

I am, Sir, very respectfully,
Your obt. servant,
(Signed)   G. W. Long
Lt. Col. & A.A.G.

ZBV to Peter Mallett   A&H:GLB

State of North Carolina
Executive Department
Raleigh May 18th 1863

Col. Mallett
Comt. of Conscripts
Camp Holmes

I was surprised to learn by your note of this morning[1] that your action in sending a portion of your troops to Weldon at the request of Genl Hill & myself was disapproved by Genl Rains. I will immediately ask Genl Hill to order them back. After the troops from this State had been ordered to Genl Lee, I proposed to Genl Hill, who was calling for help against an expected advance of the Enemy, that I would relieve all the Bridge Guards Prison & Provost Guards in the State with Militia temporarily, to which he gladly assented And as the entire Militia of this State are and have been for nine months in the service of the Conscript Bureau, I though I made but a reasonable request when I applied to you for two companies for temporary purposes and that you very properly complied. Were I to be governed by a spirit so unaccommodating, I fancy you would find the task of enrolling and bringing into Camp the Conscripts of this State quite a different job. Thanking you for the timely assistance which you have more than once rendered me and deeply regretting that it should have brought upon you the disapprobation of your superior officers,

I am
Very respectfully &c
Z. B. Vance

[1]A&H:GP.

ZBV to William D. Pender   A&H:GLB

State of North Carolina
Executive Department
Raleigh May 18th. 1863

Brig. Genl. W. D. Pender
Near Richmond

Genl

With great pleasure I acknowledge the reception of the sword of Genl Hayes U.S.A. and accompanying note by Capt Summey.[1]

I take pride in placing it among the trophies won by our gallant soldiers, and return my thanks for your remembrance of our State. I regret that so very few of our officers have followed your example. I have thought of addressing a circular to the Colonels in the field begging them to send to me some trophies of every fight, to deposit in the Capitol for our children to look at. I think yet I will do so, if you think that the assistance of our general officers could be secured. It is certainly a most proper thing to be done. You may rest assured General that North Carolina is proud of her sons in the noble army of Northern Virginia, and never had she greater occasion to be so than since the recent great battle in which they have so gallantly and conspicuous a past. I would it were in my power to tell them of the pride and admiration with which the whole state regards their noble men whose intrepid columns have so often driven back the tide of battle and swept the fields with fire, and with what great and unfeigned sorrow we mourn the gallant dead! So great was the slaughter and so noble the victories that we almost feel the sadness of defeat. May God continue his blessing upon our Soldiers. I send you a few copies of my recent proclamation which I hope may be of service. Would be pleased to have copies of your official reports for publication

Very respectfully
Z. B. Vance

[1]See Pender to ZBV, May 12, in this volume.

ZBV to James A. Seddon   A&H:GLB

State of North Carolina
Executive Department
Raleigh May 18th. 1863

Hon. Jas. A. Seddon
Secty of War
Richmond

Sir

I have been informed upon reliable authority that Col. L. M. Allen and Capt. C. N. Candler of the 64th. N.C.T. were, while recently in Madison County N.C.

guilty of the crime of seizing citizens not liable to conscription and receiving large sums of money to release them with many similar acts of oppression and corruption. These reports so injurious to the fair fame of N.C. soldiers, have obtained such general credit that I cannot pass over them in silence and therefore have the honor to request that you order an enquiry into the matter. If notified of time and place, I will have the proof which was communicated to me, placed before the Court.

> Very respectfully
> Yr. obt. Svt.
> Z. B. Vance

ZBV *to William Johnston*   A&H:GLB

> State of North Carolina
> Executive Department
> Raleigh May 18th. 1863

Col. Wm. Johns[t]on[1]
Charlotte N.C.

Sir

I have been informed by several persons, that the Charlotte and Columbia Road of which you are President has failed to respect my proclamation forbidding the exportation of certain articles from the State &c. I hope this is incorrect, as besides thwarting my earnest efforts to lower the prices of provisions—certainly a most desirable object—it would compel me either to overlook it entirely or to take steps to enforce the proclamation, which, considering the relations we have occupied would be in the last degree repugnant to my feelings. The other roads have cheerfully yielded obedience to my wishes. I should be pleased to hear from you and have the honor to be—

> Most respectfully
> Your obt. Servt.
> Z. B. Vance

[1]President of the Charlotte and South Carolina Railroad and former commissary general of North Carolina with the rank of colonel. Johnston, *Papers of Vance*, 1:242n.

ZBV to James A. Seddon   A&H:GLB

State of North Carolina
Executive Department
Raleigh May 18th. 1863

Hon. Jas. A. Seddon
Secty of War
Richmond Va

Sir

I had the honor to request of you some time since an examination into the case of Lt. Col. J. A. Keith 64th. N.C.T. charged with the murder of some un-armed prisoners and little boys during the recent troubles in the mountains of this State. I have heard by rumor only that he was brought before a Court Martial and honorably acquitted, by producing an order for his conduct from Genl Davis Comdg. in E. Tennessee. I have also been officially notified of his resignation. Will it be consistent with your sense of duty to furnish me a copy of the pro-ceedings of the Court Martial in his Case? *Murder* is a crime against the *Common law* in this state and he is now subject to that law

Very respectfully
Z. B. Vance

David A. Barnes to Haywood W. Guion   A&H:GLB

Executive Department
Raleigh May 18th. 1863

Haywood W. Guion Esqr[1]

Dear Sir

His Excellency Gov. Vance has received a communication[2] from Commander Lynch asking permission to exchange the railroad iron which he is to receive from your road, with the Petersburg railroad, as iron is needed for immediate use in completing a gunboat now building on Roanoke River. His Excellency Gov. Vance is exceedingly anxious that the boat shall be speedily completed and has consented to this exchange for the purpose indicated and he requests that you will at the earliest possible moment deliver such quantities of iron as you can to Commander Lynch.

With sentiments of great respect
Your obedient Servant
David A. Barnes
Aid de Camp to the Governor

[1]Haywood Williams Guion, president of Wilmington, Charlotte, and Rutherford Railroad Company. *Dictionary of North Carolina Biography*, s.v. "Guion, Isaac."
[2]May 14, A&H:GLB.

William Johnston to ZBV   A&H:GP

Office Charlotte and South
Carolina Railroad Co.
Charlotte N.C. May 20 1863

To His Excellency
Governor Vance

Dear Sir

I have the pleasure to acknowledge the receipt of your favor of the 18th. inst.[1] stating that you have been informed that the C & So. Ca R R has not respected your proclamations forbidding the exportations of certain articles from the state and that you hope this is incorrect &c

While I did not concur in the opinion that the constitution vested in the Governor of North Carolina the power to enforce the several proclamations issued on this subject, I nevertheless appreciated the motives & objects in view and endeavored to enforce their provisions as far as consistent with all my relations regarding the wants & dependence of our people upon the grain of a neighboring state I accordingly instructed the agent of the Road to ship from the state only in conformity to the exceptions of the proclamations. This I believe he has substantially carried into effect The instances have been numerous under the exceptions of the proclamations when the military authorities agents of towns counties or private parties for their own consumption purchased & shipped

In several instances producers—not speculators have been permitted to ship on the express understanding that the freight was to be exchanged for or proceeds invested in corn or salt to be returned to the state In my absence there may have been shipments of which I was not aware While this has been my policy in carrying into effect your proclamations, more than five loads of other freights— chiefly corn were daily arriving in the state from So. Ca for every one going out of prohibited articles /under the exceptions or otherwise/ Concurring fully in your patriotic purpose to cheapen subsistance and with every disposition to conform to your views & policy the subject has been one of much embarrassment to me. Situated near the border of the state & controling a Road constructed by private enterprise, which has created much mutual dependence in the commercial relations of the citizens of diferent states, greatly increased by the troubles of this Country I have encountered complaints from the citizens of both states on this subject.

I have again today renewed my instructions to Mr. Martin agent to ship out of the state no articles forbidden by the recent proclamation

Shall be pleased to receive any suggestions from you on this subject and while appreciating your courteous manner in calling it to my attention I have the honor to remain very

> respectfully your
> Obt. Svt.
> Wm. Johnston
> Prest.

[1]In this volume.

John White to ZBV   A&H:GP

Glasgow May 20th 1863

Honble. Z B Vance
Governor of North Carolina

Sir

After many unavoidable delays and dissapointments I have at last succeeded in obtaining a loan of money for the State from Mess. Alexr. Collie & Co.[1] of London & Manchester, which has enabled Col. Crossan[2] to purchase a Steamer and me a portion of the goods required by the State. The loan or advancement made by them is predicated upon the Sale of Cotton at 5 pence Sterling per pound. The accompanying papers and documents[3] will fully explain the nature of the transactions terms &c. I consider the Sale as proposed, at least 12 1/2 perct. better for the State, than the terms made by the Govt. at Richmond with Mess. Erlanger & Co.[4]

To enable me to carry the negotiations through successfully I found it necessary to agree to deposit here, Bonds of the State to the Amount of $1,500,000 as collateral Security without doing so I could not have effected the object of my mission. it will be necessary therefore to send me as soon as practicable the additional amount of say $1,000,000 until that shall have been done I fear I will be unable to command money to make further purchases

Col. Crossan will take out with him from 100 to 120 tons assorted merchandise, which will leave of what has now been bought I suppose about 150 tons that I expect to ship by a sailing vessel to Bermuda to be there in time for Col. Crossans second cargo—

You will see that I have also agreed to obtain from you a specific and express ratification of my acts in all matters and engagements touching the Sale of the Cotton &c, all of which I hope may meet your approbation.

At sametime I have to ask you to send me another commission the one I brought with me has by some means been misplaced it cannot be found amongst my papers or with the attorney in whose hands I at one time placed it I had retained a copy of it which I have had attested but as many of those who will buy the cotton would prefer to see the original have promised that it shall be forth comming, that the same words may be used I send a copy.

Col. Crossan and Capt. Hughes[5] will explain the difficulties and delays that has had to be encountered in making negotiations &c. hoping all may prove Satisfactory

I am Sir
Your Obt. Servt.
Jno. White

P.S. In your letter of instructions[6] to me you suggest that the vessel should not at any one time take in more than about $50,000 worth of goods, but in consideration of the great delay we have had to encounter I have in this instance exceeded that amount by about 50 prct. knowing the goods to be greatly needed & hope that in future you will allow the steamer to carry a larger amount in order to compleat the shipment of my purchases before cold weather. Col. Crossan hopes to be able to make a trip once a month, at this rate by shiping almost 150 tons each load, I will be able to ship all the 1st. of November.

I will be able to realize on the value of his return cargo of cotton in the West indies immediately upon receipt of bill of lading

Any instructions in regard to shipments please give Capt. Hughes as this department is strictly under his supervision—

J. W.

[1]Remained North Carolina's financial agent for securing supplies from Britain until the last days of the war. Barrett, *Civil War in North Carolina*, 254.

[2]Thomas Morrow Crossan, an agent accompanying White to buy a vessel for blockade-running. After the purchase of the *Lord Clyde*, he renamed the steamer *Advance* and became its captain. Barrett, *Civil War in North Carolina*, 254.

[3]Not extant.

[4]London negotiator of Confederate cotton loan. White declined to deal with that company because it charged a "higher rate of commission than I deemed advisable." Clark, *Histories of Regiments from North Carolina*, 5:455.

[5]Theodore J. Hughes, an agent with White and from whom White secured a loan for North Carolina. Clark, *Histories of Regiments from North Carolina*, 5:453, 455.

[6]Not extant among ZBV's 1863 correspondence. ZBV's original appointment of White, November 1, 1862, appears in Johnston, *Papers of Vance*, 1:288–290, but does not mention the $50,000 restriction.

ZBV to Jefferson Davis A&H:GLB

State of North Carolina
Executive Department
Raleigh May 21st. 1863

His Excellency
President Davis

Dear Sir

Captain Elliot[1] Comdg. a Company of State Troops, captured last Saturday two Steamers[2] in the Albemarle and Chesapeake Canal, one of them carrying a large mail. Upon overlooking the mail, in addition to various items of intelligence, we found a letter[3] from a man by the name of Montgomery in Washington City to Genl Foster at New Berne proposing a general negro insurrection and distruction of all rail road bridges &c in the South. I enclose you a copy of the letter giving all the minutia of the damnable scheme. You can of course make such use of it as you may think best. The necessity for increased dillegence in guarding our bridges &c is apparant. The letter has not yet been made public

Very Respectfully &c
Z. B. Vance

[1]John T. Elliott, Sixty-eighth Regiment North Carolina Troops. Clark, *Histories of Regiments from North Carolina*, 3:713; 5:17–18.
[2]*Arrow* and *Emily.*
[3]Not extant.

ZBV to William H. C. Whiting A&H:GLB

State of North Carolina
Executive Department
Raleigh May 21st. 1863

Genl. W. H. C. Whiting
Wilmington N.C.

I am applied to every day to know if the negroes at work under your command cannot be returned to their owners—

The time for which they were sent down has long since expired and you know how very greatly their services are required on the farms. Besides there is always great dissatisfaction when they are kept longer than they were told at the start. It would almost prove ruinous to Keep them after the wheat harvest begins which will be early in June. Reports have from time to time reached me that they were Employed in cleaning out the town and waiting on the officers. I directed Adjt.

Genl. Fowle to write and ask if this was true and have received no reply. Of course you must be aware that negroes could not be taken from the fields for such purposes

> Very respectfully
> Yr. obt. Servt.
> Z. B. Vance

ZBV to James A. Seddon   A&H:GP

Copy

State of North Carolina
Executive Department
Raleigh May 22d. 1863.

Hon Jas. A Seddon
Secty. of War

Sir

Col. P. Mallett Comdg. Conscripts for this State has sent me a copy of a letter[1] from your office in reference to a late decision of Chief Justice Pearson in the case of Irvin on *Habeas Corpus* concluding as follows. "The opinion of Mr cheif Justice Pearson is not regarded by the Dept. as a sound exposition of the act of Congress and you will not regard it in your official actions as such."

I do not propose to review the argument by which this conclusion was arrived at—A mere statement of the case would seem sufficeint reply. But I wish to inform you or rather /to/ remind you, that although the War Department may not be bound by the decision of the State Courts, Yet the Executive of that State is. Being sworn to execute the laws and the laws being expounded by the Courts, an attempt on the part of Confederate officers to seize Citizens in defiance of their decisions in the absence of a Supreme Court to decide between the parties, might lead to unpleasant and unprofitable consequences. It is certainly no fault of this Government that there exists no competent tribunal to decide these issues. And it is certainly not unreasonable for the State of North Carolina to object when a decision of its cheif Justice is ordered to be disregarded by a Department of the Confederate Government invested with no judicial powers whatever. Hoping and beleiving that you will not compel any resort to such unpleasant steps as might result from an adherence to such instructions as those received by Col. Mallett, I am Sir

> Very Respectfully
> Yr. obt. Servt.
> (Signed)   Z. B. Vance

[1]Enclosed in Peter Mallett to ZBV, May 18, in this volume.

Jefferson Davis to ZBV   A&H:GP

Richmond, Va.
May 22d. 1863.

His Excellency
Z. B. Vance, Govr. of N.C.
Raleigh, N.C.

Dear Sir,

I have received your letter of 13th. inst[1] and fully appreciate your efforts to check the alarming increase of desertion which threatens such danger to our cause.

Orders were long since issued for meeting one of the evils you mention and I do not understand how the impression prevails that conscripts are not allowed to select their own companies.

In general order no 82 of 3d. Novr. 1862, par 2d. Sect 5, it is expressly enjoined on the Commandant of Conscripts in each State that

"*He will consult the wishes of the Conscripts* in assigning them to companies or regiments, so far as may be consistent with their proper distribution, and will not separate men from the same county, district or parish, if it can be avoided.—The same rules will be observed by the commandants of Corps, in assigning conscripts to companies."

Under this order each conscript can select his company, (unless it be already full) and is secure from being forcibly separated from his friends and neighbors in service.

I do not think your suggestions about calling out the militia to aid in apprehending deserters would have as good an effect as the organization of exempts under the law providing for local service. If you will refer to act No. 229 of the Provisional Congress, approved August 21st. 1862, you will see that volunteers may be accepted by the Executive "for such special service as he may deem expedient." If companies of such volunteers could be organised the muster roll would set forth under the law, the special service for which they are engaged; they could not be assigned to any other duty than that specified; they would be paid and fed when called out for that service; and the great advantage would be gained of having at all times a body of men already properly organised who would be prompt to act for local defence and would be in the Confederate Service, and therefore free from the objections made by the decision of Judge Pearson. Will you inform me whether in your opinion there would be any difficulty in forming such organisations to be composed exclusively of volunteers exempt from conscription.

If it be impracticable, there would be no other resource than to call out the militia, but if feasible, I think these organisations would be more effective.

You will observe that one great advantage in the local service organisation over the militia results from the fact that when the militia is called out, it takes all classes from their labors and strips the country of those whose services are very important in other pursuits, while the local service organisation would be composed of volunteers only, and would probably leave the most valuable of the population available at home for their usual avocations.

Be assured you needed no apology for the length of your letter, the subject is too important and the tone of your remarks too public-spirited and patriotic to render your letter otherwise than most acceptable.

Very Truly & Respty Yours,
Jeffn. Davis

[1]In this volume.

ZBV to James A. Seddon   A&H:GLB

Raleigh May 22

Hon. J. A. Seddon
Richmond Va.

I send you thirteen prisoners captured by my State troops, having no place to keep them.

Please retain them until I notify you that they may be exchanged. The enemy murdered two of my men and I wish to retaliate as soon as I can communicate with Gen Foster

Z. B. Vance

ZBV to James A. Seddon   A&H:GP

State of North Carolina,
Executive Department.
Raleigh, May 23 1863.

Hon Jas A. Seddon
Sec'y of War

Sir,

Among the many persons illegally arrested in Cherokee County N.C. by order[1] of a Col Lee at Atlanta Ga. on charges of disloyalty were G. L. D. McLelland and James M Grant, both beyond the age of forty years. Nothing appearing against them they were told that if they did not volunteer in the army they should be placed in prison and kept there.

From the utterly outrageous and illegal manner in which they were seized and carried away from their homes, they were justifiable in supposing that there was no longer any protection in the country for the personal liberty of the citizens, and they yielded to this tyranny and entered Col Folks battallion in E Tennessee.

They have asked for their discharge, on the ground that they are not subject to conscription and were forced to enter the army under threats of imprisonment. Fairness, justice, and self respect on the part of the government demand it should be granted, as it is certainly not intended to recruit the army by entrapping the citizens.

> Very respectfully
> Yr. obt. svt.
> Z. B. Vance

[1]To Georgia troops scouring Cherokee County, North Carolina, for men to impress into the Confederate army. Related letters include Allen T. Davidson to James A. Seddon, April 28, A&H:GP; Davidson to ZBV, May 5, A&H:VanPC; and Seddon to ZBV, May 13, A&H:GP.

James A. Seddon to ZBV   A&H:GP

> Confederate States of America,
> War Department,
> Richmond, Va. May 23 1863

His Excellency
Z B Vance
Govr. N.C.

Sir

Your letter of the 18th. Inst.[1] has been rec'd. The resignation of Lt. Col Keith was accepted at the office of the Ad. & In. Genl the 15 Inst. No proceedings of a court Martial in his case have been rec'd. His resignation was accepted on the recommendation of Col Palmer commanding the brigade & Maj Genl Maury[2]— the examining board having reported against his competency. The Adj. & Insp. Genl was not aware of the facts of the alleged murder, as applying to this officer at the time of his action on the resignation, there being no reference to the facts in the papers before him

In a communication to the department by Lt Col Keith, he claims that Br Genl Heth gave him a verbal order to this effect "I want no reports from you about your course at Laurel. I do not want to be troubled with any prisoners & the last one of them should be killed['']—that he went on further to state, that he had been troubled with several prisoners from Laurel N.C. and he did not want any men brought to Knoxville—

This statement is supported by the deposition of a Dr Thompson, & Keith says in his letter that he can prove it by another witness

The communication of Keith & the deposition of Thompson were submitted to Br. Gen'l Heth for remarks—He says that he gave written instructions to Keith which will be found on the books of the dep't of E. Tenn.—He admits that he told Keith that those found in arms ought not to be treated as enemies & in the event of an engagement with them to take no prisoners, as he considered that they have forfeited all such claims—But he denies in strong terms the making up of any remarks which would authorise maltreatment of prisoners who had been accepted as such, or to women & children

> Very Respectfully
> Yr obt Svt
> James A Seddon
> Secy of War

¹In this volume.
²Dabney Herndon Maury, commanding Department of East Tennessee. Faust et al., *Encyclopedia of Civil War*, 481.

James A. Seddon to ZBV   A&H:GP

> Confederate States of America,
> War Department,
> Richmond, Va. May 23 1863.

His Excellency
Governor Z. B. Vance
Raleigh N.C.

Sir,

Your letter of May 1st.¹ enclosing Copy of a letter from Lt. Col S. D. Thurston, 3rd. N.C. Infantry, in regard to the organization of a brigade of North Carolina Troops, has been received, and submitted to General Lee, for his consideration.

General Lee has replied that all the troops in his army have been brigaded by States, where it was possible; and that the brigade in question consists of certain *odd* Regiments from North Carolina and Virginia, which it was impossible to assign to Brigades from their respective States, but which, being from contiguous states, he supposed would serve harmoniously; that, however, if two or three more North Carolina Regiments could be obtained he would be very glad to organize them, with the existing Regiments of this Brigade, into a separate North Carolina Brigade, which is not now possible.

Respectfully,
James A Seddon
Secretary of War

[*Endorsed*] Copy & File

Z B V

¹In this volume.

ZBV *to Peter Mallett*   A&H:GP

Copy

State of North Carolina
Executive Department
Raleigh May 23d. 1863.

Col. P. Mallett
Comdt. Conscripts
Camp Holmes

I have been informed that the man Irwin [*Irvin*] who was released by Chief Justice Pearson on Habeas Corpus as not liable to conscription, has been rearrested by you and is now in your custody. I have written to the Secretary of War protesting against the order to you to disregard Judge Pearson's decision and notifying him that I was bound by that decision and could not permit his officers to disregard it. Until his reply can be received, I have to ask you not to remove Irwin from the State. My desire is to arrange this matter amicably, which I know can be done, but you are aware that I am compelled to execute the laws of the State.

I beg to recite to you Section 8, ch: 55, of the Revised Code. "No person who shall be set at large upon any Habeas Corpus, shall be again imprisoned for the same offence by any person whatsoever, other than by the legal order and process of the Court wherein he shall be bound by recognizance to appear or other Court having jurisdiction of the Cause, under the penalty, of two thousand and five hundred dollars, to be recovered by the party agrieved"— Also a late act, Session of 1862 & 3 of the Legislature ch: 46, Section 2d., provides that a arrest of the party for the same cause upon the "former discharge appearing and if it appear that such second arrest and detention was made illegally and with the knowledge of the former discharge the party offending shall be guilty of a misdemeanor and fined and imprisoned at the discretion of the Court['"].

Beleving sir that it is not your desire to disregard the laws of the State, I am,

                                    Very Respectfully
                                    Yr. obt. Servt.
                  (signed)   Z. B. Vance

                    James A. Seddon to ZBV   A&H:GP
                    [*With enclosure*]

                                    Confederate States of America,
                                    War Department,
                                    Richmond, Va. May 23 1863

His Excellency Z. B. Vance,
Governor of North Carolina,
Raleigh, N.C.

Sir,
    I have heretofore had occasion to bring to your notice documents showing
the prevalence of desertion from our army on the Rappahannock, and I regret
now to be obliged again to invoke your earnest attention to the accompanying
copy of a letter from Genl. Lee with enclosures which show a fearful increase of
this great evil. Genl. Lee urges upon you, as well as the Department, prompt and
efficient measures to remedy the growing mischief. I have directed from such
desultory Cavalry as I can command, guards at the various ferries across the James
and Appomattox rivers, and shall take all measures in my power to intercept and
send back deserters. I feel assured you will on your part not be wanting in due
exertion to arrest the evil. A full remedy can, however, only be found in the
removal of the cause which you will excuse me for saying exists with peculiar
force among the troops from North Carolina. That cause is I fear the impression
very generally prevailing, and perhaps by designing persons disseminated among
the troops from your State, that by the decision of your highest judicial authorities, the Conscript Law has been held unconstitutional, and that they cannot
justly or legally be detained in service. They think they have only to come within
the jurisdiction of your Courts to be permanently exonerated from the perils and
hardships of military life. In addition, there seems to prevail the opinion, that if
they can reach certain Western counties of the State, they will find no repro-
bation in public sentiment, but be secure of harbor and protection. This last adds
/a/ very dangerous feature, threatening the peace and good order of your State,
to the more general mischief which follows from desertion to the common cause.
These men going off with their arms and equipment are but too apt to form
marauding bands in remote districts, which in the present condition of our population may place extensive districts at their mercy. It is not for me to suggest
to your better judgment measures of prevention or remedy, but it might be well

if your full official influence could be exercised to restrain the too ready interposition of the judicial authority in these questions of military obligation, and
that if erroneous impressions exist in regard to the true character of the decision
made by the Chief Justice or other Judge of your State, prompt means should be
adopted to publish and disseminate juster views of their opinions. A proclamation
too from yourself, making an appeal to the sober judgment and patriotic feeling
as well of the soldiers in the field as of the communities at home whom they
protect, urging the high obligations on the former to defend their country in its
greatest need and on the latter to discountenance and frown upon all influences
which spread discouragement or discontent in our army among the conscripts,
should be issued. On this latter point, however, doubt may be entertained as to
the policy of exposing by such proclamation the seriousness of the evil, which
cannot fail to give hope and comfort to the enemy. Your own judgment will best
decide about this, and to that judgment the whole matter is referred.

Yours with esteem
James A Seddon
Secretary of War

[*Enclosure*]

Robert E. Lee to James A. Seddon   A&H:GP

Copy

Head Qrs. No. Va.
21 May 1863.

Hon. James A. Seddon
Secty. of War, Richmond, Va.

Sir,
    The desertion of the No. Caro. troops from this Army is becoming so serious
an evil, that unless it can be promptly arrested I fear the troops from that state
will become greatly reduced. Brig. Genl. Lane[1] reports that on the night of the
19th. Inst. thirty two men from Co A, 37 Regt. N.C. Vols. deserted, taking with
them their arms, equipment ammunition &c: they had just been paid off. These
men are from Ashe Co N.C. bordering upon Grayson Co. Va.
    Capt. Jno. C. Gorman Co. B, 2'Regt. N.C. Troops states, that one of the men
of his Co who deserted on the 10th. of April last had voluntarily returned. From
him he learns that a great many of the deserters from his brigade cross the James
River some 40 or 50 miles above Richmond and Lumbertown, and the Roanoke
at Horse-ford mills in Amelia Co. If local troops in the neighborhood could guard
these fords and others along the rivers, a great many of our deserters might be
arrested. The deserters usually go in squads taking their arms and equipments,
and sometimes borrow from their comrades ammunition sufficient to make 100

rounds per man. I think it probable that they pass themselves off as guards or patrols in search of deserters.

I need not enlarge upon the extent to which this evil will grow if not at once stopped. I hope that you will represent the matter to his Excy. the Gov. of No. Caro. so as to induce him to take active measures in the case, and to enlist all the good men in the State to reprobate and discountenance it. I must also request that you do everything in your power to remedy the evil.

I am most respectfully
Your Obt. Servt.
(signed)   R. E. Lee
Genl.

P.S. I forward discriptive lists[2] of some of the deserters which if transmitted to the Govr. or Chief Enrolling Officer of the State might lead to their apprehension.

(signed)   R. E. Lee

[1]James Henry Lane, whose brigade comprised five North Carolina regiments including the Thirty-seventh. Faust et al., *Encyclopedia of Civil War*, 424.
[2]Not extant.

Peter Mallett to ZBV   A&H:GP

Conscript Office
Camp Holmes May 25th. 1863

His Excellency
Gov Vance

Governor

I have the honor to acknowledge the receipt of your communication of the 23rd. Inst.[1] relative to Private "Irwin" [*Irvin*] discharged on writ of Habeas Corpus, and requesting that he be retained in the State until receipt of reply to your communication to the Secty of War. I have to inform your Excellency that Irwin has been arrested and assigned to the 7th. Regt. N.C.T—near Fredericksburg to be sent on this week together with other Conscripts: Wishing to avoid the possibility of a conflict with your Excellency—I immediately telegraphed to the Superintendent for permission to comply with your request. Sincerely hoping that the matter may be amicably arranged.

I am Governor, with highest regard

Your obt. Servt.
Peter Mallett Col
Comdg Conscripts NC

¹In this volume.

ZBV to James A. Seddon   A&H:GP

Copy

State of North Carolina
Executive Department
Raleigh May 25th. 1863

Hon Jas. A. Seddon
Secty. of War
Richmond Va.

Sir
      Your letter of the 23d. inst.¹ enclosing copy of one from Genl. Lee with
descriptive rolls of deserters from Genl. Rodes² brigade, appealing to me for action
in regard to the best means of arresting desertion in the Army, has been received.
      You will see by copy of my proclamation³ enclosed, that every thing which it
is possible for me to do has been already done. The most stringent orders have
been issued to the militia to guard all fords and ferries and public highways and
every imaginable step taken to ensure activity and obedience and to avoid if
possible the danger of conflicting with the legal tribunals of the State. I have
recently written to the President suggesting that he should make a requisition
upon me for the militia for the purpose of arresting deserters &c to which letter⁴
I beg to refer you as an evidence of my great desire to put a stop to this evil. I
regret Sir that you should have deemed it necessary to adopt as an explanation
of the cause for so much desertion, an idea which has its origin solely in political
prejudice—the "too ready interposition of the Judicial Authority in these questions of Military obligation" and the false construction given to the decisions of
our Judges, in the army. That such impressions do prevail in the army, I make
no doubt—You are not the first authority I have had for that fact. But *why* it
should exist and how it was first made, I am unable to determine, except upon
the ground that there exists among our neighbors, "a too ready" desposition to
believe evil of the State, when it is known that No. Ca. is the only State in the
Confederacy which employs her militia in the arrest of Conscripts and deserters:
that she has better executed the conscript law, has fuller regiments in the field
than any other and that at the two last great battles on the Rappahannock in
Dec, and in May, she furnished over one half of the killed and wounded, it seems
strange, passing strange, that an impression should prevail that desertion would
receive official countenance and protection in her borders. The decisions of our
Judges have been published in all the papers of our State and any perversion of
their meaning must be designed and wilful—
      Neither have our Judges been "too ready" to offer them. Heavy penalties, as
you know, are annexed to the refusal of a Judge to grant the writ of Habeas

Corpus and an upright Judge, must deliver the law, as he conceives it to be, whether it should happen to comport with the received notions of the military authorities or not. I must therefore most respectfully decline to use my influence in restraining or controlling that co'ordinate branch of the Government, which intrudes upon nobody, usurps no authority, but is on the contrary, in great danger of being overlapped and destroyed by the tendency of the times. Whilst therefore it is my intention to make every possible effort to sustain the common cause, it is my firm determination to sustain the Judicial Authority of the land, the rights and privileges of the citizens, to the utmost of my power. By the action of Congress, no appeal lies from the Sup/r/eme Court of a State to that of the Confederate states and the decision of the Supreme Court of No. Ca. when formerly rendered will be binding upon all parties. I also regret to see that the impression will be made by these letters of yours and Genl Lee's, that desertion is greater among the No. Ca. Troops than those of her Sister States, which I have every reason to believe is not true. Yet has any other Executive been applied to to issue proclamations and employ the militia in arresting it? Has the "too ready interposition" of the Judiciary of So. Ca. and Ga. been rebuked for almost similar decisions rendered? Excuse me, Sir, for writing in this /strain/—I feel that our exertions are scarcely appreciated properly, and I can but speak plainly when I approach the subject

> Very Respectfully
> Yr. obt servt.
> (Signed)   Z. B. Vance

[1]In this volume.
[2]Robert Emmett Rodes, who had become commander of D. H. Hill's division in Virginia when Hill transferred to North Carolina. Rodes was promoted to major general on May 7. Wakelyn, *Biographical Dictionary of the Confederacy*, 372.
[3]May 11, in this volume.
[4]May 13, in this volume.

ZBV to William H. C. Whiting   A&H:GLB

> State of North Carolina
> Executive Department
> Raleigh May 26th 1863

Maj. Genl. Whiting
Wilmington N.C.

General

Yours[1] received in regard to the negroes. I did say to you that the first detail might remain as it would be useless to relieve them by a detail from the same

owners. But you will remember General that they have all remained far beyond
the time you told me they would be needed. I promised the owners they should
be returned in time to assist in planting the crops: they now ask them to be
returned by harvest which begins in our southern borders by 1st. June and will
continue during the month. I recognize no greater necessity to the common good,
than the safety of the coming harvest: and must therefore insist on their being
sent home next week. They can be returned immediately after harvest if desired
and in the mean time, I make no doubt but that any work absolutely necessary
to be done would be cheerfully performed by the soldiers for the extra rations
consumed by the negroes. Please give me any information you may have about
Col Crossan and his vessel

> Very respectfully
> Yr. obt. servt.
> Z. B. Vance

[1]May 23, A&H:GP.

James A. *Seddon to* ZBV   A&H:GP

> Confederate States of America,
> War Department,
> Richmond, Va. May 27 1863

His Excellency
Z B Vance
Govr. of N.C.

Your Excellency's letter of the 22nd. Ins't.[1] has been rec'd.

The opinion of Mr. Ch. Justice Pearson in the case of Irvine [*Irvin*] was submitted to this department by the Bureau of Conscription, for instructions,
whether it was to be taken as a guide for that Bureau in analogous cases, & this
department returned to the Bureau the directions which are quoted by your
Excellency. The report of the facts in the case of Irvine was not made & the
instructions of the department had no reference to the particular case (of Irvine).
Nor did the Bureau direct the arrest of Irvine It may be that the judgement of
Mr. Ch Justice Pearson may be entitled to a deference to which the department
is not willing to concede to his opinion as an exposition of the Statutes. The
opinion contradicts the practice of the department, the assent of Congress to its
orders as inferrible from the facts that they have been well known, have been
the subject of discussion in that body and remain unaltered, and also by decisions
of other Judges who have refused to discharge persons in circumstances similar
(so far as can be gathered from Ch J Pearson's statement of facts, which is not
precise, in the opinion) to those upon which he was determining. The depart-

ment has had occasion to place before your Excellency its views of the limits of the jurisdiction of the State Judiciary in such cases. If Irvine was not legally enrolled & placed in the military service by the conscription officers, the department will not claim that he was beyond the jurisdiction of the Chief Justice & will ascertain by inquiry & afford prompt relief & this without any reference to its opinion of the accuracy of his judgement. The department has submitted to the discharge of conscripts and soldiers by <that> irregular action, in cases, obviously beyond the authority of the local judges rather than incur the anger of collision between the Confederate & State jurisdictions But when desertions by hundreds & discharges in a far greater number of cases, have been occasioned by the undermining influences of judgements, made without authority the /farther/ submission would be a betrayal of its duty

The only act of Congress that relates to substitutes is found in the 9th. Section of the Act of April 1862. This act provides, "That persons *not liable for duty*, may be received as *substitutes* for those *who are*, under such *regulations* as may be *prescribed* by *the Secretary of War*"—This section suggests the question whether the substitute, must not be *continually* exempt from the military service, to be a valid substitute /for one subject/ and certainly that matter was suitable for regulation The act confers simply, a license or authority to receive substitutes, & imposes the obligation upon the Secy of War, to make regulations which shall, protect the claim of the Confederate States, to the military service of all its citizens, under any contingencies that might arise—This precise subject is matter of regulation in other military codes

The Virginia code prescribes that "Any person other, than a volunteer, who shall be detailed or drafted for duty may furnish . . an able bodied man . . well clothed . . who shall act as a substitute If such substitute while engaged for another shall be called on to perform his own tour of duty the person furnishing him shall be required to take his place, or to furnish another substitute"— The French code of conscription allows a substitute "who shall be of nonconscript age, of robust constitution, of good character, certified by his municipality He bears the surname of his principal in order that the latter may be known & compelled to march should his substitute desert, or be lost from any other cause than death or wounds received in battle within the term of two years"—

The Bureau of Conscription has ordered Col Mallett not to withdraw Irvine from the limits of NC

> Very Respectfully
> Your obt Srvt
> James A Seddon
> Secy of War

¹In this volume.

James A. Seddon to ZBV   SHC:Car

Confederate States of America,
War Department,
Richmond, Va. May 27th 1863

His Excellency Z. B. Vance
Governor of North Carolina
Raleigh N.C.

Sir

I have the honor to acknowledge the receipt of your letter of the 23rd inst[1] relative to the illegal arrest of G L D McClelland and James M Grant and to state that the communication has been referred through the Adjt and Insp Genl's Office to Genl Bragg for special attention and with the following endorsement.

"The Department has information of much violence having been committed in N.C. as stated, but has not been able to fix as the authors any save a vigilance committee of the best of whom anything evil may well be believed. If the facts be as stated let the grievance be corrected."

Very Respectfully
Your Obt Servt
James A Seddon
Secretary of War

[1]In this volume.

Peter Mallett to ZBV   A&H:GP

Conscript Office
Camp Holmes, NC May 29/63

His Excellency
Gov Vance

Governor

I have the honor to acknowledge the receipt of your letter of the 28th.[1] enclosing copy of a communication from President Davis of the 22nd.[2] relative to permitting conscripts to choose their Regiments

I take pleasure in informing your Excellency that order 82 Paragraph 2nd., Section 5th. Nov 1862 from the Adjutant & Inspector Generals Office has been strictly complied with at this Camp. No instructions to the contrary have been received from the Superintendant. Conscripts are assigned by *"Pro rata* distribution, preference being given to those Regiments that have been upon active service since the War began and whose ranks have been thined by many battles."

In accordance with instructions to Commandant of Conscription in order alluded to, and quoted by the President ("He will consult the wishes of the conscripts in assigning them to Companies and Regiments as far as may be consistent with their proper distribution and will not seperate men from the same county district or parish if it can be avoided") it is impossible to gratify the wishes of every individual. I beg most respectfully however to differ with President Davis's construction of this order. He says "under this order each conscript can select his own company (unless it be already full) and is secure from being forcibly seperated from his friends and neighbors in the service". As your Excellency is fully aware there are but few if any Regiments in service from this State "already full". If this construction is acted upon will it not interfere with the proper distribution, will not those Regiments composed originally of men from eastern counties where conscripts cannot now be had be reduced to Skeletons? Permit each conscript to select his Regiment, will not those in Virginia now greatly reduced by battle and disease be virtually broken up? Most assuredly—While those companies and Regiments retained in the State would be full to overflowing. But if this construction is intended as an order from President Davis for my guidance in future, I shall certainly comply. I shall take the liberty however of refering the correspondence to the Superintendant of Conscription for instructions and will furnish your Excellency with his reply as soon as possible. It has been, not only my duty but pleasure to consult the wishes of every conscript as far as practicable and consistent with orders, and never *have* declined a request to assign a brother or relative to the same Regiment, neither have men from the same county been seperated unless at their desire. No complaints have been made that I am aware of except possibly from those who have been brought to camp by force as recusant Conscripts or deserters, such men are not entitled to the privilege "of consulting their wishes."

> I am Governor
> With high regard
> Your Obt. Servt.
> Peter Mallett Col
> Comdg Conscription NC

[1]Not extant.
[2]In this volume.

Jefferson Davis to ZBV   A&H:GP

Richmond Va. May 30, 1863.

His Excellency:
Z. B. Vance,
Governor of North Carolina.

Sir:
     I have the honor to acknowledge the receipt of your letter of the 21st. inst.[1] covering a copy of a letter captured from the enemy, in which a plan is proposed

to Genl. Foster for a general insurrection of the Slaves on the night of August first, to destroy rail road bridges &c.

Please accept my thanks for the information conveyed. The matter has been referred to the special attention of the Secretary of War, who will communicate a warning to Generals commanding Armies in the field.

Very truly & respectfully yours
Jeffn. Davis

[*Endorsed*] File & Copy

Z B V

¹In this volume.

Leander S. Gash to ZBV   A&H:VanPC

Private (You can show this to Holden if you like)

Claytonville NC June 1st. 1863

His Exclency, Z. B. Vance,
Governor of NC—

Dear Zeb,

In your inaugural address on takeing charge of the affairs of State, I believe you stated that you needed real friends to critise your conduct more than mere place men to praise and flatter. (These are not perhaps the precise words but convey the sentiment as well as I remember) My honest opinion is that you, (and all other men of your age) do need those kind of friends, more than those friends that always Smile & praise you right or wrong

I have refrained from troubleing you thus far on account of your being pressed with more important business & the advice of wiser heads than mine. And I might /add/ of what you suppose, of better friends in this crises.

My principle object in addressing you now is in behalf of what we call the Militia in the west. They are now being called out with gun and ammunition and five days rations to hunt deserters. (A useless waste of time in my opinion) two or three such calls at this season of the year and their whole crops are lost and the Confederacy nor the public will be benefitted very little. Some are offering five dollars per day to be allowed to remain in their crops. What few deserters they succeed in captureing will be of very little service to the army, whilst their crops would be of vast importance to their families and this community generally. Could you see the straits our people are now reduced to in procuring food and clotheing for themselves and families you could better appreciate their necessity of provideing for the next years supply. Food and raiment can hardly be bought here with money. Although money is plenty there are certain classes that have very little of it. And <not a few> /half of/ the Militia are without guns, ammunition and rations that they could carry with them, consisting of milk and vegetables with a very little bread and some weeds mixed in There is another objection to the Militia being serviceable in catching deserters. The deserters are more numerous & better armed and drilled than the Militia is consequently there is more danger of their banding themselves together for armed resistance. Then there is strifes and prejudices burning in the bosoms of our people that would be easily kindled in to a flame that would be hard to extinguish if once fairly turned loose on each other. We have favoriteisms and persecutions even in the arresting of deserters. Several deserters have been wounded and some killed. I learn one soldier was killed in Henderson [County] last week by a deserter and two deserters <probably> mortally wounded. That is the first case I have heard of armed resistance. And that was probably occasioned by the same soldier haveing shot a deserter a few days before rather unnecessarily But if the war /here/ gets fairly up which it likely will do if imprudently managed, we, I fear will have dreadful times here. My impression is that prudent men should be sent from the army to arrest deserters that have no private malice to gratify, and men from other sections who have no families nor property in reach of those seeking revenge. In that event we would likely have an army quartered on us which we are unable to feed besides /our own/ armies are almost as anoying and distructive as a yankee army. But who ever are charged with the aprehension of deserters should be of a class more suitable than most of those heretofore employed in that business or we shall have more trouble than we have contracted for. But if the melitia is to attend to it do let them make their crops. Six weeks more and the present corn crop is safe so far as working it is concerned whilst the deserters caught in that time will hardly render much valuable service to any body. Millers Blacksmiths & all other exempts are dragged in to this deserter catching The first weeks work in Henderson I learn is two deserters & 1 soldier killed and none caught.

Your late Proclamation[1] to deserters I hardly think will have the effect you desired, nor is it exactly like yourself Some of your best friends doubt whether it will not do more harm than good both to yourself and the cause you so ably advocate. I imagine all good men deprecate the practice (now so common) of deserting. But that some deserters are entitled to more simpathy than is manifested in your late <message> /proclamation/ you yourself will no doubt some day or other frankly admit when the excitment of the times passes off and reason is once more enthroned. I myself am not particularly interested in the Militia nor in desertions I am (as you know) too old for any common Militia and have but one son fit for the army. I have no fears of his deserting though he might possibly deceive me. But he knows I would not approve of such a thing therefore I aprehend there is no danger of his deserting. But he also knows that if he were to desert and come home that I would feed & clothe him as heretofore and further, he well knows that if I thought his life endangered by his desertion or any thing else I would (if I *could*) harbor and conseal him, indespite of any and all the laws of the Confederacy or State of N.C. with the President and the Governor and all their Proclamations to the contray notwithstanding. How could I do otherwise and be a natural parent. Zeb. Vance I presume would do the same if he ever gets to be the father of a soldier after he is done being Governor

Some of the deserters are of good families the two young Statons killed last week were of respectable and well doing families many others are of good families. Want of food and unbearable tyranny by some of the officers are the general excuses given, numbers say they will die here sooner than go back, a little reflection may cause them to change their minds. Some are transfering themselves to other parts of the army without the knowledge or consent of their officers or any body else whilst others are concealing themselves in the mountains. The true cause in my opinion in most of the cases is they are tired of a war that they can see no hopes of ever being ended by fighting and not a few of them believe they nor the South would be benefitted by it if the North was conquered. Thousands believe in their hearts that there was no use in breaking up the old Government and that secession was wrong at the beginning and can hardly be made right by fighting. And further believe that the longer the fight is continued and kept up the more and harder the difficulties to settle That the South could have got a better settlement at the end of the first year of the war than she could at the end of the second year And further that a better settlement can be had now than can be had this time next year. The longer we continue the war the worse for us as well as the North. But more certainly worse for us as we are the owners of the property about which the pretext for the war was made. Haveing made slavery the pretext, the world /now/ recognisees it as the actual cause of it. Our pretext is accepted as a reality by the North and the balance of the civilized world, who in the main are opposed to the institution, its abolition and distruction is regarded by many sensible men as certain /& sure/. The only remaining question is as to time. And that the time depends all together on the lenth and extent of the present war The sooner peace is made /consentably/ the longer Slavery may be enjoyed by a gradual extinction, but prolong the war indefinitely and all must go together and end at the same time. Men honestly entertaining these sentiments (if honest themselves) can hardly change them if they would. Sentiments honestly formed can hardly be changed at will nor by force of law Military Statute nor mob, hence men ought not to be punished for opinions sake

Have we no men North nor South with nerve and comprehension sufficient to throttle this dreadful war insanity, (for a nation of sane men would be ashamed of it) and hold our people until reason can be restored thereby save a remnant of our people. In your Message I thought I could see the riseing star when you spoke of Habeas Corpus, and the imprisonment of North Carolinians &c. But <alas> I greatly fear you have taken the rong end of the track or found the task too hurculean for a man of your age—

Truly yours &c
L. S. Gash[2]

¹May 11, in this volume.

²Leander Sams Gash, Transylvania County farmer, merchant, postmaster, and future state senator. Otto H. Olsen and Ellen Z. McGrew, eds., "Prelude to Reconstruction: The Correspondence of State Senator Leander Sams Gash, 1866–1867," pt. 1, *North Carolina Historical Review* 60 (January 1983): 37–51.

James P. Dillard to ZBV   A&H:GP

Wentworth Rockingham Cty
June 1st./63

To his Excellency Gov Vance

Dr. Sir

Please inform me whether ex Gov John M Morehead¹ who has a large Manufacturing establisment in my Regiment, has a permit from you to let his cotton yarnes & cloth be carried in to Virginia by Citizens of that state The people of our state are made /to/ pay higher for the articles on that account, and I have been informed by his agent that the fact of his foreign trade (being from that state) heretofore that I must suffer it to continue under a permit given said Morehead by your honour. It is a channel through which much wool Cotton Cloth, & yarnes passes out it is situated very close to the Va. line I could capture a large quantity weekly please instruct me as to my duty—

Your obdent Servant
Jas. P. Dillard
Comdg. 70th. N. C M

Please instruct me what I must do with the articles taken from the Va. Speculators—

respectfuly Yours &c
J. P. D.

[*Endorsed*] I dont think he has any permit from me If he has he must show it— if not, stop the traffick—

Z B V

¹John Motley Morehead, wealthy railroad promoter, as well as textile entrepreneur, former governor, state senator, and member of Confederate Provisional Congress. *Dictionary of North Carolina Biography*, s.v. "Morehead, John Motley."

William F. Lynch to ZBV   A&H:GP

Naval Commandant's Office,
Wilmington, N.C., June 3rd., 1863.

His Excellency
Governor Z. B. Vance
Raleigh, N.C.

Dear Sir,

I received your telegram[1] respecting the prize steamers in the Blackwater, which I hope was founded upon an understanding between the Government and yourself. In order to save time, the telegram was sent to the officer in charge of the Naval detachment, but with directions that if your authority were questioned, to yield at once; as I can recognize but two parties to the present war, namely: the Government of the Confederate States, and that of the remaining States of the old Union.

> I have the honor to be,
> Very Respectfully
> Your Ob't. Serv't
> W F Lynch
> Flag Officer

[1] Not extant, but ZBV to Lynch, June 6, in this volume, provides more details on the steamers.

James A. Seddon to ZBV   A&H:GP

Confederate States of America,
War Department,
Richmond, Va. <May> /June/ 5th. 1863.

His Excellency Z. B. Vance,
Governor of North Carolina,
Raleigh, N.C.

Sir,

Under the instruction of the President, I have the honor to address you on a subject deemed by him of grave moment. The /numerically/ superior armies of the enemy, confronting us in the field at all the most important points, render essential for success in our great struggle for liberty and independence, greater concentration of our forces and their withdrawal in a measure from the purpose of local defence to our cities and least exposed States. Being the invaded country, it is impossible throughout the extent of our limits to maintain permanently without dispersion, which causes weakness every where, adequate force at the numerous points where we may be attacked. The recent raids of the enemy, in different portions of our productive but thinly populated districts, strikingly illustrate both our liability to distracting and desolating invasion, and the impracticability of affording from our armies, with sufficient promptness, the soldiers necessary for prevention or punishment. It becomes essential, therefore, that the reserves of our population capable of arms, yet required for the useful operations of society and the maintenance in the field of our embodied forces, should be relied on for employment in the local defence of important cities, and in repelling on emergencies the sudden or transient invasion of the enemy. How best to organize such reserves and make them most effective, has been the subject of consideration with the Department, and I venture to present some suggestions for your consideration and action.

The Militia of the respective States might on occasion be called out, but this would be attended with the serious evil of being dilatory in execution and by its generality be exhaustive of the already diminished population engaged in the necessary work of production and supply. The difficulty of assembling, and after discharge reassembling them, would probably induce their retention on each call beyond the time strictly necessary. Experience, too, has not shown this kind of force to be very reliable or efficient, as it is difficult, from the want of previous preparation and cooperation, to inspire them with confidence in their leaders or themselves. Local organizations or enlistments, by volunteering for limited periods and special purposes, if they can be induced, would afford more assurance of prompt and efficient action. For these the legislation of Congress has made full provision by two laws—one entitled an Act "to provide for local defence and special service", approved August 21, 1861; the other entitled "An Act to authorize the formation of volunteer companies for local defence", approved October 13, 1862, to which your attention is invoked, and of which, as they are brief, copies are appended. Under the former of these, if organizations could be effected, with the limitation prescribed in their muster-rolls of service only /at home or at specified points of importance/ within the particular State, they would be admirably adapted to obtain the desired ends of calling out those best qualified for the service, of employing them only when and so long as they might be needed, of having them animated with *esprit de corps*, reliant on each other and their selected officers, and of their securing the largest measure of activity and efficiency perhaps attainable from other than permanent and trained soldiers. After the most active and least needed portion of the reserves were embodied under the former law, the latter would allow smaller organizations, with more limited range of service, for objects of police and the pressing contingencies of neighborhood defence. Could these laws be generally acted on, it is believed as full organization of the reserve population would be secured for casual needs as would be practicable. These laws, however, contemplate only voluntary action and no compulsion or draft can be resorted to to secure organizations under them. It may well be doubted whether at this stage of the war, with the engrossing duties pressing on the limited population at home and the experience had of the priorities of military service, the spirit of volunteering would be sufficiently eager and active to secure the prompt formation of such organizations. The apprehension at least of a draft, otherwise unavoidable, would aid powerfully patriotic impulses, and by interesting all to encourage and assist such organizations might suffice to assure them. The President has therefore determined to make a requisition on the Governors of the several States to furnish by an appointed time, for service within the State, and for the limited period of six months, a number of men proportionate to the relative population of each, unless the same can be organized previously in such voluntary corps as may render them /subject/ to his call for like duty, and it is recommended to you to announce by proclamation such requisition, and that unless by a precedent day, the requisite forces can be presented by voluntary organizations under the first named law, a draft will be made on all the Militia, not engaged in voluntary organizations under that law, to furnish the requisite quota. When the need of the country for such additional service is fully presented to and realized by the patriotic population of your State, and in addition, the question is narrowed to the election between voluntary organization of special service within the State, under officers of their own selection and with the privilege of remaining at home in the pursuit of their ordinary avocations, unless when called for a temporary exigency to /active/ duty <in camp or field>, and the continuous service for an appointed time under compulsory draft as Militia men, it is confidently believed that the general preference will be promptly manifested for the former. In the formation of these organizations, it is reasonably to be expected that such portion of the population as may have seen service, but have been by detail, discharge or other cause released from the Army, will constitute an important element, and that officers in like situation will be elected to command, and then there will be afforded the untried men a confidence and an encouragement wanting to ordinary Militia. Without the general disturbance of a call on the Militia, the organizations nearest to the points of attack would always be readily summoned to meet the emergency, and the population resident in the cities and their vicinities would, without serious interruption to their business or domestic engagments, stand organized and prepared to man their intrenchments, and defend, under the most animating incitements, their property and homes.

In pursuance of the views thus imperfectly presented, and to reconcile greater concentration to our armies with adequate internal protection to your State, I am instructed by the President in his name to make on you a requisition for Seven thousand men to be furnished by your State for service therein for the period of six months from the first day of August next, unless in the intermediate time a volunteer force organized under the law for local defence and special service of a least an equal number be mustered and reported as subject to his call for service within your State.

> Very Respectfully
> Yr. Obt. Servant
> James A Seddon
> Secy. of War

ZBV to William F. Lynch   A&H:GLB

State of North Carolina
Executive Department
Raleigh June 6th. 1863

Com. W. F. Lynch
Wilmington

Sir

Your's of the 3d. inst[1] has just been received informing me that the State of North Carolina has not yet been "recognized" by the Navy Department, and that you have therefore applied to the authorities at Richmond for permission to use my boats.

The boats were captured by troops entirely in the service of this State, and are absolutely & completely her property, and it seems strange indeed that you should feel greater hesitation in accepting them than the rail road iron, which you so far recognized me as to apply for.

Should the Navy Dept. graciously permit me to use my own boats, I shall be indebted to you for the favor

Very Resptly
Yr. obt. Servt.
Z. B. Vance

[1]In this volume.

ZBV to James A. Seddon   A&H:GP

Copy

State of North Carolina
Executive Department
Raleigh June 8th. 1863.

Hon Jas. A. Seddon
Secty. of War
Richmond Va.

Sir,

Your several communications in regard to recent decisions of Chief Justice Pearson in the cases of Irwin [Irvin] & Mitchell,[1] under the operations of the Act of Conscription have been received and duly considered.

I do most sincerely regret that such a state of things should exist as a serious and important difference between the authorities of this State and those of the

Confederacy on a matter touching so vitally the efficiency of the army and the public defence. I feel however that I have no option left me as to the course I must pursue. Without pretending to controvert the arguments which you furnish me, and with my high respect for the emenant source from which it is derived, I beg leave to say that according to my conception of duty, my powers as an Executive officer are absolutely bound by the judicial decisions of the State Courts: that it is not competent for me to review them. And in the absence of a Court having a Superior and appellate jurisdiction deciding to the contrary, that they are and must of necessity be, to me the supreme law of the land.

There can be no doubt of this, it seems to me, let the argument go as it may. Having thus stated the plain path of duty which I am bound to pursue, I desire nevertheless to assure you of the great concern, which I feel in the issue, and of my earnest wish to assist the War Department in maintaining the efficiency of our armies and of avoiding conflict with the local authorities. To this end I shall endeavor to get an authoritative decision of the Supreme Court of this State, now in session in this city, in regard to the question of jurisdiction involved, and whilst declining to admit that the construction of an Executive bureau must take precedence of the decisions of the Supreme Judicial Tribunals of a State, in a matter touching the liberty of a citizen, I yet would gladly receive any suggestions as to the means of avoiding such an alternative and of Settling the difficulty temporarily or permanently.

I shall take an early opportunity of communicating with you again on this subject.

> Very Respectfully
> Yr. obt. servt.
> (signed)   Z. B. Vance.

[1]It is not certain who Mitchell was. His name appears as Nicholson in the A&H:GLB copy of this letter. Nicholson was a Guilford County miller exempted from conscription. See Memory F. Mitchell, *Legal Aspects of Conscription and Exemption in North Carolina, 1861–1865* (Chapel Hill: University of North Carolina Press, 1965), 50–52.

ZBV *to Samuel Cooper*   A&H:GLB

> State of North Carolina
> Executive Department
> Raleigh June 8th. 1863

Genl. S. Cooper
Adjt. Genl., C.S.A.

Genl

Lt. Col. John [L.] McDowell 34th. N.C.T. was some time ago dropped from the roll of officers for exceeding his leave of absence, was arrested by the enrolling officer, sent on to his regiment and immediately placed in the guard house by Gen Pender—

Considering that the President has no Earthly authority to deprive an officer of his Commission except by sentence of a Court Martial, and that the order to do so could only be intended *in terrorem*,[1] having no legality, I think such a proceeding unwarrented and tyranical. Lt. Col. McDowell only asked the privilege of volunteering in some other regiment, not wishing to serve as a private among men whom he had once commanded, which was denied him, I ask that it shall yet be granted.[2] If he consents to waive his right to a trial, to which he is entitled by law and to suffer a Commission isssued to him by the State of North Carolina taken from him in a style, so uncerimonious and so illegal, without resistance he will be certainly entitled to exemption from further punishment in the guard house and to the benefit of General Order No 82, which permits conscripts to choose their regiments

Such treatment General, believe me, is not calculated to promote the good of the service, and renders the articles of War a farce

> Very respectfully
> Yr. obt. svt.
> Z. B. Vance

[1] As intimidation.

[2] McDowell remained in the Thirty-fourth Regiment North Carolina Troops—first as a private, then as a noncommissioned officer—until the Army of Northern Virginia surrendered at Appomattox in April 1865. Manarin and Jordan, *North Carolina Troops*, 9:251, 254, 332, 337. For Secretary of War James A. Seddon's response to the McDowell affair, see Seddon to ZBV, June 15, A&H:GP, and John A. Campbell to ZBV, July 10, A&H:GP.

ZBV to James A. Seddon   A&H:GLB

> State of North Carolina
> Executive Department
> Raleigh June 8th. 1863

Hon. J. A. Seddon
Secy of War
Richmond Va.

Dr. Sir

I beg leave to suggest respectfully the propriety of permitting the great number of detailed soldiers in this State, at work for the Government, to repair to their homes for two or three weeks during harvest.

The crop is very large and promising indeed and the labor to save it very limited. These detailed men could render invaluable service in the fields, and I hope their labor could be spared a few weeks without detriment to the public interest

Please consider of it

> Very respectfully
> Yr. obt Svt
> Z. B Vance

Tod R. Caldwell to ZBV   A&H:GP

> Morganton N.C
> 8th. June 1863.

Gov Z. B. Vance.

My Dear Sir.

On day after tomorrow my son Johnny starts to the army as a private with Col. C. M. Avery,[1] who has promised me that he will if in his power give him some position which will be less laborious than that of a private—. I feel certain that Johnny cannot stand the labour and fatigue of hard service, he came very near dying with rheumatism of the heart while he was at a military school in Yorkville S.C, and as you perhaps are aware when he went to Western Va with Col. Lee[2] he had a severe attack of sickness which very nearly proved fatal, his mother and I had to go to Valley Mountain after him, I doubt not the examining board would have exempted him from the service, but he is so desirous to be in the service that I did not feel at liberty to keep him out, particularly as it might have caused complaints from persons whose sons are in the army, and who think that too many in Johnny's station are screened from duties that their sons are obliged to perform—My object in now writing to you is to request you, if you know of any good position, that would suit him, now now [sic] vacant to use your influence to get it for him, I do not ask or desire that he shall be screened from danger, he himself has too much spirit to wish to avoid any thing of that kind, nor does he know that I am writing to you, but my solicitude for an only son prompts me to endeavour to shield /him/ from a drudgery, which I feel satisfied his constitution is not able to bear—He was two years at Col. Tew's[3] school in Hillsboro, and one year in Yorkville, and persons who are competent to judge spoke highly of him as a drill-master—If you can do any thing for him it will be very grateful to me—he will be in Raleigh with Col. Avery on Thursday or Friday next—[4]

When will the committee to investigate the R. Roads be completed? I think the affairs of the W. N. C [*Western North Carolina*] R R ought to be investigated so that the report can be made before the Stockholders annual meeting, which comes off about the last Thursday in August—.

> Very Truly Yrs.
> Tod R. Caldwell[5]

[1]Clark Moulton Avery, Thirty-third Regiment North Carolina Troops. Manarin and Jordan, *North Carolina Troops*, 9:118.
[2]Stephen Lee, Sixteenth Regiment North Carolina Troops. *Dictionary of North Carolina Biography*, s.v. "Lee, Stephen."
[3]Charles Courteney Tew, who operated Hillsboro Military Academy. Hugh [T.] Lefler and Paul [W.] Wager, eds., *Orange County, 1752–1952* (Chapel Hill: n.p. 1953), 339.
[4]John Caldwell remained with his regiment, was promoted to second lieutenant, and was killed at Gettysburg on July 3, 1863. Manarin and Jordan, *North Carolina Troops*, 9:172.
[5]Tod Robinson Caldwell, lawyer, state legislator, postwar governor, and one of the founders of the Republican party in North Carolina. *Dictionary of North Carolina Biography*, s.v. "Caldwell, Tod Robinson."

ZBV to Edward J. Hale   A&H:Hale

Private

                              State of North-Carolina,
                              Executive Department.
                              Raleigh, June 10 1863.

E. J. Hale Esq

My dear Sir,

If you can possibly spare the time I would be greatly obliged to have you come up and see me.

I wish to talk with you about some matters seriously affecting the *status* of the party which elevated me to office, and perhaps the good of the Confederate cause itself, and I hardly wish to put every thing I desire to say on paper. I make this request of you, as being more nearly of [*faded*] *precise stripe* politically—past and present—than any other editor in State; and as the undisputed organ of the *war* element of the old whigs. Things are moving here in a manner calculated to give *such a whig* uneasiness and I desire advice and consultation. I hope to see Mr. Graham this week.

I know that you are [*illegible*] with your business, and that I am asking a great deal but I beg you will come if at all convenient—

                              Very truly Yours
                              Z B Vance

Proclamation by ZBV   A&H:GLB

                    By the Governor of North Carolina
                              A Proclamation

Whereas, there has arison since the adjournment of the General Assembly a very important question of finance, in the proper settlement of which the credit of the State is deeply concerned and for which settlement legislative action is required.

Now therefore, I, Zebulon B. Vance, Governor of North Carolina, do, by and with the advice of the Council of State, issue this Proclamation, convening the General Assembly in Extra Session, and calling upon the members to assemble promptly in this city on Tuesday the 30th. day of this month of June.

In witness whereof, Zebulon B. Vance, Governor, Captain General and Commander-in-Chief hath signed these presents and caused the Great Seal of the State to be affixed.

Done at the City of Raleigh, this 12th. day of June A.D. 1863, and in the eighty seventh year of American Independence

Z. B. Vance

Daniel H. Hill to ZBV   A&H:VanPC

Petersburg Va
June 13th. 1863

His Excellency Z. B. Vance
Governor of North Carolina

I was highly gratified by your kind letter[1] & delighted to hear you had hopes of over ruling Judge Pearson He is injuring the noble old State incalculably. The whole Confederacy now admits it to be the best of all the fighting States and I have been as much suprised as gratified at the frankness with which this is admitted. The Yankees declare the same thing.

It is my honest opinion that but for two or three men in the State of the Pearson stripe, she would be par excellence the honored State of the Confederacy. How sad it is that the blood bought laurels of our soldiers should be stained by these wretches in safe places.

I hope that your 7000 men can be procured for home defence.[2] There are at least 70000 fit for duty in an emergency. All the ten Regt men ought to come out now. Will they? Lip patriotism is a cheap thing & it takes just as well as with the de[ar] people as the real thing.

Genl. Fowle wrote to me in regard to an amnesty & I presumed that you wished it. My own judgment was decidedly against it.

The recent deserters have been chiefly those, who came in under the first amnesty.

All orders to the Guards at the Depots have been given in order to carry out your wishes & that of the C.S Government against the removal of supplies from the State by speculators & extortioners.

I have directed the Guard to honor all your orders for the removal of stores. I hope however that not many will be given, as the commissioners from Lee's Army tell very pitiful tales

With great respect
D H Hill
Maj Genl.

¹Not extant.
²See James A. Seddon to ZBV, June 5, in this volume.

James A. Seddon to ZBV   A&H:GP

Confederate States of America,
War Department,
Richmond, Va. June 15th. 1863.

His Excellency Z. B. Vance
Governor of North Carolina

Sir,
    Your Excellency's letter of the 8th. Inst.¹ has been duly received and respectfully considered. Where there is the unity in the aim of the Governments of the State of North Carolina and this Government, that is indicated in your Excellencys letter, it would seem that there should not be any danger of a collision which would strengthen the hands of those who are opposed to both Governments. But the Department supposes that your Excellency has not afforded to the measures which have been instituted by it, and the regulations it has from time to time published, their exact signification. This Department by the terms of its commission from Congress "exercises all its functions under "the control and direction of the President" and performs such duties in relation to the Army as "may be assigned to it" by his authority. The Supreme Court of the United States described the War Department under similar statutes as "the regular constitutional organ of the President for the administration of the military establishment of the nation: and rules and orders publicly promulgated through the Secty. of War must be received as the act of the Executive, and as such, be binding upon all within the sphere of his legal and constitutional authority. Such regulations cannot be questioned or defied because they be thought /unwise/ or mistaken". 16 Pet. 291.302. A very similar discription is given of another Executive Department in 1 Peters C.C.R.P. 466.
    The Conscription Acts of April and Sept. 1862 are addressed in a very particular and peculiar manner to the President. Under what is pronounced to be an imperious and absolute necessity for providing for the common defence of the Confederate States—a necessity that none disputes—he was authorized to call

out and place in the military service those between the ages of 18 and 45 years—that is the ordinary armsbearing population with some exceptions—"to repel the advancing columns of the enemy." The officers who were to determine <who were to be exempt, are desig> who were the class to be called out and those who were to be exempt, are designated in these laws and are to act under instructions and directions from the executive authority. Appeals from their decisions, in the nature of the case, are to be made to the agencies to be employed under the law.

Now, Sir, if State Judges can interpose to obstruct the administration or ex-ecution of these and similar Acts of the C.S., by habeas corpus, injunction or other preventive writs, it is very clear that a power similar to the liberum veto exercised by the individual members of the Polish Senate, in our Confederacy, has been placed in the hands of every State Judge or Justice having the power to issue these writs, in so far, as any Confederate administration is involved.

This was the precise claim of the abolition courts of Wisconsin, which re-ceived a solemn rebuke in the opinion of the Sup. Court of the U.S. delivered by the illustrious Chief Justice[2] only five years ago.

This Department conducts its administration with the earnest desire to avoid any thing like collision with mistaken or harmful opinions of State authorities. It wishes that the heart of the Confederacy should be engrossed but with a single sentiment—the supreme desire to drive the enemy from our soil. It has no dis-position to employ power for any other object. But when it finds that its plainest measures of legality are obstructed and thereby disorganization of the Army threatened, desertion promoted, and deserters rescued from the only authority competent to try them, by manifest exercise of undelegated authority, its silence or forbearance would be a crime against the country. For this reason it has con-sidered it to be proper to bring these measures to your notice. It trusts that the Supreme Court of No. Carolina will maintain the reputation and character that it has inherited from its Ruffins, Gastons, and Hendersons[3] and relieve us from the painful consequences that this eccentric action has occasioned.

The District Atto. has been authorized to associate with him either Mr. Badger,[4] Gov. [William A.] Graham or Mr. [George] Davis to aid him in the discussion of these questions before that tribunal.

> Very Respectfully
> Your Obt. Servt.
> James A Seddon
> Secy. of War

P.S. To the above, will you allow me to add unofficially my expression of sincere personal gratification at the spirit and temper of your Excellency's letter. I ap-preciate fully your position and the line of duty that seems prescribed to you—At the same time, with my thorough conviction of the earnest common purpose we both have to maintain our great struggle for independence and even existence, and of our mutual desire to preserve and respect in every just way the principles of law and constitutions, I cannot doubt some mode will be found of ensuring harmony & cooperation in efficient support of the Army without weakening the authority of the Confederate Executive or trenching on the dignity of your honored State & its authorities

Cordially Yrs.
James A Seddon

[*Endorsed*] Copy except the P.S. & file

Z B V

[1] In this volume.
[2] Roger Brooke Taney, chief justice of U.S. Supreme Court, in the *Dred Scott* case. Faust et al., *Encyclopedia of Civil War*, 227, 741–742.
[3] Thomas Ruffin, William Joseph Gaston, and Leonard Henderson, former justices of N.C. Supreme Court. Like Ruffin, Henderson became chief justice. *Dictionary of North Carolina Biography*, s.v. "Gaston, William Joseph" and "Henderson, Leonard."
[4] George Edmund Badger, former legislator, superior court judge, U.S. senator, and secretary of the navy. *Dictionary of North Carolina Biography*, s.v. "Badger, George Edmund."

Daniel H. Hill to ZBV   A&H:VanPC

Petersburg Va
June 15th. 1863

His Excellency Z. B. Vance
Governor of North Carolina

A [*New York*] Herald of the 12th. Inst. has been shown me claiming a reconstruction element in North Carolina upon the authority of the Standard.

You have no conception of the mischief that is being done by this paper & the unfortunate decision of Judge Pearson. These two causes are operating to cause desertion by the thousand, are poisoning the minds of the people at home, are encouraging the enemy and giving him some show of justice in his claim of restoring the union. They are tarnishing the glorious laurels of our soldiers won upon so many Bloody fields. Can nothing be done to arrest this terrible evil? Are these men really anxious to go back to Lincoln? Do they really love the Yankees better than their own people? Or is it after all a mere trick to get up popularity at home by denouncing Virginia & other Southern States? Is it possible that selfishness can go so far? The whole movement is a mystery to me. It betrays a weakness of intellect or a baseness of heart utterly incomprehensible. Surely they cannot be silly enough to suppose that the Yankees will spare them because of their toryism When have the negroes and horses of tories been spared from seisure? The Yankees ought to have been polite enough to discriminate in favor of tories, but the love given filthy greed has been too strong for policy.

Genl. Jenkins has a very fine Brigade[1] & is himself superior as an officer to Colquitt.[2] I am anxious to exchange his Brigade for Colquitt's & then I would feel safe in regard to the old State

But Jenkins is a man of rigid notions. He would offend disloyal men & then he would be denounced by the tory press as a South Carolinian. Do you think it would be safe to make the exchange? Jenkins has six Regts, all in a splendid condition Please answer on this point as soon as practicable. I don't feel safe in regard to Kinston.

Yours truly
D H Hill

[1]The brigade of Albert G. Jenkins soon left West Virginia to join the Army of Northern Virginia. The brigade fought in the Battle of Gettysburg and then returned to West Virginia. Faust et al., *Encyclopedia of Civil War*, 394.

[2]Alfred Holt Colquitt, a brigadier general under Hill's command in North Carolina, where he remained until transferred to Florida in 1864. Faust et al., *Encyclopedia of Civil War*, 151–152.

Proclamation by ZBV   A&H:GLB

By the Governor of North Carolina
A Proclamation

Whereas, the President of the Confederate States, by virtue of the authority vested in him by the constitution, has made a requisition upon North Carolina for Seven Thousand men to serve within the limits of the State, for six months from and after the first day of August next: and whereas, it is desirable that if possible the troops should be raised by voluntary enlistment, with the right to select their own officers:

Now, therefore, I, Zebulon B. Vance, Governor of North Carolina, do issue this my Proclamation, calling on the patriotic citizens of the State to volunteer for State defence, and tender their services in companies, battalions and regiments, on or before the 17th. of July.

The control and management of the troops raised under this Proclamation will be retained by the authorities of the State.

Orders for the enrollment of the militia, preparatory to a draft, in case it may be necessary, will be issued by the Adjutant General

In witness whereof, Zebulon B. Vance, Captain General and Commander-in-Chief hath signed these presents & caused the Great Seal of the State to be affixed.

Done at Raleigh this 17th. day of June A D. 1863 and in the year of American Independence the 87th.

Z. B. Vance

John A. Campbell to ZBV   A&H:GP

Confederate States of America,
War Department,
Richmond, Va. June 18 1863

Hon Z B Vance
Gov of N.C

Your letter of the 8th. Inst.[1] has been rec'd. in which you recommend that detailed soldiers may be relieved to repair to their homes to aid in gathering the crops that are now growing Instructions will be given to the Chiefs of bureaux to fulfil as far as practicable your Excellencys recommendation on this subject

Very Respectfully
Yr. obt Svt
For Secy of war
J A Campbell[2]
A.S.W

[1] In this volume.
[2] John Archibald Campbell, Confederate assistant secretary of war and former U.S. Supreme Court justice. *Dictionary of American Biography*, s.v. "Campbell, John Archibald."

Daniel H. Hill to ZBV   A&H:VanPC

Petersburg Va
June 18th. 1863

His Excellency Z. B. Vance
Governor of North Carolina

I have recd. a telegram from Presd. Davis inquiring whether I could be spared in North Carolina, as he wished to send me to Mississippi. My departure would cause great rejoicing among the exempts and speculators.

By the way, if reports be true your proclamation against the shipment of supplies is evaded every where, but especially at Weldon. Could you not keep a State Agent there and at Gaston to catch the evaders?

There has been continued fighting on my line for the last five days. So far, our troops have been eminently successful

> Yours truly
> D H Hill
> Maj Genl.

ZBV to Daniel H. Hill   A&H:Hill

> State of North Carolina,
> Executive Department.
> Raleigh, June 23 1863.

Maj Gen D. H. Hill

Dear Sir,

Allow /me/ for a moment to turn office seeker and call your attention to the claims of Sergt. W. T. Dickerson[1] of Col. Leventhorps regt—

He writes to me that he has applied to you for a situation and begs me to help him, which I can do cheerfully & conscienteously

He is a citizen of my town, Asheville, is quite an intelligent hard working, business man; and has served from Bethel down in a subordinate capacity while worthy of something better.

I have no doubt whatever that if you could find room for him in the Commissariat or Q. Masters Dept you would find him to be all I say.

> Respectfully & Truly
> Z B Vance

[1]William T. Dickerson, Eleventh Regiment North Carolina Troops. Manarin and Jordan, *North Carolina Troops*, 5:8, 96.

Joseph E. Brown to ZBV   A&H:GP

> Canton Ga. June 27th. 1863

His Excellency Z B. Vance

Dear Sir

Your dispatch of the 25th. Inst.[1] was handed to me on my way to this place and I answered it from Marietta saying that I would write you from Canton in a day or two.

The code of this State gives the governor the power to say what currency shall be excluded from the Treasury in the collection of taxes. As collections <have> have not yet commenced in this State it has not become necessary for me to give any direction in reference to the receipt of the Confederate Treasury notes which cease to be fundable in August. So long as they are bankable in this State I can use them in payment and will be willing to receive them, but when they cease to be bankable they will no longer pass currently and I shall then exclude them. Before the collections commence I expect to have an understanding with our bankers and know whether they intend to continue to receive and pay them out, after they cease to be fundable. My own opinion is that this is the proper course for each State to pursue. It cannot be expected that the States will receive uncurrent funds in payment of taxes, but they ought not to refuse to receive any of the issues of the Confederacy as long as they can use them in their own payments without loss. I regretted to see that the Banks in Richmond have detemed not to receive this class of bills, as I think it the duty of every bank as well as every good citizen to do every thing possible to sustain Confederate credit.

While I trust no one of the States will ever consent to the divesture of her sovreignty, or of the reserved rights without which her sovreignty cannot be maintained, I think it the duty of each State, and of the people of all the States, to make every other sacrifise necessary to sustain the Government of the Confederate States, and strengthen it against the powerful and unscrupulous enemy with which it has to contend.

I think it matter of regret that the legislation of Congress should have been such as to depreciate our portion of the notes issued from the Confederate Treasury below another portion. This I fear must be the necessary result of the late act[2] to which your telegram has reference. Let the States be careful not to contribute to this result, but when it can no longer be avoided, and Congress by its own act had depreciated one of its own issues below another, the States cannot be censured for demanding payment of State taxes in the current notes of the Confederate Treasury, and excluding those which are not current.

I am dear Sir,
Very Respectfully
Your obt servt.
Joseph E. Brown

[1]Not extant.
[2]The Confederate tax law of April 24, passed to overcome growing inflation in Confederate and state paper currency. The act provided for a graduated income tax and a 10 percent tax in kind on agricultural products. For discussions of the Confederacy's financial difficulties, see Richard C. Todd, *Confederate Finance* (Athens: University of Georgia Press, 1954); Coulter, *Confederate States of America*, 149–182.

Edward J. Hale to ZBV   A&H:VanPC

Fayetteville, June 27, 1863.
My Dear Sir:
I was disappointed on seeing the Standard after I left you on Thursday to find no allusion to the promised article on the currency. It was a volunteered remark

of Mr. H. [*William W. Holden*], that he was glad to see that the Observer had taken a stand in favor of sustaining the currency, & that in next Standard he would take the same ground. This was the only allusion, /I think/ in our conversation during my call, to public affairs. There were others in his office.

I hear from various parts of the State that the Treasurer's Circular[1] has produced "a panic." I do hope the Legislature will allay it. And I also most earnestly hope that there is no intention, as that wretched State Journal[2] reports, to meddle with the President's call for troops for local defense; and that there exists no reason for any interferences. I trust that our friends will not only manfully sustain the cause, but that they will afford no protest for any imputation upon their determination to do so. I trust that they are all as much in earnest as I know you & I are. I am satisfied that they are so. But to silence slander, if possible, we should make no points against the Confederate government but such as are [unanswerable].

As to the currency, I have not met with a man who does not condemn Mr. Memminger's[3] course & hope that North Carolina will not second it, as Virginia has done.

When I handed you a letter from Col. Pemberton,[4] I was not aware that he desired /a/ speedy answer, or that any such action as he asked for had been taken. But he called to see me as soon as I arrived, & said there was great anxiety on the subject, no one [knowing] what to be at. And that in other parts of the State persons were moving in the way he desired, setting up companies & regiments, either with or without authority. Can we give him any assurance that he may go ahead?

I find great difficulty—I do not know indeed that I shall succeed—in keeping my son Peter[5] out of the army. He has no military aspirations, but thinks that it is his duty; & further that he will never be willing hereafter to have it said that he stood aloof. He is unwilling to avail himself of the exemption handed me by Col. [*Adj. Gen.*] Fowle, accompanied as it is by an opinion that he is *not* exempted by law. Judge Pearson, by the way, is of a different opinion, but that is of no consequence, for he would never sue out a habeas corpus. I write you this because I do not pretend not to be aware that the Observer is useful to the cause, & because I know that if he should leave me its usefulness will necessarily be vastly impaired. I would not, however, have the matter further spoken of, or any further action taken. Please consider all this confidential.

> With great regard,
> Yours truly,
> E. J. Hale[6]

---

[1]A circular apparently referring to the provisions of the tax law of April 24. See Joseph E. Brown to ZBV, June 27, in this volume.

[2]A Raleigh newspaper.

[3]Christopher Gustavus Memminger, Confederate secretary of the treasury. *Dictionary of American Biography*, s.v. "Memminger, Christopher Gustavus."

[4]John A. Pemberton, Fifty-third Regiment North Carolina Militia. Stephen E. Bradley Jr., comp. and ed., *North Carolina Militia Officers Roster* (Wilmington: Broadfoot Publishing Co., 1992), 141–142. Pemberton's letter is not extant, but evidently it concerned organization of militia units.

[5]Peter Mallett Hale. *Dictionary of North Carolina Biography*, s.v. "Hale, Peter Mallett."

[6]Edward Jones Hale, politically influential editor and publisher of the *Fayetteville Observer*, a leading Whig newspaper before the war. *Dictionary of North Carolina Biography*, s.v. "Hale, Edward Jones."

———————

Milledge L. Bonham to ZBV   A&H:GP

State of South Carolina.
Head Quarters.
Columbia June 29, 1863

Govr. Vance

My Dear Sir

I should have written sooner in answer to your telegram[1] but have been absent.

With my views and as at present advised I cannot think it advisable to refuse to receive the non-fundable Confederate notes.

Yours Very Respectfully
M. L. Bonham

[1]Not extant.

———————

ZBV to James A. Seddon   A&H:GLB

Raleigh June 30th./63

Hon. Jas. A. Seddon
Richmond

I hope you will not remove Colquitts brigade from this State—if you do Raleigh Fayetteville and all the railroads will be at mercy of the Enemies Cavalry— The Militia cannot be got out in time

Z. B. Vance

This photograph of Zebulon B. Vance was taken around the time of his inauguration as governor in September 1862. From State Archives, Division of Archives and History, Raleigh.

Vance's brother, Robert B. Vance, who became a brigadier general in March 1863, wrote to the governor about politics and conditions in the Confederate army. Photograph from State Archives.

As solicitor of the state's Eighth District, Augustus S. Merrimon—future U.S. senator and chief justice of the state supreme court—prosecuted unionists and deserters who raided the town of Marshall in Madison County. He also informed Vance of a massacre by Confederate troops at Shelton Laurel. Photograph of engraving from State Archives.

Richmond M. Pearson, chief justice of the North Carolina Supreme Court, clashed with Vance over the issues of conscription, desertion, and habeas corpus. Photograph of portrait from State Archives.

Judge Battle,

My dear Sir,

The recent decision of Judge Pearson as you are aware, places me in an embarrassing situation.

The consequences to the country of withdrawing all the forces of the State from the arresting of deserters, who are numerous in the State, and in many places have over-awed and almost silenced the civil authorities, would be so great and alarming, that I am unwilling to assume the responsibility of so doing upon the decision of one Judge. I am therefore compelled again to trouble the Supreme court out of term time, to give me the benefit

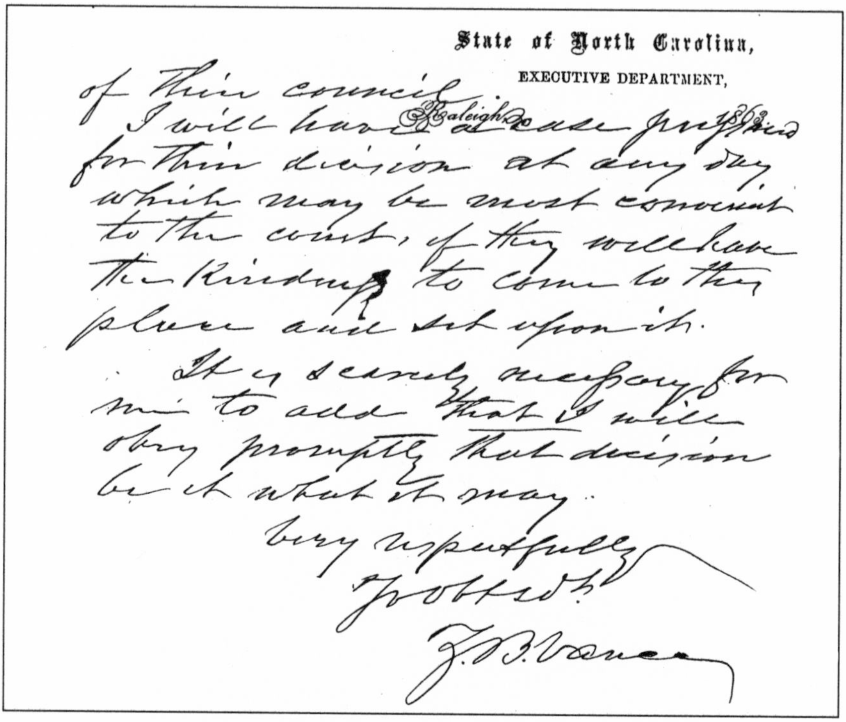

[handwritten letter]

Disagreeing with Chief Justice Pearson on the question of state authority to arrest Confederate deserters, Vance sought the counsel of the rest of the state supreme court in this March 6 letter (above and adjacent page) to Justice William H. Battle. From Governors Papers, Zebulon B. Vance, State Archives.

Amid the controversy surrounding the army's conscription of state officials, Vance adopted as his own the views of his state auditor and former law professor Samuel F. Phillips. Photograph from Phillips Russell, *The Woman Who Rang the Bell: The Story of Cornelia Phillips Spencer* (Chapel Hill: University of North Carolina Press, 1949), facing 178.

While commanding Confederate troops in North Carolina, General Daniel H. Hill complained to Vance about the progress of the war. Photograph of engraving from State Archives.

William W. Holden, editor of the *North Carolina Standard* (Raleigh), organized a movement within the state to seek peace with the Federal government. Photograph of portrait from State Archives.

Vance's chief political confidant, Edward J. Hale, editor and publisher of the *Fayetteville Observer*, initially refused the governor's request to attack publicly Holden and the peace advocates. Photograph of portrait from State Archives.

Prominent political leader William A. Graham—former governor and U.S. senator and secretary of the navy—advised Vance to restrain his denunciation of the peace movement in North Carolina. Photograph of engraving from State Archives.

Colonel William J. Clarke, commander of the Twenty-fourth Regiment North Carolina Troops, appealed to Vance to help him form a new brigade under his command. The unit, however, never was established. Emaciated from his term as a Federal prisoner of war, Clarke appeared in this photograph shortly after the war's end. Courtesy of Mrs. Graham A. Barden; copy by State Archives.

James A. Seddon to ZBV   A&H:GP

Confederate States of America,
War Department,
Richmond, Va. July 1 1863.

His Excellency Z. B. Vance,
Governor of North Carolina,
Raleigh, N.C.

Sir,

Some short time since, an application was made to me by Col. Gilmer,[1] of the Engineer Bureau, representing the slow progress made for want of labor to the construction of the Piedmont Railroad, and urging the issue of an order to the Enrolling Officers of North Carolina to impress fifty per cent of the able-bodied free negroes between 18 and 45, to be sent to Greensboro to work on that road. At the /same/ time the impression was conveyed to me, that the measure was of your suggestion and would meet your approbation. I was very reluctant to call out so large a proportion of the free negroes as fifty per cent, as recommended by Col. Gilmer, but on conference with him, he satisfied me that the needs of the road would demand that proportion. The recommendation was also made, that these negroes could be most readily collected by the Enrolling Officers, who are generally distributed throughout the State, and the plan was accordingly sanctioned. I have learned to-day with some surprise and regret, from an endorsement made by your Adjutant General upon a paper sent to Col. Mallett, that you regard as unwarranted any enrolment of free negroes without your previous order. I am not aware of the provisions of any law, either Confederate or State, which make special provision in such a case, but I certainly recognize the propriety of your concurrence and previous assent to the action which was proposed to be taken. As therefore I have acted under an erroneous impression in regard to your concurrence, I have now the honor to submit to you an application for your cooperation, or if you prefer, your own order and action to obtain the free negro laborers required. I take pleasure in assuring you there was no purpose or thought of infringing on your authority or jurisdiction in the matter; but the use of the Enrolling Officers in different parts of the State will, as you will readily perceive, aid in accomplishing the end, and if desired by you, their services will be placed at your disposition.

With esteem
Respectfully yours
James A Seddon
Secretary of War

[Endorsed] Referred to Gen Fowle
Copy & File

Z B V

[1]Jeremy Francis Gilmer, Confederate military engineer promoted to major general of engineers in August. *Dictionary of North Carolina Biography*, s.v. "Gilmer, Jeremy Francis."

William H. C. Whiting to ZBV   A&H:GLB

Head Quarters
Wilmington
July 1st. 1863
His Excellency Gov. Vance
Raleigh

Sir
    I have investigated the occurrence of Sunday evening connected with the alleged violation of the quarantine by the Steamer Advance and the refusal to allow Your Excellency to land.[1] In every point of view I regret it as most unfortunate—Technically Lt. Col. Thorburn[2] was obeying orders which were to carry out strictly the ordinances of the Wilmington Commissioners of Navigation, a civil board charged with the quarantine—But I learn as indeed he admits that under the excitement of opposition to the execution of his orders he was disrespectful in language.
    I regret exceedingly that any disrespect to the Governor should have occurred in my command and I present as the Chief Confederate officer here my apology.
    I have relieved Lt. Col. Thorburn of the command of the City which he has heretofore exercised and assigned Maj. Sparrow[3] 10 N.C. Artl. to that position.
    As to the Board of Commissioners this was a case which admitted the exercise of sound discretion. In fact if the quarantine was violated, *I alone* am to blame. The Advance arrived here some days previous to the publication of the last Quarantine orders and grounded on the Rips before inspection. On ascertaining that she was from Bermuda and with a clear bill of health and knowing also that she belonged to the State, I at once sent to her my Steamers to lighten her. This had been going on for several days and accordingly I gave readily the Steamer Flora and permission to your party to visit the Advance—To quarantine the Advance after so much previous communication and the breaking out of her Cargo was in my opinion useless and unnecessary. In this view I do not approve of the action of the Board, but over them I have no control. I much regret that circumstances prevented my presence in the City at the time, for as your Excellency well knows, this most untoward circumstance would not have occurred.
    With the sincere hope that this letter will be satisfactory to your Excellency

I am Very respectfully
W. H. C. Whiting
Maj. Genl.

[1]For an account of the incident, which occurred at the port of Wilmington, see Tucker, *Zeb Vance*, 223–226.

[2]Charles E. Thorburn, commanding city and river defenses at Wilmington. He had refused to allow ZBV to disembark from the *Advance*, which the governor had boarded for inspection in the harbor.

[3]Thomas Sparrow, Tenth Regiment North Carolina State Troops. Manarin and Jordan, *North Carolina Troops*, 1:40, 158

ZBV to Jefferson Davis   A&H:GLB

[*Telegram*]

Raleigh July 2d. 1863

President Davis

By the returns from my militia regiments there will not be men in the State to raise the Seven thousand required by you without resorting to the classes exempted from conscription, as State officers, men with substitutes &c, who would be entitled to discharge if made Confederate troops. The military committee have instructed me to ask if you will agree to the troops remaining under my control as *State* Troops, which Enables us to put in all these exempts? Please answer at once—The Legislature sits but a day or two longer

Z. B. Vance

Jefferson Davis to ZBV   A&H:GLB

[*Telegram*]

Richmond [*July*] 2 1863

To Gov. Z. B. Vance

This day recd. your dispatch[1] will receive as many as will organize under the act (of Congress) for local defence and for the residue will accept militia or State troops

Jeffn Davis

[1]July 2, in this volume.

William H. C. Whiting to ZBV   A&H:GP

Hd. Qrs. Wilmington
July 3, 1863.

To his Excellency Gov. Vance.
Raleigh—

Sir,

All but about 30 of the negro laborers here have been returned—I hope you will understand & bear in mind the great need I have for labor so as to furnish it to me as soon as possible—This is the more essential since my number of troops is so limited compared to what it was a few months ago—I shall be compelled to increase the strength of the works to compensate—The river obstructions though formidable are not sufficient—Much work remains at [*Fort*] Caswell & the whole line of city defenses together with the exterior land lines require extensive improvement & additions

Surely in the 300[,]ooo negros belonging to N.C 500 might be spared for so important a purpose.

I beg of you to consider this—There are many counties which have not furnished any.—

Respy.
W. H. C Whiting
Maj Genl.

ZBV to Richard S. Donnell   A&H:GLB

State of North Carolina
Executive Department
Raleigh 3d. July 1863

Hon. R. S. Donnell
Speaker House of Commons

Sir

Yr. note[1] communicating a Resolution of the House requesting me "to communicate any and all correspondence which I have had with the secretary of war relative to the Jurisdiction of the Judges of this state to issue writs of Habeas Corpus" &c has been received and I take pleasure in complying with the request—

The correspondence is very voluminous, about thirty letters having passed in regard to the matter referred to in the Resolution and in order not to delay the deliberations of the House and for its convenience I've thought best to submit my letter book containing a copy of the entire correspondence, rather than to wait till it could be copied from the Book, which might require several days. The various letters are referred to in an index herewith transmitted for the convenience of the reading clerk

> Very Respectfully—
> Yr. obt. Srvt.
> Z. B. Vance

[1]July 3, A&H:GP.

ZBV to James A. Seddon   A&H:GLB

> State of North Carolina
> Executive Department
> Raleigh July 3d. 1863

Hon. James A Seddon
Secretary of War

Dear Sir
    There has been much complaint among our people that the participation of our troops in the various battles, has not been noticed, with that commendation to which they are supposed by us to be entitled. This has resulted in some measure from the fact, that there [are] no Army correspondents from this State. I am exceedingly anxious of removing this ground of complaint and at the same time to provide that the deeds of daring and gallantry of our Soldiers shall be duly recorded. With this view I respectfully request that M J. McSween[1] connected with the 35th. Regiment may be detailed to attend the Army of Genl Lee as an Army correspondent and that you will give him such permission as will effect this object, with such restrictions as the public service may demand.
    Mr McSween is a gentleman of intelligence a graduate of our University and in such feeble health that he cannot render very active service in the field

> With sentiments of great respect
> Your obedient Servant
> Z. B. Vance

[1]Murdock J. McSween, lawyer, journalist, soldier, and friend of ZBV. Tucker, *Zeb Vance*, 213–215.

ZBV *to James A. Seddon*   A&H:GLB

[*Telegram*]

Raleigh July 6th [*1863*]

Hon. J. A. Seddon
Richmond

Can you send me four pieces Artillery? I have all equipments and men, but
no guns for defence of this city—Please send them to me with ammunition[1]

Z. B. Vance

[1]Colonel Josiah Gorgas, chief ordnance officer for the Confederacy, responded to ZBV's
request with two artillery pieces. See Gorgas to W. C. Duxbury, July 6, A&H:VanPC;
and Gorgas to ZBV, July 7, A&H:GP.

ZBV *to Jefferson Davis*   A&H:GLB

State of North Carolina
Executive Department
Raleigh July 6th. 1863.

His Excellency
President Davis

Dear Sir
    A great deal of harm has been done and much dissatisfaction excited by the
appointment of citizens of other states to offices and positions here that should
of right be filled by our own people
    The last appointment by the Q. Master General, of a Col. Bradford[1] of Norfolk
Va. to the Chief Collectorship of the tax in kind for this State, has given almost
universal offence, and I may be excused for, very justly. No objection that I am
aware of is made to him except that he is a citizen of another State, and we all
feel that the Offices so purely local as this, we have a right to demand that they
be bestowed upon our own people.
    I feel it my duty, out of respect to my State and people as well as to remove
any cause so far as may be, for dissatisfaction, to bring this matter to your attention and ask that you make a different appointment

Very respectfully
Yr. obt. Servt.
Z. B. Vance

[1]Edmund Bradford, a native of Pennsylvania who had settled in Virginia after graduating from West Point and serving in the U.S. Army. Tucker, *Zeb Vance*, 250–251.

ZBV to Jefferson Davis   A&H:GLB

State of North Carolina
Executive Department
Raleigh July 6th. 1863

His Excellency,
President Davis

Dear Sir
Last week the Steamer "Advance" purchased by this State in Europe arrived at Wilmington with cargo of soldiers clothing. I went down to visit her and before going on board, I obtained the permission of the Commissioners of Navigation and the Military authorities (she being below town on a sand bar) in compliance with quarrantine regulations. On returning to the Wharf Lt. Col. Thorburn, who was in command of the town, refused to permit me to land alleging that the regulations were violated. Upon showing him the permission of the Commissioner and assuring him of the assent of Genl Whiting and remonstrating with him in person, he replied that he "did not care for Gov. Vance nor Gov. Jesus Christ", that I "should not come off that boat for fifteen days"— and accordingly placed a guard on the wharf with orders to shoot any one attempting to get off. I was so detained until the Chairman of the Board of Com. came to my relief, and lost the train to Raleigh—Having thus deliberately, wilfully and without excuse, inflicted a gross insult upon the people of North Carolina through her Chief Magistrate, in their name I demand his removal from the State, and that he be no more placed in command of her troops. If it be deemed indispensable that North Carolina soldiers should be commanded by Virginians, I should regret to see the old Dominion retain all her gentlemen for her own use, and furnish us only her blackguards.

Very respectfully
Yr. obt. Servt.
Z. B. Vance

ZBV to Jefferson Davis   A&H:GLB

State of North Carolina
Executive Department
Raleigh July 9th. 1863
His Excellency
Jefferson Davis
Richmond Va

Dear Sir
    I am fearful I shall not be able to furnish the seven thousand men called for.
Upon receipt of the Secretary's /letter/[1] I immediately issued my proclamation[2]
and ordered a general enrollment throughout the State. The returns so far are
gratifying to our State pride, but sad to contemplate. The average of soldiers and
detailed men, is about Equal to the voting population, and there are very few
behind. On learning this I visited the Legislature in secret session and urged
them to draft the Magistrates and Militia officers—They declined to do so and
adopted the exemption bill of Congress, which I fear will prevent me from raising
the whole number required. I will proceed rapidly however to get out as many
as I can. I have already in Eastern Carolina some eight hundred men, raised for
local defense, which I wish you to receive as part of the number called for—
There are also some five or six small companies along the Tennessee border,
authorized by me to be raised before your requisition for defence of the citizens
against the swarms of Tories, refugees and deserters who have congregated in the
mountains and who carry pillage and murder in their path—It will be impossible
to remove them without ruin to the loyal people—I would be glad if you would
receive them and permit them to remain—

Very respectfully
Yr. obt. Servt
Z. B. Vance

[1]June 5, in this volume.
[2]June 17, in this volume.

Daniel H. Hill to ZBV   A&H:GP

Near Richmond Va
July 10 1863
His Excellency Z. B. Vance
Governor of N.C.

    I wrote you some time ago that the campaign of Lee would prolong the war
through Lincoln's administration. It has turned out as I believed it would.

God help us. "Vain is the help of man." We must meet the crisis[1] with renewed faith & firmness. A determined people inhabiting a thinly settled county cannot be conquered. A grave blunder has been committed but we must meet the calamity involved with faith and courage. The Yankees were whipped on both roads of their advance to Richmond & are /now/ hurrying off. I think that every available man ought to be sent to save Lee, but I cannot tell what counsels will prevail. I think that we have nothing to fear /in N.C./ except from raiders If the people were instructed to block up the roads & fire at the murauders the thing would soon stop. An Army of 100,000 men cannot stop a murauding band of 50 men. In fact, the smaller the party, the easier it can elude capture.

I spoke to Mr Davis about notifying our people of the contemplated insurrection on the first of August. I told him that the negroes would know it & silence only kept their masters in ignorance. I hope that you will /inform/ our people either publicly or by circulars to the colonels of militia. Humanity shudders at what may take place, should our people be unprepared. We have men enough at home to dispose of the raiders & the negroes too, if the men were only properly organised.

Genl [*James* G.] Martin can spare you a battery for the defense of Raleigh if you need it

> Respectfully
> D H Hill
> Maj Genl

[1]The Confederate defeat at the Battle of Gettysburg and the subsequent retreat of the Army of Northern Virginia.

ZBV to John White   A&H:GP

> State of North-Carolina,
> Executive Department.
> Raleigh, July 10 1863

John White Esq
Comr. for N.C.
Care of Frazer, Trenholm & Co
Liverpool

Dear Sir,

Col Crossan has arrived safely with steamer & cargo. I am much pleased with the result of your negotiations and approve most cordially of your whole conduct—You will see by the enclosed papers[1] that the legislature have also done all that was desired.

I have received full authority from the same source to run the vessel when and how I may think best, and I shall therefore keep her going until we get in the bal<l>ance of the purchases Since you left this country, many important changes have taken place and the war is evidently nearing its close. The resources of our state and the Confederacy have developed in such a degree that we have every assurance of being able to clothe our troops with our own goods, and our vast amount of captures has given us an abundance of arms. On this account I regret Col. McRae's purchase, and will only <to> continue your purchases of clothing by reason of economy. I therefore send you out the bal<l>ance of the bonds amounting to one million, but desire you to deposit them only as you need money, and to buy only as I may order, as an accident might happen to Crossan at any time. I presume from your letter[2] that you are not bound to take the whole loan at once, but may take it up from time to time, depositing bonds as you go. On the whole I will say that much being left to your descretion, <that> my desire is that you should not keep far ahead of your shipments, either in money or supplies; that you should deal cautiously & wait for advices.

I wrote you[3] before this, requesting you to purchase a lot of cotton & wool cards, and a machine for making them with a good supply of wire. If you have not acted upon this already, please buy at once fifty thousand pairs each of woolen & cotton cards and a machine & wire, & ship at once to Bermuda. I presume that by buying the teeth set in the leather without the wood finishing, this number will not be a very large bulk.

I hope Col. McRae will ship his principal cargo no further than Bermuda, as it is not needed at present and the risk need not be incurred.

Some little bills for State and private account accompany this which I hope you will attend to. As Crossans cargo was quite a well assorted one you may duplicate it once more without further orders*

I wrote Col. M. also, but lest he should not receive it I beg of you to see him & tell him not to sell the turpentine scrip or bonds. It would be bad policy to put ourselves further on the market as borrowers, and his orders are not now needed any how—In fact I did not intend for him to go to Europe to compete with you—my idea was to procure his supplies in Halifax, as people would certainly be struck with the folly of sending two agents to the same market, in part for the same object.

Your family I believe continue well & Mr. [Archibald H.] Arrington is still at home with them. The fall of Vicksburg, though creating some despondency has not discouraged us, and Gen Lee is compensating us by his invasion of Northern territory. On the whole our prospects are better than they were this time last year. Our people are adapting themselves to a state of war, our resources are developing wonderfully, our army is becoming veteran & invincible, and our crop prospects, with the harvest already in, almost exceed belief. You may assure, I think, the generous merchants who have befriended a people in their death struggle for liberty and independence, that their investment is a safe one.

Neglect no means of communicating with me.

Very truly yours
Z. B. Vance

*The Q. Masters say the shoes are too narrow in the bottoms—

P.S. I am told on reading over my letter that the proportion of the cotton to the wool cards should about four of the former to one of the latter—You will know how this should be.

Z B V

¹Not extant.
²May 20, in this volume.
³In a letter of March 12, in this volume.

ZBV to Duncan K. McRae   A&H:GP

Duplicate

State of North-Carolina,
Executive Department.
Raleigh, July-10th. 1863

Col. D. K. McRae
Care Fraser Trenholm & Co
Leverpool

Dear Sir

Yours¹ by the "Advance" was received and I reply by the same vessel.

I regret very much /that/ you did not receive my letter² in time to prevent your purchases. The increased product of our manufactories and our captures have rendered it entirely unnecessary to make further purchases in that line.³ And besides the defeat of our State project for raising troops has made it still more unnecessary. Having however purchased, if it be not possible to recant, you need ship no further than Bermuda where I desire to store for the present except the clothing which I desire deposited with Mr. White's cargos for Crossan to bring in. The enormous freights need not be incurred whilst running a Steamer of our own. If you have not sold the Scrip for Turpentine & Rosin, and I hope you have not please with-draw it from the market immediately. Having secured a loan through Mr White amply sufficient for all possible purposes, it would be injurious in the extreme not to say foolish to appear further on the market. Should Mr. Saunders [*George N. Sanders*] feel himself damaged by such a course, I pledge myself to indemnify him justly and amply

You are instructed therefore to close out immediately and return home by the first steamer. If you have not sold your bonds, *dont sell;* if you are about selling dont consumate, and if you have sold recant if possible or get off as lightly as may be*. For the loan of Mr. White will quite cover the extent of the authority given me by the Legislature

I have received nothing from you or Mr. S., since you <left> /went/ out, except a *pipe* though I believe you both took my measure for some clothes which I sadly need. Have you sent any thing which has been lost?

I suppose you continue posted on our affairs. We have lost Vicksburg by starvation of the garrison and invaded Pa. defeating the enemy, capturing large numbers of prisoners and scaring the Dutch almost into a cocked hat. We listen daily for great news. God grant it may be *good.*

Mrs. McRae I see often—she is well & doubtless writes by the same chance with this

> Very Respectfully
> Your obt. servt.
> Z. B. Vance

*I dont mean by this for you to make any sacrifice of the state interest either of money or honor, but if things are in a condition to get off reasonably to do so.

> Z B V

¹See March 6, A&H:GP, and April 18, A&H:GLB.
²March 12, in this volume.
³Arms and clothing.

ZBV *to James A. Seddon*　　　　　　　　　　　　Duke:Sed

> State of North Carolina,
> Executive Department,
> Raleigh, July 10th. 1863.

Hon. James A. Seddon
Secretary of War

Dear Sir.

Miles Dobbins a private in Captain Normans Company Dunns battalion of cavalry¹ recently committed murder upon the body of Solomon Sparks in Yadkin county. I respectfully request that he be arrested and returned for trial. Christian Shone a conscript in said county is the principal witness against Dobbins and I also request that he may be permitted to remain at home until the trial in order that his evidence may be had in the cause

A special term of the court will be held for the trial of Dobbins as soon as he is arrested and returned

> With sentiments of great respect
> Your obedient servant
> Z. B. Vance

[1]From the brigade of General Albert G. Jenkins in western Virginia. See James R. Clairborne to John H. Winder, July 14, enclosed in Winder to ZBV, July 21, in this volume.

Proclamation by ZBV   A&H:GLB

By the Governor of North Carolina
A Proclamation

Whereas, for the protection of our people, as far as possible, against the evils of speculation, there continues to be necessity to prohibit the exportation of certain articles of our products beyond the limits of our State—

Now, therefore, I, Zebulon B. Vance, Governor of North Carolina do issue this Proclamation, continuing the Proclamation of June 8th. in force for thirty days from and after the 13th. instant, in regard to Cotton & Woolen Cloth, Cotton and Woolen Yarns, Leather and Shoes, subject to such exceptions &c. as have been expressed in my proclamations heretofore on the subject of exportation—

In witness, whereof, Zebulon B. Vance, Governor, Captain General, and Commander in Chief hath signed these presents and caused the great Seal of the State to be affixed.

Done at the City of Raleigh, this 10th. day of July, A D. 1863 and in the Year of American Independence the 87th.

Z. B. Vance

Jefferson Davis to ZBV   A&H:GP

[Telegram]

Richmond July 11 1863

Gov. Vance.

Your letter[1] received and shall have attention refering to reports from Eastern part of State, I have to request that if practicable, you bring into Service as many of the local defence of the militia troops as <may> have been organized.

Jeffn Davis

---

[1]July 9, in this volume.

Jefferson Davis to ZBV   A&H:GP

Richmond Va. July 14, 1863

His Excellency
Z. B. Vance
Raleigh No. Ca.

Governor:

I regret that an accident has so long prevented an answer to your letter of March 31st.[1] in reference to the enrolment of certain state and corporation officers in North Carolina.

But I trust that no serious embarrassment has resulted to you from my delay in replying, as the attention of the Chief of the Bureau of Conscription was promptly called to the matters discussed in your letter, and the Commandant of Conscripts for the State was ordered to defer to you in every case where it could be done without positive infraction of law.

In enforcing the enrolment of conscripts, it has been my desire to comply as far as possible with the views & wishes of the Governors of the several States, in all cases where there seemed to be any fair doubt as to the intention of Congress as expressed in the several Acts relating to this subject. But when the law-making power has plainly declared its will, the Executive has no discretion & must simply enforce the law.

In cases of individual hardship the President is authorized to interfere with an order of special exemption. But with regard to classes of citizens the case is different. The Congress has explicitly designated those classes whose continued occupations with their ordinary pursuits seemed necessary to the well-being of society; and has, at the same time, declared that the danger to the country from its armed enemies is so great as to demand the presence of all other citizens, within certain ages, in the field. If, after trial, their legislation appears to have been without proper regard to the true interests of the community, in forcing into the army classes of people whom a wiser policy would have retained at home, they will probably remedy the evil at future sessions. Meanwhile, I am not justified in interfering with a full execution of their enactments. Such a course would not only be an evasion of a fair trial of the wisdom of the laws, but would imperil the successful issue of the war by withholding from the army men who have been by the competent authority declared subject to military duty.

The Government has asserted no claim to conscribe the militia officers of the States in actual commission; and the Commandants of Conscripts have been so instructed. I have also fully recognized the exemption of all State Executive and Judicial officers not made liable to ordinary militia duty by the laws of the States themselves.

In the particular case of Constables and Justices of the Peace in North Carolina, about whose liability to service there were conflicting opinions, the enrolling officers were directed to suspend action until conference could be held with you, and the laws of the State could be examined.

I have not considered it within my power, under existing laws, to extend a general exemption to the police of the corporate towns. But, in some instances, organizations in the character of home guards have been allowed to remain free from conscription temporarily, on condition of rendering local military service when called on by the Commanding General. It was supposed that many of the policemen would become attached to these companies, and thus be enabled to attend to their ordinary duties during most of the time.

As some months have now elapsed since your letter was written, and as the officers of this Government have always been instructed to confer freely with you & to insist upon a rigid construction of the laws only where it appeared necessary, it is hoped that all difficulties have been satisfactorily adjusted.

> very respectfully & truly yours,
> Jeffn. Davis

¹In this volume.

Jefferson Davis to ZBV   A&H:GP

Richmond, Va. July 18, 1863

His Excellency
Governor Vance
&c &c &c

Sir.

I have the honor to acknowledge yours of the 6th inst,¹ in relation to the appointment of Major Bradford as Quartermaster in charge of the collection of the tax in kind in North Carolina.

I caused inquiry to be made as to the circumstances of Major Bradford's appointment and have been informed that at the time he received it there was urgent need of a competent officer for the tax service in North Carolina; that there was no applicant for the office from that State, and that Major Bradford's recommendations were ample as to character and qualifications.

It is also stated that Major B. although formerly of Norfolk Va. has been for some time a resident of North Carolina, and that it was in view of this fact; of his capacity; of the absence of any application by a citizen of North Carolina, and of the pressing necessity that the appointment should be made without delay,—that Major Bradford was commissioned to superintend the collection of the tax in kind in your State.

After the receipt of your letter which first informed me of the case I have conversed with the Secty. of War with a view <to> that not only this but every impediment to your successful career should be removed.

I am aware of the embarassments you may have in carrying out your patriotic efforts to aid the Confederate government in this struggle and relying on your capacity and energy to overcome them would be very far from willingly allowing any additional obstruction to be thrown in your way

> Very Respectfully
> & truly your's
> Jeffn. Davis

[1] In this volume.

Jefferson Davis to ZBV   A&H:GP

Richmond Va. July 18, 1863.

His Excellency:
Z. B. Vance
Raleigh No. Ca.

Governor:

I have the honor to acknowledge the receipt of your letter of the 9th. inst.[1] informing me of your efforts to raise the seven thousand men I recently called for, and asking me to receive as part of this number certain companies already organised by you for local defence.

The Secretary of War has been directed to receive the companies offered and to credit them to the State, in compliance with your request.

Your zeal and energy are so well known & so highly appreciated that I am induced to hope that you will succeed in organizing the full number called for, though you do not now expect to be able to do so. Your failure to obtain the desired legislation shows how slow our people are to realize the necessities of the country.

> very respectfully & truly your's
> Jeffn. Davis

[1] In this volume.

Peter Mallett to ZBV   A&H:GP

Conscript Office,
Camp Holmes, July 20th., 1863.

His Excellency
Governor Z. B. Vance,
Raleigh, N.C.

Sir:

I am directed by the Bureau of Conscription, at your request, to grant temporary exemption to Christian Shone until he can give evidence on the trial of Miless Dobbins.

You will please inform this office when the trial will take place, that the Enrolling Officer may be instructed to grant the exemption accordingly.

I have the honor to be,
Your Obt. servant,
Peter Mallett Col.
Comdt. of Conscripts for N.C.

[*Endorsed*] Ask Col. Cowles[1] when his court is held—

Z B V

[1]Josiah Cowles, businessman, former member of the council of state, and Yadkin County justice of the peace. *Dictionary of North Carolina Biography*, s.v. "Cowles, Josiah."

ZBV to George Little   A&H:GP

[*Telegram*]

Salisbury July 20 1863

Col. Geo Little[1]

Is Genl Fowle up for duty if /so/ tell him to communicate with me I will be at home at ten tomorrow what of the enemy[2]

Z. B. Vance

[1]Aide to ZBV.
[2]Raiding toward Rocky Mount in the east. Barrett, *Civil War in North Carolina*, 164–165.

John H. Winder to ZBV   A&H:VanPC

[*With enclosure*]

Head Qrs Dpt Head
Richmond July 21, 1863

His Excellency
Gov Z B Vance
Raleigh N.C.

Governor

Upon the receipt of your telegram of the 10th. inst,[1] regarding Miles Dobbins, I immediately instituted the desired inquiry

Hearing that the man was connected with Dunns Battn, I communicated with the Comdg officer /by sending a Police officer/ and the enclosed letter contains all the information I have been able to gain, relative to the matter.

Any further information will be promptly forwarded

Very Respectfully
Your obt servt
Jno. H Winder
Brig.' Gen'l

[1]Not extant.

[*Enclosure*]

James R. Clairborne to John H. Winder   A&H:VanPC

Hd. Qrs. 37th. Batta[lion]
Camp [near] Huntsville Va
July 14th. 1863.

Brig Genl. Winder—

Genl.

Mr. Reece has arrived with your orders to arrest one Miles Dobbins of Capt Normans company—This man Dobbins deserted his company on the 12th. of April 1863 whilst on a march in N. W. Va. and has not been heard from since. Capt Norman supposes that he is in the mountains of N. Carolina with Some twenty of the same company, who deserted with Miles Dobbins.

I was requested by the Sheriff of Yadkin Co. to arrest this man and have been keeping a sharp look out for him

I have the honor to be

Very Respectfully
Your obt. Servt
Jas. R. Claiborne
Major Commdg.
37 Battalion [*illegible*]
Jenkins Brigade

Samuel Cooper to ZBV   A&H:GP

Confederate States of America,
War Department,
Adjutant and Inspector General's Office,
Richmond, Va. July 22d. 1863.

His Excellency,
Governor Vance,
Raleigh, North Carolina.

Sir:

In reply to your letter of the 9th.,[1] I am directed by the President to say that the eight hundred men organized for local defence in Eastern North Carolina, and the "five or six small companies along the Tennessee border," will be received as part of the number called for from North Carolina upon the conditions mentioned.

The muster-rolls of the several companies should be forwarded to this office, for file. Upon their receipt, certificates will be furnished to the officers.

Very respectfully, Sir,
Your Obt. Servant
S. Cooper
Adjt. & Insp'r. Gen'l.

[Endorsed] File & copy

Z B V

[1] In this volume.

James A. Seddon to ZBV   A&H:GP

Confederate States of America,
War Department,
Richmond, Va. July 23d. 1863

His Excellency Z. B. Vance
Governor of North Carolina
Raleigh N.C.

Sir

You were informed on the 7th inst that your letter[1] requesting the detail of M. J. McSween as an army correspondent to accompany Genl Lee, as it was alleged that N.C. Troops do not receive the meed of praise justly due them, was

referred to Genl Lee for consideration, and your attention is now respectfully
called to the annexed copy of his reply.

> Very Respectfully
> Your Obdt Servt
> James A Seddon
> Secretary of War
>
> "Copy"
>
> Head Quarters Bunker Hill
> 18th July 1863

"I very much regret that an impression should prevail that injustice is done to
any portion of this army. I know of no case and have heard of none. If the official
reports of the officers commanding the troops cannot be believed or relied on I
know of no way of obtaining the truth. The plan proposed by Gov Vance I think
will work great evil and produce embarrassment to the service. I cannot recommend that it be adopted. It must then be extended to all the States and it can
readily be seen what would be the result. If the officers commanding the troops
do not tell the truth they should be removed."

> Respectfully submitted
> (signed)   R E. Lee
> Genl

¹July 3, in this volume.

Edward J. Hale to ZBV   A&H:VanPC

Private & Confidential

Fayetteville, July 24 1863.

My Dear Sir:

There is a vast deal of feeling, very earnest & bitter, in various parts of the
State, against the course that the Standard is pursuing. It is regarded by calm &
prudent men, dreadfully damaging to the cause. And I cannot dissent from the
general opinion. Can nothing be done? I have been exceedingly [loth] to see you
or your friends arrayed in open antagonism to that paper, because that would be
to <would> confirm its hostility, I <can> induce it to go greater lengths in the
course we deprecate. But I am really afraid that unless it can be induced to pause,
if not to retrace its steps, there will be a necessity for your letting it be known
on all suitable occasions, & in all proper ways, that you & your friends do not
only not concur with it but most decidedly condemn its course.

Some say that he [*William W. Holden*] ought to be arrested. That is all non-
sense. That his press should be silenced, [worse] still. But cannot the considerate

men of his party be induced to remonstrate *effectually* with him: at the same time
the considerate men of the State Journal party—such men as Barringer, /Mor-
decai/ [Manly], Bragg[1] (I suppose) &c. &c., might, it seems to me, be induced to
silence that paper & the [*Raleigh*] Register, whose vile attacks upon Holden have
been, as I think, the maine cause of all this trouble, goading him on to ceaseless
assaults upon the gov't for its truly scandalous treatment of No. Ca. I should
hope, if a truce could be arranged with these papers, to see all parties have time
to come to their senses.

If things go on as at present, I think we shall not only lose more than all the
great reputation we have earned in this war, but get into serious trouble at home.

I feel sure that you will keep your skirts clear of all taint of such a policy as
the Standard is advocating.

If you be forced to separate from it, & of course from the [*Raleigh*] Progress,
which is but its sister, can you find anybody who is fit to conduct a paper <a>
in Raleigh that you can resort to? You must have such a paper there. The five
now there <are> as at present conducted are *nuisances*. The Standard is the
only one of the <other> five that was ever otherwise.

You will of course see the propriety of holding this as *strictly confidential*. In a
matter about a press, I ought not to interfere, & would not but for the imminence
of the peril, & the excuse you gave me by your late application.

Yours truly,
E. J. Hale

[1]Rufus Barringer, lawyer, legislator, and Confederate general; George Washington Mordecai, lawyer, planter, and railroad executive; Charles Manly, lawyer and governor;
Thomas Bragg, lawyer, governor, U.S. senator, and Confederate cabinet member. All four
men were prewar unionists and believed secession to be unwise. *Dictionary of North Carolina Biography*, s.v. "Barringer, Rufus Clay"; "Mordecai, George Washington"; "Manly,
Charles"; "Bragg, Thomas."

Jefferson Davis to ZBV   A&H:VanPC

Confidential

Executive Office,
Richmond, 24 July, 1863.

His Excellency
Z. B. Vance,
Governor of the
State of North Carolina.

Dear Sir:
  A letter has just been received by the Secretary of State from one of the most
distinguished citizens of your State, containing the following passage:

"I have just learned that the Union or Reconstruction party proposes holding meetings throughout the State. Trouble is fast brewing here and I fear we shall soon have open resistance to the government under the leadership of that reckless politician Holden, Editor of the Standard."

This is not the first intimation I have received that Holden is engaged in the treasonable purpose of exciting the people of North Carolina to resistance against their government, and co-operation with the enemy, but I have never received any definite statement of facts as to his conduct beyond the assertion that his newspaper which I do not read is filled with articles recommending resistance to the constituted authorities.

I know not whether his hostility and that of his accomplices is directed against the Confederate Government alone, or embraces that of his State; nor am I aware whether he has gone so far as to render him liable to criminal prosecution.

If however the facts stated in the extract of the letter which I have quoted be true, (and the author is entitled to the fullest credit) the case is quite grave enough for me to consult with you on the subject, and to solicit from you such information and advice as you may be able to give me, for the purpose of such joint or separate action as may be proper to defeat designs fraught with great danger to our common country.[1]

I write you confidentially because there may be error or exaggeration in the reports about this man, and I would be unwilling to injure him by giving publicity to the charges if there be no foundation for them.

Very respectfully,
& truly your's
Jeffn. Davis

[1]In early August ZBV traveled to Richmond to confer with Davis about Holden and the peace movement. Yates, *Confederacy and Vance*, 87–88.

John Pool to ZBV   A&H:GP

Windsor—July 25th. 1863.

Gov. Vance—
Raleigh N.C.

Dear Sir:

Mr. Bond[1] is sent as special messenger to your Excellency by order of the Col. of Bertie County,[2] & I have been requested to write to you, by several of the most prominent citizens of the County, who assembled in this place today. Information has just reached us from several distinct sources, that it /is/ arranged to land a negro regiment, or perhaps two regiments, for the purpose of inciting & sustaining a servile insurrection in this county & in Hertford. The threatening condition of affairs here has excited my attention <my attention> for several weeks past, & I have thought of calling the attention of your Excellency to some alarming circumstances, & had, indeed, prepared a letter for that purpose, but have delayed sending it, partly, from a fear that my apprehensions might prove groundless & your Excellency unecessarily disturbed. But the information received, today, makes the communication containing speculations & merely general views, out of place.

This morning, a gentleman living on the Roanoke, says, that a messenger from Plymouth went to his house & gave him warning, requesting him to send the word to W. N. H. Smith by special messenger, & not trust the uncertainty of the mails—Shortly after, those who came from Coleraine, from Chowan river, brought news that the Yankees landed there, yesterday, & one of them told the same story to Mr. Jos. H. Etheridge,[3] privately—saying that while he was willing to fight for the Union, he disapproved any proceeding of the kind indicated. From another portion of the county, distantly seperated from the above points—near the mouth of the Cashie, Mr. Thos. Bailey,[4] reports that the same warning was brought to him by a person just from Plymouth. And this afternoon, another gentleman from the Roanoke comes in & reports that the same word has been brought to him from Plymouth. Yesterday, the Yankees landed at Mr. Wm. Sutton's,[5] on Salmon Creek, burned several of his buildings, destroyed property, & carried off his overseer—the only white person on the premises. They held communication with his negroes, but went off without carrying any of the negroes. Yesterday morning, when the only white man on my plantation went out, very early, he found the Yankees there in conversation with my negroes. They went off without carrying any of them—In the afternoon, they went to Coleraine, & held communication with the negroes there, & carried none away. Last night, the barn, stables, &c. on the farm of Dr Wilson,[6] of this village, were burned—They were several miles from town. Threats & warnings against other loyal citizens, have been reported to me, today. All con[cur], in regard to the movement of the slaves, that it is to occur between the 29th. inst. & the 2nd. of August. I have carefully weighed the circumstances surrounding these reports, & listened to the opinions & suggestions of intelligent gentlemen, today—& I really think, the matter ought to claim your prompt attention. I cannot presume to indicate any measure to the attention of your Excellency because I know nothing of the means at your disposal.

Yours most respectfully,
John Pool

P.S. I have concluded to send with this, a letter[7] to your Excellency, prepared some weeks ago, & referred to above—as it may give you some additional information of the condition of this locality.

Please, excuse this rather bungling manner of communicating that letter.

[1]Apparently Captain James Bond, Eighth Regiment North Carolina Militia. Bradley, *Militia Officers Roster*, 21.

[2]Jonathan J. Rhodes, Eighth Regiment North Carolina Militia. Bradley, *Militia Officers Roster*, 21.

[3]Farmer, Colerain vicinity. Eighth Census, 1860: Bertie County, Population Schedule.

[4]Thomas Bayley, farmer, Merry Hill vicinity. Eighth Census, 1860: Bertie County, Population Schedule.

[5]William T. Sutton, farmer, Merry Hill vicinity. Eighth Census, 1860: Bertie County, Population Schedule.

[6]Turner Wilson, physician and farmer. Eighth Census, 1860: Bertie County, Population Schedule.

[7]Pool to ZBV, July 15, A&H:GP.

ZBV to John H. Winder   Mich:Sch

State of North-Carolina,
Executive Department,
Raleigh, July 25, 1863

Brig Genl Winder
Richmond Va.

Genl,

Will you have the kindness to forward the enclosed letters[1] by the first flag of truce, and oblige the father of a very noble boy[2] who fell at Gettysburg.

I dont suppose it will do any good but his father is so anxious to secure his body by learning if possible where he was buried that he procured the writer to address a relative in Pa on the subject—and I write also.

Very respectfully
Yr obt svt.
Z. B. Vance

[1]Not extant.

[2]John Caldwell, son of Tod R. Caldwell. See Tod R. Caldwell to ZBV, June 8, and B. F. Wilkins to ZBV, September 3, in this volume.

ZBV to James A. Seddon   A&H:GLB

State of North Carolina
Executive Department
Raleigh July 25th. 1863

Hon. Jas. A. Seddon,
Secty of War

Dear Sir

A large number of deserters, say 1200 are in the mountains and inaccessible wilds of the West. I have found it impossible to get them out, and they are plundering and robbing the people Through their friends they have made me propositions to come out and enlist for defence of the State alone, Shall I accept it? The effect on the Army might be injurious, but they can never otherwise be made of service, or kept from devastating the country—If you advise favorably, I think I can get at least 1000 effective men. Please answer soon

> Very respectfully
> Your obt Servt
> Z. B. Vance

ZBV to James A. Seddon   A&H:GLB

> State of North Carolina
> Executive Department
> Raleigh July 26th. 1863

Hon. J. A. Seddon
Secty of War
Richmond Va

Sir

Your note[1] in reference to the permission asked by me to send M. J. McSween to the army of N. Va. as a newspaper correspondent, with Genl Lee's reply refusing the same has been received—

It seems strange that Genl Lee and yourself should so utterly misconstrue my meaning—I had no reference of course to the "official reports" of our army officers, as doing injustice to N.C. Troops. *They* are rarely furnished to the newspapers—never except by consent of the War Dept.—I simply desired to correct as far as possible, the daily neglect and frequent slanders of a portion of the Richmond press, which has its corps of reporters in every department of the Army—by sending a similar corps to report for the press of this State—But I know that without Genl Lee's permission, they could not move with the Army or have access to any sources of reliable information. The Richmond press allege as an excuse for not speaking of N.C. Troops, that there are no correspondents from this State to report &c, and this I was in part trying to remedy—I asked for the detail of McSween, not for the purpose of giving him an official character, but simply because he is an accomplished scholar and in such feeble health, that he will soon die or be discharged from service—

I only desired Sir, in other words that newspaper correspondents from N.C. should be allowed to attend an Army, with the same protection, and the same access to information as I learn is given to others. But as Genl Lee objects to it and has seen proper to think that I object to official reports, which have never yet been published, I beg leave to withdraw the request.

The troops from N.C. can afford to appeal to history: I am confident that they have but little to expect /from/ their associates. Just after the battle of Chancellorsville notwithstanding N.C. troops furnished one half of all the killed and wounded, it was reliably reported throughout this State that Genl Lee had refused applications for furloughs, to our wounded soldiers, on the ground that they would not return when recovered—If such an endorsement was in fact made officially it would of course be credited by the historian, and injustice be done to the very men, who won that victory. The Richmond Enquirer in recent article, on the authority of its special correspondent charges our defeat at Gettysburg upon the cowardice and incapacity of the N.C. troops composing Heth's division.

Such things are hard to bear, if true, and if untrue we are denied the right of having correspondents in the Army to correct them, and must wait for the publication of official reports, which may or may not be published—

How such things can contribute to the success of the cause I am unable to say

> Very respectfully
> Your obt. Servt
> Z. B. Vance

¹July 23, in this volume.

ZBV to Edward J. Hale   A&H:Hale

Confidential.

> State of North-Carolina,
> Executive Department,
> Raleigh, July 26, 1863.

E J Hale Esq

My dear Sir,

Your note¹ recd. and as the merchants say "contract, [posted]". I assure you I am deeply concerned at the turn things have taken. I asked Mr. Graham, Gov Swain & others to talk to Holden but it has done little good—He pretends & maybe really is of opinion that 4/5ths. of the people are ready for reconstruction & says he is only *following* the people not leading them—This is not true in fact he is responsable for half this feeling at least, if it exists; of course the driver sits behind the team & yet may be said to follow his horses.

I had a long talk with him yesterday and requested him to say in his paper that he was not my organ in the matter and did not speak my sentiments He promised to do so. I think it all important that the people should know my sentiments, so [*illegible*] should there be a split, he may not be committing to him any persons under the idea that he was *my* friend, which I think it likely accounts for much of his popularity.

I dont see much help for a split I fear it must come, tho' Holden says he will not make it I wish very much you would write to our prominent men to use their influence with him. Applications to such men as Barringer & others you name I regard as useless—They are incapable of subordinating party prejudices for *any* purpose. I have talked to most of them and the only use they made of my information was to try to array Holden & myself against each other and write to Richmond urging Holdens arrest! I have no more faith in their patriotism than Holdens—not as much in fact.

I will write you again from time to time—I don't think it possible to get an Editor who could do any good in the present crisis—

Yours truly
[Z B *Vance*]

¹July 24, in this volume.

James A. Seddon to ZBV   A&H:GP

Confederate States of America,
War Department,
Richmond, Va. July 28, 1863.

His Excellency Z. B. Vance,
Governor of North Carolina,
Raleigh, N.C.

Sir,
    I have made an arrangement with the Quarter Master General by which Major Bradford, whose appointment as Quarter Master to superintend the collection of the tax in kind in North Carolina has caused some dissatisfaction,¹ <should> / will/ be removed to another field of duty. I shall thus have the opportunity of appointing some other person, who I hope will be more acceptable to yourself and the people of your State, and <*illegible*> to be assured /of/ that, I shall be pleased if you will recommend one or more persons for the position, from whom a selection may be made by the Department.

With high regard & respect
Your obdt. servt.
James A Seddon
Secretary of War

¹See ZBV to Jefferson Davis, July 6, in this volume.

Daniel Locklar to ZBV   A&H:GP

Laurinburg Richmond Co N.C
July 28th. 1863

His Excellency the Governor

Sir

If your highness will condesend to reply to my feble Note, you will confer a great favor on me, and relieve me of my troubles, my case is this I am a free man of Color, and has a large family to support, there is a man living near me, who is an Agent of the State Salt-workes appointed by [John M.] Worth, or is said to be, he took all we colored men last winter to make Salt, he is now after us to make Barrels for the State Salt-works, Comes at the dead hours of night and carries us off wherever he thinks proper, gives us one dollar and fifty Cents pr day and we find ourselves, I cannot support my family at that rate and pay the present high prices for provisions, <illegible> I can support my family very well if I were left at home to work for my neighbors they pay me or sell me provisions at the the [sic] old price for my labor, this agent says he has the power by law, to carry us where he pleases and when he pleases, if that be a law and he is ortherised by law to use that power, I am willing to su/b/mit to his Calls, for I am perfectly /willing/ to do for our Country whatever the laws requires of me, but if there be no such law and this Agent taking this power within himself perhaps speculating on the labor of <illegible> the free colored men and our families suffering for bread, I am not willing to submit to such, please let me know if this Agent *the power to use me as he does*

Daniel, Locklar

[Endorsed] He has no such authority

Z B V

ZBV to James A. Seddon   A&H:GLB

State of North Carolina
Executive Department
Raleigh, July 28th. 1863

Hon. J. A. Seddon
Secty of War
Richmond Va

I beg leave to suggest most respectfully the propriety of your forbidding positively the officers of the Government engaging in speculations on private account. Many of them have been engaged in it here to the great detriment of the community and the public service.

In addition to the temptation it offers for the misapplication of the public funds, it is corrupting in its tendencies assists in upholding prices, and excites universal prejudice in the community. It should be absolutely prohibited in my opinion—Pardon me,

> Very respectfully
> Your obt. Servt.
> Z. B. Vance

Peter Mallett to ZBV   A&H:GP

> Conscript Office,
> Camp Holmes, July 29th., 1863.

His Excellency
Gov. Z. B. Vance,
Raleigh, N.C.

Sir:
   Having frequent applications for details from Salt Commissioners of different Counties, I beg respectfully to call your attention to the fact that this Office has already furnished 500 for State Salt works, and 63 for county Commissioners.
   In consequence of the great demand for men to fill up our skeleton regiments in the field, I shall be under the necessity of declining further applications for this purpose, unless specially ordered by the Superintendent at your request.—
   I am, Governor,

> Very respectfully,
> Your obt. servant,
> Peter Mallett Col.
> Commdt. of Conscripts for N.C.

[*Endorsed*] File

ZBV

Philip Hodnett to ZBV   A&H:GP

> Caswell County N.C.
> July 30, 1863

To Hon. Governor Vance
   The undersigned respectfully represents to Your Excellency that much of the wheat in Caswell is rotten, from the Two months rain, which still continunes, the oat crop is a verry short one The corn cannot yeald more than half a crop; all the important Items of our crop has faild, except Irish Potatoes, which are

verry Good. The old supply of Grain is nearly exhausted, and many persons are complaining that they cannot buy with money. I hear threats openly made to resort to mob law to obtain Food, and there can be no doubt that civil society is in danger of being disturbed if not Broken up. It is but right and proper that the Chief Magistrate of our beloved State should be brought acquainted with these facts.

The undersigned now an old Man, a native of the South, and for the last 38 years a Citizen of Caswell County, who has never in his life had any connexion with politics, solelmly beleaves that the time has come for the orthorities of the State to take these matters into their serious consideration. The Confederate Tax in Kind will produce dissatistion if not oppersition from the people. There seems to be no escape for us from these sore troubles but to make peace with the North on the best terms we can, and I solemly beleave that three fourths of the people of Caswell desire peace now, while we have power enough to assure our constitutional rights

The extreme men in this county would represent these things in a different light from what I have done, but experience has shown that they are not safe councellors—

I am but a plain Farmer and may have made a blunder in writing these lines; but having an abideing desire for the Good of our State and for the whole South, have done so.

> I am with the highest Respect
> Philip Hodnett

Augustus S. Merrimon to ZBV   A&H:VanPC

> Asheville N.C.
> July 31st. 1863.

His Excellency
Gov. Z. B. Vance
Raleigh, N.C.

Governor;

I write to remind you to send me the affidavits &c., which Judge Ruffin promised to send you some time ago, in reference to the allegations against L't. Col. Keith. I shall read them with a view to determine what witnesses are most important for the State.

I take the liberty to state to you, that Gen'l Edney is again making an effort to induce the President to suspend the execution of the Conscript law in this Congressional District.[1] He will probably call upon you: On examining *his* Pe't. or Memorial, you will notice in it a *political complexion*, which I could not and did not, endorse. I however, gave him a statement, which you can examine and which I am quite sure takes a proper view of the matter therein mentioned. I am satisfied that no more men ought to be taken from this section, unless others are sent. There seems to be a settled purpose on the part of a *large* portion of those subject to Conscription here, not to go into the regular service. This grows out of apprehension of danger to their families and property at home and the general gloom and despondency that now over-spreds the Country. These men however, I feel sure, would do good Militia Service and police duty.

I assure you, things are not as they ought to be. A *restive spirit* is at work and may develop itself in an alarming way at any time.—I don't approve of the idea of sending an armed police into this section from the Army. There are those who would gladly seize upon an opportunity to article the approaching election by means of *force*. It would be infinitely better, to rely upon an effective "Home Guard" organization to preserve order and suppress out-laws and capture deserters.

I regret to have to say, that there is little prospect of reconcileing the conflicting claims among our political friends who want to get to Congress. I fear a *feud* will spring up among them that will be hard to quell. I fear nothing good will spring out of the Contemplated Convention at Hendersonville. It would indeed, be shameful for this District to send [*Samuel L.*] Love to Congress.

If you give Gen'l. Edney any thing for the President, contradict the statement, that a large part of our people are disloyal. Such a statement is wholly false and slanderous.

I am &c. Yrs. Truly,
A. S. Merrimon

[1]See James A. Seddon to ZBV, March 26, 1863 (no. 2), in this volume.

ZBV to James A. Seddon   A&H:GLB

State of North Carolina
Executive Department
Raleigh. August 1st 1863

Hon. J. A. Seddon,
Secty of War

Dear Sir

Yours[1] is recd. informing me that Maj. Bradford, Controlling Q. M. of the State would be removed to another field of duty, and asking me to recommend a gentlemen for the appointment.

Having anxiously sought the removal of Major Bradford for reasons purely prudential. I would not desire to run the risk of having them impugned by recommending any one for his successor. I expect however to visit Richmond on

Monday next, and if desired will give the names of several gentlemen for your information

> Respectfully
> Your obt Servt
> Z. B. Vance

¹July 28, in this volume.

James A. Seddon to ZBV   A&H:VanPC

> Confederate States of America,
> War Department,
> Richmond, Va. August 4 1863

His Excellency
Z B Vance
Governor of North Carolina
Raleigh N.C.

Sir

In reply to your letter of the 28th ult,¹ I have the honor to state, that the Acts of Congress and the Army Regulations alike prohibit officers of the Quarter Master and Commissary departments, either directly or indirectly from being concerned in the purchase or sale of articles intended for, making a part of, or appertaining to public supplies, or in making any gain for negotiating business in their departments.

The Department cannot doubt that there has been abuse in these Departments, but the investigations that have been set [o]n foot have been singularly unproductive of results. The cases of conviction have been but few, and in those cases the offence proved has fallen far short of the enormities charged on the department officers generally.

Any case of guilt will be the subject of examination whenever it may be reported, and any information apparently calling for investigation will be gladly examined

> Very Respectfully
> Your Obdt Sevt
> James A Seddon
> Secretary of War

[*Endorsed*] File

Z B V

¹In this volume.

John White to ZBV   A&H:GP

London Augt. 7/63

Gov. Z B Vance

Sir

I was very glad to learn to day from a gentleman recently arrived here from Wilmington of the safe arrival of the S.S. "Ad-Vance" Since her departure from England I have shipd. some goods to Bermuda by the "Harkaway" & "Nebula", the latter I fear will not reach there in time for the 2nd. trip of the "Ad-Vance." Messr. Collie & Co. have chartered a schooner for me which will be ready to sail on Monday, her cargo is made up of goods, mostly, for the State. She takes a few tons for the Confederate Govt. & a few tons for the firm Mr. W. Hargrave White represents. I have now ready some 50 or 60 tons more than she can take, which I will forward by first vessel up for that port, or if I can arrange to get goods enough to fill another small vessel in ten or twelve days will charter another. I have now however expended more money than I have been able to realize on the Sale of the Cotton Bonds I am relying on a bill of lading of a good cargo of Cotton, at Bermuda by the "Ad-Vance" which I trust has safely arrived there before this. I am extremely anxious to forward now, as much as possible, that they may reach home before cold weather commences—

I feel however, that I am very much crampd. for funds. Our recent reverses has sent the Confederate cotton loan down to a very great discount, & it has also had the effect to deter Capitalists from buying the N.C. cotton bonds. The whole amount issued is £150000 Sterling but not quite £100000 has yet been disposed of.

The invoices for the goods shipd. by the "Harkaway" & "Nebula" have been forwarded to you. I have also directed the invoices of the goods now shipd. to be sent forward by the regular Mail to Bermuda Via of Halifax N.S. hope all may get Safely to hand

I am Your obt. Servt.

Jno. White

P.S. I forgot to mention that in the invoice from Turner Hyde & Co. of a lot of shoes an allowance of 1/- pr pair is made in consequence of their not fully coming up to sample and representation

The invoices of all the goods first intended to go by this shipment are to day forwarded to you from Manchester, which will include the 50, or 60 tons more than she can take, duplicates will again be sent by first Mail after next shipment.

J. W.

S. S. Bingham to ZBV   A&H:GP

Concord Aug 10th. 1863

Gov. Vance,

Dear Sir:

I take the liberty, as one of your most ardent supporters, of addressing you on the subject of the peace-meetings which are now being held throughout the State. Any of those meetings, whose resolutions look to reconstruction, meet with little response here.

Our people, (unless I am much mistaken) are opposed, out & out, to reconstruction. We ask nothing more, nor will take anything else, at present, than entire separation.

We do, however, insist upon the great right of the writ of "Habeas Corpus"— that the military should be subordinate to the civil authority—that the decision of our State courts should be respected and that North Carolinians should be appointed to offices to be exercised in the State. If these points are observed by the Confederate government, there can be no difficulty here. We are a loyal people—though no secessionists—and will stand by you & the government. I hope you will pardon my impertinence in addressing you. The condition of the country is my only excuse.

Yours truly
S. S. Bingham M.D.

[Endorsed] File

Z B V

Proclamation by ZBV   A&H:GLB

By the Governor of North Carolina
A proclamation.

Whereas, it appears to me that the necessities of our people still require the continuance of the prohibition heretofore extended by proclamation to the exportation of certain articles from the State—

Now, therefore, I, Zebulon B. Vance, Governor of North Carolina do issue this Proclamation, continuing the Proclamation of July 10th., inforce for thirty days from and after the 12th. inst. in regard to the exportation of Cotton and Woolen Cloth, Cotton and Woolen Yarns, Leather and Shoes, subject to the exceptions &c., expressed heretofore—

In witness whereof Zebulon B. Vance, Governor, Captain-General and Commander in Chief hath signed these presents & caused the great seal of the State to be affixed

Done at the city of Raleigh, this 10th. day of August A.D. 1863 and in the Eighty Eighth year of our Independence.

Z. B. Vance

Richmond M. Pearson to ZBV   A&H:GP

Richmond Hill August 11th. 1863

To his excellency Governor Vance:

Dear Sir,

In the last few days I have had two applications for writs of habeas corpus presenting the same question, on the very same state of facts, that was decided by me in the matter of Irvin,[1] & in the matter of Meroney,[2] & decided by the superior court in the matter of Bryan[3] & many other cases at June term 1863—[4]

I am informed that Left [Lt.] Little the enrolling officer for the district, ordered the militia officers to make the arrests, on the ground, that he was instructed by the secretary of war not to regard the above decisions unless the party should be discharged upon writs of habeas corpus.

I will take the liberty of suggesting for your consideration, whether these instructions should not be made the subject of earnest remonstrance on your part to the president of the confederate states, as obviously in violation of the rights of citizens of our state, & disrespectful to the judicial department of the state government, & certainly not to have been expected, after the solemn decision of our supreme court, upon full argument & notice to the president.—

There is another view of the subject to which in behalf of the supreme court,— as chief justice, I feel it to be my duty to call your attention. The militia officers under your instructions to obey the orders of the enrolling officers, are required to do an act, which is oppressive to our citizens, because altho entitled to exemption, they are forced to go to the army, or to be at the expense & inconvenience of suing out a writ, (if they have an opportunity to do so)—an act, which is unlawful & violates "the peace & dignity of the state," whereby the militia officer is subjected to the payment of the costs of the proceedings under the writ of habeas corpus, is subjected to the action of the party for damages, & is liable to indictment unless he can be secured, on the ground that the confederate government "avers the act" which in the case of a foreign government would be casus belli—[5] & in case of the citizen's own government presents an anomily in the history of a free people. And an act by which, the executive of the State is made accessory to what is obviously disrespectful to the judges & courts of the state.

I trust you will pardon the freedom with which I have expressed my sentiments—but really, after reading the correspondence between the secretary of war & your excellency, on the subject of the judicial tribunals of the state, I am fearful, that the independence of the judiciary cannot be maintained, unless all encroachments are met with firmness, in [limine],.[6]

very respectfully
yours &c. &c.,
R. M. Pearson

[*Endorsed*] Col. Barnes will please answer that I anticipated his advice & made Mr. Seddon promise to revoke when at Richmond &c

Z B V

[1]See Peter Mallett to ZBV, May 18 (with enclosure), in this volume.

[2]*In re Meroney, North Carolina Reports* 60 (1863):61. For a discussion of the case, see Mitchell, *Legal Aspects of Conscription and Exemption,* 43–44.

[3]*In re* [J. C.] *Bryan, North Carolina Reports* 60 (1863):1; Mitchell, *Legal Aspects of Conscription and Exemption,* 40–43.

[4]For an indication of the number, see Hamiltion, "North Carolina Courts and the Confederacy," 369.

[5]Cause for war.

[6]Apparently meaning "in the beginning."

——————

ZBV to Sion H. Rogers   A&H:GP

State of North-Carolina,
Executive Department,
Raleigh, Augst. 11, 1863.

Col. Rogers
Atto. Genl, N.C.

Dr. Sir,

Will you please to examine the various acts of the Legislature & ordenances of the Convention relating to the manufacture of salt and give me your opinion as to the right of the County Commissioners or agents to give one part of their counties salt for hauling the other.

I refer you to the enclosed letter[1] of Mr. Woodfin, Agent at Saltville Va.

Very respectfully
Yr obt. svt.
Z B Vance

[1]July 29, A&H:GP.

ZBV to Edward J. Hale   A&H:Hale

State of North-Carolina,
Executive Department,
Raleigh, Augst. 11, 1863

E J Hale Esq

My dear Sir,

I returned from Richmond on Saturday—was much gratified with my visit indeed—I plainly told the President of the cause of his [*illegible*] popularity in this State and the injustice done us by his appointments and gave him a fair and unvarnished statement of affairs here—He promised to remove all objectionable [men] and almost gave me a *carte blanche* for the redress of grievances here—I trust things will be better now that we are understood at Richmond.

I believe however the split with Holden is decreed of the gods—I have made up my mind to it and am prepared for it any day—tho' I dont intend to "precipitate" it. He is infatuat[*torn*] [*burned*] concerted and determine[d] [*burned*] his course th[at] [*torn*] war should [ensue]. He is for submission, reconstruction or any thing else that will put him back under Lincoln & stop the war—and I might add—punish his [old] friends & [co labororers] the Secessionists—

Pitch into them—Cry aloud and spare not—My life popularity and everything shall go into this contest.

Yours most truly
Z B. Vance[1]

Confidential

[1]The letter has been torn, burned, and faded by water.

ZBV to William A. Graham   A&H:GraPC

Confidential

State of North-Carolina,
Executive Department,
Raleigh, August 13th. 1863.

My Dear Sir:

I beg to call your attention to the proceedings of many meetings in various parts of the state, in favour of *peace*—Under all the circumstances, I consider them *ruinous*, in the last degree.

They will cause the army to melt away by desertion, will create, perhaps, dissensions & civil war at home, and will defeat any & all efforts for peace, unless it be on the basis of absolute submission to our enemies—which is all that has ever been offered us—They will in short serve no purpose whatever, except to encourage our enemies, ruin our army, & hasten our subjugation—With these views, which I have not time to elaborate, my administration will take ground against any such unfortunate & premature movements, and I desire, as far as possible, to know how far, I will be sustained by *my friends* & former supporters—With this view I earnestly invite an expression of your opinion & advice, fully, freely & confidentially given—

I am anxious, at the same time, /not/ to be misunderstood as to this important issue.

No living man is more anxious for peace than I am, whenever it can, by any possibility, be obtained upon the basis of separation & our independence—I shall only oppose those clamours for peace, originating in a desire for reconstruction, or which being raised in the hour of our adversity, & in the absence of any proposition from the North, can only mean submission & a giving up of the contest.

Please, at your early leisure, give me your opinion & the sentiments of your community—

> Very Truly yours
> Z. B. Vance

Jonathan Worth to ZBV   A&H:GP

> Treasury Department
> Raleigh. Aug. 17th. 1863.

Govr. Vance

Dear Sir
I have now in the Treasury

in Con. currency	$1,650,000
in certificates for Cont. Bonds	1,289,000
in fundable N.C. Treas. notes	650,000
	3,589,000

and a large amount,—probably half a million of the taxes not yet paid in—Besides this, the Confederacy owes this State, according to the report of the board of claims, made to the last regular session of this Genl. A., between four & five millions of dollars which is now being audited at Richmond, P. H. Winston jr. being the agent of the State who reports a favorable prospect of getting the claim in caution for asking the next Congress for an appropriation to pay it.

This plethora of the Treasury has arisen from sources not foreseen by the Genl. A. at its regular session, which authorises the issue of Treasury notes, (not fundable till 1866, now worth 50 per cent more than Confederate Currency), to the amount of $3,000,000, and treasury notes not fundable to the amount of

$1,500,000. On the 1st. of January last the issue of these Treasury notes secured to furnish the best and most reliable means of meeting the drafts on the Treasury, then greatly exceeding its available means. As it takes many months to get the necessary engraving & printing done, and it was very difficult to get suitable paper, I made a contract at once for the preparation of these notes, now nearly completed. I have issued only an inconsiderable amount of them, and am now issuing only the fractional parts of a dollar and in sufficient number of the larger denominations to pay the counties in possession of the enemy the appropriation for the support of the families of indigent soldiers. This will require less than $100,000.

The Confederate notes & certificates for bonds are greatly in excess of the probable wants of the Treasury. Of the probable demands your excellency however has much better means of judging than I have, as all of them of very considerable importance arise from the expeditures of the State for clothing our troops & other military expenditures. As to the amount of drafts on State accounts State Treasurer knows nothing, either as to the amount, or the time when they will be presented, but I presume they are not likely to exceed, for the next 8 months, the amount drawn for the last 8 months. If the supply of clothing from Europe continues to succeed payment will be made for the same in cotton, much of which the State has on hand, and the Treasury will be re-imbursed from the Con. Govt., the goods being estimated at their value in Confederate currency, whereby the present redundancy of money will be greatly augmented.

It becomes necessary to inquire how this money can be used to the best advantage of the State.

I think no part of it can be used to pay the debts of the State. An act of the last regular session of the Genl. A. directs me out of the money due from the Con. Govt., when collected, to pay the 8 per cent bonds of the State, which are payable at the pleasure of the State, unless the holders will exchange them for our 6 per cent bonds, running 30 years. Not a holder of the 8 per cent bonds will receive payment in the present currency. I fear they will not exchange bonds. So none of the bonded debt can be paid.

The State owed about $3,000,000, on the 1 Jan. last, to the Banks by way of temporary loan. They loaned nearly all this sum to the State, they say, in their own currency, which they cannot pay with Con. currency. It would be suicide to accept payment in the present currency, and dishonest in the State to insist on paying it in currency worth about 1/4 th. part as much as the money they furnished us. Most of this debt I have paid in our 30 year bonds, under the act authorising me, out of the deferred debt due the State from Con Govt. or by the sale of our State bonds, to pay this debt to the Banks. As our State bonds, when the act passed, were worth about par in Con. currency, I offered them to the Banks at par. Most of them accepted them with great reluctance. Those which have declined to receive the bonds, would not receive currency. So no part of the money in the Treasury can be used to pay the debts of the State.

It is true we have a large amount in certificates for 7 per cent. Con. bonds, but this investment was not made for the interest but as a means of exchanging the old for the new issues of Con. notes. I suppose no one, in any contingency, unless he be a man whose ardor silences his reason, expects the debts of the Confederacy can ever be paid in full. I would deem it inexpedient to say this to the public, yet every day's observation shows this is the universal opinion. Its present value does not arise from any expectation of its redemption, but from the belief of the holder that he can buy with it something desirable, at some extravagant price—and still more from a consciousness that patriotism forces us to sustain it as a currency.

In view of all these things I think the best we can do, will be to invest a large part of it in the purchase of cotton as quick as possible, to be put up in the interior, in the care of men every where to be found, who would take care to protect from the weather. Whether this can be done, under existing legislation, I do not know—but if not, I think the responsibility should be assumed until the meeting of the Genl. A.

I have written this long letter to you shawdowing out my views, because you are always surrounded by such a crowd and such press of business, that I can find no chance to have an interview without danger of annoying you. When you shall have read it, I shall be glad to have an interview with you at such time as may suit you.

> Yours very truly
> Jona. Worth Pub Tr.

[*Endorsed*] File—

Z B V

Jefferson Davis to ZBV   A&H:GP

Richmond, Va, August 19, 1863

His Excellency
Z. B. Vance
Governor of N. Car.

Sir.

In the action of the 1st. of July near Gettysburg the sharpshooters of Brig. Genl. Ramseur's brigade under command of Lt. F. M. Harney[1] 14th N. Car. Vols. dispersed the 150th. Penn. Regt. That gallant officer with his own hands wrested the standard from the color bearer of the Penn. Regt, and soon afterwards fell mortally wounded.

Genl. Ramseur in communicating the above particulars informed me that it was Harneys last request that the flag should be "presented in his name to the President".

The wish of the dying hero has been complied with. The flag is in my possession and will be treasured by me as an honorable memento of the valor and patriotic devotion which the soldiers of North Carolina have displayed on many hard fought fields.

I have thought it due to the lamented officer, with whose family I have not the advantage of being acquainted, to communicate these circumstances to you as the Chief Magistrate of his State, and to express through you to his State, his comrades and his family the sincere sympathy I feel with them for the loss of one so worthy of their admiration and esteem.

Such deeds illustrate a people's history, justify a people's pride, and sustain a country's hope.

I remain
very respectfully & truly yours
Jeffn. Davis

[1]Frank M. Harney, Fourteenth Regiment North Carolina Troops. Manarin and Jordan, *North Carolina Troops*, 5:445.

ZBV to William A. Graham   A&H:GraPC

[With enclosure]

State of North-Carolina,
Executive Department,
Raleigh, Aug 19, 1863.

Gov. Graham

My dear Sir,

I take the liberty of enclosing you a letter which I had prepared for publication—I showed it to Holden who begged me to submit it to you, promising to abide by your opinion of it—

Please advise me whether it should appear in its present form or not, and make freely such criticism or such alterations as you may think wise and the great <advantage> importance of the subject will justify—Your suggestions will be considered as confidential of course—Please return as soon as possible.[1]

Very truly
Z. B. Vance

[1]Graham returned the letter to ZBV with the recommendation that the governor moderate its tone. See Graham to ZBV, August 21, 1863, in Williams and Hamilton, *Papers of Graham*, 5:522–523.

[*Enclosure*]

ZBV to John H. Haughton   A&H:VanPC

Executive Office,
Raleigh, 17th. Augst.

John H. Haughton Esq[1]

My dear Sir,

Your letter of the 15th.[2] is recd., and I take the first moment allowed me by pressing business to reply.

I feel no hesitation or delicacy whatever in giving you my opinions fully & freely in regard to our present condition, believing it /to be/ the right of the people to demand and the duty of their servants to grant such information at any time.

You ask my opinion more especially "as to the best means of obtaining a speedy, lasting just & honorable peace". National disputes can of course only be settled by negotiations or by war, by reason or by *brute force*. The former method requires the assent & concordance of both parties, and either party refusing to negotiate can force the other into hostilities, or an absolute abandonment of all its pretensions. This I conceive was precisely our case in the beginning of our troubles. The claim of the Southern states to withdraw from the union and form a separate government for themselves was deemed so inadmissible by the Federal government that no proposition whatever to negotiate would be listened to. Commissioners from the seceding states were even refused an audience of the Federal authorities. War therefore, or a total abandonment of all claim to the right of separation was the only *alternative*—Declining to yield this right / (whether, <this right> revolutionary or constitutional it matters not now/ the States then <out> /seceded/ prepared for war and the President of the United States called for volunteers to crush them into submission. North Carolina re-fused to furnish her quota of troops to murder her Southern brethren, <went out of> /severed the tie that bound her to/ the union by the unanimous voice of the peoples' delegates & solemnly pledged her blood & treasure to the common course of Southern independence. This was the issue plain & unmistakeable, then—the terms of the North were, *lay down your arms & submit;* <the terms> /those/ of the South—*let us alone.* The whole world understood it. Is it not the same today? If changed at all it is only that the North now demands more— *submission* and *emancipation of our slaves,* constituting one half the entire wealth of our country. There is therefore no escape from the conclusion, that should the North cry *peace,* it would indicate an intention to yield <the> /its/ claims <of the South>, and should the South cry *peace* it would imply submission to the North. Are we ready for this? Have the stout hearts of our soldiers and the patient sufferings of /our/ people already reached that valley of humileation which good old Bunyan located but one stage from the valley of the Shadow of Death?

God knows my dear Sir, that I would gladly lay down my life to restore peace to my country on terms of honour and safety, and would prefer the distinction to all the honors a grateful people could heap upon me. But as the matter now stands and has stood from the beginning, I can only look upon propositions of peace coming from us, no matter how pure and patriotic the motive which induces them, as involving national dishonor, ruin and disgrace. I can well appreciate the feeling of those who say they desire to talk and fight at the same time <*illegible*> /erroneous/ as I conceive it to be under all the circumstances. I can sympathise deeply with their sufferings under the desolating scourge of civil war waged with such bloody & vindictive cruelty, and do not wonder at their seeking for relief. But how /how any one can think there <*illegible*> is now/ any prospect for an honorable peace by negotiations <can now be sure>, I am at a loss to know. But recently Vice President Stevens was sent to seek an interview with the <Conf> Federal authorities to see if some more human method of conducting the war could not be devised. Even this mission of mercy & civilization was treated with <scorn> /indifference/ and he was sent back without a chance to consult the proper authorities. How much better would another embassy fare, on a mission still more important?

Suppose the state should be unanimous in the determination to make propositions to our enemies, how could it be done? <Where, when> /To whom,/ and *what* should we propose? Why sir the whole thing is <perfectly absurd> / out of the question/, except upon the supposition that we desire to submit <or reconstruct>. Then indeed the way would be easy and obvious; <[In truth] I have no doubt but that this is the intention of the knowing and> /and *there may* be/ a designing few, who desire to take advantage of the suffering and patriotic many to lead them into this enevitable ruin with hopes of peace. I trust in God my countrymen may not be led blindfold to their destruction. What would be the result of submission? To say nothing of the question of honor, it implies with absolute certainty the abolition of slavery and the turning loose of four million blacks in our midst; the confiscation of our property, the hanging of enough of our principal citizens to sate the Northern appetite for slaughter, the imposition of inordinate tariffs and a public debt greater than that of any nation on earth— In short the fate of the conquered, with the fierce and vindictive passions engendered by civil strife goading on our conquerors, is what we should expect.

Reconstruction if possible, would be little better; but it is a physical and moral imposility. As soon would I think of resurrecting the bones of our gallant soldiers scattered from Gettysburg to New Orleans and invest them with living flesh, as to undertake <reconstructing> /the task of restoring/ <an> /the/ union /as it once was/ founded on mutual good will and sustained by a constitution limiting the powers and defining the rights of each member. That mutual good will has /now/ given way to fierce hatred and bloody hostility, and th<at>e / old/ constitution torn into a thousand shreds and laughed at as waste papers. You might indeed reconstruct the territory of the old union, but the soul, the living principal of accord and nationality will not be there. And this too would for a time give our afflicted country peace, <after a fashion> /such as it would be/. Our slaves have *peace*, and could we but humble ourselves to their lowly condition we might enjoy it—The prisoner has peace in his dungeon, and if his soul be sufficiently ignoble may learn to hear complacently the rattle of his chains. Such I feel assured, is not the peace the brave and high minded people of N.C. want—With whom would we again enter into this national wedlock, and take upon ourselves these ties of /unity &/ common fellowship? With men who have slaughtered our sons & brothers in battle, murdered our citizens in cold blood, burnt our homes into cinders, stolen our property and inflicted upon our mothers /sisters/ and daughters the crowning outrage of humanity, and now send against us our own slaves armed and ready to surfeit their savage natures in brutality and murder! These people we are to receive again as brothers, red handed, reeking with the slaughter of our people and the desolation of our country, and sit as quietly down together in all peace and amity as one great and happy family! To them we are expected to say, welcome thou slayer of my son, thou <gallant> murderer of my father, <most> /thou/ <noble> /thou thief of my goods/ incendiary /of my home/, <beloved> /thou/ ravisher of my daughter, <most incorruptible thief>; right welcome to this heart you have made lonely, to this home you have made desolate and to this shelter which I have built upon the ashes of <my> /the/ <magnificent> /comfortable/ mansion you /have/ burned!! Can any true son of North Carolina be found whose crawling, creeping soul would so grovel in the dirt of degradation and /so/ lick the vile dust from the boot of a master? May God pity him /if there be/! Why is this idea even talked of? Have recent reverses cowed our people and broken their spirits, after but little over two years of war? Sir, our only hope for national honor, for happiness, for peace itself lies in a cordial undaunted & vigorous prosecution of the war until our enemies offer us peace. It is often said that peace can never be made by fighting—that you must /at last/ negotiate <last>. In one particular this is true; negotiations arrange the terms of peace, but a man has often to be well <drubbed> / beaten/ before he will even talk with you, and certainly nothing so soon inclines nations to negotiate <than> /as/ an obstinate resistance, which shows them the hopelessness of subduing their enemies. The State of North Carolina by a solemn ordinance of her convention formally and forever dissolved her connection with the old government, intered into a compact with the new, and pledged her blood and treasure to the support of the common cause—In accordance with this solemn pledge, as sacred and binding as ever was entered into by any people upon earth, the best and bravest of her sons rushed to arms and for near thirty months have met the /almost/ overwhelming numbers of the foe and driven him back upon a hundred fields of slaughter, with a gallantry and devotion which have excited the admiration of the world—<Our> /The/ equally glorious <country> women /of our country/ have woven and spun, held the plough and wielded the axe, and even tottering age and prattling childhood have shouldered the burthens of strong men—All to make good our National faith and to secure our independence from a yoke too grievous to be borne. And now with the battle half won, must all this energy, this bravery, noble devotion and patriotic self sacrifise be thrown away? Shall timid souls <be> frightened by reverses or <traitorous> /restless men/ moved by <conscription> /dissatisfaction under the necessary burdens of war/ <to> drive our people to despair and crucify afresh the spirits of our heroic dead,' and put their noble souls to open shame? God of his infinite mercy forbid!

I say the battle is half won & why? Because Sir the North gives unmistakable signs that she finds it quite as difficult to keep up the strife as we. The blood which flows through the streets of her cities, the bold and defiant tone of her press and politicians towards Lincolns administration, the thousands of Federal bayonetts gleaming throughout the land to enforce conscription and "preserve order", as they significantly term it<,>—all show that they are having their own troubles also. There is nothing in our circumstances which should induce the least sanguine to despair, and I still maintain the confident opinion that the North never /can/ conquer us, *never, never*, while our people are harmonious to resist—Our great danger and our only one <consists in the fear> /is/ that the spirit of the people may give way—We have yet five hundred thousand <acres> square miles of territory on which to fight & subsist, an area more magnificent than that of any Kingdom or empire of the old world except Russia; we have yet upon our muster rolls sufficient men were deserters and absentees returned to duty<,>—to drive back every envading enemy, like chaff before the wind. The State of North Carolina alone has twice /as many/ men /in the field/ <than> / as/ <ever> Washington /ever/ commanded against the power of the Brittish, and Napoleon never led a nobler army to battle than that of Northern Virginia. Four hundred thousand men within but little over two years, under seven different commanders have been hurled against the city of Richmond—and yet she stands A fortress formed for freedom's hands. They have indeed penetrated the Mississippi by means of their immense naval supremacy, but they have made no advance any where over fifty miles from their gun boats & water communications, and they never can, if we make such resistance as is in our power. In the darkest days of the old revolution, the Brittish had possession not only of Charleston but of every seaport on our coast /and every state capital/; they marched triumphantly through the interior of Georgia both Carolinas and Virginia driving our broken and flying forces before them—Yet for seven long years <they> /our forefathers/ <took> /bore stout/ hearts /in their bosoms/, fought on and scorned the idea of reconstructing with the Brittish empire whose monarch they had abjured with much less unanimity than we displayed in dissolving our connection with the United States. I do not think it necessary to speak extravagantly or to cite desperate examples from history to show that we must /in the end/ succeed—It is <my> /the/ sober and <logical> /deliberate/ conviction /of my mind/—"The last man and the last dollar" is a foolish phrase, more often used by men, who will not, if they can help it, make the first nor the millionth man, and /who will/ give the last dollar only when forced to do it. No one proposes, at least I do not, to obtain <liberty> /independence/ by the extermination of our citizens or soldiers. I believe it entirely possible with much less loss of life than heretofore even, owing to their greater immunity /of our troops/ from disease, & their practised steadiness and skill in battle.

If therefore it be the aim of our people to secure a lasting peace on the basis of Southern Independence (which I will not suffer myself to doubt for a moment) we may opinion there could be no better means devised to defeat its own objects and bring us to utter ruin, than the movement now going on. There could be no objection to the people instructing their representatives in Congress, to look out dilligently for any opening toward negotiations, and God knows I hold myself always ready to seize upon any tangible terms to stay the effusion of blood, and should permit no matter of punctillios or pride to stand in the way of rest to my wearried Country—But these unorganized movements of the people will not incline our enemies to listen to reason, but will on the contrary (as I learn in fact they are) be gladly seized upon as evidence that our State <has> /is/ giving up and desires to return to the Federal union, blood stained and corrupt as it is. It will encourage desertion in the army, as the soldier<s> will think with some reason, that it is not worth his while to shed his blood if the people at home will not sustain him.

There is still another great consideration which fills me with alarm, and I mention it briefly, though I fear I have already written more than your /patience/ will quietly <submit to> /endure/.

We should feel thankful to God, that in the midst of all our troubles we have so far been exempted from internal dissensions <at home>. Our people have harmonized wonderfully, and have shed only the blood of their common enemy. In the war of the Revolution our ancesters were not so blessed—Whig and tory fought each other on the field, and hung, burnt and destroyed, <each other as> /neighbor against neighbor<s>/—I fear and believe this will yet be our fate should any considerable party in favour of reconstruction be formed in the State—The conservative spirit of the country would be drowned in fierce hatred of contending factions, smarting under mutual injuries and burning for revenge. Test oaths, sedition laws, and military despotism would reign supreme; <and> Habeas Corpus would be suspended and an infamous & hellish brood of informers and witnesses would cover the land, thirsting for the blood of our wisest and best, as traitors, when an accusation would be equivalent to proof. All these horrors, compared to which [a] regular war of twenty years would be preferable are almost certain to ensue should this unfortunate division of our people be consummated.

To the men who opposed my elevation as Governor of N.C. I can scarcely have a right to appeal, except in so far as a public officer honestly endeavoring to do his duty in a period of trial and trouble has a claim to the respect of all who believe him conscientious. But my dear Sir, to you and to the thousands of my fellow citizens who with such unanimity, called me from my humble position in the army to preside over the destinies of this great State, I shall confidently appeal to prevent these great calamities. The Conservative party Sir, was born as I conceive, of the necessities of the times, and was intended to check the will and destructive spirit of revolution; to preserve the land from madly rushing into evils greater than those from /which/ it was endeavoring to escape; to maintain the rights and liberties of the citizen and the prerogatives of our judicial tribunals—the only hope of freedom in times of passion & of violence—Surely it was a noble purpose—Shall we forget it, and unintentionally or otherwise inaugurate a still more terrible state of things? Shall we cover our names with a natural suspicion of bad faith and disloyalty, and subject our State to the scornful imputations of our Southern Sisters? Shall we in other words deprive ourselves of the power to do good, and elevate our opponents over our friends by proving their accusations true? Such I believe will be the result if we look not wisely at the course of events.

If our <our> impatient but <truly> suffering people would only have more trusting faith, write cheerfully to their sons in the army, hold meetings, *all over the country*, to devise means for the assistance of the poor and to induce the <poor> tired and disheartened deserters to return to their colors, and sin no more, and <to> resolve to fight and suffer yet awhile longer, trusting the issue with God, in His own good time our deliverance will come—

Such are my impressions of our public duty, hastily given—You or any one else may see them.

very truly yours
Z. B. Vance

[1]John Hooker Haughton, lawyer, planter, and former state senator with strong unionist sympathies. *Dictionary of North Carolina Biography*, s.v. "Haughton, John Hooker."
[2]Not extant.

James A. Seddon to ZBV   A&H:VanPC

Confederate States of America,
War Department,
Richmond, Va. Aug. 21, 1863.

His Excellency Z. B. Vance,
Governor of N.C.
Raleigh, N.C.

Sir,

I take the liberty of enclosing to you a communication[1] addressed to me by the Engineer Bureau, presenting strongly the military necessity which was the adoption of the five foot guage for the Railroad connection from Danville to Greensboro. In soliciting your attention to it, I respectfully add my own conviction of the real importance of having the privilege accorded, if in your power to grant it. It will be only under the most imperative necessity, and with very great reluctance, that I should authorize even a temporary departure from the terms of the charter, unless assured that it would receive the countenance of the author-ities of your State. I venture to hope this will not be witheld, in view of the exigency dictating this application.

Very Respectfully
Your obdt. servt.
James A Seddon
Secretary of War

[*Endorsed*] File—

Z B V

[1]Not extant.

Jefferson Davis to ZBV   A&H:VanPC

Confederate States of America,
Executive Department,
Richmond, Va. August 22 1863

His Excellency
Z. B. Vance
Governor of North Carolina.

Dear Sir.

I send you herewith a sheet of the New York Herald which has been brought to my attention containing allusions to a recent article of the Raleigh Standard.

It is apparent what encouragement such publications afford to the enemy; how they tend to cause our situation to be misunderstood to our prejudice abroad, and how they are calculated to mislead a portion of our own people.

As you have been specially named as approving this publication of the Stan-dard, I have thought it proper to bring the matter to your notice that you may take such action in regard to it as your judgment may suggest.

Very Respectfully
& truly yr's.
Jeffn. Davis

Frederick J. Lord to ZBV   A&H:GP

Vice Consulate of Spain
Wilmington N C
22 Aug 1863

His Excellency
Z B Vance Gov

Dear Sir
The number of foreign citizens now claiming the protection of their Consuls being unusually large renders it necessary that the Consulates shd. be kept constantly open & under this view the Confederate Govt. has very properly exempted all foreign Consuls from military service and I have now the honor to ask from your hands exemption from the Home guards for the same reason— Shd. the exigencies of the State in your opinion render <this> the granting of my request inexpedient this Vice Consulate will be immediately closed.—
     I wd. respectfully refer you to Mr James G Burr[1] of this place, to whose care I wd. beg you to address your reply, and also to Mr P K Dickinson[2] now a resident of yr City—With the highest consideration I have the honor to remain

Yr Excellency's
Most obdt Sevt
F. J. Lord V.C. de Espa.

[*Endorsed*] Whenever it is well established that Spain has any right to a consul in the port of a government she does not recognize and having authority under an exequatur from Abraham Lincoln I will cheerfully comply—

Z B V

---

[1]Banker, railroad executive, and colonel in the Home Guards. He became director of the state insane asylum after the war. *Cyclopedia of Men of the Carolinas*, 2:334–335.
[2]Wilmington lumber dealer and railroad promoter. Johnston, *Papers of Vance*, 1:397n.

Milledge L. Bonham to ZBV   A&H:GP

State of South Carolina,
Executive Department.
Charleston Augt. 22, 1863

To His Excellency
Governor Z. B. Vance

Governor:
     I am officially advised by the Commandant of Conscripts for this State, that in the Districts of Pickens, Greenville and Spartanburg there are banded together

large numbers of Deserters and evaders of Conscription, who are armed and resolute in their purpose to resist all attempts to bring them to subordination. My advices are also that this disloyalty and disaffection is equally, if not more extended in those Counties of your State lying adjacent to the Districts named: and that those persons have across the line concerted means of communication /looking to their common protection/

This condition of affairs calls for prompt measures: and in view of the necessity which rests upon the Commanding General of this Department to direct all his resources and energies to meet the advances of the external enemy, I have felt it my duty to assume the correction, so far as may be in my power, of an evil which internally so seriously threatens our cause.

I have therefore ordered to those Districts a company of Mounted Men of State troops, well armed, who will scour those Districts and rid them of the presence of these lawless persons. This company will be sustained in their efforts by such other forces as the necessities of the case may from time to time require.

I foresee however, that their prescence and efforts may, to a great extent, serve but to drive these persons beyond the line where they will fraternize in more formidable numbers and where they may quietly remain until the withdrawal of my forces shall permit them again to return to this State. This reduces the ne-cessity that I should earnestly solicit of you concert of action, and the initiation of like measures in your Counties, with the view to simultaneous and concerted action. In the course of ten days the company which I have ordered forward will be on the ground.

May I ask to this matter your earliest attention and that I may be advised how far and in what manner your cooperation can be had. The greatest secresy and promptness seem to me desirable.

I have the honor to be
Very Respectfully
Yr. obt. servt
M. L. Bonham

Moses O. Sherrill to ZBV   A&H:GP

Aug the 23 1863
State of N C CaBarus County

to Mr govner vance

Dear Sire

I will Drop you A few lins to let you no my state of helth my helth is Bad I got wounded the forth teen Day of last DecemBer at FredicBurge and is at home and my situation is Bad me and my famlay is in nead of sum healp I have heard A old Saying and I Be leave it to Be A true one one good turn disserve an other one Dear Sir I am the man that helpe you out of the creek the /Day of the/ Battle

at New Burn[1] and I saw you the next Day and you told me that you ode me A
favor and now is the time that I need healp if I ever Did in this world I have a
wife and small children and my wife is weAkley and A levnth Dollars A month
wont Bord me and if you can Do[w] A little sum thing for me in the way of
money I will Be A thousen times A Blige to you and if ever it co[nm] in the war
againe I will Dwo all for you that I can rite to me if you pleas if you can helpe
me eney Di rect your letter to concord N c I wish you well govner vance

M. O. Sherrill[2]

[Endorsed] Send him some money & write to the comrs. of his County—

Z B V

[1]During the Battle of New Bern in March 1862, ZBV had fallen from his horse into
Bryce's Creek and almost drowned. Tucker, Zeb Vance, 126.
[2]Moses O. Sherrill, Thirty-third Regiment North Carolina Troops. Manarin and Jordan, North Carolina Troops, 9:157.

Robert B. Vance to ZBV   A&H:VanPC

Asheville N.C. Aug 24/63.

Dear Zeb;
    I got home safely after two days detention at Morganton and find the country
in a stew. There is quite a clamor to know what you will do with Holden. I tell
them nothing but to kill him off by letting him alone.
    There is a strong peace feeling in the country, but I am glad it is held in check
by the old whigs in the main. I saw James A. Patton[1] & says what ought Zeb to
do with Holden. Says he "nothing at all—wouldn't the Gov be a nice man to
get into a dirty quarrel with Holden." Whereupon I thought Jas A. had more
sense than the whole posse. Did [y]our cards get in? Write me to Chattanooga
as soon as you get this, as I am going in a few days.
    Regards to Mess Little,[2] Barnes & all the friends.
    Sister Hattie[3] is not very well to day but not dangerously ill. David Mitchell[4]
is better.

Your Bro.
Bob

[1]James Alfred Patton, lawyer, merchant, farmer, and former member of council of state.
Johnston, Papers of Vance, 1:19n.
[2]George Little, aide to ZBV and postwar commissioner of immigration for North Carolina. Johnston, Papers of Vance, 1:359n.

[3]ZBV's wife.
[4]David Mitchell Vance, the second oldest of ZBV's three living sons. Johnston, *Papers of Vance*, 1:23n, 38n, 67n.

ZBV to William A. Graham   A&H:GraPC

State of North-Carolina,
Executive Department,
Raleigh, Augst 24, 1863.

Gov. Graham,

My dear Sir,

Yours have both been recd. and I thank you sincerely for your advice.[1] I had concluded before you returned my letter to Haughton to suspend its publication at least for the present—

But Sir, I am really much distressed and harrassed—The crisis is fast approaching and hardly any two friends agree in their advice. I have some thirty or forty letters from different parts of the state—I would like much to see you and lay the matter before you in all its phases. If you can come I would be glad [*illegible*] you appoint the day most convenient for you, and write Mr. [*Edward J.*] Hale, Mr. Reade,[2] Mr. Gilmer[3] or any others to meet you here.

God knows I desire to do my duty and for the best, but the matter is one of great delicacy and a mistake might be fatal—

Very truly yours
Z. B. Vance

[1]See ZBV to Graham, August 19 (with enclosure), in this volume.
[2]Edwin Godwin Reade, lawyer and former Whig and U.S. congressman who favored peace with the North. In 1864 he served as a Confederate States senator, and after the war he became associate justice of the state supreme court. *Dictionary of American Biography*, s.v. "Reade, Edwin Godwin"; Cheney, *North Carolina Government*, 361, 362, 369n, 371n, 388, 403n, 575, 588, 689, 832.
[3]John Adams Gilmer, lawyer, large slaveholder, former state senator (Whig) and U.S. congressman strongly opposed to secession. He became a Confederate congressman in the last year of the war. *Dictionary of North Carolina Biography*, s.v. "Gilmer, John Adams."

ZBV to William P. Bynum   A&H:VanPC

State of North-Carolina,
Executive Department,
Raleigh, Augst 26 1863.

Col. Bynum,

My dear Sir,

I snatch a moment in the midst of a crowd in my office, to acknowledge your kind letter and to thank you sincerely for it—Tho' in too much haste to answer fully, I design at least to disabuse your mind of any impression unfavorable (if such an impression exists) to the character of the *"measures"* I propose to use to counteract the effect of peace meetings—Those *measures* are nothing more than persuasion, argument, & such moral force as my position may enable me to bring to bear on public opinion—These I know you will approve, and no one can easily object to—The idea of violence, possible arrests, proscription &c. never will find an advocate in me—I shall sustain the courts as heretofore, and while doing my utmost to sustain the common cause, I shall boldly maintain the rights & privileges of the citizens at all hazards—

I will try to write again more fully when I can—

> In haste
> Most truly Yours
> Z. B. Vance

Daniel G. Fowle to ZBV　　　　A&H:GP

> Executive Department, North-Carolina,
> Adjutant-General's Office,
> Raleigh, Aug: 26th., 1863.

Gov. Vance—

Governor;

As I believe that the revocation or modification of Genl Order No 17,[1] would under the circumstances be a reflection upon me, I would respectfully tender my resignation as Adjutant General of the state—[2]

> I am Governor,
> Very Respecty
> Danl. G. Fowle
> Adjt Genl

[1]That all communications to ZBV that pertained to the state's war effort should pass through the adjutant general's office. See Samuel F. Phillips to William A. Graham, August 28, 1863, in Williams and Hamilton, *Papers of Graham*, 5:525–526.

[2]ZBV immediately accepted Fowle's resignation and appointed Richard Caswell Gatlin the new adjutant general. Phillips to Graham, August 28, 1863, in Williams and Hamilton, *Papers of Graham*, 5:524–526; Cheney, *North Carolina Government*, 183; *Dictionary of North Carolina Biography*, s.v. "Gatlin, Richard Caswell."

ZBV *to Milledge L. Bonham*   A&H:GLB

[*With enclosure*]

Executive Department
Raleigh, August 26th. 1863

To His Excellency
Governor M. L. Bonham

Governor

I have received your letter[1] informing me that large numbers of deserters and evaders of conscription are banding together in your State for armed resistance and asking my cooperation in suppressing them—

I fully concur with you in the opinion that this condition of affairs calls for prompt action. I have accordingly directed my Adjutant General to order the commanding officers of the Militia for Jackson and Transylvania Counties to order out their commands and to cooperate with the State Troops of South Carolina.

I herewith enclose you a copy of the order.

I have the honor to be
Very respectfully
Your obt Servt
Z. B. Vance

[1]August 22, in this volume.

[*Enclosure*]   A&H:GLB

"Copy"

Executive Department N. Carolina
Adjutant Generals Office (Mil)
Raleigh Aug 25th 1863

His Excellency
Gov. Bonham
S.C.

Special Order
No. 93

II. The Commanding Officers of the Militia for Jackson and Transylvania counties will order out the militia and Home Guards for the purpose of arresting deserters—

They will cooperate with the State Troops of South Carolina from the Districts of Pickens, Greenville, and Spartanburg

By order of Gov. Vance
(Signed)   Danl. G. Fowle
Adjutant General.

ZBV to James A. Seddon   A&H:GLB

State of North Carolina
Executive Department,
Raleigh Aug 26th. 1863

Hon. J. A. Seddon
Secy of War
Richmond Va

Dear Sir

The vast number of deserters in the Western Counties of the State, have so accumulated lately as to set the local militia at defiance, & exert a very injurious effect upon the community in many respects—My Home Guards are poorly armed inefficient and rendered timid by fear of secret vingeance from the deserters—If Genl Lee would send one of our diminished brigades, or a good strong regiment to N.C. with orders to report to me, I could make it increase his ranks for more than the temporary loss of his brigade in a very short time—Something of this kind *must* be done.

Very respectfully
Z. B. Vance

Daniel G. Fowle to ZBV   A&H:GP

Raleigh, August 27th. 1863.

Gov. Z. B. Vance.

Governor;

Yours of the 26th.[1] was handed me to-day, and would have elicited no reply but for the concluding portion of your letter, in which you assume that General Order No. 17 was unlawful.

I beg leave to say that in this latter opinion you are mistaken, as I was prepared to demonstrate, had an opportunity been afforded me of so doing.

Your decision was rendered without hearing my side of the question, although on two occasions I endeavoured unsuccessfully to speak with you in regard thereto.

I trust that this reply, which a sense of what is due to myself, prompts me to make, will not be construed into an indication on my part of a willingness to reassume a position, which I would have resigned several months ago, but from a sense of duty—

Very respectfully &c
Yours &c
Danl. G. Fowle

[1]Not extant.

Jefferson Davis to ZBV   A&H:GP

[*Telegram*]

Richmond
Aug 27 1863

Gov Z. B. Vance

Can you send forces to defend RR from Weldon & Wilmington and to aid in defence of Wilmington—I have not learned of the arrival of any of these troops called for in June last the case is urgent

Jefferson Davis

ZBV to Jefferson Davis   Har:Van

Raleigh N.C.
Aug 28th./63

His Excellency.
Jefferson Davis—
President C.S.

Sir,
    Your letter of the 19th. inst.,[1] has been received, informing me of the gallant conduct and heroic death of Lt. F. M. Harney, 14th. N.C. Troops on the field of Gettysburg; and asking me to make known to his family your sympathy with them for the loss of one so brave and worthy of their esteem.
    I do not know Sir, that he has any relatives whatever in N.C. He was born in Kentucky and saw some service as a soldier under Gen Wm. Walker,[2] during his campaign in Central America At the commencement of hostilities he was residing in the town of Asheville N.C. pursuing his occupation of carpenter, and

joining the company which I had the honor to raise, he was made orderly Sergeant, and by good conduct and hard fighting won his way to 1st. Lieutenant—

Though without kindred in this his adopted State, I assure you She will be proud to see his name placed on the long list of her heroic dead, and all will welcome his memory among their bravest sons, and mourn him as a noble brother slain for her defence.

I am Sir,
Very respectfully yrs.
Z. B. Vance

[1]In this volume.

[2]American filibuster, who led an armed expedition in a revolution in Nicaragua in 1855. He seized control of that country, inaugurated himself president, and launched an unsuccessful scheme to unite Central American republics into a single empire. *Dictionary of American Biography*, s.v. "Walker, William."

Sewall L. Fremont to David A. Barnes   A&H:GP

Wilmington and Weldon Railroad Co.
Office Engineer and Superintendent,
Wilmington, N.C. Aug 30th. 1863

Col. D. A. Barnes
Aid. D.C. to Gov Vance
Raleigh N.C.

Colonel

Your reply[1] to my letter[2] to the Governor on the subject of shipping cotton by the "Advance" was duly received, <and was duly received>—and was in the main satisfactory but really His Excellency will not divide five bales with us & the Atlantic Road I hope. *Five* is a very small quantity, and we need very large supplies while the "Atlantic" has a good claim to some accomodation of the sort—I put our request down very low to allow them to come in above or below us not *with* us in *five* Bales—suppose we say ten Bales and then divide *pro rata* as to length of Road, and number of trains employed—I would prefer that— However we are obliged for any favours *of the kind*. Yet remember the state owns $400,000, in this road out of $1500,000 & I hope the importance of our Road as to the interests of the state either in peace or war is not underrated.

I will in this connection say if you /will/ excuse the "connection"—that we have an Engine recently purchased of the York River and Richmond Rail Road, built in Richmond before the war now thouroughly rebuilt here and in good order that will go on the road in two weeks or less that I propose to honor with the name of "Governor Vance"— Hoping his Excellency will not object to it

and that the Engine may do the company as good service and [as] the Governor
is now doing the State

> I am yours sincerely,
> S. L. Fremont
> ChfEng. & Supt.

¹Not extant.
²August 23, A&H:GP.

Robert E. Lee to ZBV   A&H:GP

[*Telegram*]

September 1 1863
Richmond

His Ex Gov Vance

I will send in response to your request for a small brigade for the purpose of acting
against certain deserters two Regiments of Infantry & a squadron of Cavalry
under either Genl Hoke or Genl Ransom please make necessary arrangements
for provisioning the troops & c and give proper instructions to the officer in
command who has been ordered to report to you

> R E Lee

ZBV to John White   A&H:GP

Executive Office
Raleigh N.C. Sep 3d./63

Mr John White,
Manchester England.

My Dear Sir,
    Yours¹ per the "Advance" was duly recd.—I regretted to learn that you were
pressed for funds, but hope the remittance of bonds which I made by the steamer
in July has enabled you to take up more of the loan and that you are now relieved.
I do not desire to touch the proceeds of our cotton shipments if it can be avoided,
except for the ships expenses. I desire you will deposit it to the credit of the State
in Bank of England. As the war progresses and our currency continues to depreciate, it may be of great advantage to the state—
    The blockade running is becoming more and more perilous, & should Charles-
ton fall soon the business will be about closed—In /view/ of this danger, you are

instructed to make no more purchases of goods for the present—The amount received and now at Bermuda—with home supplies—will keep our troops well agoing for twelve months and of course it is not desirable to have goods on hand which we can not ship—The only remaining article I am anxious about is the cotton & wool cards—I was sorry to learn—that you had not purchased them. Please make every effort to get them & send them in—Perhaps you had better purchase them through agents in New York—they are better & cheaper than the English. The card clothing I suppose you have bought—with it for our factories and plenty of cards for our housewives our people would be greatly relieved in the way of clothing and prices would greatly diminish—I can not impress too strongly upon you the importance of these articles to our people. I hope before this you have done something toward securing a supply—

I am exceedingly anxious for Col. McRae to return home—and if any business detains him, please take charge of it so that he may return. I would give almost half the amount to get his turpentine & rosin bonds out of the market—

I do not know whether to send the remainder of the bonds to you by this steamer or not—I have them ready, but you made no allusion to them in your last letter. If I send them, will advise you.

I must refer you to the papers for news—Since my last, reverses have befallen us, as was to have been expected; and we look for still others. But rest assured it will all come right—and don't believe more than one half the Federals say about our condition.

Very truly yours
Z B Vance

P.S. I send the bonds, four hundred thousand dollars worth, by same steamer.

Z.B.V.

---

[1]August 7, in this volume.

B. F. *Wilkins to* ZBV   A&H:GP

(By flag of truce)

Washington 3d. Sept. 1863.

Hon. Z. Vance,
Raleigh, N.C.

Sir:

At the request of C. F. Macdonald, Esq., acting 3d. Assistant Postmaster General, I visited Gettysburg on the 29th. ultimo, in order to make special inquiry with regard to the remains of Lieut. John Caldwell—a service requested in your note of 25th. July last,[1] addressed to Mr. Zevely.[2]

I discovered, at the outset of my mission, that much had been done in furtherance of the object desired, by Mr. S. G. Frey, a young man of intelligence
and activity, who has been commissioned by Governors Seymour and Curtin[3] to
mark the graves of New York and Pennsylvania soldiers killed in the battles near
Gettysburg. Mr. Frey was born and reared in the vicinity of the battle-field, and
is familiar with every portion thereof; was present during most of the battle, and
has been almost constantly upon the field in the performance of his duties since
the 3d. of July. Beyond consulting and questioning the authorities to whom he
referred me, my task was comparatively easy; and but little information could be
gained from other sources, although I visited the General Hospital at Gettysburg,
and conversed with many North Carolina soldiers, with a view to making my
report as satisfactory as possible.

I do not think it necessary at this time to detail the various means adopted
to make my information perfect as to the precise spot of the burial of Lieut.
Caldwell's remains. But I am confident that the grave has been found, and is
now marked in such a manner as to enable a future removal of the body. Briefly,
a wounded soldier of the same company stated that Lieut. Caldwell fell by his
side at a certain spot, near a rock of peculiar shape, and was buried within a few
feet of the same place. Mr. Frey's familiarity with the field enabled him to find
the place described, where he discovered a board indicating that 1 second lieutenant, 2 sergeants, and 21 privates of the Confederate army were buried. Upon
further inquiry among the camps and hospitals, a Union soldier who assisted in
burying the bodies was found, who stated that the soldiers were mostly if not all
from North Carolina; he was not positive with reference to the lieutenant, and
could give no other information than that he seemed quite a young man. He
further stated that no other Confederate officer was buried in that vicinity. Upon
consulting a map of the battle-field, I found the position immediately west of this
spot to have been occupied by A. P. Hill's Corps; and on inquiry of informed
persons I ascertained that a charge upon the Federal works was made on the 3d.
July by P<r>enders division, the spot in question being in a direct line from the
position where the charge was ordered and began. The grave is about 75 yards
from the Federal line.

Upon the whole, a stronger case of circumstantial evidence cannot be well
conceived.

I must not omit to state that assurance would have been made doubly sure by
opening the grave, but the provost marshal, for sanitary reasons, absolutely pro-
hibits such opening, in any case, prior to the 1st. of October next. Feeling that
for the satisfaction of the friends of the deceased, all practical proof of identity
should be given, I have made arrangements to have the grave opened for that
purpose after the 1st. of October—the further result of which will be communicated if desired. That result, however, I can predict with confidence.

I would suggest that provision be made for taking up the remains after the
date above given, placing the same in a burial case, and having the same interred

in some quiet place until such time as a removal can be made as proposed. The cost for this service, I was informed, would be about $45.

I beg leave to state that I have incurred, in making the investigation herein detailed, an expense of $16.50, which may be remitted to my address at any time suitable to your own convenience.

Very respectfully,
Your obedient servant,
B. F. Wilkins.

[1]Not extant, but see ZBV to John H. Winder, July 25, in this volume.

[2]A. N. Zevely, a native of Salem, North Carolina, and third assistant postmaster general of U.S. *People's Press* (Salem), March 29, 1888.

[3]Horatio Seymour, governor of New York, and Andrew Gregg Curtin, governor of Pennsylvania. Faust et al., *Encylopedia of Civil War*, 198, 669.

ZBV to John White   A&H:GLB

Raleigh N.C. Sept 3d. 1863

Mr. Jno. White
Care Alexander Collie & Co.
Manchester, Engd.

Sir

Capt Hughes having retired temporarily from the Pursership of the N.C. Steamer "Advance" please recognize J. H. Flanner[1] as his successor and honor his draft on account of ship expenses &c.

Respectfully
Z. B. Vance
Gov. of N.C.

[1]Joseph H. Flanner, president of the Wilmington Steamship Company and formerly an ardent Know-Nothing. Johnston, *Papers of Vance*, 1:354n.

Jason H. Carson to ZBV   A&H:GP

[*Telegram*]

Charlotte 4 Sept. 1863

Hon Z B Vance

A note from Mrs Vance of the 24th. ult. just recd. requests me to telegraph you that your Son david has diptheria & that she is sick and <that> to come up immediately

Jas. H Carson[1]

[1]Jason Hazard Carson, farmer, slaveholder, and member of the state secession convention of 1861 and the constitutional convention of 1861–1862. Johnston, *Papers of Vance*, 1:209n; Cheney, *North Carolina Government*, 387, 401, 825.

James A. Seddon to ZBV   A&H:GP

Confederate States of America,
War Department,
Richmond, Va. Sept. 4, 1863.

His Excellency Z. B. Vance
Governor of N.C.
Raleigh, N.C.

Sir,

Your letter of the 30th. ult.,[1] urging a compliance with the request of the 1st. and 3d. North Carolina Regiments to be attached to a North Carolina Brigade, has been referred to the Commanding General and commended to his special attention. I wish to be advised of his views—

Very Respectfully
Your obdt. servt.
James A Seddon
Secretary of War

[1]Not extant.

John White to ZBV   A&H:GP

Manchester September 4th. 1863

Gov. Z B Vance
Raleigh
N. Carolina

Sir

I am glad to have it in my power to acknowledge the receipt, a few days since, of your communication of the 10th of July last[1] together with other documents, all of which were indeed highly satisfactory. I am informed by letter yesterday that a package of Six Hundred Thousand dollars of the State Bonds has safely arrived in Liverpool, tomorrow I will dispatch a special messenger for it

I have placed an order with a manufacturer here, for a quantity of cotton & wool cards, and at once will attend to the purchase of a machine for making them, together with the necessary wire &c and as soon as ready will have them shipd. to Bermuda. The letter of which you speak, having before ordered cards, has not been received.

I am really gratified to know that the resources of our State are being so developed as to give us the prospect of being able to clothe our own troops I have made some progress in purchasing Cloth, Blankets & Shoes, since I last wrote you, and have chartered and sent off another schooner with about 300 tons of cargo entirely for the State. She saild. from London on the 31st. of August, /thus/ making two cargoes last month, the former of which I before advised you, sailed on the 13th. both of which I hope may reached Bermuda in safety, and in good time. I have now some goods ready for shipment, and a considerable quantity in the houses of manufacturers, the orders having been given sometime previous to the receipt of your letter, in my desire to get the goods forward as rapidly as possible so as not to delay the running of the Ad-Vance, & also that they might get home in good time to have them <ready> made up and ready by winter for the troops. I did not confine myself strictly to color. The color used in the Confederate Army can only be obtained, to any extent, by giving out the orders to the manufacturers, which would have greatly delayed the shipments. I therefore went into the market & bought out of stock such goods as I could find & that I thought would answer the purpose. I hope they may give satisfaction. I will ship what is now ready & those to come in from the manufacturers, as soon as practicable, and await further orders from you. I will endeavor to get up a statement, and enclose (if I can do so in time for this mail) of all my purchases to this time that you may see exactly what I have done what goods have been shipd. what still here and what now in the hands of the manufacturers and at sametime showing what amount of cotton bonds have been disposed of

If you have not sent out the balance of the Bonds, say $400000, I do not think it will be necessary for you to do so the $600000, which has arrived I feel assured will be fully as much as can be used, indeed I do not think they will all be required, the bonds are only deposited as collateral, as sales are made of the cotton bonds

Col. McRae had left this country for home before your letters reachd. me. I found his agent and communicated to him your wishes, and at sametime gave him your letter[2] for Col. McRae The negotiations for the Naval Store bonds the Col. had succeeded in making before leaving, and the orders for the goods his agent told me had all been placed, consequently your instructions came too late to arrest his opperations here

I will attend to the private memorandum sent, and also to that for the institution for the Deaf & Dumb & Blind.

I hope Col. Crossan may ever escape capture and succeeds in getting all of my purchases safely home.

I have letters from my family of about the same date as yours with the gratifying intelligence that all were then well.

> I am Sir
> Your obt. Servt.
> Jno. White

I found I will not be able to get the statement ready in time Will forward it by next mail

¹In this volume.
²July 10, in this volume.

James A. Seddon to ZBV   A&H:GP

Confederate States of America,
War Department,
Richmond, Va. Sept. 5, 1863.

His Excellency Z. B. Vance,
Governor of N.C.
Raleigh, N.C.

Sir,

Genl. Whiting, in several late communications, expresses grave apprehensions of the safety of Wilmington, and urges earnestly the necessity of having more troops at that point. He is, as you are aware, in command of the Department of North Carolina, and might summon the aid of the forces within it to that city, but he is unwilling to remove any of them from the long line of defence over which they are scattered, without some arrangement made to substitute them. I regret to confess, that with the formidable columns of the enemy threatening at so many vital points, the resources of the Department do not allow the withdrawal from our armies, on the command from other quarters, of the force that will be necessary to meet Genl. Whiting's requirements. Under these circumstances, remembering the confident expectation entertained by you when I had the privilege of seeing you here,¹ that you would be enabled speedily to command from ten to twenty thousand troops, either Militia or for State defence, I venture to inquire if it would not be in your power with them to undertake the defence of the Railroad line from Weldon to Wilmington, or at least so much of it as is protected by the forces under Genl. Martin, so as to allow them to be thrown at once to Wilmington. I may add, this inquiry is at the suggestion of the President himself, and if it be in your power to afford such protection to the Railroad line, I write in urging that <the> application of your State forces.

Very truly yours
James A Seddon
Secretary of War

[*Endorsed*] File & Copy.

[1]During ZBV's trip to confer with President Davis. See Davis to ZBV, July 24, in this volume.

Theodore J. Hughes to ZBV   A&H:GP

[With enclosure]

Wilmington Sept. 5th. 1863

Gov Z. B. Vance
Raleigh

Sir

I have the honor herewith to enclose a copy of Col Crossan's letter to Mr John White commissioner for the State of N. Carolina in England—

I am very Respectfully
Your Obedient Servant
Theo. J. Hughes

[Enclosure]

Thomas M. Crossan to John White   A&H:GLB

"Copy"

John White Esq.
N.C. Commissioner
Manchester England

Dear Sir

Just previous to my departure from Raleigh, I had a long interview with Gov. Vance, relative to your further purchases of goods for the State, & if in my judgment, you could not have them here in such time, as not to involve the delay of the Steamer, he wished you to make no further purchases. The fall of Vicksburg and Port Hudson together with the falling back of Generals Lee, Johnston and Bragg, has so encouraged the enemy, that they will redouble their efforts for the speedy reduction of Charleston—They have already secured a footing upon Morris' Island, from which they cannot be dislodged, and I greatly fear, that before you could receive the Bonds, purchase the goods, and have them delivered here, that Charleston will have fallen, and Wilmington either taken or so closely blockaded, as to render our efforts for running in the goods, exceedingly doubtful, if not altogether ineffectual. We are here now without a pound of goods for the State—I shall upon my arrival advise the Governor to dispose of the vessel to the Confederacy, as the number of vessels engaged in blockade running has produced such a competition as will enable the Governor to run the goods in cheaper than we can with this vessel. The goods you have already purchased will be sufficient for the immediate want of our troops. The Governor prefers that you will realize only £150.000 by sale of the State Cotton Bonds, retaining the balance of the Bonds in your hands to be disposed of as he may instruct—Unless your purchases shall have exceeded this amount, in which event, he of course expects you to sell a sufficient amount to cover all your purchases.

You will be kept regularly advised of the Governors wishes

I am
Very respectfully
T. M. Crossan

(Signed)
T. J. Hughes
Purser

ZBV to Duncan K. McRae   A&H:GLB

State of North Carolina
Executive Department
Raleigh Sept 6th. 1863

Col. D. K. McRae
care Alexander Collie & Co.
Manchester England

My dear Sir

Your letter[1] by the "Advance" was duly received informing me that you had succeeded in selling the bonds &c, and had shipped twelve hundred rifles and ammunition to suit. I regret that you sold the bonds at all, as after Mr. White had succeeded so well with his loan, it was altogether unnecessary and besides I find it exceedingly difficult to get and keep the turpentine, and it will be attended with considerable loss to the State—But let it go—

The arrival of the arms was very opportune for arming the militia. The remainder of your purchases, what, you did not say, you will ship to Bermuda and return home as soon as possible. The State ought not to maintain two agents abroad for the same purpose—

I learn you are in difficulty with Sanders,[2] but can get no particulars and therefore can give no instructions, trusting to you to see that the State suffers no damage by him. You have a copy of my contract with him—You will also remember that I advanced him $5000 in State Bonds before starting, and I believe so far, he has not complied with his agreement in any one particular—I expect him to be held *to it strictly.*

I refer you to my letter of this date[3] to Mr. White for further information.

> Very respectfully
> Your obt. Servt.
> Z. B. Vance

[1]July 10, A&H:GP.

[2]See George N. Sanders to ZBV, July 16, A&H:GLB, and McRae to ZBV, July 17, A&H:GP.

[3]September 3 (no. 1), in this volume.

ZBV to Robert F. Hoke   A&H:GLB

> State of North Carolina
> Executive Department
> Raleigh Sept 7th. 1863

Genl. R. F. Hoke

Dear Sir

You will proceed to Wilkes and adjoining counties in this State and use every effort to capture the deserters and conscripts, and break up & disperse any organized bands of lawless men to be found there, resisting the authority of the Government.[1]

You will also take out warrants before a civil magistrate for all persons who have been guilty of harboring, feeding, aiding or abetting deserters, contrary to Act of Assembly, and in default of good and sufficient security, ask that they be committed to jail in Iredell County or some other, where they would be safe— All militia officers and justices of the peace of conscript /age/, who you may be satisfied have been guilty of the same offence, or have willfully failed or neglected to execute my order for the arrest of of deserters, you will arrest & place in camp of instruction.

These instructions will also apply to any other counties which you may visit Please report frequently of your progress etc.

> Very respectfully
> Z. B. Vance

[1]R. E. Lee had dispatched Hoke to North Carolina to hunt deserters. Barrett, *Civil War in North Carolina,* 192.

Proclamation by ZBV   A&H:GLB

Sept 7, 1863

BY THE GOVERNOR OF NORTH CAROLINA
A PROCLAMATION

Whereas, a number of public meetings have recently been held in various portions of the State, in some of which threats have been made of combined resistance to the execution of the laws of Congress, in regard to conscription and the
collection of taxes, thereby endangering the public peace and tranquillity as well
as the common cause of independence, which we have so solemnly engaged to
defend: And, whereas, it is my sworn duty to see all the laws of the land faithfully
executed, and quiet and order maintained within our borders

Now, therefore I Zebulon B. Vance, Governor of the State of North Carolina,
do issue this my proclamation, commanding all such persons to renounce such
evil intentions and warning them to beware of the criminal and fatal consequences of carrying such threats into execution—The inalienable and invaluable
right of the people to assemble together and consult for the common good,
together with its necessary concomitants, the freedom of speech and the press,
are secured to you, my countrymen by the most sacred compacts. They shall
never find a disturber in me. Yet you will remember that the same instruments
which guarantee these great rights, also limit you to the exercise of them, within
the bounds of law, and impose upon me the solemn duty of seeing that these
bounds be not transgressed. The Constitution of the Confederate States and all
laws passed, in pursuance thereof, are the supreme law of the land: resistance to
them by combination is *treason*, and without combination, is a high crime against
the laws of your country. Let no one be deceived. So long as these laws remain
upon the Statute book, they shall be executed. Surely my countrymen, you would
not seek to cure the evils of one revolution by plunging the country into another.
You will not knowingly, to the present desolating war with the common enemy,
add the horrors of internal strife and entire subversion of war and civil authority!
You must not forget the enviable character which you have always maintained,
as a sober, conservative and law abiding people, nor would I have you to forget
the plain, easy and *constitutional* method of redressing your grievances. Meet and
denounce any existing laws if you think proper—you have that right—and instruct your representatives in Congress, or the State Legislature, as the case may
be, to repeal them—Your own chosen servants made those obnoxious laws, they
can repeal them, if such are your instructions. If you regard them as unconstitutional, our Supreme Court sits ready to decide upon all cases properly brought
before it. Its decisions are final in the State of North Carolina, and shall be
executed while the power remains in your Executive to enforce any law. There
is no grievance to redress and no proposition to be made, but can be most ben-
eficially effected in the way our fathers marked out by the ballot box, and the

other constitutionally appointed means. In times of great public sensibility like the present, any departure from this legal channel is revolutionary & dangerous, and tends to the division and detraction of our people.

It is my great desire, and, I hope, that of all good citizens, that our people should remain united, befall us what may. Should we triumph in the great struggle for independence let no feelings of revenge, no bitterness mar the rejoicing of that glorious day. Should we fall, & come short of that great object for which we have struggled so long and bled so freely, let not our strifes and domestic feuds add to the bitterness of defeat. Attempts suddenly to change the existing order of things would only result in bloodshed and ruin—I therefore implore you, my countrymen, of all shades of political opinion, to abstain from assembling together for the purpose of denouncing each other, whether at home or in the Army, and to avoid seeking any remedy for the evils of the times, by other than legal means & through the properly constituted authorities. We are embarked in the holiest of all causes which can stir the hearts of patriots—the cause of liberty & independence. We are committed to it by every tie that can bind an honorable people. Multitudes of our bravest and best have already sealed it with their blood, whilst others, giving up all earthly possessions, are either languishing in dungeons or are homeless wanderers through the land, and all have felt, in a greater or less degree, the iron hand of war. A great and glorious nation is struggling to be born and wondering kingdoms & distant empires are stilled with listening hope & admiration watching this greatest of human events. Let them not, I pray you, be shocked with the spectacle of domestic Strife and petty, malignent feuds. Let not our enemy be rejoiced to behold our strong arms and stronger devotion which have often made him tremble, turned against ourselves. Let us rather show that the God of Liberty is in His Holy Temple—the hearts of freemen—and bid all the petty bickerings of earth keep silence before him.

Instead of engaging in this unholy and unpatriotic strife and threatening to resist the laws of the land and endangering the peace of society, let us prepare diligently and with hopeful hearts for the hardships and sufferings of the coming winter. Heaven has blessed us with abundant crops, but thousands of the poor are unable to purchase. Let us begin in time and use every effort to provide for them and secure them against suffering—And let us exert ourselves to the utmost to return to duty the many brave but misguided men who have left their country's flag in the hour of danger, and God will yet bless us and our children, and our children's children will thank us for not despairing of the Republic in its darkest hours of disaster, and still more, for adhering to and preserving, amid the fiery trials of war, conservative sentiments and the rights and civil liberties of the young Confederacy

In witness whereof Zebulon B. Vance our Governor, Captain General and Commander in Chief, hath signed these presents and caused the Great Seal /of the State/ to be affixed

Done at the city of Raleigh, this 7th day of September, A.D. 1863, and in the year of American Independence the 88th.

Z. B. Vance

ZBV to Edward J. Hale   A&H:Hale

Raleigh, Sep 7th. [1863]

My dear Sir,

Your several communications have been recd. and "contents noted". I was very sorry you did not attend—Mr. Reade also failed but I had a letter from him—He is right but *scarery*—must not break with Holden &c. Gov Graham & Mr. Satterwaite[1] were here, and I read them letters from about thirty leading Whigs of the State—all concurring in my views of duty—We sent for Holden & Gov G—talked to him earnestly for three hours. It would do no good—he would agree to nothing & insisted that the meetings should go on and I and no one else must say a word! Modest proposition truly. I offered to keep silent if he would discourage the meetings—would not agree to it. Gov Graham was clear that I should issue a proclamation, but insisted it should be very mild and cautionary. I have accordingly written one which will appear tomorrow, but I do assure it is not the document my judgment would have dictated, but I yielded to Mr. Grahams better advice. I do not know that I [torn] pub[torn] unless my friends should think it of sufficient importance. I had prepared a lengthy letter going into the argument of the case fully, but it <would> was thought best to adopt another mode.

From my many letters, and my own knowledge of the men holding these meetings, the *metal* is very small—I expect the peace men really have a majority to start with, but the *brains* are largely with us; and brains like bottoms, will tell on the last [quarter]. I am very hopeful of the cont[es][*faded*]

I am rather surprised [torn] men who [torn] *peace* are /not/ made to say what *kind of a peace* "Under which King" &c Instead of letting them off with these Kansas-Nebraska terms, an "honorable peace" &c, you ought it seems to me, make Holden say *what* he was for & *how* he proposed to get it. In this way the issue could be forced upon him before he had the public mind read You could thus draw his fire—At present his peace, to use a old witicism, is like "the Peace of God which passeth understanding"— Dont let him deceive you—he *is for reconstruction* out & out—Write me often

Truly yours
Z B Vance

Confidential

[1]Fenner Bryan Satterthwaite, member of council of state, former Whig legislator, and delegate to state constitutional conventions of 1861 and 1865. Williams and Hamilton, *Papers of Graham*, 5:529n.

ZBV to Thomas M. Crossan   A&H:GLB

State of North Carolina
Executive Department
Raleigh Sept 9th. 1863

Col. T. M. Crossan
Commanding N.C. Steamship "Advance"

Dear Sir,

You will proceed to sea as soon as the tide will serve and sail for Bermuda—After taking in a full cargo of freight supposed to be there for the State, should any be left, you will make arrangements through Purser J. H. Flanner for shipping it all for Wilmington *as soon as possible*, leaving none for another voyage of your ship. Should more freight be expected at Bermuda from Europe, you will also instruct Mr Flanner to make arrangements with a reliable agent for shipping it immediately to Wilmington—

In the event that you should be unable to return to North Carolina I desire the ship sold and the cargo, wherever yourself and Mr Flanner shall upon consideration think best for the interest of the State and the proceeds deposited in England to credit of the State, by advice of Mr. John White our Commissioner to England.

Very respectfully
Your obt. Servt.
Z. B. Vance

John H. Winder to ZBV   A&H:GLB

Head Quarters. Dept. Henrico.
Richmond Sept 9th. 1863

His Excellency Z. B. Vance
Governor of N.C.

Sir

I have the honor to state that your communication[1] to the Secretary of War, asking for the removal of Capt. Henry McCoy, has been received—

I am instructed by the Secretary of War to say that a Court of Inquiry has been ordered to investigate all the charges preferred against Capt McCoy, as it would be unjust both to him and to the Department to remove him whilst under charges.

I am further instructed to say that as soon as the Court closes the investigation, that Capt. McCoy will be assigned to other duties, without regard to the decision of the Court, as his seems to be objectionable

Respectfully
Jno. H. Winder
Brig. Genl.

¹Not extant.

Edward J. Hale to ZBV   A&H:VanPC

Confidential

Fayetteville, Sept. 9. 1863

My Dear Sir:

Yours of the 7th¹ at hand this afternoon. We are very much pleased with your Proclamation²—it is admirable in style and temper in matter & measure. I like it so well that I would have liked "more" of it. If I had not unfortunately been kept away by a false alarm, I have no doubt that I should have give for you true full argument of the subject. Still, I have great confidence in Gov. Graham's judgment—Mr. [*George E.*] Badger was want to say that his was the soundest judgment in No. Ca.

Your account of the failure of Gov. Graham to influence Holden made me hesitate to take a step for which I had prepared myself—no less than to send a long letter to Holden. I was induced to do this by some statements of Rev. Dr. Smith³ of Va. who told me of a long conversation he had with H. I suppose you know its particulars: How a friend of the Dr. had been in Lincolnton counselling with the Northern peace men, & how he found them dispirited & the Lincolnites encouraged by the Standard. He got Holden to agree that if he could be satisfied of all this he would change his course. I think he told him enough to satisfy him. Yet he persists. It occurred to <me> /us/ that if he were hesitating, a personal appeal from me might turn the scale. So I wrote him, prefacing with the reason for it that Dr. S. told me he (H) had spoken in terms of warm respect for me & the Observer. I told him that until recently, not he, but his advisers, had been the cause of the doubts of the loyalty of No. Ca.—North & South. That I had not doubted the sincerity of his devotion to the Confederacy & its cause; but that his recent course had enabled his enemies to say: I told you so! He is disloyal, &c. I reminded him of the *effects*—the Washington meeting & the disclosures of Dr. S.—the *national results*. That his course had brought N.C. to the verge of civil war. That I knew he had reason to complain, for himself & for the state, but the bitterness & particularly of his complaints had [turned] the minds of the people, made them lukewarm, and even ready to say they might as was well be under Lincoln. That his meetings had caused desertions, as I had evidence; had produced a feeling of defiance of the laws, &c., & had arrayed our people almost in deadly strife.

He could put an end to all this. And he ought to do it. If he did not, awful would be his responsibility. The Obs. had given him an opportunity to do it; but the statements of Dr. S. presented a far more [unjust] one. He could not [intently] change his course—that would injure him <; but> & fail of effect. But a frank and bold statement of the existence of [treason] would change the whole face of affairs, settle everything, & place *him* on higher ground than he had ever occupied. The Obs. would stand by him against all enemies, if such there should be, & I didn't think that the Standard & the Obs. together, in a good cause, could be beaten.

I told him that in advising him to take this course, *I* was relinquishing more of honor & e[m]dearment than the Obs. had ever brought me before. That we were daily receiving the very highest compliments from the best & greatest men in the State, & floods of subscribers, nearly all from his region of country, to which, as a *news*-paper, we had no access. Let the Standard change its course, & all this stopped at once. The Standard would regain its accustomed circulation & influence. Compliments & subscribers were pleasant, but they could not compare with the peace of the State & the success of the cause.

I have inflicted on you this rather full outline in deference to Peter's [*Peter M. Hale*] opinion, who thinks that you ought to know, *in confidence*, of such a thing. I sent the letter this evening, thinking, upon the whole, that if it did no good it could do no harm. Of course it ought not to be spoken of, no matter what his course may be.

It is late & my eyes can't bear much night work.

> Yours truly
> E. J. Hale

[1]In this volume.
[2]September 7, in this volume.
[3]Identity unknown.

ZBV to Jefferson Davis   A&H:GP

[*Telegram*]

Copy

Raleigh Sept 10th. 1863

President Davis
Richmond

A Georgia regiment of Benning s[1] Brigade entered this city last night, at 10 o'clock and distroyed the office of the Standard newspaper.

This morning a mob of citizens distroyed the office of the State Journal, in retaliation.[2]

Please order immediately that troops passing through here shall not enter the city. If this is not done, the most frightful consequences may ensue

Respectfully
Z. B. Vance

[1]Henry Lewis Benning, in James Longstreet's command en route to Tennessee. Faust et al., *Encyclopedia of Civil War*, 55.

[2]For accounts of the riots and ZBV's response, see Barrett, *Civil War in North Carolina*, 195–196, and Tucker, *Zeb Vance*, 352–355.

Jefferson Davis to ZBV   A&H:GP

[*Telegram*]

Richmond Sep 10 1863

Gov Z B Vance

Your dispatches of this date recd. I deeply regret the occurrence you announce and have sent by telegraph the following order to Maj W W Peirce[1] Q M—You will not allow the troops in transit to be detained at Raleigh & will communicate to the commanding officer of each detachment passing there that he is instructed not to permit his men to enter the city but if transportation is not furnish to enable the detachment to proceed immedy by rail road will march halting to an encampment at safe distance from Raleigh

Jeffn Davis

[1]Stationed in Raleigh to issue clothing to returning Confederate prisoners. Tucker, *Zeb Vance*, 425.

ZBV to Jefferson Davis   A&H:GP

Copy

Raleigh Sept. 11th. 1863.

To His Excellency
President Davis
Richmond Va.

Dear Sir

This afternoon in despite of your orders to Maj. Peirce a large number of infuriated Soldiers from /an/ Alabama brigade (I did not learn whose) entered

the city and spread terror in their path by threatening murder and conflagration.
I rod with all speed to the depot and got a Col. Scruggs to march a detachment
into town and restrain them before they had done any damage. They even threatened my life if I interfered with them. This thing is becoming intolerable. For
sixty hours I have travel<l>ed up and down making speeches alternately to
citizens and soldiers without rest or sleep almost, engaged in the humiliating task
of trying to defend the laws and peace of the State against our own bayonets. Sir
the means of stopping these outrages, I leave to you, it can be easily done, if the
officers will but try. If not done I shall feel it a duty, which I owe to the dignity
and self respect of the first state in the Confederacy in point of numbers and
good conduct of her Soldiers and in all the natural resources of war, to issue my
proclamation recalling her troops from the field to the defence of their own
homes: already threats *are* loudly proclaimed of burning the bridges and destroying the Roads leading by this place. The indignation is not confined to the friends
and follows of the N.C. Standard, but its becoming general and widespread as
the insults to the State are becoming known. The matter is worth looking after
I do assure you. And I hope for the sake of the common cause of law and of
decency, it will be done

I am Sir

Your obt servt.

(Signed)   Z. B. Vance

ZBV to Jefferson Davis   A&H:GP

State of North Carolina
Executive Department
Raleigh Sept. 11th. 1863

His Excellency
Jefferson Davis
Richmond Va.

My Dear Sir

You have received by telegraph before this, information of the riots occurring
in this city. It will enable you to see what a mine I have been standing [on] and
what a delicate and embarrassing situation mine is. I am now trembling to see
its effects upon the country, though I am greatly in hopes that the mob of citizens
which destroyed the office of the state Journal will act as a counter irritant and
help to allay excitement, the damage being equal to both parties.

But Sir the country is in a dangerous excitement and it will require the utmost
Skill and tact to guide it through safely and honorably. I beg, again to impress
you with the importance of Sustaining me in every Essential particular and of
heeding my suggestions about men and things in North Carolina, concerning
which I spoke to you in Richmond.[1]

The Soldiers who orginated the mob, belonged to Benning s brigade and were led by their officers, several of whom I saw in the crowd, but heard none of their names except a Maj. Shepherd.[2] I have also reason to believe it was done with the knowledge and consent of Gen. Benning as he remarked to a gentleman an hour or two previous, that his men had threatened it. During its continuance he could not be found, a messenger sent by me to his supposed quarters at the Depot was refused admission to him and although he had ample opportunity after the occurrence, to have seen or written to me disclaiming this outrage upon the honor and peace of North Carolina, he did not do so. As it is my intention to enforce the laws rigidly against all citizens who participated in the second mob, So I feel it my duty to demand that punishment may be inflicted on the officers who assisted or countenanced the first. Should this not be done, I shall feel it my duty to demand the persons of these officers of the State of Georgia, to answer the demands of justice.

I feel very sad in the contemplation of these outrages. The distance is quite short to either anarchy or despotism, when armed Soldiers led by their officers can with impunity outrage the laws of a State. A few more such exhibitions will bring the North Carolina *troops* home to the defence of their own state and her institutions. I pray you to see that it does not occur again. Should any newspaper in this state commit *treason* I would have its Editor arrested and tried by the laws which many of us yet respect. I thank you for your prompt orders, by telegraph to Maj. Peirce, concerning the passage of the troops through this city. They are now being Enforced, and peace can be preserved if they are rigidly obeyed.

> Very Respectfully
> Yr. obt. servt.
> Z. B. Vance.

[1]See Davis to ZBV, July 24, in this volume.
[2]Lieutenant Colonel William S. Shepherd (erroneously called a major by ZBV), Second Regiment, Georgia Infantry. Tucker, *Zeb Vance*, 354.

ZBV to James A. Seddon   A&H:GLB

> State of North Carolina
> Executive Department
> Raleigh Sept 11th. 1863—

Hon. J. A. Seddon
Secty of War
Richmond, Va.

Sir

A letter received in this town from a reliable officer and gentleman, now a prisoner of war on David's Island, gives information that the thirty thousand troops in N. York, ostensibly for the enforcement of the draft, are really designed for the invasion of this State. This news obtained from good southern /men/ living in N. York and was smuggled through by their aid

Should it be true it is an alarming expedition, both to the safety of Richmond and this State, as well as to the entire Confederacy: our roads now constituting the only communication South. I beg your attention to this matter and the prompt adoption of such means, as may be in the power of the Department

Respectfully
Z. B. Vance

ZBV to Edward J. Hale   A&H:Hale

Raleigh, Sep 11 [*1863*]

My dear Sir,

Yours recd. this morning. I thank you for your kind opinion of my proclamation, and am glad you wrote to Holden—poor fellow, his time has at length come to realize the truth of the maxim, that "those who sow the wind must reap the whirlwind"— You have heard before this of the demolition of his office by the Soldiers, of the destruction of Spellmans[1] by the citizens &c. The excitement continues; troops pass every few hours and excited mobs of them rush through the streets and threaten to burn hang & destroy—For forty eight hours I have [*been*] traveling up and down, making speeches & trying to restrain both citizens & soldiers until I am almost worn out—not being well anyhow. I got the President to send orders here that no troops should enter the city, but it is of no avail, their officers secretly encouraging it. I have just telegraphed the President again to adopt more effectual means of restraining the soldiers, & have written him privately that if these great outrages upon the peace & dignity of the State were not promptly checked I would issue my proclamation recalling the N C troops to the protection of their own State—that I felt Raleigh was entitled to as much protection & respect as the abolitionists of Pa. Did I act rashly? I fear so, though I feel the outrage deeply, & I *know* it can be prevented. They threatened my life freely today, having heard that I rebuked the Georgians severely night before last. I am likely to suffer the usual fate of a reasonable man in the midst of unreasonable ones, and be crushed to powder between the two. Both sides are already denouncing me for doing too much & too little, as the one or the other wanted help Holden fled to my house for safety & is now in the country hiding like a guilty thing & old Syms[2] implored me to save his office with shaking knees, forgetting that his last edition in the State was a scurrilous fling at me. Did you /see/ the Bulletins[3] attack upon me? Founded upon a lying dispatch from this place. I asked no help from Davis except to govern his troops & help me sustain his own miserable maladministration in N.C. Britton[4] is a very contemptable puppy. I know him of old.

I fear very much the reaction in N.C. against the cause—God give us grace & strength to meet it & keep things right. I know the people will [madly] sympathise with Holden. I would feel deeply for him myself if not disgusted with his cowardice. I dread the arrival of more trains Regard this as confidential—

> Very truly yours
> Z. B. Vance

[1]John Spelman, editor of the Raleigh *State Journal.* Williams and Hamilton, *Papers of Graham*, 5:522n.
[2]John W. Syme, editor of the *Raleigh Register.* Williams and Hamilton, *Papers of Graham*, 5:115n.
[3]*Daily Bulletin* (Charlotte).
[4]Edward H. Britton, publisher of the *Daily Bulletin.*

Jefferson Davis to ZBV   A&H:GP

> Confederate States of America,
> Executive Department,
> Richmond, Va. September 13th. 1863

Govr. Z. B. Vance
Raleigh No.Ca.

My dear Sir,
Your two communications of the 11th. Inst.[1] have been received.

Upon the receipt of your telegram[2] informing me that the measures taken to put an end to the disturbances in Raleigh had not proved effective, orders were issued which it is hopeful will be sufficient to prevent further disorders.

I have referred to the Secretary of War your statements respecting particular officers alleged to have been concerned in the riot, and the matter will receive inquiry.

> Very Respectfully & truly Yours
> Jeffn. Davis

[1]In this volume.
[2]Not extant.

James A. Seddon to ZBV   A&H:GP

[*With enclosure*]

Confederate States of America,
War Department,
Richmond, Va. Sept. 14, 1863.

His Excellency Z. B. Vance,
Governor of North Carolina,
Raleigh, N.C.

Sir,
    Your Excellency's letter of the 20th. ult.,[1] with regard to the causes of dissat-
isfaction among the N.C. troops in the Army of Northern Va., was referred to
Genl. Lee, and I now have the honor to enclose a copy of his reply.

Very Respectfully
Your obdt. Servt.
James A Seddon
Secretary of War

[1]Not extant.

[*Enclosure*]

Robert E. Lee to James A. Seddon   A&H:GP

Copy.

Head Quarters, A.N.Va.
Sept. 9, 1863.

Hon. Jas. A. Seddon,
Sec'y of War,
Richmond, Va.

Sir,
    The letter of Gov. Vance of N. Carolina of Aug. 20th. with regard to the
causes of dissatisfaction among the N.C. troops in this army with your indorse-
ment has been received. I regret exceedingly the jealousies, heartburnings and
other evil consequences resulting from the crude misstatements of newspaper
correspondents who have necessarily a very limited acquaintance with the facts
about which they write and who magnify the deeds of troops from their own
States at the expense of others. But I can see no remedy for this. Men seem to
prefer sowing discord to inculcating harmony. In the reports of the officers, justice
is done the brave soldiers of North Carolina whose heroism and devotion have

illustrated the name of their State on every battlefield in which <in which> the Army of Northern Virginia has been engaged. But the publication of these reports during the progress of the war would give the enemy information which it is desirable to withhold. With regard to a correspondent for the press from North Carolina the way is open to him as to those from other States. I cannot however in my judgment, consistently with the good of the public service detail a soldier from the Army for this purpose. I believe it would be much better to have no correspondent of the press with the Army.

In the appointment of officers I do not think there is any ground for complaint. The attempt has been as far as possible to have all the regiments from the same State brigaded together under officers from their own States or old Army officers. The cavalry regiments from N.C. have been placed in a brigade to be commanded by Genl. Baker.[1] In a mixed brigade of Virginia & N.C. regiments I some time ago removed a Virginia brigadier on the representations of Govr. Vance and placed over the brigade an old Army officer from Maryland.[2] Shortly after the battle of Chancellorsville two Brigadiers from N.C. were promoted Major Generals in this Army, their former positions being filled at once by promotions from that State. Of one of these, the noble Pender the casualties of battle, alas, deprived us and the other Genl. [Matt W.] Ransom has been called to take charge of an important military Department, succeeding another distinguished North Carolinian Genl. Hill of the Army of N. Va. promoted and sent to the Department of the West. Another the lamented Pettigrew whose brigade under his skillful leadership emulated the deeds of veterans in the battles of Gettysburg fell on the banks of the Potomac. He has been succeeded by the promotion of an officer from the same State.[3] Genl. Iverson of Ga. has been transferred from the N.C. brigade which he commanded to a Louisiana brigade and his place filled by the promotion of a North Carolinian.[4] You will perceive from this statement how far I have succeeded in arranging the brigades from N.C. in conforming to the rule spoken of above, and that though the accidents of war and the wants of the service in other departments have deprived this Army of the services of many accomplished North Carolinians, they have been replaced almost entirely by promotions from that State. I need not say that I will with pleasure aid Gov. Vance in removing every reasonable cause of complaint on the part of men who have fought so gallantly and done so much for the cause of our Country. And I hope that he will do all in his power to cultivate a spirit of harmony, and to bring to punishment the disaffected who use these causes of discontent to further their treasonable designs.

> I am with great respect
> Your ob't. servt.
> (signed)   R. E. Lee
>   Genl.

[1]Laurence Simmons Baker, promoted brigadier general on July 23. *Dictionary of North Carolina Biography*, s.v. "Baker, Laurence Simmons."

[2]George Hume Steuart of Maryland replaced Raleigh Edward Colston of Virginia. Manarin and Jordan, *North Carolina Troops*, 3:137–138.
[3]William Whedbee Kirkland, promoted brigadier general on August 29. *Dictionary of North Carolina Biography*, s.v. "Kirkland, William Whedbee."
[4]Robert Daniel Johnston, promoted brigadier general on September 1. *Dictionary of North Carolina Biography*, s.v. "Johnston, Robert Daniel."

David G. Worth to ZBV   A&H:GP

Wilmington N.C
Sept 16th. 1863.

To His Excellency Govr. Vance.
Raleigh NC

Dr. Sir—

The State Salt works in this vicinity, produced during the month of Augt, about 5000 bush salt—. About 4500 bush were distributed to the counties, and the remainder exchanged for corn, fodder, bacon &c. which could not otherwise be obtained—That to the counties was billed at $6. per 50 lbs.—That exchanged yielded about the market price say $15 to $18.—

The production fell considerably short of previous months, on acct of the suspension of River Side Works, which have heretofore been producing from 1000 to 1200 bush. per month. These works were suspended because of a most malignant fever which prevailed amongst the hands & which made *all* sick. & killed many—They are now in operation again, & I hope will continue so the balance of the season—The works on the coast have been for some weeks, and still continue, much crippled, for want of hands, over half the men employed being sick. The consequence is that the supply of cut wood is becoming short, & I fear the production of salt will, in the course of a few weeks, be materially interfered with on that account—The men continue to get sick—& the sick ones recover slowly. I am compelled to let these men go home to recruit, as there is no hospital connected with the works, and no accomodations of any sort for sick men—

The time is not far off when it will again be necessary, to advance the price of salt—on account of the increasing distance to haul wood (now five miles) and advanced prices of corn, bacon &c.—It shall be put off though as long as possible—.

Most Resfully
Your obt Servt.
D. G. Worth[1]
S. Salt Comn

[1]David Gaston Worth replaced his uncle John M. Worth as salt commissioner after the latter submitted his resignation, effective on August 1. John M. Worth to ZBV, July 22, A&H:GP; Ashe, Weeks, and Van Noppen, *Biographical History*, 3:473–477.

ZBV to Edward J. Hale   A&H:Hale

State of North Carolina,
Executive Department,
Raleigh, Sep. 20th. 1863.

Mr Hale,

Dr. Sir,

Your suggestions about the telegraph shall be attended to—have heretofore urged it upon the War Dept, will do so again.[1]

Please keep your temper and dont get into a difficulty with the papers here. The Progress is ripe for it, and is urged on by some men who dont wish to be known. Dont gratify him[2]—his paper dont amount to any thing, and the whole thing is not worth quarreling about. You are mistaken in your version of the mob here, there was no altercation between the citizens & soldiers whatever—Correct it and let the matter pass quietly—I have just returned from the mountains & find to my great gratification, that the excitement about the stopping of Holdens paper is very small indeed. I met with hardly a man but was willing it should stay down, if the Journal was down with it.

Holden has been weakened by the blow, or I am vastly mistaken—He complains I hear, that you hit him whilst he is down and unable to reply and is trying to prejudice some of our friends against you on that account. I think you had best avoid this, and say nothing about him by name, until he gets up. When I last talked to him he seemed kindly disposed. I will see him again tomorrow.

Begging pardon for advising so experienced an Editor as yourself,

I remain
most sincerely &c
Z. B. Vance

Confidential

[1] See ZBV to James A. Seddon, September 24, in this volume.
[2] J. L. Pennington, editor of the Raleigh Progress. Yates, Confederacy and Vance, 86–87.

ZBV to Thomas L. Clingman   SHC:Clin

State of North Carolina,
Executive Department,
Raleigh, Sept. 21st. 1863.

Brigadier Genl T. L. Clingman[1]

Dear Sir

A quantity of cloth suitable for officers uniforms was brought by the Steamer Advance upon her first trip and has been sold to our officers upon proper requisition. The supply has been exhausted. The Steamer however is expected to make another voyage and return within 15 or 20 days. It is hoped and expected that a portion of her cargo will consist of cloth of a like kind. If so the officers of your Brigade can be supplied. In order to insure this however they had better file their requisitions with the adjutant General immediately—

> With sentiments of great respect
> Your obedient servant
> Z. B. Vance

[1] Thomas Lanier Clingman, former Whig, legislator, and U.S. congressman and senator, who commanded a brigade in eastern North Carolina. *Dictionary of North Carolina Biography*, s.v. "Clingman, Thomas Lanier."

ZBV to James A. Seddon   A&H:GLB

> State of North Carolina
> Executive Department
> Raleigh—Sept. 21st. 1863

Hon. James A. Seddon
Secty of War

My dear Sir

The occupation of East Tennessee by the enemy, and the great assemblage of tories and deserters in the mountains of the border, renders Western N. Carolina with all its supplies of beef and pork, open to the invasion of the federals and tories—It is inhabited however by quite a warlike militia, who are calling upon me to arm and organize them for a fight. I am doing so to the utmost of my ability but shall not be able to accomplish much without your assistance—

I have the honor therefore, to request that you will constitute that mountain country a District and assign a competent Brigadier to the command, with a battery or so, and a very few regular troops the various passes could be easily held with the help of some two thousand Home Guards, whom I can order to his support. If you have no suitable officer to be spared for such a purpose, I would recommend that Col. C. M. Avery of the 33d. N.C.T. or Col. Stephen Lee of the 16th. N.C.T. be made Brigadier and assigned to that duty. They are both residents of that section, acquainted with the country & people. The first named would in my opinion, be the best appointment, being younger, more active and better adapted to the management of militia and the people generally.

I cannot furnish arms to them without leaving unarmed the Home Guards on the Eastern border of the State, and so I beg you, if possible, to spare me a thousand or fifteen hundred muskets.

Please let me know if these suggestions meet your views immediately—there is no time to be lost

Very respectfully, Yours
Z. B. Vance

Robert B. Vance to ZBV   A&H:VanPC

Atlanta Ga. Sept. 21/63

Dear Brother,

Genl. Bragg has assigned me to the command of the Western Dist. of N.C. West of blue ridge with orders to organize all Troops within the Dist. both State & Confederate. I am dissatisfied. What is the prospect of getting a Brigade on N.C. coast? Please write me in full to Asheville & say what authority I have over the State Troops, if they are organized and if they go into camp etc.?

Skirmishing in front. Bragg's army in splendid fix & will whip certain. Quite well

Brother
R. B. Vance

ZBV to James A. Seddon   A&H:GLB

State of North Carolina
Executive Department
Raleigh. Sept. 24th. 1863

Hon. J. A. Seddon,
Richmond Va

Sir

Permit me to urge the importance of establishing telegraphic communication with Fayetteville N.C. and this point. I am authorized by law to do so, but can not procure the materials. No interior part in this State is of more importance, on account of the armory, the cotton factories (eight in number) and the coal, of which it is our main depot.

It is fifty miles from Raleigh and by aid of the telegraph large bodies of militia could be thrown there for its defence at any moment. Assist me in its execution if possible

Respectfully, yours
Z. B. Vance

Leander S. Gash to ZBV   A&H:GP

Claytonville NC Sept. 24th. 1863

His Exclency Z. B. Vance
Governor NC

Dear Zeb,
Yours of the 10th. inst.[1] is received And crowded as I know you are with business of more importance than than [sic] the reading of my long epistles, I have concluded to write you again with the view of setting myself right in one or two particulars and I may not anoy you soon again until you get more time In the first place you are a little mistaken if you take me to be one of your old friends that have lost confidence [in] you. There is no man in the State in whom I have more confidence than yourself, (Wrong as I believe you are on the Peace question.) It is the first and only important question that we ever differed upon and I may be wrong myself, but if so I am honestly wrong Therefore /I/ am willing to accord the same to you. I have never doubted your integrity of purpose nor doubted but what /you/ was doing, and would continue to do, what you thought was best for the State and its citizens. Nor do I believe there is a man in the state of your age whose sagasity as a statesman is superiour to your own. Yet as you are human like unto other men, I think you might once in your life be wrong. I have always found old man Hale, (Editor of Fayetteville Observer) always right before, and if I could conscienciously surrender my own judgement to that of other mens, I would like to do so on this occasion with such examples before me. Mr Graham you know is a great favorite with me. But I have always thought if he lacked any thing it was that of moral courage, though I do not know how he stands on this occasion. I like moral courage that kind that enables a man to do what he thinks is right regardless of public sentiment at the time. Individual or personal courage as known by the world I care nothing for it nor claim none of it myself Moral courage to do right regardless of friend or foe is what I like & am proud to see you possess a good share of it. I would not change your views on the question of peace if I could for you must judge for yourself and be responsible for your own course But what I have been trying to do was to inform our rulers of a few things they appear to be ignorant of. Among which is that the whole people (who are not in high office) are tired of this unfortunate war, and want it stopped in some way secondly, I have seen for months and am astonished that every body else has not seen unmistakeable signs that the poor people generally who have done a full share of the fighting were makeing up their minds to quit this war. They will either desert to the enemy or will mutinize and demand an equal distribution of property in the confederacy. Our rulers are blind to their own danger. These things were hinted at in an article in the Times [Hendersonville] sometime ago on the mobs of New York[2] prophecying they would be reenacted here. In that article I prophecyed that they would likely be put down there then & the participaters be put in the service, Only to mutinize next time with

their arms, and wreak vengeance on the heads of Abolitionists Now mark the prediction I now make: If this war is attempted to be carried through another year, between the present contending parties as they now stand, If both armies does not mutinize and turn the arms against the originators in both sections. But the prospect now is for Jefferson [Davis] to sell us out to France or attempt it at least. But the other European powers will hardly allow a thing of that kind, even if we do not object to it ourselves; Whenever other Nations touch this thing it will be apt to take a new shape. But sufficient for the day is the evil thereof

I had forgot to say to you that I should regret very much for you to resign your office. Mr Mebane³ is no doubt a good man and perhaps an older man than your/ self/. Yet, the people Elected you Governor and the great mass of them do no dou/bt/ desire you, /to/ hold the office to the end of the term. You nor no other mortal man can hope to please us all, few of us can please ourselves therefore I hope you will hold on and continue to do the best you can for us all. But my dear Sir if you could be in these mountains and mix up with the common poor people and see their real wants and distresses in almost every imaginable shape and form, their destitution of clotheing and food; bearfooted and nearly naked, with very little prospect (if any) of their being able to procure any. Then add their other troubles of loss of husbands & sons, with others in the army or deserted (which is worse) adding new troubles to all of us, You would /not/ be surprised at good men desireing peace on almost any terms that would save liberty and life to those of us left. Then we have been considerably alarmed at the prospect of a Federal raid for several days. But that is somewhat relieved by hearing that Gen Brag has routed the Federals in East Tennessee but we are a little afraid the news is too good to be all true yet we hope to hear the whole truth soon. And if my advice would be worth anything I would beg that the nearest rout be taken to bring about a peace. Would it not be a good time to offer them some honorable and liberal terms for a peace it might stiffen the back of the peace men North. Besides they might be inclined to want to make some terms that would save their friends in East Tennessee. Though I must confess that I greatly fear that Lincoln & Davis will never agree on terms of peace My only hope was that the people North & South would be able to reach the question through the ballot Box independent of of [sic] the Presidents. But you intimate that there is no hopes in that direction. Then what can we do. Fighting will never bring us a peace short of absolute subjection, which is the last thing I wanted, hence my great desire for a compromise I have nothing to do with those peace meetings except serveing as a delegate to the convention to nominate a candidate for Congress. We ad-journed to meet again next Monday. I shall attend but will not be surprised if some of us are arrested. There is a kinky headed scoundrel who lives in Ashville and draws his wages, from the state, who has from the commencement of this war been trying to [hiss] every mob and detatched solder sent to the Country on me from the commencement of this war to this day. Not that he believes what he says about me but to gratify his malice [from] and old grudge. He is a bad man at heart and my desi[re is] that he would let me alone. I do not want to commit a wrong knowingly nor do I want to be harrassed as some men has been by these little military upstarts to gratify the malice of a bad man if he is in high life. I would to God that all men could pass for their real worth and not for what they ask for themselves Some of our citizens heretofore thought to be among our best citizens have left their homes to avoid the executions of the threats of those detached soldiers some of them no doubt gone to Tennessee. A. H. Jones[4] of Hendersonville like myself had been scribbleing in the times. his life was threatened he dodged off and it is said went to Tenn. sent his nephiew back for his money His wife sent it consealed near two thousand dollars they captured the boy took his money and sent a company to capture Jones when he was to meet his nephiew. It will be quite a disappointment to Dock [A. H. Jones] to meet an armed guard in search of his body instead of his nephiew with his money. If they get him I guess they will hang him as our people are ripe for hanging somebody. I am sory for Dock and his family. he is a son of old George Jones of Hominy and his wife is a daughter of Wm. Brittain Esq. of Mills River with a large and interesting family of children one a grown daughter a maniac. I have no idea how far he has committed himself. Though he always was opposed to the war and was very near being Elected to the last legislature without being a candidate. Loftess[5] I suppose has gone through also. I should dread to see Loftess return [in power] with a raid he would more than revenge all his wrongs on the heads of his enemies. These persecutions and retaliations are all wrong and should checked if possible. I must close. If there is any possible chance for our people to get thread or cards do let them have them and for Gods sake do what you can to bring about a peace soon as possible. If we could get an armistice and parly I think we might hope for peace sometime.

With my best wishes
I am as ever yours &c
L. S. Gash

[Endorsed] File

Z B V

---

[1]Not extant.

[2]Reference to the New York draft riots of July. See Faust et al., Encyclopedia of Civil War, 225–226.

[3]Giles Mebane, speaker of the state senate and therefore in line for the governorship if ZBV resigned. Dictionary of North Carolina Biography, s.v. "Mebane, Giles."

[4]Alexander Hamilton Jones, farmer, merchant, newspaper editor, and postwar Republican congressman. Opposed to the war, he helped form a secret Union league in western North Carolina. While he was in eastern Tennessee recruiting North Carolinians for the Federal army, he was captured and imprisoned by the Confederates. Dictionary of North Carolina Biography, s.v. "Jones, Alexander Hamilton."

[5]John H. Loftis, a unionist who actively opposed the war. The Henderson County Court had convicted him of refusing to obey Confederate law, and Confederate troops operating against deserters had apparently used him as a hostage. Olsen and McGrew, "Prelude to Reconstruction," pt. 1, 54n; Gash to ZBV, September 11, A&H:GP.

Robert B. Vance to ZBV   A&H:VanPC

Asheville Sept 28/63

Dear Bro:

If it is possible to get a Regt. of regular troops for me it ought to be done at once. I do not believe that I can protect the country without them. All other troops are so uncertain until drilled. Do something for me if possible. I will go to Raleigh as soon as I can. We want some tents, cookin vessels etc.

Bro
R B Vance

ZBV to Henry A. London   A&H:GLB

State of North Carolina
Executive Department
Raleigh Sept. 29th. 1863

Henry A. London Eq.[1]
Pittsboro, N.C.

My dear Sir

Mr. S. T. Haughton wishes to lower the lock on Deep River, at Farish's first trap below the Gulf, which at present impairs the efficiency of his mill—

Not knowing anything of the matter, I must ask you to consult Mr. Ellwood Morris, the Engineer, and report to me, whether the proposed alteration can be made under the authority vested in the commissioners, and if it will impair the work &c.

Very respectfully
Your obt. servt.
Z. B. Vance

[1]Henry Adolphus London, merchant and treasurer of the Cape Fear and Deep River Navigation Company, which opened and maintained a water route from Fayetteville to the town of Gulf in central Chatham County. *Dictionary of North Carolina Biography*, s.v. "London, Henry Adolphus."

ZBV to James A. Seddon   A&H:VanPC

State of North Carolina,
Executive Department,
Raleigh Oct 1 1863

Hon J. A. Seddon
Secy. of War

Dear Sir,

I beg leave again to call your attention to the deplorable condition of Western N. Carolina. Gen R. B. Vance has arrived there and has not a single man with which to defend this country! I have ordered the militia to report to him, but have arms only for about the tenth man.

Can you possibly send a few troops there? One of our small regiments, as the 16th., and a squadron of Cavalry would be sufficient—No organized invasion is feared, but the mountains are full of tories and deserters who are burning and destroying almost at pleasure. In addition to the damage doing in this way, they are develloping all the latest tory sentiments in that country. In the County of Madison which borders on Tennesse, eighty six out of ninety conscripts have gone to the enemy. In view of all this I beg you to order all the conscripts west of the Blue Ridge to report to Gen. Vance for home service. In this way much good can be done, and men got into service who might otherwise become out-laws.

There is already a squadron of cavalry in Western N.Ca under Gen Hoke— if that cannot be sent my brother, I suggest they be taken from the 2d. N.C. Cavalry.

Capt. Rogers will give you verbally any further information you may desire—

Very resptly.
Yr. obt. srvt.
Z. B. Vance

[Endorsed} Ansr. That the Dept. would cheerfully furnish the additional force, if it could spare them—It is ascertained the 2 N C Cavalry cannot be dispensed with by Genl. Lee. It is hoped the forces now operating under Genl. Hoke in West N C together with the irregular organization constituted by the Cons Bur will prove adequate to repress the deserters & tories now threatening the peace of that section of the State

J A S

Robert F. Hoke to ZBV   SHC:Van

Wilkesboro
Octo 2nd. 1863

Hon Z. B. Vance
Raleigh N. C.

Dear Sir,

I have just received your letter of 26th.[1] I cant see why it is you have received no reports from me as I have forwarded them from each point—and have within a day or so written you—I am succeeding well and in a short time hope to complete this country—I found it necessary to accomplish anything to have troops in Yadkin, Forsyth, Surry, a portion of Davie & Iredell, Alexander, Wilkes and Allegany all at the same time and as Col Faison only has eight companies was obliged to order Maj Graham to this section[2]

Shortly I will send the whole of 56th. Regmt. to Randolph and the adjoining counties. It was not for strength that I brought forward Graham but to have troops enough to deploy over the whole country—The deserters have not made the slightest resistance but dispersed, each one taking care of himself

With the force I have to do any good one section at a time will have to be disposed of. We have sent off and have still /on hands/ to send about five hundred including those who enlisted in 21st. N C Regmt.—I sent off a number of deserters immediately to the Army with officers sent here to collect them. I was ordered by Genl. Lee to recruit my command as much as possible and have received many as the 21st. Regmt. is composed of men from the counties in which I am on duty—I have sent about twenty recruits to one company of Whistons[3] Bntt—I have taken civil action against a great many citizens—Judge B[ailey][4] gave me the necessary advice I was greatly surprised at the extent to which this trouble had grown and am sure that court could not have been held here if these "Bonds" had not been dispersed—I neglected to state that I have sent cavalry into Ashe—

This duty is a hard one and these fellows are hard to catch but I assure you no labour will be spared in a speedy accomplishment of the work—From the tone of your letter I should judge that you are not at all pleased with what I have done—

Very Respectfully Yours
R F Hoke

[1]Not extant.

[2]Paul F. Faison and John W. Graham, Fifty-sixth Regiment North Carolina Troops. Clark, *Histories of Regiments from North Carolina*, 3:318.

[3]James M. Whitson, Eighth Regiment North Carolina State Troops. Manarin and Jordan, *North Carolina Troops*, 4:521, 533.

[4]John Lawrence Bailey, superior court judge. Arthur, *Western North Carolina*, 398–399; Ashe, Weeks, and Van Noppen, *Biographical History*, 4:53–54, 6:6–8.

Richmond M. Pearson to ZBV   A&H:GP

Richmond Hill Oct 3d. 1863

Governor Vance

My Dear Sir,

Your letter of the 26th. ult.[1] was not read until last night Edwards & Baily[2] were the only two of the persons you name, in whose favor writs had issued. They were brought before me several days, before your communication came to hand—

The sheriff for cause of their imprisonment, besides the order of Col [John W.] McElroy; produced a warrant of commitment signed by their justices of the peace, & set forth that owing to the condition of things in Yancey, he had been afraid to go into that county to notify either Col McElroy or the committing magistrates

As the matter had been passed on by *justices of the peace* & no witnesses were in attendance, I felt it to be my duty to prepare the case, to be heard at Morganton, the following week—

I make it a rule when the warrant of commitment is made by one *having jurisdiction* not to dispose of the case unless the prosecuter, if there be one or the committing magistrate, has been notified—If however the matter had stood upon the order of Col. McElroy alone, I should have felt it to my duty to discharge the prisoners forthwith—for when the imprisonment is against law & in violation of the constitution, the party must be discharged without going into the evidence—

I know that you & all other good citizens of the state, feel assured, that I will at all times, discharge the duties of my office, to the best of my judgment—For this reason, I understand, that by the expression "I protest against their being tried here, without due notification of Col McElroy" you mean only to *suggest the propriety* of of a postponement—otherwise I should have felt called on, to demand, on what ground, The Governor, or anyone else, has a right to attempt by "protest" or in any other way, to interfere with the independent action of a judge in the discharge of his official duties?—

But I repeat, I have no idea you intended it in that sense, & believe you only meant to make a suggestion "amicus curiae"[3]—But as the expression admits of another meaning, it was proper to advert to it in manner I have done, as the communication seems to be in an official style.

Very respectfully &c.&c.
R. M. Pearson

[1]Not extant.

²Suspects charged with killing two members of the militia hunting deserters. On July 7 the legislature had specifically authorized the militia to arrest deserters and conscripts. Pearson released the accused on writs of habeas corpus. Hamilton, "North Carolina Courts and the Confederacy," 376–377; ZBV to Pearson, October 7, in this volume.

³As a bystander.

ZBV *to Duncan K. McRae*   A&H:GLB

State of North Carolina
Executive Department
Raleigh Oct. 3d. 1863

Col. D. K. McRae

Dear Sir

Your letter asking if you had properly construed my instructions to you, con-tained in my letter of the 12th. of March 1863,¹ in regard to taking the negoti-ation of the naval store bonds out of the hands of Mr Sanders has been received.

I enclose herewith a copy of that letter and also one written you on the 10th. July² which taken together can leave no mistake as to my meaning. I did intend for you to relieve Mr Sanders of the negotiation of these bonds, but as you will perceive, did not design to deprive him of any just and reasonable compensation, which might be due him in the premises. When entering into the contract with him, my principle inducement was the representations of Mr. S. that all the negotiations of bonds, purchases of goods etc. was to be made at Halifax, run through in sloops of slight cost &c. I had no idea of sending *another* agent to Europe, having already one there in whom I had full confidence, and knowing that it could not but hinder his negotiations and injure the credit of the State to have naval agents in the same market, higgling for the sale of our paper. Instead of repairing to Halifax however Mr Saunders and yourself made directly for Eu-rope and commenced operations side by side with Mr White, my first agent. Not liking to blast the whole project entirely and order you back home, after the journey out had been accomplished, though I claim that I would have been justifiable in annulling the whole contract, I concluded that, being a citizen of the State, alive to her interests and honor, you would be more likely to preserve both than a stranger, as was Mr. Sanders, tempted perhaps by the profits of a large contract, and that I would therefore trust the matter in your hands alone. My letter of the 12th. March was accordingly written with this view. These explanations would have been set forth therein but that I supposed you could to a great extent divine them and not knowing how Mr. S. was proceeding I thought it unjust to express any suspicion of him which might prove groundless—For proof that I did not intend also to do him pecuniary injustice I refer to my letter of July 10th., I [in] which I clothed you with an almost unlimited power to indemnify him—The honorable and loyal State of North Carolina will yet do that, to the full demand of justice

I am, Colonel
very respectfully
your obt Servt
Z. B. Vance

¹In this volume.
²In this volume.

ZBV to William H. Battle   A&H:GP

State of North Carolina,
Executive Department,
Raleigh, Oct 6th. 1863.

Judge Battle,¹

My dear Sir,

The recent decision of Judge Pearson² as you are aware, places me in an embarrassing situation.

The consequences to the country of withdrawing all the forces of the State from the arresting of deserters, who are numerous in the State, and in many places have overawed and almost silenced the civil authorities, would be so great and alarming, that I am unwilling to assume the responsibility of so doing upon the decision of one Judge. I am therefore compelled again to trouble the Supreme court out of term time, to give me the benefit of their council.

I will have a case prepared for their decision at any day which may be most convenient to the court, if they will have the kindness to come to this place and set upon it.

It is scarcely necessary for me to add that I will obey promptly that decision be it what it may

Very respectfully
Yr. obt svt.
Z. B. Vance

¹William Horn Battle, justice of North Carolina Supreme Court and former legislator and law professor. *Dictionary of North Carolina Biography*, s.v. "Battle, William Horn."

²In the case of Richard M. Austin, who refused to obey ZBV's order for the Home Guard in Davie County to arrest deserters. Austin was jailed and brought before Chief Justice Pearson, who ordered the defendant released on the ground that the governor had no authority to order home guards to arrest deserters and conscripts. The Home Guard

(or Guard for Home Defense), established by a legislative act of July 7 and composed of men not eligible for conscription, had supplanted the state militia. Hamilton, "North Carolina Courts and the Confederacy," 376–377; Mitchell, *Legal Aspects of Conscription and Exemption*, 59; *Public Laws of North Carolina*, 1863 (called session), c. 10; Louis H. Manarin, ed., *Guide to Military Organizations and Installations, North Carolina, 1861–1865* (Raleigh: North Carolina Confederate Centennial Commission, 1961), 2.

ZBV to Duncan K. McRae   A&H:GLB

State of North Carolina
Executive Department
Raleigh—Oct 6th. 1863

Col. D. K. McRae
Raleigh N.C

Col

I was perhaps as much surprised at your letter[1] as you could have been at mine—[2] I was totally unconscious of saying anything in it which would have lead you to suppose that I disapproved of your official action, except the proceeding at once to Europe instead of Halifax, in which of course you did for the best—being compelled to follow the contractor Mr Sanders—To say that this met my approbation entirely would remove a good portion of the right, which I claimed and exercised of removing the negotiations from the hands of Sanders—

I expressly avoided giving any intimation in regard to the execution of the contract or negotiations themselves, after you had relieved Sanders, for the reason that the legal gentleman to whom I submitted your charge in the form of warrants, had not rendered his opinion, and you informed me verbally that that matter might wait but you wished a confirmation in writing of your construction of my letter of the 12th. March in order to send it to Europe by the first Steamer—

I can but think therefore that you are hasty in inferring my disapprobation of your operations, which so far as I have been able to see, appear to have been advantageous to the state—Of course no blame can attach for your failing to comply with instructions never recd., as you inform me my letter of 10th. of July[3] was not.

And I am sure I did not say, or *mean to say* that any harm had been done the state by the presence of two agents in Europe operating in the same market, but only expressed what I feared would have been the case, as a reason for giving you sole charge of the bonds, and which *might* have induced me to order differently had I known originally of Mr Sanders purpose to go directly to Europe

Hoping that you may consider the matter differently with this explanation

I am Sir
very resptly Yrs
Z. B. Vance

[1]October 3, A&H:GLB.
[2]October 3, in this volume.
[3]In this volume.

James A. Seddon to ZBV   A&H:GP

[With enclosure]

Confederate States of America,
War Department,
Richmond, Va. Oct 7 1863.

His Excellency Z. B. Vance,
Governor of North Carolina,
Raleigh, N.C.

Sir,
   Your letter of the 24th. ult.,[1] urging the importance of establishing telegraphic communication between Raleigh and Fayetteville, was referred to the Postmaster General, who is by law charged with that subject, and I have the honor herewith to transmit a copy of his reply.

Very Respectfully
Your obdt. servt.
James A Seddon
Secretary of War

[1]In this volume.

[Enclosure]

John H. Reagan to James A. Seddon   A&H:GP

(Copy)

Confederate States of America,
Post Office Department,
Richmond, Oct. 5th. 1863.

Hon. Jas. A. Seddon,
Secretary of War.

   I herewith return the letter of Governor Vance asking for the building of a telegraph line from Raleigh to Fayetteville, N.C.; and also send you a copy of a report on the subject by Dr. Morris the agent for the Military Telegraph Lines. From this you will see the cost of the building of the line, it is estimated, would be $29,890. It would require in addition about $300 per month to operate the line. The receipts from Military Telegraph lines have so far been merely nominal, and hence it has been found necessary to limit the building of them to such lines as were in the judgment of the Military authorities indispensably necessary to the success of /our/ military operations.

While it is apparent that the line proposed would be useful, I am not prepared, with the information before me, to conclude that the building of it is such a military necessity as to render the heavy expenditure which it would involve proper by this Department. On similar grounds I had some time ago to decline to order the building of a line from Magnolia to Fayetteville, N.C., which was recommended by Major General Whiting.

I am informed by Dr. Morris that if the Governor should desire to have the line constructed under the authority of the State, the Southern Telegraph Co., of which he is President can furnish the requisite materials

> Very respectfully
> Your obdt. servt.
> (signed)   John H. Reagan
> P. M. General

James A. Seddon to ZBV   A&H:GP

> Confederate States of America,
> War Department,
> Richmond, Va. Oct. 7 1863.

His Excellency Z. B. Vance,
Governor of N.C.
Raleigh, N.C.

Sir,

I have received your letter[1] calling attention to the condition of Western North Carolina, and asking that a Regiment and a Squadron of Cavalry may be sent there for its protection.

In reply I have the honor to say, that the Department would cheerfully furnish the additional forces, if it could spare them. It is hoped the troops now operating under Genl. Hoke in that region, together with the irregular organizations constituted by the Conscript Bureau, will prove adequate to repress the deserters and tories now threatening the peace of that section of the State.

> Very Respectfully
> Your obdt. servt.
> James A Seddon
> Secretary of War

[1]October 1, in this volume.

ZBV to Richmond M. Pearson   A&H:GLB

State of North Carolina
Executive Department
Raleigh Oct 7th. 1863.

Judge Pearson

Sir

Yours of the 3d.[1] informing me what disposition had been made of the cases of Edwards & Bailey, in answer to mine of a previous date, has been received this morning—

You are correct in supposing that I meant no interference "with the independent action of a judge in the discharge of his official duties" by protesting against the discharge of these men without the evidence—The Sheriff of Burke County was in my office and showed me the petitions and your orders, and I was of the opinion (and am yet) that they were purposely taken before you, that the witnesses could not be present: & that two men alleged to have been found with arms in their hands in open resistance to the authority of the State, and accused of being *particeps criminis* to the murder of two of my militia, might be turned loose—

This I was anxious to prevent for various reasons, and not knowing what else to do, I addressed you that letter, not dreaming that I was trenching upon the prerogatives of the judiciary—I think therefore that reflection might have induced you to have omitted the latter part of your letter entirely—

I know that the Judiciary is exceedingly and properly jealous of the encroachments of executive authority, but as human nature is frail and the times are sadly out of joint, I can only beg you to have patience with a coordinate branch of the government, which like yourself is trying to discharge the duties of his office to the best of his judgment—

I feel, without vanity, that I might safely point you to my uncouthly self as a model of a patient officer—First it is declared incompetent for me to use my militia to arrest deserters and to execute the laws of Congress: next, when the militia have been absorbed by conscription, and the exemption Bill, the military given me in place of the militia[2] is decided out of my hands by the same process: and lastly, the Chief Justice of the State goes outside of the case to pronounce a portion of my order against law, which was not called in question by the case! And yet I have been *patient* under it all, & shall submit to it quietly without even by implication, impeaching the motives of the Judge, rendering the decision

Very respectfully, yours
Z. B. Vance

[1]In this volume.
[2]Home Guard. See ZBV to William H. Battle, October 6, in this volume.

ZBV to James A. Seddon · A&H:GLB

State of North Carolina
Executive Department
Raleigh, Oct. 8th. 1863

Hon. J. A. Seddon
Secty of War

Sir,

Last month the Steamer belonging to this State lost one trip for want of coal—the Confederate Govt. Agents at Wilmington delivering it to blockade runners in preference to my vessel and assuming to control the coal mines, so that no one else can get any without their consent. Thinking this time that I would have coals in waiting for my steamer, which is due tomorrow, I sent my agent to the mine and after much difficulty got one hundred tons, which was sent down to Wilmington, and when there, was immediately seized by some one, and put on board the "Cornubia", in defiance of the fact that it belonged to this State

Now I ask your interference in this matter—The mine from which the coal was taken, belonged to aliens, was seized by the Confederacy as confiscated property and their agents put in charge of it. As you must be aware, no title can accrue to the Confederacy in this manner, for real estate within the borders of a Soverign State. The title to this property is therefore clearly in the State of North Carolina: and whilst I am perfectly willing that the Confederacy should continue to use this mine as heretofore, I am not willing, neither do I intend to be stood aside in this manner. I must have coals when the State requires them, in preference to blockade runners or any body else—

Please therefore to give orders to this effect, or I shall be compelled to order the Attorney General to begin such legal proceedings as may be necessary, and to order coal enough for my purposes to be seized—

The loss of one trip of the Steamer alone is of consequence sufficient to justify this action, and her cargoes are of quite as much importance to the Confederacy as to the State

Very respectfully, yours
Z. B. Vance

James G. Martin to ZBV · SHC:Van

Kinston N.C.
October 9, 1863.

Governor Vance
Raleigh N.C.

Governor—

I have received your letter[1] complaining of my having violated the law, in not allowing free trade to the citizens of the State—

I have only executed the orders of the Dept. commander & thought I had been very liberal. I have never refused permission to any one who had raised produce to carry away as much as was necessary for his own use. Neither have I refused permission to persons to *buy and carry* away provisions for their own use provided they would not pay more than the Government paid.

I shall be relieved in a day or two by Genl. Barton[2] & I trust you will be better satisfied with the course he may think necessary & best.

> I am Governor
> Yours respectfully
> J. G. Martin
> Brig. Genl

[1]Not extant.

[2]Seth Maxwell Barton, ordered to North Carolina after his release from Federal imprisonment following his capture at the Battle of Vicksburg. Faust et al., *Encylopedia of Civil War*, 43.

ZBV to Shubal G. Worth   SHC:Rob

> State of North Carolina,
> Executive Department,
> Raleigh Oct 12th. 1863.

Col. S. G. Worth,[1]

Dear Sir,

You may in all cases where you think proper, promise a pardon to all men who will voluntarily come in, except such as have been concerned in any crimes or outrages upon the community and provided they have never deserted before— Those guilty of the 2d. offence I can not entercede for.

Make no publication of this, but use it privately whenever you think it judicious.

> Yrs. truly
> Z. B. Vance

[1]Shubal Gardner Worth, commanding a battalion of the Home Guard in Randolph County. Earlier he had resigned his commission from the Twenty-second Regiment North Carolina Troops. On November 27, he was appointed adjutant in the Nineteenth Regiment North Carolina Troops (Second Regiment North Carolina Cavalry) and was killed at Spotsylvania Courthouse in 1864. Clark, *Histories of Regiments from North Carolina*, 2:650; Manarin and Jordan, *North Carolina Troops*, 2:104; *Randolph County, 1779–1979* (Asheboro: Randolph County Historical Society and Randolph Arts Guild, 1980), 47,

71, 85, 90; J. G. de Roulhac Hamilton, ed., *The Correspondence of Jonathan Worth*, 2 vols. (Raleigh: North Carolina Historical Commission, 1909), 1:175–176, 246, 265.

ZBV to James A. Seddon					SHC:Ben

(Copy)

State of North Carolina
Executive Department
Raleigh, Oct. 15th. 1863.

Hon. J. A. Seddon
Sec'y. of War

Dear Sir

The letters of Genl. Benning and Lt. Col. Shepherd[1] of the 2d. Geo. Regt. in reference to the mob in this city are received. They are satisfactory so far as their denial of their own participation is concerned, though I cannot but think Gen. B is mistaken in supposing that there were any number of N.C. troops in the riot.

In my letter[2] to the President I said that Gen. Benning remarked to Col. [*John D.*] Whitford, Transportation Agent here, some hours previous to the mob that he should not be surprised if his men did tear down the "Standard" Office, as he had heard it threatened and that during the prevalence of violence, I sent for him, and he could not be found, and that my messenger sent for him, was driven away from the depot by the soldiers. This raised a suspicion in my mind that he might have connived at the conduct of his men, which was heightened by the fact that he offered no apology or regret, verbally or otherwise to me, for this great insult to the authority and laws of a Sovereign State, which I thought and still think he might and should have done. Of course I accept his denial of any knowledge of the transaction, as true.

As to Lt. Col. Shepherd, (whom the men, in the darkness called "Major") I suppose I must have fallen into a very great mistake, concerning him. If he is the officer upon whom I called at the Hotel, and who went with me to the scene of violence, then I owe him a great many thanks for his assistance, instead of an accusation of guilt. Some how, I got it into my head that the officer who assisted me was a Lt. Col. Harris, and upon arriving at the Standard Office, I heard soldiers calling for "Major Shepherd", but did not know it was the officer with me. The mistake was a very natural one, owing to the confusion and darkness, and I regret that I did Lt. Col. Shepherd injustice. His was the only name I heard called, and I did not ask any man for his name. There were several company officers in the crowd, as I judged by their swords, and by hearing men call out frequently, "Captain", "Lieutenant", &c.

This you will see was the substance of my complaint to the President. I wished no punishment inflicted upon the private soldiers, but if they really were led on and encouraged by officers, it would be highly proper and politic that *they* should be punished.

> Very respectfully
> Yr. obt. Servt.
> Z. B. Vance

[*Endorsed*] Please send copies to Gen. B. & Lt. Col. S.[3]

---

[1]See Henry L. Benning to Samuel Cooper, September 28 and John A. Campbell to ZBV, October 12, A&H:GLB.

[2]September 11 (no. 2), in this volume.

[3]This endorsement appears in the A&H:GLB copy of the letter but not in the SHC:Ben version. The last sentence in the second paragraph, however, appears only in the SHC:Ben letter, thereby making that the most complete copy and thus the one transcribed here.

ZBV to Matt W. Ransom   A&H:GLB

> State of North Carolina
> Executive Department
> Raleigh Oct. 16th. 1863

Brig. Genl. M. W. Ransom
Weldon, N.C.

Dr. Sir,

Col. [*James W.*] Hinton, commanding the troops of this State in the Chowan Country is making extensive arrangements to get out pork and corn this winter. I have issued an order that none shall be brought out of that country except by State or Confederate Agents, and to avoid imposition by speculators, have ordered that all such agents shall submit their credentials to you or Col. Hinton for verification. Please issue a similar order, as my dictum cannot bind a Confederate officer.

In order successfully to get out the vast amount of provisions said to be in the country east of the Chowan, Col. Hinton assures me it will be absolutely necessary to station a battery of artillery at Colerain or thereabouts, to protect our boats, in crossing above. Will you please to make the needed exertions to get this done? I address you instead of Gen. Pickett[1] because your thorough knowledge of the country and its resources will enable you to endorse the importance of the scheme. I hope it will meet your approbations & secure your early attention.

> Very respectfully
> Your obt. servt.
> Z. B. Vance

[1]George Edward Pickett, sent to command in North Carolina in September. Boatner, *Civil War Dictionary*, 651–652.

ZBV to Duncan K. McRae   A&H:GLB

State of North Carolina
Executive Department
Raleigh, Oct 16th. 1863

Col. D. K. McRae,

Dear Sir,

I have exhibited the "Warrant for Resin," of which that hereto appended is a copy to legal counsel for consideration as to the effect of the alteration it involves upon the "Naval Store Certificates," originally issued by me: and I hereby signify my assent, that *Warrants* of the form of said copy, may be substituted for the said "Naval Store Certificates." And I do hereby covenant and agree for & in behalf of said State of North Carolina that said Warrants when issued shall be equally as binding upon said State, as said Naval Store Certificates, for which authority is hereby given that they be substituted.

Witness my hand hand [*sic*], attested by the Great Seal of the State, this day and date above written

Z. B. Vance

Copy

No—
State of North Carolina
Warrant for Resin.
Issued in Exchange for Naval Store
Certificate No—

The Government of the State of North Carolina hereby engages to deliver to the Bearer, within thirty days after presentation of this Warrant to the said Government, at the city of Raleigh, Five Hundred Barrels of good, merchantable resin, of Three Hundred & ten pounds gross weight each such delivery to be made at the port of Wilmington or any other seaport or town, within and in possession of the said State, to be declared on presentation hereof. Such presentation must be made within six months after declaration of peace, between the present belligerents in America. The said Resin to be free from all duty, charge, or other incumbrance, save & except the excess of freight beyond that usual in times of peace. Dated this   day of   A.D. 1863

(signed)   D. K. McRae
Special commissioner of the State
of North Carolina & authorized to
issue this warrant

ZBV *to William J. Clarke*   SHC:Clar

State of North Carolina,
Executive Department,
Raleigh Oct 17 1863.

Col. W. J. Clarke[1]
24th. N.C.T.

I have induced one of your men, Private Futrell,[2] to return to duty by prom-ising your clemency if he behaves well in the future—Please make it good and receive him to duty again without some punishment.

Respectfully & truly
Z. B. Vance

[1]William John Clarke, prewar army officer, lawyer, state comptroller, and postwar Re-publican state senator and judge. *Dictionary of North Carolina Biography*, s.v. "Clarke, William John."
[2]Crawford Futrell, Company D. Manarin and Jordan, *North Carolina Troops*, 7:286.

ZBV *to John J. Guthrie*   A&H:GLB

State of North Carolina
Executive Department
Raleigh, Oct. 18th. 1863

Capt. J. J. Guthrie[1]
Wilmington

Dear Sir,
You will take command of N.C. Steamer "Advance" and proceed as soon as possible to sail for port of St. Georges, Bermuda. Take a cargo, as per directions to J. H. Flanner, Purser of this date, and return with all possible dispatch to Wilmington.
In certain contingencies you will be governed by orders heretofore given to Capt. Crossan and Mr. Purser Flanner.

Very Respectfully
Your obt. servt.
Z. B. Vance

[1]John Julius Guthrie, a Confederate navy officer. Johnston, *Papers of Vance*, 1:433n.

ZBV to John White　　　　　　　　A&H:GLB

State of North Carolina
Executive Department
Raleigh, Oct. 18th. 1863.

Mr. John White,
Manchester, England,

Sir,

Yours of 24th. August[1] was received last week. In the absence of the inventory of purchases, made so far, which you intended, but did not send, I can only say generally, that we have cloth enough and you need buy no more. The number of shoes and blankets heretofore sent is far less than I desired, though I can't tell what you have behind. I will say generally that they should far exceed in amount any other articles. The shoes are mostly too narrow and the blankets too large and heavy.

By these hints you will know what I want.

When I receive a full statement, which I expect every steamer, of your proceedings and purchases I can give you an idea about returning home. In the mean time do for the best. I do not think the "Advance" will make but one or two more trips.

Yours truly
Z. B. Vance

P.S. I have seen the manifests of the "Jane Smith" and "Rover's Bride" which are very good if we can get them in safely—

Z. B. V.

[1]Not extant.

ZBV to John H. Winder　　　　　　　　Mich:Sch

[*With enclosure*]

Ex. Dept. of N.C.
Raleigh Oct 19

Gen J. H. Winder
Richmond Va.

Gen,

The within is from the Treasurer of the State who has for some years known Mr. Ricketts. I do not know him personally my self, but presume his feelings are with his home; and if not inconsistent with public policy I trust you will permit him to leave the country.

Very respectfully
Z. B. Vance

[*Enclosure*]

Jonathan Worth to ZBV   Mich:Sch

Raleigh, Oct 19/63

Govr. Vance

The bearer Mr. Geo. R. A. Ricketts, formerly of the city of N.Y., made some four years ago, very heavy investments in mining property in Montgomery & Guilford Counties—He brought here a part of his family.—His original investment & subsequent expenditures used up all his fortune and he is now without employment. He is a brother of Genl. [*James Brewerton*] Ricketts of the Federal army. I have known him for some three years and believe him to be every way a gentleman.

He has two sons in N.Y. and some small property which his wife derives by will or inheritance from her deceased mother.

He wishes to get a pass-port to go with his family to N.Y.

I am unable to advise him whether there is any chance to get one—or how to proceed. You will oblige me by giving any information you can on the subject.

Yours very truly
Jona. Worth

ZBV to David L. Swain   A&H:VanPC

State of North Carolina,
Executive Department,
Raleigh Oct 20, 1863

Gov. Swain,

Dear Sir,

Your letter to the President[1] has been endorsed by me & forwarded through Col. Mallett—He has promised to do his best for it.

I had only 1000 prs cards on board the "Advance"; look for a full cargo next trip.

I will give Mr. Mickle[2] any possible facility for getting of supplies from the East, but have not yet heard which course the Military intend pursuing in this regard.

I have had much sickness, but all are better now—Hope you and yours are well—

> In great haste, yours
> Most truly
> Z. B. Vance

[1]Not extant, but see David L. Swain to ZBV, October 15, A&H:GP.

[2]Andrew Mickle, a Chapel Hill merchant making purchases for local families. Johnston, *Papers of Vance*, 1:396n.

ZBV to Clark M. Avery   A&H:GP

> State of North Carolina,
> Executive Department,
> Raleigh Oct 21st. 1863.

Col. C. M. Avery
33d. N.C.T.

Dr. Sir,

Mrs Jenkins of Granville Co. has a son in your regt., Co A, private E. J. Jenkins, who has been sick much of the time. She informs me that it is the opinion of her family physicians that he will not survive if kept in the field and is therefore very anxious to get him transferred to some post or garrison.

She is a most reputable and patriotic lady, has five sons in the army and another to go in soon, and if possible, consistently with the good of the service, I know you would take as much pleasure as I do in assisting her to preserve her sons life. I will feel personally obliged if you can aid her.[1]

> Very respectfully & truly
> Z. B. Vance

[1]Elias J. Jenkins remained with his company until its surrender at Appomattox Court House, April 9, 1865. Manarin and Jordan, *North Carolina Troops*, 9:129.

Robert E. Lee to ZBV   A&H:GP

Hd. Qrs. Anva
22nd. Oct 1863

His Excy. Z B Vance,
Governor of N. Carolina,
Raleigh.

Governor,

I have the honor to acknowledge the receipt of you letter[1] to the Secretary of War, respecting the 1st. & 3rd. regts. N.C. Troops.

This subject has been brought to my attention before,[2] and with every desire to comply with the wish of the troops and of your Excellency, I have been and am still unable to do so. The North Carolina brigades in this army, all have their full complement of regiments, and I cannot therefore attach the 1st. and 3rd. to any of them without prejudice to the service in my opinion. If your Excy. will send me two or three other regts., it will give me great pleasure to brigade them with the two referred to, and form a new North Carolina Brigade in this army.

Very respectfully,
[R. E. Lee]

[1]Not extant.
[2]See ZBV to James A. Seddon, May 1, and Seddon to ZBV, May 23 (no. 2), in this volume.

ZBV to Richmond M. Pearson   A&H:GLB

State of North Carolina
Executive Department
Raleigh Oct. 26th. 1863

Chief Justice Pearson,
Richmond Hill N.C.

Dear Sir,

Desiring very much to get a decision of the Supreme Court in the matter of my power to order out the "Home Guard" to arrest deserters, I have been heretofore prevented by the continued absence of the Attorney General on his circuit, and even now, had to have a case prepared without him. The petition for the writ has been sent to Judge Battle instead of yourself for the reason, as I suppose that your decision in the matter of Austin[1] <would> would prevent you from doing more than than [sic] to discharge the man upon the return, but that

you would sit on this case by my invitation and Judge Battle. I have requested
him to invite yourself and Judge Manley to sit with him and to fix upon a time
most convenient to the court for the hearing in this City. I hope it may be your
pleasure to comply and relieve me and the public service from the embarassing
situation in which I stand, to the end that the Legislature may take action if
deemed necessary.

Very Respectfully
Your obt. Servt.
Z. B. Vance

¹See ZBV to William H. Battle, October 6, in this volume.

ZBV to Edward J. Hale   A&H:Hale

Private

State of North Carolina,
Executive Department,
Raleigh, Oct 26 1863.

My dear Sir,

Some attempts are making here to injure you on account of the non-appear-
ance of Gov Graham's letter. It was pretty generally known that he had written
it, and they say it was against you and hence you declined to publish. Not knowing what it contained I cant advise as to the best course, but if it meets the war
question promptly and fully I rather think it best to publish it, tho' it does hit
hard some of the fire eaters which I judge is the case.

Our friends here think you ought to say a good word for Fuller¹ for Congress,
and as he is all right on the war question, pardon me for thinking so too. As a
matter of pure policy, you should do nothing to cut yourself off from the old
Conservative Whigs—they are largely in the majority now and to loose yr influence with them is to loose yr [power] to do good—I have found a dead set making
in certain quarters, to forestall yr influence by making the impression that you
are not a "conservative" &c, and cite as an evidence that you support Mr.
[*Thomas S.*] Ashe against Christian,² and will not support Fuller a war Whig,
though opposed by an able bodied Secessionist who has never been in the war.
Of course, I & all your friends here know how it is with you in that contest, but
I think it due to good policy that you should say a word for Fuller, that is if as I
suppose yr feelings are for him. The Secessionists have no right to complain, and
in fact need yr help too much to dare to complain if they wanted to. Think of
it. While anxious to bury party strife and subordinate everything to the common
good I have endeavored always to let my party friends know that "my heart was

in the Highlands." Doubtless however, you are better acquainted with the "Situation" in yr district than I am, and can reject the faulty points of my advice, & I trust will give it no more weight than it deserves.

I receive continued evidence of a better state of feeling in the State. [John A.] Gilmer & [Burgess S.] Gaither will both go thro' with next to no opposition tho' I fear for Mr Ashe—Deserters are pouring thro' in hundreds, really, to their colors. About ten per day report to me at my office & beg me for a letter to their officers asking pardon for their offence—Near 2000 have returned this month, by far the greater part voluntarily—God spred the good work!

No accident or misfortune befalling me, I am now in condition to ensure clothing for our troops to January 1865, shoes & blankets excepted—Our cargoes were not well assorted & sufficient of these articles were not brought in before. 18000 /prs/ shoes & boots, a quantity of leather & 17,500 blankets are at Bermuda & expected by steamer next week, God pros[per]ing her. I also expect a large supply of cotton cards—But man proposes, God disposes—

We have bad news from the west—The Yankees & tories are making I fear a serious advance from Tennessee upon Asheville. My brother who is in command of the Mountain district, has no troops but the Home Guards—He sent Maj. J W Woodfin with 240 mounted militia against them, they fought at Warm Springs and Maj. W—was killed & driven back—two privates killed & six wounded—the enemys loss unknown our men were ambushed. I have sent such help as I could today & shall go up myself tomorrow I think. Oh if Rosecrans[3] would be driven back!

In haste most truly yrs

Z. B. Vance

—over—

P.S. I have made arrangements to establish a telegraphic line from this to yr town—hope this works will be begun soon—

Z B V

---

[1]Thomas Charles Fuller, former Whig, merchant, lawyer, and Confederate army officer, who won the election and served in the Confederate Congress. *Dictionary of North Carolina Biography*, s.v. "Fuller, Thomas Charles."

[2]Samuel H. Christian, who defeated Ashe for the Confederate Congress but died before taking his seat. Williams and Hamilton, *Papers of Graham*, 5:533n.

[3]William Starke Rosecrans, commanding the Army of the Cumberland attacking in Tennessee. Apparently unknown to ZBV, Rosecrans had been relieved from that command on October 19. Faust et al., *Encyclopedia of Civil War*, 642–643.

James A. Seddon to ZBV A&H:GP

[*Telegram*]

Richmond Oct 27 186[3]

Gov Z B Vance
Raleigh Oct 27th. 1863

The Ordnance Bureau places at your disposal six hundred arms at Salisbury all that can at once be conveniently commanded in that direction Genl Hoke is acting under <orders> Genl Lee's orders but he will be instructed if not inconsistent with such orders to cooperate with you

J. A Seddon
Secty War

Alexander Collie to ZBV A&H:GP

[*With enclosure*]

17 Leadenhall Street
London 29th. Oct 1863

The Honble. Z B. Vance
Governor of North Carolina

Sir

As Mr. White returns home by the Mail Steamer of 31st. Inst. "via" Bermuda, and as he entrusts in me his power of attorney, the duty will devolve on me of informing you, during his absence, of everything that goes on here in which your State is concerned—Mr. White takes with him complete accounts of all the business that has been done through my firm for North Carolina account; and I cannot but think that the statement he will show you will prove very satisfactory in every particular—

For Mr. white individually I must say that one better adapted for the most difficult and arduous duty he has to perform it would be impossible to find— During the many months when, under most trying circumstances, he had to lie by idle at the request of Mr. Mason, in case the North Carolina loan might in any way damage that of the "Confederate States", he won the respect of all who knew him by the sound sense, the patriotic devotedness, & self denial he then displayed; and when it was at last deemed safe to make a move Mr. Whites careful prudence, & sterling honesty gained more supporters to the Cause, *and more subscribers to the Cotton Warrants*, than at one time any of us believed to be possible—"I don't know anything about North Carolina but I believe Mr White to be an honest man, so put me down for £10" was the remark made to me by more than one here, whose instinctive faith thus opened his pocket, and it would be difficult to overestimate the good effect produced in this way on the minds of business men in this quarter—Mr. white is many hundred miles away from me now—We will not meet again for many a day—if ever—but I could not let him return home after all he has gone through, and accomplished, without saying to you, and through you to his friends at home, how sincerely we appreciate his strict integrity & high moral principle & how earnestly we all hope that as his sterling worth has won the respect & esteem of all who knew him here, so may his devoted services earn him the lasting gratitude of his country—

> I remain Sir
> Very faithfully yours
> Alexr. Collie

[*Enclosure*]

Alexander Collie to John White   A&H:GP

British *Private* Hotel
Private   Edinburgh Queen Street
29 Oct 1863

My dear Sir

In case you may decide to go by Saturdays Steamer I enclose

1st. My letter to you of 1st. October proposing the business which has been agreed to between us

2nd. My letter of 28th. Octr. explaining the "agreement" &

3rd. The "agreement" duly signed by me—to which please attach your signature—

4th. My letter of 28th. Octr. on the subject of the "Cotton Warrant" which embraces the terms you already agreed to, and which needs only your signature at the end along with some such words as "the above terms meet my entire approval & are hereby ratified and agreed to"—

This done, and copies left with us, will terminate all the negotiations which have been pending between us—

I have considered it a duty to write to Governor Vance and /have/ enclosed <i[*illegible*] copy of> /for your perusal/ my letter /open/—It is right you should read it first, and, this done, please <return it to me here, as I have no other copy> close and deliver it—Enclosed you will find letters to our people in Nassau Bermuda & Wilmington—Do not forget to make enquiry into the character kept up by our people in the Confederacy & let me know confidentially—as this is a matter of much importance to all of us—I trust most sincerely you will return here soon and take charge in Liverpool of the large & important business which will be done there for account of your State. My only regret is that this business was not inaugurated six months ago—However we have all of us gained in experience in that period & therefore the business should be all the more successful now—During your absence I shall give my personal attention to the management of the business here, and I doubt not on your return you will approve of what I may do in your absence—

Please give my very kind regards to Crossan when you see him—He is a very worthy fellow, and I hope to meet him one of these days under happier auspices than those now prevaling—The feeling is general here that the war is not far from an end—God grant it may be so—but our duty clearly is to act as if the end was as far off as ever—You will find many of your friends at home whom you left in comfort very badly off now—Many of them will ask you to send them little comforts from this Country when you return to it—In this case I would say to you, as I have said to many other friends under similar circumstances I will always be very glad indeed to send over such articles in my steamers freight free—so do not hesitate to make use of me in this service—& now I must say good bye—& wish you a good voyage & all the good you can desire

> I remain my dear Sir
> very sincerely yours
> Alexr. Collie

John White to ZBV   A&H:GP

Manchester October 31st. 1863

Honble. Z B Vance
Governor of
North Carolina

Sir

I have the pleasure to acknowledge the receipt of your letter of the 3rd. Septr.[1] on the 26th. Inst. together with the $400000, of State Bonds, this with the $600000 making the whole amt. which had been desired to be forwarded. I find now, I could have gotten on without them, and will not use them, will place the whole for safe keeping in the Manchester and county Bank.

I wrote you about the first of the present month with statement of purchases made and what had been shipd. &c. Since then I have made another shipment of quite a large amount the invoice will go forward by this days mail, there are still a good many goods which had been orderd. from manufactores before your letters reach me desiring that I should not make further purchases for the present, these when ready will be forwarded with as little delay as possible. I have given out orders for cotton & wool cards and now have ready for shipment 25 or 30000 pairs, desiring that they should be forwarded without loss of time & finding no vessel up for Bermuda, I had them sent to Liverpool to go out via Halifax, but regret to say that the steamer was filld. up before they got there, they will be sent out by the first vessel up for Bermuda, either from London or Liverpool & other shipments will be made as they are ready The machines for making cards I find can be bought for about £20, each, in place of one, I have orderd. five with the wire &c. necessary to keep them going for a year. One man can attend to 10 or 12 of the machines in operation, as well as to one. They will be ready for shipment in about 2 weeks.

I notice your wishes with regard to the proceeds of the sale of the cotton, but having been able to dispose of only about £100,000 of the cotton bonds, and my expenditures having amounted to about £150000, it will require both cargos of cotton to pay the debt I have thus incured for the State.

The first cargo of cotton has just been sold & part of it has brought the highest price that the same quality has yet been sold for, the price ranged as to quality and condition from 2/. to 2/5</> pr pound, the whole averaging about 2/3d.

I have my business at present so arranged that I can leave what is unfinished in the hands of Messrs. Collie & Co. and return at least for a time, to North Carolina. The unfinished orders in the hands of Manufactores will be attended to by them & the goods inspected, packd. & shipd. A steamer will leave London about the 20th. of Novr. on which I expect to go out. I have proposals from Mr. Alexr. Collie for the State to join him in the purchase of steamers, which I desire to lay before you for your consideration. I have consented on behalf of the State to the agreement subject however to your approval in the meantime I forward with this copy of agreement letters, &c. which will explain themselves. Col. McRae I suppose reachd. home a few days after the date of your letter

> I am Your Obt. Servt.
> Jno White

[1]In this volume.

John D. Whitford to ZBV   SHC:Ben

Copy

Hillsboro, Octo 31st. 1863,

To His Exc.
Z. B. Vance
Gov. N C

Dear Sir;

I hasten to correct an error in your letter of the 15th., inst.,[1] to the Hon. James A Seddon Secretary of War, published in the Standard of the 27th. inst., with the correspondence relative to the riots in the City of Raleigh, in September last.

You say "in my letter to the President I said that Gen. Benning remarked to Col. Whitford, Transportation Agent here, some hours previous to the mob, that he should not be surprised if his men did tear down the Standard office as he had heard it threatened". Doubtless you derived this information from some one, as there were many reports circulating in the streets of the city, the day after the out break, of the complicity of Gen. Benning and other officers of his command; but you are mistaken in supposing it came from me that a word was ever said to me on the subject by Gen. Benning or by any officer or soldier of his Brigade before the outrage was perpetrated. If I had the slightest intimation such an act was contemplated, for "some hours" or for any time, previous to its occurance, and not have made it known to you or have taken some steps to aid in suppressing it, I would justly deserve the censure of all good & law abiding citizens of the State. For, whatever our opinion may be as to the course of individuals, whether right or wrong, we must all see that unless we uphold & sustain the laws of the Country "we can have no security for personal liberty, property or even exis-tence". Perhaps, if I were to see you, I could call to your recollection several incidents that would convince you that Gen. Benning did not make the state-ments, ascribed to him, to me. But I deem it useless to pursue the matter further as, I know, you are more anxious to do justice to Gen. Benning & his officers than you are to condemn them.

I am Sir
With high regard
John D. Whitford

[1]In this volume.

Richmond M. Pearson to ZBV   A&H:GP

Richmond Hill
Nov 2d. 1863

His Excellency
Gov. Vance

Dr. Sir,

    I reced by the last mail your communication of the 26th. ult.[1] in which you express a desire to get a decision of *the Supreme Court*, on the question of your power to order out the "home guards" to arrest deserters, & state that a case has been prepared & sent to Judge Battle presenting the question decided by me "in the matter of Austin"— By the same mail I recd a communication[2] from Judge Battle in reference to the case sent to him in which he expresses a wish to have the assistance of Judge Manly & myself at the hearing—I also notice an article in the Standard of the 27th. ult. which I presume is intended as an exposition of your views based on a supposed distinction between a decision of the Supreme Court & the decision of a single judge in vacation

You are mistaken in supposing that by getting up a case presenting the same question as in the matter of Austin[3] to be heard before judge Battle with the assistance of the other two judges, you can obtain a *decision of the Supreme Court* on the question—The three judges only constitute *a court* by meeting in term time—Under the Habeas Corpus Act Rev Code jurisdiction of such questions is given to a single judge "in the vacation time" without appeal—It follows that his decision in a matter properly constituted before him, is conclusive of the question & settles the law untill it is brought up to the Supreme Court by certiorari[4] & reversed or is overruled by a decision of the Supreme Court in some other case—Its binding obligation as an authority is not affected in points of law, by the circumstances that he decides the question unaided—or has the assistance of the [brother] opinion & reasoning of other judges or is aided by having the benefit of a full consultation with some or all of the other judges both of the Supreme & Superior Courts, for in either case it is the act of a single judge, who is constituted a superior judicial tribunal with full jurisdiction over the question involved in the case before him—& there is no appeal or any provision made for having the assistance of the other judges—

It is also a mistake to suppose that by the Constitution, *The Supreme Court*, is made a coordinate branch of the government. The *judiciary* is the coordinate branch of the government, and the decision of any judicial tribunal acting within the jurisdiction conferred by law, of superior jurisdiction & without appeal, is entitled to the consideration due to a coordinate branch of the government, untill it is overruled by a higher judicial tribunal, which I infer is your reason for wishing to get a decision of the Supreme Court. Allow me to refer you to my reply to Judge Battle[5] for a more full exposition of my views on this subject—

To these two errors (as I conceive them to be) & a supposed "publick necessity," must be ascribed the part that the principle decided in the matter of Austin has been disregarded and the judiciary as a coordinate branch of the government lies prostrate—God knows that I would do any thing in my power to restore it to the position assigned to it in the Constitution.—But after earnest reflection, I am satified, the plan you have adopted cannot have that effect—Should I upon the invitation of Judge Battle <& yourself> attend in Raleigh to assist him at the hearing of the case, got up for the purpose; I could not consistently with my sense of duty aid him in the labor of reversing the decision "in the matter of Austin"—I could only enter my protest against his doing so.

Upon that preliminary question I give him all the aid I can in my reply to his communication.

You remark, "The case was sent to Judge Battle because you supposed the decision "in the matter of Austin" would prevent me from doing more than to discharge the man" In other words you suppose I would feel myself bound by that decision as an authority, that is true: but Judge Battle or any other judge is as much bound by it as I am, untill it be overruled by the Supreme Court & a decision of the court cannot be obtained until its next term /As it seemed fit to the legislature to constitute a "single judge"—a superior judicial tribunal with full jurisdiction to determine such cases without appeal, & with no provision for a convocation of the other judges, no one (as it seems to me) can rightfully deny to his decision the right due to "an adjudicated case" or in any manner weaken its effect to settle the law.—/—

Very respectfully
yours &c—
R. M. Pearson

[1] In this volume.
[2] William H. Battle to Pearson, October 29, A&H:GP.
[3] See William H. Battle to ZBV, November 12, in this volume.
[4] Called up from lower court.
[5] Pearson to William H. Battle, November 2, A&H:GP.

Sion H. Rogers to ZBV   A&H:GP

Raleigh Nov. 2d. 1863.

His Excellency
Gov. Vance:

Sir:

Your letter of the 1st. Inst.[1] is just received—in which you ask my opinion as to the effect of Chief Justice Pearsons opinion in Austin's case. You ask. "Does the opinion of a single Judge in such a case bind the Executive, the other judges and settle the law of the land as an "adjudicated case" by the Supreme Court or does it simply operate in the individual case"

I shall not attempt a review of Chief Justice Pearsons opinion in Austin's case, but it strikes me that the Legislature intended and the language of the act creating and organizing the "Home Guard" admits of such a construction as to justify you in calling out this organization to arrest deserters. The State is invaded by the enemies of the Confederate Government and if arresting deserters and returning them to their commands will aid in repelling this invasion, is not the authority given so to do?

The act does not prescribe the *particular* duty the "Home Guard" is to perform, nor the *particular manner* in which their duties are to be performed, but in general terms, that the organization shall be used to repel invasion &c. of the State & as contradistinguished from the Confederate States; in other words limiting their field of action to the State. The *particular* duty to be performed as well as the manner in detail is left to your Excellency as Governor of the State and Commander in Chief of her Army whether Militia or Home Guard.

Under our Habeas Corpus act jurisdiction is given to a single judge without appeal, in cases properly constituted before him and is final in the individual cases until reversed by the Supreme Court, and it is immaterial whether the decision is made by a member of the Supreme Court or by one of the Circuit Judges as a decision of a Judge of either court is of equal authority *in law* as a decision of a Judge of the other.

Then is this dicision, whether made by a Supreme or Circuit Judge, binding upon the other Judges? and does it settle the law of the land as an adjudicated case?

My opinion upon these points is entirely in accordance with what I understand to be the opinion of all the Judges at least as far as gathered from their course of conduct, previous to the last term of the Supreme Court. Mitchells case[2] and many others, I am informed, involving an identical question, presented in Irvin's case was decided prior to the opinion in Irvin's case, and the parties were held to service whereas Irvin was discharged. Now if the opinion of a single judge binds the other judges, and the Executive and settles the law of the land until the case is reversed by the Supreme Court or overruled by the Supreme Court by the dicision of another case involving the same principles, the dicision in Irvin's case was made without authority /and against law/ and he was improperly discharged. This I cannot conclude as Irvin's case was heard by the very learned and able jurist Chief Justice Pearson

It is important to have uniformity in the decisions of our Judges; especially where the liberties of the citizens are involved, and as we have a precedent in Genl Martins, the judges of the Supreme Court I suppose upon invitation will meet and express an opinion which I have no doubt will be followed, emenating as it will from the members of the Supreme Court. Certainly no case of greater importance to the Citizen or Country has ever arisen for this unusual method of procedure.

> I am with great respect
> Your Obt Servant
> Sion H Rogers
> Att. Genl.

[1]Not extant.
[2]See ZBV to James A. Seddon, June 8, in this volume.

ZBV to Edward J. Hale   A&H:Hale

<State of North-Carolina,
Executive Department,>
Raleigh, Nov 9th. 1863.

Private

E. J. Hale Esq
[torn]

Dr. Sir,

Yrs[1] is received—in fact has been on hand some time waiting my return from the mountains.

I was pained to observe that some parts of my letter,[2] to which yours is a reply, have displeased you in some way. I assure you I regret it. My great anxiety to see your paper preserve its influence, and therefore its usefulness, with yr old party friends, caused me to advise you to support Fuller. I am free to confess however, that yr reasons for not coming out for him are amply sufficient, and I am satisfied you were *right*. I see and hear every day attempts made to destroy yr influence by placing you among the original Secessionists, and my policy was for you to avoid that if possible—You will notice recent articles in the Standard written with this intention—plainly, which show that its editor has [torn] war against you. I had hoped that /by/ the advice of Gov Graham & others, with the warning of the mob, <that> Holdens tone would be changed, and that he could be made useful to the cause. With this view, and after consultation with Gov Graham, I not only refrained from quarreling with him myself, but exerted myself to prevent a rupture between you & him. My opinion of the man has not changed "within the last month or two", but I very much fear the results of his insidious policy towards the Observer, and hence my great anxiety to warn you. But it seems you mistook the intent of my letter and took it for granted that I had changed my opinion of him and wanted to lecture you about policy &c. I assure you of yr great mistake in both respects. You are my senior [by] many years of active experience, and the advice I offered was given with great deference, and with an eye single to the good of the Cause which so much depends upon the paper which you conduct. There is the most perfect unity of sentiment between you & me in regard to the conduct of the war, and in view of the great importance of its continuance I have heretofore given you freely and frankly my whole mind. So far from desiring to give offense, I hoped that the very [prudence] with which I wrote would convince you of my sincerity and regard.

In regard to Gov. Grahams letter, I learn that he had himself told two other friends here of his having written it—Jim Taylor[3] among the number—which of course gave it publicity. The matter will die out now I suppose, and nothing more need be said. *I never supposed the letter was against you,* [torn] In my recent visit to the mountains I found an astonishing amount of disloyalty in the counties bordering on Tennessee. A regiment of 800 of the enemy, at the Warm Springs was at least 2/3 N.C. Tories! I blush to say it, but it is true. Several men who recently figured in "peace meetings" have gone off and taken arms with the enemy—Great God, what a disgrace to N. Carolina! They are more merciless and thieving than were the regular Yankees; an old & respec[table] citizen, Mr. Garrett, near Warm-Springs was basely murdered by them, several more carried off, and every portable thing in their reach stolen.

The Home Guards come out promptly and have done good service under Gen. McElroy.

Truly yours
Z. B. Vance

¹October 27, A&H:VanPC.
²October 26, in this volume.
³James Fauntleroy Taylor Jr., an anti-Confederate who cooperated with Republicans after the war and served as state librarian and a trustee of the state university. Olsen and McGrew, "Prelude to Reconstruction," pt. 3, *North Carolina Historical Review* 60 (July 1983): 351n.

ZBV to James A. Seddon   A&H:GP

State of North Carolina,
Executive Department,
Raleigh, Nov 10th. 1863.

Hon J. A. Seddon
Richmond Va.

Dr. Sir,

Lest it may not be known to you, I desire to say that the position in which the enemy have established themselves, at Winton on the Chowan river in this State, will effectually cut us off from four or five million pounds of pork which we expected to get from the counties East of that stream. It would be a terrible loss to the army & the State—

If possible for Gen Pickett to drive them off and prevent their fortifying (which I learn they are doing) it ought by all means to be done. It will be positively ruinous for our troops to stand at Weldon and surrender all the rich country below.

I beg your attention to this matter.

Very respectfully
Yr obt svt.
Z. B. Vance

[*Endorsed*] A. G. Refer to Gen Pickett inviting his attention to Gov Vance's views He will exercise his judgment as to the expediency of any movement—He of course knows that supplies of meat are very important to us

J A S Scy
16 Nov 63

[*Endorsed*] Hd. Qrs Dept N.C. Petersburg Novr. 21st. Respty returned to Gov Vance—As the enemy are not occupying Winton I suppose the anxiety of the Gov on that score is relieved—the enclosure[1] excepting the latter portion, evidently refers to something which is not contained in the letter—[2]

Should Gov Vance have any suggestion for defence to make, it will be considered with pleasure should he send it to this office

G E Pickett
Maj Genl

[1]Actually written (apparently by Seddon's staff) on back of the letter.
[2]Enlisting conscripts in western North Carolina.

ZBV to Henry T. Clark   A&H:VanPC

State of North Carolina
Executive Department,
Raleigh, Nov 10 1863

Gov. Clark
Tarboro, N.C.

My dear Sir,

Yr letter[1] was recd. in due time, and you will please accept my excuses for not replying to it sooner. I know you can well imagine what those excuses are.

I assure you that, although I felt annoyed at the time by what I thought was opposition to my [L]egion, that an actual experience of similar difficulties to those which surrounded you, has long since driven such a thought from my head. I have neither made any complaint myself, nor authorized Holden to do so in his paper; and feel sastisfied that you could scarcely have done otherwise than you did.

I feel obliged for the many kind and complimentary expressions in your letter, and feel gratified that I have been able so to steer my course as to receive them from such a source whether I merit them or not.

Accept my kind regards.

Very Truly yours
Z. B. Vance

[1]Not extant.

ZBV to John D. Whitford   A&H:GP

State of North Carolina,
Executive Department,
Raleigh, Nov 10 1863.

Col J. D. Whitford
Hillsboro N.C.

My dear Sir,
Your note of the 31st. ult[1] is recd. in which you say that I was mistaken in asserting that you had told me of having a conversation with Gen Benning on the evening of the mob in Raleigh, in which he should have said that he had heard threats made to tear down the Standard office. I accept your denial as true, as your recollection is perhaps better than mine—having less on yr mind at the time than I had.

I am perfectly confident however that such a statement was made to me by some one—You were the author of it as alluded to in my letter to the President the next day after the occurrence; in my private conversations on the subject I always mentioned yr name as the author, and never doubted it for a moment until the reception of your note. Even now I can not fix upon any other possible person who could have told me /but <in> amid the many rumors and great excitement prevailing it was easy for me to be mistaken or misled as to the person/. Still Colonel, I repeat that I accept yr denial, & take it for granted that I am mistaken

Very respectfully
Yr obt. svt.
Z B Vance

[1]In this volume.

William H. Battle to ZBV   A&H:GP

Chapel Hill Nov. 12th 1863

To his Excellency
Gov. Vance

Sir/
On or about the 25th day of October last I received from W. W. Woodell a member of the Home Guard of the County of Wake, a petition for a writ of

Habeas Corpus—A letter from your private secretary accompanied the petition, stating that, as the facts set forth therein raised the same question in relation to the power of the Governor of the State to call out the Home Guard for the purpose of arresting deserters and conscripts, which had recently been decided by Chief Justice Pearson in Austin's case, it was your wish to have the decision reviewed by all the Judges of the Supreme Court—With that view I was requested to grant the writ, make it returnable before me at Raleigh, and invite the other Judges to meet me there and assist in the hearing—I think it was also contemplated that the case should be fully argued by the Attorney General on the part of the State as well as by the counsel, G. H. [*George W.*] Haywood Esq, for the petitioner—

In compliance with your request I wrote to the Chief Justice and desired him to name a day when it would be convenient for him to attend; and I also wrote to request the attendance of Judge Manly when the day should be fixed upon—

A few days ago I received a reply[1] from Judge Pearson in which he states that he had had a letter[2] from you also on the same subject, and that he had written to you that he declined to attend the contemplated meeting. In his letter to me he fully explains the reasons for the course which he has thought proper to adopt, and I have sent it to your private secretary for your inspection—

As the question decided by Judge Pearson in Austin's case cannot now be reviewed by a hearing before all the Judges of the Supreme Court, I beg leave to suggest that the hearing of Woodell's case by myself alone, or by myself and Judge Manly, would not settle that question and, therefore, it would be better to have the application for the /writ/ withdrawn upon the release of the petitioners—It is true, as Judge Pearson says, that if all the three Judges of the Supreme Court were to meet, they could not constitute a court, and of course one or two of them alone could not—Under these circumstances it is manifest that a decision of the question, having the effect of settling it cannot now be made, until the meeting of the Supreme Court—Is not this a strong argument in favour of having the winter term of that court restored?

> I am, with high regard
> Your obt. Svt.
> Will. H. Battle

[1]November 2, A&H:GP.
[2]October 26, in this volume.

ZBV to Richmond M. Pearson   A&H:GLB

State of North Carolina
Executive Department
Raleigh, Nov. 12th. 1863

To His Honor
Judge Pearson
Ch. Justice of N.C.

Dear Sir,

Yours of the 2d. inst.[1] and also yours of same date to Judge Battle,[2] in reply to my invitation to assist him in the hearing of Woodell's case, have both been received.

Whilst regretting exceedingly that you cannot consent to comply with my request, there are some things in yr. letter to me which call for a more specific reply at my hands.

You say I am mistaken in supposing that I can get a decision of the *Supreme Court* in the manner proposed by making a case before Judge Battle, and inviting the other Judges to sit with him. I did *not* suppose I could, though my language implied as much perhaps. I have been so long from the bar that I am not always particular to speak, technically correctly, but I *did* suppose that I could get the *opinions of the Judges of the Supreme Court,* which by consent of the parties might have the effect of a *decision.* This was done in the case of the Adjutant General and I suppose, to relieve me of a great public responsibility, could be done again. You say also that the principle decided in the "Matter of Austin" has been disregarded "and the judiciary as a co-ordinate branch of the Government lies prostrate." This is rather a serious accusation, and should be made with a qualification. Your decision released Austin from the performance of Home Guard duty under my order and General Order No. 9 A & I. Genls. Office, dated May 16th. 1863, orders the militia officers to call out their commands to protect all men so discharged. Whether your decision does more, is the question. If it "settles the law" and has the same binding effect as an "adjudicated case" upon Judicial and Executive Officers, then your accusation would be true. But by the private opinions of the other Judges, the Attorney General and many of the most eminent lawyers of the State, whom I have consulted, I am forced to the conclusion that such a decision was doubtful to say the least of it. I am free to admit that even in a case of doubt and involving a difference of opinion among the Judges and the bar, under ordinary circumstances it were both safest and best to abide by the decision, as avoiding even a suspicion of disregarding an "adjudicated case" on the part of an Executive Officer.

But in this case, where the consequences were bound to be of so serious a character, when the withdrawal of the Home Guards from this Service would have been accepted as an invitation to desertion from the Army, and a license to the outrages perpetrated by those absconding soldiers, I felt clear that it was my duty to give to law and order and the Confederate cause the benefit of the doubt. I felt too that you would not have been *perfectly* alone in your position, since your had made a decision in Irwin's [*Irvin's*] case, reversing the decision made by Judge [*Robert B.*] Gilliam in Mitchell's case previously, and concurring with two others made by Judges Heath & French[3] previous to yours involving the same principle, neither of which were referred to or cited as authority in Austin's case, and not withstanding all these considerations, appreciating fully the delicacy of my position, and trusting that others would also, I endeavored to solve the difficulty by the friendly aid of the Judges of the Supreme Court, to whose opinion I proposed to submit cheerfully. You are aware how I have been thwarted in that wish, since you not only decline to assist in the hearing of the case prepared, but say that if present you could only protest against Judge Battle doing so and charge that his doing so would be surrendering the lawful power of the Judiciary to the pressure of the times.

I do not feel myself competent to combat the soundness of your reasoning in Austin's case, and in fact feel that I have no right to do so, if I were able. My conviction has always been that an Executive officer, should only enquire *if the law be so decided* & if so, he should obey it. But it is certainly both his right and his duty to know if there has been a *decision in fact*, an *adjudicated case*, such as constitutes the law of the land and determine all other like cases. Where there is an admitted doubt of this fact, I do not think an Executive officer can be fairly charged with prostrating the Judiciary by disregarding its *decisions*. I yield to no living man in respect for the courts of my country. I have labored faithfully to protect them from intrusion by military despotism whether threatened from within or without and to avoid coming to the conclusion that the restriction of any of their rights and powers was necessary to the successful prosecution of the war for independence.

Thus far my labors in both respects have been satisfactory to myself at least. I believe they will be so to my countryman

> Very Respectfully
> Yr. obt. svt.
> Z. B. Vance

[1]In this volume.

[2]A&H:GP.

[3]Robert R. Heath and Robert S. French, superior court judges. Cheney, *North Carolina Government*, 362, 371n.

William F. Lynch to ZBV A&H:GP

Head Quarters,
Naval Defences of N. Carolina,
Wilmington, November 15, 1863.

His Excellency
Z. B. Vance
Governor of N. Carolina.

Governor,
I regret not seeing you, this morning, when I called to pay my respects.

The Hon: Secretary of the Navy has asked me, by telegraph, whether something might not be done to arrest the depredations of the enemy upon vessels trading to this port.

The draft of the iron-clad "N Carolina" is too great to cross the bar, and her sister ship, the "Raleigh" is incomplete: I have therefore no means for the purpose mentioned, at my disposal, but

The "Advance" which is the fleetest and best adapted of any vessel in port, is, I am told, nearly ready for sea. With your sanction, I will attach a torpedo to her stern, put a gun, officers & crew on board, and endeavour to inflict some injury upon the foe. It will delay the departure of the "Advance" but a few days, and I trust to return her uninjured.

As such a movement requires the utmost secrecy I respectfully ask the destruction of this note and a written reply, however brief.

I have the honor to be
Your obt Serv't
W F Lynch C N
Comd'g Naval defences of N.C.

Richmond M. Pearson to ZBV A&H:GP

Richmond Hill Nov. 16th. 1863

To his excellency
Gov. Vance

Dr. Sir—
In reply to your letter of the 26th. ult.[1] expressing a wish to have the question of your authority to order out the "home guard" to arrest deserters & conscripts; decided by the *supreme court*; I informed you it could not be done by the plan you proposed—I presume no further action was taken in the case you had prepared seeing no mention of it in the newspapers

I think the habeas corpus act should be amended so as to allow an appeal & make it the duty of the chief justice when notified thereof, to call a *special term* of the court to hear it—

This would relieve the judges in vacation from great responsibility & tend "to settle the law". I suggest for your consideration the propriety of calling the attention of the Legislature to the subject & of laying before them your letter & my reply[2]—Judge Battles letter[3]—my reply[4] so as to show the necessity for some remedy, & that it was beyond the reach of the executive & judicial departments of the government. I send a copy of Judge B's letter: he will furnish you with my reply. I presume you retained a copy of yours to me.

Very respectfully
Yours &c. &c.
R. M. Pearson

[1]In this volume.
[2]Pearson to ZBV, November 2, in this volume.
[3]William H. Battle to Pearson, October 29, A&H:GP.
[4]Pearson to William H. Battle, November 2, A&H:GP.

ZBV to James W. Hinton   SHC:Yel

[*With enclosure*]

State of North Carolina,
Executive Department,
Raleigh, Novr. 24 1863.

Col James Hinton
Comdg. 6[7]th.[*sic*] N.C.T
State Line,

Dr. Sir,

You will see by the enclosed letter from the Sec'y of War that he has referred the matter of conscription beyond the Chowan to my descretion.

Whilst I freely appreciate the isolated and unprotected situation of the people of those counties, and am desirous to allow them every possible kindness, I am yet assured that there <are> /is/ quite a large per cent of the population which could well be in the army, to the great benefit of the service & without serious injury to their families. You will therefore excuse from conscription all men, heads of families, whose wives and children are absolutely and entirely dependent upon their labor for a support where there is not some male of the family beyond the age of conscription competent to take care of them. These facts you may verify by affedavit of the parties or other evidence satisfactory to your self. This exemption will not extend to any person engaged in speculation, or illicit traffic with the enemy.

As to trades, professions &c you will of course be governed by the exemption laws. The officers of the Militia will not be exempted as such, that organization being unable there to comply with calls made upon them from these Head quarters—

You can make at your discretion, details to all such men as will undertake to drive out pork for the State or Confederacy.

Trusting that may be able to compel all to do there duty without inflicting distress or suffering on the helpless—I am

Yrs. &c

Z. B. Vance

[*Enclosure*]

James A. Seddon to ZBV   A&H:GLB

Confederate States of America
War Department
Richmond Va. Nov. 3d. 1863

His Excy. Z. B. Vance
Govr. of N.C.

I owe you an apology for having allowed your letter of the 26th. Ultmo,[1] handed me some days since, respecting the effort made to enlist Troops east of the Chowan river, amid the press of other matters to escape my attention

I understand the embarassments presented by the condition of the people in the Counties east of the Chowan, for similar ones have been experienced in various Districts of this State, which without being in the actual occupancy of the enemy are at all times open to their control. It is an embarassing question in such cases to determine whether to exercise any authority over those districts and by exacting from the people manifestation of the Loyalty which fully possesses the very great majority, exposes them and their property to the insolence and ravages of the enemy, or to have them in apparent subjection to await the events of the war. I am inclined to think your Judgement suggests the best practicable course which is to draw forth as far as possible the younger & more disconnected men for service and such means and productions as can be conveniently obtained, but to leave heads of families undisturbed and such supplies as are necessary for the comfortable maintenance of the weak and dependant. The course therefore adopted by you has the concurrence of my opinion and while of course I can release no obligation the law has imposed nor relinquish the rights should more favorable circumstances be secured by the ascendancy of our arms of exacting both the service & contributions the law demands. You may expect such sanction as my authority warrants.

Very Truly Yours
James A. Seddon
Secty. of War.

[1]Not extant.

ZBV *to Edward J. Hale*   A&H:Hale

State of North Carolina,
Executive Department,
Raleigh, Nov 25th. 1863.

My dear Sir,

I am very much obliged to you indeed for a sight of the article of "M", criticizing my action in regard to Judge Pearsons decision in the "matter of Austin". As its tone is kindly and seems to be rather the rebuke of a friend than the assault of an enemy, I have no objection of your publishing it, though if really a well meaning friend is its author I think he should have reproved his brother in private rather than /before/ the whole congregation—especially for the first offence. Provided you publish it, I would be obliged if you would state, in any form you think best the substance of my answer, that ones friends may see at least I have sinned by good advice and "for cause".

In the first place, the decision in the matter of Austin *has* been respected by me. It discharged Austin, and my standing order to commanders of Militia, was to resist by force all atttempts to rearrest any man who had been so discharged. Well: did it do more than discharge Austin? Did it discharge all men falling within its scope and settle the law of the land as an "adjudicated case"? Now I have laid it down as a rule for my guidance, that an Executive officer has no right to controvert the *soundness* of a decision—he has but to obey it—else he usurps other functions than his own. But he certainly has a right to ask *has* there been a decision, and what is its extent? Under the peculiar circumstances of Austins case—alluded to by Judge P. himself—I thought it my duty and did make this enquiry. The first person I enquired of was the proper one to give me legal <office> /advice/—the Attorney General. He assured me confidently and unhesitatingly that the decision only discharged Austin and did not settle the law of the land. This was official, and can be publicly spoken of. My next application was to Mr. Phillips, the Auditor, who gave me the same advice, towit, that I was *not* bound by it as the law of the land. Then Gov. Graham, Judge Ruffin, Mr E. G. Reade, Mr. Donnel and various others of emmence in the profession were applied to for advice and all concurred in the same opinion. And finally I was informed that both the other Judges of the Supreme Court, though not able to attend with Judge Pearson at the hearing of Austins case, had written him giving <both> their opinions against him in the decision itself, and afterwards as to its binding effect!

But to relieve myself of any possible blame in the matter, I got up a special case before Judge Battle presenting the same points, and invited the other Judges to sit with him, and agreed to treat their opinions as the decision of the Supreme Court. Manly agreed but Pearson refused to attend and protested against Judge

Battle giving his opinion in the case at all! Though assured that Battle would decide against Pearson & that Manly would concur I yet forbore to press them to overrule Judge P., withdrew the case, and have referred the matter to the Legislature, treating him (Judge P.) with more forbearance & consideration than he meted out to me.

2d. The Legislature *did* contemplate using the Home Guards for the arrest of deserters, and your correspondent [is wonderfully] out as to the facts & their chronological order. The Secy of War never issued any order or made any agreement with me whatever about the militia between 40 & 45—The Presidents call for these men, and the State exemption bill—which exhausted the Militia—took place during the session of the Legislature, and that body was perfectly aware that I had no Militia and gave me the home guard in lieu of it—The exigency which your correspondent supposes to have arisen long afterwards, existed and was made known to that body before before [*sic*] its adjournment—My contest with Mr. Seddon was principally, for the reason that his officers did not want to release the man "Irvin" after the Judge had discharged him—I did not claim that Irvins case should rule all others, until confirmed by the courts—As to the conversation with the "Major" I deny it, positively—I never could with my proper senses, have said any such thing. I *did* think at one time of ordering out the Guard in those counties were there were most deserters and sending them to Kinston to watch the enemy whilst the regular soldiers went into their counties to arrest deserters, though I abandoned the idea. The "Major" may have heard something of this kind if he heard anything—

The reason why the other judges did not meet Judge P. in Raleigh as they inform me, was because they did *not* receive due notice—And yet he in a letter to me, claims that if they had met him, he would have only asked their aid but would not have been bound by any opinion of theirs, the whole responsibility of the decision being upon him, which legally is correct—

I write in great haste and imperfectly present my justification, but hope you get it substantially. I have made no "insidious attack" upon Judge Pearson though he has been neither kind or courteous to me in many things. I claim now to be as good a friend to civil liberty and legal rights as your correspondent and a better one than Judge Pearson, inasmuch as I have not only labored earnestly to maintain & uphold the courts of my State but have also done what was possible to resist that mighty aggression which is endeavoring to sweep away civil rights, home, government & everything; a matter certainly well to be remembered though neither Coke or Blackstone are volumenous about it. If you see proper you may forward this to your correspondent.

Very truly yours
Z. B. Vance

P.S. My room being piled with company last night, I could not finish this for the return mail as you desired. I desire to add this morning that which escaped me last night, that those decisions by Heath, Gilliam & French were made prior to

Judge Pearsons decision in Irvins case which were entirely disregarded—not even noticed by him in that case—If he refuses to be bound himself by a decision of equal authority with his own, he should not complain at my doing the same thing. And it only affords an argument against him to say that he did not know of the prior decisions: there was no way that they could be known, as they were not of record—except by publication in the newspapers which is unofficial—No greater absurdity or more dangerous usurpation of power can well be imagined than to say that the law of the land may be settled in a decision not of record, and the mere mention of which as a matter of news depends on the pleasure of the Judge It is a trap for the citizen—

ZBV

ZBV to Stephen R. Mallory   A&H:GLB

State of North Carolina
Executive Department
Raleigh Nov. 28th. 1863

Hon. S. R. Mallory
Secy' of the Navy
Richmond, Va.

Sir.

I beg to call your attention to the enclosed letter from Lt. G. Elliott[1] in regard to the gun boat "Albemarle", I endorse the statement fully, in regard to the delay and and [sic] blunders of Flag Officer Lynch. I am satisfied of his total & utter incapacity for the duties of his position, which has for some time been evident to the whole State. The iron furnished by the State under the express promise of both himself and you, has been applied to other purposes, and our rivers are yet at the mercy of the most contemptible boat in the Yankee Navy. The Neuse has been launched and her iron plates put in without her machinery and in the face of the known fact that it will all have to come off before the machinery does go in. Many other ridiculous things have been /done/ merely to keep the hands employed and deceive the public, for it cannot deceive the enemy. In short Sir, I am so out of heart in the matter, that if the water defences of N.C. are to continue in the hands of Commodore Lynch, I feel it useless, and will decline to furnish any more iron or other assistance whatever. It would be labor and material thrown away.*

Very Respectfully
Yr. obt. Servt.
Z. B. Vance

*I desire of course that Lt. Elliott should be allowed to finish this boat.

[1]Gilbert Elliott, adjutant of the Seventeenth Regiment North Carolina Troops, who had experience constructing "war vessels." Clark, *Histories of Regiments from North Carolina,* 5:315–323.

John McCormick to ZBV   A&H:VanPC

Raleigh Nov. 28th. 1863

To Z B Vance Gov. of N C
Gov Z B Vance

D Sir

I hope that you will pardon me for the liberty, which I have taken, in thus calling your attention to subjects which may be better understood by your Excellency, than me; I allude Gov. to the present condition of the Great Conservative Party in North Carolina, of which, you have been, and are considered to be, *The Leader.* That differences of opinion *do now exist* in a very essential degree, I must, tho. sorrowfully, Affirm: <[that]> schism is imminent in our party, and if the breach be not speedily healed, the consequences may be disastrous.

That there is a powerful Peace element in the country, no one with proper opportunities to ascertain the sentiment of the masses, will dare deny. My own observations, tho somewhat limited, (being principally in Cumberland and Harnett Counties) demonstrate to me beyond all question of doubt, that he who follows in the wake of the Fayetteville Observer will not command a Corporal's guard. Public sentiment is far in advance of Politicians, and if that sentiment is not directed in some proper channel, it will rise and sweep over us and direct the Storm, crushing us in its march. If I have come to a correct diagnosis in the case, there can possibly be but one remedy, which is readily suggestive. With much Respect Gov. I am your personal and political friend

J. McCormick[1]

[*Endorsed*] File private

Z B V

[1]John McCormick, member of the General Assembly from Cumberland County. Cheney, *North Carolina Government,* 329, 331.

ZBV to Richard C. Gatlin   A&H:GLB

Executive Department
Raleigh Nov. 30th., 1863

Gen'l. R. C. Gatlin

Gen'l.

You will order the Quartermaster to turn over to T. J. Hughes, Esqr. the sum of Three Hundred thousand dollars at various times to be expended in the purchase of Naval Stores.

Respectfully,
Z. B. Vance

Proclamation by ZBV   SHC:Yel

By the Governor of North Carolina,
A Proclamation.

Whereas it becomes a Christian People under all circumstances to acknowledge the superintending care and sovereignty of Almighty God and especially to confess our transgressions and humble ourselves before His chastening hand in seasons of affliction and calamity:

Now, therefore I, Zebulon B. Vance Governor of the State of North Carolina moved by these considerations, as also by the request of the General Assembly and to concur in the action of other Sourthern States, do issue this my proclamation, setting apart, Thursday—the 10th. day of December next as a day of Fasting, Humiliation and Prayer; earnestly requesting its sincere observance by all the good people of the State, that all worldly employments be suspended and that all Ministers and Clergy men of whatsever denomination will open their churches, and assembling their congregation make earnest and fervent supplication unto God, that He will stay His wrath, which has been heavy upon us, and especially, that He may in His wisdom open the way for the speedy restoration of peace to our desolated land, on such terms as will best promote His glory and both the spiritual and temporal welfare of His creatures.

In testimony whereof, I, Zebulon B. Vance Governor, Captain General and Commander in Chief both set my hand and caused the great seal of the State to be affixed.

Done at our City of Raleigh on the 30th. of November A.D. 1863.

Z. B. Vance

Richard C. Gatlin to ZBV   A&H:GP

Executive Department, N.C.,
Adjutant General's Office,
Raleigh, December 2d. 1863.

His Excellency,
Z. B. Vance,
Governor of N.C.

Sir:

I have the honor to submit the following estimates for funds to meet the probable wants of the various Departments of the Military Service of the State for the fiscal year commencing October 1st, 1863 and ending September 30th, 1864:

Pay Department.

Bounty to Conscripts, to soldiers unpaid, and to the Representatives of deceased soldiers	$ 700,000
Pay of [Alexander] McRae's Battalion of Artillery, [John N.] Whitfords Batt'n, Col. [James W.] Hinton's command, Officers of the Military Department, Aids to Governor & Miscellaneous	640,000
Pay of Home Guards and militia	100,000
Total	$1,440,000

Ordnance Department

Purchase of new arms.	$ 180,000
Repair of arms	20,000
Purchase of Accoutrements & horse equipments	100,000
Ammunition	80,000
Incidental	20,000
Total	$ 400,000

Commissary Department

Purchase of 500,000 lbs Bacon	$ 750,000
" 20,000 bushels corn	60,000
" 1,000 bbls. flour	50,000
" 5,000 bushels salt	75,000
Hire of Assistants, Agents & Laborers	25,000
Incidental Expenses	15,000
Total	$ 975,000

The foregoing for the support of 2,000 State Troops one year and one half the Home Guard for two months.

Quarter Master's Department

Forage for draft animals	$ 70,000
Forage for broken down Cavalry horses	25,000
Hire of teamsters and laborers	6,500
Purchase of draft horses and mules	25,000
Pay of Clerks in the several Departments	10,000
Rent of Store houses for Q. M. Stores	2,000
Incidental expenses of Home Guards, &c	30,000
Stationary and porterage	3,000
Rent of Offices	300
Transportation of troops and supplies	25,000
	$ 196,800

Clothing Department

From an examination of the transactions of the past year, it is supposed there will be required for the current fiscal year, the sum of $3,000,000

Medical Department

Medicines, Hospital Stores, &c., for the Home Guards of the State, and for such forces as may be exclusively in N.C. Service $ 50,000

Recapitulation.

Pay Department	$1,440,000
Ordnance Department	400,000
Commissary Department	975,000
Quarter Masters Department	196,800
Clothing Department	3,000,000
Medical Department	50,000
Aggregate	$6,061,800

These estimates are based upon the existing engagements of the State, and only make the necessary provision for executing the laws already in force. Should the General Assembly see proper to widen the operations of the State, such further sums will be required as may be necessary to execute its will.

The large appropriations for the support of the Clothing Department is returned to the State by the monthly sales of clothing to the Confederate Government, these sales being made at the actual cost of the articles to the State. The receipts from this source are not carried to the immediate credit of this Department, but have heretofore been paid directly into the Treasury; hence the amount here set down as an apparent, not an actual expenditure. It is designed that the Clothing Department be self-sustaining, the receipts from the sales being equal to the disbursements on that account.

It may be here added also, that the demands for the pay of troops may be diminished by their transfer to the entire control of the Confederate Government; and that, under the Act of Congress of May 1st, 1863, all payments already made for their support will be refundable to the State upon making the proper demand.

> Very Respectfully
> Your Obedient Servant
> R. C. Gatlin
> Adjutant General.

H. *Fitzhugh to* ZBV   A&H:GLB

[*Telegram*]

Wilmington Dec 2d. 1863

Gov. Vance.

Will take half the vessel on arrival here—Will deposit half a million with our Bankers at Richmond to buy bonds subject to your control at once, & more on vessels arrival if you require it. We will tender Thos. B. Power of Wilmington, with our ourselves on the agreed guarantee. If this suits telegraph us at this place accepting, or suggesting modifications & I will visit you—

> H. Fitzhugh[1]
> Care Power, Low & Co.

[1]Virginia agent for the purchase of cargo from the blockade-runner *Advance*.

ZBV *to* H. *Fitzhugh*   A&H:GLB

[*Telegram*]

Raleigh Dec. 3d.

Col. H. Fitzhugh
Wilmington

I will accept your offer, but don't know Mr. Power—wish further information as to him.

> Z. B. Vance

William F. Lynch to ZBV   A&H:GLB

Head Quarters
Naval Defences of No. Carolina
Wilmington December 4th. 1863

His Excellency
Z. B. Vance
Governor of North Carolina

Governor.

The Hon. Secretary of the Navy has sent me copies of your letter to him of the 28th. ult.[1] and of one to your Excellency from Mr. Elliott. In order to preserve harmony between yourself, the representative of the majesty of a soverign State and the head of one of the Departments of the Confederate Government.

I deem it my duty to submit the following statement.

The gunboat "Albemarle" was removed from Edward's Ferry to Halifax, by direction of Mr. Mallory a precautionary measure taken in consequence of a letter from the Military Commander of the District, a copy of which is herewith enclosed, marked A,[2] Mr. Elliott had been paid by installments; had received more than the *contract* would have justified upon a survey, and the boat was the sole property of the Government.

After repeated invitations to resume the work and three weeks had elapsed without his doing so, the matter was laid before the Navy Department and the vessel taken out of his hands. The workmen in the interim, employed by the Government, had lost no time, but put up their huts and workshops and recommenced work upon the boat. The principal delay was the want of laborers and caulkers, the application for them by Lieut. Johnston, the officer in charge having been refused.

On the 27th. ult. Mr. Mallory sent a telegram to me, a copy of which, and my reply, marked respectively B and C[3] are enclosed. They will satisfy you what was the ruling motive with the Government and myself. Your Excellency is misinformed as to the use applied by the Navy Department.

I have sent 435,000 *lbs.* of old rails to Atlanta and 125,000 *lbs.* to Richmond and have received and am receiving the plates rolled therefrom. Not one plate has been applied to any other purpose than the Naval Defences of this State, which was the agreement with your Excellency. Every order I have received from the Navy Department evinces its anxiety for the completion of the gunboats in North Carolina and to that Department I am responsible.

Your Excellency has done me great /injustice/ but self respect prevents the tending an unsought explanation. It is in my power, by written evidence with names and dates, to disprove every assertion made by Mr. Elliott. His platitudes about exalted patriotism and personal sacrifice are worse than trash—for they are untrue. When on the 10th. Febry. 1862 Elizabeth City, his place of residence, if not his native place, was attacked by the enemy, he fled and I remained to defend it. As to personal sacrifices, I can only say that his bills against the Government indicate a keen regard to individual interest.

> I have the honor to be
> Very Respectfully
> Your obt. servt.
> W. F. Lynch
> Flag Officer

[1]In this volume.
[2]Not extant.
[3]Not extant.

Alexander Collie to ZBV   A&H:GP

> 17, Leadenhall Street,
> London E.C. 7th. Decr. 1863

The Honbl. Z. B. Vance

Sir

I wrote you on 28th. Octr.[1] in the expectation that Mr. White was *then* on the eve of departure—Since that time very little has occurred here worthy of note—Mr. White goes home by this steamer; & will communicate to you personally our position & prospect. Money is likely to be very dear here for sometime; and this I think will be much in favor of your cause—

I have asked Mr. [*Theodore*] Andrea[e], my agent at Wilmington to hand you Twenty thousand dollars to be distributed among those who are suffering from the present state of things in your country. I hope this little contribution, from one who is almost a stranger, will alleviate in some degree a little of that distress which this terrible war has brought on your country—

I have taken the liberty of sending you by this same opportunity a small box which I doubt not you will find very useful—Please accept it as a mark of respect from one who has all along taken a deep interest in the fortunes of your country; and whose faith is strong that the noble efforts of yourself & of your countrymen will at no distant period be crowned with success—

Believe me

> Very faithfully yrs
> Alexr. Collie

[1]To ZBV not extant, but see Collie to John White, October 28, 29, A&H:GLB.

ZBV to Milledge L. Bonham   A&H:GLB

State of North Carolina
Executive Department
Raleigh Dec 7th. 1863

His Excellency
Gov. Bonham
Columbia S.C.

Dear Sir.

I have not until recently had time to render you my thanks, for the assistance rendered me by sending Captain Boykins Company to my brother in the mountains. He informs me they did most efficient service while with him. I trust Sir, that I may have it in my power, should you unfortunately be in a situation to ask it, to do you a similar favor.

Very respectfully,
Yr obt. servt.
Z. B. Vance

ZBV to Edward J. Hale   A&H:Hale

Private

State of North Carolina,
Executive Department,
Raleigh, Decr. 10, 1863.

E. J. Hale Esq

My dear Sir,

The report about Lincoln's letter[1] is a lie out of the whole cloth, and the man who started is an ass or a knave I dont care which. It was a pass for Miss Gaston,[2] and when I opened it I jestingly <illegible> remarked "that it was an important letter from Abe", but immediately explained what it was. I cant remember who it was in my office—*Denounce it—*

Things are gloomy here in the extreme. The Legislature will adjourn on Monday without any further demonstration from the peace men I think—thanks to the influence of Mr. Graham—But the Holdenites are making every effort to raise a row again. God help us. I fear we are on the eve of another revolution & civil war in the State

Truly yours
Z. B. Vance

[1]Not extant.

[2]Katherine Jane (Kate) Gaston, unmarried daughter of William Joseph Gaston, prominent politician and jurist. She requested the pass to visit her sister in Maryland. *Dictionary of North Carolina Biography*, s.v. "Gaston, William Joseph"; *News and Observer* (Raleigh), January 8, 1885; Kate Gaston to ZBV, November 21, A&H:GP.

ZBV to James A. Seddon   A&H:GLB

State of North Carolina
Executive Department
Raleigh Dec. 11th. 1863

Hon. J. A. Seddon
Secty of War

Dr. Sir

Referring to your letter of the 29th. Octo.[1] in relation to the petition of the 1st. and 3d. regiments N.C.T. to be put into a N.C. Brigade, in which you say that it cannot be done because all the N.C. Brigades are full. I have the honor to ask now, that the that the [sic] 1st. & 3d. & 35th. N.C. Regts. which belong to brigades from other States and the 33d. belonging to [James Henry] Lane's brigade, which has five regiments, be constituted a brigade. I have no disposition to interfere unduly with the arrangements of the Generals in the field, but so great is the desire of those brave men for this arrangement that I am induced to urge it, if it could be done without injury to the service. They have petitioned me to assist them in getting it accomplished.

Respectfully Yrs.
Z. B. Vance

[1]A&H:VanPC.

Stephen R. Mallory to ZBV   A&H:GP

Confederate States of America,
Navy Department,
Richmond, December 11th. 1863.

His Excellency
Z. B. Vance
Governor of North Carolina
Raleigh N.C.

Sir,

I have the honor to acknowledge the receipt of your letter of the 28th. ulto,[1] enclosing a statement of Mr. Gilbert Elliott, an earlier reply to which has been procluded by the necessity of making the enquiries rendered proper thereby.

Mr. Elliott, the contractor to build the "Albemarle", complains that Flag Officer Lynch took the vessel from him by force, and removed it to Halifax "for the ostensible purpose of completion". . . . "Since the removal no work has been done upon her".

It is hardly necessary to say that the "ostensible", was the real design of Flag Officer Lynch, to complete the vessel in the shortest time. This, of course, could have been done best where she was, if permitted by the enemy; but clothed with the responsibility of her completion, he made diligent and faithful enquiry, and was convinced that she would be destroyed, if not removed, there being no adequate force to protect her, and upon this point I learn that he consulted with the military commander. He may have been mistaken as to the danger to be apprehended from the enemy, but he acted upon such information as was before him.

In presenting this statement to your Excellency, upon which he expected your consideration and action, Mr. Elliott should have added certain facts, without which a correct judgement could not be arrived at. For example, he might have said that, in removing the vessel to Halifax for greater security, Flag Officer Lynch did not regard her as out of the hands of Mr. Elliott, but on the contrary expected him to complete her—, but that Mr. Elliott not only otherwise disposed of his caulkers, (who were negroes in his service) but made a return of the detailed men working with him on the boat, to the Commanding Officer whose application for their return to duty in the army was presented by the Adjutant and Inspector General of the Army to this Department, (see Flag Officer Lynch's letter of Nov. 11th. 1863 herewith enclosed, marked A[2]), though he had no right whatever to terminate their detail. Second, that on the 2nd. of November Mr. Elliott himself served written notices as "contractor &c." (copies of which are herewith enclosed, marked B. & C.[3]) to sixteen of these men to return to the army and conscript camp. Third, that when he offered, as he alleges, to complete the vessel, his offer was coupled with the condition that he should receive $25,000 for so doing, with the further condition that the expense of drilling the armour should be paid by the Government;—. Whereas he had contracted to complete the vessel including the drilling for $40,000, $30,000 of which he had already received.

His offer was regarded as a notice that he would not complete the vessel for $10,000, but would do so for $25,000.

Fourth, He should have stated that additional expense upon the vessel /became necessary/ from the inefficient manner of constructing it, the Chief Naval Constructor having examined it, and reported "that this vessel is a very rough and inferior piece of work in labor and material, she is not properly fastened".

Your remark that "the iron furnished by the state under the express promise of both himself (Capt. Lynch) and you has been applied to other purposes" requires correction. The total amount of rail road iron received at the Rolling mills up to the 30th. ulto from North Carolina—and much of which cannot be rolled for want [of] coal, is 192 tons. If this were rolled into armour plates it would produce 144 tons only to be sent back to North Carolina—; whereas 336 1/2 tons of rolled plates, requiring 420 tons to make them have been ordered back there (and are delayed only by want of transportation) 86 1/2 tons of which have already reached there—.

It is proper also to add that in addition to this iron nearly 700 tons of additional armour plates and fastening, requiring 875 tons of iron to make them have been taken from other sources and been sent to North Carolina for the ships at Wilmington.

Your Excellency will doubtless remember from my correspondence with you directly, and through Flag Officer Lynch, on the subject, my frequent and earnest efforts to obtain rail road iron in North Carolina to build iron clad vessels within the state, which efforts were fruitless up to a comparatively recent date;—so recent that much of the iron obtained it has been found impossible as yet to roll. I enclose copy of a letter from Martin & Elliott, written on January last, in which they state that you have given them assurance of enabling them to obtain rail road iron for a floating battery on the Roanoke, and the construction of which was induced by their representation and belief that they could get the iron to cover it, and had them countermand the order.

In reference to your remark that Flag Officer Lynch has placed iron plates "on the boat 'Neuse' without her machinery and in face of the fact that it will all have to come off before the machinery does go in", I beg leave to say, and only because it is stated as an evidence of Flag Officer Lynch's ignorance and incapacity, that no such proceeding will be necessary;—that the only special preparation necessary will be for the proper adjustment of the shaft and propeller, and that this will require but ordinary skill and labor.

I have, in view of your endorsement of Mr. Elliott's statements, deemed it due to Your Excellency and to this Department to state these facts, no less than to Flag Officer Lynch, who has always stood high as an intelligent, faithful, zealous and energetic officer, and who has, in his efforts to build and equip vessels in North Carolina, had to encounter difficulties and [illegible] not generally understood.

Upon receiving your letter and learning the course which the contractor had pursued, I sent the Chief Naval Constructor, Mr. Porter,[4] to Halifax with orders to adopt the best means available for the earliest completion of the vessel and he has acted accordingly.

> I am respectfully
> Your obt srvt.
> S R Mallory
> Secretary of the Navy

[1] In this volume.
[2] Not extant.

³Not extant.
⁴John Luke Porter. Faust et al., *Encylopedia of Civil War*, 595.

ZBV to Richard S. Donnell   A&H:GA

[*With enclosure*]

State of North Carolina,
Executive Department,
Raleigh, Decr. 12 1863.

Hon R S Donnell
Spr. Ho Commons,

Sir,

I enclose herewith a communication from Maj Gen W. H. C. Whiting, comdg defences of the Cape Fear, inviting of committee of both Houses to visit the fortifications of Wilmington to see how the labor furnished him by the State has been applied—

I respectfully recommend its adoption.

Very respectfully
Yr. obt. svt.
Z. B. Vance

[*Enclosure*]

William H. C. Whiting to General Assembly   A&H:GA

Hd. Qrs. Wilmington
Dec 11, 1863.

To the Honorable Senate & House of Commons of the State of North Carolina.

The undersigned commanding the defenses of the Cape Fear in this State, respectfully requests your Honorable body to appoint a committee to visit & inspect the various works upon which the labor furnished by the people of the State through his Excellency the Governor has been applied by the Confederate authorities—

In the hope that the Honorable Houses will consider this subject worthy their attention, a cordial invitation is tendered to any of the members & every facility will be afforded them either individually or as a Committee of inspection, by the officers & men of this command to examine the results produced.

With profound respect
W. H. C. Whiting
Maj Genl.
Comd. Defenses of Cape Fear

Memorandum by ZBV A&H:GP

[*December 15, 1863*]

Address a note to Col Whitford A & N. C. R. R. asking how much iron his road has delivered to Navy Dept and all the information in his possession on this subject—
Also to [*William J.*] Hawkins, if he has sold or bought any—& to [*Sewall L.*] Fremont & Sumner[1] as to how much they have bought sold or exchanged with the Confederacy &c &c

Z B V

[1]Thomas J. Sumner, superintendent of the North Carolina Railroad. Allen W. Trelease, *The North Carolina Railroad, 1849–1871, and the Modernization of North Carolina* (Chapel Hill: University of North Carolina Press, 1991), 141–142.

ZBV to James A. Seddon SHC:Clar

State of N.C.
Executive Department
Raleigh Dec. 1[6]th. 1863

Hon J. A. Seddon
Secy. of War,

Dr. Sir:
I have enlisted within and near the enemies lines in Eastern N.C. some twenty three hundred troops, raised for Local defences. Finding it impractical to properly manage them, I applied to the Legislature to turn them over to the Confederacy, which was declined. Being very anxious to make so large a body of men available for the defence of the Roanoke country, so valuable to us, I have consented to a plan of Col. Clarke's[1] for continuing and disciplining them.

If you will give him his own Regt. the 24th N.C.T. as a nucleus, I will place these State troops under his control, and give him every possible assistance in raising more. There are still many men within the lines who could be got by this arrangement.

As you will perceive this involves the necessity of conferring additional rank upon Col. Clarke. I beg leave to say particularly, that I regard him as eminently fitted for this proposed service; and generally that Col. Clarke is deserving of this promotion on account of his long and faithful services from the beginning of the war.

I have had the honor to recommend him to the Department before, having seen him on the field of battle.

Trusting that you may deem it proper to comply with this suggestion for the defense of the Roanoke Country

> I am, very resptly.
> Your obt servant
> Z. B. Vance

[Endorsed]

Richmond Dec. 18th. 1863—

His Excellency
President Davis:
    The undersigned Senators and Representatives from N. C. fully concur in the plan proposed by Col. Clarke and endorsed by Genls. Pickett & [Matt W.] Ransom, & Gov. Vance and respectfully recommend Col. Clarke for promotion— Very respectfully Wm. T. Dortch, B. S. Gaither, R.R. Bridgers,[2] A. H. Arrington, W Lander,[3] Geo. Davis, Thos. D. McDowell, J R McLean, O. R. Kenan,[4] A. T. Davidson

[Endorsed] Approved & Respt. Forwd. J. L. Manney[5] Capt.; Comdg. Fort Branch.[6]

[1]See William J. Clarke to ZBV, November 27, A&H:GP.
[2]Robert Rufus Bridgers, congressman. Dictionary of North Carolina Biography, s.v. "Bridgers, Robert Rufus."
[3]William Lander, congressman. Dictionary of North Carolina Biography, s.v. "Lander, William."
[4]Owen Rand Kenan, congressman. Dictionary of North Carolina Biography, s.v. "Kenan, Owen Rand."
[5]James L. Manney, Tenth Regiment North Carolina Troops. Clark, Histories of Regiments from North Carolina, 1:495; Manarin and Jordan, North Carolina Troops, 1:114.
[6]On the Roanoke River in northwest Martin County. Powell, North Carolina Gazetteer, 178.

ZBV to James A. Seddon   A&H:GP

Copy

> State of North Carolina
> Executive Department
> Raleigh Dec. 21st. 1863.

Hon Jas. A. Seddon
Secty. of War
Dear Sir
    I desire to call your attention to an evil which is inflicting great distress upon the people of this State and contributing largely to the public discontent. I allude

to illegal seizures of property and other depredations of an outrageous character by detached bands of Troops—chiefly Cavalry—. The Department I am sure can have no idea of the extent and character of this evil. It is enough in many cases to breed a rebellion in a loyal county against the Confederacy, and has actually been the cause of much alienation of feeling in many parts of North Carolina. It is not my purpose now to give instances and call for punishment of the offenders—that I do to their commanding officers, but to ask if some order or regulation cannot be made for the government of troops on detached service, the severe and unflinching execution of which might not check this stealing, pilfering, burning and sometimes murderous conduct. I give you my word that in North Carolina it has become a grievance, intolerable, damnable and not to be borne! If God Almighty had yet in store another plague—worse than all others, which he intended to have let loose on the Egyptians in case Pharoah still hardened his heart, I am sure it must have been a regiment or so of half-armed, half disciplined Confederate Cavalry! Had they been turned loose among Pharoah's subjects, with or without an impressment law, he would have become so sensible of the anger of God that he never would have followed the Children of Israel to the Red Sea, No Sir not an inch!!. Cannot officers be reduced to the ranks for permitting this? Can not a few men be shot for perpetrating these outrages as an example? Unless something can be done, I shall be compelled in some sections to call out my Militia and levy actual war against them. I beg your early and earnest attention to this matter

Very Respectfully Yrs.

(Signed)   Z. B. Vance

ZBV to Robert E. Lee   A&H:GLB

State of North Carolina
Executive Department
Raleigh Dec. 21st. 1863

To Genl. Robt. E. Lee
Comdg. Army N. Va.

Gen'l.

Would it be within your power to suppress the practice among soldiers of selling their clothing etc.?

I have recently /been/ much outraged to see fine English shoes, jackets and flannel shirts, which I had imported at so much risk for the comfort of our brave men, on the persons of citizens and *negroes*.

The Quartermasters too come frequently with requisitions for 800 to 1000 men to the regiment and draw for this number, when perhaps not over half is required for the troops actually in the field. The effect frequently is, when our supplies are short, that the first who apply get a double supply, others get none;

the extra amount taken to the field is an incumbrance, lost on the first hasty retreat or constitutes a dangerous temptation to the honesty of the parties in charge. In every respect it is desirable that their requisitions should come in approved only according to their actual present and not prospective wants. Confident, General, that you will fully appreciate the difficulties under which the Home Department labors in procuring supplies, constantly increasing with our diminished resources, and calculating on your assistance.

> I am most Respectfully
> Yr. obt. svt.
> Z. B. Vance

ZBV to Edward J. Hale   A&H:Hale

> State of North Carolina,
> Executive Department,
> Raleigh, Decr. 21 1863.

My dear Sir,

Your last two letters have remained unanswered for the reason that I have been confined to my /room/ for nearly a week past, partly from severe cold and partly because of a large tumor which I had cut from my neck. Six months ago you would have learned of my illness through the *newspapers*.

I did not know of young Dockery's[1] sentiments or I should not have appd. him to the office he holds—I should regret to revoke it now, but can always do so should it become necessary. Most of the appts. in the Home Guards were made before I was well aware of the spread of a feeling of reconstruction and I was not sufficiently careful in this respect—Still I dont know of many of that stamp in office, unless they develope yet which is probable. Harrison,[2] Col. of the rgt. in this County has come out full fledged & I hear of only one or two others. They can be [stripped] at any time should their opinions get in the way of their charge of duty as they hold their commissions at my pleasure.

What do you think of Holdens articles on Lincoln's message? He objects, but as you will see, *not very bitterly*. The Progress man becames a greater Ass every day. What would you say to Congress app'g Commrs. to treat for peace? Would it do any good North or South? Their terms would not be heard of course, and it *might* help to put down the clamor here.

Many of our friends here think it the only way to save N.C. and I confess I have been somewhat moved by their arguments, but am fearful to yielding my position on such without good advice. Mr. Graham was much depressed whilst here on the subject, for though we suppressed the revolution in the Caucas, yet there was much dissatifaction among men of whom you would have thought better things. Dont think me faint-hearted—I have been sick and quite gloomy. I am going to Wilkes County to make a speech as soon as invited preparations for which are now going on, then I shall go to the army if the enemy permits, and will speak wherever /& whenever/ it may be thought prudent—

Please answer my question above

Yrs

Z B Vance

[1]Oliver Hart Dockery, a unionist and former legislator, who served in the Thirty-eighth Regiment North Carolina Troops. He left that regiment in April 1862, and ZBV appointed him to the Richmond County Militia (later Home Guard). After the war Dockery became a Republican and served in Congress and as consul general in Rio de Janeiro, Brazil. He was a delegate to the state Constitutional Convention of 1875 and ran unsuccessfully for governor in 1888. He was the son of Alfred Dockery (see ZBV to Edward J. Hale, December 30, in this volume). *Dictionary of North Carolina Biography*, s.v. "Dockery, Oliver Hart"; Manarin and Jordan, *North Carolina Troops*, 10:8, 48; Bradley, *Militia Officers Roster*, 162.

[2]William H. Harrison, commander of the Wake County Home Guard. Elizabeth Reid Murray, *Wake: Capital County of North Carolina*, 1 vol. to date (Raleigh: Capital County Publishing Co., 1983—), 1:481.

Francis C. Lawley to ZBV   A&H:VanPC

Private & Confidential

Box 321. Richmond

Dec. 22. 1863

To H. E. Governor Vance

My Dear Sir

You may recollect a long conversation which I had with you at Raleigh in March last,[1] when I thought that I was about to return to England, & we spoke about a loan, to be effected in London for the State of N. Carolina. The interest of this war was such that I was unable to tear myself away from this country; but, as I am now on the point of returning to England, I cannot leave the C. S. without troubling you with these few lines. In regard to the conversation which passed between us in March, I am glad to have observed that your Agents in England have been successful in carrying out your views and it is not on this subject that I am anxious to speak to you.

I hear with great concern that there is in your State considerable dissaffection towards the Confed. Government; that there are many Unionists & some disposition to offer peace to the North on the basis of independent State action. I hope & believe that this disaffection is considerably exaggerated; but I cannot, as having long been a close & tolerably impartial observer of this struggle, omit to send to you a few words of warning, entreating you, by all means in your power, to repress, & at any rate to defer any such demonstration of N. Carolina public opinion as her independent action, reaching out after peace, would imply. For a hundred reasons, which are too lengthy to send to you in writing, I am *positive* that if the present attitude of the South is maintained for 6 months longer, the war is over. On the other hand, any such rupture in the front of the Confederacy as the splitting off from it of N. Carolina, would prolong the war indefinitely, would produce an [imminse] reaction of European & English opinion & would neutralise the representations as to the impossibility of subjugating the South, which I am about to advocate warmly & to impress upon members of Parliament, when I return to England.

This letter is written with the sole object of entreating you to do what I believe your own character & make will urge you to do: Viz. Entreat your people to have patience & long suffering for yet a few months more. It is impossible to over estimate the importance to the C. S. of keeping an undivided front for 6 months more. There is no State on this continent which has more to gain by emancipation from Yankee vassalage than North Carolina, with her magnificent raw material, & with her absence of manufactures. In a very few months that independence which is already more than three fourths gained, will be an accomplished fact.

It would be a great satisfaction & encouragement to me, before my return to England, if you would favor me with a few lines enlightening me as to the true condition of your State. I need hardly say that I shall regard your letter as entirely confidential.

With my hearty good wishes for your speedy & plenary independence

> Believe me
> My Dear Sir
> Very faithfully yours
> Francis Lawley

[1]See ZBV to Lawley, March 4, in this volume.

ZBV to Milledge L. Bonham   SHC:Law

[*Telegram*]

Raleigh Dec 22

Columbia Dec 22 1863

To Gov Bonham,

Can I possibly through your aid get any Cotton transported from Augusta to Wilmington or Charlotte [since] importing Army supplies & cannot keep Steamers in Cotton unless it comes from Augusta

Z. B. Vance

Milledge L. Bonham to ZBV SHC:Law

[*Telegram*]

Ex Dept
Columbia Dec 2[2]/63
4 1/2 P.M.

Gov Z B. Vance
Raleigh N.C.

Would with pleasure aid you if I could. It is with the greatest difficulty that I
have been able to get the smallest quantity transported for this State. I will make
an effort however & will give you the results

M. L. Bonham

ZBV to James A. Seddon A&H:GLB

State of North Carolina
Executive Department
Raleigh Dec. 23d. 1863.

To Hon. Jas. A. Seddon
Secy. of War
Richmond Va.

My Dear Sir

Some eight months since this State loaned to the Confederate Govt. some
eighteen hundred bales of Cotton upon the request of Maj. [John W.] Cameron.
Q. M. at Wilmington to load Confederate Steamers. The Cotton was to be replaced or paid for at my option. Some time /since/ I applied for the Cotton to
be replaced—the demand was replied to by a Capt. Archer of Genl. Whiting's
staff, alleging that he had *bought* the Cotton and cooly offering me 20 cents per
lb. and transportation, just what it cost the State sixteen months since. It was
bought to meet a prospective debt abroad, which I am called upon to pay in part,
and I cannot replace it for less than 80 cents per pound in South Western Ga.
and, as the Government has monopolized the rail roads, I cannot in fact get the
cotton at all to load my Steamer. In this dilema I can but appeal to you, to return
my Cotton. Justice and fair dealing requires this, to say nothing of the importance
of keeping the Steamers running with all possible despatch whilst Wilmington
remains open.

Very Respectfully
Yr. obt. servt.
Z. B. Vance

ZBV to Theodore Andreae   A&H:GLB

State of North Carolina
Executive Department
Raleigh Dec 23d., 1863

Mr. T. Andrea[e]
Wilmington N.C.

Sir.

Having purchased an interest in the Steamers of Messrs. A. Collie & Co. of London, deliverable on their arrival in the port of Wilmington, to wit, The Don and Hansa; and having by this purchase acquired the right of control over said vessels in the ports of the Confederacy, you will please act as Agent for this line at Wilmington until further orders.

You will load the Hansa now in port with Cotton as soon as possible and order her to proceed forthwith to Bermuda and take on cargo for the State of North Carolina to return

Respectfully Yours
Z. B. Vance

William J. Clarke to ZBV   A&H:GP

Weldon, December 24th. 1863.

Hon. Z. B. Vance,

Governor:

On yesterday, I had an interview with the President, and submitted to him your letter[1] to the Secretary of War. He spoke in the kindest terms of you, and approved of the plan for organizing the forces, and expressed his willingness to carry it out; but he wishes you to give him more definite information relative to the organization of the forces. He is in doubt whether they are militia or not. If they are militia he can not appoint a commanding officer for them. It is your prerogative. You say in your letter "I have enlisted, within and near the enemy's lines, in Eastern N.C. some twenty three hundred men raised for local defence. Finding it impracticable to properly manage them, I applied to the Legislature to turn them over to the Confederacy."

No light on the subject could be obtained from the War Department, and the President cannot understand the necessity of your applying to the Legislature for authority to turn them over to the Confederacy. If they were raised under the act of Congress *for local defence* there will be no difficulty in retaining them for that purpose, as is the case with quite a large number of troops in other states; but the muster rolls should be filed in the War Office. This, as I understand it, is necessary to protect the men from conscription.

It is very necessary that something should be done *immediately*, as it is very clear to me that, when active operations are resumed in the spring, if not sooner, every man now defending this section will be withdrawn, and I am fully convinced that Butler[2] intends to occupy the country as soon as he can, and we have once been admonished <from> /by/ the highest authority to "take care of ourselves" and we should prepare to do so in time. I receive very cheering accounts as to the number of men I can raise to augment the forces.

> Very respectfully
> Your obt. servant
> Wm. J. Clarke

[1]December 16, in this volume.

[2]Union general Benjamin Franklin Butler, commanding the Department of Virginia and North Carolina, later known as Department (and Army) of the James. Boatner, *Civil War Dictionary*, 109–110.

ZBV to Richmond M. Pearson   A&H:GLB

> State of North Carolina
> Executive Department
> Raleigh Dec. 26th. 1863

Chief Justice Pearson
Richmond Hill

Dear Sir.

Before the subject of Austin's case is dropped between us, I desire to say in reply to yours of the 7th. inst.,[1] that (once for all) I did not expect to get a "decision of the Supreme Court" which should "settle the law" by yourself and Judge Manley sitting with Judge Battle in the case proposed; nor did I expect it moreover to have any greater legal weight, as I knew it would still be only Judge Battle's decision. If I have failed to make myself so understood, I have been unfortunate. I did expect to "mend the matter" by *agreeing* to treat the decision so rendered as "authority" whether it was or not, and to withdraw my order to the Home Guards if the Judges of the Supreme Court so advised me. I presume that in desiring to have a consultation of all the Judges in Woodel[l]s case,[2] I was actuated by that great respect and moral weight which their opinions would and always do inspire, which induced you to ask Judges Battle and Manley to sit with you in Austin's case, though well knowing it could only be your own decision after all. And I did hope, that as it was customary for the Judges to assist each other with counsel and advice as was contemplated by yourself in the case referred to, certainly in a case involving so much embarassment to the Executive of the State, and so grave a public responsibility as imparing the efficiency of the

Army—a probability suggested by your own opinion in the case, they (the Judges) would not hesitate to extend to him their counsel and advice also! But it seems I was mistaken; legal objections bristle at every point, and for offering to defer respectfully and absolutely to the mere intimation of the Judges (if they would be good enough to give it.) I am laid open to the charge of prostrating the Judiciary! and I am expected to be bound by the decisions of eleven different Judges though they decline to be bound themselves by the decisions of each other!

You say that you had not heard of the decisions of Judge Gilliam, Heath & French alluded to in my last.[3] It is quite reasonable that you did not, and I submit most respectfully, that, that is the best reason imaginable why they did not bind. How *could* you have heard of them? They are not of record; they neither were nor could be officially reported, certainly the law does not lay a trap for the citizen and leave him to find it out after he has sinned. No other Judge besides yourself has had his decision published in a newspaper even. So in the case you cite of "Whitehart"[4] of Salem. I never heard of it until I read your letter, Never, How could I hear of it? Was it published? If so in what paper? Perhaps the Fayetteville Observer, I dont subscribe for that paper, but if I did what announcement has been made to the public that they must search its columns in order to find the law of the land? Is it the *organ* of the Chief Justice in vacation?

In regard to 3d. part of your letter, relating to a decision of the Supreme Court in the matter of [J. C.] "Bryan" & "Ritter,"[5] I have only to say that I ordered the militia, generally, to assist in arresting deserters and conscripts, meaning of course only such as were liable to conscription and unless each militia officer was a lawyer and had power to try each case as it came up, I dont see how they could avoid assisting the *enrolling officer* to seize the wrong man sometimes, though I am sure there has been no intention on my part or on theirs to do so. In such cases there are questions both of law and fact, and as the Supreme Court did *not* decide that every man *claiming* the benefit of the exemptions act between the age of 18 & 35 should be entitled to it, but those who *showed themselves by proof*, to be entitled to it, it necessarily follows that *somebody* must judge of this claim. Who shall it be? The Act of Congress provides that the Secretary of War or his officers must judge in the first place; the State laws require our Judges to do it until one or the other *does* decide—or whatever other authority be competent— I cant see how the *facts*, which are to place him within the scope of the law can be so known to the officer as to put him in the wrong. If I could frame an order which would remove even this argumentative appearance, of aiding a Confederate officer in a manner which is contrary to the decision of the Supreme Court, I would gladly do so.

But before I make this letter too long, I desire to say that I was glad to see the concluding portion of your letter wherein you express the hope that "each one of us may discharge the duties of his position without any unkind feeling toward each other," I feel none myself, and trust you do not. I hope and believe that I am actuated by as ardent a love of civil liberty and civil rights as any man living; and such a love is scarcely separable from respect and esteem for those whom the law has entrusted with the protection of those rights, with this feeling, I withdrew Woodels case from before Judge Battle, at his suggestion, though had I insisted, I am assured he would not only have decided it, assisted by Judge Manly, but decided it differently from yourself. I referred the whole matter to the Legislature and although they *amended* the law, there was no power in them to decide the issue between you and me and I am still left to bear the imputation of prostrating the Judiciary of my country with all who are so uncharitable as to believe it. I submit that you did not treat me with equal forbearance and consideration, surrounded as I was and am with a thousand difficulties, embarassments and dangers, new to the Executive Office and which none of my predecessors have felt. I thought I had a right to expect much from the kindness and forbearance of my superiors in years and legal learning. Perhaps I counted too much upon this, and have failed essentially and unpardonably in my duty. I know and all who criticize should remember, the almost unsurmountable difficulties of my position. I know that it is almost impossible to bend every energy of the State to the support of the military power which is struggling for national independence, and to maintain intact all the rights and majesty of the civil law, without offending both. Yet I told the people of North Carolina this when they unsolicited, called me to this position, and I intend to keep this promise or perish in the attempt.

Very Respectfully
Yrs. etc.
Z. B. Vance

[1]A&H:GP.
[2]See William H. Battle to ZBV, November 12, in this volume.
[3]ZBV to Pearson, November 12, in this volume.
[4]Pearson "discharged the petitioner on the ground, that a Militia officer, could not lawfully arrest a man for harboring a conscript." See Pearson to ZBV, December 7, A&H:GP.
[5]Elias Ritter. Mitchell, *Legal Aspects of Conscription and Exemption*, 47.

ZBV to Alexander Collie   A&H:GLB

State of North Carolina
Executive Department
Raleigh Dec. 28th. 1863

Alexander Collie Esq.
Manchester, England

Sir.

Your proposition to sell me for the State of North Carolina an interest in four Steamers, has been recd. and I have been specially authorized to accept it with slight alterations. I enclose herewith an agreement signed in duplicate by myself and Mr. Andrea[e] yr. Agent, which will show you the alterations I desire to make. Instead of iron, as you suggested, I propose to bring in the remainder of the State purchases of Army supplies and then bacon or such other articles as the State may desire to import.

The time required to communicate with you, has induced me to get Mr. Andrea to sign the agreement for you and put it into effect as rapidly as possible, without waiting to hear further from you.

Your endorsement of yr. Agents action will be sufficient. Please push the completion of the other Steamers with all possible despatch. Time is everything. You will please sell the States interest in the Cargoes of the Cotton, paying such expenses as may be legally incurred and depositing the remainder in some safe bank subject to the order of the Governor of No. Ca. or his Agents.

The Cotton due you according to the terms of the Cotton Warrants will be delivered in port on terms you propose, on payment by you of the extra freights now demanded by the rail roads.

> Respectfully Yours
> Z. B. Vance

ZBV to Theodore Andreae   A&H:GLB

> State of North Carolina
> Executive Department
> Raleigh Dec. 28th. 1863

Mr. T. Andrea[e]
Wilmington N.C.

Dr. Sir

I enclose duplicate letters for Alex. Collie Esqr. which please forward by Hansa and another Steamer first going out. I also send contract for sale of vessels— please sign both return one to me & forward the other to Mr. Collie. The Christmas holidays have prevented me from sending the Cotton yet, it will go down this week. The Hansa must go to Bermuda or else I shall lose one cargo inward. The State has 90 tons coal on the wharf, let her take that. My coal agent has orders to take the river boat you sell me and bring down coal as fast as possible.

> Yrs. etc.
> Z. B. Vance

ZBV to Jefferson Davis A&H:GP

Copy

State of North Carolina
Executive Department
Raleigh Dec. 29th. 1863.

His Excellency
President Davis

Dear Sir

I have been requested by a Resolution of the General assembly of this state, passed at its recent extra session to correspond with your Excellency and ascertain if one W. D. Wynns [*Wynne*][1] a citizen of Bertie County, is now confined in prison in Richmond, and if so upon what charge and if for any offence cognizable by the Courts of this state, to demand that he be delivered up to be tried according to due course of law.

In compliance with the request contained in said resolution. I have the honor to request that you will at your earliest convenience give the desired information in regard to the arrest and imprisonment of the said W. D. Wynns., I am

With great respect
Your. obt. Servt.
Z. B. Vance.

[1]William D. Wynne, arrested by Confederate soldiers. Resolution in Relation to William D. Wynne, House Resolutions, Session of November-December, A&H:GA.

ZBV to Jefferson Davis A&H:GP

Copy

State of North Carolina
Executive Department
Raleigh 29th. Dec. 1863.

His Excellency
Jefferson Davis

Dear Sir

In compliance with a Resolution of the General Assembly of North Carolina passed at its recent Session,[1] a copy of which, is herewith enclosed, I respectfully request that you direct Eli Swanner,[2] named in the Resolution to be returned to North Carolina, to be tried for the offences alleged against him. I am

Very Respectfully
Yr. obt. Servt.
Z. B. Vance.

[1]Resolution in relation to the arrest and imprisonment of Eli Swanner of Beaufort County, Senate Resolutions, Session of November-December, A&H:GA.

[2]Arrested by Confederate soldiers "without accusation or warrant" and confined in the Confederate prison at Salisbury.

ZBV to James A. Seddon   A&H:GP

Copy

State of North Carolina
Executive Department
Raleigh Dec. 29th. 1863

Hon James A. Seddon
Secty. of War

Dear Sir

I have the honor herewith to transmit to you, certain Resolutions of the General Assembly of this State passed at the recent extra session,[1] upon the subject of illegal impressments and the scarcity of provisions, to which I invite your early attention.

There is great reason to believe, that the supply of provisions is very limited and I earnestly request that the Government will impress as small quantities as possible within our borders.

Impressing agents in many instances, act in such manner as to create great dissastisfaction among our people, and I sincerely hope that you will look to their conduct and issue such instructions as will protect citizens from illegal and unjust annoyance. These agents sometimes assume the right to judge of the quantity which the citizen needs for the use of his family and impress what they regard as the surplus, thus leaving him without an adequate supply. This crying evil and injustice should be corrected without delay.

Many military officers also in violation of the laws of Congress, assume the right of impressment.

This evil cannot longer be tolerated and I invoke your aid in its suppression with sentiments of great respect.

Your obedient Servant
(Signed)   Z. B. Vance

[1]See House and Senate Resolutions, Session of November-December, A&H:GA.

ZBV to Robert Ould   A&H:GLB

State of North Carolina
Executive Department
Raleigh Dec. 29th. 1863

Judge Ould
Comr. of Exchange
Richmond Va.

Dr. Sir.

I beg to call your attention to the condition of the troops of this State on the Chowan river under the command of Col. [James W.] Hinton. As you will see by the letters from a Yankee General by the name of Wild,[1] which Col. H. will show you, they refuse to treat them as prisoners of War, although regularly commissioned by law. They have also murdered several soldiers, and have arrested two respectable ladies whom they keep handcuffed as hostages for two negro soldiers and declare their purpose to hang them in case the negroes are hung. I must ask you to see if some arrangement cannot be made to include these troops within the cartel of exchange and repress if possible this horrible, cowardly and damnable disposition on the part of enemy to put women in irons as hostages for negro soldiers! Such men as this Wild are a disgrace to the manhood of the age, not being able to capture soldiers they war upon defenceless women! Great God! What an outrage. There is no reason why those men are not entitled to be treated as prisoners of war. If it is not done and these outrages upon defenceless females continue, I shall retaliate upon Yankee soldiers to the full extent of my ability, and let the consequences rest with the damnable barbarians who begun it

Very respectfully
Yr. obt. svt.
Z. B. Vance

[1]Edward Augustus Wild, commanding Federal black troops on a raid in northeastern North Carolina. Barrett, *Civil War in North Carolina*, 177–181.

ZBV to Jefferson Davis   A&H:VanPC

State of North Carolina
Executive Department
Raleigh, Dec. 30th. 1863

His Excellency
President Davis

My dear Sir:

After a careful consideration of all the sources of discontent in North Carolina, I have concluded that it will be perhaps impossible to remove it except by making some effort at negotiation with the enemy. The recent action of the Federal House of Representatives, though meaning very little, has greatly excited the public hope that the Northern mind is looking towards peace. I am promised by all men who advocate this course, that if fair terms are rejected it will tend greatly to strengthen and intensify the war feeling and will rally all classes to a more cordial support of the government. And although our position is well known, as demanding only to be let alone yet it seems to me that for the sake of humanity, without having any weak or improper motives attributed to us, we might with propriety constantly tender negotiations.

In doing so we would keep conspicuously before the world a disclaimer of our responsibility for the great slaughter of our race and convince the humblest of our citizens, who sometimes forget the actual situation, that the government is tender of their lives and happiness and would not prolong their sufferings unnecessarily one moment. Though Statesmen might regard this as useless, the people will not, and I think our cause will be strengthened thereby. I have not suggested the method of these negotiations or their terms, the *effort* to obtain peace is the principal matter. Allow me to beg your earnest consideration of this suggestion.

> Very respectfully Yours
> Z. B. Vance

ZBV *to Robert R. Heath*   A&H:GLB

State of North Carolina

To the Honorable Robt. R. Heath, Greeting,

By virtue of authority vested in the governor, by an Act of the General Assembly, ratified on the 12th. day of December A.D. 1863, good cause having been shown why a Court of Oyer and Terminer shall be held in the County of Halifax, for the speedy trial of certain persons accused of crimes against the laws of the State, you are hereby nominated appointed and commissioned to hold such Court of Oyer /and/ Terminer in said County, at such early time as you may be pleased to designate.

In witness whereof Zebulon B. Vance our Governor, Captain General and Commander-in-chief, hath signed these presents, and caused the great seal to be affixed Done at our city of Raleigh this 30th. Dec. A.D. 1863, and in the Eighty Seventh year of Independence.

> Z. B. Vance

ZBV *to Edward J. Hale*   A&H:Hale

Confidential

Raleigh Decr. 30th./63

E J Hale Esq

My dear Sir,

I wrote Mr Dortch in regard to the propriety of some terms of peace in Congress—He saw the President about it, who was not quite convinced of its propriety but said he would consult about it. Since the reception of yr letter, I am more than ever convinced that it could do no harm and would silence the clamor of a certain fear in N.C. or *force* them to take sides against their country which most of them are afraid to do while we still have two great armies in the field.

Another great reason is this. The plan is all arranged to advocate a convention in the Spring. The Legislature will attempt to call it and Holden in the mean time is to prepare the public [*burned*] In his last issue he announced [*burned*] This is a short article [*burned*] you doubtless noticed. This program was arranged here after due consultation, and it was concluded that no issue could be possibly made with me on my record so far. The convention question is to be my test and I am to be beaten if I oppose it. I have this from a man who was in the caucas & you may depend on it. My desire [*is*] to make a record showing *every* desire for peace except at the expense of my countrys ruin and dishonor; and I want the question narrowed down to *Lincoln or no Lincoln*, & dont intent to fritter away my strength on any minor issue. I advise you therefore to make no fight on the substitute question—the courts will settle that—on taxation schemes or any thing of that kind. Judge [*Edwin* G.] Reade will not oppose me—he privately assured me of his support last month when here—Holden & [*Daniel* G.] Fowle are both out of the question. Gen. Dockery[1] E. J. Warren[2] or Settle[3] will furnish [*burned*] Lincoln candidate. [More] [*burned*] you should write to Mr. Seddon in regard [*burned*] offering terms—It would have weight with him—

Yr [burned]
[Z. B. Vance]

[1]Alfred Dockery, former Whig legislator, congressman, unsuccessful gubernatorial candidate, and member of the state's postwar Reconstruction government. He never served in the military, and the nickname or title "general" was merely given him by friends and associates. *Dictionary of North Carolina Biography*, s.v. "Dockery, Alfred."

[2]Edward J. Warren, delegate to state Secession and Constitutional conventions, 1861–1862, legislator, superior court judge, and member of the state's postwar Reconstruction government. Cheney, *North Carolina Government*, 329, 330, 332, 362, 386, 450, 824.

[3]Thomas Settle, planter, legislator, state solicitor, and Confederate army officer. After the war he helped establish North Carolina's Republican party, became a state senator

and supreme court justice, then served as federal ambassador to Peru and district court judge in Florida. He ran unsuccesfully against ZBV for governor in 1876. *Dictionary of American Biography*, s.v. "Settle, Thomas."

ZBV to James A. Seddon   A&H:GLB

State of North Carolina
Executive Department
Raleigh Dec. 31st. 1863.

Hon. Jas. A. Seddon
Secy. of War
Richmond Va.

Dear Sir.

I learn that large distillaries are in operation at Charlotte & Salisbury in this State, making spirits of the tithe grain by order of the War Dept. Upon application to the office of Maj. Badham, Chief Collector of Tithe for this State, I learn that he has orders to deliver 30,000 bushels of grain to the distilleries for this purpose.

In addition to the many and weighty reasons which could be urged against the abstraction of this much bread from the Army or the poor, I beg to inform you that the laws of this State positively forbid the distillation of any kind of grain within its borders under heavy penalties. It will therefore be my duty to interpose the arm of civil law to prevent and punish this violation hereof, unless you will order it to cease.

It seems to me if spirits are so absolutely requisite to the Medical Department, that grain sufficient might be found in remote and plentiful districts, and leave for the use of the people every grain which is accessible. Be this as it may, I am sure you will agree with me in saying that no person can under authority of the Confederate Government violate State laws with impunity.

Very respectfully
Yr. obt. Servt.
Z. B. Vance

CALENDAR OF PAPERS NOT PRINTED IN THIS VOLUME

Correspondents	Date	Subject	Repository
John P. Rascoe to ZBV	Jan 1	passport	A&H:GP
Thomas W. Ritter to ZBV	Jan 1	jury verdict	A&H:GP
J.L. McLean to ZBV	Jan 1	transfer	A&H:GP
John A. Bradshaw to ZBV	Jan 1	shoes	A&H:GP
William W. Morrison to ZBV	Jan 1	slaves	A&H:GP
Francis E. Shober to ZBV	Jan 2	introduction	A&H:GP
Thomas J. Foster to ZBV	Jan 2	appointment	A&H:GP
R.W. Rest to ZBV	Jan 2	destitution	A&H:GP
George W. Munford to ZBV	Jan 2	Charlotte Co.	A&H:GP
David P. Langley to ZBV	Jan 2	appointment	A&H:GP
Scott & Scott to ZBV	Jan 2	hearing	A&H:GP
F&H Fries to ZBV	Jan 2	cloth	A&H:GP
John Frazer & Co. to ZBV	Jan 2	shipment	A&H:GP
William H.C. Whiting to ZBV	Jan 3	r.r. iron	A&H:GP
Beverly H. Robertson to ZBV	Jan 3	gunboats	A&H:GP
Samuel W. Melton to ZBV	Jan 3 (1)	troop transport	A&H:GP
Samuel W. Melton to ZBV	Jan 3 (2)	Federal threat	A&H:GP
John D. Whitford to ZBV	Jan 3	pork	A&H:GP
Hiram V. Houston to ZBV	Jan 3	appointment	A&H:GP
Samuel J. Wheeler to ZBV	Jan 3	appointment	A&H:GP
Matthias E. Manly to ZBV	Jan 3	R.J. Graves	A&H:GP
S. Sidney Carter to ZBV	Jan 3	discharge	A&H:GP
Urial J. Cate to ZBV	Jan 3	prohibit export	A&H:GP
B. McKenne to ZBV	Jan 4	ambulances	A&H:GP
Clement Dowd to ZBV	Jan 4	habeas corpus	A&H:GP
J.W. Whitworth to ZBV	Jan 4	detail	A&H:GP
Octavius H. Blocker to ZBV	Jan 4	appointment	A&H:GP
John W. Woodfin to ZBV	Jan 4	appointment	A&H:GP
J.C.M. Justice to ZBV	Jan 4	conscription	A&H:GP
T.B. Maury to ZBV	Jan 4	yarn	A&H:GP

Correspondents	Date	Subject	Repository
C.E. Thompson to ZBV	Jan 5	desertion	A&H:GP
E.W. Hoyle to ZBV	Jan 5	appointment	A&H:GP
R.A. Hamilton to ZBV	Jan 5	check	A&H:GP
Hugh M. May to ZBV	Jan 5	conscription	A&H:GP
Nicholas W. Woodfin to ZBV	Jan 5	salt	A&H:GP
Delia W. Jones to ZBV	Jan 6	appointment	A&H:GP
William H.C. Whiting to ZBV	Jan 6	r.r. iron	A&H:GP
S.W. Wallace to ZBV	Jan 6	distilling	A&H:GP
Elizabeth Nance et al. to ZBV	Jan 6	detail	A&H:GP
Thomas Carter to ZBV	Jan 6	blockade	A&H:GP
Jere Smith to Isaac Smith	Jan 6	disaffection	A&H:GP
Thomas Evans to ZBV	Jan 6	prohibit export	A&H:GP
William W. Williamson to ZBV	Jan 6	pork	A&H:VanPC
Hiram E. Stilley to ZBV	Jan 7	plunder	A&H:GP
Matthias E. Manly to ZBV	Jan 7	R.J. Graves	A&H:GP
Otis F. Manson to ZBV	Jan 7	hospital	A&H:GP
ZBV to Edward J. Hale	Jan 8	appointment	A&H:GP
T.J. Dula to ZBV	Jan 8	transfer	A&H:GP
G.W. Chipley to ZBV	Jan 8	hospital	A&H:GP
Sidney Nixon to ZBV	Jan 8	detail	A&H:GP
N.A. Marlow to ZBV	Jan 8	appointment	A&H:GP
L.T. Beardsley to ZBV	Jan 9	salt	A&H:GP
Braxton Craven to ZBV	Jan 9	commission	A&H:GP
W. Dunn Jr. to ZBV	Jan 9	appointment	A&H:GP
S.R. Hawly to ZBV	Jan 9	destitution	A&H:GP
R.S. Abrams to ZBV	Jan 9	murder	A&H:GP
W.R. Ward to ZBV	Jan 9	salt	A&H:GP
Thomas L. Clingman to ZBV	Jan 10	attack	A&H:GP
Thomas A. Wynne to ZBV	Jan 10	debt	A&H:GP
Edward J. Hale to ZBV	Jan 10	appointment	A&H:GP
Richard Sterling to ZBV	Jan 10	literary fund	A&H:GP
Gabriel Johnston to ZBV	Jan 10	gift	A&H:GP
M. Cooke to ZBV	Jan 10	appointment	A&H:GP
David A. Barnes to James A. Seddon	Jan 10	R.J. Graves	A&H:GLB
Lizzie T. Mebane to ZBV	Jan 11	transportation	A&H:GP
Thomas Carter to ZBV	Jan 11	*Advance*	A&H:GP
John Pool to ZBV	Jan 11	assistance	A&H:GP
William B. Richardson to ZBV	Jan 11	disaffection	A&H:GP
James Boroughs to ZBV	Jan 11	habeas corpus	A&H:GP
William Beal to ZBV	Jan 12	charts	A&H:GP
Tira T. Gantt to ZBV	Jan 12	detail	A&H:GP
J.H. Robbins to ZBV	Jan 12	conscription	A&H:GP
William Core to ZBV	Jan 12	destitution	A&H:GP
James W. Hinton to ZBV	Jan 12	appointment	A&H:GP
N.N. Mills to ZBV	Jan 12	detail	A&H:GP
H. Reynoldson Curtis to ZBV	Jan 12	discharge	A&H:GP
William Eaton Jr. to ZBV	Jan 12	appointment	A&H:GP
Marcus Erwin to ZBV	Jan 13	militia	A&H:GP
Daniel G. Taylor to ZBV	Jan 13	detail	A&H:GP
George Howard Jr. to ZBV	Jan 13	conscription	A&H:GP
Diliard Lucas et al. to ZBV	Jan 13	discharge	A&H:GP

Correspondents	Date	Subject	Repository
Samuel G. Schenck to ZBV	Jan 13	appointment	A&H:GP
M.E. Rudasill to ZBV	Jan 13	mfg. profits	A&H:GP
Albert H. Campbell to ZBV	Jan 13	map	A&H:GP
Ransom Gulley to ZBV	Jan 14	appointment	A&H:GP
John Blackburn to ZBV	Jan 14	furloughs	A&H:GP
R.F. Hackett to ZBV	Jan 15	horses	A&H:GP
B.B. Marley to ZBV	Jan 15	civil unrest	A&H:GP
G.W. Nicholson to ZBV	Jan 15	corn	A&H:GP
Hugh Hicks et al. to ZBV	Jan 15	blacksmith	A&H:GP
A.R. Eaves to ZBV	Jan 15	detail	A&H:GP
R.H. Skeen to ZBV	Jan 15	appointment	A&H:GP
T.J. Dula to ZBV	Jan 15	transfer	A&H:GP
McCoy Johnson to ZBV	Jan 15	conscription	A&H:GP
Catherine Hunt to ZBV	Jan 15	conscription	A&H:GP
Blanton Dunton to ZBV	Jan 15	cotton	A&H:GP
ZBV to Blanton Dunton	Jan 15	cotton	A&H:GP
Edwin M. Holt to ZBV	Jan 15	yarn	A&H:GP
ZBV to Milledge L. Bonham	Jan 15	extradition	SHC:Law
E.L. Cunningham to ZBV	Jan 16	appointment	A&H:GP
E.D. Snead to ZBV	Jan 16	prohibit export	A&H:GP
Benjamin R. Moore to ZBV	Jan 16	appointment	A&H:GP
Ralph P. Buxton to ZBV	Jan 16	disaffection	A&H:GP
Matthias E. Manly to ZBV	Jan 16	R.J. Graves	A&H:GP
L.K. Walker to ZBV	Jan 16	tobacco	A&H:GP
Magnolia Lee & Co. to ZBV	Jan 16	distilling	A&H:GP
Daniel W. Courts to ZBV	Jan 16	resignation	A&H:VanPC
James G. Martin to M. Erwin	Jan 17	militia	A&H:GP
D. McD. Yount to ZBV	Jan 17	distilling	A&H:GP
George W. Blount to ZBV	Jan 17	conscription	A&H:GP
John H. Stephens to ZBV	Jan 17	militia	A&H:GP
Henry Heth to ZBV	Jan 17	disaffection	A&H:GP
Gustavus W. Smith to ZBV	Jan 17	militia	A&H:GP
James A. Seddon to ZBV	Jan 17	D.H. Hill	A&H:GP
Burton N. Harrison to ZBV	Jan 17	cotton	A&H:GP
Edward J. Hale to ZBV	Jan 18	disaffection	A&H:GP
James A. Washington to ZBV	Jan 18	desertion	A&H:GP
John W. Evans to ZBV	Jan 18	discharge	A&H:GP
J.E. Wiles to ZBV	Jan 18	appointment	A&H:GP
Fielding G. Brown to ZBV	Jan 19	pension	A&H:GP
Thomas J. Sumner to ZBV	Jan 19	r.r. & troops	A&H:GP
J.C. Turner to ZBV	Jan 19	railroad	A&H:GP
Soloman Hathcock to ZBV	Jan 19	flour	A&H:GP
Donald MacRae to ZBV	Jan 19	steamboat	A&H:GP
Pharaoh Richardson to ZBV	Jan 19	impressed slaves	A&H:GP
Henry Hardie to ZBV	Jan 19	poor relief	A&H:GP
R.S. Gage to ZBV	Jan 19	money deal	A&H:VanPC
Jacob Siler to ZBV	Jan 19	Cherokee land	SHC:Sil
John W. Autry to ZBV	Jan 20	conscription	A&H:GP
W.O. Harrelson to ZBV	Jan 20	conscription	A&H:GP
M.H. Hoke to ZBV	Jan 20	r.r. engines	A&H:GP
J.A. Claywell to ZBV	Jan 20	poor relief	A&H:GP

Correspondents	Date	Subject	Repository
Richard S. Donnell to ZBV	Jan 20	reports	A&H:GP
James H. Foote to ZBV	Jan 20	appointment	A&H:GP
William T. Ennett et al. to ZBV	Jan 20	3rd Reg't.	A&H:GP
R.A. Loughter to ZBV	Jan 20	appointment	A&H:GP
Thomas L. Clingman to ZBV	Jan 20	attack	A&H:GLB
William G.M. Davis to General	Jan 20	Shelton Laurel	A&H:GLB
Jesse Bunn to ZBV	Jan 21	conscription	A&H:GP
Ralph P. Buxton to ZBV	Jan 21	disaffection	A&H:GP
R.D. Hart to ZBV	Jan 21	destitution	A&H:GP
John M. Worth to ZBV	Jan 21	salt	A&H:GP
T.B. Gilliam to ZBV	Jan 21	appointment	A&H:GP
Henry Heth to ZBV	Jan 21	Shelton Laurel	A&H:GLB
John M. Worth to ZBV	Jan 21	salt	A&H:GLB
Allen T. Davidson to ZBV	Jan 21	Congress	A&H:VanPC
Kemp P. Battle to ZBV	Jan 21	railroad	Duke:Van
William W. Woodhouse to ZBV	Jan 22	shipment	A&H:GP
Tolivar Davis to ZBV	Jan 22	provisions	A&H:GP
James J. Daniel to ZBV	Jan 22	conscription	A&H:GP
Violette to ZBV	Jan 22	peace	A&H:VanPC
L.R. Gibson to ZBV	Jan 23	appointment	A&H:GP
James T. Cuthrell to ZBV	Jan 23	tents	A&H:GP
John M. Bingham to ZBV	Jan 23	contract	A&H:GP
Stephen R. Mallory to William F. Lynch	Jan 23	iron clads	A&H:GP
Joseph C. Pinnix to ZBV	Jan 24	militia	A&H:GP
Pinckney Warlick to ZBV	Jan 24	appointment	A&H:GP
G.W.M. Neil to ZBV	Jan 24	conscription	A&H:GP
William E. Mann to ZBV	Jan 24	appointment	A&H:GP
Eugene Grissom et al. to ZBV	Jan 24	conscription	A&H:GP
William H.C. Whiting to ZBV	Jan 24	habeas corpus	A&H:GLB
W.T. Flynt to ZBV	Jan 24	Daniel G. Fowle	A&H:VanPC
L. Greene et al. to ZBV	Jan 24	Daniel G. Fowle	A&H:VanPC
C. Wilson to ZBV	Jan 24	Union Society	A&H:VanPC
ZBV to Richard S. Donnell	Jan 24	railroad	Duke:Van
James Bailey to ZBV	Jan 25	discharge	A&H:GP
George A. Makepeace to Jonathan Worth	Jan 25	cotton cards	A&H:GP
George V. Strong to ZBV	Jan 25	R.J. Graves	A&H:GP
B.B. Marley to ZBV	Jan 25	disaffection	A&H:GP
S.L. Carter to ZBV	Jan 25	appointment	A&H:GP
E.H. Burton to ZBV	Jan 26	conscription	A&H:GP
Nancy J. Long et al. to ZBV	Jan 26	destitution	A&H:GP
D.B. Rea to ZBV	Jan 26	appointment	A&H:GP
Mollie C. Ballard to ZBV	Jan 26	furlough	A&H:GP
Henry A. Gilliam to ZBV	Jan 26	conscription	A&H:GP
Catherine A. Culpepper to ZBV	Jan 26	conscription	A&H:GP
W.J. Cohoon to ZBV	Jan 26	appointment	A&H:GP
D.F. Ramsour to ZBV	Jan 26	poor relief	A&H:GP
William F. Lynch to ZBV	Jan 26	iron	A&H:GP
David L. Swain to ZBV	Jan 26	argument	A&H:VanPC
Thomas H. Modlin et. al to ZBV	Jan 27	conscription	A&H:GP
W.W. Spain to ZBV	Jan 27	conscription	A&H:GP
T.D. Gay to ZBV	Jan 27	conscription	A&H:GP

Correspondents	Date	Subject	Repository
Mary C. Williams et al. to ZBV	Jan 27	destitution	A&H:GP
M.J. McDuffie to ZBV	Jan 27	conscription	A&H:GP
Benjamin A. Wade to ZBV	Jan 27	appointment	A&H:GP
John S. McElroy to ZBV	Jan 27	NC Reg't.	A&H:GP
John Spelman to ZBV	Jan 27	disaffection	A&H:GP
John C. Hallburton to ZBV	Jan 27	imprisonment	A&H:GP
Eliza A. Lamb to Dr. Murphy	Jan 27	discharge	A&H:GP
Jasper Spruill to ZBV	Jan 28	conscription	A&H:GP
N.R. Mendenhall to ZBV	Jan 28	appointment	A&H:GP
W.M. Pickett to ZBV	Jan 28	desertion	A&H:GP
John R. Rose to ZBV	Jan 28	appointment	A&H:GP
John J. Whitehead to ZBV	Jan 28	impressed slaves	A&H:GP
Charles F.M. Garnett to R.H. Cowan	Jan 28	railroad	A&H:GP
J.J. Badwines to ZBV	Jan 28	flour	A&H:GP
Duncan K. McRae to ZBV	Jan 28	blockade	A&H:GP
Thomas L. Clingman to ZBV	Jan 28	r.r. attack	A&H:VanPC
James H. Ward to ZBV	Jan 29	conscription	A&H:GP
James M. Alexander to ZBV	Jan 29	appointment	A&H:GP
John P. Bailey to ZBV	Jan 29	conscription	A&H:GP
Joseph Keener to ZBV	Jan 29	pardon	A&H:GP
Isaiah Craven to ZBV	Jan 29	conscription	A&H:GP
H.W. Long to ZBV	Jan 29	arrest	A&H:GP
Samuel F. Phillips to ZBV	Jan 29	finances	A&H:GP
ZBV to Walter Brown & Joseph Keener	Jan 29	appointments	A&H:GLB
"Friend" to ZBV	Jan 29	disaffection	A&H:VanPC
Peter Mounger et al. to ZBV	Jan 30	conscription	A&H:GP
D. Thompson Sims to ZBV	Jan 30	desertion	A&H:GP
James A. Seddon to ZBV	Jan 30	address	A&H:GP
Raiford Fisher to ZBV	Jan 30	conscription	A&H:GP
William R. Bass to ZBV	Jan 30	conscripts	A&H:GP
E.W. Foster to ZBV	Jan 30	conscription	A&H:GP
James Sinclair to ZBV	Jan 30	conscription	A&H:GP
Mrs. J.H. Hawley to ZBV	Jan 30	donation	A&H:GP
William G.M. Davis to ZBV	ca. Jan 30	Shelton Laurel	A&H:GLB
Samuel Forkner to ZBV	Jan 31	desertion	A&H:GP
Owen Holmes to ZBV	Jan 31	desertion	A&H:GP
J.W. Davis to ZBV	Jan 31	salt peter	A&H:GP
B.F. Tripp to ZBV	Jan 31	conscription	A&H:GP
E. Murrell, Jr., to ZBV	Jan 31	militia	A&H:GP
Henson F. Murphy to ZBV	Jan 31	discharge	A&H:GP
Tod R. Caldwell to ZBV	Jan 31	impressment	A&H:GP
William T. Dortch to ZBV	Jan 31	commandant	A&H:VanPC
William J. Nelson to ZBV	Jan n.d.	appointment	A&H:GP
John W. Woodfin to ZBV	Feb 1	violence	A&H:GP
William H. Pilkinton to ZBV	Feb 1	desertion	A&H:GP
N.A. Ramsey to ZBV	Feb 1	disloyalty	A&H:GP
B.W. Ivey to ZBV	Feb 1	desertion	A&H:GP
George V. Strong to ZBV	Feb 1	request	A&H:GP
Mrs. E. McCallum to ZBV	Feb 1	discharge	A&H:GP
Samuel G. French to Gustavus W. Smith	Feb 1	discharge	A&H:GLB
J.P. Whisnant to ZBV	Feb 2	desertion	A&H:GP

Correspondents	Date	Subject	Repository
Samuel P. Arrington to ZBV	Feb 2	detail	A&H:GP
T. Brown Venable to ZBV	Feb 2	slaves	A&H:GP
T.B. Johnson to ZBV	Feb 2	desertion	A&H:GP
R.F. Simonton to ZBV	Feb 2	appointment	A&H:GP
Richard Anderson et al. to ZBV	Feb 2	appointment	A&H:GP
R.A. Myrick to ZBV	Feb 2	appointment	A&H:GP
Clement Dowd to ZBV	Feb 2	militia	A&H:GP
Charles Manly to David L. Swain	Feb 2	argument	A&H:VanPC
Lt. Troy to ZBV	Feb 3	enlistments	A&H:GP
P.J. Sinclair to ZBV	Feb 3	resignation	A&H:GP
J.J. Jackson to ZBV	Feb 3	distilling	A&H:GP
Wesley N. Freeman to ZBV	Feb 3	conscription	A&H:GP
John W. Cameron to ZBV	Feb 3	cotton	A&H:GP
James C.S. McDowell to ZBV	Feb 3	transfer	A&H:GP
Joshua L. Moore to ZBV	Feb 3	hardship	A&H:GP
Abel Hartsoe to ZBV	Feb 3	destitution	A&H:GP
J.J.D. Lucas to ZBV	Feb 3	complaint	A&H:GP
Henry Berrier to ZBV	Feb 3	desertion	A&H:GP
T.H. Campbell to ZBV	Feb 3	pork	A&H:GP
Lander Johnson et al. to ZBV	Feb 3	conscription	A&H:GP
D.G. Morrow to ZBV	Feb 3	conscription	A&H:GP
A.F. Cook to Samuel Jones	Feb 3	forage	A&H:VanPC
David L. Swain to ZBV	Feb 3	argument	A&H:VanPC
D. Styers to ZBV	Feb 4	detail	A&H:GP
Thomas Miller to ZBV	Feb 4	salt	A&H:GP
Maurice A. Vaughan to ZBV	Feb 4	appointment	A&H:GP
J. Cathey to J.M. Lyle	Feb 4	appointment	A&H:GP
Joseph H. Flanner to ZBV	Feb 4	blockade	A&H:VanPC
E.R. Norton to ZBV	Feb 5	bounty	A&H:GP
D.M. Gudger to ZBV	Feb 5	thanks	A&H:GP
James M. Sinclair to ZBV	Feb 5	transfer	A&H:GP
James Sloan to ZBV	Feb 5	gift	A&H:VanPC
John N. Whitford to ZBV	Feb 6	transfer	A&H:GP
Mary A.V. Carroll to ZBV	Feb 6	clothing & schools	A&H:GP
Edward B. Cohen to ZBV	Feb 6	appointment	A&H:GP
James T. Gough to ZBV	Feb 6	shoemaker	A&H:GP
Samuel F. Phillips to ZBV	Feb 6	audit	A&H:GP
Stephen D. Wallace to ZBV	Feb 6	r.r. iron	A&H:GP
Robert B. Vance to ZBV	Feb 6	appointment	A&H:VanPC
William N.H. Smith to ZBV	Feb 6	NC command	A&H:VanPC
Elias A. Vogler to ZBV	Feb 7	destitution	A&H:GP
Margaret Perry to ZBV	Feb 7	hardship	A&H:GP
Edward W. Fonvielle to ZBV	Feb 7	conscription	A&H:GP
John V. Jordan to ZBV	Feb 7	recommendation	A&H:VanPC
G.W. Stancel to ZBV	Feb 8	volunteer	A&H:GP
E.S. Swindell to ZBV	Feb 8	physician	A&H:GP
J.A. Harris to ZBV	Feb 8	appointment	A&H:GP
Cornelia G. Daniel to ZBV	Feb 9	hardship	A&H:GP
William H. Graves to ZBV	Feb 9	transfer	A&H:GP
James T. Reid to ZBV	Feb 9	card mfg.	A&H:GP
G.C. Moses to ZBV	Feb 9	speculation	A&H:GP

Correspondents	Date	Subject	Repository
John A. Graves to ZBV	Feb 9	conscription	A&H:GP
J.L. Wright to ZBV	Feb 9	corn	A&H:GP
W.D. Smith to ZBV	Feb 9	salt	A&H:GP
D.C. Harden to ZBV	Feb 9	conscription	A&H:GP
Milledge L. Bonham to ZBV	Feb 9	SC bonds	A&H:GP
Margaret M. Smith et al. to ZBV	Feb 9	destitution	A&H:GP
Thomas H. Modlin to ZBV	Feb 9	conscription	A&H:GP
M.W. Buffkin et al. to ZBV	Feb 10	physician	A&H:GP
George V. Strong to ZBV	Feb 10	treason	A&H:GP
Robert C. Hill to ZBV	Feb 10	disaffection	A&H:GP
James W. Hinton to ZBV	Feb 10	black raids	A&H:GP
William M. Shipp to ZBV	Feb 10	appointment	A&H:GP
George N. Folk to ZBV	Feb 10	appointment	A&H:GP
Mrs. M. Everitt to ZBV	Feb 10	destitution	A&H:GP
Thomas P. Clapp et al. to ZBV	Feb 10	yarn	A&H:GP
C.W. Bradshaw to ZBV	Feb 10	speculation	A&H:GP
William M.S. McKay to ZBV	Feb 10	transfer	A&H:GP
James Hardison to ZBV	Feb 10	troops	A&H:GP
James A. Seddon to ZBV	Feb 10	r.r. transport	A&H:GP
William M. Swann to ZBV	Feb 11	lawlessness	A&H:GP
James K. Gibson to ZBV	Feb 11	cotton	A&H:GP
O.S. Hanner to ZBV	Feb 11	discharge	A&H:GP
Robert H. Mann to ZBV	Feb 11	executions	A&H:GP
James P. Boyce to ZBV	Feb 11	Confed. bonds	A&H:GP
C.A. Church to ZBV	Feb 11	affidavits	A&H:GP
Catherine Parsons to ZBV	Feb 11	discharge	A&H:GP
J.S. Brooks et al. to ZBV	Feb 11	discharge	A&H:GP
V. Lash to ZBV	Feb 11	distilling	A&H:GP
Samuel G. French to ZBV	Feb 11 (1)	amnesty	A&H:GP
Samuel G. French to ZBV	Feb 11 (2)	amnesty	A&H:GP
J. Vance, Jr., to ZBV	Feb 11	cloth	A&H:GP
S.P. Ivey to ZBV	Feb 12	speculation	A&H:GP
Riley Hill to ZBV	Feb 12	miller	A&H:GP
Jesse M. Green to ZBV	Feb 12	conscription	A&H:GP
W.W. Dunn to ZBV	Feb 12	detail	A&H:GP
T.L. Barlow to ZBV	Feb 12	shoemaker	A&H:GP
Thomas J. Boykin to ZBV	Feb 12	yellow fever	A&H:GP
John A. McMannen to ZBV	Feb 12	card mfg.	A&H:GP
Burton N. Harrison to ZBV	Feb 12	conscription	A&H:GP
Thomas M. Walker to ZBV	Feb 13	conscription	A&H:GP
James K. Gibson to ZBV	Feb 13	cotton	A&H:GP
James Baker to ZBV	Feb 13	speculation	A&H:GP
James Blanton to ZBV	Feb 13	conscription	A&H:GP
ZBV to J.J. Pettus	Feb 13	resolutions	A&H:GP
James C. Webb to ZBV	Feb 13	recruiting	A&H:GP
James G. Martin to ZBV	Feb 13	enemy	A&H:GP
V.N. Seawell to ZBV	Feb 13	transfer	A&H:GP
T.L. Hargrove et al. to ZBV	Feb 13	distilling	A&H:GP
Mrs. T. King et al. to ZBV	Feb 13	soldiers' relief	A&H:GP
Stephen R. Mallory to ZBV	Feb 13	gunboats	A&H:GP
Alfred L. Rives to ZBV	Feb 13	weapon	A&H:VanPC

Correspondents	Date	Subject	Repository
ZBV to Thomas D. McDowell	Feb 13	resolutions	SHC:McD
William P. Parker	Feb 14	detail	A&H:GP
A.C. Ferrell to ZBV	Feb 14	cloth	A&H:GP
R.G. Tuttle et al. to ZBV	Feb 14	recommendation	A&H:GP
Sewall L. Fremont to ZBV	Feb 14	r.r. pass	A&H:GP
James G. Dickson to ZBV	Feb 15	miller	A&H:GP
Martha E. Curtis to ZBV	Feb 15	discharge	A&H:GP
William H.C. Whiting to ZBV	Feb 15	free blacks	A&H:GP
Mary H. Williams to ZBV	Feb 15	destitution	A&H:GP
Alfred M. Waddell to ZBV	Feb 15	recommendation	A&H:GP
John M. Hancock to ZBV	Feb 15	conscription	A&H:GP
E.D. Hawkins to ZBV	Feb 15	distilling	A&H:GP
W.W. Stafford to ZBV	Feb 16	desertion	A&H:GP
Augustus S. Merrimon to ZBV	Feb 16	Shelton Laurel	A&H:GP
Christopher A. Cameron to ZBV	Feb 16	desertion	A&H:GP
Uriah Vaughan to ZBV	Feb 16	impressed slaves	A&H:GP
James W. Hinton to ZBV	Feb 16	appointment	A&H:GP
Joseph M. Edwards to ZBV	Feb 16	conscription	A&H:GP
William B. Rodman to ZBV	Feb 16	refugee	A&H:GP
T. Howard to ZBV	Feb 16	conscripts	A&H:GP
Robert Liles to ZBV	Feb 16	conscription	A&H:GP
John W. Cameron to ZBV	Feb 16	cotton	A&H:GP
W.A. Joyce to ZBV	Feb 16	conscripts	A&H:GP
Samuel G. French to ZBV	Feb 16	r.r. transport	A&H:GLB
John D. Hyman to ZBV	Feb 16	*Spectator*	A&H:VanPC
William B. Carter to ZBV	Feb 16	safe conduct	A&H:VanPC
Confederate Friends to ZBV	Feb 17	disaffection	A&H:GP
John Dellinger et al. to ZBV	Feb 17	physician	A&H:GP
John A. Murray to ZBV	Feb 17	desertion	A&H:GP
W.S. Ramsey to ZBV	Feb 17	desertion	A&H:GP
James Sloan to George Little	Feb 17	hides	A&H:GP
John Fraser & Co to ZBV	Feb 17	D.K. McRae	A&H:GP
G.W. Shackleford to ZBV	Feb 17	account	A&H:GP
L.P. Olds to ZBV	Feb 17	prohibit export	A&H:GP
Henry Ledbetter to ZBV	Feb 17	farm hands	A&H:GP
F.B. Price to ZBV	Feb 17	prohibit export	A&H:GP
A.M. Johnson to ZBV	Feb 17	bounty	A&H:GP
Mrs. T. Reid et al. to ZBV	Feb 17	destitution	A&H:GP
James A. Seddon to ZBV	Feb 17	detail	A&H:GP
Robert B. Vance to ZBV	Feb 17	peace	A&H:VanPC
Regulators to ZBV	Feb 18	disaffection	A&H:GP
C.W. Styron to ZBV	Feb 18	cotton	A&H:GP
Nathaniel R. Jones to John H. Fleming	Feb 18	free blacks	A&H:GP
Beady M. Alley to ZBV	Feb 18	discharge	A&H:GP
W.H. Bailey to ZBV	Feb 18	Shelton Laurel	A&H:GP
Joshua Bradley to ZBV	Feb 18	conscription	A&H:GP
Henry A. Gilliam to ZBV	Feb 18	conscripts	A&H:VanPC
John W. Cameron to ZBV	Feb 19	adjutant general	A&H:GP
Jacob Brookfield to ZBV	Feb 19	promotion	A&H:GP
John A. Murray to ZBV	Feb 19	corn	A&H:GP
William C. Askew to ZBV	Feb 19	salt	A&H:GP

Correspondents	Date	Subject	Repository
A.C. Williamson et al. to ZBV	Feb 19	speech invitation	A&H:GP
J.C. West et al. to ZBV	Feb 19	conscription	A&H:GP
L.W. Boynes to ZBV	Feb 19	appointment	A&H:GP
R.F. Armfield to ZBV	Feb 19	conscripts	A&H:GP
A.C. Williamson to ZBV	Feb 20	official seal	A&H:GP
Bates B. Hardison to ZBV	Feb 20	discharge	A&H:GP
D.[Y].P. Clark to ——	Feb 20	Union sentiment	A&H:GP
Thomas Webb to ZBV	Feb 20	NCRR directors	A&H:GP
Calvin Deans to ZBV	Feb 20	discharge	A&H:GP
A.J. Pollock to ZBV	Feb 20	appointment	A&H:GP
Sewall L. Fremont to ZBV	Feb 20	r.r. iron	A&H:GP
W.W. Peirce to ZBV	Feb 20	stable & well	A&H:GP
N. Kelsey to ZBV	Feb 20	peace	A&H:GP
William H.C. Whiting to ZBV	Feb 20	free blacks	A&H:GP
J.W. Leckie to ZBV	Feb 21	appointment	A&H:GP
John Jarratt to ZBV	Feb 21	prohibit export	A&H:GP
H.B. Guthrie to ZBV	Feb 21	slave murders	A&H:GP
A Lieutenant to ZBV	Feb 21	conscripts	A&H:GP
George H. Kelley to ZBV	Feb 21	prohibit export	A&H:GP
Owen Davis et al. to ZBV	Feb 21	schoolteacher	A&H:GP
Caleb Phifer to ZBV	Feb 21 (1)	card mfg.	A&H:GP
Caleb Phifer to ZBV	Feb 21 (2)	card mfg.	A&H:GP
R.S. McDonald to ZBV	Feb 21	free blacks	A&H:GP
H.T. McLelland to ZBV	Feb 22	impressment	A&H:GP
C.W.L. Edney to ZBV	Feb 22	appointment	A&H:GP
T. McKinson to ZBV	Feb 22	discharge	A&H:GP
Isaac Jarratt to ZBV	Feb 22	distilling	A&H:GP
S.J. Wheeler to David A. Barnes	Feb 22	transfer	A&H:GP
John McDonald to ZBV	Feb 23	militia	A&H:GP
Alfred W. Bell to ZBV	Feb 23	prohibit export	A&H:GP
William H.C. Whiting to ZBV	Feb 23	slave labor	A&H:GP
George Laws to ZBV	Feb 23	slave murders	A&H:GP
Mary G. Garrett to ZBV	Feb 23	substitution	A&H:GP
John S. McElroy to ZBV	Feb 23	flag	A&H:GP
J.C. Watkins to ZBV	Feb 23	endorsement	A&H:GP
J.M. Lyle to ZBV	Feb 23	Cherokee land	A&H:GP
William H. Henry to ZBV	Feb 23	remains	A&H:GP
James Simmons to ZBV	Feb 23	prohibit export	A&H:GP
Peter Mallett to ZBV	Feb 23	conscripts	A&H:VanPC
William Poisson to ZBV	Feb 23	speculation	A&H:VanPC
Charles S. Carrington to Abraham C. Myers	Feb 24	provisions	A&H:GP
L.M. Dillard to ZBV	Feb 24	yarn	A&H:GP
Frank Nissen to ZBV	Feb 24	deserters	A&H:GP
Thomas Webb to ZBV	Feb 24	NCRR board	A&H:GP
Richard Hobson to ZBV	Feb 24	transfer	A&H:GP
Braxton Craven to ZBV	Feb 24	destitution	A&H:GP
J.A. Bitting to ZBV	Feb 24	poor relief	A&H:GP
G.C. Stowe to ZBV	Feb 24	promotion	A&H:GP
Augustus S. Merrimon to ZBV	Feb 24	Shelton Laurel	A&H:GP
Nicholas W. Woodfin to ZBV	Feb 24	salt	A&H:GP

Correspondents	Date	Subject	Repository
Samuel Cooper to ZBV	Feb 24	appointment	A&H:VanPC
Andrew C. Cowles to ZBV	Feb 24	destitution	A&H:VanPC
John W. Woodfin to ZBV	Feb 24	crops	A&H:VanPC
William Brooks et al. to ZBV	Feb 25	discharge	A&H:GP
David F. Caldwell to ZBV	Feb 25	speculation	A&H:GP
John Gill Shorter to ZBV	Feb 25	support	A&H:GLB
R.S. Gage to ZBV	Feb 25	money deal	A&H:VanPC
William J. Brown to ZBV	Feb 25	Union refugees	A&H:VanPC
James M. Grant to ZBV	Feb 26	impressment	A&H:GP
J.H. Brinkley to ZBV	Feb 26	detail	A&H:GP
J.M. Lyle to ZBV	Feb 26	Cherokee lands	A&H:GP
Zeba Gibson et al. to ZBV	Feb 26	distilling	A&H:GP
G.W. Godwin to ZBV	Feb 26	desertion	A&H:GP
Robert L. Abernethy to ZBV	Feb 26	impressment	A&H:GP
Thomas A. Norment to ZBV	Feb 26	promotion	A&H:GP
R.J. Ashe to ZBV	Feb 26	cotton	A&H:GP
John McRae to ZBV	Feb 26	council meeting	A&H:GP
Truman Jones to ZBV	Feb 26	transfer	A&H:GP
John [N] Kirkland to ZBV	Feb 26	recommendation	A&H:GP
Ivey Foreman to ZBV	Feb 26	appointment	A&H:GP
B.N. Kerns to ZBV	Feb 26	conscripts	A&H:GP
Jesse G. Shepherd to ZBV	Feb 26	introduction	A&H:GP
Mily Barker to ZBV	Feb 27	poor relief	A&H:GP
Samuel P. Arrington to George Little	Feb 27	meeting	A&H:GP
Richard C. Swain to ZBV	Feb 27	appointment	A&H:GP
O. Goddin to ZBV	Feb 27	destitution	A&H:GP
James K. Gibson to ZBV	Feb 27	cotton	A&H:GP
Samuel P. Moore to ZBV	Feb 27	medical board	A&H:GP
L.J. Johnson to ZBV	Feb 27	prisoners	A&H:GP
A.D. Banks to ZBV	Feb 27	correspondent	A&H:VanPC
Alexander R. Boteler to ZBV	Feb 27	introduction	A&H:VanPC
Thomas Webb to ZBV	Feb 28	r.r. agreement	A&H:GP
Spiers Singleton to ZBV	Feb 28	transfer	A&H:GP
R.R. Crawford to ZBV	Feb 28	disloyalty	A&H:GP
James N. Conrad to ZBV	Feb 28	discharge	A&H:GP
Bettie A. Folk to ZBV	Feb 28	boots	A&H:GP
T.H. Smith to ZBV	Feb 28	speculation	A&H:GP
William Eggleston to ZBV	Feb 28	poor relief	A&H:GP
J.C. Watkins et al. to ZBV	Feb 28	free blacks	A&H:GP
G.W. Joyner to William A. Pugh	Feb 28	Union sentiment	A&H:GP
Joseph H. Flanner to ZBV	Feb 28	blockade	A&H:VanPC
William Gardner to ZBV	Mar 1	gunboats	A&H:GP
Jesse Needham to ZBV	Mar 1	yarn	A&H:GP
James J. Johnston et al. to ZBV	Mar 1	Edward Wood	A&H:GP
B.E.L. Wilfong to ZBV	Mar 1	distilling	A&H:GP
Thomas R. Roberson to ZBV	Mar 1	discharge	A&H:GP
Robert Rice to ZBV	Mar 1	destitution	A&H:GP
G.S. McClintock to ZBV	Mar 2	speculation	A&H:GP
S.J. Neal to ZBV	Mar 2	appointment	A&H:GP
Elizabeth Weadon to ZBV	Mar 2	discharge	A&H:GP
James T. Reid to ZBV	Mar 2	appointment	A&H:GP

Correspondents	Date	Subject	Repository
William Pickens to ZBV	Mar 2	disaffection	A&H:GP
S.P. Dula to ZBV	Mar 2	appointment	A&H:GP
E.H. Dockery to ZBV	Mar 2	detail	A&H:GP
Samuel F. Phillips to ZBV	Mar 2	distilling	A&H:GP
L.F. Siler to ZBV	Mar 2	transfer	A&H:VanPC
A.H.E. Scheck to ZBV	Mar 3	conscription	A&H:GP
R.J. Townes to ZBV	Mar 3	Confed. debt	A&H:GP
Michael Bollinger to ZBV	Mar 3	speculation	A&H:GP
G.P. Formyduval to ZBV	Mar 3	complaint	A&H:GP
D.H. Starbuck to ZBV	Mar 3	letter	A&H:GP
Thomas Webb to ZBV	Mar 3	NCRR	A&H:GP
P. Black to ZBV	Mar 3	disaffection	A&H:GP
Walter Gwynn to ZBV	Mar 3	laborers	A&H:GP
J.T. Shell to ZBV	Mar 3	millwright	A&H:GP
Mordecai Williams et al. to ZBV	Mar 3	millwright	A&H:GP
Walter Gwynn to ZBV	Mar 4	laborers	A&H:GP
Victor C. Barringer to ZBV	Mar 4	passport	A&H:GP
Michael Bollinger to ZBV	Mar 4	Confed. money	A&H:GP
Richard Barnes to ZBV	Mar 4	transfer	A&H:GP
William L. Saunders to ZBV	Mar 4	desertion	A&H:GP
Willis Childers to ZBV	Mar 4	discharge	A&H:GP
M.F. Freeland to ZBV	Mar 4	seal	A&H:GP
John R. Williams to ZBV	Mar 4	transfer	A&H:GP
W.P. Moore to ZBV	Mar 4	substitution	A&H:GP
William H. Oliver to ZBV	Mar 5	cotton	A&H:GP
James A. Seddon to ZBV	Mar 5	Shelton Laurel	A&H:GP
J. Hawkins Simpson to ZBV	Mar 5	hospitals	A&H:GP
R.T. Bennett to ZBV	Mar 5	recommendation	A&H:GP
John W. Woodfin to ZBV	Mar 5	gift box	A&H:VanPC
James G. —— to ZBV	Mar 5	support	A&H:VanPC
John White to ZBV	Mar 6	cotton bonds	A&H:GP
Duncan K. McRae to ZBV	Mar 6	supplies	A&H:GP
Thomas A. Harvey to ZBV	Mar 6	commission	A&H:GP
William S. McDonald to ZBV	Mar 6	discharge	A&H:GP
A. Reid to ZBV	Mar 6	destitution	A&H:GP
Bedford Brown to ZBV	Mar 6	speculation	A&H:GP
John W. Hunt to ZBV	Mar 6	militia	A&H:GP
Margaret Phelps et al. to ZBV	Mar 6	discharge	A&H:GP
Thomas W. Cooper to ZBV	Mar 7	pilot	A&H:GP
L.J. Deupree to ZBV	Mar 7	cotton bonds	A&H:GP
[Robert B.] Vance to ZBV	Mar 7	battle news	A&H:GP
Daniel H. Hill, special order	Mar 7	deserters	A&H:GP
James A. Seddon to ZBV	Mar 7	cavalry	A&H:GP
A. McDowell to ZBV	Mar 7	destitution	A&H:GP
William A. Graham to ZBV	Mar 7	distilling	A&H:VanPC
Ezekiel Blizard to ZBV	Mar 8	discharge	A&H:GP
William T. Faircloth to ZBV	Mar 8	desertion	A&H:GP
Andrew J. Busick to ZBV	Mar 8	transfer	A&H:GP
Stephen R. Mallory to ZBV	Mar 9	r.r. iron	A&H:GP
Otis Porter to ZBV	Mar 9	furlough	A&H:GP
E.J. Crowson to ZBV	Mar 9	evidence	A&H:GP

Correspondents	Date	Subject	Repository
John H. Martin to ZBV	Mar 9	detail	A&H:GP
Donald MacRae to ZBV	Mar 9	wreck	A&H:GLB
James L. Henry to ZBV	Mar 9	*Spectator* sale	A&H:VanPC
T.D. Love to ZBV	Mar 10	conscription	A&H:GP
John D. Whitford to ZBV	Mar 10	r.r. transport	A&H:GP
James W. Strickland to ZBV	Mar 10	furlough	A&H:GP
G.W. McNeil to ZBV	Mar 10	deserters	A&H:GP
Francis E. Shober to ZBV	Mar 10	conscription	A&H:GP
M.L. Stransbury to ZBV	Mar 10	prisoner	A&H:GP
G.N. Bristol to ZBV	Mar 10	salt	A&H:GP
James C. Johnston to ZBV	Mar 10	war views	A&H:GP
Charles R. King to ZBV	Mar 10	appointment	A&H:GP
W. W. Ayer to ZBV	Mar 10	distilling	A&H:GP
John Withers to ZBV	Mar 10	furlough	A&H:VanPC
Isaac E. Avery to ZBV	Mar 11	recommendation	A&H:GP
Joseph E. Brown to ZBV	Mar 11	cultivation law	A&H:GP
Elizabeth Nalon to ZBV	Mar 11	destitution	A&H:GP
Ann McComicke to ZBV	Mar 11	destitution	A&H:GP
W.W. Deatherage to ZBV	Mar 11	yarn	A&H:GP
John R. Williams to ZBV	Mar 11	transfer	A&H:GP
James W. McDaniel to ZBV	Mar 11	detail	A&H:GP
David H. Sherrill to ZBV	Mar 11	desertion	A&H:GP
James C. Johnston to ZBV	Mar 11	plantations	A&H:GP
James L. Shoemaker to ZBV	Mar 11	cotton	A&H:GP
David A. Barnes to Donald MacRae	Mar 11	wreck	A&H:GLB
David A. Barnes to Henry A. London	Mar 11	wreck	A&H:GLB
Allen T. Davidson to ZBV	Mar 11	cavalry	A&H:VanPC
Collett Leventhorpe to ZBV	Mar 11	lands	Mich:Sch
J.L. Mills to ZBV	Mar 12	substitution	A&H:GP
Z.W. Davidson to ZBV	Mar 12	yarn	A&H:GP
H.P. Eidson et al. to ZBV	Mar 12	recommendation	A&H:GP
Victor C. Barringer to ZBV	Mar 12	assistance	A&H:GP
Mrs. H. Hammarskold to ZBV	Mar 12	letters	A&H:GP
Joseph Thompson to ZBV	Mar 12	impressed slaves	A&H:GP
M.J. McSween to ZBV	Mar 12	appointment	A&H:GP
Branch A. Merrimon to ZBV	Mar 12	appointment	A&H:GP
Oscar G. Parsley to ZBV	Mar 12	advice	A&H:GP
ZBV to James M. Mason	Mar 12	power of attorney	A&H:GLB
C.D. Smith to ZBV	Mar 12	disaffection	A&H:VanPC
L.J. Johnson to David A. Barnes	Mar 13	prisoners	A&H:GP
R.C. Holmes to ZBV	Mar 13	discharge	A&H:GP
Thomas M. Allen to ZBV	Mar 13	commissions	A&H:GP
S.J. Wheeler to ZBV	Mar 13	appointment	A&H:GP
W.A. Helms to ZBV	Mar 13	furlough	A&H:GP
N.A. Cherry to ZBV	Mar 13	poor relief	A&H:GP
ZBV to Daniel G. Fowle	Mar 13	commission	A&H:GLB
John C. Winder to ZBV	Mar 13	resignation	A&H:GLB
Allen T. Davidson to ZBV	Mar 13	quartermaster	A&H:VanPC
J.A. Thorn to ZBV	Mar 14	appointment	A&H:GP
John D. Whitford to ZBV	Mar 14	visit	A&H:GP
Robert C. Lindsay to ZBV	Mar 14	corn	A&H:GP

Correspondents	Date	Subject	Repository
Calvin H. Wiley to ZBV	Mar 14	funeral	A&H:GP
John D. Whitford to ZBV	Mar 14 (1)	summons	A&H:GP
John D. Whitford to ZBV	Mar 14 (2)	battle report	A&H:GP
Daniel G. Fowle to ZBV	Mar 14	paymasters	A&H:GP
Francis Lawley to John White	Mar 14	loan	A&H:GP
George White et al. to ZBV	Mar 14	discharges	A&H:GP
David L. Swain to ZBV	Mar 14	visit	A&H:GP
Alexandre Jones to ZBV	Mar 14	desertion	A&H:GP
Lewis Hanes to ZBV	Mar 14	desertion	A&H:GP
David A. Barnes to George V. Strong	Mar 14	habeas corpus	A&H:GP
ZBV to John C. Winder	Mar 14	resignation	A&H:GLB
Mrs. C.W. Kallam to ZBV	Mar 15	destitution	A&H:GP
Cotton Blaine to ZBV	Mar 15	gifts	A&H:GP
George T. Atkin to ZBV	Mar 15	appointment	A&H:GP
James Johnson et al. to ZBV	Mar 15	discharges	A&H:GP
John D. Whitford to ZBV	Mar 15	Kinston battle	A&H:VanPC
James C. Whitson to ZBV	Mar 15	cotton	A&H:VanPC
C.J. Hammarskold et al. to ZBV	Mar 16	slave murder	A&H:GP
Lady's Tableaux Society to ZBV	Mar 16	donation	A&H:GP
Joseph Keener to ZBV	Mar 16	appointment	A&H:GP
John L. Johnson & John S. Fullam to ZBV	Mar 16	transfer	A&H:GP
Robert V. Blackstock to ZBV	Mar 16	conscription	A&H:GP
James G. Wiseman to ZBV	Mar 16	impressment	A&H:GP
Andrew C. Cowles to ZBV	Mar 16	impressment	A&H:GP
W.A. Newell to ZBV	Mar 16	detail	A&H:GP
William H. Graves to ZBV	Mar 16	transfer	A&H:GP
Henry J. Morgan to ZBV	Mar 16	yarn	A&H:GP
Samuel Wilkins to ZBV	Mar 16	resignation	A&H:VanPC
—— Brown to ZBV	Mar 17	illegible	A&H:GP
E.N. Peterson to ZBV	Mar 17	prisoner	A&H:GP
Isaac H. Foust to ZBV	Mar 17	impressment	A&H:GP
Joseph H. Flanner to ZBV	Mar 17	salt	A&H:VanPC
E.N. Peterson to ZBV	Mar 18	prisoner	A&H:GP
Jed H. Singdray to ZBV	Mar 18	corn	A&H:GP
Michael Brown to ZBV	Mar 18	Salisbury riots	A&H:GP
W.A. Pearson to ZBV	Mar 18	distilling	A&H:GP
William Core to ZBV	Mar 19	assistance	A&H:GP
Eliza J. Gilmore to ZBV	Mar 19	discharge	A&H:GP
Robert H. Garratt to ZBV	Mar 19	transfer	A&H:GP
James F. Murray to ZBV	Mar 19	desertion	A&H:GP
Daniel H. Hill to ZBV	Mar 19	r.r. cars	A&H:GP
Thomas Webb to ZBV	Mar 19	r.r. train	A&H:GP
William E. Mastin to ZBV	Mar 19	conscription	A&H:GP
Henry J. Morgan to ZBV	Mar 19	yarn	A&H:GP
David A. Barnes to Daniel G. Fowle	Mar 19	paymaster	A&H:GLB
Sidney P. Clark to A. Anderson	Mar 20	powder mill	A&H:GP
Richard C. Freeman to ZBV	Mar 20	appointment	A&H:GP
Elizabeth Thomasson to ZBV	Mar 20	discharge	A&H:GP
N.A.G. Goode to ZBV	Mar 20	distilling	A&H:GP
Thomas Webb to ZBV	Mar 20	r.r. engine	A&H:GP
Joshua Boner to ZBV	Mar 20	conscription	A&H:GP

Correspondents	Date	Subject	Repository
David A. Barnes to William A. Blount	Mar 20	land rental	A&H:GLB
David A. Barnes to William Grimes	Mar 20	land rental	A&H:GLB
Robert V. Blackstock to ZBV	Mar 21	appointment	A&H:GP
John Grissom to ZBV	Mar 21	transfer	A&H:GP
Mary C. Moore et al. to ZBV	Mar 21	food riots	A&H:GP
William A. Pugh to ZBV	Mar 21	distilling	A&H:GP
William P. Henley to ZBV	Mar 21	corn	A&H:GP
William Grimes to David A. Barnes	Mar 21	land rental	A&H:GP
Charles S. Carrington to ZBV	Mar 21	r.r. transport	A&H:GP
R.C. Pearson to ZBV	Mar 21	gift	A&H:VanPC
Marcus Erwin to ZBV	Mar 22	impressment	A&H:GP
A.W. Zackary to ZBV	Mar 22	desertion	A&H:GP
Otis F. Manson to ZBV	Mar 22	furloughs	A&H:GP
E.J. Green to ZBV	Mar 22	detail	A&H:GP
S.H. Miller to ZBV	Mar 23	roads	A&H:GP
James C. Turner to ZBV	Mar 23	free blacks	A&H:GP
John D. Whitford to ZBV	Mar 23	r.r. train	A&H:GP
Samuel L. Love to ZBV	Mar 23	George Swepson	A&H:GP
John M. Worth to ZBV	Mar 23 (1)	salt	A&H:GP
John M. Worth to ZBV	Mar 23 (2)	salt	A&H:GP
Daniel H. Hill to ZBV	Mar 23	atrocities	A&H:GP
F.A. Bobbin & J.A. Faulcon to ZBV	Mar 23	impressment	A&H:GP
Thomas A. Nomient to ZBV	Mar 23	promotion	A&H:GP
ZBV to Robert R. Heath	Mar 23	special court	A&H:GLB
E.D. Hale to ZBV	Mar 23	promotion	A&H:VanPC
Allen T. Davidson to ZBV	Mar 23	Robert B. Vance	A&H:VanPC
Samuel O. Deaver to ZBV	Mar 24	desertion	A&H:GP
John W. McElroy to ZBV	Mar 24	militia	A&H:GP
William H.C. Whiting to ZBV	Mar 24	prohibit export	A&H:GP
William M. Harvey to ZBV	Mar 24	transportation	A&H:GP
T.C. Parks to ZBV	Mar 24	distilling	A&H:GP
Joseph C. Rudder to ZBV	Mar 24	prisoner	A&H:GP
Andrew C. Cowles to ZBV	Mar 24	disaffection	A&H:GP
J.R. Stubbs to ZBV	Mar 25	appointment	A&H:GP
C.T. Eidson to ZBV	Mar 25	appointment	A&H:GP
M.P. Lytle to ZBV	Mar 25	hospital	A&H:GP
Minutes	Mar 25	NCRR meeting	A&H:GP
William P. Bynum to ZBV	Mar 25	Capt. Cole	A&H:VanPC
Lizzie J. Carter to ZBV	Mar 26	money	A&H:GP
J. Newton Bryson to ZBV	Mar 26	appointment	A&H:GP
G.M. Green to ZBV	Mar 26	exemption	A&H:GP
J.G. Hardy to ZBV	Mar 26	appointment	A&H:GP
A. Porter to ZBV	Mar 26	discharge	A&H:GP
Ezra Bullock to ZBV	Mar 26	destitution	A&H:GP
John C. Russell to ZBV	Mar 26	discharge	A&H:GP
Stokely Martin to ZBV	Mar 26	poor relief	A&H:GP
Allen T. Davidson to ZBV	Mar 26	arrests	A&H:VanPC
Benjamin Meithkan to ZBV	Mar 27	conscription	A&H:GP
James C. Fowler to ZBV	Mar 27	destitution	A&H:GP
Jesse A. Cahoon to ZBV	Mar 27	guerrillas	A&H:GP
Henry T. Perkinson to ZBV	Mar 27	pass	A&H:GP

Correspondents	Date	Subject	Repository
Rufus Y. McAden to ZBV	Mar 27	pass	A&H:GP
L.N. Brasfield to ZBV	Mar 27	speculation	A&H:GP
Catherine Wortman to ZBV	Mar 27	discharge	A&H:GP
Nat M. Taylor to ZBV	Mar 27	loan	A&H:VanPC
John K. Connally to ZBV	Mar 27	promotion	A&H:VanPC
Jonathan Worth to ZBV	Mar 28	bonds	A&H:GP
Joseph H. Flanner to ZBV	Mar 28	gift	A&H:GP
J.A. Goode & J.W. Harris to ZBV	Mar 28	distilling	A&H:GP
Sewall L. Fremont to ZBV	Mar 28	railroad	A&H:GP
W.W. Green to ZBV	Mar 28	discharge	A&H:GP
Elizabeth Lunsford et al. to ZBV	Mar 28	exemption	A&H:GP
J.A. McDowell to ZBV	Mar 28	appointment	A&H:GP
J.R. Siler to ZBV	Mar 28	payment	A&H:VanPC
Milledge L. Bonham to ZBV	Mar 29	export	A&H:GP
James J. Osborne to ZBV	Mar 30	appointment	A&H:GP
Annie Dickie to ZBV	Mar 30	cotton	A&H:GP
S.A. Allen to ZBV	Mar 30	appointment	A&H:GP
Lucinda Johnson to ZBV	Mar 30	yarn	A&H:GP
Sewall L. Fremont to ZBV	Mar 30	railroad	A&H:GP
Henry Johnson to ZBV	Mar 30	destitution	A&H:GP
Robert Hall to ZBV	Mar 30	exemption	A&H:GP
William G.W. Davis to ZBV	Mar 30	Shelton Laurel	A&H:GLB
George W. Logan to ZBV	Mar 31	special court	A&H:GP
Nicholas Dalton et al. to ZBV	Mar 31	provisions	A&H:GP
A.M. Erwin to ZBV	Mar 31	desertion	A&H:GP
George Williamson to ZBV	Mar 31	testimony	A&H:GP
Martin Brown et al. to ZBV	Mar 31	exemption	A&H:GP
Oscar G. Parsley to ZBV	Mar 31	appointment	A&H:GP
Markus Woodlieff to ZBV	Mar 31	pass	A&H:GP
Samuel F. Phillips to ZBV	Mar 31	railroad	A&H:GP
James J. McDougald to ZBV	Mar 31	appointment	A&H:GP
Elihu Chambers to ZBV	Mar 31	transfer	A&H:GP
J.M. Wilson to ZBV	Mar 31	salt	A&H:VanPC
D.H. Christie to ZBV	Mar 31	Alfred Iverson	A&H:VanPC
John G. Shorter to ZBV	Mar 31	cloth	SHC:Pea
M.E.F. to ZBV	Mar n.d.	praise	A&H:GP
E. Toms to ZBV	Mar n.d.	special court	A&H:GP
Nathaniel Boyden to ZBV	Mar n.d.	disaffection	A&H:VanPC
S.W. Watts to ZBV	Apr 1	exemption	A&H:GP
William Johnston to ZBV	Apr 1	destitution	A&H:GP
T.J. Corpening to ZBV	Apr 1	distilling	A&H:GP
Henry Best to ZBV	Apr 1	exemption	A&H:GP
B.L. Bitting to ZBV	Apr 1	conscription	A&H:GP
N.G. Allman to ZBV	Apr 1	turnpike	A&H:GP
Hiram Weatherspoon to ZBV	Apr 1	appointment	A&H:GP
B.M. Enloe to ZBV	Apr 1	transfer	A&H:GP
Bartlet Y. Allen to ZBV	Apr 1	transfer	A&H:GP
Hardy Brown et al. to ZBV	Apr 1	theft	A&H:GP
J.H. McIntosh to ZBV	Apr 1	distilling	A&H:GP
G.D. Wilson to ZBV	Apr 1	transfer	A&H:GP
Peter Mallett to ZBV	Apr 1	conscription	A&H:GP

Correspondents	Date	Subject	Repository
H.H. Robinson to ZBV	Apr 2	r.r. transport	A&H:GP
John H. Winder to ZBV	Apr 2	Union deserters	A&H:GP
Andrew C. Cowles to ZBV	Apr 2	conscription	A&H:GP
Tolivar Davis to ZBV	Apr 2	appointment	A&H:GP
Robert Ransom Jr. to ZBV	Apr 2 (1)	transportation	A&H:GP
Robert Ransom Jr. to ZBV	Apr 2 (2)	transportation	A&H:GP
William H. James to ZBV	Apr 2	provisions	A&H:GP
Daniel G. Fowle, special order	Apr 2	impressed slaves	SHC:Gra
L.P. Olds to ZBV	Apr 3	appointment	A&H:GP
Milledge L. Bonham to ZBV	Apr 3	distilling	A&H:GP
G.K. Moore to ZBV	Apr 3	appointment	A&H:GP
William A. Houck to ZBV	Apr 3	conscription	A&H:GP
Thomas Stradley to ZBV	Apr 3	discharge	A&H:GP
C.D. Foy to ZBV	Apr 3	transfer	A&H:GP
R.R. Bearden to ZBV	Apr 3	NC bonds	A&H:GP
C.H. Burge to ZBV	Apr 3	transfer	A&H:GP
Joseph Keener to ZBV	Apr 3	impressment	A&H:VanPC
William L. Love to ZBV	Apr 3	Confed. Congress	A&H:VanPC
Augustus S. Merrimon to ZBV	Apr 4	special court	A&H:GP
David M. Furches to ZBV	Apr 4	special court	A&H:GP
H.D. Bird to David A. Barnes	Apr 4	supplies	A&H:GP
Benajah Wooten et al. to ZBV	Apr 4	discharge	A&H:GP
S. Roberts et al. to ZBV	Apr 4	discharge	A&H:GP
James A. Seddon to ZBV	Apr 4	commissions	A&H:VanPC
John D. Whitford to ZBV	Apr 5	railroad	A&H:GP
John J.C. Gore to ZBV	Apr 5	postmaster	A&H:GP
E.S. Morris to ZBV	Apr 5	tobacco	A&H:GP
Lizzie J. Carter to Harriette E. Vance	Apr 5	dress	A&H:VanPC
Nicholas W. Woodfin to ZBV	Apr 6	r.r. transport	A&H:GP
Milledge L. Bonham to ZBV	Apr 6	attack	A&H:GP
Sarah E. Dicken to ZBV	Apr 6	poor relief	A&H:GP
J.A. Coston to ZBV	Apr 6	prisoner	A&H:GP
C.S. Croom to ZBV	Apr 6	parolees	A&H:GP
Benjamin Askew to ZBV	Apr 6	justices peace	A&H:GP
J.A.C. Brown to ZBV	Apr 6	appointment	A&H:GP
H.J. Mitchell to ZBV	Apr 6	transfer	A&H:GP
E.J. Warren to ZBV	Apr 6	introduction	A&H:GP
E.F. Ashe to ZBV	Apr 6	discharge	A&H:GP
Catherine Cowan to ZBV	Apr 6	discharge	A&H:GP
James W. Osborne to ZBV	Apr 6	salt	A&H:VanPC
James K. Gibson to ZBV	Apr 6	cotton	A&H:VanPC
E.B. Drake to ZBV	Apr 6	letter	A&H:VanPC
Mrs. L.K. Shryock to ZBV	Apr 7	speculation	A&H:GP
John Bumgarner et al. to ZBV	Apr 7	discharge	A&H:GP
J.C. Peirce to ZBV	Apr 7	exemption	A&H:GP
J. Newton Bryson to ZBV	Apr 7	poor relief	A&H:GP
John M. Worth to ZBV	Apr 7	salt	A&H:GP
T.B. Kingsbury to ZBV	Apr 8	destitution	A&H:GP
William M. Wadley to ZBV	Apr 8	salt	A&H:GP
Nicholas W. Woodfin to ZBV	Apr 8	salt	A&H:GP
D. Coble to Peter Mallett	Apr 8	deserters	A&H:GP

Correspondents	Date	Subject	Repository
J.W. Cooper & T.F. Midgett to ZBV	Apr 8	prohibit export	A&H:GP
Peter Mallett to ZBV	Apr 9	conscription	A&H:GP
Richmond M. Pearson to			
Peter Mallett	Apr 9	John N. Irvin	A&H:GP
James C. McRae to ZBV	Apr 9	conscription	A&H:GP
L.K. Walker to ZBV	Apr 9	tobacco	A&H:GP
Mary Owens to ZBV	Apr 9	hardship	A&H:GP
Milledge L. Bonham to ZBV	Apr 9	SC battle	A&H:GP
David A. Barnes to James Longstreet	Apr 9	Alfred Brown	A&H:GP
U. Wells to ZBV	Apr 9	locomotive	A&H:GP
Eliza J. Gupton to ZBV	Apr 9	allotment	A&H:GP
James Roberts to ZBV	Apr 9	appointment	A&H:GP
Samuel F. Phillips to ZBV	Apr 9	surgeon general	A&H:GP
Henry T. Clark et al. to ZBV	Apr 9	poor relief	A&H:GP
Nancy —— to ZBV	Apr 9	destitution	A&H:GP
A. Carmichael to ZBV	Apr 9	gratitude	A&H:VanPC
A.H. Temple to ZBV	Apr 10	transfer	A&H:GP
Young Jordan et al. to ZBV	Apr 10	postmaster	A&H:GP
Benjamin Gurley to ZBV	Apr 10	discharge	A&H:GP
James Sloan to ZBV	Apr 10	speculation	A&H:GP
J.W. Hunter to ZBV	Apr 10	recommendation	A&H:GP
T.J. Farrar to ZBV	Apr 10	detail	A&H:GP
William T. Muse to ZBV	Apr 10	pilot	A&H:GP
Joseph J. Baxter to ZBV	Apr 10	transfer	A&H:GP
John A. Averett to ZBV	Apr 10	food transport	A&H:GP
A.D. Childs to ZBV	Apr 10	distilling	A&H:GP
Samuel F. Phillips to ZBV	Apr 10	legal opinion	A&H:GP
Elnori Ca[u]ble et al. to ZBV	Apr 10	exemption	A&H:GP
R. Street to ZBV	Apr 10	deserters	A&H:GP
Mahata Bell Boykin to ZBV	Apr 11	discharge	A&H:GP
Ralph P. Buxton to ZBV	Apr 11	slave murder	A&H:GP
William H.C. Whiting to ZBV	Apr 11	new battalion	A&H:GP
J.B. Church to ZBV	Apr 12	shoes	A&H:GP
Marcus Erwin to ZBV	Apr 12	disagreement	A&H:GP
Mrs. E.J. Edney to ZBV	Apr 12	appointment	A&H:GP
B.S. Guion to ZBV	Apr 12	railroad	A&H:GP
Thomas G. Pugh to ZBV	Apr 12	corn	A&H:GP
Rufus W. Collins to ZBV	Apr 12	r.r. timber	A&H:GP
William T. Muse to ZBV	Apr 13	pilot	A&H:GP
Perry & Witty to ZBV	Apr 13	corn transport	A&H:GP
J.T.P.C. Cohoon to ZBV	Apr 13	appointment	A&H:GP
Elizabeth Throwere to ZBV	Apr 13	allotment	A&H:GP
James H. White to ZBV	Apr 13	transfer	A&H:GP
William Hodges to ZBV	Apr 13	discharge	A&H:GP
Isaac Miller to ZBV	Apr 13	civil violence	A&H:GP
Daniel H. Hill to ZBV	Apr 13	Federal attack	A&H:VanPC
George N. Penland to ZBV	Apr 13	debt	A&H:VanPC
Joseph E. Brown to ZBV	Apr 14	soldiers' pay	A&H:GP
Perry Godwin & B.A. Wellons to ZBV	Apr 14	magistrates	A&H:GP
John J. Hickman to ZBV	Apr 14	detail	A&H:GP
Jeremiah Phillips & Phillip			

Correspondents	Date	Subject	Repository
Wilson to ZBV	Apr 14	torture	A&H:GP
A.W. Cummings to ZBV	Apr 14	destitution	A&H:GP
Mary Hester to ZBV	Apr 14	clothing	A&H:GP
Thomas A. Baker to ZBV	Apr 14	conscription	A&H:GP
D & W McLaurin to L.G. Pate	Apr 14	account	A&H:GP
George McNeill to ZBV	Apr 14	poor relief	A&H:GP
Stephen D. Wallace to ZBV	Apr 14	r.r. transport	A&H:GP
George F. Hurst to ZBV	Apr 14	desertion	A&H:GP
John G. Shorter to ZBV	Apr 14	cassimere	A&H:GP
Luke Blackmer to ZBV	Apr 14	arrest	A&H:GP
R. Wooten to ZBV	Apr 14	transfer	A&H:GP
Thomas J. Boykin to ZBV	Apr 14	NC reg'ts	A&H:GP
K.C. Washburn to ZBV	Apr 14	salt	A&H:GP
G.W. Goldston to ZBV	Apr 15	impressed slaves	A&H:GP
William T. Muse to ZBV	Apr 15	pilot	A&H:GP
T.M. Shoffner to ZBV	Apr 15	file mfg.	A&H:GP
Ellen Congleton to ZBV	Apr 15	confiscation	A&H:GP
Levi Thorne to ZBV	Apr 15	Quakers	A&H:GP
Martha Weman to ZBV	Apr 15	poor relief	A&H:GP
Caleb Phifer to ZBV	Apr 15	prohibit export	A&H:GP
S.R. Hawley to ZBV	Apr 15	destitution	A&H:GP
Stephen D. Wallace to ZBV	Apr 15	r.r. transport	A&H:GP
Oscar G. Parsley to ZBV	Apr 15	rice	A&H:GP
James A. Patton to ZBV	Apr 15	council of state	A&H:VanPC
A.W. Cochran to ZBV	Apr 16	meat	A&H:GP
J.M. Corn to ZBV	Apr 16	discharge	A&H:GP
Jason H. Carson to ZBV	Apr 16	prohibit export	A&H:GP
W.G. Boudinot to ZBV	Apr 16	pilot	A&H:GP
Sterling H. Gee to ZBV	Apr 16	battalion	A&H:GP
Daniel Hoffman to ZBV	Apr 16	speculation	A&H:GP
William T. Muse to ZBV	Apr 16	pilot	A&H:GP
A. M. Powell to ZBV	Apr 16	eggs	A&H:VanPC
William Sutton to ZBV	Apr 17	exemption	A&H:GP
R.M. Stafford to ZBV	Apr 17	yarn	A&H:GP
O.S. Hanner to ZBV	Apr 17	civil violence	A&H:GP
D.J. Gilbert to ZBV	Apr 17	corn	A&H:GP
R.S. Gage to ZBV	Apr 17	appointment	A&H:GP
D.P. McEachern to ZBV	Apr 17	provisions	A&H:GP
Mrs. E. Walters to ZBV	Apr 17	cloth	A&H:GP
F. Munroe P[ik]e to ZBV	Apr 17	civil violence	A&H:GP
W.M.R. Johns to ZBV	Apr 17	appointment	A&H:GP
C.C. Hines to ZBV	Apr 17	transfer	A&H:GP
S.W.S. Kimbro to ZBV	Apr 17	disaffection	A&H:GP
E. H. Rabbits to Dr. Warren	Apr 17	bill	SHC:Van
W.M. Pickett to ZBV	Apr 18	speculation	A&H:GP
A.A. Sheek to ZBV	Apr 18	appointment	A&H:GP
John W. Cole to ZBV	Apr 18	produce	A&H:GP
F.P. Williams to ZBV	Apr 18	discharge	A&H:GP
J.H. Deheny to ZBV	Apr 18	enemy trade	A&H:GP
Many Citizens to ZBV	Apr 18	impressment	A&H:GP
Duncan K. McRae to ZBV	Apr 18	bonds	A&H:GLB

Correspondents	Date	Subject	Repository
— Morrison to ZBV	Apr 18	appointment	A&H:VanPC
Bryant Williams to ZBV	Apr 19	conscription	A&H:GP
— Yellan to ZBV	Apr 19	destitution	A&H:GP
Eli H. Girkins to ZBV	Apr 19	habeas corpus	A&H:GP
Daniel F. Summey to ZBV	Apr 19	resignation	A&H:VanPC
Archer Anderson to ZBV	Apr 20	civil violence	A&H:GP
A.C. Freeman to ZBV	Apr 20	prohibit export	A&H:GP
Thomas G. Addington to ZBV	Apr 20	conscription	A&H:GP
Samuel Jones et al. to ZBV	Apr 20	pay	A&H:GP
G.C. Moore to ZBV	Apr 20	disloyalty	A&H:GP
William J. McMillan to ZBV	Apr 20	transfer	A&H:GP
A.W. Coleman to ZBV	Apr 20	appointment	A&H:GP
B.C. Washburn to ZBV	Apr 20	salt	A&H:GP
Thomas J. Forney to ZBV	Apr 20	provisions	A&H:GP
W.L. Bryan to ZBV	Apr 20	disloyalty	A&H:GP
K.T. Exum to ZBV	Apr 20	transfer	A&H:GP
Bayles M. Edney to ZBV	Apr 20	conscription	A&H:GP
John D. Hyman to ZBV	Apr 20	*Spectator* sale	A&H:VanPC
Daniel H. Hill to ZBV	Apr 20	disloyalty	A&H:VanPC
Blanton Duncan to ZBV	Apr 21	contract	A&H:GP
Toanna Downs to ZBV	Apr 21	discharge	A&H:GP
John Lonon to ZBV	Apr 21	discharge	A&H:GP
A.S. Murdock to ZBV	Apr 21	detail	A&H:GP
John A. Reid to ZBV	Apr 21	prohibit export	A&H:GP
Allan Macfarlan to ZBV	Apr 21	prohibit export	A&H:GP
John L. McDowell to ZBV	Apr 21	court martial	A&H:GP
Emily Branson to ZBV	Apr 21	civil violence	A&H:GP
L.H. Edney et al. to ZBV	Apr 21	recommendation	A&H:GP
James A. Patton to ZBV	Apr 21	Eagle Hotel	A&H:VanPC
Joseph H. Flanner to ZBV	Apr 22	appointment	A&H:GP
Sallie Wright to ZBV	Apr 22	poor relief	A&H:GP
John M. Worth to ZBV	Apr 22	salt	A&H:GP
Jesse T. Alexander to ZBV	Apr 22	Union sentiment	A&H:GP
John E. Hunt & Co. to ZBV	Apr 22	travel permit	A&H:VanPC
Lizzie J. Carter to ZBV	Apr 22	loan	A&H:VanPC
Pat H. Vance to ZBV	Apr 23	prohibit export	A&H:GP
Daniel H. Hill to ZBV	Apr 23	deserters	A&H:GP
William T. Muse to ZBV	Apr 23	pilot	A&H:GP
Bryant Williams to ZBV	Apr 23	conscription	A&H:GP
George W. Cameron to ZBV	Apr 23	release	A&H:GP
J.S. Gibbs to ZBV	Apr 23	conscription	A&H:GP
John A. Fuquay et al. to ZBV	Apr 23	discharge	A&H:GP
D.E. Ridenhower to ZBV	Apr 23	transfer	A&H:GP
Anonymous to ZBV	Apr 24	Union occupation	A&H:GP
J.R. Hargrave to ZBV	Apr 24	defense plan	A&H:GP
James Boggan to ZBV	Apr 24	defense plan	A&H:GP
Susan L. Johnston to ZBV	Apr 24	exemption	A&H:GP
William T. Muse to ZBV	Apr 24	pilot	A&H:GP
Franklin J. Moses to ZBV	Apr 24	prohibit export	A&H:GP
Joseph T. Cathey to ZBV	Apr 24	transfer	A&H:GP
William H.C. Whiting to ZBV	Apr 25	impressed slaves	A&H:GP

Correspondents	Date	Subject	Repository
James Sloan to ZBV	Apr 25	flour	A&H:GP
W.M. Hicks to ZBV	Apr 25	prohibit export	A&H:GP
James A. Keith to L.M. Allen	Apr 25	Shelton Laurel	A&H:GP
John Partiz to ZBV	Apr 25	iron works	A&H:GP
James L. Henry to ZBV	Apr 25	*Spectator*	A&H:VanPC
Dennis D. Ferebee to William W. Hammond	Apr 25	Federal threat	A&H:VanPC
William C. Rough to ZBV	Apr 26	substitution	A&H:GP
Henry K. Burgwyn Jr. to Nicholas C. Hughes	Apr 26	battles	A&H:GP
John A. Newton to ZBV	Apr 26	desertion	A&H:GP
William L. Love to ZBV	Apr 26	John D. Hyman	A&H:GP
Daniel H. Hill to ZBV	Apr 26	disaffection	A&H:VanPC
Joseph J. Young to ZBV	Apr 26	transfer	A&H:VanPC
William R. Young to ZBV	Apr 27	yarn	A&H:GP
J.L. Marsh to ZBV	Apr 27	discharge	A&H:GP
William Lankford to ZBV	Apr 27	prohibit export	A&H:GP
James H. Hunter to ZBV	Apr 27	prohibit export	A&H:GP
James R. Duncan to ZBV	Apr 27	destitution	A&H:GP
William J. Robinson et al. to ZBV	Apr 27	allegiance oath	A&H:GP
Stephen D. Thurston to ZBV	Apr 27	3rd Reg't	A&H:GP
John L. Caddell to ZBV	Apr 27	soap	A&H:GP
G.H. Blalock to ZBV	Apr 27	exemption	A&H:GP
Wilburn Gurren to ZBV	Apr 27	exemption	A&H:GP
Charles Barrien to ZBV	Apr 27	discharge	A&H:GP
William H. Tripp to ZBV	Apr 27	transfers	A&H:GP
Allen T. Davidson to James A. Seddon	Apr 28	arrests	A&H:GP
James Sinclair to David A. Barnes	Apr 28	conscription	A&H:GP
C.O. Sanford to ZBV	Apr 28	prohibit export	A&H:GP
William A. Allen to ZBV	Apr 28	appointment	A&H:GP
Abner Harrington to ZBV	Apr 28	appointment	A&H:GP
James G. Williamson to ZBV	Apr 28	transfer	A&H:GP
D.C. Coggins to ZBV	Apr 28	transfer	A&H:GP
John H. Hall to ZBV	Apr 29	prohibit export	A&H:GP
William A. Hammer to ZBV	Apr 29	transfer	A&H:GP
J.M. Brown to ZBV	Apr 29	appointment	A&H:GP
Jacob S. Atlee to ZBV	Apr 29	slave clothing	A&H:GP
David Carpenter et al. to ZBV	Apr 29	prohibit export	A&H:GP
John J. Whitehead to ZBV	Apr 29	special court	A&H:GP
William H. Powell to ZBV	Apr 29	arrests	A&H:GP
Eli Branson et al., affidavit	Apr 29	bond	A&H:GP
E.R. West to ZBV	Apr 29	prohibit export	A&H:GP
Newton Wright to ZBV	Apr 29	transfer	A&H:GP
C.P. Green to ZBV	Apr 30	appointment	A&H:GP
Thomas Branch to ZBV	Apr 30	prohibit export	A&H:GP
H.C. Lee to ZBV	Apr 30	salt	A&H:GP
M.B. Creekmun to ZBV	Apr 30	transfer	A&H:GP
John S. Gibson et al. to ZBV	Apr 30	exemption	A&H:GP
William J. Martin to ZBV	Apr 30	deserters	A&H:GP
J.A. Tarwater to ZBV	Apr 30	prohibit export	A&H:GP
W.A.C. Doggett to ZBV	Apr 30	prohibit export	A&H:GP

Correspondents	Date	Subject	Repository
Richard S. Donnell to ZBV	Apr 30	disloyalty	A&H:GP
W.J. Brown to ZBV	Apr 30	safe conduct	A&H:VanPC
John H. Koon[tz] to ZBV	Apr n.d.	discharge	A&H:GP
Daniel H. Hill to ZBV	May 1	conscription	A&H:GP
William H. Wright to ZBV	May 1	bank	A&H:GP
Elizabeth Clemmons to ZBV	May 1	discharge	A&H:GP
Many Citizens to ZBV	May 1	distilling	A&H:GP
B.S. Martin to ZBV	May 1	appointment	A&H:GP
Henry K. Burgwyn Jr. to ZBV	May 1	band	A&H:GP
Daniel H. Hill to ZBV	May 2	raids	A&H:GP
Lucinda Snyder to ZBV	May 2	destitution	A&H:GP
George H. Taylor to ZBV	May 2	transfer	A&H:GP
Camden Lewis to ZBV	May 2	transfer	A&H:GP
Peter Mallett to ZBV	May 2	conscription	A&H:GP
J.W. Bitting to ZBV	May 2	appointment	A&H:GP
J.S. Lucas to ZBV	May 3	militia	A&H:GP
G.M. Roberts to ZBV	May 3	substitution	A&H:GP
Benjamin H. Sugg to ZBV	May 3	conscription	A&H:GP
C.D. Smith to ZBV	May 4	saltpeter	A&H:GP
James A. Seddon to ZBV	May 4	appointment	A&H:GP
John D. Whitford to ZBV	May 4	r.r. accident	A&H:GP
Peter Mallett to ZBV	May 4	conscription	A&H:GP
William P. Heath to ZBV	May 4	prohibit export	A&H:GP
J.W. Alspaugh to ZBV	May 4	r.r. transport	A&H:GP
Henry K. Burgwyn Jr. to ZBV	May 4	detail	A&H:GP
John H. Haughton to ZBV	May 4	prohibit export	A&H:GP
A.M. Record to ZBV	May 4	transfer	A&H:GP
David McDaniel to ZBV	May 5	desertion	A&H:GP
Augustus S. Merrimon to ZBV	May 5	substitution	A&H:GP
A.H. McNeill to ZBV	May 5	special court	A&H:GP
Dista Swindell to ZBV	May 5	discharge	A&H:GP
Mary Johnson to ZBV	May 5	poor relief	A&H:GP
James R. Duncan to ZBV	May 5	poor relief	A&H:GP
J.B. Smith to ZBV	May 5	conscription	A&H:GP
Daniel H. Hill to ZBV	May 5	loyalty	A&H:GP
Allen T. Davidson to ZBV	May 5	conscription	A&H:VanPC
George V. Scott to ZBV	May 6	prohibit export	A&H:GP
James C. Johnston to ZBV	May 6	thanks	A&H:GP
E.B. Jeffreys to ZBV	May 6	prohibit export	A&H:GP
Thomas Goldhwaite to Peter Mallett	May 6	conscription	A&H:GP
Bryan Tyson to ZBV	May 6	compliments	A&H:GP
Henry E. Colton to ZBV	May 6	promotion	A&H:GP
James Cook to ZBV	May 6	recovery	A&H:GP
William C. Dawson et al. to ZBV	May 6	cotton yarn	A&H:GP
Martha A. Allen to ZBV	May 6	poor relief	A&H:GP
Victor C. Barringer to ZBV	May 6	prohibit export	A&H:GP
John T. Harris to ZBV	May 6	prohibit export	A&H:GP
Daniel H. Hill to ZBV	May 6	loyalty	A&H:GP
James K. Gibson to ZBV	May 6	cotton	A&H:VanPC
Allen T. Davidson to ZBV	May 6	tax collectors	A&H:VanPC
George Seeman to ZBV	May 7	letters	A&H:GP

Correspondents	Date	Subject	Repository
John H. Winder to ZBV	May 7	passports	A&H:GP
G.H. Blalock to ZBV	May 7	conscription	A&H:GP
Cape Fear Bank to ZBV	May 7	meeting	A&H:GP
H.D. Stowe to ZBV	May 7	tax collectors	A&H:GP
Henry McCoy to ZBV	May 7	detail	A&H:GP
T.J. Bicknell to ZBV	May 7	distilling	A&H:GP
Jesse G. Shepherd to ZBV	May 7	appointment	A&H:GP
Daniel H. Hill to ZBV	May 7 (1)	deserters	A&H:GP
Daniel H. Hill to ZBV	May 7 (2)	troops	A&H:GP
Henry A. Dowd, address	May 7	yarn	SHC:Rob
J.M. Stepp to ZBV	May 8	appointment	A&H:GP
James K. Gibson to ZBV	May 8 (1)	cotton	A&H:GP
James K. Gibson to ZBV	May 8 (2)	provisions	A&H:GP
T.B. Stimpson to ZBV	May 8	speculation	A&H:GP
Joseph Bobbitt to B.F. Moon	May 8	court case	A&H:GP
James Burke to parents	May 8	court martial	A&H:GP
A.J. & W. Greenwood to ZBV	May 8	powder mill	A&H:GP
William T. Muse to ZBV	May 8	gunboats	A&H:GP
James Buchanan to ZBV	May 8	deserters	A&H:GP
Daniel G. Fowle, Order No. 4	May 8	militia	SHC:Rob
J. Krider et al. to ZBV	May 9	prohibit export	A&H:GP
Sol. G. Bryan to ZBV	May 9	conscription	A&H:GP
Henry McCoy to ZBV	May 9	prison guards	A&H:GP
Charles Osborn to ZBV	May 9	discharge	A&H:GP
Martha Ann Oakley to ZBV	May 9	poor relief	A&H:GP
Edward Warren to ZBV	May 9 (1)	wounded troops	A&H:GP
Edward Warren to ZBV	May 9 (2)	wounded troops	A&H:GP
W.W. Townes to ZBV	May 9	slave murder	A&H:GP
John W. Stephenson to ZBV	May 9	slave murder	A&H:GP
Peter Mallett to ZBV	May 9	conscription	A&H:GP
Daniel H. Hill to ZBV	May 9	desertion	A&H:GP
A.J. Whitehurst et al. to ZBV	May 9	conscription	A&H:GP
William J. Brown to ZBV	May 9	passport	A&H:VanPC
Bacchus J. Smith to ZBV	May 9	prohibit export	A&H:VanPC
Daniel G. Fowle, Order No. 5	May 9	militia	SHC:Rob
John F. Poindexter et al. to Theophilus H. Holmes	May 10	furlough	A&H:GP
S.L. Blackwell to ZBV	May 10	transfer	A&H:GP
Loyd T. Jones to ZBV	May 10	appointment	A&H:GP
Rufus Y. McAden to ZBV	May 10	prohibit export	A&H:GP
John C. McDowell to ZBV	May 10	prohibit export	A&H:GP
M. Williams to ZBV	May 10	transfer	A&H:GP
Daniel H. Hill to ZBV	May 10	war progress	A&H:GP
Daniel H. Hill to ZBV	May 11 (1)	war progress	A&H:GP
Daniel H. Hill, order	May 11 (2)	prohibit export	A&H:GP
A.G. Moore to ZBV	May 11	poor relief	A&H:GP
James H. Caul to ZBV	May 11	discharge	A&H:GP
M.J. Carroll to ZBV	May 11	discharge	A&H:GP
James Sloan to ZBV	May 11	appointment	A&H:GP
Daniel H. Hill to ZBV	May 11	NC reg't.	A&H:GP
John A. Gilmer to ZBV	May 11	slaves	A&H:GP

Correspondents	Date	Subject	Repository
George S. Johnson to ZBV	May 11	militia	A&H:GP
James D. Pardue to ZBV	May 11	salt	A&H:GP
Clinton Utley to ZBV	May 11	arrival	A&H:GP
Richard Leevens to ZBV	May 11	desertion	A&H:GP
S.J. Neal to ZBV	May 11	poor relief	A&H:GP
John A. Campbell to Peter Mallett	May 11	substitution	A&H:VanPC
James A. Seddon to ZBV	May 12	East Tenn.	A&H:GP
Alexander Collie & Co., warrants	May 12	cotton	A&H:GP
John White, declaration	May 12	cotton warrants	A&H:GP
Jason C. Harris to ZBV	May 12	conscription	A&H:GP
James Southgate, Jr., to ZBV	May 12	speech	A&H:GP
Jones Watson to David L. Swain	May 12	promotion	A&H:GP
P. [Powers] to ZBV	May 12	passport	A&H:GP
M.F. Arendell to ZBV	May 12	wounded troops	A&H:GP
William Pannill to ZBV	May 12	provisions	A&H:GP
Albert T. Summey to ZBV	May 12	bank notes	A&H:VanPC
Daniel H. Hill to ZBV	May 12	proclamation	A&H:VanPC
John A. Fleming to ZBV	May 13	transfer	A&H:GP
Joseph W. Tate to ZBV	May 13	promotion	A&H:GP
David L. Swain to ZBV	May 13	appointment	A&H:GP
George W. Mumford to ZBV	May 13	slave murder	A&H:GP
James Burk to ZBV	May 13	desertion	A&H:GP
James A. Seddon to ZBV	May 13 (1)	discharge	A&H:GP
James A. Seddon to ZBV	May 13 (2)	recommendation	A&H:GP
James A. Seddon to ZBV	May 13 (3)	arrests	A&H:GP
Oscar G. Parsley to ZBV	May 14	cargo	A&H:GP
R.H. Hicks to ZBV	May 14	copper mines	A&H:GP
A.B. Porter to ZBV	May 14	discharge	A&H:GP
W.M. Crisp et al. to ZBV	May 14	conscription	A&H:GP
William F. Lynch to ZBV	May 14	r.r. iron	A&H:GLB
George V. Strong to ZBV	May 15	arrival	A&H:GP
Simmons B. Staton to ZBV	May 15	appointment	A&H:GP
M. London to ZBV	May 15	introduction	A&H:VanPC
C. Armstrong to ZBV	May 16	destitution	A&H:GP
Hirum Green et al. to ZBV	May 16	conscription	A&H:GP
Thomas Carroll to William J. Hawkins	May 16	prohibit export	A&H:GP
Nelson Slough to ZBV	May 16	battle flag	A&H:GP
William R. Toone to ZBV	May 16	prohibit export	A&H:GP
Seaton Gales to ZBV	May 16	transfer	A&H:GP
George W. Logan to ZBV	May 16	murder appeal	A&H:GP
Mrs. Edward Warren to ZBV	May 16	husband	A&H:VanPC
Daniel H. Hill to ZBV	May 17 (1)	desertion	A&H:GP
Daniel H. Hill to ZBV	May 17 (2)	bridge guard	A&H:GP
G.H. Blalock to David A. Barnes	May 17	discharge	A&H:GP
James A. Seddon to ZBV	May 17	order	A&H:GP
Green Burk to ZBV	May 17	guardhouse	A&H:GP
S.S. Crisco to ZBV	May 17	proclamation	A&H:GP
Daniel V. Etheridge to ZBV	May 17	disloyalty	A&H:GP
N.G. Allman to ZBV	May 18	resignation	A&H:GP
Daniel H. Hill to ZBV	May 18	visit	A&H:GP
J.A. Henley to ZBV	May 18	salt	A&H:GP

Correspondents	Date	Subject	Repository
J. Atwater to ZBV	May 18	poor relief	A&H:GP
William P. Fortune to ZBV	May 18	transfer	A&H:GP
Peter Mallett to ZBV	May 18	conscription	A&H:GP
John McKeil to ZBV	May 18	desertion	A&H:GP
Rufus Y. McAdem to ZBV	May 18	prohibit export	A&H:GP
Mathew Maning et al. to ZBV	May 18	discharge	A&H:GP
Braxton Craven to ZBV	May 18	commission	A&H:GP
David A. Barnes to William F. Lynch	May 18	r.r. iron	A&H:GLB
Daniel F. Summey to ZBV	May 18	departure	A&H:VanPC
David A. Barnes to ZBV	May 19	steamers	A&H:GP
E.J. Arthur to ZBV	May 19	pardon	A&H:GP
P.W. Hennessee to ZBV	May 19	transfer	A&H:GP
J. Myrick to ZBV	May 19	conscription	A&H:GP
J.M. Smith to ZBV	May 19	bacon	A&H:GP
Walter Gwynn to ZBV	May 19	militia	A&H:GP
Daniel H. Hill to James A. Seddon	May 19	desertion	A&H:VanPC
F.A. Newbury to ZBV	May 20	contract	A&H:GP
William T. Muse to ZBV	May 20	boats	A&H:GP
E.S. Pendleton to ZBV	May 20	prohibit export	A&H:GP
Elizabeth Glover to ZBV	May 20	discharge	A&H:GP
J.B. Sil[es] to ZBV	May 20	desertion	A&H:GP
William M. Shipp to ZBV	May 20	court trial	A&H:GP
W.G. Boudinot to ZBV	May 20	signal stations	A&H:GP
Robert R. Heath to ZBV	May 20	murder case	A&H:GP
Alexander Beck to ZBV	May 20	transfer	A&H:GP
Thomas J. Green to ZBV	May 20	appointment	A&H:GP
John J. Shaver to ZBV	May 20	discharge	A&H:GP
W. Taylor to ZBV	May 20	r.r. shipment	A&H:GP
Spier Whitaker to ZBV	May 20	r.r. commission	A&H:GP
William T. Muse to ZBV	May 20	steamers	A&H:GP
Blanton Duncan to ZBV	May 20	photograph	A&H:VanPC
James Calloway to ZBV	May 21	discharge	A&H:GP
Daniel H. Hill to ZBV	May 21	communication	A&H:GP
Edward J. Warren to ZBV	May 21	Salisbury Prison	A&H:GP
David A. Barnes to W.G. Boudinot	May 21	signal station	A&H:GLB
Proclamation by ZBV	May 21	pardon	A&H:GLB
Albert T. Summey to ZBV	May 21	destitution	A&H:VanPC
William H.C. Whiting to ZBV	May 22	iron clad	A&H:GP
Duncan McNeill to ZBV	May 22	appointment	A&H:GP
S.P. Dula to ZBV	May 22	discharge	A&H:GP
William M. Barbour to ZBV	May 22	appointment	A&H:GP
D. McN. McKay to ZBV	May 22	impressment	A&H:GP
Martha Ann Oakley to ZBV	May 22	destitution	A&H:GP
Giles Leitch to ZBV	May 22	appointment	A&H:GP
William B. Carter to ZBV	May 22	Col. Ludlow	A&H:GP
H.A. Boone et al. to ZBV	May 22	distilling	A&H:GP
John Heart to H. Cabaniss	May 22	conscription	A&H:GP
J.H. Greene to ZBV	May 22	office seal	A&H:GP
John L. McDaniel to ZBV	May 22	appointment	A&H:GP
Mary Reid et al. to ZBV	May 22	destitution	A&H:GP
William P. Bynum to ZBV	May 22	Cap't. Cole	A&H:VanPC

Correspondents	Date	Subject	Repository
Samuel G. French to ZBV	May 23	mail	A&H:GP
Thomas J. Sumner to ZBV	May 23	lumber	A&H:GP
James A. Seddon to ZBV	May 23	disbanding	A&H:GP
William H.C. Whiting to ZBV	May 23	slaves	A&H:GP
James A. Seddon to ZBV	May 23	habeas corpus	A&H:GP
J.A. Barnett to ZBV	May 23	commission	A&H:GP
A[hi] C. Robbins to ZBV	May 23	conscription	A&H:GP
Francis E. Shober to ZBV	May 23	Salisbury Prison	A&H:GP
B.S. Young to ZBV	May 23	appointment	A&H:GP
Samuel B. Farmer to ZBV	May 23	substitution	A&H:GP
James J. Pettigrew to ZBV	May 23	desertion	A&H:GLB
W.C. McGimsey to ZBV	May 23	transfer	A&H:VanPC
Samuel L. Holt to ZBV	May 24	disaffection	A&H:GP
A.O. Warren to ZBV	May 24	transfer	A&H:GP
J.B. Teeter to ZBV	May 24	transfer	A&H:GP
J.W. James to ZBV	May 24	slaves	A&H:GP
A.W. Jenkins to ZBV	May 24	detail	A&H:GP
William T. Muse to ZBV	May 25	gunboats	A&H:GP
Henry McCoy to W.S. Winder	May 25	desertion	A&H:GP
S.J. Neal to ZBV	May 25	conscription	A&H:GP
Jesse W. Wells to ZBV	May 25	desertion	A&H:GP
W.N. Tillinghast to ZBV	May 25	navigation co.	A&H:GP
D.B. McLauchlin to ZBV	May 25	discharge	A&H:GP
Walter Gwynn to ZBV	May 25	militia	A&H:GP
G.W. Dobson to ZBV	May 25	deserters	A&H:GP
Henry E. Colton to ZBV	May 25	discharge	A&H:GP
Asa Biggs to ZBV	May 25	appointment	A&H:GP
Benjamin P. Martin to ZBV	May 25	desertion	A&H:GP
John D. Hyman to ZBV	May 25	election	A&H:VanPC
Carrie Bowie to ZBV	May 25	transfer	A&H:VanPC
Daniel H. Hill to ZBV	May 25	deserters	Har:Hill
J.M. McCorkle to Samuel Cooper	May 26	bounties	A&H:GP
William H.C. Whiting to ZBV	May 26	report	A&H:GP
Thomas J. Green to ZBV	May 26	prohibit export	A&H:GP
Thomas D. Snead to ZBV	May 26	appointment	A&H:GP
W.G. Boudinot to ZBV	May 26	blockade	A&H:GLB
James A. Seddon to ZBV	May 27	desertion	A&H:GP
James J. Pettigrew to ZBV	May 27	desertion	A&H:GP
Adrian B. Wanet to ZBV	May 27	gunboats	A&H:GP
B.F. Pearce to ZBV	May 27	appointment	A&H:GP
John R. Moore to ZBV	May 27	prohibit export	A&H:GP
G.G. Gulley to ZBV	May 27	conscription	A&H:GP
Sophia E. Bowen et al. to ZBV	May 27	destitution	A&H:GP
A.H. McLeod to ZBV	May 27	substitution	A&H:GP
N.M. Green to ZBV	May 28	conscription	A&H:GP
Hugh C. Harden to ZBV	May 28	impressment	A&H:GP
A.B. McGregor to ZBV	May 28	transfer	A&H:GP
C.D. Junkin to ZBV	May 28	prohibit export	A&H:GP
S.J. Neal to ZBV	May 28	contract	A&H:GP
Ben Bailey to ZBV	May 28	slaves	A&H:GP
P.W. Hennessee to ZBV	May 28	transfer	A&H:GP

Correspondents	Date	Subject	Repository
W.H. Croom to ZBV	May 28	bridge	A&H:GP
Archy Brown to ZBV	May 28	appointment	A&H:GP
John W. Brock to ZBV	May 28	furlough	A&H:GP
John M. Worth to ZBV	May 28	salt workers	A&H:GP
D.T. Towles to ZBV	May 28	transfer	A&H:GP
Alexander Walker to ZBV	May 28	slaves	A&H:GP
G.W. Walker to ZBV	May 28	furlough	A&H:GP
H. Cabarriss et al. to ZBV	May 28	conscription	A&H:GP
Robert Strange to Richard H. Battle	May 29	commission	A&H:GP
Judah Shelton et al. to ZBV	May 29	poor relief	A&H:GP
R.N. Cannon to ZBV	May 29	desertion	A&H:GP
J.F. Murrils to ZBV	May 29	impressment	A&H:GP
James Johnson to ZBV	May 29	discharge	A&H:GP
L.A.L. Roberson to ZBV	May 29	desertion	A&H:GP
Asa Clapp to ZBV	May 29	conscription	A&H:GP
William Eaton Jr. to ZBV	May 29	meeting	A&H:GP
Augustus S. Merrimon to ZBV	May 29	Shelton Laurel	A&H:VanPC
B.W. Forohel to ZBV	May 30	promotion	A&H:GP
Hackley Norton, testimony	May 30	Shelton Laurel	A&H:GP
Joseph C. Richey to ZBV	May 30	contract	A&H:GP
Amos F. Johnston to ZBV	May 30	substitution	A&H:GP
G.G. Hege to ZBV	May 30	substitution	A&H:GP
William H.C. Whiting to ZBV	May 30	promotion	A&H:GLB
William F. Farished to Capt. Robbins	May 30	militia	SHC:Rob
Jacob Satterfield to ZBV	May 31	discharge	A&H:GP
P.C. Hoge to ZBV	May 31	discharge	A&H:GP
William J. Houston to ZBV	May 31	brigade	A&H:GP
Amelia E. Jones to ZBV	May 31	destitution	A&H:GP
Daniel H. Hill to ZBV	May 31	disloyalty	A&H:GP
William J. Headen to ZBV	May 31	slaves	A&H:GP
Allen T. Davidson to ZBV	May 31	election	A&H:VanPC
A.S. Perkins et al. to ZBV	May n.d.	clemency	A&H:GP
Daniel H. Hill to ZBV	May n.d.	raid	A&H:GP
George Little to J.F. Murrill	Jun 1	desertion	A&H:GP
Leonard Stubbs to ZBV	Jun 1	conscription	A&H:GP
Moses Young et al. to ZBV	Jun 1	conscription	A&H:GP
W.L. Ledbetter to ZBV	Jun 1	appointment	A&H:GP
Marier Eler to ZBV	Jun 1	poor relief	A&H:GP
Caleb Eller to ZBV	Jun 1	appointment	A&H:GP
Lucy A. Walker to ZBV	Jun 1	conscription	A&H:GP
James L. Welch to ZBV	Jun 1	homicide	A&H:GP
Isabella Kennedy to ZBV	Jun 1	peace	A&H:GP
W.P. Andrews to ZBV	Jun 1	discharge	A&H:GP
William Gulick, appointment	Jun 1	horses	A&H:GLB
Albert T. Summey to ZBV	Jun 1	yarn	A&H:VanPC
Joseph Kenner to ZBV	Jun 1	Thomas's Legion	A&H:VanPC
H. Cabarriss to ZBV	Jun 2	conscription	A&H:GP
J. Hiatt to ZBV	Jun 2	slaves	A&H:GP
Marget Holder to ZBV	Jun 2	discharge	A&H:GP
John Norfleet to ZBV	Jun 2	conscription	A&H:GP
Sarah A. Metcalf to ZBV	Jun 2	Shelton Laurel	A&H:GP

Correspondents	Date	Subject	Repository
A.R. Harriss to ZBV	Jun 2	desertion	A&H:GP
Ben Bailey to ZBV	Jun 2	impressed slaves	A&H:GP
Washington C. Kerr to ZBV	Jun 2	salt	A&H:GP
Stephen R. Mallory to ZBV	Jun 2	appointment	A&H:VanPC
James A. Seddon to ZBV	Jun 2	transfer	A&H:VanPC
John Norfleet to ZBV	Jun 3	commission	A&H:GP
S. Greene to ZBV	Jun 3	prohibit export	A&H:GP
Robert F. Armfield to ZBV	Jun 3	appointment	A&H:GP
G.W. Shackleford to ZBV	Jun 3	transfer	A&H:GP
Elias Bryan et al. to ZBV	Jun 3	impressed slaves	A&H:GP
James A. Seddon to ZBV	Jun 3	artillery	A&H:VanPC
Samuel B. French to ZBV	Jun 3	merchant	A&H:VanPC
J.G. Moore to ZBV	Jun 4	prohibit export	A&H:GP
M. Overcourt to ZBV	Jun 4	harvest	A&H:GP
B.A. Kittrell to ZBV	Jun 4	prohibit export	A&H:GP
William T. Dickerson to ZBV	Jun 4	appointment	A&H:GP
Isaac Sharkey to ZBV	Jun 4	impressed slaves	A&H:GP
Lawrence M. Allen to W.N. Garrett	Jun 4	habeas corpus	A&H:GP
S.J. Neal et al. to ZBV	Jun 4	conscription	A&H:GP
John H. Hall to ZBV	Jun 4	prohibit export	A&H:GP
John A. Campbell to ZBV	Jun 4	passport	A&H:VanPC
Daniel H. Hill to ZBV	Jun 4	NC generals	A&H:VanPC
Jordan Tyson to ZBV	Jun 5	impressed slaves	A&H:GP
John A. Gilmer to ZBV	Jun 5	impressed slaves	A&H:GP
Samuel Garrard to ZBV	Jun 5	desertion	A&H:GP
John Boothe to ZBV	Jun 5	prohibit export	A&H:GP
Samuel B. French to ZBV	Jun 5	Jackson statue	A&H:VanPC
John W. Graham to ZBV	Jun 6	conscription	A&H:GP
A. Van Derhorst to ZBV	Jun 6	Advance	A&H:GP
William H.C. Whiting to ZBV	Jun 6	militia	A&H:GP
A.H. Greenway to ZBV	Jun 6	conscription	A&H:GP
Robert G.A. Love to ZBV	Jun 6	bounty	A&H:GP
L. Chapman to ZBV	Jun 6	appointment	A&H:GP
R.F. Lehman to ZBV	Jun 6	passport	A&H:GP
William Eaton, Jr., to ZBV	Jun 6	resignation	A&H:GP
W.N. Garrett to ZBV	Jun 6	desertion	A&H:GP
James W. Osborne to ZBV	Jun 6	special court	A&H:GP
Charles Evans to ZBV	Jun 6	conscription	A&H:GP
S.M. Collis to ZBV	Jun 6	destitution	A&H:GP
Bryan Tyson to ZBV	Jun 6	peace	A&H:GP
John McDuffie to ZBV	Jun 7	conscription	A&H:GP
R.A. Edmonston to ZBV	Jun 7	desertion	A&H:GP
Nancy Grady to ZBV	Jun 7	destitution	A&H:GP
Mary K. Walker to ZBV	Jun 7	discharge	A&H:GP
James Tyson to ZBV	Jun 8	harvest	A&H:GP
John H. Dillard to ZBV	Jun 8	impressed slaves	A&H:GP
Anzilla May to ZBV	Jun 8	conscription	A&H:GP
William West to ZBV	Jun 8	discharge	A&H:GP
William H. Lyon to ZBV	Jun 8	prohibit export	A&H:GP
Virgil S. Lusk to ZBV	Jun 8	desertion	A&H:GP
Nicholas W. Woodfin to ZBV	Jun 8	salt	A&H:GP

Correspondents	Date	Subject	Repository
James E. Parker to ZBV	Jun 8	destitution	A&H:GP
A.J. Mills to ZBV	Jun 8	transfer	A&H:GP
James J. Benfrow to ZBV	Jun 8	transfer	A&H:GP
Samuel J. Wheeler to S.K. Edwards	Jun 8	transfer	A&H:GP
James A. Seddon to ZBV	Jun 8	Ramseur's brigade	A&H:GP
B.A. Kittrell to George Little	Jun 8	prohibit export	A&H:GP
Aaron Learey to ZBV	Jun 8	desertion	A&H:GP
Proclamation by ZBV	Jun 8	prohibit export	A&H:GLB
John A. Boyett to ZBV	Jun 9	discharge	A&H:GP
Wiley F. Parker to ZBV	Jun 9	appointment	A&H:GP
Samuel A. Walkup to ZBV	Jun 9	habeas corpus	A&H:GP
Anonymous to ZBV	Jun 9	destitution	A&H:GP
James Wilson et al. to ZBV	Jun 9	conscription	A&H:GP
Hillary Taylor to ZBV	Jun 9	salt	A&H:GP
A.G. Lentz to ZBV	Jun 10	conscription	A&H:GP
John Phelan to ZBV	Jun 10	speculation	A&H:GP
Eugene M. Williams to ZBV	Jun 10	appointment	A&H:GP
W.G.B. Morris to ZBV	Jun 10	Shelton Laurel	A&H:GP
Jesse Rankin to ZBV	Jun 10	cotton cards	A&H:GP
Bettie A. Folk to ZBV	Jun 10	boots	A&H:VanPC
Edward D. Hall to ZBV	Jun 10	recommendation	A&H:VanPC
T.R. Egerton to ZBV	Jun 11	prohibit export	A&H:GP
Loyd T. Jones to ZBV	Jun 11	appointment	A&H:GP
William Lamb to ZBV	Jun 11	Ft. Fisher	A&H:GP
J.M. McCorkle to ZBV	Jun 11	bounty	A&H:GP
Mark Nelson to ZBV	Jun 11	desertion	A&H:GP
Betty Wimbish to ZBV	Jun 11	relief society	A&H:GP
J.B. Tilghman to ZBV	Jun 11	prohibit export	A&H:GP
Otis F. Manson to ZBV	Jun 11	removal	A&H:VanPC
Richard M. Pearson to ZBV	Jun 11	Confed. notes	A&H:VanPC
ZBV to Joseph H. Saunders	Jun 11	commission	SHC:Sau
T.C. Horton, certification	Jun 12	surveyor	A&H:GP
T.D. Guy to ZBV	Jun 12	prohibit export	A&H:GP
Mary A. Fuller to ZBV	Jun 12	transportation	A&H:GP
Francis E. Shober to ZBV	Jun 12	impressed slaves	A&H:GP
Mrs. George N. Sanders to ZBV	Jun 12	invoice	A&H:VanPC
David A. Barnes to Daniel H. Hill	Jun 12	salt	A&H:VanPC
Milledge L. Bonham to ZBV	Jun 12	petition	A&H:VanPC
R.B. Miller to ZBV	Jun 13	violence	A&H:GP
R.A. Jenkins to ZBV	Jun 13	conscription	A&H:GP
Abagail Propst to ZBV	Jun 13	Confed. money	A&H:GP
William K. Lane to ZBV	Jun 13	resignation	A&H:GP
S.W. Kenner to ZBV	Jun 13	destitution	A&H:GP
James M. Black to ZBV	Jun 13	transfer	A&H:GP
E.L. Dockrey to ZBV	Jun 13	Shelton Laurel	A&H:GP
A.A. Duees to ZBV	Jun 13	Shelton Laurel	A&H:GP
Daniel McMonroe to ZBV	Jun 13	passport	A&H:GP
Henry R. Strong to ZBV	Jun 13	passport	A&H:GP
ZBV to Wake Co. Sheriff	Jun 13	special election	A&H:GLB
J.L. Little to ZBV	Jun 14	desertion	A&H:GP
James M. Brown to ZBV	Jun 14	desertion	A&H:GP

Correspondents	Date	Subject	Repository
[Intha] McGraw to ZBV	Jun 14	transfer	A&H:GP
William R. Sparks to ZBV	Jun 15	peace	A&H:GP
Henry Summit to ZBV	Jun 15	Confed. money	A&H:GP
A.M. Fuller to ZBV	Jun 15	impressed slaves	A&H:GP
M.E. Lazarus to ZBV	Jun 15	ZBV's house	A&H:GP
Thomas Johnston to ZBV	Jun 15	r.r. wool	A&H:GP
G.W. Nicholson to ZBV	Jun 15	prohibit export	A&H:GP
J.S. Patterson to ZBV	Jun 15	poor relief	A&H:GP
Catherine M. Riley to ZBV	Jun 15	destitution	A&H:GP
S[illegible] to ZBV	Jun 15	violence	A&H:GP
Levi R. Hill to ZBV	Jun 15	conscription	A&H:GP
"Female Sect." to ZBV	Jun 15	destitution	A&H:GP
Thomas Ruffin, Jr. to ZBV	Jun 15	Shelton Laurel	A&H:GP
James A. Seddon to ZBV	Jun 15	John McDowell	A&H:GP
Hugh Simpson to ZBV	Jun 15	salt	A&H:GP
J.H. Gooch to ZBV	Jun 15	salt	A&H:GP
John A. Campbell to ZBV	Jun 15	furlough	A&H:GLB
William K. Lane to ZBV	Jun 15	resignation	A&H:GLB
John H. Winder to ZBV	Jun 15	court martial	A&H:VanPC
James A. Seddon to ZBV	Jun 15	discharge	A&H:VanPC
Samuel P. Arrington to ZBV	Jun 16	blockade	A&H:GP
George A. Dancy to ZBV	Jun 16	conscription	A&H:GP
William T. Muse to ZBV	Jun 16	pilot	A&H:GP
James McLure to ZBV	Jun 16	desertion	A&H:GP
R.C. Belden to ZBV	Jun 16	detail	A&H:GP
D.A. Cameron et al. to ZBV	Jun 16	detail	A&H:GP
Thomas Webb to ZBV	Jun 16	appointment	A&H:GP
William J. Clarke to ZBV	Jun 16	appointment	A&H:GP
Joseph Russell to ZBV	Jun 16	discharge	A&H:GP
James C. McRae to George Little	Jun 16	conscription	A&H:GP
William H.C. Whiting to ZBV	Jun 16	shipment	A&H:GP
A.M. Powell to ZBV	Jun 17	discharge	A&H:GP
James C. Johnston to ZBV	Jun 17	conscription	A&H:GP
Lavina Mathews to ZBV	Jun 17	poor relief	A&H:GP
R.S. Marks to ZBV	Jun 17	poor relief	A&H:GP
Jeremy F. Gilmer to ZBV	Jun 17	address	A&H:GP
W.B. Stipe to ZBV	Jun 17	conscription	A&H:GP
Elander Gibson to ZBV	Jun 17	discharge	A&H:GP
Asa Eubanks et al. to ZBV	Jun 17	detail	A&H:GP
Philip B. McLaurin, testimony	Jun 17	theft	A&H:GP
Fenner B. Satterthwaite to ZBV	Jun 17	war support	A&H:VanPC
James L. Henry to ZBV	Jun 17	appointment	A&H:VanPC
B.W. Baber to ZBV	Jun 18	discharge	A&H:GP
Elbert W. Jones to ZBV	Jun 18	appointment	A&H:GP
William Myers et al. to ZBV	Jun 18	conscription	A&H:GP
Blewfore Lucas to ZBV	Jun 18	discharge	A&H:GP
Daniel H. Hill to ZBV	Jun 18	speculation	A&H:VanPC
John A. Williams to ZBV	Jun 18	recommendation	A&H:VanPC
Anonymous to ZBV	Jun 19	desertion	A&H:GP
William A. Lash to ZBV	Jun 19	impressed slaves	A&H:GP
W.J. Price to ZBV	Jun 19	transfer	A&H:GP

Correspondents	Date	Subject	Repository
S.M. Green et al. to ZBV	Jun 19	conscription	A&H:GP
R.H. Lueen to ZBV	Jun 19	desertion	A&H:GP
Hackley Norton to ZBV	Jun 19	Shelton Laurel	A&H:GP
"Many Citizens" to ZBV	Jun 19	civil unrest	A&H:GP
William Davis, testimony	Jun 20	Shelton Laurel	A&H:GP
William H.C. Whiting to ZBV	Jun 20	impressed slaves	A&H:GP
W.E. Demill to ZBV	Jun 20	check	A&H:GP
James T. Rogers to ZBV	Jun 20	transfer	A&H:GP
S.J. Buchanan to ZBV	Jun 20	desertion	A&H:GP
John Helms to ZBV	Jun 20	destitution	A&H:GP
John D. Whitford to ZBV	Jun 20	r.r. company	A&H:GP
Emily D. Moore to ZBV	Jun 20	conscription	A&H:GP
James Ledford to ZBV	Jun 20	transfer	A&H:GP
S.J. Townsend to ZBV	Jun 20	extradition	A&H:VanPC
Daniel H. Hill to ZBV	Jun 20	fortification	A&H:VanPC
J.N. Ballenton to ZBV	Jun 21	detail	A&H:GP
John W. Francis to ZBV	Jun 21	election	A&H:GP
Joseph Robeson to ZBV	Jun 21	conscription	A&H:GP
James Vance to ZBV	Jun 21	family	A&H:VanPC
John A. Gilmer to ZBV	Jun 22	conscription	A&H:GP
Tolivar Davis to ZBV	Jun 22	war support	A&H:GP
A.F. Lewis et al. to ZBV	Jun 22	transfer	A&H:GP
Rufus K. Spruill to ZBV	Jun 22	prohibit export	A&H:GP
James H. Bryson to ZBV	Jun 22	resignation	A&H:GP
S.A. Chamberland et al. to ZBV	Jun 22	transfer	A&H:GP
H.A. Davis to ZBV	Jun 22	conscription	A&H:GP
D. William McDonald to ZBV	Jun 22	conscription	A&H:GP
Charles E. Johnson to E.M. Covey	Jun 22	hospitals	A&H:GP
Daniel H. Hill to ZBV	Jun 22	militia	A&H:VanPC
James F. Moore to James Sloan	Jun 23	leather	A&H:GP
Thomas Edwards to ZBV	Jun 23	wts./measures	A&H:GP
William H.C. Whiting to ZBV	Jun 23	cotton cards	A&H:VanPC
William A. Askew to ZBV	Jun 24	conscription	A&H:GP
David Rankin to ZBV	Jun 24	appointment	A&H:GP
Chesley Jones to ZBV	Jun 24	civil unrest	A&H:GP
Harrit Dickey to ZBV	Jun 24	conscription	A&H:GP
W.C. Troy to ZBV	Jun 24	supplies	A&H:GP
A.E. Baird to ZBV	Jun 24	conscription	A&H:GP
A.J. Morey to W.N. Garrett	Jun 24	Shelton Laurel	A&H:GP
Hester T. Rowden to ZBV	Jun 24	discharge	A&H:GP
David Kahnweiler to ZBV	Jun 25	letters	A&H:GP
William N. Thrower to ZBV	Jun 25	discharge	A&H:GP
Thomas Springer to ZBV	Jun 25	transfer	A&H:GP
Kenneth M. McDonald to ZBV	Jun 25	discharge	A&H:GP
James O. Paxton to ZBV	Jun 25	appointment	A&H:GP
E.H. Fulenwider to ZBV	Jun 25	conscription	A&H:GP
John W. Roberts to ZBV	Jun 25	substitution	A&H:GP
Thomas M. Moore to ZBV	Jun 25	civil unrest	A&H:GP
Thomas L. Bayne to David A. Barnes	Jun 25	cotton cards	A&H:VanPC
Daniel H. Hill to ZBV	Jun 25 (1)	militia	A&H:VanPC
Daniel H. Hill to ZBV	Jun 25 (2)	conscription	A&H:VanPC

Correspondents	Date	Subject	Repository
Daniel H. Hill to ZBV	Jun 25 (3)	appointment	A&H:VanPC
J.M. Albertson to ZBV	Jun 26	speculation	A&H:GP
Joseph H. Flanner to ZBV	Jun 26	steamers	A&H:GP
Benjamin Ammon to ZBV	Jun 26	prohibit export	A&H:GP
[F] H. Hughes to ZBV	Jun 26	supplies	A&H:GP
Edmund B. Haywood to ZBV	Jun 26	ice	A&H:VanPC
Daniel H. Hill to ZBV	Jun 27	letter	A&H:GP
Francis E. Shober to ZBV	Jun 27	impressed slaves	A&H:GP
Murdock J. McSween to ZBV	Jun 27	appointment	A&H:GP
St. Clair Dearing to ZBV	Jun 27	troop trains	LC:CSA
"J.C." to ZBV	Jun 28	W.W. Holden	A&H:GP
Daniel H. Hill to Samuel J. Wheeler	Jun 29	marauders	A&H:GP
Sarah A. Tillinghast to ZBV	Jun 29	conscription	A&H:GP
Frank J. Wilson to ZBV	Jun 29	appointment	A&H:GP
J.M. Bryan to ZBV	Jun 29	desertion	A&H:GP
J.B. Locket to ZBV	Jun 29	transfer	A&H:GP
Abraham C. Myers to ZBV	Jun 29	steamer	A&H:VanPC
James McDeyck to ZBV	Jun 30	transfer	A&H:GP
Allen T. Davidson to ZBV	Jun 30	militia	A&H:GP
Jonathan Worth to ZBV	Jun 30	salt works	A&H:GP
B.D. Austin to ZBV	Jun 30	Confed. money	A&H:GP
Joseph H. Flanner et al. to Jefferson Davis	Jun 30	dismissal	A&H:GP
John A. Gilmer to ZBV	Jun 30	desertion	A&H:GP
A.M. Hawkins to ZBV	Jun 30	conscription	A&H:GP
N. McKay to William W. Holden	Jun 30	river works	A&H:GP
John Russell to ZBV	Jun 30	conscription	A&H:GP
A.H. Horton to ZBV	Jun 30	conscription	A&H:GP
Thomas C. Evans to ZBV	Jun 30	appointment	A&H:GP
Murdock J. McSween to ZBV	Jun 30 (1)	conscription	A&H:GP
Murdock J. McSween to ZBV	Jun 30 (2)	appointment	A&H:GP
William H.C. Whiting to ZBV	Jun n.d.	prohibit export	A&H:GP
Williams and Gray to ZBV	Jun n.d.	speculation	A&H:GP
Nicholas W. Woodfin to ZBV	Jul 1	salt	A&H:GP
William A. Pugh to ZBV	Jul 1	deserters	A&H:GP
Mary A. Walker to ZBV	Jul 1	hardship	A&H:GP
James Green et al. to ZBV	Jul 1	conscription	A&H:GP
Edwin Barnes to ZBV	Jul 1	deprivation	A&H:GP
Josiah Coats to ZBV	Jul 1	commission	A&H:GP
F.E. Proctor to ZBV	Jul 1	discharge	A&H:GP
Samuel B. French to ZBV	Jul 1	Jackson statue	A&H:GP
Moses A. Smith to B.N. Clements	Jul 1	militia	A&H:VanPC
G.W. Joyner to Samuel J. Wheeler	Jul 2	impressment	A&H:GP
B. Griffith to ZBV	Jul 2	desertion	A&H:GP
William F. McKesson to ZBV	Jul 2	tax in kind	A&H:GP
G.D. Moore et al. to ZBV	Jul 2	impressment	A&H:GP
A.J. Mills to ZBV	Jul 2	hardship	A&H:GP
William H. Wright to ZBV	Jul 2	blockade	A&H:GP
Joseph Harper to ZBV	Jul 2	discharge	A&H:GP
John M. Worth to ZBV	Jul 2	salt	A&H:GP
H. Baker to ZBV	Jul 2	dissension	A&H:GP
Tod R. Caldwell to ZBV	Jul 2	appointment	A&H:GP

Correspondents	Date	Subject	Repository
A.S. Kemp to ZBV	Jul 2	furlough	A&H:GP
John D. Whitford to ZBV	Jul 3	r.r. bonds	A&H:GP
Lambert W. Hall to ZBV	Jul 3	conscription	A&H:GP
E.G. Gray to ZBV	Jul 3	appointment	A&H:GP
M. London et al. to ZBV	Jul 3	conscription	A&H:GP
John H. Hays to ZBV	Jul 3	furlough	A&H:GP
D. McD. Yount to ZBV	Jul 3	tax in kind	A&H:GP
Thomas W. Dewey to General —	Jul 3	resignation	A&H:GP
Lucy B. Hunt to ZBV	Jul 3	poor relief	A&H:GP
Edward W. Jones to ZBV	Jul 3	recommendation	A&H:GP
William N. Brice to ZBV	Jul 3	pass	A&H:GP
Joseph H. Flanner to ZBV	Jul 3	dismissal	A&H:GP
Richard S. Donnell to ZBV	Jul 3	habeas corpus	A&H:GP
Walter L. Steele to ZBV	Jul 4	peace	A&H:GP
[Birza] Williams to ZBV	Jul 4	desertion	A&H:GP
Virgil S. Lusk to ZBV	Jul 4	habeas corpus	A&H:GP
John H. Roberts to ZBV	Jul 4	conscription	A&H:GP
S.M. Chestnutt to ZBV	Jul 4	prohibit export	A&H:GP
J.W. Killian to ZBV	Jul 4	conscription	A&H:GP
Silas K. Edwards to ZBV	Jul 4	transfer	A&H:GP
Nathaniel A. Boyden to ZBV	Jul 4	salt	A&H:GP
Richard S. Donnell to ZBV	Jul 4	resolution	A&H:GP
Eliza C. Hedgeth to ZBV	Jul 4	deprivation	A&H:GP
Joseph J. Young to ZBV	Jul 4	Gettysburg	A&H:GP
Q.A. Ward to ZBV	Jul 4	conscription	A&H:GP
James Hicks to ZBV	Jul 5	desertion	A&H:GP
William J. Saunders to ZBV	Jul 5	artillery	A&H:GP
R.W. Freeman et al. to ZBV	Jul 5	disaffection	A&H:GP
M.J. Hogan to ZBV	Jul 5	desertion	A&H:GP
Henry Popplin to ZBV	Jul 6	discharge	A&H:GP
Richard S. Donnell to ZBV	Jul 6	requisition	A&H:GP
Thomas Ruffin, Jr., to ZBV	Jul 6	volunteers	A&H:GP
John D. Whitford to ZBV	Jul 6 (1)	transport cotton	A&H:GP
John D. Whitford to ZBV	Jul 6 (2)	transport	A&H:GP
James G. Martin to ZBV	Jul 6	artillery	A&H:GP
James A.J. Bradford to ZBV	Jul 6 (1)	artillery	A&H:GP
James A.J. Bradford to ZBV	Jul 6 (2)	Union troops	A&H:GP
James A.J. Bradford to ZBV	Jul 6 (3)	Union raid	A&H:GP
Thomas J. Sumner to ZBV	Jul 6 (1)	arrival	A&H:GP
Thomas J. Sumner to ZBV	Jul 6 (2)	departure	A&H:GP
William H.C. Whiting to ZBV	Jul 6 (1)	Union raid	A&H:GP
William H.C. Whiting to ZBV	Jul 6 (2)	retreat	A&H:GP
Albert W. Barksdale to ZBV	Jul 6	prohibit export	A&H:GP
Giles Mebane to ZBV	Jul 6	troops	A&H:GP
Stephen Pilkington to ZBV	Jul 6	desertion	A&H:GP
J. Metcalf to ZBV	Jul 6	Shelton Laurel	A&H:GP
Josiah Gorgas to W.C. Duxbury	Jul 6	artillery	A&H:VanPC
Josiah Gorgas to ZBV	Jul 7	artillery	A&H:GP
W.M. Gordon to ZBV	Jul 7	cadets	A&H:GP
Robert F. Davidson to ZBV	Jul 7 (1)	weapons	A&H:GP
Robert F. Davidson to ZBV	Jul 7 (2)	defense	A&H:GP

Correspondents	Date	Subject	Repository
Capt. Lockhard to ZBV	Jul 7	Union raid	A&H:GP
L.G. Watson to ZBV	Jul 7	blockade	A&H:GP
A.F. Shaw et al. to ZBV	Jul 7	hospital	A&H:GP
R.S. Deportes to Josiah Gorgas	Jul 7	artillery	A&H:GP
William P. Carson to ZBV	Jul 7	conscription	A&H:GP
John D. Whitford to ZBV	Jul 7	cotton	A&H:GP
William H.C. Whiting to ZBV	Jul 7	bridge guard	A&H:GP
Joel G. Anderson et al. to ZBV	Jul 8	conscription	A&H:GP
Samuel McD. Tate to ZBV	Jul 8	Gettysburg	A&H:GP
Joseph H. Flanner to ZBV	Jul 8	cotton	A&H:GP
F. George et al. to ZBV	Jul 8	conscription	A&H:GP
Charley Cisson to ZBV	Jul 8	distilling	A&H:GP
John D. Coble to ZBV	Jul 8	cotton cards	A&H:GP
John H. Reagan to ZBV	Jul 8	postmaster	A&H:VanPC
R. Henry Glenn to ZBV	Jul 9	commission	A&H:GP
Enoch Ward to ZBV	Jul 9	detail	A&H:GP
A.J. Johnston to ZBV	Jul 9	coroner	A&H:GP
Thomas J. Boykin to ZBV	Jul 9	prohibit export	A&H:GP
J.G. Reynolds to ZBV	Jul 9	conscription	A&H:GP
Joseph H. Flanner to ZBV	Jul 9	blockade	A&H:GP
George N. Sanders to John White	Jul 9	D.K. McRae	A&H:GP
William H. Oliver to ZBV	Jul 9	cargo	A&H:GP
James J. Pettigrew to ZBV	Jul 9	26th Reg't.	A&H:GLB
William F. Green to ZBV	Jul 10	desertion	A&H:GP
D.B. Black to ZBV	Jul 10	militia	A&H:GP
Stratton Burton to ZBV	Jul 10	militia	A&H:GP
E.A. Parks et al. to ZBV	Jul 10	conscription	A&H:GP
Archibald H. Arrington to ZBV	Jul 10	passport	A&H:GP
James W. Conley et al. to ZBV	Jul 10	conscription	A&H:GP
Kenneth M. Murcheson to ZBV	Jul 10	transfer	A&H:GP
Duncan K. McRae to ZBV	Jul 10	bonds	A&H:GP
George N. Sanders to John White	Jul 10	D.K. McRae	A&H:GP
John A. Campbell to ZBV	Jul 10	John McDowell	A&H:GLB
John A. Campbell to ZBV	Jul 10	transfer	A&H:VanPC
Mattie Hubbard to ZBV	Jul 10	appointment	A&H:VanPC
Mary C. Clayton To ZBV	Jul 11	poor relief	A&H:GP
Joshua H. Stanly et al. to ZBV	Jul 11	conscription	A&H:GP
Joseph B. Cherry to ZBV	Jul 11	conscription	A&H:GP
Alethea A. Crowell to ZBV	Jul 11	poor relief	A&H:GP
Sarah Ann Willoughby to ZBV	Jul 11	disaffection	A&H:GP
Josiah Turner, Jr., to ZBV	Jul 11	habeas corpus	A&H:GP
Henry T. Clark to E. Burke Haywood	Jul 11	hospital	A&H:GP
William L. Love to ZBV	Jul 11	appointment	A&H:VanPC
S.P. Duncan to ZBV	Jul 12	desertion	A&H:GP
B. Griffith to ZBV	Jul 12	desertion	A&H:GP
J.G. Reynolds to ZBV	Jul 12	civil unrest	A&H:GP
B.P. Currie to ZBV	Jul 12	appointment	A&H:GP
E. Burke Haywood to Samuel P. Moore	Jul 13	hospital	A&H:GP
John W. McElroy to ZBV	Jul 13	civil unrest	A&H:GP
William Martin to ZBV	Jul 13	militia	A&H:GP
John S. Livingston to ZBV	Jul 13	conscription	A&H:GP

Correspondents	Date	Subject	Repository
William H.C. Whiting to ZBV	Jul 13	artillery	A&H:GP
W.W. Parker to ZBV	Jul 13	conscription	A&H:GP
William G. Webb to ZBV	Jul 13	forgery	A&H:GP
S.P. Frederick to ZBV	Jul 13	appointment	A&H:GP
John L. Doggett to ZBV	Jul 13	recommendation	A&H:GP
Joseph Smith to ZBV	Jul 13	provisional gov.	A&H:GP
James A. Seddon to ZBV	Jul 13	desertion	A&H:GP
Richard Harris to ZBV	Jul 13	prohibit export	A&H:GP
Goodwyn Harris to ZBV	Jul 13	desertion	A&H:GP
A. Andrews to ZBV	Jul 13	transfer	A&H:GP
N.A. Cherry to ZBV	Jul 13	refugee	A&H:GP
John A. Campbell to ZBV	Jul 13	passports	A&H:VanPC
James C. McRae to ZBV	Jul 13	factory case	A&H:VanPC
Murray & Brothers to ZBV	Jul 14	cotton cards	A&H:GP
Otis F. Manson to ZBV	Jul 14	hospital	A&H:GP
A. McNeill to ZBV	Jul 14	desertion	A&H:GP
James G. Martin to ZBV	Jul 14	Union troops	A&H:GP
H.K. Patton to ZBV	Jul 14	appointment	A&H:GP
W.A.E. Roberts to ZBV	Jul 14	transfer	A&H:GP
P.N. Heilig to ZBV	Jul 14	impressed slaves	A&H:GP
Archibald H. Arrington to ZBV	Jul 14	appointment	A&H:GP
G.M. Roberts to ZBV	Jul 14	transfer	A&H:GP
Bedford Brown to ZBV	Jul 14	appointment	A&H:GP
J. H. Coltrane to ZBV	Jul 14	conscription	A&H:GP
Jesse G. Shepherd to ZBV	Jul 14	recommendation	A&H:VanPC
James A. Seddon to ZBV	Jul 14	discharge	A&H:VanPC
Edward Warren to ZBV	Jul 15	surgeons	A&H:GP
A.J. Holt to ZBV	Jul 15	transfer	A&H:GP
Bayles M. Edney to ZBV	Jul 15	praise ZBV	A&H:GP
Abner Feimster to ZBV	Jul 15	conscription	A&H:GP
James G. Ramsay to ZBV	Jul 15	impressed slaves	A&H:GP
John Pool to ZBV	Jul 15	civil unrest	A&H:GP
James B. Slaughter to ZBV	Jul 15	desertion	A&H:GP
W.G. Hall to ZBV	Jul 15	transfer	A&H:GP
Francis B. Smith to ZBV	Jul 15	prohibit export	A&H:GP
Edward F. Woolard to ZBV	Jul 15	appointment	A&H:GP
Perry Forrest to ZBV	Jul 15	discharge	A&H:GP
David W. Siler to ZBV	Jul 15	conscription	A&H:GP
[Tom] to ZBV	Jul 15	transfer	A&H:GP
Robert D. Melvin to ZBV	Jul 15	appointment	A&H:GP
John White to ZBV	Jul 15	blockade	A&H:GP
James L. Henry to ZBV	Jul 15	transfer	A&H:VanPC
Richard Morton to ZBV	Jul 15	conscription	A&H:VanPC
Kenneth Raynor to ZBV	Jul 16	impressed slaves	A&H:GP
Jesse G. Shepherd to ZBV	Jul 16	arsenal	A&H:GP
Allen Miller to ZBV	Jul 16	discharge	A&H:GP
Josiah Woody to ZBV	Jul 16	conscription	A&H:GP
George Little to ZBV	Jul 16	summons	A&H:GP
Daniel G. Fowle to ZBV	Jul 16	conscription	A&H:GP
E. Beckersdell to ZBV	Jul 16	disaffection	A&H:GP
Mahala W. Hundley to ZBV	Jul 16	conscription	A&H:GP

Correspondents	Date	Subject	Repository
James Vance to ZBV	Jul 16	ZBV	A&H:GP
George N. Sanders to ZBV	Jul 16	purchases	A&H:GLB
Thomas Settle Jr. to ZBV	Jul 16	slave rape	A&H:Set
George P. Collins to ZBV	Jul 17	appointment	A&H:GP
Ambrose M. Johnson to ZBV	Jul 17	appointment	A&H:GP
Phineas Horton to ZBV	Jul 17	appointment	A&H:GP
Daniel Reap et al. to ZBV	Jul 17	conscription	A&H:GP
Thomas Symons et al. to ZBV	Jul 17	detail	A&H:GP
Duncan K. McRae to ZBV	Jul 17	bonds	A&H:GP
J.L. Houland et al. to ZBV	Jul 17	desertion	A&H:GP
G.C. Askew to ZBV	Jul 17	conscription	A&H:GP
W.W. Gilbert to ZBV	Jul 17	appointment	A&H:GP
J.M. Hamlin to ZBV	Jul 17	transfer	A&H:GP
P.N. Wheeler to George Little	Jul 17	letter	A&H:GP
Samuel McLeod to ZBV	Jul 17	transfer	A&H:GP
Thomas J. Patrick to ZBV	Jul 17	prohibit export	A&H:GP
Louis G. Young to ZBV	Jul 17 [1]	J.J. Pettigrew	A&H:GP
Louis G. Young to ZBV	Jul 17 [2]	J.J. Pettigrew	A&H:GP
N.A. Cameron et al. to ZBV	Jul 17	civil unrest	A&H:GP
Phifer Neisler to ZBV	Jul 18	prohibit export	A&H:GP
G.C. Beasley to ZBV	Jul 18	appointment	A&H:GP
E.S. Blackwood to ZBV	Jul 18	transfer	A&H:GP
John A. Gilmer to George Little	Jul 18	conscription	A&H:GP
H.T. Farmer et al. to ZBV	Jul 18	conscription	A&H:GP
B.C. Lankford to ZBV	Jul 18	detail	A&H:GP
Bayles M. Edney to ZBV	Jul 18	conscription	A&H:GP
William D. Whitted to ZBV	Jul 18	conscription	A&H:GP
M. Fain to ZBV	Jul 18	disloyalty	A&H:GP
E.H. Hornaday to ZBV	Jul 18	appointment	A&H:GP
Louis G. Young to ZBV	Jul 18	J.J. Pettigrew	A&H:GP
Wilson L. Temple to ZBV	Jul 18	discharge	A&H:GP
N.L. Williams to ZBV	Jul 19	passport	A&H:GP
W.H. McNeil to ZBV	Jul 19	desertion	A&H:GP
D.F. Ramsour to ZBV	Jul 19	disloyalty	A&H:GP
Elizabeth Sampson to ZBV	Jul 19	poor relief	A&H:GP
Robert R. Heath to ZBV	Jul 19	civil unrest	A&H:GP
Theodore J. Hughes to ZBV	Jul 19	blockade	A&H:GP
James G. Gibbes to ZBV	Jul 19	prohibit export	A&H:GP
Jesse P. Williams to ZBV	Jul 19	troops	A&H:GP
Joseph Rosser to ZBV	Jul 19	conscription	A&H:GP
James A.J. Bradford to ZBV	Jul 20 (1)	Federal raid	A&H:GP
James A.J. Bradford to ZBV	Jul 20 (2)	Federal raid	A&H:GP
James A.J. Bradford to ZBV	Jul 20 (3)	Federal raid	A&H:GP
James A.J. Bradford to ZBV	Jul 20 (4)	Federal raid	A&H:GP
James A.J. Bradford to ZBV	Jul 20 (5)	Federal raid	A&H:GP
Elizabeth J. Garrison et al. to ZBV	Jul 20	slave patrol	A&H:GP
Hugh Rice to ZBV	Jul 20	lathe	A&H:GP
James Hicks to ZBV	Jul 20	desertion	A&H:GP
Richard Harris et al. to ZBV	Jul 20	conscription	A&H:GP
George Little to ZBV	Jul 20	Federal raid	A&H:GP
Edward D. Hall to ZBV	Jul 20	promotion	A&H:GP

Correspondents	Date	Subject	Repository
J.S. Timberlake to ZBV	Jul 20	appointment	A&H:GP
G.W. Cox to ZBV	Jul 20	habeas corpus	A&H:GP
D. Maxwell to ZBV	Jul 20	conscription	A&H:GP
William M. Brooks to ZBV	Jul 20	appointment	A&H:GP
William Richardson to ZBV	Jul 20	discharge	A&H:GP
William J. Saunders to ZBV	Jul 20	Federal raid	A&H:GP
David A. Barnes to ZBV	Jul 20	Federal raid	A&H:GP
Louis G. Young to ZBV	Jul 20	J.J. Pettigrew	A&H:GP
John L. Doggett to ZBV	Jul 20	appointment	A&H:GP
S.P. Frederick to ZBV	Jul 20	appointment	A&H:GP
William Flanekin to ZBV	Jul 20	conscription	A&H:GP
James A.J. Bradford to ZBV	Jul 21	Federal raid	A&H:GP
James G. Martin to ZBV	Jul 21	Federal raid	A&H:GP
N. Bowen et al. to ZBV	Jul 21	conscription	A&H:GP
J. Cline to ZBV	Jul 21	salt	A&H:GP
Nathaniel A. Boyden to ZBV	Jul 21	conscription	A&H:GP
John L. Roberts to ZBV	Jul 21	furlough	A&H:GP
Thomas J. Dark to ZBV	Jul 21	conscription	A&H:GP
Clement Dowd to ZBV	Jul 21	appointment	A&H:GP
Mrs. Nathaniel M. Hill to ZBV	Jul 21	conscription	A&H:GP
A.J. Troy to ZBV	Jul 21	conscription	A&H:GP
Martha W. Nowell et al. to ZBV	Jul 21	poor relief	A&H:GP
N.A. Miller to ZBV	Jul 21	desertion	A&H:GP
J.B. McKinnon to ZBV	Jul 21	transfer	A&H:GP
James E. Griffith et al. to ZBV	Jul 21	conscription	A&H:GP
John C. Lamb to ZBV	Jul 21	Federal raid	A&H:GP
C.D. Smith et al. to ZBV	Jul 21	conscription	A&H:GP
Richard S. Donnell to ZBV	Jul 21	conscription	A&H:GP
James A.J. Bradford to ZBV	Jul 21	Federal raid	A&H:GP
Jennette E. Loudermilk et al. to ZBV	Jul 21	civil unrest	A&H:GP
Hillsboro cadets to ZBV	Jul 21	volunteer	A&H:GP
W.G. White to Charles S. Carrington	Jul 21	horse thieves	A&H:GP
T.S. Lindsay to Joel Griffin	Jul 21	horses	A&H:GP
James A. Seddon to ZBV	Jul 21	discharge	A&H:VanPC
W.W. Smith to ZBV	Jul 22	appointment	A&H:GP
John M. Worth to ZBV	Jul 22 (1)	conscription	A&H:GP
John M. Worth to ZBV	Jul 22 (2)	resignation	A&H:GP
John M. Worth to ZBV	Jul 22 (3)	recommendation	A&H:GP
John C. Tynes & George T. Darden to ZBV	Jul 22	appointment	A&H:GP
David A. Barnes to Thomas C. Rickes	Jul 22	cotton export	A&H:GP
Murchison Reid Co. to ZBV	Jul 22	yarn	A&H:GP
Oscar G. Parsley to ZBV	Jul 22	conscription	A&H:GP
Samuel P. Moore to ZBV	Jul 22	hospitals	A&H:GP
Samuel F. Phillips to ZBV	Jul 22	clerk	A&H:GP
Duncan K. McRae to ZBV	Jul 22	bonds	A&H:GLB
Francis E. Shober to ZBV	Jul 23	conscription	A&H:GP
Mrs. Joseph Graham to ZBV	Jul 23	appointment	A&H:GP
H.L. Steed to ZBV	Jul 23	desertion	A&H:GP
Mrs. Thomas J. Womack to ZBV	Jul 23	conscription	A&H:GP
James A.J. Bradford to ZBV	Jul 23	Federal raid	A&H:GP

Correspondents	Date	Subject	Repository
Anonymous to ZBV	Jul 23	disloyalty	A&H:GP
Berry Thomas to ZBV	Jul 23	transfer	A&H:GP
James M. Leach to ZBV	Jul 23	conscription	A&H:GP
Preston Wilson to ZBV	Jul 23	petition	A&H:GP
W.D. Barkley to ZBV	Jul 23	appointment	A&H:GP
Amos J. Battle to ZBV	Jul 23	Federal raid	A&H:GP
A.R. Bryan to ZBV	Jul 23	C. Leventhorpe	A&H:GP
Allen T. Davidson et al. to ZBV	Jul 23	conscription	A&H:GP
James Hollomon to ZBV	Jul 24	discharge	A&H:GP
T.C. Hooper to ZBV	Jul 24	appointment	A&H:GP
James Patton to ZBV	Jul 24	conscription	A&H:GP
William P. Bynum to ZBV	Jul 24	conscription	A&H:GP
Anonymous to ZBV	Jul 24	hospital	A&H:GP
Richard Morton to ZBV	Jul 24	conscription	A&H:GP
Richard Anderson to ZBV	Jul 24	discharge	A&H:GP
H.K. Patton to ZBV	Jul 24	appointment	A&H:GP
Garrison Green to ZBV	Jul 24	note	A&H:GP
W.R. Moore Jr. et al. to ZBV	Jul 24	volunteer	A&H:GP
Samuel B. French to ZBV	Jul 25	Jackson statue	A&H:GP
William Long to ZBV	Jul 25	conscription	A&H:GP
Jesse P. Brown to ZBV	Jul 25	Federal raid	A&H:GP
Charles E. Cosley to ZBV	Jul 25	horse theft	A&H:GP
H.M. Dewers to ZBV	Jul 25	discharge	A&H:GP
Louena Cates to ZBV	Jul 25	cotton yarn	A&H:GP
J.G. Lockhart to ZBV	Jul 25	prohibit export	A&H:GP
John Faucett, certification	Jul 25	cotton export	A&H:GP
Daniel H. Hill to ZBV	Jul 25	Federal raids	A&H:VanPC
Robert Graham, commission	Jul 25	lieutenant	SHC:Gra
D.N. Gore to ZBV	Jul 26	conscription	A&H:GP
W.W. Gaither to ZBV	Jul 26	appointment	A&H:GP
Lloyd T. Jones to ZBV	Jul 26	appointment	A&H:GP
G.H. Boman to ZBV	Jul 26	appointment	A&H:GP
Harris Tyson to ZBV	Jul 26	peace	A&H:GP
J.H. Gadsby to ZBV	Jul 26	furlough	A&H:GP
J. Cline to ZBV	Jul 27	salt workers	A&H:GP
Mary Anne Osborne to ZBV	Jul 27	special court	A&H:GP
Oscar G. Parsley to ZBV	Jul 27	salt comm.	A&H:GP
W.P. Taylor to ZBV	Jul 27	conscription	A&H:GP
J.W. Johnson to ZBV	Jul 27	Federal raid	A&H:GP
William H.C. Whiting to ZBV	Jul 27	Federal attack	A&H:GP
T. Brown Venable to ZBV	Jul 27	Federal raid	A&H:GP
James H. Hill to ZBV	Jul 27	artillery	A&H:GP
James A.J. Bradford to ZBV	Jul 27	Federal raid	A&H:GP
Samuel McLeod to ZBV	Jul 27	transfer	A&H:GP
Richard Sterling to ZBV	Jul 27	bonds	A&H:GP
C.G. Perkins to ZBV	Jul 27	habeas corpus	A&H:GP
Thomas V. Roberts to ZBV	Jul 27	prohibit export	A&H:GP
Stephen B. Evans to ZBV	Jul 27	Reg't transfer	A&H:GP
William R. Utley & Joseph H. Flanner to ZBV	Jul 27	salt comm.	A&H:GP
Joshua Carman Jr. to ZBV	Jul 27	desertion	A&H:GP

Correspondents	Date	Subject	Repository
Urial J. Cates Jr. to ZBV	Jul 27	arrest	A&H:GP
Mary M. Gaines to ZBV	Jul 27	father	A&H:GP
Jeremiah Glover to ZBV	Jul 27	discharge	A&H:GP
A.G. Halyburton to ZBV	Jul 27	appointment	A&H:GP
W.C. Walker to ZBV	Jul 27	civil unrest	A&H:GP
B.J. Smith et al. to James A. Seddon	Jul 27	disloyalty	A&H:GP
Travis H. Smith to ZBV	Jul 28	cadets	A&H:GP
A.D. Bracy to ZBV	Jul 28	conscription	A&H:GP
D. McD. Lindsey to ZBV	Jul 28	Federal raid	A&H:GP
Mary Ann Buie to ZBV	Jul 28	soldiers' aid	A&H:GP
Joseph Kenner et al. to ZBV	Jul 28	conscription	A&H:GP
William A. Graham Jr. to ZBV	Jul 28	Reg't comm.	A&H:GP
Mrs. Peyton Atkinson to ZBV	Jul 28	Federal raid	A&H:GP
James Page et al. to ZBV	Jul 28	civil unrest	A&H:GP
Randal M. Moore to ZBV	Jul 28	hardship	A&H:GP
M.O. Dickerson to ZBV	Jul 29	elections	A&H:GP
William J. Clarke to ZBV	Jul 29	Federal raid	A&H:GP
Martha H. Williams to ZBV	Jul 29	poor relief	A&H:GP
J.G. Lockhart to ZBV	Jul 29	Federal raid	A&H:GP
Simon Watson to ZBV	Jul 29	conscription	A&H:GP
Amos J. Battle to ZBV	Jul 29	Federal raid	A&H:GP
Nicholas W. Woodfin to ZBV	Jul 29	salt	A&H:GP
M.F. Puckett to ZBV	Jul 29	conscription	A&H:GP
W.J. Hogan to ZBV	Jul 29	prohibit export	A&H:GP
M.O. Dickerson to ZBV	Jul 29	resignation	A&H:GP
Ed C. Fisher to ZBV	Jul 29	insane asylum	A&H:GP
John H. Winder to ZBV	Jul 29	letters	A&H:VanPC
A.M. Powell to ZBV	Jul 30	prohibit export	A&H:GP
D.B. Bell to ZBV	Jul 30	Federal raid	A&H:GP
J.G. Lockhart to ZBV	Jul 30	Federal raid	A&H:GP
Blackman H. Culbreth to ZBV	Jul 30	appointment	A&H:GP
Elizabeth Chamberlain to ZBV	Jul 30	discharge	A&H:GP
W.F. Hunt to ZBV	Jul 30	petition	A&H:GP
Thomas M. Crossan to John White	Jul 30	blockade	A&H:GP
A. Hobson et al. to ZBV	Jul 30	volunteers	A&H:GP
A.G. McCray to ZBV	Jul 30	poor relief	A&H:GP
R.N. Hager to ZBV	Jul 31	desertion	A&H:GP
A.J. Moses to ZBV	Jul 31	prohibit export	A&H:GP
T.A. Allen to ZBV	Jul 31	unfit soldier	A&H:GP
William P. Bynum to ZBV	Jul 31	peace	A&H:GP
Elizia Godward to ZBV	Jul 31	discharge	A&H:GP
Jesse G. Shepherd to ZBV	Jul 31	son	A&H:VanPC
Calvin H. Wiley to ZBV	Jul 31	manuscript	A&H:VanPC
W.C. Morris et al. to ZBV	Jul n.d.	conscription	A&H:GP
R.W. Hill to ZBV	Jul n.d.	disaffection	A&H:GP
Louis G. Young to ZBV	Jul n.d.	J.J. Pettigrew	A&H:GP
Ellen Rivenbark et al. to ZBV	Jul n.d.	conscription	A&H:GP
E.Q.M.C. Robbins to ZBV	Jul n.d.	conscription	A&H:GP
J.M. Wilson to ZBV	Jul n.d.	Robert Vance	A&H:VanPC
M.W. Campbell to Daniel G. Fowle	Aug 1	conscription	A&H:GP
John M. Galloway et al. to ZBV	Aug 1	63rd Reg't	A&H:GP

Correspondents	Date	Subject	Repository
Thomas Webb to ZBV	Aug 1	r.r. arms	A&H:GP
William G. Jordan to ZBV	Aug 1	prohibit export	A&H:GP
Daniel I. Dreher to ZBV	Aug 1	speculation	A&H:GP
Wesley McIver to ZBV	Aug 1	conscription	A&H:GP
Joseph S. Pender to ZBV	Aug 1	blockade	A&H:GP
D.M. Hicks to ZBV	Aug 1	detail	A&H:GP
Stephen B. Evans to James H. Hill	Aug 1	63rd Reg't	A&H:VanPC
Stephen Lee to ZBV	Aug 2	home guards	A&H:GP
Horace R. Chappell to ZBV	Aug 2	transfer	A&H:GP
E.R. Liles to ZBV	Aug 2	habeas corpus	A&H:GP
Devoted Friend to Dearest Friend	Aug 2	hardship	A&H:VanPC
N.P. Beck to ZBV	Aug 3	personal grudge	A&H:GP
J.P. McPherson to ZBV	Aug 3	substitution	A&H:GP
John H. Haughton to ZBV	Aug 3	substitution	A&H:GP
James Sloan to David A. Barnes	Aug 3	complaint	A&H:GP
Aaron Peterson to ZBV	Aug 3	conscription	A&H:GP
John A. Sykes to ZBV	Aug 3	conscription	A&H:GP
John J.C. Steele to ZBV	Aug 3	shoes	A&H:GP
O.S. Hanner to ZBV	Aug 3	desertion	A&H:GP
B.J. Egerton to ZBV	Aug 3	appointment	A&H:GP
William Medlock to ZBV	Aug 3	distilling	A&H:GP
Otis F. Manson to ZBV	Aug 3	hospital	A&H:GP
T.P. Thomas to ZBV	Aug 4	prohibit export	A&H:GP
Bayles M. Edney to ZBV	Aug 4	faded	A&H:GP
E.H. Fulenwider to ZBV	Aug 4	salt	A&H:GP
John W. Patton to ZBV	Aug 5	desertion	A&H:GP
Jesse Jackson to ZBV	Aug 5	conscription	A&H:GP
John D. Hudson to ZBV	Aug 5	discharge	A&H:GP
Jesse Towns to ZBV	Aug 5	discharge	A&H:GP
Octavius H. Blockers to ZBV	Aug 5	desertion	A&H:GP
James F. Dean to ZBV	Aug 5	desertion	A&H:GP
Henry Eubank to ZBV	Aug 6	distilling	A&H:GP
William M. Sutton to ZBV	Aug 6	appointment	A&H:GP
Betty Norman to ZBV	Aug 6	speculation	A&H:GP
N.S. Patterson to ZBV	Aug 6	support	A&H:GP
I.C. Sinclair to ZBV	Aug 7	foreigners	A&H:GP
P.J. Sinclair to ZBV	Aug 7	foreigners	A&H:GP
J.M. Happoldt to ZBV	Aug 7	transfer	A&H:GP
J. Johnston to ZBV	Aug 7	conscription	A&H:GP
J.A. Weston to ZBV	Aug 7	appointment	A&H:GP
M.A. Gay to ZBV	Aug 8	conscription	A&H:GP
Samuel B. French to ZBV	Aug 8	Jackson Statue	A&H:GP
James A. Seddon to ZBV	Aug 8	conscription	A&H:GP
Jones Mendenhall & Co. to ZBV	Aug 8	iron works	A&H:GP
George N. Sanders to ZBV	Aug 8	naval stores	A&H:GP
N. Dunn to ZBV	Aug 8	prohibit export	A&H:GP
Alfred Gibson to ZBV	Aug 9	conscription	A&H:GP
William G. Thomas to ZBV	Aug 9	transfer	A&H:GP
Nancy Royal to ZBV	Aug 9	violence	A&H:GP
J.M. Happoldt to ZBV	Aug 10	transfer	A&H:GP
Mrs. M.M. Warner to ZBV	Aug 10	furlough	A&H:GP

Correspondents	Date	Subject	Repository
John B. Herring to ZBV	Aug 10	discharge	A&H:GP
Elijah Ames to ZBV	Aug 10	discharge	A&H:GP
Zebedee Barnes to ZBV	Aug 10	appointment	A&H:GP
N.T. Bowdon to ZBV	Aug 10	desertion	A&H:GP
S. Barron to ZBV	Aug 10	resolutions	A&H:GP
Jacob C. Barnhardt to ZBV	Aug 10	prohibit export	A&H:GP
T.J. Dula to ZBV	Aug 10	transfer	A&H:GP
John C. Boyd to ZBV	Aug 10	substitution	A&H:GP
A.A. McKethan to ZBV	Aug 10	poor relief	A&H:GP
W.B. Lane to ZBV	Aug 11	civil unrest	A&H:GP
Hugh Rice to ZBV	Aug 11	gratitude	A&H:GP
Thomas A. Branson to ZBV	Aug 11	desertion	A&H:GP
Soldier to ZBV	Aug 11	hospital	A&H:GP
Nancy Hall et al. to ZBV	Aug 11	conscription	A&H:GP
John Herring to ZBV	Aug 11	pardon	A&H:GP
Thomas P. Johnston to ZBV	Aug 12	appointment	A&H:GP
W. Murdock to ZBV	Aug 12	disaffection	A&H:GP
W.H. Stone to ZBV	Aug 12	buttons & lace	A&H:GP
Francis E. Shober to ZBV	Aug 12	Salisbury Prison	A&H:GP
Edward J. Hale to ZBV	Aug 12 (1)	peace	A&H:VanPC
Edward J. Hale to ZBV	Aug 12 (2)	civil unrest	A&H:VanPC
James A. Hague to ZBV	Aug 13	passport	A&H:GP
Alethea A. Crowell to ZBV	Aug 13	speculation	A&H:GP
W.M. Munday to ZBV	Aug 13	passport	A&H:GP
W.W. Gaither to ZBV	Aug 13	peace	A&H:GP
John Letcher to ZBV	Aug 13	free blacks	A&H:GP
D.H. Hamilton Jr. to ZBV	Aug 14	appointment	A&H:GP
A.G. Halyburton to ZBV	Aug 14	appointment	A&H:GP
James Cassius L. Gudger to ZBV	Aug 14	25th Reg't	A&H:GP
Bayles M. Edney to ZBV	Aug 14	civil unrest	A&H:GP
Penninah Dixon to ZBV	Aug 14	conscription	A&H:GP
A.C. Wentz to ZBV	Aug 14	passport	A&H:GP
Y.W. Johnstone to ZBV	Aug 14	peace	A&H:GP
Eli Starr to ZBV	Aug 14	detail	A&H:GP
Jackson T. Taylor to ZBV	Aug 14	prohibit export	A&H:GP
W.F. French to ZBV	Aug 15	desertion	A&H:GP
Issac Arledge to ZBV	Aug 15	yarn	A&H:GP
Soldier to ZBV	Aug 15	hospital	A&H:GP
Edrith Odaniel to ZBV	Aug 15	deprivation	A&H:GP
Alexander R. Lawton to ZBV	Aug 15	appointment	A&H:VanPC
Joseph H. Flanner to ZBV	Aug 16	*Advance*	A&H:GP
William Lamb to ZBV	Aug 16	*Advance*	A&H:GP
M.D. Laney to ZBV	Aug 16	furlough	A&H:GP
Jesse Sentell et al. to ZBV	Aug 16	teacher	A&H:GP
Samuel E. Wilson, oath	Aug 16	corn	A&H:GP
H.P. Langley to ZBV	Aug 17	transfer	A&H:GP
F.R. Holland to ZBV	Aug 17	passport	A&H:GP
Richmond M. Pearson, court order	Aug 17	discharge	A&H:GP
Nancy Green to ZBV	Aug 17	discharge	A&H:GP
W.B. Gainey to ZBV	Aug 17	conscription	A&H:GP
Peter Newton to ZBV	Aug 17	desertion	A&H:GP

Correspondents	Date	Subject	Repository
Calvin H. Wiley to ZBV	Aug 17	publishing	A&H:GP
James A. Seddon to ZBV	Aug 18	passport	A&H:GP
J.F. Forman to ZBV	Aug 18	disability	A&H:GP
A.M. Powell to ZBV	Aug 18	prohibit export	A&H:GP
J.H. Pless to ZBV	Aug 18	transfer	A&H:GP
J. William Barnes to ZBV	Aug 18	steamer passage	A&H:GP
Richard H. Northrop to ZBV	Aug 18	passport	A&H:GP
R.M. Smith to ZBV	Aug 18	W.W. Holden	A&H:VanPC
John D. Whitford to ZBV	Aug 19	r.r. iron	A&H:GP
William H. Harvey to John D. Whitford	Aug 19	r.r. iron	A&H:GP
Thomas J. Hughes to ZBV	Aug 19	blockade	A&H:GP
Thomas M. Egerton to ZBV	Aug 19	prohibit export	A&H:GP
Mary E. Edwards to ZBV	Aug 19	poor relief	A&H:GP
S.W. Pittman to ZBV	Aug 19	discharge	A&H:GP
Thomas M. Neely to ZBV	Aug 19	conscription	A&H:GP
Robert W. Taylor to ZBV	Aug 19	steamer berth	A&H:GP
Otis F. Manson to ZBV	Aug 19	recommendation	A&H:GP
Sally A. Long to ZBV	Aug 20	deprivation	A&H:GP
Joseph H. Flanner to ZBV	Aug 20	*Advance*	A&H:GP
Jesse H. Lindsay to ZBV	Aug 20	conscription	A&H:GP
Stephen D. Pool to Daniel G. Fowle	Aug 20	Robert Griffin	A&H:GP
W.F. Sandford to ZBV	Aug 20	poor relief	A&H:GP
William H.C. Whiting to ZBV	Aug 20	impressed slaves	A&H:GP
John H. Hall to ZBV	Aug 20	prohibit export	A&H:GP
G.W. Nicholson to ZBV	Aug 20 (1)	salt	A&H:GP
G.W. Nicholson to ZBV	Aug 20 (2)	r.r. transport	A&H:GP
Thomas Allen to ZBV	Aug 20	prohibit export	A&H:GP
John White, invoices	Aug 20	purchases	A&H:GP
Thomas Fodamead to ZBV	Aug 20	salt	A&H:GP
E.R. Harrington to ZBV	Aug 20	desertion	A&H:GP
Benjamin C. Rush to ZBV	Aug 21	passport	A&H:GP
B.G. Steele et al. to ZBV	Aug 21	detail	A&H:GP
Rebecak Sellers to ZBV	Aug 21	discharge	A&H:GP
David J. Corpening to Peter Mallet	Aug 21	conscription	A&H:GP
Jannie Jones to ZBV	Aug 21	cotton cards	A&H:GP
William A. Graham to ZBV	Aug 21	advice	A&H:VanPC
Theodore Sikes to ZBV	Aug 22	conscription	A&H:GP
W. Murdock to ZBV	Aug 22	black soldiers	A&H:GP
Francis H. Smith to ZBV	Aug 22	prohibit export	A&H:GP
James R. McDonald to ZBV	Aug 22	transfer	A&H:GP
A.A. Scroggs to ZBV	Aug 22	distilling	A&H:GP
William M. Hannah, certification	Aug 22	cotton thread	A&H:GP
Joseph H. Flanner to ZBV	Aug 22	*Advance*	A&H:VanPC
Calvin H. Wiley to ZBV	Aug 22	peace	A&H:VanPC
David J. Corpening to ZBV	Aug 23	conscription	A&H:GP
Temperance Tise to ZBV	Aug 23	discharge	A&H:GP
Sewall L. Fremont to ZBV	Aug 23	*Advance*	A&H:GP
A.D. Lamont to ZBV	Aug 23	discharge	A&H:GP
William Huffman to ZBV	Aug 24	desertion	A&H:GP
John H. Wheeler to ZBV	Aug 24	documents	A&H:GP
W.W. Phelan to ZBV	Aug 24	appointment	A&H:GP

Correspondents	Date	Subject	Repository
John Knote to Joseph Hierholzer	Aug 24	leather	A&H:GP
R.H. Morence to ZBV	Aug 24	prohibit export	A&H:GP
John C. Carson to ZBV	Aug 24	appointment	A&H:GP
John Brown to ZBV	Aug 24	desertion	A&H:GP
William H.C. Whiting to ZBV	Aug 24	Wilmington	A&H:GP
Edward J. Warren to ZBV	Aug 24	steamer passage	A&H:GP
William J. Martin to ZBV	Aug 24	desertion	A&H:GP
Francis E. Shober to ZBV	Aug 24	Western NCRR	A&H:GP
Mrs. George N. Sanders to ZBV	Aug 24	letters	A&H:GP
William T. Dortch to ZBV	Aug 24	steamer passage	A&H:GP
William L. Love to ZBV	Aug 24	appointment	A&H:GP
Charles S. Carrington to ZBV	Aug 24	recommendation	A&H:VanPC
William H.C. Whiting to James A. Seddon	Aug 24	Wilmington	A&H:VanPC
Robert V. Blackstock to ZBV	Aug 24	peace	A&H:VanPC
Samuel Barron to ZBV	Aug 24	appointment	A&H:VanPC
Lucius H. Smith to ZBV	Aug 25	requisition	A&H:GP
Edwin Shelton to ZBV	Aug 25	prohibit export	A&H:GP
R.H.D. Bullock to ZBV	Aug 25	special pass	A&H:GP
Edward J. Hale to ZBV	Aug 25	letter	A&H:GP
A. Sinclair to ZBV	Aug 25	appointment	A&H:GP
Mrs. T. Atkinson to ZBV	Aug 25	protection	A&H:GP
M.M. Miller to ZBV	Aug 25	appointment	A&H:GP
Samuel N. Mc[illegible] to ZBV	Aug 25	prohibit export	A&H:GP
Pride Jones to ZBV	Aug 25	cotton cards	A&H:GP
David G. Cuthbertson to ZBV	Aug 25	disloyalty	A&H:GP
Matt W. Ransom to ZBV	Aug 26	free blacks	A&H:GP
Daniel G. Fowle to ZBV	Aug 26	home guards	A&H:GP
Edward Warren to ZBV	Aug 26	recommendation	A&H:GP
Mrs. M.L. Pearson to ZBV	Aug 26	appointment	A&H:GP
Henry O. Dixon to ZBV	Aug 26	transfer	A&H:GP
W.G. Boudinot to ZBV	Aug 26	command	A&H:GP
Alexander R. Lawton to ZBV	Aug 26	yarn	A&H:GP
Thomas J. Pitchford et al. to ZBV	Aug 26	support	A&H:GP
Charles B. Mallett to ZBV	Aug 27	coal	A&H:GP
Dorsett Brown to ZBV	Aug 27	Jackson statue	A&H:GP
John Roberts to ZBV	Aug 27	discharge	A&H:GP
J.M. Galloway to ZBV	Aug 27	Confed. currency	A&H:GP
James H. Foote, special order	Aug 27	home guards	SHC:Rob
J.C. Kirkman to ZBV	Aug 27	desertion	SHC:Rob
W.R. Smith to ZBV	Aug 28	desertion	A&H:GP
J.W. Zimmerman to ZBV	Aug 28	appointment	A&H:GP
C.D. Foy to ZBV	Aug 28	rangers	A&H:GP
John H. Poindexter to ZBV	Aug 28	transfer	A&H:GP
John B. Griswold to ZBV	Aug 28	Robert Griffith	A&H:GP
Nancy Braxton to ZBV	Aug 28	destitution	A&H:GP
J.F. Foreman to ZBV	Aug 28	impressment	A&H:GP
H.H. Robinson to ZBV	Aug 28	cotton	A&H:GP
William J. Martin to ZBV	Aug 29	recommendation	A&H:GP
John M. Tate to ZBV	Aug 29	appointment	A&H:GP
E.W. Faucette to ZBV	Aug 29	resignation	A&H:GP
Joseph Hierholzer to John Letcher	Aug 29	leather	A&H:GP

Correspondents	Date	Subject	Repository
J. Walter Browne to ZBV	Aug 29	appointment	A&H:GP
William H.C. Whiting to ZBV	Aug 29	Federal raid	A&H:GP
Isaac H. Foust to ZBV	Aug 29	desertion	A&H:GP
Wake Co. document	Aug 29	Robert Griffith	A&H:GP
Nathaniel R. Jones to ZBV	Aug 29	prohibit export	A&H:GP
Thomas D. Hogg to ZBV	Aug 29	ordnance	A&H:GP
Thomas J. Boykin to ZBV	Aug 30	meeting	A&H:GP
Murdock J. McSween to ZBV	Aug 30	complaint	A&H:GP
Anonymous to ZBV	Aug 30	home guards	A&H:GP
Rufus Y. McAden to ZBV	Aug 30	conscription	A&H:GP
Jonas P. Levy to ZBV	Aug 30	*Advance*	A&H:GP
George W. Highsmith to ZBV	Aug 31	transfer	A&H:GP
A.J. Davis to ZBV	Aug 31	appointment	A&H:GP
David Outlaw to ZBV	Aug 31	prohibit export	A&H:GP
J.C. Whitson to ZBV	Aug 31	disaffection	A&H:GP
Joseph B. Boteholtz to ZBV	Aug 31	speech	A&H:GP
Joseph B. Boteholtz et al. to ZBV	Aug 31	speech	A&H:GP
R.T. Steele to ZBV	Aug 31	conscription	A&H:GP
A.P. Aldrich to ZBV	Aug 31	Charleston	A&H:GP
Isaac H. Foust to ZBV	Aug 31	desertion	A&H:GP
Charles H. Thomas to brother	Aug n.d.	disaffection	A&H:GP
Anonymous to ZBV	Aug n.d.	destitution	A&H:GP
J.W. Hayes to ZBV	Sep 1	home guards	A&H:GP
W.J.S. Miller to ZBV	Sep 1	appointment	A&H:GP
Tolivar Davis to ZBV	Sep 1	peace	A&H:GP
P. Babcock to ZBV	Sep 1	conscription	A&H:GP
John H. Lee to ZBV	Sep 1	disaffection	A&H:GP
J. Brinkley et al. to ZBV	Sep 1	conscription	A&H:GP
Thomas D. Williams to ZBV	Sep 1	appointment	A&H:GP
George Johnson et al. to ZBV	Sep 1	desertion	A&H:GP
William P. Tucker to ZBV	Sep 1	prohibit export	A&H:GP
James W. Strange to ZBV	Sep 1	horse thief	A&H:GP
Alexander Sprunt to Jonathan Worth	Sep 1	*Advance* berth	A&H:GP
John D. Whitford to ZBV	Sep 1	Richard C. Gatlin	A&H:GP
Stephen R. Mallory to ZBV	Sep 2	naval officer	A&H:GP
Elizabeth Jones to ZBV	Sep 2	destitution	A&H:GP
Alex M. Searcy to ZBV	Sep 2	detail	A&H:GP
K.M. McIntyre to ZBV	Sep 2	discharge	A&H:GP
Susan M. Daniel to ZBV	Sep 2	cotton cards	A&H:GP
Mrs. A.E.W. Jones to ZBV	Sep 2	soldier's pay	A&H:GP
Jeptha M. Israel to ZBV	Sep 2	salt	A&H:GP
Nathan H. Gwyn to ZBV	Sep 2	appointment	A&H:GP
Samuel Lander to ZBV	Sep 2	appointment	A&H:GP
Edward J. Hale to ZBV	Sep 2	W.W. Holden	A&H:VanPC
Shubal G. Worth to ZBV	Sep 3	desertion	A&H:GP
W.D. Royster to ZBV	Sep 3	commission	A&H:GP
John D. Whitford to ZBV	Sep 3	r.r. cotton	A&H:GP
T. Brown Venable to ZBV	Sep 3	*Advance*	A&H:GP
J.W. Archer to ZBV	Sep 3	*Advance*	A&H:GP
Azariah G. McCray et al. to ZBV	Sep 3	home guards	A&H:GP
Mary Pilloon to ZBV	Sep 3	desertion	A&H:GP

Correspondents	Date	Subject	Repository
Samuel B. French to ZBV	Sep 4	Jackson statue	A&H:GP
Hiram H. Webb to ZBV	Sep 4	conscription	A&H:GP
John T. Sykes to ZBV	Sep 4	conscription	A&H:GP
James Hemby to ZBV	Sep 4	disaffection	A&H:GP
Thomas Carter to ZBV	Sep 4	coal	A&H:GP
Thomas B. Bailey to ZBV	Sep 4	desertion	A&H:GP
M.A. Bledsoe to ZBV	Sep 4	slavery	A&H:GP
William H. Neave to ZBV	Sep 4	army band	A&H:GP
Commission by ZBV	Sep 4	Samuel M. Tate	SHC:Tate
Beverly Rose to ZBV	Sep 5	coal	A&H:GP
Thomas K. Thomas to ZBV	Sep 5	appointment	A&H:GP
J.H. Gooch to ZBV	Sep 5	conscription	A&H:GP
R.H. Glass to ZBV	Sep 5	prohibit export	A&H:GP
John H. Wheeler to ZBV	Sep 5	*Advance*	A&H:GP
26th Reg't. Band to ZBV	Sep 5	furloughs	A&H:GP
Thomas Miller to ZBV	Sep 5	rice crop	A&H:GP
Amanda M. Nelson to ZBV	Sep 5	destitution	A&H:GP
Edward G. Haywood et al. to ZBV	Sep 5	disloyalty	A&H:GP
John A. Campbell to ZBV	Sep 5	passport	A&H:VanPC
Thomas Ruffin Jr. to ZBV	Sep 6	clothes	A&H:GP
Eli W. Hall to ZBV	Sep 6	conscription	A&H:GP
Eliza Ormon et al. to ZBV	Sep 6	destitution	A&H:GP
Thomas D. Williams to ZBV	Sep 6	appointment	A&H:GP
Augustus S. Merrimon to ZBV	Sep 7	Federal invasion	A&H:GP
Leander S. Gash to ZBV	Sep 7	disaffection	A&H:GP
Thomas Ruffin Jr. to ZBV	Sep 7	supply permit	A&H:GP
Edwin Fulghum to ZBV	Sep 7	poor relief	A&H:GP
Martin Isenhower to ZBV	Sep 7	notes	A&H:GP
W.W. Hampton to ZBV	Sep 7	peace	A&H:GP
W. Howard to ZBV	Sep 7	destitution	A&H:GP
C.P. Gibson to ZBV	Sep 7	desertion	A&H:GP
J.P. Speight to ZBV	Sep 7	conscription	A&H:GP
W.S.B. Mathews to ZBV	Sep 7	printing	A&H:GP
Theodore Andreae to ZBV	Sep 7	conscription	A&H:GP
Rufus K. Speed to ZBV	Sep 7	prohibit export	A&H:GP
Permission by ZBV	Sep 7	passport	Har:Van
Robert F. Hoke to ZBV	Sep 8	cavalry	A&H:GP
Edwin Whitifield to ZBV	Sep 8	conscription	A&H:GP
William H.C. Whiting to ZBV	Sep 8	laborers	A&H:GP
H.A. Troutman to ZBV	Sep 8	prohibit export	A&H:GP
James S. Bridgers to ZBV	Sep 8	desertion	A&H:GP
A.R. Eaves to ZBV	Sep 8	discharge	A&H:GP
Robert C. Hill to ZBV	Sep 8	disaffection	A&H:GP
Soldier's wife to ZBV	Sep 8	desertion	A&H:GP
Henry Peacock to ZBV	Sep 8	discharge	A&H:GP
Richard A. Sterling to ZBV	Sep 8	rosin	A&H:GP
Sarah P. Bowden to ZBV	Sep 8	discharge	A&H:GP
Spicy W. Rhodes to ZBV	Sep 8	poor relief	A&H:GP
Sterling, Campbell & Albright to ZBV	Sep 9	books	A&H:GP
J.M. Seixas to ZBV	Sep 9	coal	A&H:GP
Peter Mallett to ZBV	Sep 9	desertion	A&H:GP

Correspondents	Date	Subject	Repository
A.M. Nesbit to ZBV	Sep 9	desertion	A&H:GP
Rosean Phillips to ZBV	Sep 9	destitution	A&H:GP
Joseph H. Flanner to ZBV	Sep 9	steamer	A&H:GP
Jonathan Smith to ZBV	Sep 9	home guards	A&H:GP
Henry Sewell to ZBV	Sep 9	poor relief	A&H:GP
James Q. McRae to ZBV	Sep 9	free blacks	A&H:GP
Thomas Carter to ZBV	Sep 9	coal	A&H:GP
David G. Worth to ZBV	Sep 9	salt	A&H:GP
Richard C. Gatlin to Lt. Col. Worth	Sep 9	home guards	SHC:Rob
Mrs. M.B. Moore to ZBV	Sep 10	desertion	A&H:GP
J.P. Hand to ZBV	Sep 10	conscription	A&H:GP
Albert T. Summey to ZBV	Sep 10	detail	A&H:GP
John S. McElroy to ZBV	Sep 10	Federal invasion	A&H:GP
John W. McElroy to ZBV	Sep 10	John S. McElroy	A&H:GP
W.S.B. Mathews to ZBV	Sep 10	type machine	A&H:GP
Peter Mallett to ZBV	Sep 10 (1)	R.F. Hoke	A&H:GP
Peter Mallett to ZBV	Sep 10 (2)	riot	A&H:GP
"A non-resident" to ZBV	Sep 10	W.W. Holden	A&H:GP
Leon F. Sensabaugh to ZBV	Sep 10	Federal invasion	A&H:GP
Samuel Cooper to ZBV	Sep 11	24th Reg't	A&H:GP
D. Pinckney Johnston to ZBV	Sep 11	reconstruction	A&H:GP
Alexander Collie to John White	Sep 11	finances	A&H:GP
Pride Jones to ZBV	Sep 11	conscription	A&H:GP
Leander S. Gash to ZBV	Sep 11	disaffection	A&H:GP
Francis M. Parker to ZBV	Sep 11	home guards	A&H:GP
Calvin S. Brown to ZBV	Sep 12	resignation	A&H:GP
Calvin W. Wiley to ZBV	Sep 12	common schools	A&H:GP
Lewis E. Harris to ZBV	Sep 12	r.r. stock	A&H:GP
R.W. Rest to ZBV	Sep 12	poor relief	A&H:GP
John F. Logan to ZBV	Sep 12	appointment	A&H:GP
James H.O. Daniel to ZBV	Sep 12	desertion	A&H:GP
J.A. Poor to ZBV	Sep 12	home guards	A&H:GP
William Dedman to ZBV	Sep 13	suppression	A&H:GP
W.L. James to ZBV	Sep 13	discharge	A&H:GP
Stephen D. Pool to ZBV	Sep 14	supply detention	A&H:GP
W.F. Cowan to ZBV	Sep 14	desertion	A&H:GP
Pro. A. Jones to ZBV	Sep 14	slaves	A&H:GP
Thomas J. Meroney to ZBV	Sep 14	Henry McCoy	A&H:GP
Mary F. Dixon to ZBV	Sep 14	destitution	A&H:GP
James C. Gibson to ZBV	Sep 14	discharge	A&H:GP
Samuel F. Patterson to ZBV	Sep 14	Federal raid	A&H:GP
Edward J. Hale to ZBV	Sep 14	telegraph	A&H:VanPC
James B. Slaughter to ZBV	Sep 15	recommendation	A&H:GP
Alpheus M. Erwin to ZBV	Sep 15	cloth	A&H:GP
Samuel B. French to ZBV	Sep 15	cotton	A&H:GP
Joseph Thompson to ZBV	Sep 15	conscript arrest	A&H:GP
Joseph H. Flanner to ZBV	Sep 15	*Advance*	A&H:GP
William H.C. Whiting to ZBV	Sep 16	engineer	A&H:GP
R.W. Pulliam et al. to ZBV	Sep 16	Federal raid	A&H:GP
William Murdock to ZBV	Sep 16	unionists	A&H:GP
Augustus S. Merrimon to ZBV	Sep 16	conscription	A&H:GP

Correspondents	Date	Subject	Repository
James Sinclair to ZBV	Sep 16	reputation	A&H:GP
Mary J. Strickland to ZBV	Sep 16	desertion	A&H:GP
Henry B. Constable to Coln.	Sep 16	appointment	A&H:GP
Moses L. Holmes to ZBV	Sep 16	detail	A&H:GP
James W. Satchwell to ZBV	Sep 16	Alfred Stanly	A&H:GP
Essay by Hezekiah G. Spruill	Sep 16	war politics	A&H:VanPC
J.L. McKee to ZBV	Sep 17	gift	A&H:GP
William F. Lamkin to ZBV	Sep 17	tax in kind	A&H:GP
S.W. Brewer to ZBV	Sep 17	desertion	A&H:GP
F.A. Collier to ZBV	Sep 17	discharge	A&H:GP
B. Duncan to ZBV	Sep 17	steamer	A&H:GP
James A. Seddon to ZBV	Sep 17	63rd Reg't	A&H:VanPC
William Murdock to ZBV	Sep 18	Federal raid	A&H:GP
Augustus S. Merrimon to ZBV	Sep 18	Shelton Laurel	A&H:GP
Samuel Cooper to ZBV	Sep 18	riots	A&H:GP
Joseph R. Blanton to ZBV	Sep 18	appointment	A&H:GP
Sarah D. to —	Sep 18	conscription	A&H:GP
Jesse Coppedge to ZBV	Sep 18	discharge	A&H:GP
Julia Graham to ZBV	Sep 18	photograph	SHC:Van
William M. Pickett et al. to ZBV	Sep 19	desertion	A&H:GP
John A. Murray to ZBV	Sep 19	prohibit export	A&H:GP
Alfred W. Dockery Jr. to ZBV	Sep 19	cloth	A&H:GP
James W. Satchwell to ZBV	Sep 19	Alfred Stanly	A&H:GP
Anna J. Sanders to ZBV	Sep 20	pamphlet	A&H:GP
William Murdock to ZBV	Sep 20	Federal raid	A&H:GP
Sophia C. Turner to ZBV	Sep 20	cotton cards	A&H:GP
Allen Jordan to ZBV	Sep 20	desertion	A&H:GP
Sanders M. Ingram to ZBV	Sep 20	conscription	A&H:GP
J.G. Cave to ZBV	Sep 20	petition	A&H:GP
Moses O. Sherrill to ZBV	Sep 20	thanks	A&H:VanPC
William Murdock to ZBV	Sep 21	desertion	A&H:GP
J.F. Palmer to ZBV	Sep 21	discharge	A&H:GP
Anonymous to Edward J. Hale and Sons	Sep 21	disaffection	A&H:GP
Ann E. Hodges to ZBV	Sep 21	discharge	A&H:GP
Moses B. Joyner to ZBV	Sep 21	home guards	A&H:GP
James W. Hinton to ZBV	Sep 21	artillery	A&H:GP
Joseph C. Bradshaw, certification	Sep 21	constable	A&H:GP
Commission by ZBV	Sep 21	James A. Graham	SHC:Gra
P.J. Phelps to ZBV	Sep 21	David Orrell	A&H:GP
John W. Blackburn to ZBV	Sep 22	transfer	A&H:GP
Julia A. Hale to ZBV	Sep 22	poor relief	A&H:GP
N. Hunter to ZBV	Sep 22	certification	A&H:GP
Alanson Capehart to ZBV	Sep 22	transfer	A&H:GP
Edward J. Hale to ZBV	Sep 22	W.W. Holden	A&H:VanPC
Robert B. Vance to ZBV	Sep 23	assignment	A&H:GP
Alexander Kelly to ZBV	Sep 23	resignation	A&H:GP
Mrs. Brown & Co. to ZBV	Sep 23	speculation	A&H:GP
W.W. Peirce to ZBV	Sep 24	horse	A&H:GP
Maria L. Lamkin to ZBV	Sep 24	destitution	A&H:GP
George Little to ZBV	Sep 24	poor relief	A&H:GP
Samuel B. French to ZBV	Sep 25	cotton	A&H:GP

Correspondents	Date	Subject	Repository
James W. Hinton to ZBV	Sep 25	conscription	A&H:GP
James A. Seddon to ZBV	Sep 25	local companies	A&H:GP
C.C. Whitehurst to ZBV	Sep 25	appointment	A&H:GP
Richard C. Gatlin, exemption	Sep 25	home guards	SHC:Rob
Theodore Andreae to ZBV	Sep 26	delay	A&H:GP
J. Marshall McCue to ZBV	Sep 26	wool	A&H:GP
Thomas Sparrow to ZBV	Sep 26	Alfred Stanly	A&H:GP
G.W. Philips to W.H. Ash	Sep 26	desertion	A&H:GP
Henry Reed to ZBV	Sep 26	treason	A&H:GP
Abraham C. Myers to ZBV	Sep 26	lard & flour	A&H:VanPC
Rufus C. Barringer to ZBV	Sep 26	cavalry reg't	A&H:VanPC
Stephen Huff et al. to ZBV	Sep 26	unionist	A&H:VanPC
John M. Sides to ZBV	Sep 27	desertion	A&H:GP
John S. McElroy to ZBV	Sep 27	conscript co.	A&H:GP
J.L. Henry to ZBV	Sep 27	commission	A&H:GP
Samuel Tate to ZBV	Sep 27	son	A&H:GP
H.F. Wasley to ZBV	Sep 28	recommendation	A&H:GP
Anonymous to ZBV	Sep 28	speculation	A&H:GP
Henry A. London to ZBV	Sep 28	soldiers' relief	A&H:GP
Robert P. Dick to ZBV	Sep 28	conscription	A&H:GP
Peter E. Hines to ZBV	Sep 28	hospital	A&H:GP
A.W. Harrill to ZBV	Sep 28	conscription	A&H:GP
William Woodward to ZBV	Sep 28	distilling	A&H:GP
Thomas J. Wilson & D.H. Starbuck to ZBV	Sep 28	home guards	A&H:GP
William H.C. Whiting to ZBV	Sep 28	command	A&H:GLB
Henry L. Benning to Samuel Cooper	Sep 28	riots	A&H:GLB
Robert B. Vance to ZBV	Sep 28	equipment	A&H:VanPC
Otis F. Manson to ZBV	Sep 28	appointment	A&H:VanPC
John B. Herring to ZBV	Sep 29	conscription	A&H:GP
David Outlaw et al. to ZBV	Sep 29	local defense	A&H:GP
Robert F. Webb to ZBV	Sep 29	clothing	A&H:GP
Rufus Froneberger to David A. Barnes	Sep 29	aid society	A&H:GP
Lucius B. Northrop to ZBV	Sep 29	subsistence	A&H:GP
Ann E. Hodges to ZBV	Sep 29	discharge	A&H:GP
James A. Seddon to ZBV	Sep 29	passport	A&H:VanPC
Silas A. Sharpe to James C. McRae	Sep 29	John Templeton	SHC:Sha
C.L. Banner to ZBV	Sep 30	distilling	A&H:GP
F.J. Lord to ZBV	Sep 30	desertion	A&H:GP
James Sinclair to ZBV	Sep 30	reputation	A&H:GP
J.W. Ellis to ZBV	Sep 30	discharge	A&H:GP
Dennis J. Calihan to ZBV	Sep 30	desertion	A&H:GP
John L. Morehead to ZBV	Sep 30	gift	A&H:VanPC
George F. Bahnson to ZBV	Sep n.d.	conscription	A&H:GP
N.V. Durham et al. to ZBV	Sep n.d.	tableaux	A&H:VanPC
T.P. Wells et al. to ZBV	Sep n.d.	tableaux	A&H:VanPC
N.V. Durham et al. to Rufus Froneberger	Sep n.d.	tableaux	A&H:VanPC
Mary Knox Woodward to Rufus Froneberger	Sep n.d.	tableaux	A&H:VanPC
Nicholas W. Woodfin to ZBV	Oct 1	salt	A&H:GP
Alexander Collie to John White	Oct 1	blockade	A&H:GP

Correspondents	Date	Subject	Repository
Henry D. Carson to ZBV	Oct 1	destitution	A&H:GP
Lucian Brown to ZBV	Oct 1	desertion	A&H:GP
J. Fields to ZBV	Oct 1	stolen horses	A&H:GP
Edward J. Hale to ZBV	Oct 1	desertion	A&H:GP
Warner Lewis to ZBV	Oct 1	passport	A&H:GP
ZBV to David G. Worth	Oct 1	commission	Duke:Wor
James T. Pearson to ZBV	Oct 2	appointment	A&H:GP
G.L. Mardre to ZBV	Oct 2	cotton cards	A&H:GP
David P. Glass to ZBV	Oct 2	speculation	A&H:GP
Josiah Gorgas et al., agreement	Oct 2	blockade	A&H:GP
James A. Weston to ZBV	Oct 2	blockade	A&H:GP
Matt W. Ransom to ZBV	Oct 2	Capt. Roberts	A&H:GP
Alfred Stanly to ZBV	Oct 2	Federal arrest	A&H:GP
G. M. Roberts to ZBV	Oct 3	appointment	A&H:GP
E.D. Mathews to ZBV	Oct 3	destitution	A&H:GP
L.E. Thompson to ZBV	Oct 3	desertion	A&H:GP
James W. Hinton to ZBV	Oct 3	bacon	A&H:GP
Jabez W. Be[torn] to ZBV	Oct 3	destitution	A&H:GP
James Roberts et al. to ZBV	Oct 3	conscription	A&H:GP
Joseph H. Flanner to John White	Oct 3	blockade	A&H:GP
John V.B. Rogers to Sec. of War	Oct 3	civil unrest	A&H:GP
Murdock J. McSween to ZBV	Oct 3	commission	A&H:GP
Duncan K. McRae to ZBV	Oct 3	bonds	A&H:GLB
Thomas J. Boykin to ZBV	Oct 3	resignation	A&H:VanPC
F.A. Weaver to ZBV	Oct 4	appointment	A&H:VanPC
Warner Lewis to ZBV	Oct 5	passport	A&H:GP
W.G. Hix to ZBV	Oct 5	conscription	A&H:GP
B.W. Alison, statement	Oct 5	R.B. Fulenwiden	A&H:GP
R.B. Fulenwiden to ZBV	Oct 5	prohibit export	A&H:GP
George W. Logan to ZBV	Oct 5	son	A&H:GP
John Templeton to ZBV	Oct 5	arrest	A&H:GP
Samuel McD. Tate to ZBV	Oct 5	promotion	A&H:GP
S.V. Paken to ZBV	Oct 5	appointment	A&H:GP
T.B. Harris to ZBV	Oct 5	slave	A&H:GP
Joseph C. Fincher to ZBV	Oct 6	discharge	A&H:GP
M.L. Brittain to ZBV	Oct 6	home guards	A&H:GP
Murdock J. McSween to ZBV	Oct 6	commission	A&H:GP
J.D. Baker to ZBV	Oct 6	detail	A&H:GP
L.D. McMannen to ZBV	Oct 6	cloth	A&H:GP
Ira R. Gasten to ZBV	Oct 6	blockade	A&H:GP
B.L. Furgurson to ZBV	Oct 6	prohibit export	A&H:GP
J.C. Ives to ZBV	Oct 6	appointment	A&H:GP
Joseph S. Pender to ZBV	Oct 6	blockade	A&H:GP
James T. Roper to ZBV	Oct 6	desertion	A&H:GP
C. Capehart to ZBV	Oct 6	imprisonment	A&H:GP
John A. Craven to ZBV	Oct 6	nephew	A&H:GP
Thomas J. Morrisy to ZBV	Oct 6	desertion	A&H:GP
Samuel F. Phillips to ZBV	Oct 6	script	A&H:VanPC
Lee Dudley Jr. to ZBV	Oct 7	impressment	A&H:GP
James C. Gibson to ZBV	Oct 7	conscription	A&H:GP
N.S. Walker to ZBV	Oct 7	*Advance*	A&H:GP

Correspondents	Date	Subject	Repository
J.R. Bradford to ZBV	Oct 7	prohibit export	A&H:GP
Mrs. M.P. Caudle to ZBV	Oct 7	discharge	A&H:GP
Nancy M. Caldwell to ZBV	Oct 8	desertion	A&H:GP
Joseph H. Flanner to ZBV	Oct 8	*Advance*	A&H:GP
Silas Heady to ZBV	Oct 8	impressment	A&H:GP
N.A. Ramsey to ZBV	Oct 8	desertion	A&H:GP
Sallie A. Carter to ZBV	Oct 8	detail	A&H:GP
William S. Shepherd to ZBV	Oct 8	riots	A&H:GP
William Warren to ZBV	Oct 8	destitution	A&H:GP
W.W. Thomason to ZBV	Oct 8	conscription	A&H:GP
B.H. Lassiter et al. to ZBV	Oct 8	desertion	A&H:GP
James A. Seddon to ZBV	Oct 8	cavalry	A&H:GP
J.L. Henry to ZBV	Oct 8	resignation	A&H:GP
A. Myers to ZBV	Oct 8	gift	A&H:VanPC
Francis E. Shober to ZBV	Oct 8	promotion	A&H:VanPC
F.R. Holland to ZBV	Oct 8	passport	Duke:Van
Richard C. Gatlin, general order	Oct 8	home guards	SHC:Rob
Delphina E. Mendenhall to ZBV	Oct 9	destitution	A&H:GP
Calvin J. Cowles to ZBV	Oct 9	discharge	A&H:GP
J.C. Blocker to ZBV	Oct 9	poor relief	A&H:GP
David A. Barnes, order	Oct 9	James M. Blanton	A&H:GP
C.F. Sussdorff to ZBV	Oct 9	prohibit export	A&H:GP
Anonymous to ZBV	Oct 9	destitution	A&H:GP
Tod R. Caldwell to George Howard	Oct 9	conscription	A&H:GP
Samuel F. Phillips to ZBV	Oct 9	cotton yarn	A&H:GP
John B. Simpson to ZBV	Oct 9	desertion	A&H:GP
J.L. Scott, receipt	Oct 9	flour	A&H:VanPC
John L. Morehead to ZBV	Oct 9	gift	A&H:VanPC
Robert B. Vance to ZBV	Oct 9	conscription	LC:RBV
William E. Barden to ZBV	Oct 10	detail	A&H:GP
William R. Bass to ZBV	Oct 10	local company	A&H:GP
L.G. Jones to ZBV	Oct 10	appointment	A&H:GP
W.T. Davis to ZBV	Oct 10	prohibit export	A&H:GP
Warner Lewis to ZBV	Oct 10	passport	A&H:GP
W.F. Owen to ZBV	Oct 10	desertion	A&H:GP
Ira J. Moss to ZBV	Oct 10	transfer	A&H:GP
J.C. Washington to ZBV	Oct 10	prohibit export	A&H:GP
David Whitaker to ZBV	Oct 10	appointment	A&H:GP
James H. White to ZBV	Oct 10	resignation	A&H:GP
James Sloan to ZBV	Oct 10 (1)	sugar	A&H:GP
James Sloan to ZBV	Oct 10 (2)	*Advance*	A&H:GP
Robert R. Heath to Henry Berrier	Oct 10	habeas corpus	A&H:GP
John W. Blackburn to ZBV	Oct 10	desertion	A&H:GP
Anonymous to ZBV	Oct 10	parole	A&H:GP
Charles D. Sides to ZBV	Oct 11	desertion	A&H:GP
Wiley P. Hampton to ZBV	Oct 11	transfer	A&H:GP
M.M. Williams to ZBV	Oct 11	detail	A&H:GP
Daniel W. Kirkman to ZBV	Oct 12	home guards	A&H:GP
Betsy Lury to ZBV	Oct 12	desertion	A&H:GP
J.W. Archer to J.M. Seixas	Oct 12	cotton	A&H:GP
Mont. Patton to ZBV	Oct 12	cloth	A&H:GP

Correspondents	Date	Subject	Repository
Joseph H. Flanner to ZBV	Oct 12	steamer	A&H:GP
Jacob Herring to ZBV	Oct 12	desertion	A&H:GP
A.M. Powell to ZBV	Oct 12	desertion	A&H:GP
John A. Campbell to ZBV	Oct 12	riots	A&H:GLB
Robert V. Blackstock to ZBV	Oct 12	tax collector	A&H:VanPC
Thomas Waller to ZBV	Oct 13	desertion	A&H:GP
Joseph T. Worff to ZBV	Oct 13	conscription	A&H:GP
H.A. D[ew] to ZBV	Oct 13	blockade	A&H:GP
Benjamin Deboard et al. to ZBV	Oct 13	conscription	A&H:GP
William R. Skinner to ZBV	Oct 13	substitution	A&H:GP
Robert R. Heath to A.S. Wagoner	Oct 13	habeas corpus	A&H:GP
David M. Young, receipt	Oct 13	beef	A&H:GP
P.R. Harden to ZBV	Oct 13	disloyalty	A&H:VanPC
Albert T. Summey to Harriette Vance	Oct 13	Asheville house	A&H:VanPC
Elijah Ladd to ZBV	Oct 14	malfeasance	A&H:GP
Anonymous to ZBV	Oct 14	speculation	A&H:GP
Harling Falkner to ZBV	Oct 14	transportation	A&H:GP
Delphina E. Mendenhall to ZBV	Oct 14	poor relief	A&H:GP
A. Myers to ZBV	Oct 14	flour	A&H:VanPC
David L. Swain to ZBV	Oct 15	destitution	A&H:GP
David F. West to ZBV	Oct 15	desertion	A&H:GP
William G.M. Davis to ZBV	Oct 15	readiness	A&H:GP
D.S. Latham to ZBV	Oct 15	transfer	A&H:GP
Thomas Sparks to ZBV	Oct 15	land sale	A&H:GP
Henry A. London to ZBV	Oct 15	poor relief	A&H:GP
William H. Harrison to ZBV	Oct 15	endorsement	A&H:GP
Henry A. Dowd to ZBV	Oct 15 (1)	steamer	A&H:GP
Henry A. Dowd to ZBV	Oct 15 (2)	steamer	A&H:GP
George Little to ZBV	Oct 15	Advance	A&H:GP
A.M. Veazey to David A. Barnes	Oct 15	poor relief	A&H:GP
Sarah D. Jones to ZBV	Oct 15	disloyalty	A&H:GP
James A. Seddon to ZBV	Oct 15	Advance	A&H:VanPC
A.W. Gilliam to Tod Caldwell	Oct 16	conscription	A&H:GP
Thomas Miller to ZBV	Oct 16	speculation	A&H:GP
John D. Whitford to ZBV	Oct 16	cotton	A&H:GP
Pattie Vernon to ZBV	Oct 16	desertion	A&H:GP
Joseph H. Flanner to ZBV	Oct 16	steamer	A&H:GP
Joseph H. Flanner to ZBV	Oct 17	steamer	A&H:GP
James Sloan to ZBV	Oct 17	detail	A&H:GP
E. Morgan et al. to ZBV	Oct 17	detail	A&H:GP
Jesse Kinley to ZBV	Oct 17	desertion	A&H:GP
G.C. Moses to ZBV	Oct 17	Federal raid	A&H:GP
Andrew McMillan to ZBV	Oct 17	transfer	A&H:GP
J. Cline to ZBV	Oct 17	conscription	A&H:GP
R.A. Russell to ZBV	Oct 17	conscription	A&H:GP
James B. Hope to Thomas Crossan	Oct 17	recommendation	A&H:VanPC
Giles Leitch to ZBV	Oct 18	M.J. McSween	A&H:GP
Jacob Shipton to ZBV	Oct 18	desertion	A&H:GP
Andrew C. Cowles to ZBV	Oct 18	cloth	A&H:GP
Tod R. Caldwell to ZBV	Oct 18	Gilliam & Dalton	A&H:GP
B.D. Rice et al. to ZBV	Oct 19	home guards	A&H:GP

Correspondents	Date	Subject	Repository
Henry A. Dowd to ZBV	Oct 19	permission	A&H:GP
James Anderson to ZBV	Oct 19	r.r. engine	A&H:GP
Sterling, Campbell & Albright to ZBV	Oct 19 (1)	textbooks	A&H:GP
Sterling, Campbell & Albright to ZBV	Oct 19 (2)	textbooks	A&H:GP
Joseph H. Flanner to ZBV	Oct 19	surgeon's pay	A&H:GP
A.B. Romano to ZBV	Oct 19	*Advance*	A&H:GP
ZBV to Peter Mallett	Oct 19	conscription	A&H:GP
John F. Cotton to ZBV	Oct 19	desertion	A&H:GP
Joseph J. Hales to ZBV	Oct 19	poor relief	A&H:GP
F.M. McNeely to ZBV	Oct 19	conscription	A&H:GP
William F. Lynch to James W. Cooke	Oct 19	gunboat materials	A&H:GP
William H. Moize to ZBV	Oct 19	cotton yarn	A&H:GP
J.P. Mabry to ZBV	Oct 19	cotton cards	A&H:GP
Fred G. Roberts to ZBV	Oct 19	appointment	A&H:GP
Thomas M. Crossan to ZBV	Oct 19	conscription	A&H:GP
Calvin J. Cowles to ZBV	Oct 19	disaffection	A&H:VanPC
Veturia A. Drake to ZBV	Oct 20	poor relief	A&H:GP
W.E. Peirce to ZBV	Oct 20	transfer	A&H:GP
John A. Murray to ZBV	Oct 20	slave laborers	A&H:GP
James Anderson to Edward Warren	Oct 20	cotton	A&H:GP
George Hobbs to ZBV	Oct 20	conscription	A&H:GP
S.F. Holder to ZBV	Oct 20	desertion	A&H:GP
Minnie P. Murdock to ZBV	Oct 20	uniform	A&H:GP
John F. Cotton to ZBV	Oct 20	desertion	A&H:GP
James A. Seddon to ZBV	Oct 20 (1)	riots	A&H:VanPC
James A. Seddon to ZBV	Oct 20 (2)	W.H. Marshall	A&H:VanPC
John A. Campbell to ZBV	Oct 20	passports	A&H:VanPC
Thomas E. Skinner to ZBV	Oct 21	arrangements	A&H:GP
Ladies of Goldsboro Soldiers Aid Society to ZBV	Oct 21	soldiers' home	A&H:GP
William Sexton to ZBV	Oct 21	desertion	A&H:GP
Thomas J. Sumner to ZBV	Oct 21	r.r. engine	A&H:GP
J.M. Roper to ZBV	Oct 21	blankets	A&H:GP
Stephen Johnson to ZBV	Oct 21	conscription	A&H:GP
Eli W. Hall to ZBV	Oct 21	r.r. iron	A&H:GP
Robert F. Hoke to ZBV	Oct 21	requisition	A&H:GP
James W. Cooke to ZBV	Oct 21	*Albemarle*	A&H:GP
John Hunt to ZBV	Oct 21	home guards	A&H:GP
Clement Dowd to ZBV	Oct 21	cotton cards	A&H:GP
G.W. Dobson to ZBV	Oct 21	conscription	A&H:GP
J.M. Seixas to ZBV	Oct 21	cotton vouchers	A&H:GP
William F. Lynch to ZBV	Oct 21	r.r. iron	A&H:GP
John H. Haughton to ZBV	Oct 21	appointment	A&H:VanPC
John H. Winder to ZBV	Oct 21	casualty list	A&H:VanPC
C.D. Smith to ZBV	Oct 21	disaffection	A&H:VanPC
James McGaffey to ZBV	Oct 22	desertion	A&H:GP
T.T. Slade to ZBV	Oct 22	cloth	A&H:GP
John J. Guthrie to ZBV	Oct 22	*Advance*	A&H:GP
Donald MacRae to ZBV	Oct 22	iron works	A&H:GP
William T. Joyner to ZBV	Oct 22	prohibit export	A&H:GP
W.S. Foreman to ZBV	Oct 22	command	A&H:GP

Correspondents	Date	Subject	Repository
Richard Vanlandingham et al. to ZBV	Oct 22	conscription	A&H:GP
James R. Dodge to ZBV	Oct 22	conscription	A&H:GP
E.J. Thompson to ZBV	Oct 22	cotton cards	A&H:GP
Gaston Vance to ZBV	Oct 22	transfer	A&H:GP
R.G. Mangum & G.T. Mangum to ZBV	Oct 22	desertion	A&H:GP
Ellis Malone to ZBV	Oct 22	impressed slaves	A&H:GP
Joseph Keener to ZBV	Oct 23	cloth	A&H:GP
Silas A. Sharpe, memorandum	Oct 23	desertion	A&H:GP
S.E. Estes to ZBV	Oct 23	desertion	A&H:GP
D.V. McCracken to ZBV	Oct 23	salt	A&H:GP
Lucius P. McGee to ZBV	Oct 23	pass	A&H:GP
Bartlett Nixion to ZBV	Oct 23	desertion	A&H:GP
John A. Murray to ZBV	Oct 23	desertion	A&H:GP
George E. Pickett to ZBV	Oct 23	desertion	A&H:GP
B.W. Young to ZBV	Oct 24	commission	A&H:GP
James Sloan to ZBV	Oct 24	impressment	A&H:GP
William H.C. Whiting to ZBV	Oct 24	troops	A&H:GP
Clark M. Avery to ZBV	Oct 24	NC brigade	A&H:GP
Richard C. Blankenship to ZBV	Oct 24	desertion	A&H:GP
Bently Yearwood to ZBV	Oct 25	desertion	A&H:GP
Temperance Tise to ZBV	Oct 25	discharge	A&H:GP
Cicero H. Harris to ZBV	Oct 25	transfer	A&H:GP
Elizabeth Herrell to ZBV	Oct 25	discharge	A&H:GP
Branch A. Merrimon to ZBV	Oct 26	urgent business	A&H:GP
B.T. Winston to ZBV	Oct 26	desertion	A&H:GP
Thomas D. Johnson to ZBV	Oct 26	clothing	A&H:GP
Peter E. Hines to ZBV	Oct 26	recommendation	A&H:GP
James W. Hinton to ZBV	Oct 26	Federal raid	A&H:GP
A.R. Homesly to ZBV	Oct 26	mill machinery	A&H:GP
George W. Seagle to ZBV	Oct 26	transfer	A&H:GP
N.L. Griffin to ZBV	Oct 26	detail	A&H:GP
Asa Phelps to ZBV	Oct 26	conscription	A&H:GP
J.M. Blackwood to ZBV	Oct 26	recommendation	A&H:GP
John H. Bryan Jr. to ZBV	Oct 26	bonds	A&H:GP
William R. Raby to ZBV	Oct 27	desertion	A&H:GP
A. Coffey to ZBV	Oct 27	desertion	A&H:GP
William F. Jones et al. to ZBV	Oct 27	pardon	A&H:GP
C.L. Partee to ZBV	Oct 27	cotton cards	A&H:GP
Sue A. Hyman to ZBV	Oct 27	cotton cards	A&H:GP
E.C. Townsend to ZBV	Oct 27	transfer	A&H:GP
Martin V. Moore to ZBV	Oct 27	murder	A&H:GP
Rufus C.D. Beamon to ZBV	Oct 27	impressed slaves	A&H:GP
Alexander Piggott to ZBV	Oct 27	provisions	A&H:GP
John O'Brian to ZBV	Oct 27	train	A&H:GP
Mary Overman to ZBV	Oct 27	arrest	A&H:GP
John S.W. Pearce to ZBV	Oct 27	impressed slaves	A&H:GP
W.E. Peirce to ZBV	Oct 27	transfer	A&H:GP
E. Bryan to ZBV	Oct 27	peace	A&H:VanPC
Edward J. Hale to ZBV	Oct 27	peace	A&H:VanPC
John W. McElroy to ZBV	Oct 28	western NC	A&H:GP

Correspondents	Date	Subject	Repository
Stuart Buchanan & Nicholas W. Woodfin, agreement	Oct 28	salt	A&H:GP
Bettie Coleman to ZBV	Oct 28	M.J. McSween	A&H:GP
A.G. Brenizer to ZBV	Oct 28	ammunition	A&H:GP
Joshua Smith to ZBV	Oct 28	transfer	A&H:GP
R.R. McKissick to ZBV	Oct 28	desertion	A&H:GP
Thomas L. Johnston et al. to ZBV	Oct 28	NC brigade	A&H:GP
William N. Thomas to ZBV	Oct 28	conscription	A&H:GP
Robert B. Sutton to ZBV	Oct 28	free black	A&H:GP
Charles S. Croom to ZBV	Oct 28	reorganization	A&H:GP
Murdock J. McSween to ZBV	Oct 28	trial	A&H:GP
Alexander Collie to John White	Oct 28 (1)	blockade	A&H:GLB
Alexander Collie to John White	Oct 28 (2)	cotton warrants	A&H:GLB
E. Wilkes & Bros. to ZBV	Oct 29	home guards	A&H:GP
John Hall to ZBV	Oct 29	conscription	A&H:GP
Lucinda Glenn to ZBV	Oct 29	cotton yarn	A&H:GP
Betsy Lury to ZBV	Oct 29	desertion	A&H:GP
Chauncey Watson to ZBV	Oct 29	Ebenezer Emmons	A&H:GP
Isaac Thompson to ZBV	Oct 29	desertion	A&H:GP
William H. Battle to Richmond M. Pearson	Oct 29	supreme court	A&H:GP
Henry E. Colton to ZBV	Oct 29	sulphuric acid	A&H:GP
James I. Philips to ZBV	Oct 29	support	A&H:GP
James A. Weston to ZBV	Oct 29 (1)	blockade	A&H:GP
James A. Weston to ZBV	Oct 29 (2)	gift	A&H:VanPC
James A. Seddon to ZBV	Oct 29	NC Brigade	A&H:VanPC
Sewall L. Fremont to ZBV	Oct 30	salt	A&H:GP
Thomas S. Ashe to ZBV	Oct 30	district election	A&H:GP
Mrs. Stephen B. Evans to ZBV	Oct 30	clothing	A&H:GP
James M. Walker to ZBV	Oct 30	poor relief	A&H:GP
William Robinson to ZBV	Oct 30	transfer	A&H:GP
Nancy J. Boyette et al. to ZBV	Oct 30	detail	A&H:GP
John W. McElroy to ZBV	Oct 30	resign threat	A&H:GP
John S. Morgan to ZBV	Oct 30	cong. election	A&H:GP
J.M. Henson to ZBV	Oct 30	family news	A&H:VanPC
Samuel Handy et al. to ZBV	Oct 31	discharge	A&H:GP
John White, account	Oct 31	supplies	A&H:GP
William H.C. Whiting, order	Oct n.d.	clothing	A&H:GP
[torn] Quick to Col. Roper	Oct n.d.	desertion	A&H:GP
An[stis] Carver to ZBV	Oct n.d.	poor relief	A&H:GP
William M. Shipp to ZBV	Nov 1	prohibit export	A&H:GP
Jacob Shipton to ZBV	Nov 1	transfer	A&H:GP
J.M. Gentry to ZBV	Nov 1	remains	A&H:GP
George C. Compton to ZBV	Nov 1	desertion	A&H:GP
T.D. Crawford to ZBV	Nov 1	appointment	A&H:GP
James & B.F. Houston to ZBV	Nov 1	home guards	A&H:GP
Thomas P. Oldham et al. to ZBV	Nov 1	desertion	A&H:GP
William Williams to ZBV	Nov 1	desertion	A&H:GP
Clark M. Avery to R.C. Chilton	Nov 1	transfer	A&H:GP
Clark M. Avery to ZBV	Nov 1	NC Brigade	A&H:GP
M.L. Brittain to ZBV	Nov 1	Goldman Bryson	A&H:GP
J.H. Draughan to ZBV	Nov 2	return reg't.	A&H:GP

Correspondents	Date	Subject	Repository
J.S. Bennick to ZBV	Nov 2	transfer	A&H:GP
M.T. & J. Davidson to ZBV	Nov 2	prohibit export	A&H:GP
C.S. Harris to ZBV	Nov 2	free blacks	A&H:GP
J.K. & M.H. Pinnix to ZBV	Nov 2	prohibit export	A&H:GP
Richard M. Pearson to William H. Battle	Nov 2	Austin decision	A&H:GP
E.D. Snead to ZBV	Nov 2	cloth	A&H:GP
Moses Evens, affidavit	Nov 2	conscription	A&H:GP
Lucas Eastrady to George Little	Nov 2	desertion	A&H:GP
John F. Hoke to ZBV	Nov 2	certification	A&H:GP
Jacob Tise to Richmond M. Pearson	Nov 2	conscription	A&H:GP
Thomas H. Ervin to ZBV	Nov 3	conscription	A&H:GP
James C. McRae to ZBV	Nov 3	conscription	A&H:GP
S.S. Horney to ZBV	Nov 3	poor relief	A&H:GP
S.W. Wallace to Peter Mallett	Nov 3	conscription	A&H:GP
James D. Wilson to ZBV	Nov 3	furlough	A&H:GP
David McAdams to ZBV	Nov 3	impressed slaves	A&H:GP
J.S. Lemmon to Duncan K. McRae	Nov 3	blockade	A&H:GP
George P. Heath to ZBV	Nov 3	furlough	A&H:GP
Oscar R. Hough to ZBV	Nov 3	soldiers' vote	A&H:GP
W.J.T. Miller to ZBV	Nov 3	hogs	A&H:GP
William T. Muse to James B. Hoke	Nov 3	CSA navy	A&H:VanPC
Richard C. Gatlin to Shubal G. Worth	Nov 3	home guards	SHC:Rob
John Withers to ZBV	Nov 4	furlough	A&H:GP
Shubal G. Worth to ZBV	Nov 4	desertion	A&H:GP
Lewis Bond, statement	Nov 4	cong. election	A&H:GP
Stark B. Smith et al., statement	Nov 4	cong. election	A&H:GP
William P. Mitchell, statement	Nov 4	cong. election	A&H:GP
Elizabeth Burmon to ZBV	Nov 4	destitution	A&H:GP
John W.M. Abernathy to ZBV	Nov 4	desertion	A&H:GP
John Letcher to ZBV	Nov 4	extradition	A&H:GP
G.C. Askew et al. to ZBV	Nov 4	conscription	A&H:GP
D.A. Dellers to ZBV	Nov 5	desertion	A&H:GP
William Marshall & William A. Brindell to ZBV	Nov 5	desertion	A&H:GP
Jane Tilley to ZBV	Nov 5	desertion	A&H:GP
Jacob Tise, affidavit	Nov 5	conscription	A&H:GP
John Fraser to ZBV	Nov 5	freight bill	A&H:VanPC
Arthur Charlton to ZBV	Nov 6	salt	A&H:GP
W.H. Collins to ZBV	Nov 6	conscription	A&H:GP
E.J. Aston to ZBV	Nov 6	appointment	A&H:GP
William Murdock to ZBV	Nov 6	mill machinery	A&H:GP
J.L. [Sleney] to ZBV	Nov 6	conscripts	A&H:GP
J.J. Guy & J.M. Harrell to ZBV	Nov 6	transfer	A&H:GP
Shubal G. Worth to ZBV	Nov 6	desertion	A&H:GP
Willie Walston to ZBV	Nov 6	impressed slaves	A&H:GP
Noah Bowman to ZBV	Nov 6	desertion	A&H:GP
Sewall L. Fremont to David A. Barnes	Nov 6	*Advance*	A&H:GP
John T. Kennedy to ZBV	Nov 7	volunteers	A&H:GP
David G. Worth to ZBV	Nov 7	salt	A&H:GP
Oliver H. Looper to ZBV	Nov 7	desertion	A&H:GP
William F. Martin to ZBV	Nov 7	gunboat	A&H:GP

Correspondents	Date	Subject	Repository
Henry F. Miller to ZBV	Nov 7	conscription	A&H:GP
R.B. Bryan to ZBV	Nov 7	conscription	A&H:GP
Beckwith West to ZBV	Nov 7	commission	A&H:GP
Fanny Roulhac Hamilton to ZBV	Nov 7	cloth	A&H:GP
John M. Guyther to ZBV	Nov 7	appointment	A&H:GP
John V.B. Rogers to ZBV	Nov 7	ZBV letter	A&H:GP
William P. Bynum to ZBV	Nov 7	appointment	A&H:GP
David G. Worth to ZBV	Nov 7	salt	A&H:GLB
L.C. Turner to ZBV	Nov 9	passport	A&H:GP
R.F. Simonton to ZBV	Nov 9	poor relief	A&H:GP
Joshua Smith to ZBV	Nov 9	hospital	A&H:GP
Henry Watson to ZBV	Nov 9	appointment	A&H:GP
Thomas J. Wilson to ZBV	Nov 9	conscription	A&H:GP
Joseph Williams to ZBV	Nov 9	magistrate	A&H:GP
J.A.C. Brown to ZBV	Nov 9	appointment	A&H:GP
Jefferson Thomas to ZBV	Nov 9	conscription	A&H:GP
John H. Wheeler to ZBV	Nov 9	documents	A&H:GP
Billy Carter to ZBV	Nov 10	discharge	A&H:GP
Drury Lacy to ZBV	Nov 10	cloth	A&H:GP
Piety King to ZBV	Nov 10	desertion	A&H:GP
Clement Dowd to ZBV	Nov 10	desertion	A&H:GP
Celia A. Taylor to ZBV	Nov 10	discharge	A&H:GP
Peter Mallett to ZBV	Nov 10	furlough	A&H:GP
William A. Wright to ZBV	Nov 11	stockholders	A&H:GP
Henry A. Dowd to ZBV	Nov 11	cargo	A&H:GP
Robert F. Hoke to ZBV	Nov 11	brigade	A&H:GP
Louisa Reaves to ZBV	Nov 11	poor relief	A&H:GP
John A. Oates et al., returns	Nov 11	cong. election	A&H:GP
Nathaniel R. Jones to ZBV	Nov 11	prohibit export	A&H:GP
W.H. Smith et al., returns	Nov 11	cong. election	A&H:GP
Thomas P. Walker to ZBV	Nov 11	*Advance*	A&H:GP
William Hicks to ZBV	Nov 11	troop co.	A&H:GP
Joseph J. Young to ZBV	Nov 12	26th. Reg't.	A&H:GP
William H. Oliver to John Devereux	Nov 12	cotton	A&H:GP
Robert B. Vance to ZBV	Nov 12	hostages	A&H:GP
James C. McRae to ZBV	Nov 12	troops	A&H:GP
John P. Campbell to ZBV	Nov 12	peace	A&H:GP
Rufus Galloway et al., returns	Nov 12	cong. election	A&H:GP
Edward D. Hall to ZBV	Nov 12	transfer	A&H:GP
T.J. Lee to ZBV	Nov 12	appointment	A&H:GP
Nathaniel Boyden to ZBV	Nov 12	appointment	A&H:VanPC
D.L. May to ZBV	Nov 13	home guards	A&H:GP
William R. West to ZBV	Nov 13	transfer	A&H:GP
Samuel H. Walkup to ZBV	Nov 13	cloth	A&H:GP
Flora D. Godwin to ZBV	Nov 13	speculation	A&H:GP
P.K. Dickinson to ZBV	Nov 13	stockholders	A&H:GP
J.S. Hanekel to ZBV	Nov 13	cotton cards	A&H:GP
Jasper Etheridge to ZBV	Nov 13	desertion	A&H:GP
Nathaniel Boyden to ZBV	Nov 13	appointment	A&H:GP
Abraham Myers (Capt.) to ZBV	Nov 13	*Advance*	A&H:GP
Ancram W. Ezzell to Samuel Cooper	Nov 13	transfer	A&H:GP

Correspondents	Date	Subject	Repository
G.W. Blacknall to ZBV	Nov 13	appointment	A&H:GP
Thomas J. Boykin to ZBV	Nov 13	cloth	A&H:GP
J.S. Burnett to ZBV	Nov 13	western NC	A&H:GP
Whit. H. Anthony et al. to ZBV	Nov 13	conscription	A&H:GP
Robert R. Heath to ZBV	Nov 13	judges	A&H:GP
James W. Hinton to ZBV	Nov 13	conscription	A&H:VanPC
John L. Morehead to ZBV	Nov 13	provost guard	A&H:VanPC
Mary J. Cashwell to ZBV	Nov 14	desertion	A&H:GP
William S. Seinbach to ZBV	Nov 14	slaves	A&H:GP
R.W. Rest to ZBV	Nov 14	cotton cards	A&H:GP
William T. Muse to ZBV	Nov 14	appointment	A&H:GP
D.A. Carter to ZBV	Nov 14	appointment	A&H:GP
John J. Guthrie to ZBV	Nov 14	visit	A&H:GP
Nathaniel Knight et al. to ZBV	Nov 14	desertion	A&H:GP
C.O. Sanford to ZBV	Nov 14	supplies	A&H:GP
William Warren to ZBV	Nov 14	furlough	A&H:GP
Josiah Nelson to ZBV	Nov 14	cotton/wool cards	A&H:GP
A.C. McIntosh et al. to ZBV	Nov 14	desertion	A&H:GP
Fannie J. Liles to ZBV	Nov 14	discharge	A&H:GP
M.P. Ashe to ZBV	Nov 15	seed	A&H:GP
Thomas J. Sumner to ZBV	Nov 15	r.r. wood	A&H:GP
William L. Love to ZBV	Nov 15	home guards	A&H:GP
John Deal et al. to ZBV	Nov 15	desertion	A&H:GP
Henry M. Drane to Thomas D. Walker	Nov 15	r.r. stock	A&H:GP
James A. Seddon to George W. Mordecai	Nov 16	poor relief	A&H:GP
E.B. Cranford to ZBV	Nov 16	civil unrest	A&H:GP
William J. Chapel, statement	Nov 16	loyalty	A&H:GP
George W. Logan to ZBV	Nov 16	election returns	A&H:GP
Thomas J. Sumner to ZBV	Nov 16	cotton	A&H:GP
J.A. Parks to ZBV	Nov 16	desertion	A&H:GP
L.J. Siler to ZBV	Nov 16	destitution	A&H:GP
Rebeca Varner to ZBV	Nov 16	civil unrest	A&H:GP
R.C. Young to ZBV	Nov 16	Confed. money	A&H:GP
Daniel J. Bradshaw to ZBV	Nov 16	transfer	A&H:GP
Alethea A. Crowell to ZBV	Nov 16	poor relief	A&H:GP
G.M. Roberts to ZBV	Nov 16	appointment	A&H:GP
Eli J. Hester et al. to ZBV	Nov 16	appointment	A&H:GP
Alexander Gilbreath, statement	Nov 16	loyalty	A&H:GP
George E. Pickett to ZBV	Nov 17	amnesty	A&H:GP
Almiry Cross to ZBV	Nov 17	desertion	A&H:GP
C.W. Carlton to ZBV	Nov 17	corn	A&H:GP
George D. Pool et al. to ZBV	Nov 17	conscription	A&H:GP
Cader Perry et al. to ZBV	Nov 17	conscription	A&H:GP
John W. McElroy to ZBV	Nov 17	western NC	A&H:GP
Sarah M. Cox to ZBV	Nov 17	discharge	A&H:GP
Eliza Johnson to ZBV	Nov 17	poor relief	A&H:GP
Sewall L. Fremont to ZBV	Nov 17	stockholders	A&H:GP
Joseph Cook et al. to ZBV	Nov 17	detail	A&H:GP
George S. Hooper to ZBV	Nov 17	resignation	A&H:GP
James C. Harrison to ZBV	Nov 17	transfer	A&H:GP
William House to ZBV	Nov 17	conscription	A&H:GP

Correspondents	Date	Subject	Repository
W.T. Dickenson to ZBV	Nov 17	appointment	A&H:GP
Shubal G. Worth to ZBV	Nov 17	special court	A&H:GP
B.A. Berry et al., returns	Nov 18	cong. election	A&H:GP
Robert F. Smith to ZBV	Nov 18	desertion	A&H:GP
J. Cline et al., returns	Nov 18	cong. election	A&H:GP
Charles M. Sudderth to ZBV	Nov 18	appointment	A&H:GP
William Howard to ZBV	Nov 18	conscription	A&H:GP
R. Stegall to ZBV	Nov 18	free black	A&H:GP
J.B. Ferguson Jr. to ZBV	Nov 18	clothing	A&H:GP
Arthur C. Smith to ZBV	Nov 18	salt	A&H:GP
Shubal G. Worth to ZBV	Nov 18	desertion	A&H:GP
W.T. Crawford et al., returns	Nov 19	cong. election	A&H:GP
J.S. Snow et al., returns	Nov 19	cong. election	A&H:GP
Samuel B. French to ZBV	Nov 19	Jackson statue	A&H:GP
James A. Seddon to ZBV	Nov 19	Cap't. Graham	A&H:GP
A. Heath to ZBV	Nov 19	habeas corpus	A&H:GP
John H. McGilvary to ZBV	Nov 19	cloth	A&H:GP
William A. Eaton to ZBV	Nov 19	impressed slaves	A&H:GP
Jacob Shipton to ZBV	Nov 19	transfer	A&H:GP
Nathan Bagley et al. to ZBV	Nov 19	conscription	A&H:GP
Robert B. Vance to ZBV	Nov 19	western NC	A&H:VanPC
James C. Norman to ZBV	Nov 20	cotton/wood cards	A&H:GP
Clarinday Hulin to ZBV	Nov 20	civil unrest	A&H:GP
Richard C. Puryear to ZBV	Nov 20	appointment	A&H:GP
T.H. Hart to ZBV	Nov 21	free black	A&H:GP
Kate Gaston to ZBV	Nov 21	passport	A&H:GP
James G. P[ower] to ZBV	Nov 21	foreigner	A&H:GP
T.J. Dunsom to ZBV	Nov 21	transfer	A&H:GP
George N. Sanders to ZBV	Nov 21	D.K. McRae	A&H:GP
Thomas J. Boykin to ZBV	Nov 21	resignation	A&H:GP
Joseph Brendle to ZBV	Nov 21	toll	A&H:GP
W.H. George to ZBV	Nov 21	impressment	A&H:GP
John L. Bailey to ZBV	Nov 21	resignation	A&H:GP
James M. Stevenson to ZBV	Nov 22	appointment	A&H:GP
James L. Henry to ZBV	Nov 22	conscripts	A&H:GP
James F. Johnston to ZBV	Nov 22	recommendation	A&H:GP
George W. Johnson to ZBV	Nov 22	imprisonment	A&H:GP
John F. Cotton to ZBV	Nov 23	desertion	A&H:GP
William D. Ellis to ZBV	Nov 23	sugar	A&H:GP
Ralph P. Buxton, certificate	Nov 23	slave murder	A&H:GP
C.K. Baldwin to ZBV	Nov 24	detail	A&H:GP
Jesse R. Combs to ZBV	Nov 24	distilling	A&H:GP
James L. Henry to ZBV	Nov 24	desertion	A&H:GP
Thomas B. Lyon to ZBV	Nov 24	impressed slaves	A&H:GP
Jeptha M. Israel to ZBV	Nov 24	salt	A&H:GP
Shubal G. Worth to ZBV	Nov 24	desertion	A&H:GP
Soloman S. Satchwell to ZBV	Nov 24	distilling	A&H:GP
Edward J. Hale to ZBV	Nov 24	supporter	A&H:VanPC
ZBV to General Assembly	Nov 24	letter & vacancy	A&H:GA
S.R. Hawly to ZBV	Nov 25	desertion	A&H:GP
Peter Mallett to ZBV	Nov 25	"orange factory"	A&H:GP

Correspondents	Date	Subject	Repository
S.A. Baldwin to ZBV	Nov 25	reward	A&H:GP
S. Lane Hayman to ZBV	Nov 25	appointment	A&H:GP
Thomas P. Devereux to ZBV	Nov 25	gunboat	A&H:GP
William M. Lyon to ZBV	Nov 25	impressed slaves	A&H:GP
James H. Whitaker to ZBV	Nov 25	special court	A&H:GP
Mrs. John T. Wheat to ZBV	Nov 26	cotton machine	A&H:GP
Maryan Arrowood to ZBV	Nov 26	destitution	A&H:GP
C. Cloud & Mary McDaniel to ZBV	Nov 26	transfer	A&H:GP
Thomas H. Saintclair et al. to ZBV	Nov 26	arrest	A&H:GP
John A. Richardson to ZBV	Nov 26	resignation	A&H:GP
Edward Kidder to ZBV	Nov 26	salt	A&H:VanPC
Ephriam Mitchell to ZBV	Nov 27	discharge	A&H:GP
Isaac H. Foust to ZBV	Nov 27	desertion	A&H:GP
William J. Clarke to ZBV	Nov 27	troop plan	A&H:GP
John A. Flemming to ZBV	Nov 27	distilling	A&H:GP
S.P. Smith to ZBV	Nov 27	cong. election	A&H:GP
John Pool to ZBV	Nov 27	discharge	A&H:GP
Ralph P. Buxton to William H.C. Whiting	Nov 27	prisoner release	A&H:GP
Sarah A. Cook to ZBV	Nov 27	desertion	A&H:GP
E.B. Steele to ZBV	Nov 27	cotton cards	A&H:GP
Thomas Atkinson to ZBV	Nov 27	cotton cards	A&H:GP
G.W. Sharpe to ZBV	Nov 27	desertion	A&H:GP
J.Y. Munden to ZBV	Nov 28	speculation	A&H:GP
Theodore Andreae to ZBV	Nov 28	cargo agents	A&H:GP
William J. Clarke to ZBV	Nov 28	eastern NC	A&H:GP
William Whitley to ZBV	Nov 28	conscription	A&H:GP
John W. Lane to ZBV	Nov 28	r.r. delay	A&H:GP
William R. Gordon to ZBV	Nov 28	conscription	A&H:GP
Richard J. Donnell to ZBV	Nov 28	cotton/wood cards	A&H:GP
John L. Phifer to ZBV	Nov 28	yarn mfg.	A&H:GP
Lizzie Lee to ZBV	Nov 29	disloyalty	A&H:GP
William A. Ellis et al. to ZBV	Nov 29	poor relief	A&H:GP
Henry T. Clark to ZBV	Nov 29	eastern NC	A&H:GP
Thomas Long to ZBV	Nov 29	tax in kind	A&H:GP
Rhoda Tedder to ZBV	Nov 29	habeas corpus	A&H:GP
Mary E.T. Beasley to ZBV	Nov 29	poor relief	A&H:GP
George Howard et al. to ZBV	Nov 30	eastern NC	A&H:GP
William Bingham to ZBV	Nov 30	desertion	A&H:GP
T. Stanly Beckwith to ZBV	Nov 30	Alfred Stanly	A&H:GP
James W. Osborne to ZBV	Nov 30	special court	A&H:GP
Richard F. Langdon to ZBV	Nov 30	cloth	A&H:GP
William J. Clark to ZBV	Nov 30	eastern NC	A&H:GP
Fenner B. Satterthwaite et al. to ZBV	Nov 30	recommendation	A&H:GP
Alexander Collie, accounts	Nov 30	expenditures	A&H:GP
J.J. Ferrell to ZBV	Nov n.d.	special court	A&H:GP
Sarah Shipton to ZBV	Dec 1	transfer	A&H:GP
William M. Shipp to ZBV	Dec 1	appointment	A&H:GP
Alexander Barrett to ZBV	Dec 1	M.J. McSween	A&H:GP
L.J. Moore to ZBV	Dec 1	transfer	A&H:GP
Daniel Hilton to ZBV	Dec 1	cotton/wool cards	A&H:GP
Joseph J. Young to ZBV	Dec 1	clothing	A&H:GP

Correspondents	Date	Subject	Repository
William O. Harrelson to ZBV	Dec 1	distilling	A&H:GP
M.H. Gilreath to ZBV	Dec 1	conscription	A&H:GP
Thomas Williams to ZBV	Dec 1	poor relief	A&H:GP
E. Griswolde to ZBV	Dec 1	T.H. Webb	A&H:VanPC
William T. Dortch to ZBV	Dec 1	*Advance*	LC:CSA
J.A. Thompson to ZBV	Dec 2	furlough	A&H:GP
George C. Moses to ZBV	Dec 2	orders	A&H:GP
Halifax Co. Chairman to Stephen R. Mallory	Dec 2	gunboat	A&H:GP
Ladies of Chowan to ZBV	Dec 2	conscription	A&H:GP
Alfred Dockery to ZBV	Dec 2	transfer	A&H:GP
Robert McFarland et al., returns	Dec 2	cong. election	A&H:GP
G.H. Brown to ZBV	Dec 2	Federal raid	A&H:GP
George C. Moses to ZBV	Dec 3	Federal threat	A&H:GP
John T. Dodson to ZBV	Dec 3	impressed slaves	A&H:GP
D. Gordon to ZBV	Dec 3	impressment	A&H:GP
J.C. Fowler to ZBV	Dec 3	desertion	A&H:GP
Henry T. Clark to ZBV	Dec 3	home guards	A&H:GP
Julius Wilcox to ZBV	Dec 4	prohibit export	A&H:GP
Thomas L. Clingman to ZBV	Dec 4	home guards	A&H:GP
Stephen D. Pool to ZBV	Dec 4	Federal raid	A&H:GP
Samuel Cooper to ZBV	Dec 4	R.B. Vance	A&H:GP
A.M. Roc[ure] to ZBV	Dec 4	cotton cards	A&H:GP
W.W. Birkell to ZBV	Dec 4	impressment	A&H:GP
Charles Goddard to ZBV	Dec 4	disloyalty	A&H:GP
Milledge L. Bonham to ZBV	Dec 4	cotton	SHC:Law
Alexander H. Jones to ZBV	Dec 5	discharge	A&H:GP
Ralph P. Buxton to ZBV	Dec 5	habeas corpus	A&H:GP
Robert C. Pearson to ZBV	Dec 5	conscription	A&H:GP
Giles Mebane to ZBV	Dec 5	medical relief	A&H:GP
W.P. Wilkins to ZBV	Dec 5	impressed slaves	A&H:GP
D. Spruill to ZBV	Dec 5	prohibit export	A&H:GP
M.R. Cooke to ZBV	Dec 5	conscription	A&H:GP
David G. Worth to ZBV	Dec 5	salt	A&H:GP
W.S. Williams to ZBV	Dec 5	cloth	A&H:GP
Henry T. Clark to ZBV	Dec 5	Federal raid	A&H:GP
Elias J. Jenkins, certificate	Dec 5	disability	A&H:GP
James E.B. Stuart to ZBV	Dec 5	murder case	A&H:GLB
James W. Hinton, order	Dec 5	day of fasting	SHC:Yel
John W. Graham to ZBV	Dec 6	impressment	A&H:GP
John P. Lockhart to ZBV	Dec 6	recommendation	A&H:GP
James E. Gadd to ZBV	Dec 6	clothing	A&H:GP
Walter W. Lenoir to ZBV	Dec 7	appointment	A&H:GP
Theodore Andreae to ZBV	Dec 7	letter	A&H:GP
Robert DeSchweinitz to ZBV	Dec 7	Salem Academy	A&H:GP
Samuel R. Huntt to ZBV	Dec 7	desertion	A&H:GP
Shadrach Radford to ZBV	Dec 7	transfer	A&H:GP
Anny Beck to ZBV	Dec 7	civil unrest	A&H:GP
William J. Clarke to ZBV	Dec 7	defense plan	A&H:GP
Richmond M. Pearson to ZBV	Dec 7	Austin case	A&H:GP
Sophia E. Downing to ZBV	Dec 7	desertion	A&H:GP

Correspondents	Date	Subject	Repository
James H. Everitt to ZBV	Dec 7	conscription	A&H:GP
J.J. Winton to ZBV	Dec 7	desertion	A&H:GP
George N. Sanders to ZBV	ca. Dec 7	D.K. McRae	A&H:GLB
J.T. Hancock to ZBV	Dec 8	poor relief	A&H:GP
F.A. Belsher to ZBV	Dec 8	cotton cards	A&H:GP
Milledge L. Bonham to ZBV	Dec 8	prohibit export	A&H:GP
J.M. McConkle to Edward J. Hale	Dec 8	Austin case	A&H:VanPC
R.L. Patterson to ZBV	Dec 8	taxation	A&H:VanPC
R.C. Blankenship to J. Carson	Dec 9	desertion	A&H:GP
F.T. Bolton to ZBV	Dec 9	destitution	A&H:GP
Roger P. Atkinson to Robert H. Cowan	Dec 9	r.r. iron	A&H:GP
Robert H. Cowan to ZBV	Dec 9	letter delay	A&H:GP
T.J. Fandler to ZBV	Dec 9	appointment	A&H:GP
H.C. Baldwin to ZBV	Dec 9	passport	A&H:GP
Elizabeth Beal to ZBV	Dec 9	detail	A&H:GP
Peter Mallett to ZBV	Dec 9	discharge	A&H:GP
L.M. Hill et al. to ZBV	Dec 9	cotton yarn	A&H:GP
J.G. Reynolds to ZBV	Dec 9	Federal raid	A&H:GP
Calvin J. Cowles to ZBV	Dec 10	cavalry horses	A&H:GP
J.S. Lemmon to ZBV	Dec 10	blockade	A&H:GP
David G. Worth to ZBV	Dec 10	salt	A&H:GP
William S. Morris to ZBV	Dec 10	telegraph	A&H:GP
A Woman to ZBV	Dec 10	money	A&H:GP
J.D. Flanner to ZBV	Dec 10	*Advance*	A&H:GP
A. McDowell to ZBV	Dec 10	slavery	A&H:GP
S.G. Barrett et al., statement	Dec 10	killing	A&H:GP
Robert C. Pearson to ZBV	Dec 10	mule	A&H:GP
Edward J. Hale to ZBV	Dec 10	disloyalty	A&H:VanPC
W.F. Loftin to ZBV	Dec 11	furlough	A&H:GP
T. George Walton to ZBV	Dec 11 (1)	appointment	A&H:GP
T. George Walton to ZBV	Dec 11 (2)	overcoat	A&H:GP
James B. Robinson to J.A. Young	Dec 11	conscription	A&H:GP
J.D. Flanner to ZBV	Dec 11	blockade	A&H:GP
Theodore Andreae to ZBV	Dec 11	blockade	A&H:GP
Robert H. Cowan to ZBV	Dec 11	r.r. iron	A&H:GP
Giles Leitch et al. to ZBV	Dec 11	appointment	A&H:GP
Maria E. Hawkins to ZBV	Dec 11	impressed slave	A&H:GP
Henry A. London to ZBV	Dec 11	claim	A&H:GP
Thomas W. Lindsey to ZBV	Dec 12	uniform bill	A&H:GP
Walter F. Leak to Edward J. Hale	Dec 12	peace	A&H:GP
Franklin White to ZBV	Dec 12	prisoners	A&H:GP
Duncan K. McRae to ZBV	Dec 12	recommendation	A&H:GP
Catherine Cruise to ZBV	Dec 12	assignment	A&H:GP
Leonidas L. Polk (2nd Lt.) to ZBV	Dec 12	promotion	A&H:GP
James G. Ramsay to ZBV	Dec 12	resignation	A&H:GP
John Cooper to ZBV	Dec 12	impressment	A&H:GP
John H. Lee to ZBV	Dec 12	destitution	A&H:GP
Richmond M. Pearson to Gaither Walser	Dec 12	habeas corpus	A&H:GP
D.P. Paschall et al. to ZBV	Dec 13	discharge	A&H:GP
John A. Young to ZBV	Dec 13	conscription	A&H:GP
L.J. Durham to ZBV	Dec 13	poor relief	A&H:GP

Correspondents	Date	Subject	Repository
E.H. Lyon to ZBV	Dec 14	desertion	A&H:GP
James S. Amis to ZBV	Dec 14	financial advice	A&H:GP
George Tait to ZBV	Dec 14	appointment	A&H:GP
Mrs. T. Atkinson to ZBV	Dec 14	conscription	A&H:GP
Joseph Hollinsworth to ZBV	Dec 14	prohibit export	A&H:GP
Theodore Andreae to ZBV	Dec 14	route	A&H:GP
A. Chatham to Mr. Jarett	Dec 14	appointment	A&H:GP
Abraham Myers (Capt.) to ZBV	Dec 14	lard	A&H:VanPC
S.B. Taylor to ZBV	Dec 15	provisions	A&H:GP
Lewis P. Olds to ZBV	Dec 15	cotton	A&H:GP
W. Murdock to ZBV	Dec 15	sheep	A&H:GP
Andrew Parker to ZBV	Dec 15	poor relief	A&H:GP
C.O. Sanford to ZBV	Dec 15	appointment	A&H:GP
Sander Simmons to ZBV	Dec 15	desertion	A&H:GP
P.S. Rogers to ZBV	Dec 15	distilling	A&H:GP
William T. Shipp to ZBV	Dec 15	desertion	A&H:GP
W.W. Sides to ZBV	Dec 15	desertion	A&H:GP
James M. Lackey to ZBV	Dec 16	shoes & blanket	A&H:GP
William H.H. Conner to ZBV	Dec 16	desertion	A&H:GP
James M. Warren to ZBV	Dec 16	furlough	A&H:GP
Lewis Webb to ZBV	Dec 16	appointment	A&H:GP
T.J. Sawner to George Little	Dec 17	r.r. iron	A&H:GP
J.R. Sikes to ZBV	Dec 17	passport	A&H:GP
Robert B. Gilliam to ZBV	Dec 17	slaves	A&H:GP
D.B. McSween to ZBV	Dec 17	brother	A&H:GP
Samuel A. Warren to ZBV	Dec 17	murder	A&H:GP
John Phelan, claim	Dec 17	bounty	A&H:GP
Hezekiah G. Spruill to ZBV	Dec 17	praise	A&H:GP
Cooper Huggins to ZBV	Dec 17	volunteer co.	A&H:GP
Mary C. Batchelor to ZBV	Dec 18	destitution	A&H:GP
Sophia E. Downing to ZBV	Dec 18	desertion	A&H:GP
James H. Hill, special order	Dec 18	disrespect to ZBV	A&H:GP
John A. Young to ZBV	Dec 19	cards	A&H:GP
Daniel F. Summey to ZBV	Dec 19	medical supplies	A&H:GP
Otis F. Manson to ZBV	Dec 19	cloth	A&H:GP
John S. Delap, affidavits	Dec 19	shoemaker	A&H:GP
T. L. Delozier to ZBV	Dec 19	transfer	A&H:GP
James Sloan to ZBV	Dec 19	cloth	A&H:VanPC
E.R. Liles to ZBV	Dec 20	substitution	A&H:GP
John A. McKay to ZBV	Dec 20	transfer	A&H:GP
George C. Moses to ZBV	Dec 20	surgeon	A&H:GP
Henry T. Clark to ZBV	Dec 20	eastern NC	A&H:GP
Bennett Flanner Jr. to ZBV	Dec 20	recommendation	A&H:GP
Joshua Hill to ZBV	Dec 21	horse	A&H:GP
Martha A. Veazey to ZBV	Dec 21	cotton yarn	A&H:GP
William H.C. Whiting to Samuel Cooper	Dec 21	letter	A&H:GP
John Letcher to ZBV	Dec 21	introduction	A&H:GP
Rufus Y. McAden to ZBV	Dec 22	Quakers	A&H:GP
Frank J. Wilson to ZBV	Dec 22	appointment	A&H:GP
James L. Tait to ZBV	Dec 22	clothing	A&H:GP
L.A. Johnson to ZBV	Dec 22	resignation	A&H:GP

Correspondents	Date	Subject	Repository
William M. Poisson to ZBV	Dec 22	conscription	A&H:GP
William A. Graham to ZBV	Dec 23	resignation	A&H:GP
J.J. Coner et al. to ZBV	Dec 23	impressment	A&H:GP
Jane Bryan to ZBV	Dec 23	impressment	A&H:GP
George W. Mordecai to Literary Fund	Dec 23	taxes	A&H:GP
John W. Leak to ZBV	Dec 23	distilling	A&H:GP
B.F. Arthur to ZBV	Dec 23	M.L. Bonham	SHC:Law
William H. Harp to ZBV	Dec 24	desertion	A&H:GP
Peter Mallett to ZBV	Dec 24	*Daily Progress*	A&H:GP
John A. Carpenter et al. to ZBV	Dec 24	blankets & coats	A&H:GP
James A. Seddon to ZBV	Dec 24	impressment	A&H:VanPC
George W. Ruffty to ZBV	Dec 25	paroled prisoner	A&H:GP
Robert C. Pearson to ZBV	Dec 25	friend's visit	A&H:GP
D.M. Carter to ZBV	Dec 25	liquor	A&H:GP
John D. Whitford to ZBV	Dec 25	r.r. iron	A&H:GP
J.K. Baldwin to ZBV	Dec 25	discharge	A&H:GP
Edward D. Walsh to ZBV	Dec 25	troop co.	A&H:GP
Leander S. Gash to ZBV	Dec 25	home guards	A&H:GP
Augustus S. Merrimon to ZBV	Dec 25	prisoner of war	A&H:GP
Alfred G. Foster to David A. Barnes	Dec 26	appointment	A&H:GP
Sewall L. Fremont to George Little	Dec 26	r.r. iron	A&H:GP
S.R. Townsend to ZBV	Dec 26	appointment	A&H:GP
Lewis Vance to ZBV	Dec 26	conscription	A&H:GP
R.R. Collier to ZBV	Dec 26	pamphlet	A&H:GP
J. Luther to ZBV	Dec 27	conscription	A&H:GP
John W. McElroy to ZBV	Dec 27	new reg't.	A&H:GP
S.A. Wicker et al. to ZBV	Dec 27	conscription	A&H:GP
William J. Hardee to ZBV	Dec 27	clothing	A&H:GP
Thomas B. Powers to ZBV	Dec 27	*Advance*	A&H:GP
Kemp P. Battle to ZBV	Dec 28	r.r. provisions	A&H:GP
Augustus S. Merrimon to ZBV	Dec 28 (1)	special court	A&H:GP
Augustus S. Merrimon to ZBV	Dec 28 (2)	special court	A&H:GP
James B. Wallington to ZBV	Dec 28	Confed. currency	A&H:GP
John Manning Jr. to ZBV	Dec 28	habeas corpus	A&H:GP
Sewall L. Fremont to George Little	Dec 28	shooting	A&H:GP
A.E. Wright to Sewall L. Fremont	Dec 28	shooting	A&H:GP
Francis T. Hank to Sewall L. Fremont	Dec 28	shooting	A&H:GP
John W. Wilson to ZBV	Dec 28	detail	A&H:GP
R. Bradley to ZBV	Dec 28	appointment	A&H:GP
Power Low & Co. to ZBV	Dec 28	express box	A&H:GP
James J. Palmer to Sewall L. Fremont	Dec 28	wounded	A&H:GP
Sion H. Rogers to ZBV	Dec 28	special court	A&H:GP
W.J. Magrath to Milledge L. Bonham	Dec 28	locomotives	A&H:GP
W.F. Craig to ZBV	Dec 28	conscription	A&H:GP
William Collie to ZBV	Dec 28	Theodore Andreae	A&H:GP
Many Soldiers to ZBV	Dec 28	destitution	A&H:GP
Theodore Andreae to ZBV	Dec 28	authority	A&H:GP
J.P. McConell to ZBV	Dec 28	detail	A&H:GP
William A. Smith to ZBV	Dec 29	cotton factory	A&H:GP
H. Walser to ZBV	Dec 29	habeas corpus	A&H:GP
W.H. Powell et al. to ZBV	Dec 29	conscription	A&H:GP

Correspondents	Date	Subject	Repository
John T. Bellamy to ZBV	Dec 29	cotton	A&H:GP
James H. Ward to ZBV	Dec 29	mail	A&H:GP
Thomas Webb to ZBV	Dec 29	cotton	A&H:GP
M.D. Gibbons to ZBV	Dec 29	speculation	A&H:GP
R.A. Jenkins to ZBV	Dec 29	eastern NC	A&H:GP
A. McN. Leach to ZBV	Dec 29	conscription	A&H:GP
John Pool to ZBV	Dec 29	Bertie Co.	A&H:VanPC
Winnyford Battin & Mahata B. Boykin to ZBV	Dec 30	speculation	A&H:GP
J.M. Center to ZBV	Dec 30	transfer	A&H:GP
W.D. Whitted to ZBV	Dec 30	conscription	A&H:GP
James S. McCubbins to ZBV	Dec 30	cotton cards	A&H:GP
John W. Young to ZBV	Dec 30	appointment	A&H:GP
B.F. Arthur to ZBV	Dec 30	letter	A&H:GP
Edwin G. Reade to ZBV	Dec 30	judgeship	A&H:VanPC
J.H. Forest to ZBV	Dec 30	desertion	SHC:Rob
William H. Bagley to ZBV	Dec 31	resignation	A&H:GP
D.D. McBryan to ZBV	Dec 31	disaffection	A&H:GP
Nancy Waler to ZBV	Dec 31	destitution	A&H:GP
List of Dortch District	Dec n.d.	slaves	A&H:GP
Anonymous to ZBV	Dec n.d.	destitution	A&H:GP
E.M. Carpenter to ZBV	Dec n.d.	refugees	A&H:GP
Jefferson Davis to ZBV	n.m. 2	NC troops	A&H:GP
J.D. Flanner to ZBV	n.m. 3	Advance	A&H:GP
John W. Cameron to ZBV	n.m. 4	cotton	A&H:GP
George Little to ZBV	n.m. 6	news	A&H:GP
William H.C. Whiting to ZBV	n.m. 7	labor	A&H:GP
William H. Oliver to ZBV	n.m. 7	cotton	A&H:GP
K. Thigpen to Jesse H. Powell	n.m. 7	commission	A&H:GP
James A. Seddon to ZBV	n.m. 7	artillery	A&H:GP
W.C. Duxbury to ZBV	n.m. 8	artillery	A&H:GP
William H.C. Whiting to ZBV	n m. 8	desertion	A&H:GP
Joseph H. Flanner to ZBV	n.m. 11	cotton	A&H:GP
James W. Wilson to ZBV	n.m. 11	r.r. car	A&H:GP
William Lamb to ZBV	n.m. 12	Advance	A&H:GP
James A. Seddon to ZBV	n.m. 13	Salibury command	A&H:GP
S.S. Williams to ZBV	n.m. 14	wool	A&H:GP
Thomas Slade to ZBV	n.m. 17	small pox	A&H:GP
Nicholas W. Woodfin to ZBV	n.m. 19	salt	A&H:GP
Joseph H. Flanner to ZBV	n.m. 19	arrival	A&H:GP
William H.C. Whiting to ZBV	n.m. 21	quarantine	A&H:GP
Norman & Sloan to ZBV	n.m. 22	recommendation	A&H:GP
James A.J. Bradford to ZBV	n.m. 22	Federal raid	A&H:GP
J.D. Flanner to ZBV	n.m. 23	Advance	A&H:GP
William H.C. Whiting to ZBV	n.m. 23	desertion	A&H:GP
Joseph E. Brown to ZBV	n.m. 23	transportation	A&H:GP
W.E. Dul[in] to George Little	n.m. 25	permit	A&H:GP
Thomas M. Crossan to ZBV	n.m. 26	Advance	A&H:GP
Jefferson Davis to ZBV	n.m. 26	visit	A&H:GP
Thomas J. Boykin to ZBV	n.m. 26	Raleigh arrival	A&H:GP
Stephen D. Pool to ZBV	n.m. 27	Raleigh arrival	A&H:GP

Correspondents	Date	Subject	Repository
William H.C. Whiting to ZBV	n.m. 27	Federal raid	A&H:GP
James L. Henry to ZBV	n.m. 28	commission	A&H:GP
Alexander Barrett to ZBV	n.m. 28	McSween trial	A&H:GP
William H.C. Whiting to ZBV	n.m. 28	black laborers	A&H:GP
Milledge L. Bonham to ZBV	n.m. 29	notes	A&H:GP
George Little to ZBV	n.m. 29	order	A&H:GP
R.W. Wharton to Abraham Myers (Capt.)	n.m. 30	Robert F. Hoke	A&H:GP
William H.C. Whiting to ZBV	n.m. 30	apology	A&H:GP
James A. Seddon to ZBV	n.m. n.d.	Braxton Bragg	A&H:GP
Robert F. Davidson to ZBV	n.m. n.d.	fortifications	A&H:GP
Resolutions	n.m. n.d.	peace	A&H:GP
Mary Moody to ZBV	n.m. n.d.	destitution	A&H:GP
Legislative bill	n.m. n.d.	deceased soldiers	A&H:GP
E.L. Roberts to Nicholas W. Woodfin	n.m. n.d.	tax	A&H:GP
Daniel G. Fowle to ZBV	n.m. n.d.	militia	A&H:VanPC
Conservative to ZBV	n.m. n.d.	disaffection	A&H:VanPC
Kemp P. Battle, essay	n.m. n.d.	conscription	A&H:VanPC

ufacture, 62; advises ZBV re courts, 62, 64; advises ZBV re W. W. Holden, 318; advises ZBV re proclamation, 270; dissuades ZBV re peace letter, xix; district attorney's association with, 193; L. S. Gash's opinion of, 285; identified, 63n; influences General Assembly, 133, 338; nonappearance of letter by, 308; on peace negotiations, 346; talks with W. W. Holden, 226, 270; ZBV hopes for meeting with, 190, 252; ZBV seeks advice of, re peace movement, 237–238; ZBV seeks advice of, re public letter, 241

Grant, James M., 166–167, 177
Graves, Robert J., 1–3
Guerrilla warfare. See Uncivilized warfare
Guion, Haywood W., 159–160
Gunboats, 32–33, 77, 82n, 159, 325, 330, 336, 340–341
Guthrie, John J., 303

H

Habeas corpus: dissatisfaction with suspension of, 113; General Assembly inquires about, 204–205; law concerning, 315, 316–317, 325–326; public support for, 234; refusal to extend suspension of, 132; suspension of, suggested, 48; War Department's reponse to writs of, 155, 235; writs of, issued, 144n, 150–151, 321–322; ZBV's position on, xx, 42–43, 100, 164, 169, 173–174
Hale, Edward J.: cautions ZBV re W. W. Holden, 220–221, 272–273; on Confederate currency, 198–199; L. S. Gash's opinion of, 285; identified, 200n; informed by ZBV re court cases, 328–330; informed by ZBV re W. W. Holden, 226–227, 237, 270, 282, 318; informed by ZBV re Lincoln's letter, 338; informed by ZBV re political situation, 308–309, 318–319, 346–347, 359; informed by ZBV re riots, 277–278; ZBV seeks meeting with, 190, 252. See also *Fayetteville Observer*
Hale, J. C., 94–95

Hale, Peter M., 199, 200n, 273
Hall, Edward D., 117, 118n
Ha[neberr]y, Henry, 125
Hansa, 350, 354
Harkaway, 233
Harney, Frank M., 240–241, 256–257
Harris, Lt. Col., 300
Harrison, Burton N., 56
Harrison, William H., 346, 347n
Haughton, John H., 242–247, 252
Haughton, S. T., 288
Hawkins, William J., 30, 343
Hays, William, 149–150, 157
Haywood, George W., 322
Heath, Robert R., 324, 329–330, 352, 358
Henderson, Leonard, 193, 194n
Henry Adderly and Co., 17
Heroes of America, xvii
Heth, Henry, 20–21, 167–168
Hill, Daniel H.: advises ZBV re militia, 141; assumes command in N.C., 11, 12, 22, 56; on conditions in N.C., 77, 191–192, 209; denounces reconstruction advocates, 194–195; on desertion, 151; enacts conscription, 127; gathers troops, 145; on progress of war, 208–209; recommendation from, 117; request of, denied, 156; transfer of, 196; on troops to hunt deserters, 126; ZBV advises re troops, 89; ZBV asks favor from, 197; ZBV complains to, re impressment, 128; ZBV responds to, re troops, 129
Hillsborough Military Academy, 189
Hine, Joseph, 79
Hinton, James W., 101, 102n, 301, 326–327, 333, 357
Hodges, William, 125
Hodnett, Philip, 229–230
Hogg, Thomas D., 37, 38n
Hoke, Robert F., 16, 89, 90n, 258, 267, 289, 290, 310
Holden, William W.: articles by, re Lincoln, 346; called coward by ZBV, 278; on Confederate currency, 198–199; flees to safety, 277; identified, 110n; leads peace movement, xviii, xix, 222; refuses to discourage peace meetings, 270, 272–273; relationship of, with ZBV, xix,